D0483949

A

PEOPLE'S HISTORY

OF THE

SUPREME

COURT

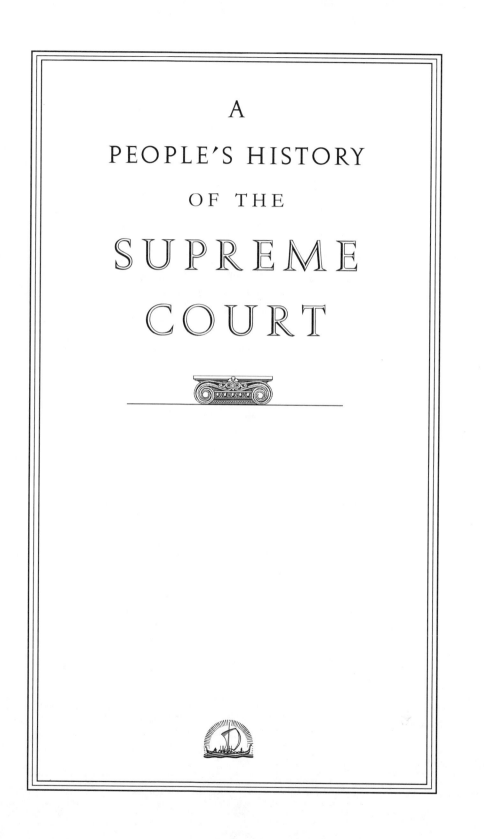

PREVIOUS BOOKS BY PETER IRONS

THE NEW DEAL LAWYERS (1981)

JUSTICE AT WAR:
The Story of the Japanese American
Internment Cases (1982)

THE COURAGE OF THEIR CONVICTIONS:
Sixteen Americans Who Fought Their Way to the
Supreme Court (1988)

JUSTICE DELAYED:
The Record of the Japanese American
Internment Cases (1989)

MAY IT PLEASE THE COURT:
The Most Significant Oral Arguments Made Before the
Supreme Court Since 1955
(edited with Stephanie Guitton, 1993)

BRENNAN VS. REHNQUIST:
The Battle for the Constitution (1994)

MAY IT PLEASE THE COURT:
Arguments on Abortion
(edited with Stephanie Guitton, 1995)

MAY IT PLEASE THE COURT:
The First Amendment (1998)

A
PEOPLE'S HISTORY
OF THE
SUPREME
COURT

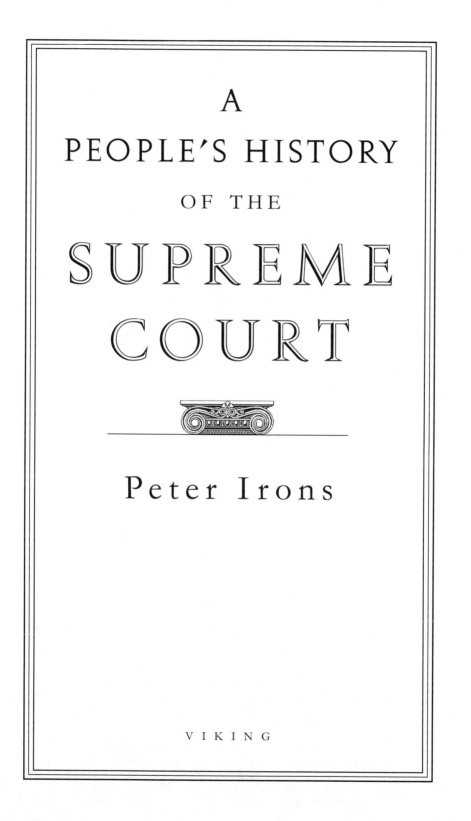

Peter Irons

VIKING

HOUSTON PUBLIC LIBRARY

R0117 76473

Dedicated to my daughters,

Haley Ellen Fox and
Maya Grace IronFox

VIKING
Published by the Penguin Group
Penguin Putnam Inc., 375 Hudson Street, New York, New York 10014, U.S.A.
Penguin Books Ltd, 27 Wrights Lane, London W8 5TZ, England
Penguin Books Australia Ltd, Ringwood, Victoria, Australia
Penguin Books Canada Ltd, 10 Alcorn Avenue,
Toronto, Ontario, Canada M4V 3B2
Penguin Books (N.Z.) Ltd, 182–190 Wairau Road,
Auckland 10, New Zealand

Penguin Books Ltd, Registered Offices:
Harmondsworth, Middlesex, England

First published in 1999 by Viking Penguin,
a member of Penguin Putnam, Inc.

1 3 5 7 9 10 8 6 4 2

Copyright © Peter Irons, 1999
Foreword copyright © Howard Zinn, 1999
All rights reserved

LIBRARY OF CONGRESS CATALOGING-IN-PUBLICATION DATA
Irons, Peter H., 1940–
A people's history of the Supreme Court / by Peter Irons.
p.   cm.
Includes bibliographical references.
ISBN 0-670-87006-4
1. United States. Supreme Court—History.   2. Law and politics.
I. Title.
KF8742.I76   1999
347.73'26'09—dc21   98–53706

This book is printed on acid-free paper. ∞

Printed in the United States of America
Set in Garamond MT
Designed by Kathryn Parise

Without limiting the rights under copyright reserved above, no part of
this publication may be reproduced, stored in or introduced into a retrieval
system, or transmitted, in any form or by any means (electronic, mechanical,
photocopying, recording or otherwise), without the prior written permission
of both the copyright owner and the above publisher of this book.

FOREWORD

Although the Preamble to the United States Constitution begins with the words "We the People . . . ," the volumes upon volumes that deal with constitutional law are remarkably devoid of human beings. How many Americans, of the huge number who have heard of *Brown v. Board of Education,* know that "Brown" refers to Oliver Brown and his eight-year-old daughter Linda in Topeka, or know anything about the long struggle of their family to bring the case before the highest court in the land?

How many, even if they have studied constitutional law and argued the case of *Tinker v. Des Moines,* know (unless they have read Peter Irons's wonderful book *The Courage of Their Convictions*) the human story of Mary Beth Tinker, the thirteen-year-old suspended from school in 1965 for wearing a black armband in school to protest the war in Vietnam?

It is this situation that Peter Irons has set out to remedy, with a history of the Supreme Court that breathes life into the dry language of the judicial system, that looks behind the cases to the human beings crucial to the cases but long forgotten, that examines the realities of social conflict beneath the surface of legal argument.

The document created by the Founding Fathers was born of intense conflicts of race and class, yet there has always been a certain aura of disinterestedness around the decisions of the Supreme Court, notwithstanding the adversarial character of the cases before it.

Sharp divisions of interest are concealed behind abstract legal arguments. Substantive issues are obscured and arguments advanced, decisions made, based on technicalities of law. In the austere chambers of the Court, life-and-death matters are decided in an atmosphere of genial academic debate. It is a contribution of this book that the human beings behind these legal arguments are brought to the fore, giving the debates their proper significance.

At the highest levels of legal discourse, and embedded in popular belief, is the notion that something called "precedent" has ironclad power. The result of holding to this was long ago observed by Jonathan Swift in *Gulliver's Travels*:

> *It is a maxim among lawyers, that whatever hath been done before may legally be done again: and therefore they take special care to record all the decisions formerly made against common justice and the general reason of mankind. These, under the name of precedents, they produce as authorities, to justify the most iniquitous opinions; and the judges never fail of directing accordingly.*

Swift's irony is an exaggeration of course, but with a great deal of truth in it. The deference to precedent, without regard to "common justice," will be found again and again in these pages, as Professor Irons takes us through the fascinating history of the Supreme Court and its decisions.

Yet, precedents are broken when the social forces demand it. Thus, it took more than half a century to overturn the principle of "separate but equal" enunciated in the case of *Plessy v. Ferguson*. Its overturn came not, as it might seem from a superficial reading of the arguments, from a reconsideration of the language of the Fourteenth Amendment, but from tumultuous changes in the United States and in the world: the disintegration of old colonial empires, the legacy of war, and the emergence of a movement among black people for equal rights.

The justices of the Supreme Court are not simply black-robed repositories of objective wisdom; rather, as Professor Irons reminds us, they come out of the political system, out of a social context, and each brings to the Court legal philosophies and moral attitudes that come out of his or her background. To understand this is to demystify the pronouncements of the courts, even the words of the Founding Fathers, and to recognize the Constitution as a living, changing document. "The Constitution," he has said, "should adapt to the changing needs of a society, based on core values like the dignity of the individual."

Thus, while Peter Irons is aware of the power of law, he is not deferential to it. He understands its magnetic hold on the public, but also its limitations. He knows, for instance, having been jailed as a result of his refusal to serve in an unconstitutional war, what the Roman statesman Cicero said a long time ago: *"Silent enim leges inter arma"* (The law is silent in wartime).

His resistance to the draft and the war in Vietnam came out of his involvement in the civil rights movement, and the pacifist philosophy of Gandhi and Martin Luther King. He came out of prison armed with a social conscience tempered by years of observing how the law can serve immoral ends. He was determined to turn law to good ends. After receiving his doctorate in political science at Boston University he went on to Harvard Law School, distinguishing himself in both endeavors. Almost immediately, he began turning out books, much admired by both specialists and general readers, on issues involving the intersection of law and politics.

His first book, *New Deal Lawyers*, based on untapped litigation files in the National Archives and on interviews with the lawyers who worked for Franklin D. Roosevelt, was very well received. He then became interested in the legal battles surrounding the internment of Japanese-Americans in World War II. He used the Freedom of Information Act to uncover the behind-the-scenes deceptions involved in FDR's infamous order and the Supreme Court decisions affirming the constitutionality of that order. The result was his prizewinning book *Justice at War*.

The documents that Professor Irons uncovered in the course of his research on the internment cases became the basis for legal action, in which he was a crucial participant. He was now in his favorite mode, that of a lawyer-researcher-activist. He enlisted volunteer lawyers, many of them children of detention-camp inmates, and in 1983 drafted petitions asking the courts to vacate the wartime decisions; and one by one, starting with the case of Fred Korematsu and ending dramatically with the case of Gordon Hirabayashi, the convictions were overturned.

The Hirabayashi case then became one of sixteen cases Professor Irons wrote about in his book *The Courage of Their Convictions,* cases where ordinary Americans pursued their convictions all the way to the Supreme Court. Some won, some lost, but all displayed remarkable bravery in insisting on their constitutional rights, and the result is a wonderfully inspiring book.

In the early 1990s, Peter Irons achieved an extraordinary victory for the principle of free expression when he went into the National Archives, where the arguments made before the Supreme Court were housed. They had been recorded, put on tape, since 1955. He copied twenty-three of the tapes, dealing with critical issues of civil liberties, and then, with the help of the legal scholar Stephanie Guitton, edited them for publication, defying a National Archives rule. The resulting volume, and its accompanying tapes, were published in 1993 as *May It Please the Court*. There was a flurry of threats from the government, but Irons and Guitton held to their belief that it was the right of everybody to know what happened before the Court. The government yielded, and now the tapes were open to the public.

Contemplating Peter Irons's record, we may then know what to expect from *A People's History of the Supreme Court*—scrupulous legal scholarship, bold ideas, and an abiding concern for human rights, sometimes violated by the law, sometimes upheld, but always depending on the courage of ordinary citizens.

HOWARD ZINN

CONTENTS

Section VI: "A Right of Personal Privacy"   421

INTRODUCTION

"The Genius of the Constitution"

A People's History of the Supreme Court begins in the early years of the seventeenth century, with the arrival of a few hundred British emigrants on the shores of a vast continent. These first settlers of a New World left behind most of their belongings, but they brought with them the English common law and the rights it granted "freemen" who vowed allegiance to God and King. This book ends in the final years of the twentieth century, with the descendants of those English "freemen" now a small fraction of the quarter billion citizens of a diverse and divided nation, governed by a constitution that requires no profession of allegiance to any deity or secular ruler to enjoy its protections.

Between the "Body of Liberties" of the Puritan colonists and the American Constitution of today lies a dramatic story of efforts to secure "the blessings of liberty" to a people who have never reached agreement on what that evocative term really means. Too often in our history, Americans who have claimed the Constitution's protection of their own "liberty" have denied that it equally protects fellow Americans who differ in race, religion, class, gender, or politics. For some two centuries, since the Constitution was ratified in 1789, disputes over the meaning of its broadly worded provisions have been decided by the Supreme Court of the United States, whose unelected members have often wielded the power to strike down the acts of elected lawmakers. Just over a hundred people have served on the Supreme Court in just over two hundred years. All but two have been white, all but two have been men, and all but seven have been Christian. Many of the landmark cases these justices have decided were brought by blacks, women, and religious and political dissenters. In a very real sense, the history of the Supreme Court reflects the appeals of powerless "outsiders" to the powerful "insiders" who have shaped the Constitution's meaning over the past two centuries.

Viewed through a narrow lens, we can read the history of the Supreme Court through the judicial opinions of famous men like John Marshall, Roger Taney, Oliver Wendell Holmes, Louis Brandeis, Hugo Black, Felix Frankfurter, and Earl Warren. Their landmark decisions track the first exercises and the final triumph of judicial power in the American political system and trace the shifting course of constitutional doctrine. But a people's history of the Court requires a broader lens and a wider focus. We need to remember that each landmark decision stemmed from a "case or controversy" that began with claims to constitutional protection by ordinary Americans like Dred Scott, Homer Plessy, Lillian Gobitas, Fred Korematsu, Harry Briggs, Norma McCorvey, and Michael Hardwick. Each of these individual litigants faced a legal adversary who asserted the power to enforce the laws: a judge, school principal, army general, or district attorney. Each of their cases, in turn, brought into the courtroom an unresolved political conflict: slavery, racial segregation, patriotic conformity, military power, abortion, or gay rights. And the outcome of each case reflected the composition of a Court whose members had most often been active in the political party of the president who placed them on the bench.

A People's History of the Supreme Court takes account of the interlocking factors of personality, principle, and politics. We will look closely at the people who played leading roles in framing and interpreting the Constitution, and at those whose cases brought its important provisions before the Court. The people in these two groups differ widely in background: many among the Framers and justices were wealthy and wellborn, while most of those who sought their rights in the Court had little money or social status. We will explore the differing principles these people expressed, some in articulate and thoughtful judicial opinions, others in simple words or forceful acts.

It is difficult to place labels on the wide range of principles we will encounter, but they fall broadly into two conflicting viewpoints in American history. One looks first at the individual; the other at the community. One values personal rights; the other stresses social responsibility. One believes that the Constitution—as Justice Robert Jackson wrote—was designed to place fundamental rights "beyond the reach of majorities." The other argues—in the words of Jackson's former law clerk Chief Justice William Rehnquist—that "it is the majority who will determine what the constitutional rights of the minority are." The recurring conflict between these sets of principles has roiled American politics ever since the Constitution was drafted, and those political battles have often produced skirmishes in the Supreme Court. This book takes for its epigraph the words of a perceptive and prescient foreign observer, Alexis de Tocqueville, who visited America in the 1830s and remarked: "Scarcely any political question arises in the United States that is not resolved, sooner or later, into a judicial question."

A People's History of the Supreme Court is the culmination of thirty years of teaching, writing, speaking, and practicing in the field of constitutional law. It also reflects some forty years of involvement in movements and campaigns for social change. These two aspects of my life are inseparable; I chose a career in law—

later than most lawyers—because it offered a chance to combine my personal values and professional interests. I have no desire to conceal those values behind a mask of scholarly "objectivity" or a veil of "neutrality" in recounting the legal battles this book examines. No book on constitutional history I have ever read has failed to conceal its author's personal values or political stance, despite the disclaimers of some.

Every book has a point of view, and I think it fair to disclose mine at the outset. I believe firmly that the Constitution's basic command is that every person must be accorded the dignity he or she deserves as a human being. All people must be treated fairly and equally, without discrimination because of any characteristic they were born with or have chosen to express their identity, including race, religion, nationality, gender, sexual orientation, politics, disability, and any other distinguishing quality by which we label people. It is the job of every government official—from police officer to president—to treat each person with respect. This may sound more like the Golden Rule than the rule of law, but the same idea lies behind each.

I also believe firmly that the Framers—despite their flaws—shaped the Constitution as a "living" document, whose basic principles would endure but whose separate provisions would grow in meaning as American society grew in size and diversity. Justice William Brennan, who remains my judicial ideal and inspiration, expressed this notion when he wrote in 1986 of constitutional interpretation: "We look to the history of the time of framing and to the intervening history of interpretation. But the ultimate question must be: What do the words of the text mean in our time? For the genius of the Constitution rests not in any static meaning it may have had in a world that is dead and gone, but in the adaptability of its great principles to cope with current problems and current needs." In less resonant words, I made the same point in 1957, responding as a high school senior to a right-wing columnist in the *Cincinnati Enquirer* who almost daily attacked the Warren Court's rulings on school integration. I replied that "the duty of the Supreme Court is to redefine the purport of the law in light of changing social trends." That remains my belief, reinforced by changing social trends in areas like gender equality, gay rights, abortion, and death with dignity. My positions on these issues are "liberal" by most standards, but I consider myself a true conservative in holding fast to the principles best expressed in the Declaration of Independence, the enduring principles of liberty and equality.

Let me explain the genesis of this book, whose title and approach I modeled on Howard Zinn's exciting and provocative *A People's History of the United States*. My first contact with Howard came in 1967, when I wrote to him at Boston University, seeking his help in gaining admission to graduate study in political science. I was then Inmate No. 21341 at the Federal Correctional Institution in Danbury, Connecticut, serving a three-year sentence for refusing military induction in 1963. I wound up in prison as the result of my involvement in the sit-in movement and my pacifist beliefs. In October 1960, as a student at Antioch College, I attended a conference in Atlanta of the Student Nonviolent Coordinating Committee, where I was inspired by two young black ministers, Martin Luther King, Jr., and James Lawson. King's ringing call to practice nonviolence in our lives and Lawson's powerful challenge to risk jail for our beliefs prompted me to return my draft card and tell my local board in Cincinnati that I could not fight for a country that practiced racial segregation.

My draft board returned my card, along with an invitation to apply for conscientious objector status. The form they sent me required that I affirm my belief in a Supreme Being, with duties "superior to those arising from any human relationship." Not only did I not hold this belief, but I felt that it violated the Constitution's provision that "no religious test shall ever be required as a qualification to any office or public trust under the United States." Serving my country through "alternative service" seemed to me like an office or public trust. I made this argument to a federal judge in 1965, after my indictment for refusing induction, but I failed to convince him. Before I started my prison sentence, I worked for three years in the Washington legislative office of the United Auto Workers, where I often took breaks from boring congressional hearings and crossed the street to hear arguments in the Supreme Court chamber. These experiences spurred an interest in law and politics, and I decided to pursue a career that would combine them. "My special interests are in civil liberties and American politics," I wrote to Howard Zinn from prison. He responded promptly and warmly, sending me books over the eighteen months before we first met in February 1969. Howard became a friend, mentor, and inspiration as a "committed scholar" whose books recount the struggles of ordinary people with extraordinary courage.

After completing my political science doctorate at Boston University in 1973, I held several part-time teaching jobs in Boston while I worked against the Vietnam War. Howard also helped arrange a job with the law firm representing Daniel Ellsberg, who was under federal prosecution for "stealing" the Pentagon Papers, which revealed decades of presidential lies about the war. Ellsberg's lawyers put me to work documenting the release of "secret" records by government officials—including Henry Kissinger and President Lyndon Johnson—who had escaped prosecution. My research ended when a federal judge dismissed Ellsberg's indictment because of prosecutorial misconduct, but I had caught the legal bug and decided to get a law degree. Much to my surprise, Harvard Law School admitted an ex-convict in his mid-thirties, and I delved into constitutional law with Laurence Tribe and American legal history with Morton Horwitz. I also volunteered with Harvard Defenders in Boston criminal courts and helped to edit the *Harvard Civil Rights–Civil Liberties Law Review*.

After graduating in 1978, I taught at Boston College Law School and then in the Legal Studies Program at the University of Massachusetts at Amherst, before moving to the University of California at San Diego in 1982. At UCSD, I established the Earl Warren Bill of Rights Project, designed to produce innovative curricular materials for high school and college classes. My book *The Courage of Their Convictions* was the first product of the Warren Project, followed by the *May It Please the Court* series of Supreme Court oral arguments on tape. During these years, I also helped to reopen the wartime internment cases of Fred Korematsu, Min Yasui, and Gordon Hirabayashi and served on the national board of the American Civil Liberties Union.

I offer this brief personal history for two reasons. First, my experiences help explain my approach to constitutional law. My involvement in movements for civil rights and liberties—in jails and prisons, picket lines and courtrooms—has taught me more about how law affects people's lives than have graduate study and law school. Equally important, this book starts with the experiences of people whose lives have helped to shape our Constitution's meaning over the past two centuries. Each person's story forms the backdrop to a Supreme Court decision that resulted from some personal decision to take a stand. These stories, which are rarely told in the Court's opinions or in books on constitutional history, help us to understand the connections between individuals and the historical forces that shaped their lives and, in turn, shape our own.

Let me also explain why, unlike most writers of constitutional casebooks or histories, I have focused on relatively few cases—I examine only eighty-five in some detail—and have filled in their backgrounds with political, economic, and social history. This book was not designed to be encyclopedic or exhaustive in coverage, but to illustrate the connections of law and politics in areas of civil rights and liberties. I have left out many important cases and have slighted important issues like capital punishment and voting rights. One reader of this book in manuscript form professed "shock" that I left out the Pentagon Papers and Watergate Tapes cases. Other readers will surely wonder why I failed to discuss one or more of their "favorite" cases. I can only reply that these omissions, however painful for me and puzzling for readers, reflect my decision to pursue greater depth in coverage at the expense of breadth. The brief sketches I included of every Supreme Court justice from John Jay to Stephen Breyer and the personal stories of the litigants in landmark cases took up space that a different author might have used for more case citations or doctrinal exposition. When you finish this book, I hope you will feel that you met some real people in its pages—some admirable, some not—and perhaps some whose examples you may follow in your own life. That, to me, is what our Constitution's history is about: the people whose lives have given it meaning over the years since it became our nation's charter.

Finally, let me thank some of the many people who helped make this book come to life. My agent, Sandy Dijkstra, found my editor, Jane von Mehren, whose meticulous and thoughtful editing has improved the book immeasurably. Bill Bookheim and Linda Weathers of the California Western Law School library were invariably helpful, as were Larry Cruse and Renata Coates of the

UCSD library. Jeff Fritsch and Mike O'Hagan solved the computer problems that seem to plague me more than anyone else I know. My discussions over the years with many colleagues—including Ken Karst, Michal Belknap, Glenn Smith, Nadine Strossen, and Harry Hirsch—planted seeds of thought that have finally sprouted in this book. I have also learned much from the works of scholars like Leonard Levy, Don Fehrenbacher, Richard Polenberg, Sanford Levinson, Mark Tushnet, G. Edward White, Richard Kluger, and David Garrow. On the home front, my wife, Bonnie Fox, took care of our two girls, twenty-odd pets, and me while I worked on this book. She is a wonderful person and shares the values that make my life meaningful. Our daughters, Haley and Maya, to whom this book is dedicated, are simply delightful. Now that "Daddy's book" is done, they will get more time with me, which makes all my work more rewarding.

SECTION I

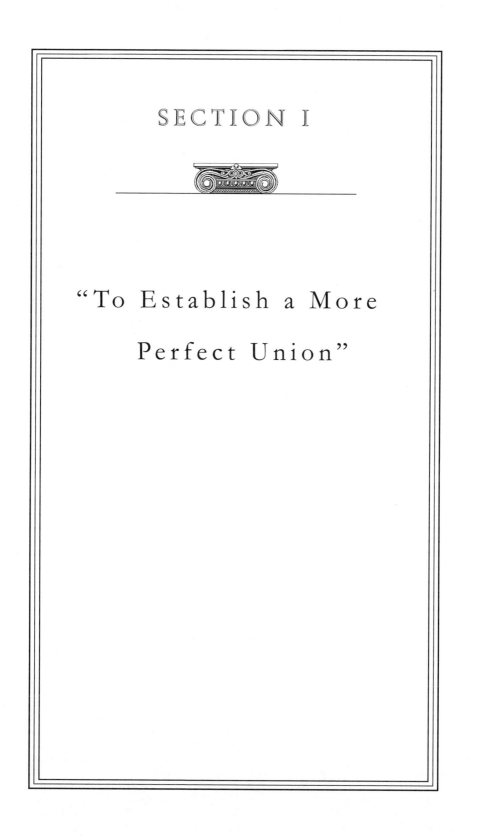

"To Establish a More
Perfect Union"

1

"Morally Sinful by the Word of God"

The Constitution of the United States was framed and ratified by men who had launched a successful revolution to free the American colonies from British rule. Throughout recorded history, most revolutionaries—those who succeed and those who fail alike—have been determined to uproot and replace the political and legal systems against which they fought at risk of life and property. The American revolutionaries were an exception to this general rule. They based their opposition to British rule not on rejection of British law but on the repeated failure of the king and his governors to abide by that law. In his final draft of the Declaration of Independence, Thomas Jefferson listed twenty-seven counts of an indictment of King George; thirteen accused the king of violating British law in subjecting the colonies to "tyranny." Jefferson pointed to "the free system of English laws" as the foundation of governments that derive "their just powers from the consent of the governed." The men who signed the Declaration were schooled in English law and simply wanted to rid the colonies of arbitrary enforcement of laws they had no voice in shaping.

British law came to the American colonies with the first settlers, most of whom brought with them a fierce determination to protect the rights of English "freemen" against the religious and political persecution that many had suffered as dissenters in their native land. Not all those who joined the growing wave of immigrants shared this respect for British law; some rejected entirely the notion of secular law and sought to impose on their fellow colonists a "theocracy" of biblical law, while others were "outlaws" who had been exiled for violating criminal or civil laws in England. But the colonists, in the main, wanted to retain the basic forms and substance of a legal system that had governed them and their forebears for centuries.

British law could not, of course, be lifted bodily from London and the

English counties and transplanted without change into "New" England or Maryland or Virginia or any other colonial province. Legal structures and rules that reflected the feudal system of land tenure and servitude in England could not easily be adapted to colonies in which land was plentiful and laborers could bargain with employers over terms of work and wages. Change was necessary, in law as well as in the social relations that law governed. At the same time, tradition had a powerful pull on the colonists who grew up under English law. They copied, often with little change, the complex and archaic system of English courts that enforced the system of royal justice: courts of common pleas, courts of chancery, courts of admiralty, and others with jurisdiction over special matters.

The colonists also brought with them a judicial system that gave local "justices of the peace" the authority to bring disputants before the bench and settle most criminal and civil matters. These judicial officers, of course, acted in the king's name and could enforce their judgments with the king's power. With few exceptions, they were men of means and stature who were chosen to hold the king's commission because they supported the monarchy and protected the "peace" of the community against dissent and disruption. However, these local justices knew most of the people who came before them and rarely applied the full force of the law against those whose transgressions did not threaten the fabric of the community. Most criminal sentences or civil judgments were modest and admonitory rather than harsh and crippling. One reason for this relative "softness" was that labor was scarce in the colonies and anyone willing and able to work was valuable to the community. The exceptions were punishments of those considered unrepentant or irredeemable, or whose crimes violated the biblical injunctions that had been enacted into law. For example, a few men in Massachusetts who were convicted of bestiality or buggery (the old term for homosexual sodomy) were executed, and a handful of women were whipped for bearing bastards. In these cases, sentences were imposed and executed by higher courts than local justices, whose jurisdiction was generally limited to misdemeanors.

Criminal law in the colonies varied from one jurisdiction to another, but in many respects it provided more rights to the accused than in the mother country. Most colonies allowed defendants to be represented by lawyers, a right not extended to English felony defendants until 1836. During the seventeenth and eighteenth centuries, colonial lawyers developed thriving criminal practices, and courtrooms were often packed with spectators who flocked to enjoy the thrust and parry of adversarial combat. Waitstill Avery, a prominent North Carolina lawyer, successfully defended Paul Crosby against a petty larceny charge and boasted in his diary that he was quickly "surrounded with a flood of clients and employed this term in no less than 30 actions."

The colonists also jealously protected their right to trial by jury, a practice often ignored or dismissed in England, where summary decisions by justices of the peace displaced a right first stated in the Magna Carta. Not all colonial defendants took advantage of this right, preferring (often with good reason) to place their fate in the hands of judges, who were usually educated and relatively impartial, thus avoiding the verdict of a jury of neighbors who knew, through direct observation or gossip, facts in the case that had not come out during trial. In addition, jurors could be influenced by their knowledge of the defendant's other (and usually unpunished) personal flaws and foibles.

On the other side of the ledger, local jurors could protect defendants who were clearly guilty from penalties that many felt were excessive, or from laws that jurors considered arbitrary and unfair. The practice of "jury nullification" of laws, against which judges and prosecutors have railed for centuries, took root in the colonies as a protest against unfair prosecutions by English officials. The most famous instance of nullification took place in 1735, when jurors in New York found John Peter Zenger not guilty of seditious libel. An outspoken newspaper publisher, Zenger had printed articles that accused colonial governor William Cosby of trampling on the legal rights of New York's residents. Zenger's lawyer, Andrew Hamilton, appealed to the jurors to disregard the direct instructions of Judge James Delaney (a political ally of Governor Cosby) that the "truth" of the published accusations was no defense under English law. The jurors heeded Hamilton's passionate argument and promptly acquitted Zenger, a verdict that not only set a precedent for later American law but also encouraged other appeals for jury nullification in cases of lesser import. Defending a client in a debt collection case in 1771, John Adams told jurors that if they disagreed with a judge's instructions on the law, each juror with "any feeling or conscience" should consider it "not only his right but his duty in that case to find the verdict according to his own best understanding, judgment and conscience, tho in direct opposition to the direction of the court."

Even though the colonists took pains to provide fair and impartial legal procedures for those accused of criminal behavior, the substance of their laws reflected the stern morality of their Puritan faith, tempered by concern for the rights of "freemen" to be treated equally. The settlers of Plymouth Colony enacted their first legal code in 1636, and were followed by their neighbors to the north in the Massachusetts Bay Colony, who adopted a "Body of Liberties" in 1641 that added protections for "freeman" to the Plymouth code. In many respects, these early legal codes foreshadowed the protections against arbitrary governmental power that were enshrined in the Constitution through adoption of the Bill of Rights in 1791, a century and a half later. The Body of Liberties spoke with the spirit, and even much of the language, of the Due Process Clause of the Fifth Amendment and of the Equal Protection Clause of the Fourteenth Amendment, which was not added to the Constitution until the nation had suffered a bloody Civil War.

Governor John Winthrop of Massachusetts Bay Colony delegated his friend Nathanial Ward to draft the Body of Liberties. Ward brought to this task ten years of experience as a lawyer in the common-law courts of England, but he later entered the ministry and served the Plymouth Bay town of Ipswich as a testy, outspoken Puritan pastor. He denounced from his pulpit and in pamphlets all dissenters from Puritan orthodoxy, warning them "to keep away from us; and such as will come, to be gone; the sooner the better." The document he drafted, and the colonists adopted to govern themselves, reflected the tension between Ward's secular and sectarian roles. The Body of Liberties first proclaimed the colonists' intention to provide "such liberties, immunities and privileges as humanity, civility, and Christianity call for as due to every man in his place and proportion" and to guarantee that these rights will be "impartially and inviolably enjoyed and observed throughout our jurisdiction for ever." In words that were later echoed in the Bill of Rights, the Body of Liberties pledged: "No man's life shall be taken away, no man's honor or good name shall be stained, no man's person shall be arrested, restrained, banished, dismembered, nor any ways punished, no man's goods or estate shall be taken away from him, nor in any way indamaged under color of law or countenance of authority, unless it be by virtue or equity of some express law of the country warranting the same. . . ." The colonists also promised: "Every person within this jurisdiction, whether inhabitant or foreigner shall enjoy the same justice and law, that is general for the plantation, which we constitute and execute one towards another without partiality or delay."

It would be hard to find a comparable legal code of that time, or even today in many parts of the world, that established in such clear terms the principles of fair and equal treatment that the Supreme Court only began to enforce for all Americans in the latter half of the twentieth century. The Body of Liberties even provided the protections now found in the Double Jeopardy Clause of the Fifth Amendment and the Cruel and Unusual Punishment Clause of the Eighth Amendment. The colonists stated: "No man shall be twice sentenced by civil justice for one and the same crime, offence, or trespass," and "For bodily punishments we allow amongst us none that are inhumane, barbarous or cruel."

However, in drafting those parts of the criminal code that set out "Capitall Crimes" and punishments, Nathaniel Ward abandoned the noble sentiments and legal protections of the English law and turned for guidance to the stern morality and severe penalties of the Mosaic Code in the Old Testament. In this respect, the Puritans of New England were heeding the admonition of John Calvin, the sixteenth-century Swiss preacher and theologian to whose writings they looked for guidance. Calvin wrote in 1559: "God hath put the sword into the hands of magistrates to suppress crimes against . . . the law of God." The Puritans feared the God of vengeance more than they sought the warmth of the God of forgiveness. Ward heeded the admonition of Governor Winthrop to base the laws on "the fundamentals which God gave to the Commonwealth of Israel" in the biblical commands to Moses. Stating his purpose as punishing "anything that can be proved to be morally sinful by the word of God," Ward took pains to note in the margin of each provision of the criminal code he drafted the book, chapter, and verse in the Bible that gave divine sanction to the crime and punishment in the Puritan code.

Ward began his listing of capital crimes not with murder but with the most serious affront to Puritan orthodoxy, that of idolatry: "If any man after legal conviction shall have or worship any other god, but the lord god, he shall be put to death." The biblical citations that Ward provided for this provision included the verses in Chapter 17 of Deuteronomy in which Moses told the Israelites that any person who has "served other gods and worshipped them" shall be brought before the people "and you shall stone them to death." In a break with biblical commands, the Puritans recoiled from this form of execution and substituted hanging from a public gallows.

Second on the list of capital crimes was witchcraft, a law applied with a vengeance in the Puritan town of Salem in 1692. Nathaniel Ward had warned in his preaching and pamphlets against "Familists," by which he meant those who communed in their worship not with the "Lord God" of the Bible but with "familiar spirits" who were considered to be the Devil's agents on earth. The law he drafted stated: "If any man or woman be a witch (that is, hath or consulteth with a familiar spirit), they shall be put to death." There was more than a whiff of misogyny in Ward's attacks on witchcraft; all but one of those accused in Salem and other towns of consulting with "familiar spirits" were women. The records in the witchcraft cases suggest that their crimes had less to do with biblical injunctions against "sorcery" or "calling up the dead" than with challenges to male control of the Puritan faith and state, which subjugated women to men in churches and government. Whether or not he foresaw its consequences, the witchcraft law that Ward drafted led to the executions of nineteen women, who were all hanged, and one man, Giles Corey, who was pressed to death with heavy stones.

The Puritan obsession with "familiar spirits" and witchcraft did not, of course, set the New England colonies apart from England and continental Europe in the sixteenth and seventeenth centuries. Periodic frenzies of "witch trials" resulted in the executions, often by burning at the stake, of hundreds—perhaps thousands—of suspected and actual "witches." There is evidence that some women in Salem did practice various kinds of "witchcraft" by performing occult rituals and casting spells. But most of those accused were girls and young women who were simply the victims of religious paranoia and fanaticism. The fact that witchcraft was made a capital crime in the Body of Liberties reflected the Puritan zeal to extirpate every dissident and unorthodox religious practice, in particular those led by women who challenged the male control of church and state.

The Body of Liberties also prescribed capital punishment for sexual practices that were condemned in the Mosaic Code. Nathaniel Ward included bestiality, homosexual sodomy, and adultery as crimes punishable by death. Again, the marginal citations to Old Testament books provided biblical sanction. Executions for these sexual crimes were infrequent, but a few offenders did suffer the ultimate penalty; one young man was hung for having sex with a sheep, and the animal was also killed, as both the Bible and the Puritan law required. The records of the colony show that although prosecutions for fornication and adultery were common, penalties were generally light and only two married persons were executed for this crime. Today, many Americans are shocked and sickened by news accounts of public executions in countries such as Afghanistan or Saudia Arabia, often carried out by stoning or beheading, for crimes such as adultery and homosexual sodomy. We tend to forget that those Islamic countries that have enacted the religious law of the Koran into their criminal codes are separated only by time and distance from the religious moralists of the New England colonies.

Looking at the Body of Liberties as a whole, and the records of the colonial courts, it is clear that the Puritans did not intend or attempt to create a literal "New Jerusalem" in New England. Incorporating much of the Mosaic Code into law served more to impress upon the residents of this wilderness outpost their need to "purify" their lives than to exact the biblical sanctions in every case. Holding in reserve the ultimate penalty of death, and its occasional use as a warning to others, served the function of social control in a society based on outward conformity but with fairly high levels of "morally sinful" behavior. The work of modern historians shows that many colonists, even those who sat through endless Puritan sermons, were just as likely to violate the social and sexual taboos of their "Bible-based" society as are contemporary Americans, despite the extreme penalties they faced for their transgressions.

The criminal laws and penalties of the New England colonies, at least in the statute books, were more harsh than those of other colonies. But they were decidedly less severe than those of England, where in the seventeenth century more than a hundred crimes were punishable by death. In this area of law, factors such as the need for labor, the absence of rigid social roles based on feudal distinctions between "serfs" and "lords," and the granting of "freeman" status to most males who owned some property, produced in the colonies a greater emphasis on community norms of behavior and shared religious beliefs. The civil laws and court procedures of the colonies also reflected a more fluid and egalitarian social structure than that of England, where feudal laws of inheritance, land tenure, and commercial transactions had created and maintained an archaic legal system more suited for the Middle Ages than for a time of exploration, expansion, and emigration. The American colonies, in contrast to the mother country to whose monarchs the colonists swore allegiance, believed in the promise of the Body of Liberties of Massachusetts Bay that "every person shall enjoy the same justice and law."

The promise of equal justice, however, extended only to the "freemen" of the colonies. This favored group, in fact, made up only a small minority of the colonial population. The ranks of freemen were generally limited to white males who owned some property and who belonged to the dominant religious denomination of the colony. In short, the freemen were the precursors of the WASP (or White Anglo-Saxon Protestant) elite that owned and operated American business, government, and culture for more than three centuries, and that still maintains a disproportionate share of power in these areas. In the process of taking power for themselves, the freemen of colonial America consciously employed the legal system to keep the members of other groups in subordinate roles. Four groups in particular were excluded from the ranks of "every person" to whom the colonists gave their promise of equal justice. Those who received less justice—in some cases, none at all—included religious dissenters, women, African slaves, and the Indians who occupied the land before the colonists arrived.

There is a powerful irony in the disparity between the myth of colonial America as a haven for religious dissenters from the orthodoxy of the Church of England and the reality of intolerance toward those who challenged the new orthodoxy of the colonists. It was an awareness of this irony, and a revulsion at religious intolerance, that prompted the men who framed the Bill of Rights to provide in the First Amendment that Congress "shall make no law respecting an establishment of religion, or prohibiting the free exercise thereof." During the century and a half that separated the Body of Liberties of the Massachusetts Bay Colony from the adoption of the Bill of Rights in 1791, religious conflict affected virtually every village and town in every colony.

Two episodes in Massachusetts illustrate the divisive effects of religious intolerance. The first was the expulsion of Roger Williams from the colony in 1636, which led to the establishment of the new colony of Rhode Island. Williams had come to Boston in 1631 as a Puritan pastor; he soon became minister of the church in Salem. During his formative years in England, Williams studied under the great jurist Edward Coke, who defended both political and religious freedom within the narrow confines of laws against "seditious libel." Williams became a controversial figure in Salem, from whose pulpit he denounced the notion that civil authorities could enforce religious edicts. These views so offended his parishioners and the political leaders of the colony that Williams left Salem after a few months for the relative tolerance of the church in Plymouth, where he continued his attacks on the Puritan theocracy. "Let any man show me a commission given by the Son of God to civil powers in these spiritual affairs of His Christian kingdom and worship," Williams demanded in a pamphlet that enraged Puritan leaders. For this heresy, the General Court of Massachusetts expelled Williams from their midst.

The second religious dissident was poles apart from Roger Williams in theology, but equally a threat to Puritan orthodoxy. Williams was, in some ways, more of a Puritan than those who condemned and expelled him. He argued against admitting to worship those "unregenerant" Puritans who attended Church of England services on visits to England. Anne Hutchinson, on the other hand, resisted Puritan worship altogether. She held services in her home and preached to those who attended her "study" sessions—mostly women— the heretical doctrines that salvation comes through grace and not through work, and that the Holy Spirit can dwell within every person through individual revelation. Despite her social prominence—her husband was a close friend and ally of Governor John Winthrop—Anne Hutchinson so directly challenged Puritan orthodoxy that she found herself facing trial before the General Court in 1637, with Governor Winthrop as the chief prosecutor and interrogator.

The transcript of this historic trial offers an insight into the conflict between individual conscience and state power that continues to divide Americans. Far more knowledgeable than Winthrop on biblical scripture, Hutchinson continually bested him in debates over fine points of theology. She turned the tables on Winthrop, questioning him so relentlessly that he finally admitted that Hutchinson had biblical support for the main charge against her, that of preaching a doctrine of personal revelation of God's word. "How did Abraham know that it was God that bid him offer his son" for sacrifice? she demanded to know from Winthrop. "By an immediate voice," he responded. Hutchinson pounced on the governor. "So to me by an immediate revelation," she said of her views on salvation by grace. "By the voice of his own spirit to my soul." Winthrop was so enraged at falling into Hutchinson's trap that he quickly called a vote on the heresy charges and secured a conviction with only three dissents. The penalty was banishment from the colony. Anne Hutchinson and John Winthrop had one last exchange. "I desire to know wherefore I am banished," she asked. The governor's answer spoke volumes about colonial limits on the rule of law. "Say no more," Winthrop replied; "the court knows wherefore and is satisfied." Anne Hutchinson left the colony in 1637 and settled in Rhode Island, the tiny outpost of religious tolerance in New England.

The expulsions of Roger Williams and Anne Hutchinson took place early in the colonial era, and they exemplify the extremes of religious intolerance in the most intolerant colony. By the time of the Revolution, advocates of toleration spoke with louder voices and demanded the "disestablishment" of the churches that controlled most of the colonies. James Madison of Virginia, the primary author of the Bill of Rights, deserves the greatest credit for moving the country toward religious toleration of dissenters. In 1774, Madison wrote to a friend that the "diabolical, hell-conceived principle of persecution rages among some" in Virginia. "There are at this time in the adjacent county not less than five or six well-meaning men in close jail, for publishing their religious sentiments, which in the main are very orthodox. . . . I have squabbled and scolded, abused and ridiculed so long about it, that I am without common patience."

Madison continued his crusade for religious toleration through the Revolution and into the period of independence. His patience was still taxed by efforts of the Church of England in Virginia, renamed the Episcopal Church, to retain its status as the established denomination. Working closely with his friend and mentor Thomas Jefferson, Madison drafted and the Virginia legislature enacted in 1785 "An Act Establishing Religious Freedom." The law provided that "no man shall be compelled to frequent or support any religious worship, place, or ministry whatever, ... nor shall otherwise suffer on account of his religious opinions or belief; but that all men shall be free to profess, and by argument to maintain, their opinions in matters of religion, and that the same shall in no wise diminish, enlarge, or affect their civil capacities." Jefferson later wrote that Madison's law was "meant to comprehend within the mantle of its protection the Jew and the Gentile, the Christian and Mahometan, the Hindu and Infidel of every denomination."

Jefferson's words reveal an attitude toward religious diversity that the Puritans had totally rejected. But it took another century and a half before the Supreme Court first began to enforce Madison's crowning achievement, the religion clauses of the First Amendment. And even today, despite Jefferson's words, Jews and Muslims, Hindus and atheists, the "infidels" of our time, face hostility in communities across the country in which latter-day Puritans try to enforce their opposition to "anything that can be proved to be morally sinful by the word of God."

The exclusion of women from government, church, and the courts did not set the colonies apart from England, or from any other country at that time. Their legal status as "wards" of husbands stemmed from centuries of English common law and biblical precepts that reflected male domination of every institution in society. Saint Paul laid down as Christian doctrine in his letter to the Ephesians the attitude toward women that became written into English and colonial law: "Wives, be subject to your own husbands, as to the Lord. For the husband is the head of the wife, as Christ also is the head of the church, He himself being the Savior of the body. But as the church is subject to Christ, so also the wives ought to be to the husbands in everything."

The legal term for the status of married women was "coverture," which meant that wives were "covered" by their husbands in all areas of life, especially the control of property. With few exceptions, husbands could buy and sell property of any kind, real or personal, without the wife's permission. In turn, wives could rely on courts to force husbands to provide them with the necessities of food, clothing, and shelter. An English resolution, submitted to Parliament in 1632 at the time of the Puritan settlement of Plymouth Bay, set out "women's rights" in these terms: "Eve, because she had helped to seduce her husband, had inflicted upon her a special bane. See here the reason ... that women have no voice in Parliament. They make no laws, they consent to none, they abrogate none. All of them are understood either married, or to be married, and their desires are to their husbands. The common laws here shaketh hands with divinity."

In one respect the laws of most colonies provided women with a right not shared by their sisters in England. Although a Protestant country, England retained the Catholic attitude toward divorce and made it virtually impossible to obtain. Perhaps because of Puritan abhorrence of Catholicism, the Plymouth Bay colony and most others allowed for divorce in cases of adultery and desertion. The Connecticut law of 1656 provided that "if any married person [be] proved an adulterer or an adulteress, . . . a separation or divorce shall, by sentence of the Court of Magistrates, be granted and published, and the innocent party shall in such case have liberty to marry again. . . . That if any husband shall, without consent, or just cause shown, willfully desert his wife, or the wife her husband, . . . the husband or wife so deserted may justly seek and expect help and relief, according to I Corinthians 7:15." The reference in this law to Saint Paul's command that if an "unbelieving" spouse leaves a "believer" in Christ, "the brother or the sister is not under bondage in such cases" reflects again the colonial coupling of law and scripture, even though most colonists regarded marriage as a civil contract, with legal remedies available for its breach.

The court records of the colonies show both the legal status of women as a form of property and regard for their well-being in cases of husbandly neglect or abuse. The Plymouth Bay court in 1659 ordered "the wife of John Spring of Watertown," who had deserted him several years earlier, "to return with all convenient speed to her husband. . . . In case she shall refuse to attend this order, the court will take a speedy course to send her to her said husband." On the other side, a jury in the same court in 1666 found that John Williams had defamed his wife, Elizabeth, by calling her a "whore" and ruled, "It is not safe or convenient for her to live with her husband, and gives her liberty at present to depart from him. . . . The court orders him to apparel her suitably at the present, to furnish her with a bed and bedding and such like necessaries, and to give her ten pounds yearly while she shall be thus absent from him."

The voices of women who chafed under the bonds of paternalism in the colonial period were few and faint. Even Abigail Adams, the strong-willed wife of John Adams, the revolutionary leader and future president, confined her feminist complaints to letters to her husband. Shortly before John Adams helped in drafting the Declaration of Independence in 1776, Abigail wrote to him: "I long to hear that you have declared an independency—and by the way, in the new code of laws which I suppose it will be necessary for you to make I desire you would remember the ladies, and be more generous and favorable to them than your ancestors. Do not put such unlimited power into the hands of the husbands. Remember, all men would be tyrants if they could. If particular care and attention is not paid to the ladies we are determined to foment a rebellion, and will not hold ourselves bound by any laws in which we have no voice and no representation."

This early (and private) appeal for women's suffrage fell on deaf ears. After the Revolution, the legal status of women slowly improved, particularly in the reformation of property laws. The New York legislature passed a law in 1849 that discarded the doctrine of coverture and provided that "Any married female may . . . convey and devise real and personal property, and any interest on estate therein, and the rents, issues and profits thereof in same manner and with like effect as if she were unmarried." But women were still denied a voice in making the laws until Congress and the states amended the Constitution in 1920 and granted women the right to vote. And not until 1971 did the Supreme Court, in striking down a state law that gave preference to men over women in administering estates, rule that women were covered by the Equal Protection Clause that granted legal rights to former slaves.

Slaves, of course, had no legal rights in colonial America. They were ruled by law, but they had no recourse to the courts to enforce the rights that white "freemen" enjoyed. The importation of Africans into the colonies began in 1619 (some accounts say 1620) with the arrival in Virginia of a "Dutch man of war" that carried a cargo of twenty blacks. These first African Americans were not, in fact, brought as slaves but as indentured servants, who would be freed after serving their masters for a term of years. Some of these early black arrivals later showed up on the colony's rolls as free men. Although court records and statutes in Virginia and other southern colonies mentioned blacks in the forty years after 1619, their legal status was unclear before 1659, when the Virginia legislature first passed laws that used the term "slave" and applied it solely to blacks. After that time, virtually all blacks imported into the colonies arrived as slaves and were generally sold at auction.

The differences between northern and southern colonies over the legal status of blacks were slight, since all the colonies (even the Quaker colony of Pennsylvania) accepted the institution of slavery. The colonies differed largely in the number of persons held in slavery and the harshness of the southern "black codes" that provided for the whipping and execution of slaves who tried to escape or had the audacity to disobey or assault their owners or other white people. The Body of Liberties of Massachusetts Bay colony stated in 1641: "There shall never be any bond slavery . . . amongst us unless it be lawful captives taken in just wars, and such strangers as shall willingly sell themselves or are sold to us." These loopholes, of course, allowed for slavery in Massachusetts, and the colonial census of 1754 listed 2,445 black slaves over sixteen years of age. At that time, slaves made up almost 20 percent of the male laborers in New York City and Philadelphia.

The southern colonies had far more slaves than their northern neighbors and far more problems with "refractory" slaves who resisted their masters. The "black codes" of the South were designed to keep slaves "in their place" by force and violence. The Virginia legislature passed a law in 1669 that acknowledged the difficulty of dealing with "the obstinacy of many of them by other than violent means" and provided that "if any slave resist his master . . . and by the extremity of the correction should chance to die," the owner would be "acquit from molestation" and suffer no penalty. Southern colonists also feared, with some reason, that their slaves might plot or actually rebel against their condition. To prevent and punish such rebellions, the Virginia legislature provided in 1723 that "if any number of negroes" shall "consult, advise, or conspire, to rebel or make insurrection, . . . they shall suffer death."

Surprisingly, one of the harshest applications of law against slaves took place not in the South but in New York City in 1741. The greatest danger in the cities of that time was fire, since most buildings were constructed of wood and firefighting equipment was rudimentary. A series of eight fires in the span of five days spread fear throughout the city, and suspicion centered on a group of slaves who congregated at an alehouse on the waterfront. After a roundup of slaves and quick trials, thirteen blacks were convicted of "treason" and burned at the stake, sixteen slaves were hanged for arson (along with four whites), and another seventy blacks were banished from the colony. The fevered reaction to the supposed Slave Conspiracy of 1741, particularly in the convictions and executions for "treason" against masters, illustrated the role of law in keeping slaves in subjugation.

The institution of slavery, and the "black codes" that enforced white rule, endured for almost a century after the Declaration of Independence proclaimed that "all men are created equal" and are equally endowed with the rights of life and liberty. Even after the Thirteenth Amendment to the Constitution abolished slavery and the Fourteenth Amendment extended the "equal protection of the laws" to the former slaves, the Supreme Court in the 1880s and 1890s struck down civil rights laws and upheld the Jim Crow laws that replaced the "black codes" of the colonial era. The legacy of slavery and efforts to redress its impact on African Americans continue to divide Americans, including those nine Americans who sit on the Supreme Court.

The people who received the worst treatment from the Puritans and other colonial settlers, and the least protection from their laws, were the Native Americans—known as "Indians" at the time, because Columbus was searching for India in 1492. From the very beginning of English settlement, relations between the Indians and settlers were marked by conflict. Even during times of relative peace and accommodation, the relentless search for new lands by the settlers created animosity on both sides, which flared into open warfare that lasted more than three centuries before the last resisting Indians finally succumbed to armed force near the end of the nineteenth century. The schoolbook myth of Pilgrims living in peaceful harmony with their Indian neighbors, sharing Thanksgiving feasts and native festivals, illustrates the fact that official history is written by the winners. Indians were the losers in virtually every battle with the colonists who forced them from their lands.

The first English settlers in Virginia built their village of Jamestown in the midst of an Indian confederacy led by Chief Powhatan. During the brutal winter of 1610, the "starving time" for the English, Powhatan maintained an attitude of coolness toward the settlers, but his people fed the whites who fled into the wilderness in search of food. When the governor asked Powhatan the next summer to return the refugees, he replied—according to the English account— with "noe other than prowde and disdaynefull Answers." The governor then sent English soldiers "to take Revendge" on the Indians. They burned an Indian village, cut down the corn around it, killed fifteen or sixteen Indians, forced the tribe's queen and her children into boats, and then threw the children overboard and took sport in "shoteinge owtt their Braynes in the water." After this massacre, the Indians waited twelve years before exacting their own revenge, killing 347 English settlers in a bloody rampage through the colony.

From that time on, open warefare raged between the Indians and colonists. A noted historian of the colonial period wrote of the English response to the 1622 massacre: "Since the Indians were better woodsmen than the English and virtually impossible to track down, the method was to feign peaceful intentions, let them settle down and plant their corn wherever they chose, and then, just before harvest, fall upon them, killing as many as possible and burning the corn. . . . Within two or three years of the massacre the English had avenged the deaths of that day many times over."

The settlers of Plymouth Bay colony waged their own wars against the Indians with equal violence, fueled by biblical conviction that God had given the land to them. The Puritans employed the legal fiction that land on which Indians grew crops was "virgin" land because the Indians did not use proper (that is, English) methods of farming. In reality, the Indians employed a slash-and-burn agriculture better suited to the land than English plowing and planting. Governor John Winthrop, however, argued that because the Indians had not "subdued" the land for fields and meadows, the entire colony was legally a "vacuum" and that Indians had only a "natural" right to their lands and not a "civil right" that could be legally enforced. The Puritan settlers poured into this "vacuum" and took legal title to lands they "purchased" from Indians with deeds that were full of archaic English legal terms the Indians did not understand. The greatest source of misunderstanding was over the English concept of absolute possession of property. English common law provided that holders of land in "fee simple" could evict and prosecute any trespasser. Indians believed they had only given the colonists in these deeds the right to hunt and "traverse" the land, not to make permanent settlements. Over this legal misunderstanding—which the colonists did nothing to erase—much blood was shed on both sides.

Conflicts with the Pequot Indians of southern New England simmered until 1636, when the murder of a white trader accused of kidnapping Indians led Governor Winthrop to give his troops a "commission to put to death" the Indian men of Block Island and to seize "some of their children as hostages" for the surrender of the murderers. The Puritan soldiers not only killed the Pequot men of Block Island but went up and down the coast of Long Island Sound, burning villages and crops. Winthrop's military commander, Captain John Mason, decided to avoid facing Pequot warriors in open combat and instead to burn all the villages and massacre those who could not escape. William Bradford, former governor of the colony, celebrated the results in these words: "Those that scaped the fire were slaine with the sword; some hewed to peeces, others rune throw with their rapiers, so as they were quickly dispatchte, and very few escaped. It was conceived they thus destroyed about 400 at this time. It was a fearful sight to see them thus frying in the fyer, and the streams of blood quenching the same, and horrible was the stincke and sente there of, but the victory seemed a sweete sacrifice, and they gave the prayers thereof to God, who had wrought so wonderfuly for them, thus to inclose their enemise in their hands, and give them so speedy a victory over so proud and insulting an enemie."

The colonial period ended with another bloody war, this one waged by rebellious colonists against their English rulers. Ironically, the colonists who had deprived most of the population—religious dissenters, women, slaves, and Indians—of legal rights and voices in governance based their Declaration of Independence on pious claims that "all men are created equal" and that governments must derive "their just powers from the consent of the governed." Those who drafted and signed this solemn declaration in 1776 firmly believed in its principles and protestations, but they were all white men of property who simply did not comprehend that people unlike them had been equally "endowed by their Creator" with the same "inalienable rights" they claimed for themselves. And so, when another group of white men of property met in Philadelphia in 1787 to draft a constitution for the United States, they brought to this task the same lack of comprehension. The dispossessed and disenfranchised groups that had no voices in the Constitutional Convention were forced to wait almost two centuries until their own declarations of independence were heard—if not always heeded—by the Supreme Court.

2

"The Exigencies of the Union"

On May 14, 1787, a dozen men gathered at the red-brick State House in Philadelphia, Pennsylvania. This was the same building in which another group of
men assembled in 1776 and signed a Declaration of Independence that set in
motion the revolution against English rule. Seven years of war had sapped the
strength and resolve of British troops and their military and political leaders,
and the rebellious American colonies won their independence in 1783. But the
victorious revolutionaries, united in their rejection of English "tyranny," had
not united to replace the thirteen colonies with a new nation. All they had accomplished was to form a "confederation" of thirteen sovereign states, each
one jealous of its prerogatives and unwilling to relinquish any of its powers to a
national government.

The men who gathered at the State House in 1787 were keenly aware of the
failure of the Articles of Confederation, which had been ratified in 1781, to
bind the thirteen states into a workable union. The "United States" of the Confederation were anything but united. The Articles did nothing more than establish "a firm league of friendship" among the states. But in the six years since
they formed this league, the states had acted in decidedly unfriendly ways
toward one another. They fought over trade and commerce, over recognition of
their separate currencies, over boundaries between the states, over the creation
of new states in the burgeoning western territories. In short, they acted more
like quarreling European principalities than like "united states" with common
purposes. The Confederation had been created in reaction to the arbitrary rule
of a powerful government, but the men who drafted and ratified the Articles of
Confederation erred in the opposite direction: the government they designed
was weak, divided, and unable to resolve conflicts between warring interests and
regions.

The flaws in the Articles were built into the governmental structure they created. Each state retained "its sovereignty, freedom and independence, and every power, jurisdiction, and right, which is not by this Confederation expressly delegated to the United States, in Congress assembled." The only powers that the drafters had delegated to the Confederation Congress were those to conduct foreign affairs, make treaties, and declare war. These were powers that no individual state could exercise by itself, although political leaders in each state continued to squabble over the ways in which Congress conducted the nation's foreign affairs. Congress itself was an ineffective governing body. Members did not vote by themselves; each state had one vote, and nine of the thirteen states had to agree on each piece of legislation. The drafters of the Articles, determined to avoid lodging power in a single executive, created instead a president of Congress, who had no power to enforce the laws passed by its members. No state, in fact, was required to abide by the decisions of Congress; they were, in effect, merely advisory, and states often rejected that advice. The Articles also did not provide for a national judiciary; there was no body to adjudicate conflicts between states or citizens of different states. The drafters, in understandable reaction to the tyrannical rule against which they revolted, had replaced one of the strongest governments in the Western world with one of the weakest.

Well before the 1787 meeting in Philadelphia, leaders of the emerging "Federalist" bloc in politics began to criticize the ineffective Confederation and to call for revision of the Articles. Noah Webster, who had served in the revolutionary army and who was a lawyer as well as a lexicographer, wrote in 1785: "So long as any individual state has power to defeat the measures of the other twelve, our pretended union is but a name, and our confederation, a cobweb." John Jay, who later served as the first Chief Justice of the United States, expressed his fears of disunion to George Washington: "Our affairs seem to lead to some crisis, some revolution—something I cannot see or conjecture. I am uneasy and apprehensive; moreso than during the war." Whatever their concerns about the deficiencies of the Confederation, however, few men of stature wanted to scrap the Articles entirely; most agreed with Benjamin Franklin, widely admired for his wit and wisdom, that "we discover some errors in our general and particular constitutions; which it is no wonder they should have, the time in which they were formed being considered. But these we shall mend."

Despite Franklin's optimism, "mending" the Articles would not be an easy task. First, all thirteen states had to agree on any amendment of the Articles. The prospects for unanimous agreement on any proposal to expand the powers of Congress or to create executive or judicial branches of government were slim. Second, the interests of the separate states, divided by geography along northern and southern lines and by population into larger and smaller, had diverged so rapidly since the Articles were ratified that further division seemed more likely than unification. Few men, however, saw much harm in meeting to discuss possible revisions of the Articles; unanimity might be forged on proposals to "mend" those parts that most leaders thought amenable to minor revision. There were, to be sure, men in various states who desired a strong "federal" government, but they were by no means a majority in numbers or influence. Between 1785 and 1787, those who advocated a convention to revise the Articles of Confederation assured skeptics that they had no larger agenda than tinkering and talk.

As the weaknesses of the Articles became more evident, and as pressure built for a convention to revise them, one of the oldest laws of politics began to operate. Those who are most satisfied with the status quo, which in the Confederation era meant those who felt that the states should remain "sovereign" and only loosely federated, generally sit back and let the "hotheads" blow off steam. Conversely, those who desire rapid and radical change often conceal their designs behind clouds of soothing rhetoric, until they feel confident that they can control events. This law operated perfectly in 1787. James Madison, the scholarly young Virginian whose designs would powerfully shape both the new Constitution and the Bill of Rights that followed its ratification, shared his real views with his friend and fellow Virginian George Washington: "Temporizing applications will dishonor the Councils which propose them, and may foment the internal malignity of the disease. . . . Radical attempts, though unsuccessful, will at least justify the authors of them." But Madison wrote in disarming words to Edmund Randolph, Virginia's governor and an opponent of any major alteration of the Articles: "I think with you that it will be well to retain as much as possible of the old Confederation, though I doubt whether it may not be best to work the valuable articles into the new system, instead of engrafting the latter on the former."

James Madison had begun hatching plans for a new constitution long before he arrived in Philadelphia in May 1787. Born in 1751, the eldest of ten children, Madison grew up on a Virginia plantation whose fields were plowed and planted by slaves. From early childhood, he buried himself in books and relished talk of philosophy and public affairs. Madison's father sent him north for an education at the College of New Jersey, later known as Princeton. Here the young scholar came under the tutelage of John Witherspoon, a Presbyterian minister who drilled his students in the writings of David Hume, the Scottish philosopher who argued for the "utilitarian" principle of promoting "the greatest good for the greatest number." Witherspoon also preached against slavery in passionate sermons; Madison later echoed his teacher in the Philadelphia convention when he denounced slavery as "the most oppressive dominion ever exercised by man over man." He also told the delegates that he "thought it wrong to admit in the Constitution the idea that there could be property in men." But the "utility" of the Constitution outweighed his personal moral views, and Madison signed a document that recognized slavery as a lawful institution.

The Philadelphia convention actually grew out of a meeting at George

Washington's estate at Mount Vernon in 1785. Disputes over fishing and navigation rights along the Potomac River, down to its outlet in Chesapeake Bay, had created tensions between all four states—Maryland, Virginia, Pennsylvania, and Delaware—bordering those waterways. The colonial grant to Lord Baltimore in 1632 had given Maryland all of the Potomac, up to the high-water point on Virginia's side. The conflict over the "oyster war" dragged on for years, before and after the Revolution, and the Continental Congress did nothing to settle the dispute. Finally, representatives from all four states met at Mount Vernon, hoping that Washington could lend his name and prestige to a settlement. But the meeting did not succeed, and those who attended resolved to met with delegates from all the other states at Annapolis, Maryland, in September 1786. The Virginia legislature invited the other states to send delegates to "take into consideration the trade of the states" and to draft, if possible, a "uniform system in their commercial regulations."

Not enough delegates showed up in Annapolis to make up a quorum, and nothing was done to end the "oyster war" along Chesapeake Bay. But the delegates who did attend passed a resolution, urged by James Madison and Alexander Hamilton, a wealthy lawyer and strong Federalist from New York, calling upon all state legislatures to send delegates to another meeting to consider "the situation of the United States" and to "devise such further provisions as shall appear to them necessary to render the constitution of the federal government adequate to the exigencies of the Union." The Annapolis delegates set the meeting time for the second Monday of May 1787 and the place in Philadelphia. Whether enough states would send delegates to yet another meeting was far from certain.

James Madison was the first delegate to arrive in Philadelphia for the meeting to "devise" alterations to the Articles of Confederation. During the preceding months, he had buried himself in books, reading widely in political philosophy and histories of republics and confederacies from ancient Greece to the current states of Europe, with special attention to the Swiss Confederation of independent cantons and the United Provinces of the Netherlands. Madison filled one notebook with his gleanings on the topic "Of Ancient and Modern Confederacies," and another with a list of the "Vices of the Political System of the United States." Not a single delegate arrived in Philadelphia after Madison who matched him in knowledge of the world's governments and constitutions, or with equal determination to frame a new system that would forge the disunited states of America into a real federal union, one with powers "adequate to the exigencies of the Union."

Madison not only had ideas about the new system he envisioned, but he had a plan. While delegates from other states were trickling into Philadelphia, Madison shared his plan with Washington, who arrived a few days later. Determined to create a strong national government, but also aware that the states would not willingly cede their cherished "sovereignty" over their own affairs, Madison wrote to Washington: "I have sought for some middle ground, which may at once support a due supremacy of the national authority, and not exclude the local authorities wherever they can be subordinately useful." Both the sentence structure and choice of words left no doubt of Madison's views on the primacy of federal power. He underscored this position in telling Washington that his plan would invest the federal government "with positive and complete authority in all cases which require uniformity; such as the regulation of trade, including the right of taxing both exports and imports." Madison then confided to Washington that his plan would place, "over and above this positive power, a negative in all cases whatsoever on the legislative acts of the states. . . . Without this defensive power, every positive power that can be given on paper will be evaded and defeated." This was a radical—even revolutionary—proposal that would in effect reduce the "sovereign" states to a subordinate role in the new federal system.

The convention resolution of the Virginia legislature had set a quorum of seven states to begin deliberations. Eleven days passed between the opening session on May 14 and the first official session on May 25, when the quorum was finally met with twenty-nine delegates from seven states in attendance. During this time, Madison met almost daily with his fellow Virginians, whose seven members formed the largest delegation. He circulated among them copies of the fourteen points in his plan for a new government. His first, and most delicate, task was to convince Edmund Randolph, the powerful and persuasive Virginia governor, to set aside his objections to a new constitution. Madison won Randolph over with a brilliant strategem, allowing him to add to the "Virginia Plan" a fifteenth resolution, elevated to first place above Madison's fourteen. Randolph proposed, and Madison accepted, a resolution that "the Articles of Confederation ought to be so corrected and enlarged as to accomplish the objects proposed by their institution; namely, 'common defense, security of liberty and general welfare.' " This was decidedly *not* what Madison had in mind, but he viewed Randolph's resolution as harmless and his support of the other fourteen as essential.

With that strategic concession in hand, Madison prevailed on Randolph to introduce the Virginia Plan as soon as the convention elected officers and adopted rules. One May 25, the delegates unanimously elected George Washington as the presiding officer, and he took his seat in a high-backed mahogany chair behind a table covered in green baize. Washington assumed a tone of humility in telling the delegates that he "lamented his want of better qualifications, and claimed the indulgence of the House towards the involuntary errors which his inexperience might occasion."

Washington's words were recorded by Madison, although the delegates had elected William Jackson of Pennsylvania as secretary. Madison had decided to keep his own account of the proceedings, later explaining that he was not "unaware of the value of such a contribution to the fund of materials for the history of a Constitution on which would be staked the happiness of a people great even in its infancy, and possibly the cause of liberty throughout the world." To record the debates, Madison wrote, "I chose a seat in front of the presiding member" and from "this favorable position for hearing all that passed, I noted in terms legible and in abbreviations and marks intelligible to myself what was read from the chair or spoken by the members." Madison's *Notes of Debates in the Federal Convention of 1787*, recorded in his spidery handwriting, covered more than six hundred printed pages when published in 1840, four years after his death at eighty-six, the last surviving delegate, who once wryly commented that "I may be thought to have outlived myself." Madison had resisted every entreaty to publish his notes, feeling himself bound—until all had died—to protect his fellow delegates from attacks on what they may have said on one day and repented or regretted on another.

Madison also carried to his grave the rule adopted by the convention that "nothing spoken in the House be printed, or otherwise published or communicated without leave." Only one delegate slipped from the secrecy rule, dropping a copy of convention proceedings on the floor outside the chamber. They were returned to Washington, who dramatically threw the document onto his table. "I know not whose paper it is, but there it is. Let him who owns it take it." The miscreant did not come forward, but there were no further breaches of the secrecy rule. No delegate wished to risk the general's wrath again.

The secrecy rule produced much discomfort among the delegates, as the State House windows were sealed during convention sessions to prevent eavesdropping and the Philadelphia summer of 1787 was sweltering. But the rule had the salutary effect—as Madison recognized in protecting his notes from publication—of allowing delegates to voice opinions, float proposals, and cast votes they would later alter or abandon. Edmund Randolph's opening speech on the Virginia Plan, delivered with the gestures and flourishes of the practiced orator, set the standard for this changeable pattern. He first enumerated "the defects of the confederation" and of its Articles; he later played an active role in drafting what he described as a "fundamental constitution" to replace the Articles; and he finally refused to sign the document that emerged from the convention's four months of deliberation.

The Virginia Plan that Randolph presented to the convention drew upon Madison's exhaustive study of other governments, and his conviction that a strong federal system required a dispersal of power among several branches, to avoid both the "monarchical" tendencies of unchecked executive power and the "instability" of governments based on legislative supremacy. Madison proposed, and Randolph presented, a system that included a "National Legislature" of two houses, one "elected by the people of the several states," the other chosen by the elected members of the first house from "persons nominated by the individual legislatures" of each state. The Virginia Plan also called for a "National Executive" with "a general authority to execute the national laws," and a "National Judiciary" to consist of "one or more supreme tribunals, and of inferior tribunals to be chosen by the National Legislature," with a jurisdiction that included "piracies and felonies on the high seas, captures from an enemy; cases in which foreigners or citizens of other states applying to such jurisdictions may be interested, or which respect the collection of the National revenue; impeachments of any National officers, and questions which may involve the national peace and harmony." The Virginia Plan included many features of the Constitution that the delegates later adopted and the states ratified, including a two-house legislature, a "national executive," and a federal judiciary. The principle of "checks and balances" among the branches of the national government reflected Madison's studies of the deficiencies of governments that lodged power in either legislative bodies or executive officers.

Throughout their four months of deliberation, with few exceptions, the delegates listened carefully and respectfully to one another and spoke in measured, thoughtful words. As in any other deliberative body, of course, there were those who spoke rarely or rashly. William Blount of North Carolina did not utter a recorded word until he announced on the final day his intention to sign the document he had taken no part in drafting. William Bassett of Delaware also remained silent during the convention, signing the Constitution without a word. Others ruffled feathers with endless, rambling speeches or thinly veiled attacks on the character or motives of fellow delegates. Luther Martin of Maryland spoke for two whole days on the evils of a strong national government in which small states would be overpowered by those of larger population and wealth. Even Madison, who rarely inserted critical remarks in his notes, recorded that Martin spoke "with much diffuseness and considerable vehemence." Oliver Ellsworth of Connecticut, a firm nationalist who fumed during Martin's discourse, later blasted him as "a specimen of eternal volubility."

But the delegates, however hot and bothered from the humid roasting they endured in the State House chamber or from the heated words of their fellows, mingled amicably in the nearby taverns and lodging houses and generally enjoyed each other's company. Everyone admired Benjamin Franklin for his wit and sagacity, even those few who found him a bit supercilious and pontifical. And General Washington, who had entertained many of the delegates at his Mount Vernon estate, was a prized dinner companion and was sought after for horseback excursions into the Pennsylvania countryside.

The day after Randolph proposed the Virginia Plan, the delegates voted to consider it not as a convention but as a "Committee of the Whole"; this parliamentary device allowed for debate and preliminary votes without binding the convention to any final decisions. The delegates first agreed "without debate or dissent, except that of Pennsylvania," Madison noted, to his proposal "that the national legislature ought to consist of two houses." Benjamin Franklin "was understood to be partial to a single house of legislation," but no other delegation deferred to him on this issue.

After that initial agreement, the delegates quickly moved to the most fundamental issue in government: democracy. The Virginia Plan stated that members of the lower house of the national legislature "ought to be elected by the people of the several states." This raised a fundamental question: Can people be trusted to elect their own lawmakers? The first delegate to speak on this issue, Roger Sherman of Connecticut, firmly and bluntly said no. He insisted that all national lawmakers should be chosen by state legislatures. The people, he argued, "should have as little to do as may be about the government. They want information and are constantly liable to be misled." Sherman used the term "want" in the old-fashioned meaning of "lack" rather than "desire." But his point reflected the perspective of the New England town-meeting member that Sherman had been for many years. He came to the convention as mayor of New Haven, a blunt, outspoken man who had signed both the Declaration of Independence and the Articles of Confederation. Sherman spoke for those "localists" who believed in grassroots government but who felt that democracy should stop at the state level. He distrusted those who would seek national office and the powers they would exert over the states.

Sherman was seconded by another New Englander, Elbridge Gerry of Massachusetts. His state had recently experienced an armed uprising by the "people" of western Massachusetts against their state lawmakers during Shays' Rebellion. Formed into ranks by a former revolutionary officer, Daniel Shays, two thousand farmers had formed a blockade of courthouses from which judges had issued foreclosure orders. Farmers had been heavily taxed to pay off the state's war debts, and many could not meet the tax burden. While the state militia had routed the rebellious farmers, Gerry feared that allowing the "people" to elect national lawmakers might encourage a revival of the insurrectionary spirit of Shays' Rebellion and that a national legislature might yield to pressure to curb state powers over taxation.

Gerry's attack on popular election of national legislators took the "too much of a good thing" approach. "The evils we experience flow from the excess of democracy," he argued. "The people do not want virtue, but are the dupes of pretended patriots," he continued, using the term "want" as Roger Sherman had. Without mentioning Shays' Rebellion, Gerry claimed that his distrust of the "people" had been "fully confirmed by experience that they are daily misled into the most baneful measures and opinions by the false reports circulated by designing men, and which no one on the spot can refute." Gerry, who like Sherman had signed the Declaration of Independence, confessed to his fellow delegates that he had "been too republican heretofore: he was still however republican, but had been taught by experience the danger of the levelling spirit."

No sooner did Gerry sit down than George Mason of Virginia jumped to his feet to answer the New Englanders. Mason spoke as a plantation owner from a state that allowed slavery, but he had drafted Virginia's Declaration of Rights and took the most radical position of any delegate on the question of democracy. Madison noted that Mason "argued strongly for an election of the larger branch by the people. It was to be the grand depository of the democratic principle of the government." Speaking as one property owner to another, Mason took Gerry to task for his distrust of democracy. "He had often wondered," Madison recorded Mason as saying, "at the indifference of the superior classes of society" to those on the bottom. Mason admonished Gerry and his supporters on this issue that their "selfish motive" of protecting their property would best be served by providing "no less carefully for the rights and happiness of the lowest than of the highest orders of citizens." A host of ironies surround this exchange between Sherman and Gerry, speaking as New Englanders, and Mason, the Virginia planter. With its tradition of town-meeting government, one would expect New England to send delegates to Philadelphia who would support popular election of all legislators, at whatever level of government. For more than a century and a half, the "freemen" of New England had voiced their opinions and voted their convictions, with few restrictions on the franchise. New England had its share of wealthy farmers and merchants, and of landless workers and servants, but the gap between rich and poor was fairly narrow. In contrast, Virginia was governed largely by wealthy planters and merchants, who formed an aristocracy of power and privilege. Only a handful of Virginians could vote for their local and state officials; close to half the population had no rights at all, living in slavery and subject to laws that treated them as property. But Roger Sherman of Connecticut supported the "Great Compromise" that recognized slavery in the Constitution as lawful, while Mason vehemently denounced the "infernal traffic" in slaves. "Every master of slaves is born a petty tyrant," he declaimed.

James Madison took the most populist approach on the issue of electing lawmakers. He first argued, on May 31, that he "considered the popular election of one branch of the national legislature as essential to every plan of free government." Madison also urged that members of the Senate—the delegates had begun referring to the upper house by this term, borrowed from the Romans—be elected by the people. If senators were chosen by the state legislatures, "the people would be lost sight of altogether; and the necessary sympathy between them and their rulers and officers, too little felt." When the delegates returned to this question on June 6, John Dickinson of Delaware spoke against popular election of senators. The next day, Dickinson moved that senators be elected by the state legislatures, explaining that "he wished the Senate to consist of the most distinguished characters, distinguished for their rank in life and their weight of property, and bearing as strong a likeness to the British House of Lords as possible." Dickinson admired the House of Lords not only for its "family weight," as he put it, but for its numbers; he argued that the Senate "ought to be composed of a large number," as many as 160 members.

This was too much for Madison, who finally spoke up. He noted that the Roman senators "lost their influence and power, in proportion as their number was augmented." The larger the legislative body, the more likely its members would "fall into factions among themselves." Not only should the Senate be small in numbers, Madison argued, but "election by the people" would provide a "useful check" on the state legislatures. Elbridge Gerry took the floor after Madison and "insisted that the commercial and monied interest would be more secure in the hands of the state legislatures, than of the people at large." When the delegates voted on this question, every state supported Dickinson's motion. Madison could not even persuade a majority of his own delegation. Not until 1913 did the state legislatures give up their power to pick senators, by ratifying the Seventeenth Amendment to the Constitution.

3

"Dishonorable to the
National Character"

Debates in the Philadelphia convention did not proceed in any orderly or logical fashion, such as beginning with the structure and powers of the Congress, moving to the executive branch, and finally to the federal judiciary. The delegates instead jumped back and forth, debating motions as they were made, setting up committees to refine proposals and report back when they were ready, voting for motions one day and against them the next. The convention lacked a steering committee, or anything like the Rules Committee in the House of Representatives. There were no formal "parties" or party leaders. Delegates asked for the floor to introduce motions or to speak whenever they wished, on whatever subject they pleased. Because of this formless structure, the convention discussed the powers of Congress well before it decided on election procedures, the size of each house, or methods of representation.

The first debate on the powers of Congress took place on May 31, near the end of a long day of long speeches on how members of each house should be chosen. The delegates then moved to Edmund Randolph's proposal in the Virginia Plan—which was really Madison's plan—that Congress should have power "to legislate in all cases to which the separate states were incompetent." The debate on this proposal was surprisingly brief. It was also surprising—to those delegates who did not know of Madison's hand in the Virginia Plan—that Randolph spoke vigorously against his own proposal. He "disclaimed any intention to give indefinite powers to the national legislature, declaring that he was entirely opposed to such an inroad on the state jurisdictions, and that he did not think any considerations whatever could ever change his determination." Madison recorded Randolph's emphatic conclusion: "His opinion was fixed on this point."

As soon as Randolph took his seat, Madison put down his pen and took the floor to answer his fellow Virginian. He told the delegates that "he had brought with him into the convention a strong bias in favor of an enumeration and definition of the powers necessary to be exercised by the national legislature; but also brought doubts concerning its practicability. His wishes remained unaltered; but his doubts had become stronger. What his opinion might ultimately be he could not tell. But he should shrink from nothing which should be found essential to such a form of government as would provide for the safety, liberty and happiness of the community. This being the end of all our deliberations, all the necessary means for attaining it must, however reluctantly, be submitted to." After these heartfelt words, all but one state delegation—Connecticut was divided on the question—voted for the proposal Randolph had made and then opposed. On this issue, Randolph could not sway even his own delegation.

Madison's admission of "doubts" that the Constitution should include an enumeration of congressional powers may have been sincere, but he later gave in to his "wishes" and pressed the convention for a detailed listing of these powers. The delegates spent several steamy days in August debating proposals on congressional powers from the Committee on Detail—whose name aptly described its function—and motions by individual delegates. Many of these motions were to add or delete just one word or phrase, although sometimes adding or deleting a few words made a considerable change in the meaning of a constitutional provision. For example, when the delegates considered the provision of the Virginia Plan that limited the grounds for impeaching the president to "treason and bribery," George Mason of Virginia proposed adding the word "maladministration" after "bribery." Madison promptly objected. "So vague a term will be equivalent to a tenure during pleasure of the Senate," he complained. Mason thought for a moment, and then suggested the phrase "other high crimes and misdemeanors" as a substitute. By a vote of eight to three, with no recorded discussion, the state delegations agreed. Almost two centuries later, Richard Nixon resigned as president in 1974 to avoid certain impeachment, and Bill Clinton survived an impeachment trial in 1999 for "high crimes and misdemeanors" whose definition the Framers never discussed. The brief colloquy between Mason and Madison is the entirety of the Framers' "original intent" on this crucial provision.

When the delegates finally agreed to an "enumeration" of congressional powers, they debated for several days before agreeing on a listing, which became Section 8 of Article I in the Constitution. Many of the eighteen grants of power were narrow and specific: Congress was authorized to "establish post offices and post roads," to "fix the standards of weights and measures," and to "grant letters of marque and reprisal" for the arming of ships to capture enemy cargo in wartime. Others were broad and momentous: Congress was empowered to "lay and collect taxes" in order to "provide for the common defense and general welfare of the United States," to "borrow money on the credit of the United States," to "regulate commerce with foreign nations, and among the several states," and—after much debate over the respective powers of Congress and the president—to "declare war." On this last point, Madison and Elbridge Gerry—who differed on almost everything else, including support for the final Constitution—joined in a motion to change the wording of the Committee on Detail, which had proposed granting Congress the power to "make war," to the more limited power to "declare war." Gerry spoke for both men in stating that he "never expected to hear in a republic a motion to empower the Executive alone to declare war."

The most divisive issue in the convention, even more than the powers of Congress, arose from the great disparties in population between the large and the small states. The question resolved around representation in the two houses of Congress. One group of delegates pressed for proportional representation in both houses, based on the total population of each state. Another faction argued strenuously that representation in both houses should be based on a combination of population and "wealth," which became a euphemism in convention debates for slaves. A third group, largely but not exclusively from the smaller states, agreed with representation by population in the lower houses, but insisted that each state deserved equal representation in the Senate. Over the course of the summer, the heat of debate on these issues often matched the broiling temperatures in the convention chamber.

The question of representation in Congress, or any legislative body, can be argued from differing principles of political philosophy. Radical democrats are generally loath to allow any deviation from the "one person, one vote" standard in every lawmaking body. Those of more "aristocratic" or elitist leanings are suspicious of popular government and advocate the allocation of legislative seats on such bases as geographic area—counting acres rather than voters—or interests such as farming, logging, or mining. Other issues often lurk in the background when these conflicting positions are debated. During the Philadelphia convention of 1787, the real division was not between democrats and aristocrats, between delegates from rural or urban areas, or even between those from large or small states. The real issue was slavery.

James Madison, perhaps more than any other delegate, understood the positions of each group and worked diligently to forge a workable compromise. His political philosophy, shaped by John Witherspoon at Princeton, and his own temperament as a compassionate person, combined to make Madison an advocate of radical democracy. On the other hand, as the son of a planter and slave owner from Virginia, he knew that delegates from states large in the "wealth" of slaves would insist that their interests be protected in Congress. Madison was also determined that the Philadelphia convention not end without agreement on a Constitution that established and empowered a strong national government. From these differing perspectives, and with his ultimate goal in mind, he sensed—from one day to the next—the shifting coalitions on the question of congressional representation and tried to maneuver each side toward the "Great Compromise" that finally broke the impasse on this issue.

Madison first urged compromise on July 9, after William Paterson of New Jersey had urged that each state have just one vote in the Senate. Paterson had earlier introduced a plan for a national government that called for modest revisions in the Articles of Confederation and the retention of sovereignty in each state. Madison considered the New Jersey Plan, as it came to be called, as the most serious threat to his Virginia Plan, and he considered Paterson a formidable rival in the convention. Both men were Princeton graduates, but Paterson epitomized the elitism that Madison deplored; he wrote favorably of the "good breeding" that produced the "true gentlemen" who were best fitted to govern the masses. Paterson had no deep-rooted objection to slavery, but he appealed to its opponents in seeking to maintain the powers of the smaller states. Madison recorded Paterson as stating that "he could regard negro slaves in no light but as property. They have no free agents, have no personal liberty, no faculty of acquiring property, but on the contrary are themselves property, and like other property entirely at the will of the master."

Paterson made these remarks as matters of fact, with no moral judgment attached. He went on to pose a rhetorical question about representation in state legislatures: "Has a man in Virginia a number of votes in proportion to the number of his slaves?" The answer was obvious: he did not. "And if Negroes are not represented in the states to which they belong," Paterson continued, "why should they be represented in the general government?" His point was clear, but his purpose was devious. Paterson sounded like a true democrat when he asked another rhetorical question: "What is the true principle of representation?" He answered that it was based on "the expedient" of choosing a small number of representatives "in place of the inconvenient meeting of the people themselves." Paterson had only disdain for "the people" themselves—at least those without property—but he wanted to prevent states with small white populations but large numbers of slaves, such as Georgia and South Carolina, from outvoting states like New Jersey and New Hampshire in the federal Congress.

Sensing the dangerous appeal of Paterson's words, Madison felt compelled to respond on the spot. His purpose—keeping the large and small states together in the Congress—was clear, but his words were devious. Madison first "reminded Mr. Paterson that his doctrine of representation which was in its principle the genuine one, must forever silence the pretensions of the small states to an equality of votes with the larger ones." He turned Paterson's democratic pretensions against him. The states should vote in Congress "in the same proportion in which their citizens would do, if the people of all the states were collectively met." But principle gave way to practicality as Madison "suggested as a proper ground of compromise, that in the first branch the states should be represented according to their number of free inhabitants; and in the second, which had for one of its primary objects the guardianship of property, according to the whole number, including slaves."

This first effort at compromise did not succeed, for Madison had misjudged the determination of Paterson and his allies in the small northern states to prevent the southern states—with equally small white populations—from outvoting them in Congress. Following Madison's speech, the delegates voted to refer the question of representation to a committee on which each state had a member. This group, called the Committee of Eleven, replaced the Committee of Five, which the delegates had earlier set up to propose a representation plan. The numbers game on this question illustrated the intransigence on both sides: no committee—however small or large—could fashion a compromise that would satisfy a majority of the state delegations. When the Committee of Eleven reported back on July 10, the delegates spent most of the day haggling over whether New Hampshire should have two or three representatives in the House.

After this contentious session, Hugh Williamson of South Carolina—who had spoken very little on any issue—presented his own compromise, offering a choice between those who wanted to count all inhabitants in apportioning House seats and those who wanted to count only whites. Williamson was a man of moderation, drawn to compromise rather than confrontation. He moved that "a census shall be taken of the free white inhabitants and three fifths of those of other descriptions" and that "representation be regulated accordingly."

Williamson's proposal had the advantage of seeming a reasonable position between two extremes. Pierce Butler and Charles Cotesworth Pinckney of South Carolina, adamant defenders of slavery, promptly "insisted that blacks be included in the rule of representation, equally with the whites," and moved to strike the words "three fifths" from Williamson's motion. Butler argued that "the labor of a slave in South Carolina was as productive and valuable as that of a freeman in Massachusetts" and that "an equal representation ought to be allowed for them in a government which was instituted principally for the protection of property, and was itself to be supported by property." But only two other states voted with the South Carolinians on this motion.

On the other side, those who argued against proposals to count slaves did so not on moral grounds but simply from expedience. Roger Sherman of Connecticut "thought the number of people alone the best rule" for representation, but he opened the door for compromise by endorsing Edmund Randolph's proposal that some ratio between all or none "ought to be fixed by the Constitution." Rufus King of Massachusetts voiced the sentiments of many delegates who simply wanted to settle the issue and move on to other questions. He found "great force" in the objections of Gouverneur Morris of Pennsylvania, the most insistent opponent of compromise on slavery, but he would vote for Williamson's motion "for the sake of doing something." The debate on representation became complicated by disputes over the number of years between each census; Madison's motion to add the words "at least" after "15 years" was defeated on a tie vote. By the day's end the delegates were so testy that Williamson's "three fifths" motion, weighted down with amendments, was rejected by every state.

What seemed to many weary delegates as the death knell for compromise spurred others to redouble their efforts. After a weekend of private meetings and caucuses, the delegates returned to the State House on Monday, July 16, ready to vote on what soon came to be called the Great Compromise. Over the previous week, debate on the representation issue made clear that the small states would rather bolt from the convention than agree to proportional representation in the Senate. The southern states were also adamant that slaves be counted, either equally with whites or in some substantial ratio, in apportioning House seats. Pierce Butler of South Carolina told the convention that "the security the southern states want is that their Negroes may not be taken from them, which some gentlemen within or without doors, have a very good mind to do." He was answered by James Wilson of Pennsylvania, who proclaimed that "all men wherever placed have equal rights" and that "he could not agree that property was the sole or the primary object of government and society."

James Madison made one last appeal for his principle of population as the basis of representation in the session on Saturday, July 14. He "expressed his apprehensions that if the proper foundation of government was destroyed, by substituting an equality in place of a proportional representation, no proper superstructure would be raised." His last-ditch effort at a compromise that would satisfy him was the proposition that "In all cases where the general government is to act on the people, let the people be represented and the votes be proportional. In all cases where the government is to act on the states as such, in like manner as Congress now act on them, let the states be represented and the votes be equal. This was the true ground of compromise if there was any ground at all." But Madison then retreated to his principle and "denied that there was any ground" for compromise.

Madison's words became increasingly sharp and bitter. He challenged his opponents to show "a single instance in which the general government was not to operate on the people individually." He leveled a veiled insult at Delaware, whose five delegates outnumbered both Massachusetts and New York. "No one would say that either in Congress or out of Congress Delaware had equal weight with Pennsylvania," Madison said. He repeated his earlier disquisition on the Dutch confederacy, and then outlined five objections to equality of states in the Senate, arguing that small states "could extort measures" from the larger states and frustrate "the will of the majority of the people." He finally lashed out at the southern states as the fomenters of discord and division. "It seemed now to be pretty well understood," Madison said, "that the real difference of interest lay, not between the large and small but between the northern and southern states. The institution of slavery and its consequences formed the line of discrimination." Giving the slave states extra weight in Congress by counting, even at three fifths, persons who were barred from voting struck Madison as unjust, on both moral and practical grounds.

Madison used strong words in the Saturday session. By Monday morning, the battle was over. The Great Compromise, allowing the southern states to count slaves as three fifths of a person for House seats and providing for equal votes for each state in the Senate, was adopted without further debate. Four of the small states—Connecticut, New Jersey, Delaware, and Maryland—found an ally in North Carolina, a large state in population but also a slave state. These five states outvoted Pennsylvania, Virginia, South Carolina, and Georgia. Four of the thirteen states in the Confederation were divided or did not vote. The four delegates from Massachusetts were split, two on each side; Rhode Island did not send delegates to Philadelphia; and New York and New Hampshire each lacked a quorum. Based on the white population, states with less than one third of the total population prevailed over those with two thirds. The outcome was hardly a ringing endorsement of democracy; in fact, it represented a victory for slavery, aristocracy, and elitism. But the rules of the convention had been followed, and five was a larger number than four.

Edmund Randolph was the first to speak after this momentous decision. He voiced the concerns of those from the larger states who felt the closeness of the vote robbed the convention of legitimacy. "The vote of this morning had embarrassed the business extremely," he began. Randolph then spoke of the Constitution the delegates had assembled in Philadelphia to draft. "It will probably be in vain to come to any final decision with a bare majority on either side." He proposed that the convention adjourn, "that the large states might consider the steps proper to be taken in the present solemn crisis of the business, and that the small states might also deliberate on the means of conciliation."

William Paterson of New Jersey, who had opposed counting slaves in any representation plan but whose delegation had voted for the Great Compromise, took Randolph's remarks a step further. He thought "it was high time for the convention to adjourn, that the rule of secrecy ought to be rescinded, and that our constituents should be consulted." Paterson challenged Randolph to move for adjournment "sine die"—that is, without specifying a day to reconvene—which would have ended the convention for good. Randolph replied that he had not proposed an indefinite adjournment, and "was sorry that his meaning had been so readily and strangely misinterpreted." John Rutledge of South Carolina did not wish to "abandon everything to hazard" and wanted to proceed. He was adamant on this issue. "The little states were fixed," he said. "All that the large states then had to do, was to decide whether they would yield or not."

And yield they did. The delegates voted to adjourn until the next day. That morning, before the convention resumed, Madison attended a meeting of delegates from several states—large and small—to discuss the seeming impasse. "The time was wasted in vague conversation," he noted, "without any specific proposition or agreement." Some delegates from large states held firm against the Great Compromise, but others "seemed inclined to yield to the smaller states" and move on. When the delegates met on July 17 in the State House, the battle was over. Counting slaves as "three fifths" of a person for House seats and providing equal votes for each state in the Senate were now parts of the Constitution.

Flushed with victory, the slave states pressed for even greater protection of their "property" in fellow humans. Before the convention ended, they succeeded in securing two additional provisions. Pierce Butler and Charles Cotesworth Pinckney of South Carolina moved on August 28 "to require fugitive slaves and servants to be delivered up like criminals." Roger Sherman of Connecticut objected that he "saw no more propriety in the public seizing and surrendering a slave or servant, than a horse." The South Carolinians withdrew their motion, and came back the next day with a longer, more detailed motion providing that—even in free states—fugitive slaves "shall be delivered up to the person justly claiming their service or labor." The delegates agreed to this provision by voice vote, with no recorded debate. The final version in the Constitution, polished by the Committee on Style, differed only slightly in wording and was adopted once more without debate.

The third provision about slavery did provoke debate, much of it heated. Luther Martin of Maryland, himself the owner of "domestic" slaves as household help, moved on August 21 that Congress be allowed to prohibit the further importation of slaves. He argued that slavery "weakened one part of the Union which the other parts were bound to protect: the privilege of importing them was therefore unreasonable." He also objected that slavery "was inconsistent with the principles of the Revolution and dishonorable to the American character to have such a feature in the Constitution." John Rutledge of South Carolina immediately responded for the slave states. "Religion and humanity had nothing to do with this question," he said dismissively. "Interest alone is the governing principle with nations." He felt that "If the northern states consult their interest, they will not oppose the increase of slaves which will increase the commodities of which they will become the carriers." Rutledge issued an implied threat, reminding Martin that the convention had not yet adopted a Constitution and that the "true question" was whether the slave states "shall or shall not be parties to the Union."

The debate over slavery consumed most of the next day. Roger Sherman of Connecticut "disapproved of the slave trade" but found it "expedient to have as few objections as possible" to the Constitution. He proposed allowing the southern states to continue importing slaves and "urged on the convention the necessity of dispatching its business." Sherman wanted to move on to such pressing issues as the number of days each house of Congress could adjourn without consent from the other. George Mason, the Virginia radical, jumped to his feet and answered Sherman with indignation. Despite being a slave owner

himself, he denounced the "infernal traffic" in slaves and rebuked those northern states that allowed a "lust of gain" from commerce to cloud their moral vision. Mason added that "the judgement of heaven" fell on countries that
allowed the "nefarious traffic" in slaves. "As nations cannot be rewarded or
punished in the next world they must be in this," he continued. "By an inevitable chain of causes and effects providence punishes national sins, by national calamities." Mason spoke like an Old Testatment prophet, but his fellow
delegates did not "incline their ear" to his words, as Jeremiah had lamented of
those who ignored his prophecy that "the land will become a ruin" if they did
not repent "the evil of their ways."

Oliver Ellsworth of Connecticut was deaf to moral appeals. "Let us not in-
termeddle," he replied to Mason, and "be unjust" toward the states whose commerce depended on slavery. Delegates from the slave states warned those who
would prohibit further importation that intransigence on this question would
imperil the Constitution. "If the convention thinks," said John Rutledge, that
the slave states "will ever agree to the plan, unless their right to import slaves be
untouched, the expectation is vain. The people of those states will never be
such fools as to give up so important an interest."

Despite the southern threats, enough delegates voiced support for allowing
Congress to ban the slave trade that both sides agreed with the proposal of
Gouverneur Morris of Pennsylvania that the issue be sent to a committee that
"may form a bargain among the northern and southern states." The committee
returned on August 24 with a bargain in hand: Congress would be allowed to
prohibit the importation of slaves, but could not exercise this power before
1800, thirteen years later. When the delegates reached this provision the next
day, Charles Cotesworth Pinckney of South Carolina moved to extend the
time to 1808. James Madison was the only voice in opposition. "Twenty years
will produce all the mischief that can be apprehended from the liberty to
import slaves," he warned. "So long a term will be more dishonorable to the
national character than to say nothing about it in the Constitution." The delegates ignored Madison's counsel and adopted the provision with Pinckney's
amendment.

Slavery was not the only issue that divided the delegates in Philadelphia. But
there was, in retrospect, no issue that more affected the Union over the next
two centuries—and into the next millennium—than slavery and its legacy in
racial segregation and discrimination. Every branch of the government the
delegates fashioned in Philadelphia—Congress, the executive, and the judiciary—
has struggled to resolve the conflicts that stemmed from the Great Compromise in 1787. Those who praise the Framers as farsighted statesmen and
champions of democracy tend to ignore or brush aside the slavery provisions
of the Constitution. Not one delegate refused to sign the document because of
moral objections to these provisions. And, as George Mason had warned, national sins were punished by national calamities.

4

"The Supreme Law of the Land"

The adoption of the Great Compromise by delegates to the Philadelphia convention in 1787, with its legitimation of slavery in the Constitution, did not end debate over other contentious issues. Divisions over the structure of Congress, how members of the House and Senate would be elected, and what powers they could exercise largely reflected conflicts between larger and smaller states, compounded by the demands of states—both small and large—whose "wealth" depended on slavery. Even while debate continued over the provisions of what finally became Article I of the Constitution, vesting "all legislative powers" in Congress, the delegates argued over the structure and powers of the executive and judicial branches of the national government.

The Virginia Plan, drafted by James Madison, provided for a "national executive" with "general authority to execute the national laws" and for a "national judiciary" with jurisdiction over "questions which may involve the national peace and harmony." More questions were raised than answered by Madison's proposals for these two branches of government. Madison himself, who prepared for the convention with months of reading on different forms of government, had no inflexible positions on how to choose executive and judicial officers, what powers they should wield in their respective spheres, and their relations with Congress. In his first speech to the convention on "executive authority," delivered on June 1, Madison professed doubt in deciding whether that department should be "administered by one or more persons." He then proposed that executive officers, in addition to their authority to "carry into effect the national laws," also exercise "such other powers" which were "not legislative nor judiciary in their nature." Madison's remarks added nothing of substance to the vague contours of his plan. His first comments on the judicial branch, made on June 13, were equally vague. Along with his fellow Virginian Edmund Randolph, Madison moved that "the jurisdiction of the national judiciary" should include "questions which involve the national peace and harmony." Sitting as the Committee of the Whole, the delegates adopted this motion without debate or dissent, leaving questions of federal judicial power for further deliberation.

One reason that Madison avoided taking strong positions on these questions in early debate was that he really had none. His wide reading and diligent research had convinced him of the necessity for a strong national government, with three branches of separate but equal powers. Beyond this, he was open to persuasion from other delegates with experience in executive and judicial positions. Seven delegates had served as chief executives of their states; several others held state judicial offices. Some of these delegates expressed strong opinions on the questions that Madison left open in his early remarks; others shifted between one position and another as various proposals came up for debate and decision. In the end, Madison's "Federalist" vision of a strong national government with three branches of extensive and equal powers prevailed over the "localist" view that wished to retain state sovereignty in a slightly restructured Confederation, with limited powers for Congress and no national executive or judicial officers.

The convention first took up the question of executive power on June 1, in an atmosphere of gravity and anticipation. The session opened with a motion by James Wilson of Pennsylvania that "the executive consist of a single person." Madison recorded in his *Notes* that a "considerable pause" followed the motion, as delegates hesitated to commit themselves on this issue. Benjamin Franklin, who had been assisted to his special chair to attend a session he considered vital, finally broke the silence. Franklin "observed that it was a point of great importance and wished that the gentlemen would deliver their sentiments on it" before they voted. John Rutledge of South Carolina obliged the elder statesman. He spoke of the "shyness of gentlemen" on this question, suggesting that delegates who, "having frankly disclosed their opinions" on choosing the executive, might feel precluded from "afterwards changing them." Rutledge supported "vesting the executive power in a single person, though he was not for giving him the power of war and peace."

During the debate that followed Rutledge's speech, Edmund Randolph of Virginia—himself the chief executive of a large and powerful state—chafed in his seat and finally jumped to his feet. Randolph "strenuously opposed a unity in the executive magistracy," Madison reported. "He regarded it as the fetus of monarchy." Randolph "could not see why the great requisites for the executive department, vigor, despatch, and responsibility, could not be found in three men, as well as in one man." James Wilson answered that "unity in the executive instead of being the fetus of monarchy would be the best safeguard against tyranny."

With the delegates unable to agree on how many men should occupy the "executive magistracy," debate shifted to the method of election. Again, divisions on this issue reflected attitudes toward "the people" as participants in the political process. During the session on June 9, Elbridge Gerry of Massachusetts moved that the state governors select the national executive, with each state having the same number of votes as it had senators. He reasoned that governors "would be most likely to select the fittest men" for the post, whether one or more. Not a single delegate rose to support Gerry's motion, and not a single state—including his own—voted for his motion.

Over the weeks that followed this first inconclusive debate and vote, the question of choosing the national executive came up in several sessions, but without any resolution. Delegates spent most of their time making speeches and motions about the legislative branch; deciding who made the national laws concerned them more than who executed them. The era of the "imperial presidency" would not begin for another century and a half, and the Framers of 1787 worried less about presidential power—or abuse of power—than about congressional power and relations between the states and federal government.

One remarkable aspect of the American political system is that most citizens believe they can vote directly for officials at all levels of government. From city councils to Congress, voters cast their ballots for the candidate they prefer. But many are unaware they cannot vote directly for the president and vice president of the United States. Instead, they vote indirectly for candidates to these high offices through "electors" whose names often do not appear on the ballot and who are usually obscure party loyalists. For two centuries, proposals to amend the Constitution and provide for direct election of the president and vice president have failed to change this anachronistic system.

During the Philadelphia convention, a few delegates did urge that "the people" be allowed to elect the president directly. On July 17, after the states voted without dissent that the "national executive consist of a single person," the delegates took up the proposal in the Virginia Plan that the executive "be chosen by the national legislature." Gouverneur Morris of Pennsylvania spoke "pointedly" against this motion, Madison noted in recording his speech. "He ought to be elected by the people at large," Morris said of the president. "If the people should elect, they will never fail to prefer some man of distinguished character, or services; some man, if he might so speak, of continental reputation." Madison did not record in his notes whether heads turned in the chamber toward General Washington, seated before them in the presiding chair. Virtually all the delegates assumed that Washington would be elected by acclamation as the first "national executive" by whatever method they chose; it was the question of who would follow Washington that led most delegates to question the proposal for direct election.

Morris outlined his objections to the Virginia Plan. "If the legislature elect," he argued, "it will be the work of intrigue, of cabal, and of faction; it will be like the election of a pope by a conclave of cardinals; real merit will rarely be the title to the appointment." Roger Sherman of Connecticut voiced the concern of the smaller states on this question. He countered Morris that "the people at large ... will never be sufficiently informed of characters" of the candidates. "They will generally vote for some man in their own state, and the largest state will have the best chance for the appointment." George Mason of Virginia, who fervently supported the rights of "the people" on most issues, and who represented both the largest state in delegates and the home of George Washington, surprisingly sided with Sherman. "He conceived it would be as unnatural," Madison recorded, "to refer the choice of a proper character for Chief Magistrate to the people, as it would to refer a trial of colors to a blind man. The extent of the country renders it impossible that the people can have the requisite capacity to judge of the respective pretensions of the candidates." When the delegates voted, only Morris's home state of Pennsylvania supported his motion for "an election by the people" of the president.

Debate over varying proposals for the election of the president—although that title for the chief executive was not widely used until the convention neared its end—dragged on throughout the summer, with no agreement in sight. On July 19, Gouverneur Morris restated his position that "the executive magistrate should be the guardian of the people, even of the lower classes, against legislative tyranny, against the great and the wealthy who in the course of things will necessarily compose the legislative body." His long and eloquent speech fell on deaf ears. Even Madison, who supported direct election of the president in principle, yielded to sentiment against it and observed that electors chosen by state legislatures "seemed on the whole to be liable to fewest objections."

Frustration on this issue mounted to such levels that George Mason, speaking on July 26, listed seven different proposals that had been moved and rejected, from direct election by the people to choosing a president by lottery. Mason opposed direct election because a choice which should be made "by those who know most of eminent characters" should not be made "by those who know least." About the lottery proposal, which was totally facetious, Mason wryly remarked that "the tickets do not appear to be in much demand."

Not until September did the delegates take any real steps toward settling this vexing issue. Opinions seemed to be moving toward proposals for a single presidential term of seven years, with the president elected by Congress, and with a provision for impeachment. But the convention refused to make a decision, and the weary delegates finally dumped the issue on a newly created Committee on Postponed Matters. When that group reported on September 4, it laid before the convention a proposal that became—with minor changes—the text of Article II of the Constitution. The country would not only have a president, elected for a term of four years, but a vice president as well, chosen by electors who were themselves chosen by the state legislatures. The election plan was complex, giving both houses of Congress a role in choosing the president in case a majority of state electors could not agree; the vice president would be the man with the second-largest number of electoral votes.

By September 12, after dozens of motions to amend the committee's report had been debated and voted up or down, the convention finally adopted a detailed plan for election of the "national executive" that Madison had proposed in vague outline on May 29. The president was now designated as "commander in chief" of the armed forces, was empowered to "make treaties" with the concurrence of two thirds of the Senate, and was authorized to appoint "judges of the Supreme Court, and all other officers of the United States," subject to approval by a Senate majority. The provisions of Article II did not satisfy Gouverneur Morris's plea that "the people" directly elect the president, but the sharing of powers with Congress muted Edmund Randolph's fears of an executive "monarchy" that might impose a "tyranny" on the country. In the end, the Framers of 1787 adopted yet another compromise that diluted the principles of democracy. But this compromise on presidential election and powers—like the Great Compromise on congressional structure and powers in Article I—allowed the Framers to submit to the states for ratification a constitution that established a strong national government.

Looking back from the perspective of more than two centuries, it seems astounding that delegates to the Philadelphia convention of 1787 spent so little time—and so few words—debating the structure and powers of the "national judiciary" that Madison first proposed in the Virginia Plan. Since its establishment by Article III of the Constitution, the Supreme Court has exercised "the judicial power of the United States" in thousands of cases that have decided whether state and federal laws conform to the Constitution, which is sanctified by Article VI as the "supreme law of the land." This awesome power—limited only by the equally awesome power of Congress and the states to amend the Constitution—appears at first glance to have been granted as an afterthought by the Philadelphia delegates.

On closer inspection, however, it seems clear that the delegates who drafted the final version of the Constitution's judicial provisions were united in supporting a "national judiciary" with expansive powers over state and federal legislation. They arrived at this destination by varied routes, but the notion of "judicial review" of legislation was not foreign to them. Once the concept of an independent judiciary gained majority support, the delegates did not shrink from vesting the Supreme Court with the powers needed for its role as the dominant branch of the national government.

As we have seen, the vague outlines of the Virginia Plan provided for "one or more supreme tribunals" and for "inferior tribunals" with jurisdiction over "questions which may involve the national peace and harmony." Madison proposed that judges for these courts be chosen by the "national legislature," but the initial debate on this proposal showed that other delegates supported a selection by the "national executive." Speaking on June 5, James Wilson of Pennsylvania "opposed the appointment of judges by the national legislature," Madison reported. "Intrigue, partiality, and concealment were the necessary consequences" of allowing lawmakers to choose judges, Wilson argued. Born in Scotland and a signer of the Declaration of Independence, Wilson spoke now as a prosperous Philadelphia lawyer and member of the Confederation Congress. Although he supported popular election of federal officials, the savvy Scotsman recognized that politicians were tempted to reward their backers with such prizes as judicial office. Wilson won such a prize just two years later in 1789, when George Washington rewarded him with a Supreme Court seat for supporting ratification of the Constitution.

John Rutledge of South Carolina spoke for other delegates who supported appointment of judges by the legislative branch. He was "by no means disposed to grant so great a power to any single person," Madison recorded. "The people will think we are leaning too much towards monarchy." Although he differed with Wilson on this issue, Rutledge also won appointment from Washington to the Supreme Court, not once but twice. He served for one year, in 1790 and 1791, but resigned without hearing or deciding a single case; when Washington nominated him as Chief Justice in 1795, he was rejected by the Senate for political reasons. Benjamin Franklin, who attended the session to hear the debate on "a point of great moment," as he put it, listened to Wilson and Rutledge and then spoke from his special seat. Expressing his hope that "other modes" of choosing judges would be proposed, Franklin delighted the delegates in his "entertaining manner" with a story—perhaps with glances at his friend James Wilson—of the "Scotch mode" of choosing judges. Lawyers made the choice in Scotland, Franklin said, and "always selected the ablest of the profession in order to get rid of him, and share his practice among themselves."

Madison could not match Franklin in humor, but he took advantage of this opening to suggest that judicial appointments be made not by "any numerous body" such as the entire Congress or by a single executive but rather by the "Senatorial branch," which he argued would be "sufficiently stable and independent to follow their deliberate judgment." These remarks, of course, came well before the convention voted to give each state an equal vote in the Senate, a part of the Great Compromise that Madison opposed until its final passage. His motion to defer the question of judicial appointment to another day, to allow for "maturer reflection" by the delegates, passed by a vote of nine states to two.

The question next arose on June 13, when Charles Pinckney of South Carolina and Roger Sherman of Connecticut jointly moved for appointment of judges by the "national legislature." Madison restated his objections, arguing that candidates for judicial office "who had displayed a talent for business in the legislative field, who had perhaps assisted ignorant members in business of their own, or of their constituents, or used other winning means, would without any of the essential qualifications for an expositor of the laws prevail over a competitor not having these recommendations, but possessed of every necessary accomplishment." Madison then moved for "appointment by the Senate" of federal judges. Overwhelmed—at least for the moment—by Madison's eloquence, Pinckney and Sherman promptly withdrew their motion. Sitting as the Committee of the Whole and hence not bound to any later decision, the delegates agreed to Madison's proposal without dissent.

More than a month passed before the convention resumed its debate on judicial appointments. While his fellow delegates argued over the legislative and executive branches, Madison devoted some of his spare time to pondering this unresolved question. After listening on July 18 to half a dozen familiar speeches by advocates of legislative or executive appointment, Madison tried to break the impasse. He proposed that federal judges "be appointed by the executive with the concurrence of one-third at least" of the Senate. Madison argued that his proposal "would unite the advantage of responsibility in the executive with the security afforded in the second branch against any incautious or corrupt nomination by the executive." After listening to half a dozen more speeches on the issue, Madison realized that his proposal had no chance of approval. Without a recorded vote, the delegates agreed "by common consent" to defer the question for later decision.

When the convention returned to his proposal on July 21, Madison eagerly seized on movement toward compromise on the election of Congress, in which supporters of popular election to the House would agree to give every state equal votes in the Senate. Urging that "the spirit of compromise which had prevailed" on this question should extend to judicial appointments, Madison suggested "a concurrence of two authorities, in one of which the people, in the other the states, should be represented." On this issue, the convention rejected his plea for compromise, and Madison trimmed his sails. Professing that he was "not anxious" to allow a Senate minority to block a judicial nomination by the executive, Madison revised his motion "to let a majority reject." On this day, Madison lost by a vote of six states to three.

Having failed to resolve this issue, Madison took a low profile and deferred his next move for more than seven weeks. During this time, the delegates adopted the Great Compromise that legitimated slavery and gave the smaller states equal votes in the Senate. Between July 21 and September 12, when the convention neared its end, not a single delegate rose to speak on the issue of judicial appointments. On August 6, however, the Committee on Detail, which had worked diligently for weeks to prepare a draft of the Constitution, based on the tentative votes of the Committee of the Whole, reported its efforts to the delegates. This draft included the language that became, with little change, the wording of Article III of the Constitution, establishing the Supreme Court and outlining its jurisdiction. On the issue that had most divided the delegates— whether members of the Supreme Court should be chosen by the president or the Senate—the committee placed this power in the Senate. Madison was a member of the Committee on Detail, but he obviously failed to persuade his fellow members that judicial appointments should be shared by the president and Senate.

During the weeks that followed the submission of the draft Constitution by the Committee on Detail, the delegates laboriously slogged their way through every clause of every article, taking literally hundreds of votes on motions to strike or add words and phrases. The convention devoted little of its time to the Supreme Court, which was dealt with in Article III, about halfway through the lengthy document. The delegates finally reached this article on August 27, and almost hurried their way through it, with little discussion or debate. They agreed to vesting "the judicial power of the United States" in a Supreme Court "and in such inferior courts" as Congress might create. They also agreed to give the Supreme Court jurisdiction over "all cases under laws passed by the legislature of the United States," and to "controversies" between states, "between a state and citizens of another state," and "between citizens of different states." Through this jurisdictional scheme, the delegates intended to place all cases that did not arise solely within a single state into a federal judicial forum. Although only a few delegates voiced their underlying concerns on this issue, these jurisdictional provisions obviously reflected fears that state judges might be biased against out-of-state litigants or against the federal government itself.

During the debate on August 27, William Johnson of Connecticut, a noted scholar with degrees from Yale and Harvard, who would shortly become president of Columbia, offered an amendment to change the provision to give the Court jurisdiction over "all cases arising under this Constitution and laws" enacted by Congress. Some delegates may have considered this a trivial change, or simply one that was assumed, but Madison rose to object. He recorded himself as doubting "whether it was not going too far to extend the jurisdiction of the Court generally to cases arising under the Constitution and whether it ought not to be limited to cases of a judiciary nature. The right of expounding the Constitution in cases not of this nature ought not to be given to that department." Madison did not define what he meant by "cases of a judiciary nature," but he presumably intended to prevent the Supreme Court from issuing advisory opinions on constitutional questions, a power that some delegates had suggested giving the Court in earlier sessions. At any rate, the delegates promptly passed Johnson's motion without dissent, "it being generally supposed that the jurisdiction given was constructively limited to cases of a judiciary nature," Madison recorded approvingly.

With hardly any debate, the delegates approved the creation of a branch of the national government with sweeping jurisdiction and awesome—if still untested—powers to strike down laws of both the states and Congress. Many delegates, in fact, seemed unaware that they had granted these powers to the national judiciary. During the extended debate over proposals to join the president and Supreme Court into a "Council of Revision" with power to veto laws passed by Congress, Madison proposed on August 15 a complicated scheme to allow Congress to override such vetoes. His motion, by far the most complicated of any on this issue, would have entangled members of all three branches in the business of the others.

During the debate that followed, as Madison reported, John Mercer of Maryland "disapproved of the doctrine that judges as expositors of the Constitution should have the authority to declare a law void. He thought laws ought to be well and cautiously made, and then to be uncontrollable." John Dickinson of Delaware was "strongly impressed" with Mercer's comment. "He thought no such power ought to exist. He was at the same time at a loss what expedient to substitute." No other delegate rose to suggest a substitute for Madison's proposal, but his notion of involving the Supreme Court in deciding the constitutionality of legislation before it took effect—giving it, in other words, the power of issuing advisory opinions—never came close to passage. On this particular motion, Madison lost by a vote of eight states to three. Later on, the convention voted to give Congress the power to override presidential vetoes by a two-thirds vote of both the House and Senate. The delegates left the Supreme Court out of these battles among the other two branches of the national government.

A majority of the delegates in Philadelphia shared Madison's "Federalist" belief in a strong national government, with varying degrees of intensity. At the same time, every delegate represented his state and was loath to hand over to the new government they were framing the essential powers of the states. Yet in designing the judicial branch of government, the delegates added to its sweeping jurisdiction in Article III the additional power to make the Constitution and federal laws "the supreme law of the land," binding every state judge to their enforcement.

This provision, which became the Supremacy Clause of Article VI, first took shape in Madison's proposal in the Virginia Plan to give the national legislature a "negative" over state laws that contravened the "articles of Union." Debate over this proposal continued for almost three months, from its introduction on May 29 until August 23, when the delegates finally buried it. During that final debate, Roger Sherman of Connecticut proclaimed a congressional veto power over state laws to be "unnecessary; the laws of the general government being supreme and paramount to the state laws according to the plan, as it now stands." That plan, submitted by the Committee on Detail on August 6, provided that federal laws "shall be the supreme law of the several states" and would prevail over contrary state laws. Madison finally gave up. "He had been from the beginning a friend to the principle" of a congressional veto, he recorded himself as saying, but he now agreed to the "modification" in the draft Constitution. Hugh Williamson of North Carolina added, in words that Madison might have taken as a slight, that further discussion of his proposal "was a waste of time."

There is some irony in the fact that the strongest statements on judicial review, on both sides of the question, came from delegates who did not sign the final document. John Mercer of Maryland, who first took his seat on August 6, the day the Committee on Detail submitted its draft Constitution, rose to speak for the first time two days later. Madison recorded his short and sour remarks: "Mr. Mercer expressed his dislike of the whole plan, and his opinion that it never could succeed." Shortly after declaring on August 15 that he "disapproved of the doctrine" that judges could declare laws unconstitutional, Mercer left Philadelphia without any farewell remarks, and later campaigned—without success—against ratification of the Constitution in Maryland.

The leading proponent of the "doctrine" that Mercer rejected was Elbridge Gerry of Massachusetts, a professed opponent of the "excesses" of democracy. Early in the convention, Gerry argued strenuously against Madison's proposal that the Supreme Court take part along with the president in a "Council of Revision" to pass on all state laws. Gerry insisted that judges should be independent of the other branches of government in "their exposition of the laws, which involved a power of deciding on their constitutionality. In some states the judges had actually set aside laws as being against the Constitution" of the state. "This was done too with general approbation," Gerry added.

From the perspective of political theory, it makes sense that an opponent of democratic "excesses" made the strongest defense of judicial veto power over laws passed by democratically elected legislators. Not a single state at the time of the Philadelphia convention elected the judges of its highest court; most often, the men who received judicial appointments represented the social and financial elite whose interests they furthered. But it made far less sense that the first delegate who proposed making the Constitution and statutes passed by Congress the "supreme law" of the land was a leading advocate of state sovereignty. William Paterson, a lawyer trained at Princeton, and a dandy who emulated the manners and dress of the emergent American aristocracy, submitted the New Jersey Plan to the convention on June 15. His nine resolutions to "revise, correct, and enlarge" the Articles of Confederation included the formation of a national government with a single legislative body, in which each state would have one vote. This was simply a duplicate of the Congress established under the Articles of Confederation. Paterson also proposed an executive of several men—he left the number blank—whose members could be removed by Congress "on application by a majority" of state governors. These provisions of the New Jersey Plan were directly opposed to the "Federalist" notion of the Virginia Plan and were intended to maintain state control over a weak national government. But for reasons that Paterson never explained to the convention, he also proposed that "all acts" of Congress "shall be the supreme law of the respective states" and that "the judiciary of the several states shall be bound thereby in their decisions, anything in the respective laws of the individual states to the contrary notwithstanding."

Paterson clearly had no intention of placing the federal judiciary in a position of "supremacy" over the states. He envisioned a Congress in which the states—particularly the smaller states like New Jersey—dominated the federal government, and in which the national executive had very limited powers. Paterson's proposal that "all acts" of Congress would be the "supreme law" of the states hardly threatened state power, especially since his plan limited the jurisdiction of federal judges to cases that involved impeachments, piracies, treaties, and "collection of the federal revenue." But in his choice of words, Paterson—unwittingly for sure—gave the advocates of a strong national government the design of a judicial battering ram that would knock down hundreds of state laws over the next two centuries.

When the Committee on Detail submitted its draft Constitution to the delegates on August 6, it adopted Paterson's "supreme law" wording with little change. But the committee's draft, of course, also proposed a Congress with sweeping powers over the states. With hardly another word on the convention floor, the delegates approved the Supremacy Clause in their final vote on September 12, 1787. The ultimate irony of the Constitution is that the provision giving the Supreme Court a veto power over state laws, the most important power it exercises, was first proposed by a vehement advocate of state sovereignty. To compound this irony, George Washington nominated William Paterson to the Supreme Court in 1793, a position he held until his death in 1806. Paterson remained a firm advocate of constitutional supremacy during his judicial service, ruling in one case that "every act of the legislature repugnant to the constitution is absolutely void."

Over the past two centuries, historians have debated and politicians have declaimed over the question of "judicial review" of federal and state laws. Exercising this power, the Supreme Court has struck down hundreds of laws as contrary to the Constitution. Depending on the prevailing political winds, critics of "judicial supremacy" have come from both the left and right. During the early New Deal years of Franklin Roosevelt's presidency, the "Nine Old Men" on the Supreme Court were excoriated by the left for striking down state and federal laws designed to revive an economy crippled by the Great Depression. Two decades later, critics on the right mounted a campaign to "Impeach Earl Warren" and curb the Court's jurisdiction, to punish the Chief Justice and his colleagues for "putting Negroes in the schools and taking God out," as one southern politician complained. More recently, critics of "judicial activism" have come from both sides of the political spectrum. Opponents of abortion rights denounced the Supreme Court for exercising the power of judicial review to strike down criminal abortion laws, while supporters of affirmative action programs criticized the Court for ruling that cities cannot "set aside" a portion of public construction funds for minority-owned firms. Judicial review of legislation is a sword that cuts on both sides of its sharp blade, a fact the Framers clearly understood when they inserted the Supremacy Clause in the Constitution.

5

"The Country Must

Finally Decide"

Surprisingly, it was not until August 20, after three months of deliberation, that any delegate raised the question of including a bill of rights in the Constitution. Many had thought about this issue, and talked about it over dinners in the surrounding taverns and in meetings of state delegations. All but two of the state constitutions that were adopted after the states declared their independence from England in 1776 contained "bills of rights" that protected citizens against arbitrary governmental power. Many of these constitutions included specific guarantees for rights of speech, press, and religion. The Virginia constitution, which James Madison had helped to draft, offered protection against unreasonable search or seizure, provided that defendants in criminal trials could not be forced to testify against themselves, and barred the state from infringing the freedom of the press. Pennsylvania, where the first colonial newspaper was published and which was settled by Quakers, who preached and practiced religious toleration, protected the freedoms of press and religion in its constitution.

Although a large majority of delegates came to Philadelphia with the resolve to create a strong federal union—one with "positive" powers to make and execute national laws—most also believed that the state governments should be primarily responsible for protecting citizens in the "negative" sense of barring legislators and executive officials from infringing their basic rights. Many of these "inalienable" rights—summed up as "life, liberty, and the pursuit of happiness" in the Declaration of Independence—had first been "enumerated" in the Magna Carta. The notion of listing such rights in a written constitution gained many supporters before and after the American Revolution. Few of those who advocated bills of rights in state constitutions, however, felt that the federal constitution they were creating should add to—or subtract from—the rights provided by the states.

Ironically, it was a delegate from the slave-owning state of South Carolina who first proposed a federal bill of rights. When the session opened on August 20, Charles Cotesworth Pinckney submitted thirteen "propositions" to the convention, asking that they be referred to the Committee on Detail. Pinckney, who rose the very next day to denounce proposals to give Congress the power "of meddling with the importation of negroes," proposed that "the liberty of the press shall be inviolably preserved," and that "no soldier shall be quartered in any house in time of peace without consent of the owner." With changes only of wording, Pinckney's proposals were incorporated—four years later—into the Bill of Rights as parts of the First and Third Amendments. But the delegates in 1787 referred them "without debate or consideration" to the Committee on Detail, from which they never emerged.

On September 12, three weeks after Pinckney offered his proposal, the Committee on Style submitted its draft of the Constitution, laying out in detail the "positive" powers of the three branches of the national government. Along with its draft, the committee appended a letter to the delegates. Noting that "the full and entire approbation of every state is not perhaps to be expected," the committee expressed its hope that the draft Constitution "may promote the lasting welfare of that country so dear to us all, and secure her freedom and happiness." George Mason of Virginia was not happy with the result. "He wished the plan had been prefaced with a Bill of Rights," Madison recorded his Virginia colleague as saying. Mason added that such a provision "would give great quiet to the people; and with the aid of the state declarations, a bill might be prepared in a few hours." Elbridge Gerry of Massachusetts "concurred in the idea and moved for a committee to prepare a Bill of Rights."

Only two delegates addressed Gerry's motion. Roger Sherman of Connecticut spoke for the "localists" in the convention. "The state Declarations of Rights are not repealed by this Constitution," he argued, "and being in force are sufficient." Mason rose from his seat again. "The laws of the United States are to be paramount to state Bills of Rights," he replied. These brief remarks, on both sides of this momentous question, barely scratched the surface of a question that later divided those who supported or opposed the ratification of the Constitution. Eager to conclude their deliberations, the state delegations—with the abstention of Gerry's colleagues from Massachusetts—unanimously rejected his motion.

Three days after deciding not to include a bill of rights in the Constitution, the delegates took their final vote on the provisions of the document they had labored to produce. On September 15, George Mason offered a motion that no "navigation act" regarding the shipping trade be enacted without the concurrence of two thirds of each house of Congress, rather than a simple majority as provided by the draft Constitution. Mason lost on this issue by a vote of seven states to three. Within seconds of the tally, Edmund Randolph sought and received George Washington's permission to address the convention. Almost four months earlier, Randolph had yielded to Madison's entreaties to introduce the Virginia Plan to the convention, prefaced by his own proposal that the Articles of Confederation "be so corrected and enlarged as to accomplish" their objectives of ensuring the "common defense, security of liberty and general welfare" of the confederated states. Randolph was bitterly disappointed with the results of the succeeding four months of debate and deliberation. Scribbling furiously to record his friend's remarks, Madison wrote that Randolph denounced the "dangerous power given by the Constitution to Congress" and expressed "the pain he felt at differing from the body of the convention, on the close of the great and awful subject of their labors."

Randolph knew that his fellow delegates were eager to submit the Constitution to the states for final ratification. Keenly aware that he spoke for a small minority, he nonetheless moved that "amendments to the plan might be offered by the state conventions, which should be submitted to and finally decided on by another general convention." Should his motion be rejected, Randolph said with obvious sadness, it would "be impossible for him to put his name to the instrument." Randolph spoke to the convention not only as a single delegate but as the governor of Virginia, the state whose legislature had called for the Philadelphia convention. His introduction of the Virginia Plan had carried special weight because of his position.

George Mason, who followed Randolph in addressing the delegates, enjoyed his own eminence as the author of Virginia's Declaration of Rights and from his indefatigable labors in framing the Constitution he now rose to reject. Mason spoke in even stronger words than Randolph. The "dangerous power" given to Congress in the Constitution, he predicted, "would end either in monarchy, or a tyrannical aristocracy; which, he was in doubt, but one or other, he was sure." Mason complained that the Constitution "had been formed without the knowledge or idea of the people." He followed Randolph in proposing another convention, one that could add a bill of rights to the version before the delegates. "It was improper to say to the people, take this or nothing," Mason argued.

The arguments of Randolph and Mason, made by delegates who were widely respected by their fellows, did not fall on deaf ears in the State House chamber. But they did not sway any votes that were not already committed. Charles Pinckney of South Carolina responded to his fellow southerners. "These declarations from members so respectable," he said, "give a particular solemnity to the present moment." But Pinckney saw no reason for a second convention. "Nothing but confusion and contrariety could spring from the experiment," he predicted. "He was not without objections as well as others to the plan," Pinckney said of the draft Constitution. "But apprehending the danger of a general confusion, and an ultimate decision by the sword, he should give the plan his support."

The last delegate to speak before the convention took its final votes on the Constitution had, like Randolph and Mason, labored hard over the past four months. Elbridge Gerry had risen to speak more than a hundred times, most often to denounce the "Federalist" provisions that Madison had drafted, which Gerry considered incursions on the rights of the states. In his speech of September 15, Gerry listed in detail his accumulated objections to the Constitution. Some points were minor, such as "the power of Congress over the places of election." Others were substantial, such as the Great Compromise on counting slaves as three fifths of a "person" in allocating House seats. But on each of Gerry's objections, other delegates had voted with him in the minority and then swallowed their doubts when the time came for a final vote on the Constitution.

Gerry assured his fellow delegates that he, too, could "get over all these" objections. But he could not sign a document in which "the rights of the citizens" had been "rendered insecure by the general power of the legislature to make what laws they please to call necessary and proper." Gerry was not a diehard on the states' rights issue; he had earlier spoken in favor of a federal union as "an umpire to decide controversies" between the states. Neither did he support "the people" as best qualified to make political decisions, as shown by his remarks about the "excesses" of democracy. But Gerry equally distrusted legislative supremacy, and his advocacy of a national bill of rights fit into his political philosophy, which sought a broad dispersal of power between the states and federal government, and between their separate branches. Having opened his speech by stating that he felt compelled "to withhold his name from the Constitution," Gerry ended with a plea for "a second general convention," as Randolph had moved.

As soon as Gerry sat down, the convention voted on Randolph's motion for "another general convention" to consider amendments "offered by the state conventions" when they met to consider ratification of the Constitution. Madison recorded the verdict on Randolph's motion: "All the states answered—no." Madison then scribbled in his notes: "On the question to agree to the Constitution, as amended. All the states aye. The Constitution was then ordered to be engrossed. And the House adjourned."

The delegates met on this Saturday until six o'clock, and left the State House for dinners in their rooming houses or taverns while the product of their labors was copied in a fine hand on four sheets of parchment and printed by the firm of Dunlap and Claypoole for their final session on Monday, September 17. Sunday may have been a day of rest for many of the weary delegates, but some worked in their rooms with pen and ink, putting onto paper their final words on the document over which they had labored for the past four months. Not a single delegate was pleased with every provision of the Constitution. George Washington, who rarely spoke from his presiding chair, expressed his thoughts in a letter to Patrick Henry, his friend and fellow revolutionary soldier. "I wish the Constitution which is offered had been made more perfect," Washington confessed, "but I sincerely believe it is the best that could be obtained at this time." Henry, who would soon lead the Virginia campaign against ratification of the Constitution, revered Washington as a military leader but rejected the product of the Philadelphia convention as providing "no checks, no real balances, in this government."

The question of checks and balances had consumed the delegates in Philadelphia over the entire summer of 1787. How should they check the powers of government over the rights of the citizens? And how should they balance the powers of the separate branches of the national government? These were questions that had provoked four months of debate, and that produced a document based on many compromises, both large and small. When the delegates returned to the State House on Monday morning, September 17, they first listened while the convention secretary, William Jackson, read the engrossed copy of the Constitution, which had been placed on each desk in the chamber. During this reading, which consumed at least an hour, a dozen of the delegates looked down at their notes and rehearsed their final speeches to the convention.

The first to rise, slowly and with helping arms, was Benjamin Franklin, the oldest delegate at the age of eighty-one. Crippled by gout, Franklin handed the pages of his speech to his fellow Pennsylvanian James Wilson and sat down to hear his words read to the convention. "I confess that there are several parts of this Constitution which I do not at present approve," Wilson read from Franklin's speech, "but I am not sure I shall ever approve them." Franklin made light of his advanced age. "The older I grow, the more apt I am to doubt my own judgment, and to pay more respect to the judgment of others." Franklin continued with a joking reference to theological debate. An Episcopalian divine, he recounted, once told the Pope that the only difference between their denominations was that "the Church of Rome is infallible and the Church of England is never in the wrong."

James Madison did not indicate in his notes whether the delegates responded with laughter to Franklin's little joke. He did, however, record Franklin's next jest, about "a certain French lady, who in a dispute with her sister said, I don't know how it happens, sister, but I meet with nobody but myself, that's always in the right—Il n'y a que moi qui a toujours raison." Madison got the French right, and Franklin got his point across. "For when you assemble a number of men to have the advantage of their joint wisdom," Franklin continued, "you inevitably assemble with those men, all their prejudices, their passions, their errors of opinion, their local interests, and their selfish views. From such an assembly can a perfect production be expected?" This was, in almost the same words, the question George Washington had posed to Patrick Henry.

Benjamin Franklin answered his own rhetorical question about the Constitution. "The opinions I have had of its errors, I sacrifice to the public good," he told his fellow delegates. Franklin concluded with his "wish that every member of the convention who may still have objections to it, would with me, on this occasion doubt a little of his own infallability, and to make manifest our unanimity, put his name to this instrument." Franklin made one final effort to achieve unanimity on the Constitution. He proposed that "the Constitution be signed by members" not as individuals but "by the unanimous consent of the states present" at the convention.

Franklin's motion to adopt the Constitution by vote of the states ran into a minor roadblock. Nathaniel Gorham of Massachusetts, who rose to speak on almost every issue the delegates considered, made one final motion. Expressing his wish "of lessening objections to the Constitution," Gorham proposed changing the provision that apportioned House seats from "every forty thousand" inhabitants to thirty thousand. This motion would have given Massachusetts another House seat in Congress. Gorham's motion struck one delegate, perhaps the most influential in the convention, as "of so much consequence that it would give much satisfaction to see it adopted." With this blessing from George Washington, Gorham's motion passed without dissent.

James Madison then recorded the convention's final action. "On the question to agree to the Constitution enrolled in order to be signed. It was agreed to, all the states answering aye." But even this unanimous vote did not end debate on the Constitution. Edmund Randolph rose from his seat, asked George Washington for permission to speak, and then looked directly at Benjamin Franklin, almost three times his age. Randolph "apologized for his refusing to sign the Constitution," he said, "notwithstanding the vast majority and venerable names that would give sanction to its wisdom and its worth." Randolph had not decided "that he should oppose the Constitution" after the convention ended, he assured Franklin. "He meant only to keep himself free to be governed by his duty as it should be prescribed by his future judgment," he continued. Randolph then pledged to take "such steps as might appear to him most consistent with the public good." With these equivocal words, Randolph nodded to Franklin and took his seat.

Once again, and with great effort, Franklin rose to address the convention. "He expressed a high sense of obligation to Mr. Randolph for having brought forward" the Virginia Plan, Madison recorded, "and hoped that he would yet lay aside his objections, and by concurring with his brethren, prevent the great mischief which the refusal of his name might produce." Randolph was deeply moved by Franklin's remarks. Madison recorded his colleague's final words to the convention. "He repeated that in refusing to sign the Constitution, he took a step which might be the most awful of his life, but it was dictated by his conscience, and it was not possible for him to hesitate, much less, to change." Once again, Randolph appealed to the delegates to allow the state conventions to propose amendments, and for a second national convention to consider them before final ratification. Failure to do this, he predicted, "would really produce the anarchy and civil convulsions which were apprehended from the refusal of individuals to sign it."

Elbridge Gerry then rose to describe "the painful feelings of his situation, and the embarrassment" he felt at Franklin's remarks, which he considered as "levelled at himself and the other gentlemen who meant not to sign." But Gerry felt even more strongly that "a civil war may result from the present crisis of the United States," a crisis that would only worsen under the proposed Constitution. Franklin's motion, that the Constitution be signed by individual delegates but sent for ratification "by the unanimous consent of the states," was adopted without dissent. The delegates then took their final vote, to deposit the Journal of the Convention with the president, with directions that "he retain the Journal and other papers, subject to the order of the Congress, if ever formed under the Constitution." However confident the delegates were that a new Congress would be formed, they knew that ratification by nine states—required by Article VII—was not a foregone conclusion.

Madison recorded the next step in his notes: "The members then proceeded to sign the instrument." The parchment copy of the Constitution was laid on the small table, covered with green baize, that stood before Washington's chair as presiding officer. George Washington signed first, as president of the convention. While he placed his signature on the parchment, dipping his pen in a silver inkwell, the remaining delegates lined up, as they had in voting on motions, in geographical order, north to south—beginning with New Hampshire and ending with Georgia. John Langdon of New Hampshire was the first to sign after Washington, and Abraham Baldwin of Georgia the last; ironically, neither man had contributed much to the convention. The name of John Dickinson of Delaware, who was ill and had returned home the day before, was signed by his colleague George Read.

While the last signatures were being affixed, Madison recorded a touching scene. Benjamin Franklin, who had been helped forward to sign the Constitution, looked at the wall behind the president's chair, on which a bright yellow sun had been painted. Franklin spoke to the delegates who surrounded him. "I have, said he, often in the course of a session, and the vicissitudes of my hopes and fears as to its issue, looked at that behind the President without being able to tell whether it was rising or setting: But now at length I have the happiness to know that it is a rising and not a setting sun."

With that last remark in their minds, the delegates voted to adjourn "sine die." And then, as George Washington reported in his diary, "the members adjourned to the City Tavern," the meeting and eating place of Philadelphia's elite, for a dinner hosted by Washington. Most likely, even the three delegates who refused to sign the Constitution trooped along with the men they had argued with for an entire summer. Indeed, scarcely a delegate had not made at least one passionate speech on an issue about which he felt strongly.

Fifty-five men attended at least part of the Philadelphia convention. Some, like John Lansing and Robert Yates of New York, departed soon after they arrived, convinced that the convention's real purpose was to discard the Articles of Confederation and impose a strong national government on the states. Others who opposed the "Federalist" plan, like Luther Martin of Maryland, remained in Philadelphia until shortly before the convention ended, but left without a farewell speech. Martin's last words, spoken on August 31, warned that "the people would be against" the Constitution, and "would not ratify it unless hurried into it by surprise." Six of the delegates, including the three who stayed through the final session and refused to sign the Constitution, became leaders of the Antifederalist movement against ratification. Of the thirty-nine delegates who did sign the final document, only a handful were men of national reputation and renown: Alexander Hamilton of New York, Benjamin Franklin, Robert Morris, and Gouverneur Morris of Pennsylvania, and James Madison and George Washington of Virginia. Other signers, of course, held positions of influence in their states, and several gained eminence after the Constitution was ratified, as members of Congress, cabinet officers, or justices of the Supreme Court.

The men who sat through the long and often tedious sessions of the Philadelphia convention in 1787 constituted, with some exceptions, a notable collection of political thinkers and practitioners. Measured by their prior and subsequent public service, both in state and federal government, no comparable group has contributed more to the American system of government. For more than two centuries, scholars have debated the motivations of the men who framed the Constitution. In a book that shattered the conventional view of the Framers, historian Charles Beard of Columbia University argued in 1913 that the Philadelphia delegates were motivated primarily by economic self-interest. He computed—down to the last dollar—the amount of wealth that each delegate held in public securities, land speculation, "mercantile, manufacturing, and shipping" businesses, and ownership of slaves. Beard claimed that the "overwhelming majority" of the Framers were "economic beneficiaries from the adoption of the Constitution." His book, *An Economic Interpretation of the Constitution*, came at the height of the "progressive" era in American politics, a time in which "muckrakers" such as Lincoln Steffens, Ida Tarbell, and Upton Sinclair exposed the greed and corruption of American capitalism.

Historians, much like politicians, move with the currents of public opinion. Beard's depiction of the Framers as self-interested capitalists was countered in 1928 by Charles Warren of Harvard, who had already won the Pulitzer Prize for his three-volume work, *The Supreme Court in United States History*. Warren, a lawyer and scion of a patrician Boston family, argued in his book, *The Making of the Constitution*, that the Framers were farsighted statesmen who abandoned their parochial interests to forge a Grand Compromise that created a strong national union as the only alternative to the disunity of the confederated states. Basing his research largely on the correspondence of the Framers, Warren wrote that the "patriotic sincerity" of these men was based on "principles which were distinctively American and little connected with economics." Warren, of course, wrote in a decade that celebrated the achievements of American capitalism, which soon crumbled in the Great Depression that followed the Crash of 1929.

Which historian—Beard or Warren—correctly identified the underlying motivations of the men who framed the Constitution? There is no question, as Beard concluded, that most of the Framers had some personal stake in the outcome of their deliberations. But evidence of economic motivation does not necessarily contradict Warren's claim that the Framers also acted from "such motives as patriotism, pride in country, unselfish devotion to the public welfare, desire for independence, inherited sentiments, and convictions of right and justice."

Politicians often act from motives that reflect a mixture of interests. Some are personal, some are philosophical, and others respond to public opinion. It would be difficult to identify a single delegate to the Philadelphia convention in 1787 who voted—on hundreds of motions—with a consistency of motivation. James Madison himself, who could aptly be called the first of the Framers, advocated a plan of popular election for all members of Congress and the president. But Madison finally agreed to equal votes for states in the Senate, to indirect election of the president, and to counting slaves as three fifths of a person in allocating House seats.

Madison later shared with Thomas Jefferson—who observed the Philadelphia convention from his diplomatic post in Paris—his concern that the Constitution, "should it be adopted, will neither effectually answer its national object nor prevent the local mischiefs which everywhere excite disgust against the state governments." In this gloomy assessment of his labors, Madison took little account of the combination of principle and practicality that he brought to the monumental task of framing the Constitution. There is, in retrospect, significance in the fact that Madison's last words to the convention—spoken on September 15—responded to a motion that every state have an equal vote in the Senate, a proposal he had consistently opposed. "Begin with these special provisos," he said, "and every state will insist on them." When the convention ended, Madison had agreed to this provision in the Constitution. More than any delegate in Philadelphia, Madison knew that ratification of the Constitution depended on the many compromises that he had initially opposed and then grudgingly accepted.

One of these compromises dealt with the number of states necessary to ratify the Constitution. The delegates resolved this question near the end of their deliberations. This was, they all recognized, an important and delicate issue, since the Articles of Confederation they were supposedly "revising" provided that amendments must be approved by unanimous vote of the states. It was almost certain that at least one state, and probably two or three, would vote in the Confederation Congress to reject the Constitution. Rhode Island, after all, had refused to send any delegates to Philadelphia, and its political leaders had denounced the whole notion of a new constitution. New York's governor, George Clinton, also opposed the idea, and two of the state's three delegates to the Philadelphia convention had walked out in July, leaving Alexander Hamilton with a voice but no vote.

To lessen the risk of rejection, the delegates voted on August 31 that ratification by nine of the thirteen states "shall be sufficient" to establish the Constitution as binding among the ratifying states. During the debate on what became Article VII, motions were made to set the number at seven, eight, nine, ten, and thirteen of the states. Ironically, two delegates who refused to sign the Constitution helped to assure its final ratification. Edmund Randolph proposed nine as "a respectable majority" of the states, and George Mason agreed this was the "preferable" number. Compounding the irony, Madison and the other Virginia delegates voted against the motion, placing their state in the minority on this motion, which passed by a vote of eight states to three.

The delegates also decided to bypass the Confederation Congress and submit the Constitution to conventions in each state. This was also a risky move, since they could not dictate to the states how to choose the members of these conventions. Madison urged this move, rather than allowing the state legislatures to vote on ratification, for the quite pragmatic reason that, as he put it, "the powers given to the general government being taken from the state governments, the legislatures would be more disinclined" to ratify the Constitution. Madison ended on a loftier note: "The people were in fact," he proclaimed, "the fountain of all power, and by resorting to them, all difficulties were got over."

The difficulties of securing ratification by conventions of at least nine states would not easily be "got over," as Madison well knew. The day after they adjourned, the Philadelphia delegates sent the Constitution to New York, on a stagecoach with Major Jackson, for submission to the Confederation Congress. Considering that the delegates had voted to bypass that body, this step was largely, as Madison confessed to George Washington, "a matter of form and respect." Along with eight other signers, Madison was a member of Congress, and he hoped that it would send the Constitution to the states without delay. He also hoped to secure a resolution from Congress that endorsed the ratification of the Constitution by the state conventions.

Madison accomplished his first goal, but only after his fellow Virginian Richard Henry Lee—who listened to George Mason's objections after the convention's veil of secrecy had been lifted—urged that the Congress amend the

Constitution to add a bill of rights. Ironically, Madison, the man we now honor as "the Father of the Bill of Rights," argued strenuously against Lee's motion and prevailed. On September 28, 1787, the Confederation Congress—with eleven states voting—unanimously agreed that the Constitution "be transmitted to the several legislatures, in order to be submitted to a convention of delegates chosen in each state by the people thereof." His fellow congressmen, however, frustrated Madison's second goal, withholding any endorsement of the Constitution. After all, the document they sent to the states would replace their body with another, more powerful Congress, one that would wield enormous powers over the states they had been chosen to represent.

Two days after this vote, Madison wrote from New York to George Washington, who had returned to his Mount Vernon estate. The refusal of Congress to endorse the Constitution pained Madison. "A more direct approbation would have been of advantage" in securing ratification, he lamented. The man who accepted many compromises in Philadelphia was now afraid that too many compromises might doom his ultimate goal of a strong national government. "The country must finally decide," he wrote to Washington, "the sense of which is as yet wholly unknown."

6

"The Plot Thickens Fast"

James Madison and other Framers of the Constitution feared that the document they had labored so hard to create might be ripped to shreds in the state conventions to which it was sent—without endorsement—by the Confederation Congress. Their deliberations in Philadelphia had been conducted behind closed doors and sealed windows, raising suspicions that the delegates had conspired to impose an executive "monarchy" or a legislative "tyranny" on the people. Many delegates were regarded—quite rightly—as representatives of the old colonial aristocracy or the newer economic elite. The "Federalists" who dominated the Constitutional Convention were largely from the cities of the Eastern Seaboard, spread from Boston in Massachusetts to Charleston in South Carolina. More than half of the Framers were lawyers or had legal training, which raised more suspicions among those who distrusted "pettifoggers" in the courts. Only a handful worked the land as farmers, although many of the southern delegates owned or lived on plantations, where the land was plowed, planted, and harvested by slaves. In short, the Framers had little in common with the backcountry farmers, small-town tradesmen, and urban "mechanics" who made up a majority of the American population in 1787. To be more correct, the white, male population that owned enough property or paid enough taxes to vote in most states.

Factors that might seem to hobble the Framers and their supporters in the ratification debate also became sources of political strength. First—and very important in their campaign for the Constitution—the Framers took the initiative and adopted the "Federalist" name for themselves. This left their opponents with the weak and negative label "Antifederalist," despite the efforts of some to call themselves "Federal Republicans" or some more appealing name.

Second, the Federalists enjoyed the support of most of the country's newspapers, which were largely published in cities like Boston, New York, and Philadelphia. Access to the media has always been a crucial factor in political success. Third, the Federalists had the advantage of having a concrete proposal—a detailed Constitution—while their opponents had nothing to offer except criticism. The text of the Constitution was widely published and avidly read by those who voted for delegates to the state ratifying conventions. The Antifederalists, among them men of great oratorical and rhetorical skill, made speeches and wrote pamphlets that presented their case with logic and polish. But their only alternatives to the Constitution were amendment and delay.

The Federalists moved quickly to capitalize on their advantages. Most important, they only needed the support of nine states, the number proposed for ratification by Edmund Randolph. In the first three months after the Confederation Congress sent the document to the states, conventions in three of the smaller states voted unanimously for ratification. Delaware took first place in the race (its license plates now boast "The First State") on December 7, 1787. John Dickinson and George Read, two of the most active and articulate delegates in Philadelphia, persuaded the Delaware convention to ratify by a vote of thirty to zero. Led by James Paterson, who swallowed his states'-rights objections and signed the Constitution, the New Jersey convention ratified by a vote of thirty-eight to zero on December 18. Georgia, the most southern state and probably the most in need of national protection to fend off Indian attacks and predatory land speculators, ratified on the last day of 1787 by a vote of twenty-six to zero. George Washington said of Georgia that "if a weak state with the Indians on its back and the Spaniards on its flank does not see the necessity of a general government, there must I think be wickedness or insanity in the way."

The victories in these small states produced a welcome momentum for ratification. But the larger states posed greater problems for the Federalists. The first major obstacle was Pennsylvania, which seemed on the surface an easy state to persuade. After all, the state's most eminent citizen, Benjamin Franklin, had signed the Constitution and urged its adoption before the state legislature. Another of the Framers, James Wilson, helped to draft the Pennsylvania constitution and was widely respected around the state. But the Constitution's supporters faced two serious problems in Pennsylvania. First, although Federalists controlled the one-house state legislature, the Antifederalist bloc—mostly from the western and rural areas—held more than a third of the sixty-nine seats. If the Federalists could not muster a quorum of forty-six members, their opponents could block a vote to send the Constitution to a state convention. Second, the ratification debate, waged primarily in the state's newspapers, had become ferocious and fevered.

The Federalists solved the first problem with strongarm tactics. When the roll call in the legislative session, called to propose a ratification convention, turned up only forty-four members, the Pennsylvania Assembly sent its sergeant at arms to round up at least two of the Antifederalist members, who had boycotted the meeting to prevent a vote they knew they would lose. Surrounded by a self-appointed posse, the sergeant canvassed the taverns and lodging houses near the State House and finally located two of the boycotters, James M'Calmont and Jacob Miley. A later report by the dissenting members described their treatment by the Federalist posse: "Their lodgings were violently broken open, their clothes torn, and after much abuse and insult, they were forcibly dragged through the streets of Philadelphia to the State House, and there detained by force." Federalist members held M'Calmont and Miley in their seats while the Assembly—with its press-gang quorum—voted forty-six to twenty-three to hold elections for a ratification convention. This was hardly a victory for democracy, but neither side in the ratification debate played by the rules of genteel debate. For them, the stakes were too high.

The rhetoric of the debaters reached equally violent levels. Many of those who penned essays in the newspapers employed pseudonyms to conceal their identity, perhaps fearing the wrath of another partisan mob. Writing under the name "Centinel," one Pennsylvania Antifederalist argued in the *Independent Gazetteer* of Philadelphia that the "most perfect system of local government in the world" would be replaced under the Constitution by "the supremacy of the lordly and profligate few." Centinel could see "no alternative between adoption and absolute ruin." He even insinuated that "the weakness and indecision attendant on old age" had influenced Benjamin Franklin to sign the Constitution.

These charges against his dear friend, and the publication in the *Pennsylvania Packet* of George Mason's objections to the Constitution, prompted James Wilson to fight back. He was particularly stung by criticism that the Constitution did not include a bill of rights, which the Pennsylvania charter provided in detail. Wilson argued in the state ratification debate that "such an idea never entered the mind" of the Framers. "To every suggestion concerning a Bill of Rights, the citizens of the United States may always say, 'We reserve the right to do what we please.' "

Remarks like these did not please those who agitated for a constitution that would provide a federal bill of rights. Wilson upset his "democratic" critics by arguing that it was "the nature of man to pursue his own interests in preference to the public good." However accurate, this statement enraged one writer, who claimed that Wilson "has always been tainted with the spirit of high aristocracy; he has never been known to join in a truly popular measure, and his talents have ever been devoted to the patrician interest."

Despite these attacks on his character, Wilson prevailed in the Pennsylvania convention, which ratified the Constitution by a vote of forty-six to twenty-three on December 12, 1787. By the end of that fateful year, four of the nine states required for final ratification had given their assent to the Constitution. But ratification by three of the larger states—Massachusetts, Virginia, and New York—lay ahead. Without the approval of all three, the Constitution had little chance of success. It would be possible, of course, to secure final ratification with the votes of smaller states. But the ultimate goal of the Federalists—the creation of a powerful national government—would be frustrated if even one of these crucial states rejected the Constitution. Political reality, far more than principle, dictated the Federalist strategy of securing unanimous support in the state conventions.

The Massachusetts convention posed more problems for the Federalists. The town meetings that elected delegates sent a large number of farmers to Boston, and the western part of the state still harbored résentment at the politicians— many of them Federalists—whose tax laws had fueled Shays' Rebellion. And, in contrast to Pennsylvania, the Massachusetts Antifederalists were well organized, boasting the leadership of Elbridge Gerry, the renowned patriot and pamphleteer Sam Adams, and men like James Winthrop, James Warren, and Benjamin Austin, whose family roots went deep in the state's rocky soil. The Antifederalists also offered their own proposal: if the convention did ratify the Constitution, it should attach amendments to secure a federal bill of rights.

Passions ran high as the Massachusetts convention began on January 9, 1788. The delegates first elected Governor John Hancock as president, but Hancock—who looked at the political weathervane and saw it swinging wildly— pled an attack of gout and stayed home until the convention's final days. The debate in Massachusetts, which the public followed avidly in the state's newspapers, revolved around Antifederalist calls for a bill of rights. Writing under the name "Agrippa," one opponent published sixteen essays against the Constitution in the *Massachusetts Gazette.* "There is no bill of rights, and consequently a continental law may control any of those sacred principles" the state's constitution provided its citizens, Agrippa complained. The Federalist answer to this argument, made at the convention by Joseph Varnum, did little to mollify the opponents. The powers granted to Congress in the Constitution, Varnum claimed, were the sole extent of federal power; therefore, a bill of rights as a check on these powers would be superfluous. The problem with this response, as Antifederalists quickly noted, lay in the provision which gave to Congress the additional power "to make all laws which shall be necessary and proper" to implement the specified powers, which included a broad authority to provide for the "general welfare of the United States."

Antifederalists voiced their fears that Congress could use these clauses to ride roughshod over the states. Amos Singletary, a farmer from Worcester County, spoke bluntly: "These lawyers and men of learning, and moneyed men that talk so finely, and gloss over matters so smoothly, to make us poor illiterate people swallow down the pill, expect to get into Congress themselves. They expect to be the managers of the Constitution, and get all the power and all the money into their own hands. And then they will swallow up us little fellows."

This poor-mouthing by a longtime member of the state legislature provoked a fellow farmer, Jonathan Smith of western Berkshire County. "I am a plain man," he replied to Singletary, "and get my living by the plough. I am not used to speak in public, but I beg your leave to say a few words to my brother ploughjoggers in this house." Smith alluded to the "anarchy" of Shays' Rebellion, and the "cure" he found in the Constitution. "I got a copy and read it over and over," he continued. "I formed my own opinion, and was pleased with this constitution." Smith gestured toward Singletary. "My honorable old daddy there won't think that I expect to be a congressman and swallow up the liberties of the people. I never had any post, nor do I want one. But I don't think the worse of the constitution because lawyers and men of learning and monied men are fond of it."

Exchanges like these may not have swayed votes, but they revealed the views that each side in the ratification debates had of the other. Those in the middle recognized that compromise was necessary to avoid a bitter conflict. William Heath, a moderate Federalist, suggested that the convention "ratify the Constitution, and instruct our first Members of Congress, to exert their utmost endeavors to have such checks, and guards provided as appears to be necessary" to the delegates. Talk of compromise brought Governor Hancock from his sickbed to the convention, where he asked to "hazard a proposition" that would bridge the differences. Hancock quickly drafted nine proposed amendments—he probably had them ready—and put them before the convention. The first, and most important, provided "that all powers not expressly delegated by the aforesaid Constitution are reserved to the several states, to be by them exercised."

The response to Hancock's move exceeded his expectations. Sam Adams, perhaps the most respected Antifederalist, rose to announce that he now supported ratification. The delegates then voted by the narrow margin of 187 to 168 to ratify the Constitution, directing the state's future congressmen to "exert all their influence" in pressing for the amendments Hancock had drafted. As a reward, the Federalists promised to support Hancock's reelection as governor. Watching from Mount Vernon, George Washington expressed his qualified relief. "The decision of Massachusetts would have been more influential had the majority been greater," he wrote, "and the ratification unaccompanied by the recommendatory Act. As it stands, however, the blow is severely felt by antifederalists in the equivocal states."

Another three of the smaller states were not equivocal. By a vote of 128 to 40, Connecticut had ratified the Constitution a month before Massachusetts. Maryland held its convention in April 1788. The delegates listened for hours to the vituperative Antifederalist railings of Luther Martin, who had walked out of the Philadelphia convention in disgust. George Washington's secretary wrote that Martin "is a man whose character is so infamous that anything advanced by him against the Constitution, would where he is known, bias the people in favor of it." This proved an accurate prediction. After Martin sat down, the delegates voted for ratification by a tally of sixty-three to eleven. South Carolina followed in May by a vote of 149 to 73, although it joined Massachusetts in proposing amendments that would reserve to the states the powers not granted to Congress.

Five days after South Carolina became the eighth state to ratify the Constitution, George Washington wrote to his French friend the Marquis de Lafayette: "The plot thickens fast. A few short weeks will determine the political fate of America for the present generation, and probably no small influence on the happiness of society through a succession of ages to come." Although his prose was portentous, Washington did not exaggerate. Ratification by any of the remaining five states was far from certain. From New Hampshire to North Carolina, Antifederalists were determined to fight to the finish.

Washington hoped, of course, that Virginia would provide the crucial ninth vote for the Constitution. He remained aloof from the fray, and did not stand for election to the state convention, which opened in Richmond on June 2, 1788. Each county elected two delegates, and the western regions of Kentucky and Trans-Allegheny (then part of Virginia) sent sixteen, for a total of 170. A tally by a Federalist delegate showed eighty-five in his camp, with sixty-six Antifederalists and three "doubtful." The leanings of the western delegates were unknown, but they were the kind of "backwoods" men who in other states had opposed ratification. One Antifederalist delegate wrote that "both sides are contending" for their votes "by every means in their power." James Madison confessed to Washington that the outcome in Virginia "may depend on the Kentucky members; who seem to lean more against than in favor of the Constitution."

The delegates in Richmond included some of the most illustrious men in American political and judicial history. Among the Federalists were James Madison; George Wythe, the state's chancellor and its most noted lawyer; and John Marshall, a brilliant young lawyer who everyone knew was destined for national prominence. Their opponents were equally distinguished. George Mason had published his objections to the Constitution in a widely read pamphlet, Edmund Randolph was the state's governor, and Richard Henry Lee was a respected member of the Confederation Congress. These eminent men, however, had little of the luster of Patrick Henry, the golden-tongued orator who stirred the country to revolution in 1775 with his cry, "Give me liberty, or give me death!"

The former revolutionary was now a wealthy man, rich in landholdings, and he no longer spoke for the ordinary people he had spurred to fight the British. Ironically, Henry accused the Federalists of speaking for the people without their consent. The preamble to the Constitution began with the words "We the people of the United States" and spoke of their resolve to "form a more perfect union" of the states. Henry, whose speeches consumed more than a fifth of the convention record, vented his anger on Madison and the other Philadelphia delegates. "Who authorized them to speak of We the people, instead of We the states," he demanded to know. "The people gave them no power to use their name."

Henry waved a rhetorical copy of the Declaration of Independence before the delegates. The document "which separated us from Great Britain," he declaimed, had asserted the rights of the people against arbitrary governmental power. But the Constitution protected none of these rights. "The rights of conscience, trial by jury, liberty of the press," he thundered, "all pretensions to human rights and privileges, are rendered insecure, if not lost, by this change." Echoing his stirring call to rebellion against the British, Henry urged the delegates to rebel against the Federalists. "Liberty, greatest of all earthly blessings— give us that precious jewel, and you may take everything else!"

Despite his rhetorical excesses, Patrick Henry made a point that appealed to many delegates. Virginia had enshrined in its constitution in 1776 a Declaration of Rights, drafted by George Mason, that protected rights of religion, speech, and press. James Madison, who sat quietly during Henry's lengthy speeches, listened carefully and decided to take the wind out of his opponent's billowing sails. Madison, who had publicly opposed any amendments to the Constitution as a condition of ratification, conferred with Edmund Randolph and proposed a compromise. If Madison agreed to amendments, would Randolph support ratification? The two former adversaries in Philadelphia reached agreement in Richmond. Speaking in quiet tones, Randolph told the convention that he would support the Constitution if the delegates asked Congress to adopt a bill of rights.

Randolph's defection to the Federalist camp enraged Patrick Henry. "It seems to me very strange and unaccountable," he said with a glare at Randolph, that the Constitution "which was the object of his execration, should now receive his encomiums. Something extraordinary must have operated to produce so great a change in his opinions." The soft-spoken Randolph could not contain his outrage. "I disdain his aspersions and his insinuations," he shot back at Henry. "His asperity is warranted by no principle of parliamentary decency, nor compatible with the least shadow of friendship: and if our friendship must fall—let it fall, like Lucifer, never to rise again." Henry was so incensed by his comparison to the devil that he challenged Randolph to a duel, but tempers soon cooled and the two men never cocked their pistols.

Just before the Virginia convention voted to ratify the Constitution, by the close vote of eighty-nine to seventy-nine, Patrick Henry conceded defeat in a gracious speech. "If I shall be in the minority," he said, "I shall have those painful sensations which arise from a conviction of being overpowered in a good cause. Yet I will be a peaceable citizen." Henry spoke wistfully of his revolutionary efforts. He expressed the hope "that the spirit which predominated in the revolution is not yet gone, nor the cause of those who are attached to the revolution yet lost. I shall therefore patiently wait in expectation of seeing that government changed, so as to be compatible with the safety, liberty, and happiness, of the people."

Patrick Henry lost the battle in Virginia, but he won the war he waged against the Federalists. James Madison agreed, as a condition for ratification, to press the new Congress to adopt a bill of rights. With that concession, the debate over the Constitution shifted from the "positive" powers of Congress to the "negative" limitations that would protect "the people" from their federal lawmakers.

As it turned out, Virginia was not the ninth state to ratify. That honor went to New Hampshire, whose convention first met in February 1788. When the state's Federalists realized they had been outvoted in the town meetings that elected delegates, they pulled all their parliamentary strings and succeeded in postponing the convention until June 17, two weeks after Virginia began its sessions. By that time, the New Hampshire Federalists had flexed their political muscles—promising federal offices to their opponents—and they prevailed on June 21 by the narrow margin of fifty-seven to forty-seven. New Hampshire bested Virginia by four days in the race for ratification, but neither side in this political battle could claim victory until New York decided to adopt or reject the Constitution.

Without New York, there could be no United States. Not only in population but in commerce and finance, this was the largest state, the linchpin of the union. Alexander Hamilton, New York's sole delegate in Philadelphia after Robert Yates and John Lansing departed, turned his immense talents and energy to the ratification campaign. He had founded the Federalist Party in New York before the Constitutional Convention, and its members represented the state's landowning, mercantile, banking, and legal interests. Governor George Clinton headed the Antifederalist forces, which drew support—as in most states—from farmers and "upstate" voters.

Hamilton turned the momentum for ratification to his advantage, maneuvering to delay the state convention until adoption of the Constitution seemed assured. This put the burden on his opponents to either accept or destroy the union. He also waged a masterful propaganda campaign, through the eighty-five essays that were published in the New York press under the name "Publius." Hamilton recruited John Jay, who became the first Chief Justice of the United States, and James Madison to help write the essays, which the authors churned out every two or three days between October 1787 and May 1788. The Publius essays gained later fame, and wide circulation, as *The Federalist Papers*, but they had little circulation or influence outside New York at the time.

The men who wrote the Publius essays were actually responding to

"Brutus," a pseudonymous Antifederalist who was never identified but may have been Robert Yates. Brutus wrote sixteen essays during the same months as the Publius letters. His attack on the Constitution stressed the country's size— "it now contains near three millions of souls"—and its diverse and discordant interests, from north to south. "Now, in a large, extended country," Brutus wrote, "it is impossible to have a representation, possessing the sentiments, and of integrity, to declare the minds of the people, without having it so numerous and unwieldy, as to be subject in great measure to the inconveniency of a democratic government." A national legislature, Brutus concluded, "would be composed of such heterogenous and discordant principles, as would constantly be contending with each other."

In a brilliant essay, later known as "Federalist No. 10," Madison—disguised as Publius—answered Brutus by accepting his premise and turning his logic around. "A landed interest, a manufacturing interest, a mercantile interest, a moneyed interest, with many lesser interests, grow up of necessity in civilized nations," Madison wrote, listing the groups that dominated Hamilton's Federalist Party, "and divide them into different classes, actuated by different sentiments and views." However, the existence of these "factions" was not a vice but a virtue in a national government. In a large and diverse country, Madison argued, no single faction was likely to control a legislative majority. "If a faction controls less than a majority," he wrote, "relief is supplied by the republican principle, which enables the majority to defeat its sinister views by regular vote." The more "factions" the better, he claimed. The "increased number of parties comprised within the Union" would better protect the people from "local prejudices," Madison concluded, and "make it less probable that a majority of the whole will have a common motive to invade the rights of other citizens."

The essays of Publius and Brutus, which powerfully and persuasively stated the arguments for and against a strong national government, probably changed few votes in the New York convention. What did change votes was the defection of a prominent Antifederalist to Hamilton's side. Sam Adams in Massachusetts and Edmund Randolph in Virginia had switched sides and swayed votes in their conventions. Melancton Smith—an upstate merchant—played this role in New York, although he had secretly changed sides before the convention began, convinced that his state's interests could not be protected outside the Union. Without revealing his true feelings, Smith debated the Constitution with Hamilton. He pointed out that a majority of a quorum in Congress would be twenty-four. "Can the liberties of three millions of people be securely trusted in the hands of twenty-four men," Smith asked. He charged Hamilton with proposing an "aristocratic" government. Hamilton, in fact, hardly concealed his admiration for an aristocracy of the wellborn and wealthy.

Sensing defeat on an up-or-down ratification vote, the New York Antifederalists—unaware of Smith's secret defection—adopted the strategy of their Massachusetts and Virginia compatriots and pressed for amendments to the Constitution. John Lansing proposed adding a bill of rights, including an amendment providing that "no person" could be deprived of "life, liberty, or property but by due process of law." With only minor changes in wording, Lansing's proposal later formed the basis of the Fifth Amendment to the Constitution, which has protected Americans from arbitrary governmental power since the Supreme Court "rescued" the Liberty Clause from corporations—which had used it as a weapon against workers—in the 1930s.

Lansing also proposed an amendment providing that all powers not expressly granted to Congress "shall be reserved to the respective states, to be by them exercised." This proposal, which echoed the words of Governor Hancock in Massachusetts, later formed the basis of the Tenth Amendment to the Constitution. That last—but certainly not least—article in the Bill of Rights provided that all powers not delegated to Congress "are reserved to the states respectively, or to the people." The nature and extent of these "unenumerated" powers have caused much debate in the Supreme Court's chambers over the past two centuries.

Lansing's move, endorsed by the Federalists, paved the way for Melancton Smith's motion that the Constitution be ratified with "confidence" that the proposed amendments would be adopted by Congress. Smith brought several wavering delegates with him to the Federalist side. On July 26, 1788, the convention voted thirty to twenty-seven to ratify the Constitution.

The New York vote sealed the victory of the Federalists, even though North Carolina and Rhode Island stubbornly refused to join the ratification parade. North Carolina, in fact, initially voted in August 1788 to reject the Constitution by a decisive vote of 184 to 84. The delegates to this first convention heatedly denounced the failure of the Framers to include a bill of rights. In November 1789, a month after the first Congress sent twelve proposed amendments to the states for ratification, North Carolina held a second convention and ratified the Constitution by the more decisive vote of 194 to 77. And the stubborn Rhode Islanders—who boycotted the Philadelphia convention—finally and grudgingly joined the Union in May 1790 by the closest vote of any state, thirty-four to thirty-two. Ironically, the only state with no constitution of its own was now subject to one it played no role in framing.

7

"The Nauseous Project of

Amendments"

James Madison and his fellow Federalists rejoiced at the final ratification of the Constitution they had labored to produce in Philadelphia and later guided through the state conventions. Their efforts had come perilously close to disaster; the switch of two votes in New York, six in Virginia and New Hampshire, or ten in Massachusetts could have doomed the Constitution. And the jubilation of the victorious Federalists was tempered by political reality. They had promised, as a campaign strategy during the ratification debates, to propose a bill of rights to the First Congress. Madison and other leading Federalists, who had opposed adding a bill of rights in Philadelphia, now found themselves under pressure to fulfill their campaign promise.

Despite the slowness of the mails in the age of sailing ships—it took weeks, sometimes months, for a letter to cross the Atlantic—one keen observer kept up a voluminous correspondence from his diplomatic post in Paris. Before and after ratification, Thomas Jefferson sent dozens of letters to America, all with the same message: the Constitution must contain a bill of rights. "I do not like," he wrote to Madison in December 1787, "the omission of a bill of rights providing clearly and without the aid of sophisms for freedom of religion, freedom of the press," and other guarantees against governmental oppression. Jefferson pounded his drum for more than a year. Writing in March 1789, just before the First Congress began its first session, Jefferson replied to Madison's letter of the previous October: "How it happened to be four months on the way," he wrote, "I cannot tell, as I never knew by what hand it came."

Madison had raised in this letter—reporting, he said, the sentiments of others—several objections to a bill of rights. Jefferson answered them point by point. "1. That the rights in question are reserved [to the states] by the manner in which the federal powers are granted. Answer. A constitutive act ... which leaves some precious articles unnoticed, and raises implications against others, a declaration of rights becomes necessary by way of supplement. This is the case of our new federal constitution." Jefferson moved on. "2. A positive declaration of some essential rights could not be obtained in the requisite latitude. Answer. Half a loaf is better than no bread. If we cannot secure all our rights, let us secure what we can." Jefferson reminded Madison of the "tyranny of the legislatures" and of executives. "In the arguments in favor of a declaration of rights," he noted, "you omit one which has great weight with me, the legal check which it puts into the hands of the judiciary." The third objection Madison raised—whether for himself or others—was that the "limited powers of the federal government" could not compel the states to protect their citizens' rights. Although Jefferson did not mention the Supremacy Clause of Article VI, his answer reflected its premise. "The declaration of rights will be the text whereby they will try all the acts of the federal government," he wrote. "In this view it is necessary to the federal government also: as by the same text they may try the opposition of the subordinate governments." In other words, state and federal governments alike would be bound to enforce the Constitution as "the supreme law of the land."

Once he became president, Jefferson would repent his support for judicial review of legislation. He wrote in 1803 of Chief Justice John Marshall's decision in *Marbury v. Madison* that the Constitution had become "a mere thing of wax in the hands of the judiciary, which they may twist and shape into any form they please." But in 1803, Jefferson was a powerful government official, whose assertion of power had been rejected by the judiciary; in 1789 he wrote as an advocate of the political principle that governmental power must be checked by the Constitution, enforced and interpreted by an independent judiciary. Like most officials, Jefferson's attachment to principle was tempered by political reality. The Supreme Court ruled against him in *Marbury*, and he responded as a partisan, just as other presidents—including Jackson, Lincoln, and both Roosevelts—complained about judicial decisions they disliked.

Keenly aware of Madison's ambivalence on the need for a bill of rights, Jefferson made a final appeal in his letter of March 1789. "There is a remarkable difference between the characters of the inconveniences which attend a declaration of rights, and those which attend the want of it," he wrote. "The inconveniences of the declaration are that it may cramp government in its useful exertions. But the evil of this is shortlived, moderate, and reparable. The inconveniences of the want of a declaration are permanent, afflicting, and irreparable: they are in constant progression from bad to worse."

Just at the time he received this letter from his mentor and friend, Madison was taking his seat in the First Congress—which met in the nation's first capital, New York City—as a representative from Virginia. Presidential electors had already been chosen under the Constitution's indirect plan, and they voted unanimously on February 4, 1789, for George Washington, with John Adams of

Massachusetts as vice president. On the same day, Madison faced the voters in Virginia. It had been a tough campaign, in which he faced James Monroe, a young protégé of Patrick Henry's and like Madison a future president. The state legislature, controlled by Antifederalists, sent two of its members, Richard Henry Lee and William Grayson, to the Senate.

Madison faced attack for his failure to support a bill of rights. He had "never thought the omission a material defect" in the Constitution, Madison explained, and was "not anxious to supply it even by subsequent amendments." But his election over Monroe by a scant 366 votes, and the fact that both Virginia and New York had called on Congress for a second—and wide-open—constitutional convention persuaded Madison to honor his promise, made in Virginia's ratifying convention, to press Congress for a bill of rights. Jefferson's letter provided the final push that Madison needed to begin the amendment process he had long resisted.

Looking back from the perspective of more than two centuries, the emergence of the Bill of Rights from the First Congress in 1789 has as many ironies as the events in Philadelphia that produced the Constitution in 1787. Much like football teams that shift from offense to defense when they lose the ball, the contending sides in the debate over the Bill of Rights switched positions as they fought for control of a brand-new political system. Federalists in the new Congress who had deprecated the need to declare the "rights" of the people now pushed for limits on their own powers. Antifederalists who had insisted on a bill of rights to protect the people against legislative "tyranny" suddenly turned around and claimed that Congress had more pressing business.

The First Congress met in New York City on March 4, 1789, but it lacked a quorum, with only eight senators and thirteen representatives on hand; another month passed before the House held its first official session and elected its speaker, Frederick Muhlenberg of Pennsylvania. The Senate lagged behind, conducting business with temporary officers until both chambers met on April 30 for the inauguration of President Washington, who spoke to members of Congress and a cheering throng of citizens from the balcony of Federal Hall, at the corner of Wall and Broad Streets in lower Manhattan.

Near the end of his inaugural address, Washington spoke directly to the members of Congress. They would need to "decide how far an exercise of the occasional power" conferred on them to propose amending the Constitution "is rendered expedient at the present juncture by the nature of objections which have been urged against the system, or by the degree of inquietude which has given birth to them." With this florid language, Washington seemingly hinted that Congress should respond to popular pressure for a bill of rights. Disclaiming "any particular recommendations on this subject," he nonetheless expressed hope that "a reverence for the characteristic rights of freemen and a regard for public harmony will sufficiently influence your deliberations on the question" of amendments.

The new president did not propose any particular amendment. He left that job to Madison, who had already begun the laborious task of sifting through some two hundred proposed amendments that eight of the state ratifying conventions had submitted. After eliminating duplicates, the list still approached a hundred. Even when Madison eliminated amendments he considered outside the Constitution's scope, there still remained dozens from various states. Madison imposed his own rule of thumb on the stack that remained; he would only consider amendments that had been proposed—with allowance for different wording—by at least four states. This made his task much easier, and reduced the pile to twenty-two potential amendments.

Madison informed the House on May 4 that he planned to introduce the final list of proposed amendments within the month. He hurried to complete this task, worried that Antifederalist calls for a second Constitutional Convention would spread from Virginia and New York to other states. The prospect of a second convention horrified Madison, who confessed his fear that such a convention would "mutilate" the Constitution that had emerged from Philadelphia. Another concern was that Congress had already bogged down in debate over "tonnage duties" and other revenue measures. Several representatives responded to Madison's announcement on May 4 with arguments that the House had more pressing business than debating a bill of rights. He made a conciliatory reply, expressing hope that the people would "wait with patience" until the House was "at leisure" to consider the issue.

Madison did not meet his self-imposed deadline, but he finally rose in the House chamber on June 8, 1789. Facing his fellow representatives, who numbered sixty-five, he placed a substantial pile of paper on his desk. Over the past several days, Madison had laboriously written in longhand a speech that would take him at least three hours to deliver. He knew that this might well be the most important address of his political life, certainly one that might rescue the Constitution from its enemies. The men who sat before Madison included Elbridge Gerry, his adversary in Philadelphia, and a bloc of Antifederalists who had switched positions and no longer supported a bill of rights. Their goal now was to press for a second convention and return to the Articles of Confederation, dressed up in new clothes.

Madison began with an apology. "I am sorry to be accessory to the loss of a single moment of time by the House," he said. But he did not rise for a trivial purpose. Madison usually spoke in measured, matter-of-fact terms, but he rose to unusual rhetorical heights on this momentous occasion. Harking back to the Revolution, he proclaimed his desire "to extinguish from the bosom of every member of the community, any apprehension that there are those among his countrymen who wish to deprive them of the liberty for which they valiantly fought and honorably bled." Looking beyond the House chamber, Madison asked "the doubting part of our fellow citizens" to credit the Federalists with "that spirit of deference and concession for which they have hitherto been distinguished." And the Federalists had, in fact, deferred to their adversaries in Philadelphia and made concessions that Madison had opposed in 1787 and now endorsed. Admitting that there remained "a great number of our constituents who are dissatisfied" with the Constitution, Madison continued that the campaign for a bill of rights, "though mistaken in its object, is laudable in its motive." Since he rarely spoke offhandedly, Madison must have meant to rebuke the Antifederalists whose ardor for this goal had cooled. He went on in this dismissive tone. It was primarily a desire for "amity and moderation" between the Federalists and their opponents, Madison implied, that led him "to conform to their wishes, and expressly declare the great rights of mankind secured under this Constitution."

His lengthy speech contained not a hint that Madison himself considered a bill of rights essential or even necessary. His goal was simply "to satisfy the public mind that their liberties will be perpetual," and to accomplish this "without endangering any part of the Constitution, which is considered as essential by those who promoted its adoption." Madison painted those who had pressed for state bills of rights as desiring to "raise barriers against power in all forms and departments of the Government," a vast exaggeration of their aims. Lumping together the state bills and the amendments he was introducing, Madison damned both with faint praise, saying that "although some of them are rather unimportant, yet, upon the whole, they will have a salutary tendency." Many declarations of rights "do no more than state the perfect equality of mankind," he sniffed. "This, to be sure, is an absolute truth, yet it is not absolutely necessary to be inserted at the head of a Constitution."

Madison clearly resented those who stirred up fears of an omnipotent and oppressive national government. In his mind, "the great danger lies rather in the abuse of the community than in the Legislative body," referring to Congress. The real danger, he argued, "is not found in either the Executive or Legislative departments of government, but in the body of the people, operating by the majority against the minority." The majorities he meant by this phrase were not those which elected members of Congress, but those which elected local and state lawmakers. Madison implied that the people had little to fear from the body he addressed, stating that the powers granted to Congress by the Constitution were "circumscribed" and "directed to particular objects" that were limited to those listed in Article I. He conceded that these powers "may admit of abuse to a certain extent," and even pointed to the "necessary and proper" clause as tempting Congress to exceed its powers. His concessions over, Madison concluded with a triumphant flourish, pointing to the federal courts as "independent tribunals of justice" that "will be an impenetrable bulwark against every assumption of power in the Legislative and Executive" branches.

Madison made no secret of his disdain for state governments, which he said "are as liable to attack" their citizens' rights "as the General Government is, and therefore ought to be as cautiously guarded against." Why, then, did he make the effort to draft a bill of rights, if he saw the states as more dangerous than Congress? His answer to this unstated question was smoothly phrased, but revealed his true feelings. It would be "highly politic," he said, "for the tranquility of the public mind, and the stability of the government, that we should offer something, in the form I have proposed, to be incorporated in the system of Government, as a declaration of the rights of the people." Soothing the public with a bill of rights he considered "unnecessary" was good politics, and Madison was certainly a good politician. The "something" he offered, after all, was better than nothing. And giving Congress nothing to consider might stir more calls to scrap the Constitution.

What *did* Madison offer to Congress as a bill of rights? He listed "the amendments which have occurred to me" in order from "firstly" to "ninthly." His first proposed amendment took inspiration from the Declaration of Independence, suggesting that "there be prefixed to the Constitution a declaration, that all power is originally vested in, and consequently derived from, the people." Madison continued with words borrowed from Thomas Jefferson. Governments existed to protect "the enjoyment of life and liberty, with the right of acquiring and using property, and generally of pursuing and obtaining happiness and safety." He went on to state—in words that only a lawyer could love—that "the people have an indubitable, unalienable, and indefeasible right to change their Government" when they find it "adverse" to their interests. This was precisely the kind of language that Madison considered "unnecessary" in a Constitution. Perhaps he hoped with this verbiage to placate Jefferson, who considered a bill of rights essential, which Madison clearly did not.

Madison's second proposed amendment responded to complaints by the smaller states, like Delaware and Rhode Island, that the Constitution penalized them by granting one representative for every thirty thousand inhabitants. These two states, in fact, each had just one House member in the First Congress. Madison considered this a petty issue, but he nonetheless proposed that each state have "at least two Representatives" in Congress. His third amendment proposed that changes in congressional salaries could not take effect "before the next ensuing election of Representatives."

Not until his fourth proposed amendment did Madison address the real concerns of those who pressed for a bill of rights. He suggested inserting several new clauses in the Constitution, after the provisions in Article I that barred Congress from enacting any "bill of attainder" or "ex post facto" law. It had been Elbridge Gerry of Massachusetts—who had vainly pressed for a bill of rights in 1787—who convinced the delegates in Philadelphia to include in the

Constitution these protections against governmental power to punish individuals without trial and for acts that were lawful when they were committed. Madison had not spoken a word in support of Gerry's motion in Philadelphia. Now he spoke in New York to press for additional rights in the Constitution.

Madison's fourth proposed amendment had ten separate paragraphs and included all but a few of the provisions adopted in the Bill of Rights that was later ratified by the states. The first paragraph dealt with religion: "The civil rights of none shall be abridged on account of religious belief or worship, nor shall any national religion be established, nor shall the full and equal rights of conscience be in any manner, or on any pretext, infringed." The next two paragraphs provided that the "right to speak" and "freedom of the press" should remain "inviolable," and that "the people shall not be restrained from peaceably assembling" and petitioning the government "for redress of their grievances." These paragraphs formed the basis of what later became the First Amendment.

The next paragraph in the proposed amendment had three clauses. The first provided that "The right of the people to keep and bear arms shall not be infringed" by the federal government. The second clause—separated by a semicolon from the first—stated that this right stemmed from the need for "a well armed and well regulated militia" to protect the "security of a free country," presumably from insurrection or invasion. The third clause provided that "no person religiously scupulous of bearing arms shall be compelled to render military service in person." This last clause did not survive the congressional gauntlet, but the first two were blended into the Second Amendment, with their order reversed and the semicolon replaced by a comma.

In recent years, advocates on both sides of the "gun control" issue have debated the "original intent" of those who framed the Second Amendment. Elbridge Gerry, Madison's adversary in both Philadelphia and New York, offered this defense of the proposed amendment: "What, sir, is the use of a militia? It is to prevent the establishment of a standing army, the bane of liberty." Arming the citizens who belonged to state militias, Gerry argued, would deter Congress from establishing a federal army that might oppress or invade the states. Those who now advocate the constitutional "right" of every citizen to "bear arms" of any kind—from cheap handguns to assault rifles—are well advised to read the debates that led to adoption of the Second Amendment. Not a single member countered Gerry's argument that the "right to bear arms" was limited to members of a state militia. The current opponents of gun control legislation pay little heed to the Framer who spoke most clearly to the "intent" of Congress on this controversial issue.

Madison followed this proposed amendment with one that reflected old resentments at the British army's practice of forcing the American colonists to house and feed its red-coated soldiers. The First Congress debated no more than ten minutes before adopting Madison's proposal that "No soldier shall in time of peace be quartered in any house without the consent of the owner; nor at any time, but in a manner warranted by law." With only minor wording changes, this became the Third Amendment to the Constitution.

The next four paragraphs that Madison read to Congress dealt with the rights of criminal defendants. Politicians today—responding to the "majority" against which Madison warned—are quick to denounce as "soft on crime" anyone who questions the need for quicker trials, longer sentences, and bigger prisons. More than two centuries ago, Madison spoke for most Americans in urging protections for ordinary citizens against the arbitrary practices of British officials that provoked their colonial subjects to revolt. He proposed that no person be subjected to more than "one trial for the same offence," which became the Double Jeopardy Clause of the Fifth Amendment. Madison also proposed that no person be "compelled to be a witness against himself," be "deprived of life, liberty, or property without due process of law," or be "obliged to relinquish his property, where it may be necessary for public use, without a just compensation." With minor wording changes, these proposals became part of the Fifth Amendment.

Madison also proposed the protection of criminal defendants against "excessive bail" before trial and "excessive fines" after conviction. These provisions, which became part of the Eighth Amendment, raised no opposition. But his proposal that Congress ban the infliction of "cruel and unusual punishments" prompted Samuel Livermore of New Hampshire to reply. He argued that "it is sometimes necessary to hang a man, villains often deserve whipping, and perhaps even having their ears cut off; but are we in future to be prevented from inflicting these punishments because they are cruel?" Madison's proposed amendment passed by a "considerable majority," but Delaware allowed whipping into the 1950s, and the Supreme Court has upheld capital punishment against charges that it is both "cruel and unusual." No state, however, now permits cutting off ears as a criminal penalty. In this sense, Madison's proposed amendment had the "salutary effect" he hoped for.

Madison included a provision that citizens be "secured in their persons, their houses, their papers, and their other property, from all unreasonable searches and seizures." He went on to propose jury trials in civil cases, the right to an "impartial jury" in criminal cases, and—near the bottom of the list—a guarantee that "no state" shall abridge "the freedom of the press." From this hodgepodge emerged parts of the First, Fourth, Sixth, and Seventh Amendments.

Another proposed amendment was phrased in convoluted words, but in the middle was a provision that the Bill of Rights—if adopted—"shall not be so construed as to diminish the just importance of other rights retained by the people." Madison stated his final proposal in clear words: "The powers not delegated by this Constitution, nor prohibited by it to the States, are reserved to the States respectively." These two provisions emerged from Congress, after polishing by committees and debate on the floor, as the Ninth and Tenth Amendments to the Constitution.

Madison outlined in his lengthy speech almost every provision that later became part of the Bill of Rights. He worked long hours, for more than a month, to perfect his list of proposed amendments and polish the words he spoke to Congress. But his heart was not really behind his careful preparation. Ending his speech, Madison confessed to his fellow representatives that his work "may be deemed unnecessary," but he saw "no harm in making such a declaration" of rights. "I am sure I understand it so," he concluded, "and do therefore propose it." With that ambivalent endorsement of his labors, Madison sat down.

Madison's halfhearted speech to Congress seems at odds with the accolades showered on him since his death—and even during his lifetime—as the "Father of the Bill of Rights." The facts are that he did *not* consider a federal bill of rights essential, and that he proposed amendments partly to placate his political mentor, Thomas Jefferson, and partly to blunt the Antifederalist campaign for a second constitutional convention. He even referred to "the nauseous project of amendments" in a letter to a Federalist friend. Nonetheless, Madison loyally and diligently performed the task he had assumed, and pressed ahead for adoption of the Bill of Rights by Congress and ratification by the states.

The immediate response to Madison's speech and list of proposed amendments was compounded of apathy and annoyance. Representative James Jackson of Georgia stated his opinion that "we ought not be be in a hurry with respect to altering the Constitution." He urged that his colleagues "not neglect the more important business which is now unfinished before them." Madison shot back that Jackson was "unfriendly to the object I have in contemplation," but assured the House that "I only wish to introduce the great work" of the Bill of Rights, and that "I do not expect it will be decided immediately."

Roger Sherman of Connecticut, who had often sparred with Madison at the Philadelphia convention, noted that his state ratified the Constitution "by a very great majority, because they wished for the Government; but they desired no amendments." He suggested to the House that "it will therefore be imprudent to neglect much more important concerns for this." Sherman had signed the Constitution in Philadelphia, and he saw no need for amendments. "I have strong objections to being interrupted in completing the more important business" of Congress, he complained, "because I am well satisfied it will alarm the fears of twenty of our constituents where it will please one." Madison seemed discouraged by these remarks. He replied to Sherman, in plaintive words, that he was "compelled to beg a patient hearing to what I have to lay before you."

Madison's patience was sorely tested over the month that followed his speech. Hardly any member of the House offered full support for the Bill of

Rights, and Madison struggled to put his proposals into better shape. On July 21, he "begged the House to indulge him in the further consideration of Amendments to the Constitution." Once again, House members claimed they had more pressing business, although Madison succeeded in having the project sent to a select committee with a member from each state.

The Committee of Eleven reported back on July 28. It made few substantive changes to the list Madison had proposed on June 8. Busy with revenue bills, the House promptly tabled the report. Madison faced a constant struggle during the summer of 1789 to force his reluctant colleagues to consider the amendments. Debate did not begin in earnest until August 14. Antifederalists heaped scorn on the whole project. Representative Aedanus Burke of South Carolina dismissed the proposals as "not those solid and substantial amendments which the people expect" but "frothy and full of wind." He thought "we have done nothing but lose our time, and that it will be better to drop the subject now, and proceed to the organization of the Government." Even the representative who chaired the Committee of Eleven, John Vining of Delaware, apologized for diverting the House from considering "the bill for establishing a Land Office for the disposal of the vacant lands in the Western Territory."

When the debate finally began, Roger Sherman of Connecticut moved that the amendments be placed at the end of the Constitution, rather than scattered throughout its existing articles. "The Constitution is the act of the people," he argued, "and ought to remain entire. But the amendments will be the act of the state governments." Expecting that Congress would approve at least some of the proposed amendments, Sherman wanted to keep them out of the Constitution itself. Madison opposed this motion, responding that the Constitution should "remain uniform and entire." The House first defeated Sherman's motion, but later adopted it. Had the House agreed with Madison, the Bill of Rights—which we now read as a package—would have been scattered through the Constitution. Roger Sherman deserves credit for the form of the amendments whose paternity we credit to Madison. This is ironic, because Sherman worked hard and successfully to prevent the Connecticut legislature from ratifying the Bill of Rights, something it put off until 1939.

The House debates on the Bill of Rights did not rise to the rhetorical heights, or rival the political passions, of those in the Philadelphia convention in 1787. In truth, they were dull and dispiriting. At one point, John Vining ridiculed a motion by Roger Sherman as reminding him of "an act to amend a supplement to an act entitled an act for altering part of an act entitled an act for certain purposes therein mentioned." The substantive provisions of the amendments submitted by the Committee of Eleven underwent numerous wording changes, and finally emerged on August 24 as a resolution to the Senate. The House recommended seventeen amendments; the first and longest revised the apportionment of House seats by a complicated formula, designed to keep the total number in check as the nation's population grew. The second, to which little objection was voiced, prevented laws that raised congressional salaries from taking effect before the next House elections.

The ten amendments we now call the Bill of Rights began in the House resolution with the third, which stated that "Congress shall make no law establishing religion or prohibiting the free exercise thereof, nor shall the rights of conscience be infringed." The fourth on the list contained the rest of what became the First Amendment, protecting freedom of speech and of the press, and rights of assembly and petition. Those dealing with the rights of criminal defendants were presented in forms that emerged in the final Bill of Rights with minor wording changes. The House list also included what are now the Ninth and Tenth Amendments, guaranteeing to "the people" those "rights" not enumerated in the Constitution, and reserving to the states those powers not granted to Congress by the Constitution.

The Senate began consideration of the House resolution on September 2. But that body met in closed session until 1794, and no record exists of its debates on the Bill of Rights, although the *Senate Journal* includes a record of motions and votes. We do know that the Senate tinkered with the apportionment proposal and removed protection against military service by conscientious objectors to war. In their most significant action, the senators dropped the article in the House resolution that Madison considered "the most valuable" of the lot. This proposed amendment, fourteenth on the House list, read: "No state shall infringe the right of trial by jury in criminal cases, nor the rights of conscience, nor the freedom of speech, or of the press." Had it remained, and been adopted, the rights of the people against oppression by the states would have been secured well before the Supreme Court finally began applying the Bill of Rights to the states. That did not happen until 1925, when it ruled that the First Amendment was binding on the states as part of the "liberty" protected against state infringement by the Fourteenth Amendment, ratified in 1868.

The Senate concluded its debates on the Bill of Rights on September 10, sending back to the House a revised and pared-down list of twelve amendments. Since it was clear the House would not accept the Senate version without further revision, the two bodies each named three members to a conference committee, which Madison chaired. The most significant change to emerge from this committee was that Madison succeeded in restoring the House version of what became the first clause of the First Amendment, providing that "Congress shall make no law respecting an establishment or religion." Madison had labored for years in Virginia against state support for established religions, and he now imposed the same ban on the national government.

The House adopted the final version of the twelve proposed amendments by a vote of thirty-seven to twenty-four on September 24, and the Senate followed suit the next day, without a recorded vote. On October 2, President Washington sent copies to each state governor, with a brief letter of transmittal.

There remains virtually no record of debates over the Bill of Rights in the state legislatures. Few lawmakers spoke from written texts, and speeches were not transcribed by reporters. We must rely on letters by partisans and on newspaper accounts, which often reflected personal or political bias. We do know that ratification of the Bill of Rights, which required the assent of eleven states, dragged on for more than two years.

New Jersey was the first to ratify, on November 20, 1789, although it rejected the second proposed amendment, dealing with congressional salaries. Before the process was completed, the first two of the twelve amendments adopted by Congress were defeated in the states. In recent years, many people—including Supreme Court justices—have noted that the protections of religion, speech, press, and assembly were placed in the First Amendment. They argue from this fact that the Framers intended to elevate these rights to a "preferred position" in the Bill of Rights, to underscore their primacy in protecting the people's rights. Of course, had the states not rejected the first two proposed amendments, the First Amendment would now be the Third. Claims that "my rights are protected by the Third Amendment" do not have quite the force of invoking the First.

Maryland, the two Carolinas, New Hampshire, and Delaware approved the Bill of Rights with little dissent. North Carolina actually first joined the Union when it finally ratified the Constitution on November 21, 1789. One month later, its legislature adopted all twelve proposed amendments. New York, with Antifederalist George Clinton still its governor, ratified all but the second proposed amendment in February 1790. Clinton had rallied his troops against the Constitution with appeals for a bill of rights, and he was stuck with that record. Privately, he regretted his earlier enthusiasm. After his state's ratification, he wrote to a relative that his legislature "has transacted no business of very great consequence, unless the adoption of the trivial and equivocal amendments may be so styled."

After the New York vote, Pennsylvania and Rhode Island joined the parade. That made nine of the required eleven states; the Constitution required ratification by three fourths of the states, which now numbered fourteen. Vermont gave up its status as an independent republic and joined the Union in 1791. Its legislature ratified all thirteen proposed amendments in November 1791, two years after President Washington submitted them to the states. One state was still needed before the Bill of Rights became part of the Constitution. Connecticut and Georgia, which were both Federalist strongholds, refused to ratify the amendments, largely because their political leaders felt that the Constitution left such matters to the states. Massachusetts also withheld its vote, the result more of legislative bumbling than clear intent. The two houses of the "Great and General Court" of Massachusetts bickered over the amendments and never joined in a final vote. As a result, the failure of Connecticut, Georgia, and Massachusetts to ratify the Bill of Rights made Virginia the crucial eleventh state.

Virginia actually took up the proposed amendments shortly after President Washington submitted them in October 1789. But the state senate, in which Patrick Henry served, was firmly in Antifederalist hands. The state's two federal senators, Richard Henry Lee and William Grayson, sent a letter to Governor Beverly Randolph—the brother of Edmund—stating that "it is with grief that we now send forward propositions inadequate to the purpose of real and substantial Amendments, and so far short of the wishes of our Country." Amazingly, the Virginia senate even rejected the proposed Third Amendment—now the First—which drew its inspiration from that state's Declaration of Religious Freedom. The Virginia Antifederalists were so consumed with hostility to the national government that they would deny federal protection of rights they jealously claimed for themselves.

The legislative logjam was finally broken when Senator Lee and George Mason—who had refused to sign the Constitution in Philadelphia—changed their minds and grudgingly agreed to support ratification of the Bill of Rights. Both men feared that the Antifederalists, who looked ahead to the next congressional elections, would be tarred as opponents of the people's rights. Mason, who had first blasted Madison's proposals as "milk and water propositions," now found "much satisfaction" in the Bill of Rights. Even the oratory of Patrick Henry could not overcome these defections, and the Virginia legislature finally ratified all twelve proposed amendments on December 15, 1791, a day now celebrated by federal proclamation as "Bill of Rights Day."

James Madison had stated in the Virginia convention that ratified the Constitution his belief that amendments to that document would be both "unnecessary and dangerous—unnecessary, because it was evident that the general government had no power but what was given it" by the Constitution, and "dangerous, because an enumeration which is not complete is not safe." He also dismissed the need for "parchment barriers" against the powers of Congress. Two years later, after the states ratified ten of the twelve proposed amendments, Madison wrote that adoption of the Bill of Rights "will kill the opposition everywhere, and by putting an end to dissatisfaction with the Government itself, enable the Administration to venture on measures not otherwise safe." The primary advocate in Congress of a bill of rights displayed an attitude toward the "nauseous project" that moved, grudgingly and solely for political reasons, from hostile opposition to lukewarm support.

Considering the ambivalence of its sponsor, why should Americans now celebrate—even venerate—the Bill of Rights? The reasons have much to do with the survival of the Constitution over more than two centuries, despite a bloody Civil War and continuing discord between the "factions" that Madison felt were inevitable in a democratic society. Adoption of the Bill of Rights was the price we paid for the Constitution, and its protections of fundamental freedoms—for religious and political dissenters, even for those charged with serious crimes—have been applied by the Supreme Court to reach every government official in the land. As Justice Robert Jackson wrote in 1943, "The very purpose of a Bill of Rights was to withdraw certain subjects from the vicissitudes of political controversy, to place them beyond the reach of majorities and officials and to establish them as legal principles to be applied by the courts." With the ratification of the Constitution in 1789 and the Bill of Rights in 1791, it became the task of the Supreme Court to breathe life into their "parchment" provisions.

SECTION II

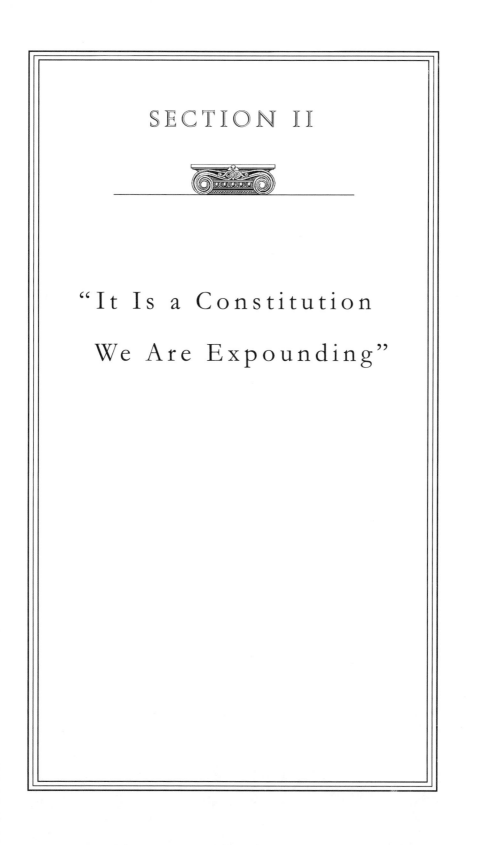

"It Is a Constitution
We Are Expounding"

8

"The Court Is Now Sitting"

The first session of the Supreme Court of the United States was hardly an auspicious or momentous occasion. On February 1, 1790, three men gathered at the Royal Exchange Building, an undistinguished two-story brick edifice at the foot of Broad Street in New York City. With a population of 33,000, New York was the nation's mercantile center and had more than its share of lawyers. Many leaders of the city's bar attended the "uncommonly crowded" Supreme Court session in a makeshift courtroom. The audience buzzed with anticipation as the Chief Justice of the United States, attired in a flowing black-and-red robe, took his seat behind the bench. The court clerk readied his quill pen to record the Court's business, and the court crier prepared to still the crowd with a stentorian call to order.

The mood in the courtroom quickly turned from anticipation to anticlimax. In addition to the Chief Justice, only two of the five associate justices appeared that morning. Congress had set the Court's membership at six in the Judiciary Act of 1789, which meant that four justices must be present to constitute a quorum. With only three justices behind the bench, the Court was unable to transact any business that first day, and the Chief Justice quickly adjourned the session. The disappointed spectators drifted away, most to their offices in the legal and financial district of lower Manhattan. With no assurance that a quorum would appear the next day, few returned to witness the first official meeting of the nation's highest judicial tribunal.

When the Court convened the following morning, a fourth justice took his seat to make up a quorum. The court crier opened the proceedings with a ritual invocation that has remained unchanged for more than two centuries: "Oyez! Oyez! Oyez! All persons having business before the honorable, the Supreme

Court of the United States, are admonished to draw near and give their attention, for the Court is now sitting. God save the United States and this Honorable Court." Whatever anticipation remained from the previous day's abortive session was quickly dissipated. No person had business before the Supreme Court that day. No lawyer approached the bench to argue a case. The Court's docket was completely bare. The justices bore no responsibility for their lack of judicial business. After all, the primary business of judges is hearing and deciding cases, and courts cannot manufacture them. Judges on appellate courts must wait for cases to proceed through the lower courts, a process that has always been time-consuming, and frustrating to impatient litigants. Lacking any cases to decide, the four justices busied themselves with the adoption of procedural rules and the admission of lawyers to the Court's bar. Few lawyers sought admission during this session, since very few members of state bars represented clients whose cases fit within the Court's jurisdiction.

Hardly anything about the first meetings of the Supreme Court would have impressed anyone who had witnessed the proceedings of English courts, with their bewigged and powerful judges who laid down the principles of the common law that formed the foundation of the American legal system. Many of England's judges—men like Sir Edward Coke and Lord Edward Mansfield—enjoyed great prominence. Even the "common people" in England recognized the "Law Lords" as men of power and privilege. But in the new United States, hardly anyone who did not move in legal circles was likely to recognize a single one of the eleven men George Washington chose for the Supreme Court during his eight years as president. Only Franklin Roosevelt, who occupied the White House for twelve years, approached this record; he selected eight justices and elevated one sitting justice to the Chief's seat. Roosevelt's choices included some of the most illustrious names in American legal history: Hugo Black, Felix Frankfurter, William O. Douglas, Robert Jackson, and Chief Justice Harlan Fiske Stone. The men Washington placed on the Court, in contrast, were a thoroughly undistinguished lot. One spent time in debtors' prisons for defaulting on loans; one returned his commission after five days to serve in state office; one never attended a single Court session; one was impeached for political bias on the bench; one was insane; and another was senile. The first Chief Justice campaigned for state office from the bench and spent much of his tenure on diplomatic missions abroad. The second had already resigned once from the Court to take a state judicial post, and was rejected by the Senate after serving five months as Chief Justice. The third made no secret of his boredom in the post and left for a more exciting career in state politics.

One reason for Washington's sorry record was that he limited his selections to men whose common attribute was loyalty to the Federalist cause. But almost every justice has come from the party of the president who nominated him—or, in two cases, her—to the Court. The major reason Washington picked such poor justices stemmed from the Court's poor reputation in its early years. Almost as many men turned down offers to serve on the Court as those who accepted. The Court had little business; the salary was low; "circuit-riding" duty was burdensome; and the Court's quarters—as the nation's capital shifted between three cities—were cramped and uncomfortable. In truth, service on the Court held few inducements for lawyers of eminence and esteem.

Washington's first choice for the Supreme Court, and the first Chief Justice, was John Jay of New York. Jay was born into the American aristocracy of mercantile wealth, and he married into the landed wealth of the Livingston family, the richest in the country. His favorite maxim was that "those who own the country ought to govern it," and he advocated stringent property qualifications on voting. Jay also stated that "the wise and the good never form the majority" of society and that, consequently, government must guard against the "never ceasing union of the wicked and the weak."

Jay brought to his position as Chief Justice a lucrative legal practice, an extensive political background, and very little judicial experience. He had been elected to the First Continental Congress in 1775, in which he spoke against separation from Great Britain. But he switched sides and supported the Revolution once Congress adopted the Declaration of Independence. Several years before the states ratified the Constitution, he served as New York's chief judge, deciding cases that primarily involved property and contract disputes. Jay had more interest in national politics than he did in minor legal squabbles. He resigned his judicial post after less than two years to return to the Confederation Congress, which elected him president in 1778. With the hard-won victory of General Washington's army over the British in sight, Congress appointed Jay in 1781 to the delegation that negotiated a peace treaty with Great Britain.

His appetite whetted by this diplomatic success, Jay eagerly accepted his appointment by Congress in 1784 as secretary for foreign affairs, and he spent five years in this post before President Washington offered him the choice of serving the new federal government as Chief Justice or secretary of state. Jay chose the former post, for reasons that are hard to explain. One colleague in Congress wrote to a friend that Jay "is waiting to see which salary is best, that of Lord Chief Justice or Secretary of State." The former job paid $500 more per year, a sum unlikely to entice the wealthy lawyer. Most likely, Jay realized that disputes between the United States, England, and France had reached an impasse that threatened further warfare. He may have anticipated—or even hoped—that Thomas Jefferson, who accepted the post as secretary of state, would become so entangled in these disputes that Washington would ask Jay to step in and negotiate another treaty to resolve these dangerous conflicts. That is, in fact, what happened. Jay received national acclaim for negotiating the "Jay Treaty" with Great Britain in 1795, settling the commercial disputes between the two countries. New York's voters rewarded Jay's diplomatic victory the next year by electing him governor, the job he always wanted.

With the post as Chief Justice open after Jay's resignation, President

Washington turned to the second man he had named to the Supreme Court in 1790, John Rutledge of South Carolina. Washington made a particularly bad choice, not once but twice. As a delegate to the Constitutional Convention, Rutledge had vehemently defended slavery. But support for slavery, in Washington's mind, did not disqualify a man for the Supreme Court. Rutledge was a loyal Federalist and had lobbied hard for appointment as Chief Justice. He was disgruntled that John Jay got the post, but agreed to serve as an associate justice. Rutledge had little attachment to democratic principles. During the Revolution, he resigned as South Carolina's governor because its constitution did not include stringent property restrictions on voting. Rutledge returned as governor after the legislature limited the post to those who owned plantations worth at least 10,000 pounds in British currency. After the Senate confirmed his Supreme Court nomination in 1789, Rutledge did not attend a single session, and he resigned in 1791 to become chief justice of South Carolina.

Because the Senate was not in session when President Washington selected Rutledge in 1796 to replace Jay, the new Chief Justice held a "recess" appointment until the Senate resumed its business. Most senators were appalled at this nomination. Shortly before Washington sent Rutledge's name to the Senate, Attorney General Edmund Randolph advised the president that "it is very seriously whispered" that the prospective Chief Justice was "deranged in his mind." Perhaps he was a victim of what we now call Alzheimer's disease. On the other hand, Rutledge might have been a victim of political distemper. He violently denounced in 1795 the treaty that Jay negotiated with Great Britain. After his nomination as Chief Justice, Rutledge delivered an inflammatory speech in South Carolina against the Jay Treaty, denouncing it as a "puerile production" and "a surrender of our rights and privileges" to the British. This act of political disloyalty prompted Randolph to caution Washington that Rutledge's speech was "proof of the imputation of insanity." Randolph warned the president a week later that Rutledge's "attachment to his bottle, his puerility, and extravagances, together with a variety of indecorums and imprudencies multiply daily."

Rutledge's political blunders doomed his nomination, which the Senate rejected by a vote of fourteen to ten. John Adams wrote to his wife, Abigail, that Rutledge deserved his rejection. "Chief Justices must not go to illegal meetings and become popular orators in favor of sedition," wrote Adams, who later prosecuted his own political enemies for sedition. Nonetheless, Rutledge served—however briefly—as Chief Justice of the United States, and wrote opinions in two cases that involved claims against foreign ships under admiralty law. These cases had no impact on constitutional law, and John Rutledge had no impact on the Supreme Court.

President Washington had decided—and later presidents followed his example—that the Supreme Court should reflect the nation's geography. His first two nominees, Jay and Rutledge, represented the North and South. With six positions to fill, Washington maintained this regional balance in his remaining choices. He awarded the Court's third seat in 1790 to William Cushing of Massachusetts. Cushing was almost bred for judicial service; his father and grandfather had both served the British crown as judges before the Revolution. He had become chief judge of the Massachusetts courts in 1780, and later ruled in several cases against debtors, including the farmers who took up arms against the state government in Shays' Rebellion. After Jay resigned as Chief Justice in 1795, and the Senate rejected Rutledge, President Washington turned to Cushing, after his first choice—Patrick Henry of Virginia, the Antifederalist firebrand whose distrust of the federal government had cooled—declined the offer. The Senate confirmed Cushing, but he declined to serve, citing illness and age—he was then sixty-three years old—as the reasons. Despite his reservations, Cushing proved to be remarkably healthy and remained on the Court until his death in 1810. But he did not put his fading energy into judicial opinions; during his twenty-one years on the Court, Cushing wrote just nineteen opinions, all of them brief. From beginning to end, he remained a true-blue Federalist, voting in virtually every case to uphold the powers of the federal government against the states.

Washington picked two other southerners for the first Supreme Court. The president's first choice from his own state was George Wythe, a noted lawyer and chancellor of Virginia. But Wythe declined and Washington turned to John Blair, Jr., an old friend who had been a delegate to the Constitutional Convention in 1787 and said virtually nothing during the debates. Blair remained on the Court for five years and wrote almost nothing of significance. The president's next choice, Robert Harrison of Maryland, served for only five days before returning his commission to become chancellor of Maryland. Washington then turned to James Iredell, a leading North Carolina Federalist who became the youngest justice, at thirty-eight, although he died after nine years on the Court. As a lawyer, he represented plantation owners and wealthy merchants. Of all the Federalist justices, Iredell was the only one who displayed any concern for the rights of states against the federal government.

The best lawyer of those Washington picked for the Supreme Court turned out the worst in personal terms. James Wilson of Pennsylvania had played a major role in framing the Constitution and was perhaps second only to James Madison as a force at the Philadelphia convention. Although he dressed and lived like an aristocrat, he supported popular election of both houses of Congress and the president and opposed property qualifications on voting. Born and educated in Scotland, Wilson had an incisive mind and a firm belief in national power over the states. But he also had serious character flaws. For one, his personal vanity was matched by overweening ambition. Wilson sought the office of Chief Justice through shameless flattery and self-promotion. He wrote to President Washington that "I commit myself to your Excellency without reserve and inform you that my aim rises to the important office of Chief Justice of the United States. But how shall I proceed? Shall I enumerate reasons in justification of my high pretensions? I have not yet employed my pen in my own praise." Washington answered with an implied rebuke: "I presume it will be unnecessary for me to say that I have entered upon my office without the constraint of a single engagement and that I never wish to depart from that line of conduct which will always have me at full liberty to act in the manner which is befitting an impartial and disinterested Magistrate." Nonetheless, Washington admired Wilson's legal skills and prevailed on him to accept the post of associate justice under John Jay.

Wilson had a more serious flaw than ambition. He was also a reckless speculator in land and finance, which proved to be his downfall. Before and after he joined the Supreme Court, Wilson borrowed heavily to invest in bank stock and land grants in states from Pennsylvania to Georgia. Unable to pay his mounting debts and hounded by creditors, he became the first—and, so far, the only—justice to be jailed while serving on the Court, not once, but twice. Humiliated by his first term in debtors' prison, Wilson traded circuit-riding duties with Justice Iredell in 1798 and took refuge in North Carolina, where another creditor had him jailed for two months. Wilson died shortly after his release, penniless and stripped of the power he had once wielded on the Supreme Court.

The first six men who actually decided cases on the Supreme Court differed in background, experience, and personality. But they shared four attributes. All were staunch Federalists; all had participated in framing the Constitution or campaigned for its ratification; all belonged to or represented the creditor class with wealth in land or finance; and all believed that government's primary function was protecting property rights from the debtor class of workers and small farmers. In these respects, they shared little with "the people" in whose name the Constitution was framed. But they met the test Washington imposed on his judicial choices: loyalty to his party and its nationalistic goals. The first justices shared another attribute: none had any experience in applying and construing the Constitution of the new nation. How, then, did they approach this task?

The Court's first answer to this important question did not come until the justices had spent almost three years waiting for a case that raised constitutional issues. Chief Justice Jay had adjourned the Court's first three terms—two in 1790 and one in 1791—without issuing a single legal decision. (During these early years, the Court held two "terms" each year, in February and August.) Not until the August term of 1792 did the justices actually decide a case and issue opinions. They had no need to consult the Constitution for guidance in the first case, *Georgia v. Brailsford*, which began in 1774 during the colonial period and grew out of efforts to collect debts owed by American citizens to British subjects whose property had later been confiscated during the Revolution. The legal issues before the Supreme Court were entirely procedural and involved the state of Georgia's effort to intervene in the case and lay claim to the confiscated funds. The legal briefs in the case bristled with terms like "treason" and "fraud," but this was really just a debt-collection case that raised no issues of constitutional interpretation. The six justices, who finally had work to do, dug into the procedural niceties and decided, by a vote of four to two, that Georgia was entitled to an injunction to keep the disputed funds in state hands until a lower court tried the claim.

The only significance of the *Brailsford* case was that the Court adopted the practice of each justice delivering an opinion in each case, known in legal parlance as *seriatim* opinions. The *Brailsford* opinions were brief, ranging from one to three paragraphs in length, and were framed in the language of equity, the branch of law based on notions of fairness between the parties. Chief Justice Jay put the question in these words: Would it be "equitable to stay the money in the hands of the marshal until the right to it is fairly decided?" He and three colleagues agreed that it would, over the dissenting opinions of two justices. The Court's decision sent the case back for trial on the merits, with the disputed funds in the state's hands.

Three days before the Court decided the *Brailsford* case, the *Gazette of the United States* alerted its readers that "Business of great importance it is said is pending" before the justices. The decision itself, however, passed without comment. The *Gazette* and other newspapers had little to report of the Court's business during its first three years of operation. This did not reflect any lack of diligence by the justices, who in fact were kept busy—too busy for some—by the circuit-riding duties imposed on them by Congress in the Judiciary Act of 1789. Congress had required in this bill that two Supreme Court justices sit with each federal district judge in four judicial terms each year. The nation was divided into three circuits (thus the initial number of six justices) with the idea of bringing federal judges closer to the people. Given the deplorable state of roads and inns of the time, most justices resented their duty of "riding circuit" around the country. Justice Thomas Johnson, who joined the Court in 1792, resigned the following year because, as he wrote to the president, "I cannot resolve to spend six months in the year of the few I may have left from my family on roads at taverns chiefly and often in situations where the most moderate desires are disappointed; my time of life, temper and other circumstances forbid it." Chief Justice Jay complained that his circuit-riding duty "takes me from my family half the year, and obliges me to pass too considerable a part of my time on the road, in lodging houses, & inns."

The justices decided many cases during their circuit-riding tours, but the vast majority were the kind of mundane contract and property squabbles that today would be relegated to small-claims courts. One circuit court case, however, placed the justices in the uncomfortable position of feeling compelled to rebuke—politely but firmly—both the president who nominated them and the Congress that confirmed them. The legal dispute that became known as *Hayburn's Case* began in 1792, when Congress granted pensions to disabled and invalid revolutionary soldiers. The law provided that pension claims would first be decided by the circuit courts on which the justices sat with district judges; their rulings could be reviewed by the secretary of war, who could modify or deny any pension award. That same year, William Hayburn applied for a pension in Pennsylvania. Justices James Wilson and John Blair, sitting on circuit court, refused to consider Hayburn's claim, even after Attorney General Randolph urged them to take off their judicial robes and decide the claim as "commissioners," deputized by him.

Wilson and Blair explained their plight in a letter to President Washington. Reminding him of his constitutional obligation to "take care that the laws" of the United States "be faithfully executed," they apologized for the "painful occasion" of refusing a request from the attorney general. But "the business directed by this act is not of a judicial nature," they wrote. Asking the justices to perform an executive task violated the "important principle" of separation of powers between the branches of government. Wilson and Blair assured Washington that their position "was far from being pleasant. To be obliged to act contrary either to the obvious directions of Congress, or to a constitutional principle, in our judgment equally obvious, excited feelings in us, we hope never to experience again." Despite this letter, feelings of compassion persuaded five justices to rule on pension claims as "commissioners," although Wilson still refused to act in an "extra-judicial" role.

This whole episode was embarrassing to the Court, which had yielded to entreaties to act outside its delegated powers. But the decision in *Hayburn's Case*, even if expressed in letters to the president, was "the first instance in which a Court of Justice had declared a law of Congress to be unconstitutional," as Representative Elias Boudinot told the House. This was not a ruling of the Supreme Court as an institution, but the first justices paved the way in *Hayburn's Case* for their successors—most notably Chief Justice John Marshall—to exercise the power of judicial review over acts of Congress. The judicial refusal in *Hayburn's Case* to breach the constitutional separation of powers between the branches of the federal government prompted congressional denunciation and even calls for impeachment, the first of many efforts to punish the justices for decisions that federal or state lawmakers considered judicial "usurpation" of their legislative powers. Ironically, the congressional bluster about impeachment over *Hayburn's Case*—which quickly died down—came largely from the Federalist majority, which had confirmed all the justices and now felt insulted by their rebuke.

The Court's first real foray into constitutional law provoked an even greater furor than *Hayburn's Case*. This dispute began in 1792 when Alexander Chisholm, a citizen of South Carolina, filed suit against the state of Georgia. Chisholm was acting as executor of the estate of Robert Farquhar, who had sold cloth and uniforms to Georgia during the Revolution but was never paid. The amount Chisholm sought was substantial for that time, nearly $70,000 in damages. Georgia's attorney general, acting for Governor Edward Telfair, responded in federal district court that his "sovereign" state was immune from suit by citizens of other states. The case of *Chisholm v. Georgia* became tangled in legal brambles, but rather quickly wound up in the Supreme Court.

Alexander Chisholm made a smart move when he hired Attorney General Edmund Randolph to represent him as a private lawyer. Congress then allowed government lawyers to supplement their meager salaries with outside work; even today, district attorneys in rural counties of several states work only part-time and are permitted to maintain private practices. The state of Georgia made a dumb move in defending itself against Chisholm's suit. The Supreme Court's reporter, Alexander Dallas, noted that the state's lawyers presented a "written remonstrance and protestation" that the Court lacked jurisdiction to hear the case, "but in consequence of positive instructions, they declined taking any part in arguing the question."

Dallas did not mention in his notes, however, that Georgia had hired *him* to represent the state in the Supreme Court. He sat quietly in the chamber and recorded Randolph's argument, which consumed several hours of oratory. Randolph first admitted that his position was "unpopular" in the states. Even his home state of Virginia, "whose will must always be dear to me," had denied that states could be sued by citizens of other states. But Randolph held firm on this issue. Asking him to surrender for the federal government "a constitutional right, supported by my own conviction," would justly subject him to "official perfidy." Stripped of rhetorical excess, Randolph's argument was simple: Article III of the Constitution gave the Supreme Court jurisdiction over "controversies between a state and citizens of another state."

Randolph dismissed Georgia's claim that "state sovereignty" made it immune from suit by "foreigners" like Chisholm. The Constitution had replaced the Articles of Confederation, under which states "retained their exemption" from suits by other states of their citizens. It was now "the people" of the United States, not the individual states, who were sovereign. The "new order of things" under the Constitution required "diminutions of sovereignty" by the states. Randolph professed "horror" at Georgia's argument: "Shall the tranquility of our country be at the mercy of every state?" The clear words of the Constitution provided "an easy and usual construction" of the answer to this rhetorical question. When Randolph sat down, Chief Justice Jay asked if any lawyer present wished "to take up the gauntlet in opposition to the attorney general." Alexander Dallas recorded Jay's words and remained silent.

Those who search today for the "original intent" of the Framers would cheer the Court's decision in *Chisholm v. Georgia*. All the justices who decided the case had been Framers, in various roles, and all but one of the five sitting justices agreed that the Constitution granted the Court jurisdiction in this case. Their separate opinions allow an insight into each justice's mind. John Blair considered—and quickly dismissed—Georgia's claim that the Court could only decide cases in which states brought suit as plaintiffs against citizens of other states. "A dispute between A. and B. is surely a dispute between B. and A.," he wrote. The "clear and positive directions" of the Constitution governed this case for Blair.

James Wilson, whose opinion rambled on for thirty pages, concluded after many pedantic digressions that "the term sovereign is totally unknown" to the Constitution. Wilson not only played a leading role in drafting Article III at the Philadelphia convention, but he was the Court's leading advocate of federal supremacy over the states. "As to the purposes of the Union," Wilson declared, "Georgia is not a sovereign state." Justice William Cushing and Chief Justice John Jay wrote much shorter opinions and reached the same conclusion.

Only Justice James Iredell picked up the "gauntlet" of state sovereignty. But his opinion took a detour around the Constitution. Iredell argued that "judicial authority" depended on "acts of the legislature, appointing courts, and prescribing their methods of proceeding." Congress had not, in Iredell's view, given the Supreme Court jurisdiction in cases of "assumpsit," the common-law "writ" on which Chisholm based his claim against Georgia. "Writs" are simply "writings" that allow parties in lawsuits to ask for judicial relief; the "writ of habeas corpus" is the most famous example. Congress had, in fact, provided in the Judiciary Act of 1789 an "all-writs" section that allowed the Court to issue orders "agreeable to the principles and usages" of the common law. This clearly anticipated writs such as assumpsit, which means in plain English an order to perform an agreement such as a contract.

Justice Iredell, whose opinion was picky on issues of judicial procedure, totally ignored the wording of Article III. He simply claimed that states were "totally independent" of federal control unless Congress passed a "new law" to carry out its delegated powers. Iredell did not consider the Judiciary Act a "new law" on the subject of writs of assumpsit, since it did not mention this writ by name. His reasoning seems weak in retrospect. Most likely, Iredell was responding to the political backlash from states that had ratified the Constitution with reluctance to give up their "sovereign" powers. His own state of North Carolina had initially rejected the Constitution, ignoring Iredell's pleas to join the federal union. Even though he now wore a judicial robe, Iredell realized as an astute politician that the Court's decision in *Chisholm* would be as "unpopular" as Attorney General Randolph had predicted.

Reaction from the states was swift and ferocious. Within days of the *Chisholm* decision in February 1793, state legislatures—led by Virginia and Massachusets— besieged Congress with resolutions demanding a constitutional amendment to overturn the Court's ruling. Virginia's resolution attacked the decision as threatening "a general consolidation of these confederated republics," reflecting lingering Antifederalist sentiment. But this was a temperate response compared to the action of the Georgia house, which passed a bill providing that any federal official who attempted to enforce Chisholm's judgment would be "guilty of felony and shall suffer death, without benefit of clergy, by being hanged." The bill never became law, but it expressed the bitter reaction by states which faced a multitude of suits by citizens of other states, most of them filed to recover property and money confiscated from British Loyalists during the Revolution.

Even though Federalists controlled both houses of Congress and held off action on the state resolutions for another year, the intense pressure threatened political damage. Congress adopted the Eleventh Amendment in March 1794, providing that the "judicial power of the United States" did not extend to suits "against one of the United States by citizens of another State" or by subjects of foreign nations. But the amendment was not finally ratified until January 1798. Having fired their shots at the Supreme Court, which promptly retreated and dismissed the pending suits against states, the victors took their time in leaving the battlefield.

The furious reaction to *Chisholm* shocked the Supreme Court, which had undertaken its new tasks with fortitude, standing up to Congress, the president, and the states. Chastened by passage of the Eleventh Amendment, and by calls for impeachment in the wake of *Hayburn's Case*, the justices ducked their heads for the next decade and avoided further confrontations. Service on the Court became less and less attractive.

President Washington found it difficult to find anyone to fill the post of Chief Justice after John Jay resigned in 1795 and the Senate rejected John Rutledge to replace him. Patrick Henry and Justice William Cushing both declined the post, and Washington finally selected Oliver Ellsworth of Connecticut, a delegate to the Philadelphia convention in 1787 and later a Federalist stalwart in the Senate. His colleagues quickly confirmed Ellsworth, an extremely wealthy, arrogant, and aristocratic man whose four-year tenure as Chief Justice was marked only by his success in persuading the Court to abandon the practice of separate opinions in each case. The Court's majority now spoke in one voice. But that voice, until John Marshall succeeded Ellsworth in 1801, was weak and cautious. The emphatic reversal of *Chisholm* by constitutional amendment eroded whatever resolve the justices had mustered to assert their influence and independence. The Supreme Court ended its first decade anything but supreme in public estimation.

9

"To Say What the Law Is"

During George Washington's second presidential term, which ended in 1797, the Supreme Court tried hard to avoid stirring up controversy. The uproar over *Chisholm v. Georgia* in 1793, which led to adoption of the Eleventh Amendment, weakened the Court's already shaky prestige and made the justices wary of exercising their power to strike down state and federal laws. There were few public arguments over the Constitution during these four years; most politicians—and the public as well—simply ignored the Court and turned to more pressing issues. Passions ran high over the war between England and France and its impact on American shipping and trade. The dominant Federalists, who controlled both houses of Congress, sided with the British, while their opponents—led by Thomas Jefferson and calling themselves Republicans—favored the French.

President Washington, who stayed aloof from the loud and sometimes vitriolic debates in Congress over foreign policy, devoted most of his energies to keeping the United States from entanglement in foreign wars. Having been lectured by three Supreme Court justices in *Hayburn's Case* for trespassing on their turf, Washington avoided further conflict with the Court before he retired to his Mount Vernon estate. Washington did, however, nominate two more justices before he left office. Both met his basic test of supporting the Federalist Party, but they were polar opposites in temperament and legal talent.

After the resignation in 1793 of Justice Thomas Johnson, who complained bitterly about his "circuit-riding" duties, Washington replaced him with William Paterson of New Jersey, a much younger man at forty-seven. Paterson had been a prominent figure in the Constitutional Convention, defending the rights of small states but also proposing a strong federal judiciary. He married into an extremely wealthy family, the van Rensselaers, and dressed in the velvet-and-lace

fashion of the British aristocracy whose manners he adopted. Despite his fop-
pish appearance, Paterson was a solid lawyer, having served as New Jersey's attorney general for seven years. During his term in the first Senate, he helped
Oliver Ellsworth draft the Judiciary Act of 1789. Among Washington's Supreme Court choices, Paterson was the workhorse, and he plowed his Federalist
furrow with little deviation from its plotted course until his resignation in 1806.

In contrast to Paterson, Samuel Chase of Maryland was the Court's bucking
bronco, untamed and unbridled. Washington selected Chase to replace John
Blair, who resigned in 1795 after five undistinguished years as a justice. The
president never revealed his reasons for this choice; most likely, he rewarded
Chase for his fervent support of Washington during the Revolution as a member of the Continental Congress. Hardly anyone else spoke well of Chase. Even
Washington, three months before he nominated him to the Supreme Court,
wrote to Alexander Hamilton that Chase had "opposed the adoption of the
Constitution" and had been "accused of some impurity in his conduct." Chase,
in fact, had been forced to resign from Congress in disgrace for trying to corner
the flour market by corrupt means.

Much like James Wilson, Chase had lobbied President Washington for nomination to the Court in 1789, promising that he would "execute so honorable a
station with integrity, fidelity, and diligence, and I flatter myself, that you will
never have occasion to regret the confidence reposed in me." Washington did
not respond to this letter, but seven years later he elevated Chase from chief
justice of Maryland to the Supreme Court. After this decision, several people
questioned Chase's character and integrity. One observer reported that Chase
"takes beer aboard" and that his drinking had caused a "scandal" that made his
Maryland colleagues "very glad to get rid of him which is a very bad symptom."

John Adams, who obviously heard these reports, wrote to his wife, Abigail,
that Chase's "corpulency" would prevent "his riding Circuit very long." Adams
added that his "character has a mist about it of suspicion and impurity which
gives occasion to the enemy to censure." The enemies Adams had in mind were
Jefferson and his Republican allies. James Madison expressed his view to Jefferson, not in words but in punctuation marks. "Chase in the place of Blair!!!!"

President Washington's Supreme Court nominations illustrate the central importance of foreign affairs to all branches of the national government—including
the Supreme Court—during this early period of American history. Chief Justice John Jay eagerly left his judicial duties to negotiate a commercial treaty with
Great Britain. Criticism of the Jay Treaty cost John Rutledge his brief tenure as
Jay's successor. Chief Justice Oliver Ellsworth, who finally replaced Jay, spent
the last months of his judicial career on a diplomatic mission to France. Justice
Chase dropped his judicial duties in 1796 to campaign for John Adams, who

rode a pro-British tide of public opinion to a slim victory by three electoral votes over Thomas Jefferson. Under the Constitution, Jefferson became vice president and used his office to torment Adams and support the French cause.

Adams tried to steer a middle course between the extreme Federalists in his own party, led by Alexander Hamilton, who feared the French Revolution as little more than "rule by rabble," and the Jeffersonian Republicans, who denounced the president as a British tool. Adams was a born-and-bred aristocrat in social outlook, but he did not want to involve the country in costly and dangerous warfare. So he decided to send a diplomatic mission to France, as Washington earlier had dispatched Chief Justice Jay to England. He chose two former delegates to the Constitutional Convention of 1787, Elbridge Gerry and Charles Cotesworth Pinckney, and a younger Virginia lawyer, John Marshall.

The neophyte diplomats arrived in Paris in October 1797, expecting to meet with Foreign Minister Talleyrand. But the imperious Talleyrand refused to meet with the Americans for several months, finally sending three men— who would not reveal their names—to their hotel after dark. The mysterious Frenchmen demanded an American apology for past (and unspecified) misdeeds, a $10 million loan to France, and a $1 million bribe to Talleyrand and his friends. After months of haggling with the still-anonymous Frenchmen, the American delegation indignantly refused to accept these conditions for a treaty. Marshall reported these events to Adams in March 1798, and the president promptly sent his letter to Congress, labeling Talleyrand's extortioners as "Messr. X, Y, and Z." When Marshall returned to Philadelphia (still the nation's capital) from Paris, he received a hero's welcome and found the country inflamed over what everyone called the "XYZ affair."

Riding a wave of nationalistic and anti-French sentiment, the Federalists put the Republicans on the defensive. The Rev. Timothy Dwight, president of Yale, delivered a sermon in which he claimed that Jeffersonian Republicanism would make "our wives and daughters the victims of legal prostitution" as Frenchmen supposedly encouraged their wives and daughters to practice. A Federalist writer urged that Republicans should be treated "as we should a TURK, A JEW, A JACOBIN, OR DOG." Diatribes like these turned the voters—white men with property, many with wives and daughters—against the Republicans, and swept the Federalists to an overwhelming victory in the 1798 congressional elections.

The Federalist victory emboldened the party's leaders to push through Congress in 1798 a set of three laws that reflected popular fears of the "alien" French and their "seditious" American supporters. The Naturalization Act lengthened the time of residence needed for American citizenship from five to fourteen years. The Alien Act allowed the president to direct the deportation of "all such aliens as he shall judge dangerous to the peace and safety of the United States" or who engaged in "secret machinations against the government." Two shiploads of French citizens promptly sailed for their homeland to escape jailing and forced deportation.

The Federalist law that most directly affected American citizens was the Sedition Act, which directly confronted the First Amendment's provision that "Congress shall make no law . . . abridging freedom of speech, or of the press." This law authorized criminal prosecution, with fines or imprisonment as penalties, for the utterance or publication of any "false, scandalous and malicious" statements that might expose Congress or the president to "contempt or ridicule." Republicans in Congress denounced the Sedition Act as a clear violation of the First Amendment, but they were voted down in both houses.

Federalist prosecutors, placed in office by President Adams, immediately began a witch-hunt that rivaled those of colonial Salem and the more recent McCarthy era. Their first victim was Mathew Lyon of Vermont, his state's Republican congressman. Lyon had written and published a letter to his constituents which accused Adams of "a continuous grasp for power" and an "unbounded thirst for ridiculous pomp, foolish adulation and selfish avarice." Under the law of the time, based on the English common law of "seditious libel," establishing the truth of a statement was a defense against conviction. Representative Lyon had the bad luck to appear before Supreme Court Justice William Paterson for trial, while Paterson was sitting as a circuit judge. And he had the bad judgment to ask Paterson from the witness stand if the justice had not dined with Adams and observed his "ridiculous pomp and parade." Paterson replied that the president had always displayed "much plainness and simplicity" at dinner. Adams was, in fact, a pompous man, but Paterson was determined to send Lyon to jail, regardless of the president's conduct at the dinner table.

Paterson did not even allow Lyon's lawyer, Anthony Haswell, to present a defense, over Haswell's strenuous objections. The justice instructed the jurors to find Lyon guilty, which they promptly did, and Paterson sentenced him to four months in jail. Paterson later convicted Haswell of sedition for charging that federal marshals had mistreated Lyon during his jail term. Lyon got some measure of revenge against Paterson and the Federalists. While he sat behind bars, his loyal and admiring constituents returned him to Congress by a landslide over his Federalist opponent.

Justice Samuel Chase not only rivaled but exceeded Paterson in zealous persecution of Republicans. Chase had publicly urged Congress to adopt the Sedition Act, and he gained the sobriquet of the "hanging judge" for his conduct in trying John Fries for "treason" in 1800. Fries, a militia captain, led a troop of armed farmers against federal tax collectors in Pennsylvania. His mutinous acts reminded Federalists of Daniel Shays, who had led a similar rebellion in 1787. Justice Chase, sitting as a circuit judge, was so determined to punish Fries that he dispensed with even the rudiments of fair trial. Explaining that he wanted to speed up the proceedings, Chase showed the hapless defendant's lawyers—before the trial even began—his ruling that Fries could not challenge the constitutionality of the Sedition Act. Since this claim was the basis of their defense of Fries, the muzzled lawyers were so outraged they withdrew from the case. Chase rushed through the trial and sentenced Fries to death. John Adams, however, faced a presidential campaign against Thomas Jefferson and did not wish to stain his hands with his opponents' blood. He pardoned Fries and avoided being labeled the "hanging president."

Justice Chase made many enemies during his trials of Republicans for "seditious libel" of President Adams. His bullying of lawyers dismayed even his political allies. District judge Richard Peters, a loyal Federalist, complained, "I never sat with him without pain, as he was forever getting into some intemperate and unnecessary squabbles." Chase missed the entire Supreme Court term that began in August 1800 because he was campaigning across Maryland for President Adams, denouncing Jefferson as a dangerous "Jacobin" who would impose the terrors of the French Revolution on his American opponents. Jefferson would not forget Chase's attacks on his character and policies.

Before the Sedition Act prosecutions ended in 1800, every Supreme Court justice had presided at trials and had sentenced Republicans to fines or imprisonment. Flushed with victory in the "XYZ affair," the Federalists misjudged the public's attachment to the Constitution and squandered their support in prosecuting their Republican critics. President Adams lost his office to Thomas Jefferson and the Federalists lost control of both houses of Congress. Only in Abraham Lincoln's presidential campaign against Stephen Douglas in 1860 and Franklin Roosevelt's attacks on the Supreme Court's "Nine Old Men" in 1937 did judicial power become national issues that matched the debate between Federalists and Republicans over the Sedition Act prosecutions.

But the Federalists did not lose everything in the 1800 elections. During his single term in office, Adams had the opportunity to place three justices on the Supreme Court. The first opening came in 1798, with the death of James Wilson. Adams chose Bushrod Washington, the first president's favorite nephew, to fill the seat. His uncle had sent the younger Washington in 1782 to Wilson's law office in Philadelphia, where he studied law and absorbed Federalist politics for two years. He then returned to Virginia and practiced law for another decade, often facing another young lawyer, John Marshall, in courtroom battles over property and contract cases.

Adams did not reveal his reasons for picking Washington, but Virginia had not been represented on the Supreme Court since John Blair had resigned in 1796, and the president owed many debts to his predecessor. Bushrod Washington owed debts as well; he wrote his uncle after his nomination that "I could not upon a small piece of poor land in Westmoreland have paid debts which I owe, and supported my family." Only thirty-six when he took his seat, Washington served for thirty years before his death in 1829, all but the first two under the tutelage of Chief Justice John Marshall, his former legal adversary. One fellow justice observed that Washington and Marshall "are commonly estimated as one judge," and Washington disagreed with his formidable Chief in just three cases over three decades.

The second justice Adams picked also came from his predecessor's home state. James Iredell died in 1799, and Adams replaced him with another North Carolina lawyer, Alfred Moore, the state's attorney general and a prominent Federalist. The best any friend could say of Moore was that he was among the "ornamental members of society." President Adams had nothing to say about why he chose Moore for the Court. During four years of judicial service, Moore wrote just one opinion, in a maritime case than raised no constitutional issues. He left the Court in 1804 with hardly a ripple in his wake.

The third and final Supreme Court choice of President Adams, John Marshall of Virginia, served as Chief Justice for thirty-four years and transformed the Court from a trickling stream into a mighty river in American law and politics, in more than a metaphorical sense. Marshall and the Court he commanded swept away every dam and levee that state lawmakers, the Congress, and five presidents constructed in his path. What prompted President Adams to choose Marshall, a man with no prior judicial experience, as Chief Justice in 1801, an act that changed the course of American constitutional history?

Marshall did not ride to the Supreme Court on a wave of acclamation, as his later reputation might suggest. He was not, in fact, among the candidates that Adams first considered for the post. Adams turned to Marshall, then serving as his secretary of state, largely to escape the crossfire of political and personal battles within the Federalist ranks. The resignation of Chief Justice Oliver Ellsworth in October 1800, just before Adams lost his office to Jefferson, offered the chance to place the Court under Federalist tutelage for years to come. But the most prominent candidates for the post were disabled by age, infirmity, or political wounds. The first problem Adams confronted stemmed from the machinations of Alexander Hamilton and his allies. Hamilton's objections to the president's policies, both foreign and domestic, led him to publish a widely circulated pamphlet, "Concerning the Public Conduct and Character of John Adams," arguing that Adams was unfit to be president. Adams was notoriously thin-skinned, and took his revenge by dismissing three cabinet members who sided with Hamilton.

The Hamiltonian attacks on the president also doomed their campaign to replace Ellsworth with Justice William Paterson, who later wrote to a friend that "if the president had put my name in nomination I should have considered it a complimental thing, a mere feather, which might tickle a vain mind, but which I neither wished nor wanted." Paterson was exceedingly vain and clearly wanted the job, but Adams had no intention of elevating him to the Chief's post. Moving to deflect the pressure for Paterson, Adams nominated John Jay, although the former Chief Justice had announced his decision to retire from public office. There is no record that Adams even consulted with Jay before sending his name to the Senate for confirmation in December 1800. Most likely, Adams hoped to avoid a bitter partisan battle before the presidential electors cast their votes. The electors were evenly split between Jefferson and Aaron Burr, who both ran as Republicans. Both men had earned Hamilton's enmity, although he considered Jefferson more dangerous to the Federalists. John Marshall incurred Hamilton's wrath as well by refusing his entreaties to support Burr and block Jefferson's election. President Adams was determined to stay out of these political battles.

On his part, Jefferson feared that Adams would nominate a Federalist firebrand like Paterson as Chief Justice, and expressed relief when Adams chose Jay. "We were afraid of something worse," he wrote to James Madison. But something worse *did* happen to Jefferson and the Republicans. The Senate confirmed Jay, but he returned his commission and forced Adams to choose again. Jefferson had earlier expressed fear to Madison that the Federalists in Congress, having lost the election, would push through a bill "giving the government" to the Chief Justice or "to Marshall as Secretary of State." Rumors of a Federalist plot to circumvent the electoral college proved unfounded, but Adams turned to Marshall as Chief Justice after Jay declined to serve. The extreme Federalists remembered that Marshall had refused to help block Jefferson's election and reacted bitterly to his selection. Jonathan Dayton, a New Jersey senator, expressed his "grief, astonishment and almost indignation" to Justice Paterson. Conceding that Marshall was a lawyer of "respectable talents and standing," Dayton questioned "the propriety of making a stand" against his confirmation. Dayton could only lament that Adams had displayed "such debility or derangement of intellect" in choosing Marshall.

Paterson's diehard supporters made one last appeal, sending a delegation of Federalist senators to meet with Adams. Dayton reported to Paterson that Adams "was inflexible, and declared that he would never nominate you. Under those circumstances we thought it advisable to confirm Marshall, lest another not so well qualified, and more disgusting to the bench, should be substituted" for him. Dayton could not resist denouncing Adams as a "wild freak of a man, whose administration, happily for this country, is soon to terminate."

Dayton and his Federalist colleagues need not have protested Marshall's nomination, which the Senate confirmed without dissent. Marshall gave far more to their nationalist cause, in more than three decades as Chief Justice, than Paterson—who left the Court in 1806 because of injury and illness—could possibly have accomplished. What distinguished Marshall from other competent lawyers like Alfred Moore, and made his reputation as the greatest Chief Justice in our history?

Four factors—aside from good health and longevity—helped Marshall to turn the Supreme Court from what Hamilton called the "least dangerous branch" of government into a judicial leviathan. First, he possessed an iron will and fierce determination to have his way. Marshall's portraits show a piercing gaze that reflects his solid inner core. Second, he placed his legal skills at the service of Federalist politics. He firmly believed in a strong national government whose primary objectives were the promotion of economic growth and the protection of property. Third, Marshall joined the grant of "judicial power" to the Supreme Court in Article III of the Constitution with the Supremacy Clause of Article VI to fashion the sword of judicial review, wielding it to cut down state laws that offended his views of the Constitution. Fourth, and perhaps most important, Marshall's commanding personality allowed him to shape every justice—fifteen in all—who served with him into his mold. The Marshall Court produced no "Great Dissenter" like Oliver Wendell Holmes. Dissents from Marshall's decisions were few, and he only once voted with the Court's minority in a significant case.

Marshall's background gives some clues to his later achievements. Born in 1755, he was the oldest of fifteen children in one of the leading families of Fauquier County in Virginia. His father was a planter and managed part of the great Fairfax estate, whose British owners controlled more than five million acres in twenty-one counties. Like his father, Marshall became skilled at land surveying, and he worked as a teenage assistant to his boyhood friend George Washington. When the Revolution began, he became a lieutenant in the Culpepper Minute Men at the age of nineteen, and rose to the rank of captain. Marshall distinguished himself in battle and endured the harsh winter at Valley Forge with General Washington.

After his military service, Marshall studied law—for less than a year—at the College of William and Mary, was admitted to the bar in 1780, and practiced in Fauquier County and then Richmond for almost twenty years. He specialized in representing the owners of landed estates and used his legal fees to purchase a large chunk of the Fairfax estate, which made him a wealthy man in land and slaves. Like many ambitious lawyers, Marshall also played at politics, winning election to the Virginia legislature and the state convention that ratified the Constitution, at which he argued for a strong national judiciary. Following his triumphant return from France after the XYZ affair, Marshall turned his sights to national office and won election to Congress in 1798. President Adams chose him as secretary of state in 1800, and during the last month of the Adams administration—after his confirmation as Chief Justice—Marshall served in both posts until Thomas Jefferson became president on March 4, 1801.

Four months elapsed between the national election in November and the change of administration the following March, a delay provided by the first Congress out of concern for bad roads and winter storms, which might keep electors from meeting and sending their votes to Congress. Hardly anyone foresaw the potential mischief that lame-duck lawmakers and presidents could create for their successors, particularly when control of Congress and the White

House changed parties. The defeated Federalists in Congress met for their last session in December 1800 and passed a Judiciary Act that President Adams signed in February 1801. The law's most notable provision would reduce the Supreme Court from six to five members after the next vacancy. Many people expected the elderly and frail Justice Cushing to retire soon, and the Federalists wanted to prevent Jefferson from choosing a Republican to replace him. Cushing, although noticeably senile, depended on his judicial salary and hobbled to the Court until 1810.

The Judiciary Act also created twenty-six new posts in the federal district and circuit courts, to relieve the Supreme Court of the detested burden of circuit-riding. With the nation's capital moved to the District of Columbia, Congress established forty-five positions as "justice of the peace," a minor judicial office that provided a small salary and fees for notarizing papers and handling small claims. Washington was still a small city in 1801 and hardly needed forty-five new judges. But as one Republican paper accurately noted, Congress had passed "a bill providing sinecure places and pensions for thoroughgoing Federal partisans." President Adams and Congress spent considerable time picking and confirming the new district and circuit judges in the weeks before Jefferson took office. Faced with a deadline of midnight on March 3, Congress met into the night and rushed through confirmations of the new justices of the peace. Clerks quickly delivered their commissions to Secretary of State Marshall, who signed the parchment documents and stacked them on his desk.

In the last-minute rush, however, Marshall neglected to have the commissions delivered to the "midnight judges," as Republicans derisively called them. One account—probably apocryphal—had the incoming attorney general, Levi Lincoln, dramatically striding into Marshall's office with Jefferson's watch in his hand. Pointing to the timepiece, Lincoln informed Marshall that midnight had arrived and directed him to leave the office. Humiliated by this order, Marshall laid down his pen and departed. Whether or not this actually happened, Marshall did keep signing judicial commissions until at least nine o'clock that night. Shortly after Jefferson took his oath as president on March 4, 1801, James Madison took Marshall's office as secretary of state and sat behind the desk on which the undelivered commissions rested.

This was the odd beginning of the famous case of *Marbury v. Madison*, which started with Marshall's oversight in 1801 as secretary of state and culminated in 1803 with his forceful assertion of judicial review as Chief Justice. The two years in between were marked by Republican efforts to hobble the federal courts that remained as Federalist redoubts. "The Federalists have retired into the judiciary as a stronghold," Jefferson complained after taking office, "and from that battery all the works of republicanism are to be beaten down and erased." He directed Madison to deliver only twenty-five of the forty-two commissions Marshall left on his desk, perhaps to cut expenses for judicial salaries, even the small amount for these minor posts.

Of the seventeen slighted judges, only four—including William Marbury—took their claims to court, filing suit in the Supreme Court and asking for a "writ of mandamus" against Secretary Madison. This common-law writ, with roots in English practice, empowers judges to order recalcitrant officials to carry out their duties; the Latin term comes from the word for "hand." In effect, the judge issuing the writ is forcing the official to move his hand. Marshall had not lifted his hand to deliver Marbury's commission and Madison now refused to complete the task.

Marbury's suit against Madison languished in the Supreme Court clerk's office for two years before it was argued. The Court, in fact, did not conduct any business for more than a year, as the Republican majority in Congress exacted revenge on the Federalists for passing the Sedition Act in 1798 and for packing the federal courts in 1801. Over Federalist protests, Congress repealed the Judiciary Act of 1801 and then passed a law moving the Court's next term, scheduled for June 1802, to February 1803. This move did not remove any sitting judges from their posts, but the Republicans wanted to prevent the Court from striking down the repeal bill as unconstitutional while they prepared impeachment charges against federal judges (and perhaps even Supreme Court justices) for partisan bias in Sedition Act prosecutions.

Although some extreme Federalists implored Marshall to convene the Court in June 1802 as originally scheduled, he prudently decided to avoid a confrontation with Congress that might have provoked even further efforts to cripple the Court. But when the justices did meet in February 1803, for the first time in fourteen months, Marshall was ready to respond. Both sides in *Marbury v. Madison* expected the justices to issue the requested writ of mandamus, which would likely have precipitated the constitutional crisis that political moderates feared and that extremists in both parties welcomed as an overdue showdown between the Republican "Jacobins" and the Federalist "Tories."

Anticipating defeat, James Madison did not even send a lawyer to defend him, passing up the chance to blame Marshall for the entire mess. William Marbury's lawyer, former attorney general Charles Lee, brimmed with confidence as he addressed the justices. The Court had three simple questions before it, Lee argued, and the answer to each was obvious. First, was Marbury entitled to his commission? Article I of the the Constitution empowers Congress to create federal offices. Marbury was duly nominated for the post that Congress established, he was duly confirmed by the Senate, and his commission was duly signed by the secretary of state, as the law provided. The answer to Lee's first question was obviously yes. Second, did the law provide Marbury a remedy for Madison's refusal to deliver his commission? The answer came from the old maxim "Every wrong provides a remedy." Otherwise, courts would have no power or even purpose.

The only remaining question was whether mandamus provided the remedy in Marbury's suit. Lee did not even consider this a question but a settled fact.

The First Congress had authorized the Supreme Court in Section 13 of the Judiciary Act of 1789 to issue writs of mandamus against "persons holding office under the authority of the United States." Secretary Madison was such a person, and the writ of mandamus was necessary to force his compliance with a clear legal duty to Marbury. Lee stated his case as if he were reciting a simple syllogism.

Chief Justice Marshall issued the Court's opinion in *Marbury v. Madison* on February 24, 1803, just two weeks after Lee's argument. Given the rhetorical polish of this momentous opinion, Marshall had most likely decided the case and begun writing before Lee opened his mouth. He wrote for himself and three other justices; because of illness, William Cushing and Alfred Moore did not hear argument or vote in the case. Marshall posed the three questions Charles Lee had asked, and answered each in turn. The first and second gave Marshall no trouble. It was "the opinion of the Court," he wrote, that "by signing the commission of Mr. Marbury, the president of the United States appointed him a justice of the peace" and that "the seal of the United States, affixed thereto by the secretary of state," conferred on Marbury "a legal right to the office" he sought. Madison's refusal to deliver that commission "is a plain violation of that right, for which the laws of his country afford him a remedy."

Marbury won the right to his commission, but could the Court order Madison to deliver it? Marshall's answer to this question surprised everyone, and cleverly defused the constitutional crisis he hoped to avoid. Congress had authorized the Supreme Court to issue writs of mandamus, but Article III of the Constitution limited the Court's "original jurisdiction" to cases involving ambassadors, foreign consuls, and states. In all other cases, the Court had only "appellate jurisdiction" over decisions of lower courts, both state and federal. William Marbury made the fatal mistake of filing his suit in the Supreme Court, wrongly assuming that it had jurisdiction under Section 13 of the Judiciary Act to decide his claim. Marshall concluded that "the jurisdiction must be appellate, not original," for the Court to authorize writs of mandamus.

With that conclusion, Marbury's suit against Madison was over. He could, of course, ask a lower court to issue the writ; Marshall had not offered this advice in his opinion, but a good lawyer like Charles Lee would know how to remedy the error. Normally, if a judge decides that his (or her) court lacks jurisdiction over a case, the judge refrains from expressing an opinion on the merits of that case. But Marshall did not stop with his holding that Marbury had filed suit in the wrong court. He continued with a stern lecture to Congress, asserting the Court's power to declare the offending Section 13 unconstitutional. His words rang with certitude and confidence. He began with a rhetorical question. "If an act of the legislature, repugnant to the Constitution, is void, does it, notwithstanding its invalidity, bind the courts, and oblige them to give it effect?" Answering yes to this question, Marshall wrote, would be "an absurdity too gross to be insisted on."

Marshall's next question was implied by the first. Who decides if a law is unconstitutional? His answer was clear and simple. "It is emphatically the province and duty of the judicial department to say what the law is," he wrote. Because "the Constitution is superior to any ordinary act of the legislature," the provisions of the Constitution "must govern the case to which they both apply." Arguments that "courts must close their eyes on the Constitution, and see only the law," Marshall wrote, "would subvert the very foundation of all written constitutions."

In going beyond the questions raised in *Marbury* and proclaiming the Supreme Court's power to strike down congressional acts, Marshall deliberately threw down a gauntlet before Congress. He took a calculated risk, knowing that President Jefferson had recently asked Congress to impeach a Federalist judge, John Pickering of New Hampshire, for partisan bias in Sedition Act prosecutions. Marshall must have known that if Pickering—who was both alcoholic and insane—was removed from office, the Republicans might turn their guns on the Supreme Court. The political stakes were high, but Marshall did not flinch.

Several generations of historians have elevated Marshall to the pantheon of judicial greatness, and have annointed his *Marbury* opinion as the most important in American constitutional history. Marshall certainly led the Supreme Court from obscurity to a position of power. But his *Marbury* opinion did not break new legal ground. The doctrine of judicial review had been stated by several Framers of the Constitution in 1787, was refined in *The Federalist Papers* during the ratification debates, and was forcefully restated by Justice Paterson in 1795, when he wrote in a circuit court decision that "every act of the legislature repugnant to the Constitution is absolutely void." What transformed *Marbury* from a simple "jurisdiction" case, sending the plaintiff back to a lower court, into a constitutional landmark was John Marshall's determination to force a showdown with Thomas Jefferson—his political foe and personal enemy— over the most basic question in politics: Who rules?

The *Marbury* case presented this question in its clearest form. If Congress ruled in authorizing the Supreme Court to issue writs of mandamus, then Congress could expand or contract the Court's jurisdiction at will. And if the president ruled in directing James Madison to withhold judicial commissions that Congress had confirmed and Marshall had signed, the executive branch could evade judicial orders. But if the Supreme Court could strike down legislative acts, and invalidate executive actions based on such laws, the justices would hold the power "to say what the law is" and bind the Congress and president to their decisions.

Marshall's opinion in *Marbury* is best understood not as a legal opinion but as a political act. As a committed Federalist, he knew that his nationalist views could only survive Jefferson's "Jacobin" regime if the Supreme Court employed the power of judicial review to keep the president and Congress in check. Marshall won his first duel with Jefferson in the *Marbury* case. There were, in fact, no more shots fired in public before Marshall died in 1835.

10

"These Jarring and
Discordant Judgments"

Chief Justice Marshall's opinion in *Marbury v. Madison* left both sides in the lawsuit with a partial victory, but the Supreme Court emerged as the real winner in this first clash between the three branches of the federal government. Republicans in Congress, and perhaps President Jefferson, would have loudly denounced Marshall if the Court had ordered Secretary Madison to deliver Marbury's commission. But he "sophisticated" his opinion so cleverly that no one had grounds for complaint. The only remaining obstacle in Marshall's path, as he sought to fashion the Court into a powerful institution, was the prospect of impeachment of one or more justices. The House had impeached Judge John Pickering in 1803 for his partisan bias in Sedition Act prosecutions, and the Senate convicted him on March 12, 1804. Pickering had become an embarrassment to the bench, since he was clearly insane, and his conviction prompted no Federalist outcry.

Within an hour of Pickering's conviction, the House voted to impeach Justice Samuel Chase. The intemperate justice might have been forgiven his hectoring of lawyers and defendants in Sedition Act prosecutions, since the law had expired in 1800, but he offended Jefferson with a bitter attack on the repeal of the Judiciary Act of 1801. He told a grand jury in 1803 that Jeffersonian "Mobocracy" threatened to destroy "peace and order, freedom and prosperity." Jefferson asked his party's House leader to consider impeaching this "insolent and overbearing man." The president wanted to avoid Federalist charges of conducting a personal vendetta against Chase, so he cautioned that "it is better that I should not interfere." But he clearly *had* interfered in the case, determined to punish his judicial foes.

The Constitution provides in Article II that "civil officers of the United States" can be impeached only for "treason, bribery, or other high crimes and misdemeanors." But Article III states that Supreme Court justices shall hold office "during good behavior." Justice Chase had not violated any criminal laws, but his judicial behavior was clearly not good. Which clause should prevail in deciding his impeachment charges? Judge Pickering was not guilty of criminal offenses, but was removed for exceedingly bad behavior. Chase's offenses were also political in nature, despite his obvious partisan bias and injudicious behavior.

Chase was hardly the only federal judge who showed prejudice on the bench; President John Kennedy paid his political debts to southern Dixiecrats by appointing several vicious racists to federal district courts. One judge he placed in Mississippi, Harold Cox, routinely insulted blacks, calling them "chimpanzees" from the bench, and refused to obey direct orders from appellate judges and the Supreme Court in segregation cases. Were Justice Chase and Judge Cox both unfit for judicial office? The answer is clearly yes. Were they guilty of "high crimes and misdemeanors" and subject to impeachment? The answer depends on whether this phrase, inserted into the Constitution by the Framers with no discussion of its meaning, refers only to criminal offenses. The wording suggests that it does, but the English common-law interpretation of the phrase arguably (a word that lawyers love) encompassed political offenses as well as crimes. Political attacks on the British crown were criminal acts under the law of "seditious libel," which was incorporated into American law after the Revolution.

Justice Chase entered the Senate chamber for his trial on January 3, 1805, anticipating his conviction and removal from office. Republicans outnumbered Federalists by twenty-five to nine in the Senate, two more than the two thirds required for conviction. Chief Justice Marshall and all of Chase's colleagues attended the proceedings to show their support. The political basis of the charges—the House had filed eight articles of impeachment—was clear from the start. Senator William Giles, who headed the Republicans, boasted to John Quincy Adams during the trial, "We want your offices, for the purpose of giving them to men who will fill them better." The younger Adams reported to his father that Chase's impeachment "was unquestionably intended to pave the way for another prosecution, which would have swept the Supreme Judicial Bench clean at a stroke."

Faced with an overwhelming Republican Senate majority, and saddled with Chase's widespread unpopularity, Chief Justice Marshall considered striking a deal with his political enemies. "I think the modern doctrine of impeachment should yield to an appellate jurisdiction in the legislature," he wrote to Chase before the trial began. "A reversal of those legal opinions considered unsound by the legislature would certainly better comport with the mildness of our character than a removal of the judge who has rendered them unknowing of his fault."

This was an astonishing proposal by the forceful Chief Justice. Marshall was suggesting that the Supreme Court, which two years earlier had wielded the power of judicial review over Congress in the *Marbury* case, now allow Congress to overrule the Court. Members of Congress, from both the left and right, have often proposed legislative reversal of Court decisions, but Marshall was the only justice who ever floated such an idea, even in a private letter. Fortunately for Marshall, his letter to Chase—suggesting in effect a "plea bargain" to avoid his conviction—never reached the press or the Senate floor. If it had, the course of American constitutional history might have been profoundly changed. Giving Congress a veto power over Supreme Court decisions would have reduced the Court to the insignificant role it had played before Marshall became Chief Justice.

Chase's trial dragged on for a month. Marshall was called as a witness and struck observers as nervous and evasive in his testimony. The Chief Justice was not accustomed to hostile interrogation, but he should not have lost his customary composure. The Republican Senate voted to acquit Chase on all eight charges. Five did not even gain a simple majority. Only the charge based on Chase's harangue in 1803 against Jefferson's "Mobocracy" came close, but the nineteen votes for conviction fell short of the twenty-three required to remove him from the Court. Six Republican senators, in fact, voted to acquit Chase on every charge. These defections prompted one Republican leader to ask why "there should be any class of men in society in any office that should be treated like gods, placed so far above the reach of censure and almost dignified with papal infallibility?"

President Jefferson reacted in calmer words, predicting to a friend that "impeachment will not be tried again" against Supreme Court justices, but lamenting that "we have no law but the will of the judge." Although Jefferson finally patched up his quarrels with John Adams, he never forgave Marshall for clipping his presidential wings. Writing in 1820, more than a decade after he returned to his Monticello estate, Jefferson complained that the "judiciary of the United States is the subtle corps of sappers and miners constantly working underground to undermine the foundations of our confederated fabric." He deplored Supreme Court opinions issued "with the silent acquiescence of lazy and timid associates, by a crafty chief judge who sophisticates the law to his own mind by the turn of his own reasoning." What Jefferson neglected to add was that he had chosen three of Marshall's associates, and that the justices he placed on the Court all joined Marshall in most of the decisions that upheld federal power over the states and judicial power over the legislative and executive branches of government. William Johnson, Jefferson's first nominee to the Court in 1804, was a loyal Republican when he took the bench, but soon fell under Marshall's sway. He later confessed that "I found that I must either submit to circumstances or become such a cypher ... as to effect no good at all. I therefore bent to the current." Johnson served until 1834, almost the entire length of Marshall's tenure as Chief Justice; although his thirty-four dissents (slightly more than one per year) set the record for the Marshall Court, Johnson never influenced enough fellow justices to challenge Marshall's dominance. Jefferson's other two justices, Brockholst Livingston of New York and Thomas Todd of Kentucky, served on the Court for thirty-six years between them and left no visible mark on constitutional law.

Between his bold assertion in 1803 of judicial supremacy in *Marbury v. Madison* and his death in 1835, John Marshall wielded more influence over national affairs than any of the four presidents who followed Thomas Jefferson. During this period of expansive growth in territory, population, and technology, Marshall read the Constitution as a charter for his nationalistic vision of an American empire. Emboldened by his early victories, the Chief Justice enlisted his compliant associates into a political force—the Marshall Party, in effect—that could ignore the electorate and bypass the ballot box.

During the first third of the nineteenth century, while Marshall held office, the number of Americans tripled, from five to fifteen million. The nation's territory also tripled in size, through the Louisiana Purchase of 1803 and the acquisition of Florida from Spain. The national economy boomed as well, spurred by construction of canals, turnpikes, and railroads. The Erie Canal opened in 1825, and one thousand miles of railroad track had been laid by 1835. The expanding national transportation network—financed largely with state and federal funds—speeded the products of farms and factories to domestic consumers and spurred a growing foreign trade. The rapid growth of manufacturing gave rise to corporations as instruments for raising capital, and the steady development of a national economy led to calls for a national currency and a centralized banking system.

This almost explosive growth in population, area, and wealth did not come without conflict, some of it violent. Thomas Jefferson, who wrote that "all men are created equal," adopted a policy of Indian removal to pave the way for westward expansion. American soldiers pushed the Indians from their native lands at bayonet point, forcing them into desolate "reservations" and killing thousands of those who resisted. The federal government was so determined to take Indian lands that it defied a ruling in 1831 by Chief Justice Marshall that Indian tribes were "dependent domestic nations" with rights to lands they did not voluntarily cede to the United States. After the Court issued its decision in *Worcester v. Georgia*, President Andrew Jackson reportedly answered, "John Marshall has made his decision; now let him enforce it." Jackson defied the Court's ruling and federal troops began expelling the Creek, Chickasaw, and Cherokee tribes from their lands, to which they held title by treaties the government refused to honor. This sorry episode ended in 1838 with the forced march of seventeen thousand Cherokees to western territory in what is now Oklahoma. More than four thousand died on the "Trail of Tears" from disease, exhaustion, and starvation.

Other groups suffered from the growth of American capitalism. The replacement of household weaving with the factory system in textiles brought whole families into noisy, dusty mills. Children as young as four or five labored with their parents, tending looms from dawn to dusk. Railroad workers and miners died by the thousands under the wheels of trains or in rockfalls and explosions. There were no laws to protect the health or safety of America's industrial workers, and they had no legal right to join unions, which state courts—following English common law—outlawed as "criminal conspiracies." It is hardly a radical notion to note that those who reaped the profits of American expansion—merchants, financiers, manufacturers, and plantation owners—did so at the expense of the workers, small farmers, and slaves who outnumbered the economic elite but could not outvote them. Even the presidential victories of Andrew Jackson in 1828 and 1832, riding a populist wave of protest against bankers and businessmen, did not dislodge—or even threaten—those who controlled the economy and took the biggest share of the national wealth.

No provision of the Constitution held more importance for those who invested in American expansion than the clause in Section 10 of Article I that bars states from passing any law "impairing the obligation of contracts." Protecting private bargains from state interference had motivated many of the Constitution's framers, most notably James Madison. "In the internal administration of the states," he wrote in the preface to his convention notes, "a violation of contracts had become familiar," a problem compounded by "occulsions of the Courts of Justice" in deciding contract disputes. Providing "more effectively for the protection of private rights," he also noted, "more perhaps than anything else, produced this convention."

Contract law became a crucial issue during the first third of the nineteenth century because of the frenzied land speculation as the nation's boundaries and population marched south and west. Title to land changed hands frequently; private owners bought and sold land with contracts whose enforcement depended on state law; and state legislatures sold public land with grants that formed binding contracts. A considerable number—figures are hard to find—of land transactions wound up in court, and judges struggled to interpret contract terms that were often poorly drafted and imprecise in meaning. Yielding to political pressure, state legislatures passed many laws that upset the contracted bargains of buyers and sellers, and pressure mounted on the Supreme Court to stop legislative incursions into this common-law field.

The Court first interpreted the Contract Clause in *Fletcher v. Peck* in 1810. It would be hard to imagine a lawsuit more tainted with corruption and collusion. The case began in 1795 with the participation of a Supreme Court justice in land speculations that smelled of fraud. Justice James Wilson put up $25,000 for ten shares in the Georgia Company, which entitled him to 750,000 acres of land in a huge tract—about 35 million acres—west of the Yazoo River, including most of what is now Alabama and Mississippi. The Georgia legislature granted this land to four companies, all loosely associated, for less than two cents an acre. The land speculators then sold chunks of their holdings for ten cents an acre, reaping enormous profits. The sudden rise in land values reflected the recent invention of the cotton gin by Eli Whitney; the Yazoo lands were ideal for raising cotton.

There is nothing wrong with buying low and selling high; the stock market is based on this principle. But there is everything wrong with contracts obtained through bribery and fraud. Many of the Georgia lawmakers who made the Yazoo land grants to Justice Wilson and his fellow speculators were paid for their votes. One state senator later testified that a colleague gave him $2,000 for his vote. "I asked him how he got it," Senator Clayton said. Senator Thomas replied that "it is nothing to you, take care of it, and smiled." Another senator offered a state representative "ten likely negroes" for his vote.

The bribery of Georgia's lawmakers was so obvious that the state's voters threw all out but two in the next election. Residents of Augusta actually marched on the state capital, determined to lynch the corrupt lawmakers. The reform legislature passed a law in 1796 that recited the "self evident proof of fraud" in the Yazoo land grants and annulled the contracts held by the corrupt purchasers. Robert Morris, the wealthy Pennsylvania merchant who financed George Washington's ragtag Continental Army and helped to frame the Constitution, spent three years in debtors' prison for his role in the Yazoo scandals. Justice James Wilson, whose land speculations also landed him in prison, participated in a scheme to block Georgia's annullment law by selling land grants to "innocent" purchasers.

The evidence of collusion in the Yazoo lands case is circumstantial but strong. Robert Fletcher of New Hampshire, one of the "innocent" purchasers, filed suit against John Peck of Massachusetts in 1803 to "quiet" the title to his land, which would remove any legal barriers to its resale. The Eleventh Amendment barred Fletcher, an investor in the New England Mississippi Company, from suing Georgia for annulling his purchase from Peck, and the Georgia legislature had forbidden state judges to hear cases stemming from the land sales. But Article III of the Constitution gives federal courts jurisdiction over suits "between citizens of different states." The evidence points to an agreement between Fletcher and Peck to use the federal courts to undo the Georgia law and uphold the land sales to buyers who had "innocently" purchased land originally secured through fraud and bribery.

The case of *Fletcher v. Peck* bounced through lower courts for several years before it landed in the Supreme Court in 1809. The speculators who sold the tainted Yazoo land—including John Peck—hired the biggest guns of the American bar to argue this case. For reasons that remain obscure, the case was argued twice. In the first round, John Quincy Adams—a future president—represented Peck. Adams was replaced in 1810 by by Joseph Story, an illustrious lawyer who then represented Massachusetts in Congress, and who was placed on the Court the following year by President James Madison.

Fletcher, who apparently hoped to lose his case, chose the same lawyer for each argument. He could not have found a better—or worse—lawyer for the task. Luther Martin, who had loudly opposed ratification of the Constitution, appeared before the Court in 1809 so drunk that the justices adjourned the argument until he sobered up. Whether Martin was drunk or sober the next year made no difference in the outcome. Joseph Story was not only a far superior lawyer, but he boasted of his access to the justices. "The scene of my greatest amusement is the Supreme Court," he wrote to a friend in 1808. "I daily spend several hours there, and generally when disengaged, dine and sup with the judges." During the first decade of the Marshall Court, the justices shared the same boardinghouse in Washington; eating and drinking with them gave Story an advantage over Martin, who was not invited to these convivial gatherings.

The Court's decision in *Fletcher v. Peck* did not surprise either party in this collusive suit. Chief Justice Marshall, writing for the Court, ignored the case's tawdry history. "The importance and difficulty of the questions" raised in this case, he piously stated, "are deeply felt by the court." The Georgia legislature that made the original grants "was fully competent" to convey land "to those who were willing to purchase," he ruled. Marshall then moved to the question of Robert Fletcher's purchase of Yazoo lands from John Peck. Who was the "innocent" party in this case? Peck had originally bought land from those who bribed the Georgia lawmakers, and Fletcher then bought this land from Peck. Given the national publicity about the Yazoo land frauds, it is hard to believe that neither man had knowledge of his tainted purchase.

But Marshall covered his judicial eyes, like the blindfolded statue of Liberty. His opinion absolved both Fletcher and Peck of legal blame. "If the original transaction was infected with fraud," he wrote, "these purchasers did not participate in it, and had no notice of it. They were innocent." This statement was, in truth, the rankest form of the "sophistical" reasoning that Thomas Jefferson had earlier accused Marshall of employing to justify the doctrine of judicial supremacy. Under Marshall's reasoning in *Fletcher*, "when a law is in its nature a contract" and creates "vested rights" in purchasers of property, "a repeal of the law cannot divest those rights" in derogation of the Constitution.

The original fraud of the Yazoo land grants did not bother Marshall. Just one question concerned him: "What is a contract?" The answer was simple: "A contract is a compact between two or more parties," whether private parties or states. Proceeding from this premise, the only obstacle in Marshall's path was Georgia's claim that "sovereign" states could revise contract laws without regard for constitutional limitations. Marshall declared that Georgia was not a "sovereign power" and could not pass laws "impairing the obligations of contract." His ruling stemmed from the statement of Justice James Wilson in *Chisholm v. Georgia* in 1793 that "Georgia is not a sovereign state." Judicial nationalism reached new heights in the *Fletcher* decision, but states' rights advocates could only deplore Marshall's decision; his opponents knew that efforts to reverse the outcome through constitutional amendment would be futile.

Marshall's opinion in *Fletcher* relied less on legal reasoning than on political factors. The Chief Justice admitted as much when he wrote that "the people of the United States" had adopted the Constitution "to shield themselves and their property from the effects of those sudden and strong passions to which men are exposed." The "passions" that Marshall obviously had in mind were those of lawmakers who responded to political pressures for easy money and bankruptcy laws. But in the Yazoo case, the "passions" of the Georgia lawmakers in 1795 were clearly motivated by personal greed. In ruling that Robert Fletcher and John Peck were both "innocent" purchasers of Yazoo land, Marshall refused to hold up a judicial "shield" to protect those whose property titles were tainted by corruption and fraud.

The stench of the Yazoo land scandal lingered in the courtroom for years, as the public suspected the justices of complicity in the frauds. Marshall's refusal to examine the real issue—whether a law enacted through widespread bribery could be repealed by subsequent legislation—struck most observers as judicial evasion of duty. His claim that the case was simply a contract dispute between two private parties ignored the collusion between Fletcher and Peck.

Justice William Johnson agreed with the outcome of Marshall's opinion, but he could not remain quiet in this malodorous case. "I have been very unwilling," he wrote in reluctant concurrence, "to proceed to the decision of this cause at all. It appears to me to bear strong evidence on the face of it of being a mere feigned case." Only his admiration for John Quincy Adams and Joseph Story "has induced me to abandon my scruples in the belief they would never consent to impose a mere feigned case upon this Court." Hardly anyone outside the Court shared Johnson's professed belief. But Marshall was determined to block a possible deluge of contract fraud cases stemming from shady land deals. Voiding a law passed by honest lawmakers and upholding the actions of their dishonest predecessors gave the Chief Justice no pause. The end of protecting the "absolute rights" of property against state interference justified the means of enforcing fraudulent contracts in a feigned case.

Marshall was himself involved in another land title case, which came before the Supreme Court twice, first in 1813 under the caption *Fairfax's Devisee v. Hunter's Lessee* and finally in 1816 as *Martin v. Hunter's Lessee.* Two new justices, placed on the Court by President James Madison, participated in deciding this complex and costly lawsuit. Gabriel Duvall of Maryland and Joseph Story of Massachusetts took their seats on the same day in 1812 and served for a total of fifty-six years. Both replaced men from their home states, and in many ways each resembled his predecessor. Duvall took the seat of Samuel Chase, the irascible and vindictive Federalist who survived an impeachment trial in 1805 but faded into obscurity during his final six years on the bench. Duvall, who joined the Court at the age of fifty-nine, was quieter than Chase; in fact, he became totally deaf and wrote only seventeen opinions for the Court in twenty-three years. His colleagues, their work hindered by Duvall's deafness and senility, finally prevailed on him to resign in 1835, shortly before Marshall's death. Neither Chase nor Duvall, who between them occupied the Court's "Maryland seat" for almost forty years, wrote anything of significance on constitutional law while they served under John Marshall.

Joseph Story, the son of a Massachusetts physician who had been one of the "Indians" at the Boston Tea Party, replaced William Cushing, whose twenty-one years on the Court made him the longest-serving of George Washington's eleven justices. Cushing and Story both attended Harvard, and both opposed slavery on moral grounds. Story occupied the Court's "Massachusetts seat" for thirty-four years, and proved as loyal to Marshall's nationalist views as Cushing. Much like Justice William Brennan under Chief Justice Earl Warren, Story became Marshall's "brain," adding his legal acumen to the Chief's political goals. Story was the Court's leading scholar of the nineteenth century; his three volume *Commentaries on the Constitution*, published in 1833, influenced several generations of judges, lawyers, and law professors. The story is probably apocryphal that Marshall would often hand Story the draft of an opinion and say, "This is the law; now you find the precedents." But Story knew all the precedents, and his opinions bristled with citations to decisions that had long gathered dust in the Court's library.

The facts behind *Martin v. Hunter's Lessee* are incredibly tangled, but they deserve recounting to illustrate the problems caused by conflicting land claims in the early years of American law. This legal snarl began during the colonial period in Virginia, with a grant by King Charles II to Lord Fairfax of a huge estate in northern Virginia, along the banks of the Potomac River. During the Revolution, the Virginia legislature passed a law that "sequestered" the estates of British subjects and placed them under state control. Lord Fairfax, a prominent Tory Loyalist who feared for his life, had earlier fled to England, where he died in 1781. Before his death, however, Fairfax had willed his estate to his nephew, Denny Martin, who was a British subject. In 1782, the Virginia legislature passed another law that barred aliens such as Martin from inheriting property in the state.

Some time between 1777 and 1782, David Hunter obtained a grant of eight hundred acres of the Fairfax estate from Virginia. But when he tried to occupy the land, he was warned off by Thomas Martin, the younger brother of Denny Martin and a citizen of Virginia, who claimed that he held title to the land under another Virginia law, passed in 1779. Thomas Martin claimed that this statute, poorly drafted and difficult to unravel, restored title to the original owners of confiscated estates. The conflict over this land was further complicated by the Jay Treaty of 1783 between England and the United States. Under this treaty, Congress agreed to recommend to the states that they return confiscated property to Loyalists such as Lord Fairfax. The treaty, however, did not bind the states to its terms, and Virginia ignored this provision.

Long before Hunter and Martin took their dispute over the Fairfax estate to court, the heirs of an earlier claimant named Joist Hite filed suit for title to 140,000 acres that Virginia had granted to Hite in 1731, land also claimed by Lord Fairfax. Litigation between the Hite and Fairfax families dragged on for more than fifty years, and finally came before the Virginia Court of Appeals in 1786. The lawyer for the Fairfax estate was John Marshall, whose father had been a plantation supervisor for Lord Fairfax. Marshall argued that the "long and quiet possession" of the disputed land by Lord Fairfax and the "various acts" of the state legislature recognizing his title were sufficient to defeat Hite's claim. But Hite had in fact vigorously disputed the Fairfax claim and the Virginia legislature had granted the land to Hite. Marshall lost this case, and Governor Edmund Randolph later granted part of Hite's land to David Hunter.

Two factors made the suit between Denny Martin and David Hunter significant. First, John Marshall had a personal stake in this case. He and his brother James had bought Denny Martin's claim to the Fairfax estate, a tract of some 300,000 acres of prime tobacco-growing land. Marshall stood to make a fortune if Martin's claim to the land was upheld by the courts. Second, the case directly tested the power of the Supreme Court to reverse decisions of state courts. The Court had struck down a state law in *Chisholm v. Georgia* because it conflicted with the Constitution, but that case did not involve a ruling by a state court. The suit between Martin and Hunter dragged on for years in the Virginia courts, until Spencer Roane, the state's chief justice, ruled in 1810 that John Marshall and his brother Thomas had violated "the principles of justice" in pressing Martin's claim. Roane came close in his opinion, which ruled in Hunter's favor, to accusing the Marshalls of fraud and unethical behavior.

Denny Martin appealed the Virginia court's decision to the Supreme Court. Chief Justice Marshall wisely decided to absent himself from the arguments in *Fairfax's Devisee v. Hunter's Lessee*, as the case was known in 1813. He need not have worried about the outcome. Justice Story picked his way carefully through a maze of English common law, colonial statues, state laws, and treaties. He emerged with a deed to the Fairfax estate in Denny Martin's name. What his opinion did not say was that John Marshall and his brother had bought a large chunk of this deed and now held title to that part of the Fairfax estate known as "Leed's Manor."

Story sent the case back to the Virginia court with instructions to enter judgment for Denny Martin's "devisees," who included John Marshall. Spencer Roane, a longtime political and personal enemy of Marshall (and the son-in-law of Patrick Henry), first consulted with Thomas Jefferson and President James Madison. He then wrote an opinion that denied the Supreme Court's power to review the decisions of state courts. Roane ruled that Section 25 of the Judiciary Act of 1789, which conferred this power on the Supreme Court, violated the Constitution because it infringed the "sovereignty" of the states, and that "everything done in this cause" by the Supreme Court was "unconstitutional and void, and should be entirely disregarded by this court." For a state court to rule that a federal law was unconstitutional was akin to a man biting a dog. In this case, the dog bit back.

Spencer Roane's act of defiance brought the case back to the Supreme Court in 1816. Marshall again stepped down from the bench and Story again wrote for the Court. Story tiptoed up to the central issue, noting the "great importance and delicacy" of the questions posed in the case and bowing to the "great respectability" of the Virginia Court of Appeals, to which he expressed the "entire deference" of the Court "for the learning and ability" of its judges. After these polite words, Story moved in for the kill. He showed no deference to Roane's arguments against federal supremacy over state courts. The Constitution was not established "by the states in their sovereign capacities," Story wrote, but by "the people of the Untied States." And the people withheld from the states any powers they granted to Congress, which had given the Supreme Court jurisdiction over cases that began in state courts and raised questions under the Constitution or federal law. "It is the case, then, and not the court, that gives the jurisdiction" to the Supreme Court, Story wrote with emphasis.

Having lectured Judge Roane in a schoolmaster's tone, Story proceeded to impugn his integrity. "The Constitution has presumed," he wrote, "that state attachments, state prejudices, state jealousies, and state interests, might sometimes obstruct" the "administration of justice" by state judges. What Story really meant to say was that Roane and other state judges would uphold their state's interests against claims based on the Constitution, federal law, or treaties. "This is not all," Story continued. "A motive of another kind" had prompted Congress to enact Section 25 of the Judiciary Act. "That motive is the importance, and even necessity of uniformity of decisions throughout the whole United States, upon all subjects within the purview of the constitution." In other words, state judges like Roane might block the Supreme Court's drive for national judicial supremacy. "If there were no revising authority to control these jarring and discordant judgments," Story continued, the "public mischiefs that would attend such a state of things would be truly deplorable."

Justice Story was clearly correct in holding that Section 25 of the Judiciary Act rested firmly on the Supremacy Clause of the Constitution. State judges could not defy the rulings of the Supreme Court. But Story was less clearly correct in upholding Denny Martin's claim—in reality, John Marshall's claim—to the Fairfax estate. Traversing the maze of colonial grants, state laws, and treaties was a daunting task, but the Virginia legislature had confiscated the estates of British Loyalists such as Lord Fairfax and granted their lands to Virginia citizens like David Hunter. Nothing in the Constitution prohibited this exercise of state power; Congress had not passed any laws in this field, and the Jay Treaty did not bind the states to its provisions. The Supremacy Clause clearly required state judges to obey the Constitution. But the Constitution was silent on the questions raised in *Martin v. Hunter's Lessee*. Justice Story's contention that Spencer Roane and other state judges were "bound by obedience to the letter of the Constitution" begged the question; Story could point only to a strained reading of the Jay Treaty to support his claim that Virginia could not control the property rights of its citizens.

Five years after the *Martin* decision, Marshall added the final blow to the nail that Story had driven into the coffin of state "sovereignty." The Court ruled in 1821 in *Cohens v. Virginia* that states as well as individuals were subject to Section 25 of the Judiciary Act of 1789. In this case, the Virginia courts held that a state law prohibiting lotteries barred the sale of tickets for the District of Columbia lottery, which had been authorized by Congress. The Cohen brothers, Philip and Mendes, appealed their conviction under the state law to the Supreme Court, arguing that the federal statute allowed them to sell lottery tickets in Virginia.

This should have been an easy case for any judge, since the federal statue did not authorize the sale of lottery tickets in states that prohibited lotteries. The Cohen brothers should have paid their fine and stayed out of Virginia, but they stubbornly persisted and presented Chief Justice Marshall with the chance to slap down his home state's refusal to show proper deference to his Court. His opinion displayed the same combination of legal brute force and political dexterity that he had employed much earlier in *Marbury v. Madison*. Virginia's lawyers argued in the *Cohens* case that principles of "state sovereignty" barred the Supreme Court from reviewing the decisions of state courts. They further argued that states could not be sued without their consent.

Marshall answered both questions with single assertion of constitutional supremacy over state laws. He first conceded the "general proposition" that states must consent to being sued by anyone. But that consent, he continued, "may be given in a general law." And what was that general law? The Constitution, of course. By ratifying that document, the states had "surrendered" their sovereignty to the "great empire" of the United States. The Constitution included the provision in Article VI that "the judges in every state shall be bound" to defer to federal laws, "anything in the constitution or laws of any state to the contrary notwithstanding." Those federal laws included Section 25 of the Judiciary Act. Marshall answered the defiant Virginia judges with a sterner lecture than

Story had administered in his *Martin* opinion. "The constitution and laws of a state," Marshall wrote, "so far as they are repugnant to the constitution and laws of the United States, are absolutely void."

What did this high-flown rhetoric have to do with the mundane questions in the *Cohens* case? Absolutely nothing, in fact. Having decided that state court rulings were reviewable by the Supreme Court, a conclusion that flowed inexorably from the *Marbury* and *Martin* cases, Marshall upheld the decision of the Virginia court that the state could bar the sale of "foreign" lottery tickets within its borders. This was a simple matter of statutory construction, one that judges generally perform without recourse to the Supremacy Clause of the Constitution. But Marshall was determined to force the surrender of his judicial enemies on state courts to the "supreme" power of the federal government, and to his Court's "power of revising the decisions of local tribunals" when they conflicted with his nationalist reading of the Constitution.

Marshall sounded like Victor Hugo in *Les Misérables* in sympathizing with the underdog who faced the bias of state judges. Even as he ruled against the Cohen brothers, Marshall turned them into compatriots of Jean Valjean. "However unimportant his claim might be," he wrote of litigants in state courts, "however little the community might be interested in its decision, the framers of our constitution thought it necessary for the purpose of justice, to provide a tribunal as superior to influence as possible, in which that claim might be decided." But were Supreme Court justices more "superior to influence" than state judges when their interests—both personal and political—were at stake? Cases such as *Martin v. Hunter's Lessee* suggest that judges on courts from the lowest to highest are equally subject to the influence of their interests. John Marshall was not the only justice to profit from the rulings of the Supreme Court. And the interests of his political party certainly profited from the Marshall Court's decisions.

11

"The Good and the Wise"

The Marshall Court read the Constitution to promote economic expansion in the "empire" of the United States, as the Chief Justice characterized the growing nation in his *Fletcher* and *Cohens* opinions. The most important provision in pursuing this goal was the clause in Article I that prohibits states from "impairing the obligation of contracts." But the Court's interpretation of this clause in the *Fletcher* case, which upheld corrupt and fraudulent contracts, proved damaging to the national economy. Encouraged by the Court's ruling, land speculators borrowed huge sums for their investments from state banks, which operated virtually without governmental controls. Nine years after the *Fletcher* decision in 1810, the Supreme Court faced three cases that all stemmed from the financial panic that followed the collapse of the land speculation boom.

The cases the Court decided in 1819 were hurried to argument and decision, with the looming economic crisis on everyone's mind. The facts in each were quite different, but they all threatened the interests of those who controlled property. Each case raised the question of whether states could pass laws to benefit those with less property. These issues included state power to tax the national bank, state control over corporate charters, and state relief to "insolvent" debtors. But they all rested on the Supreme Court's assertion of judicial supremacy over state lawmakers.

The most important of these cases was *McCulloch v. Maryland*, which grew out of political battles—almost thirty years earlier—between Alexander Hamilton and Thomas Jefferson. Hamilton, secretary of the treasury under George Washington, had campaigned tirelessly for a national bank, viewing a strong federal bank as a source of capital for "national" projects like roads, canals, and ports. He succeeded in 1791, over the objections of Jefferson, then secretary of state, that creation of such a bank exceeded the powers delegated to Congress by the Constitution. Hamilton won this battle of cabinet members, and Washington signed a bill establishing a national bank for a term of twenty years.

The first charter expired in 1811, during James Madison's first presidential term. Both the president and the Republicans in Congress opposed a second charter. But the War of 1812 with England had badly damaged the nation's economy, and Congress now viewed a national bank as a source of capital for repairing the damage. A second national bank was chartered in 1816 with a capital of $35 million. Madison signed the bank charter in recognition, he explained, of "the general will of the nation." In reality, he bowed to pressure from those who wanted to refuel the nation's stalled economy.

The rechartering of the Bank of the United States soon created an economic crisis, as the bank's managers tightened credit in 1819, calling in loans and foreclosing thousands of farm mortgages. When hard-pressed debtors paid the bank in easy-money notes from state banks, the bank demanded payment from these banks in cash. With little money in their vaults, most of these state banks closed their doors. The Panic of 1819 swept across the country and provoked calls for relief from state legislatures. Several states passed laws that imposed taxes on the federal bank's operations. Maryland levied an annual tax of $15,000 on banks not chartered by the state, a law that applied only to the Bank of the United States. When James McCulloch, cashier of the bank's Baltimore branch, refused to pay the tax, state officials sued him to collect. Not surprisingly, judges in the Maryland courts ruled against McCulloch, who promptly appealed to the Supreme Court.

Dozens of congressmen, federal officials, and lawyers crowded into the Court's modest chamber in the Senate wing of the Capitol building to witness the oral arguments in *McCulloch v. Maryland*. They anticipated a clash of orators that would rival the best of Washington's theaters for dramatic spectacle, and they were not disappointed. Daniel Webster headed the cast of lawyers for the Bank of the United States. No lawyer ever argued more times before the Supreme Court—he appeared in 168 cases—and no lawyer approached Webster in eloquence and confidence. During a public career that spanned fifty years, he served in both the House and Senate, first as a Federalist and then as a Whig. He also ran for president in 1836 (finishing a distant fourth in electoral votes) and later served under three presidents as secretary of state. By any measure, Webster was also the greatest corporate lawyer who ever lived.

(The change in party labels requires a brief digression to avoid confusion. The Federalists changed their name to the Whig Party between 1836 and 1856, when they became the second Republican Party, adopting the name of their former opponents. The Jeffersonians who first called themselves Republicans abandoned that name in 1828—after using the hybrid title of Democratic-Republican for several years—to become the Democrats. If this sounds confusing, it is. But the nineteenth century saw a proliferation of party labels, including Free-Soil, Liberty, Union, American, and Anti-Mason.)

Today, the Supreme Court limits argument in most cases to one hour, divided equally between the opposing parties. But the Court had a smaller docket in those days, and a greater taste for oratory. The arguments in *McCulloch* spanned nine days, and Webster spoke at greater length than any other lawyer. He covered familiar ground, expounding the ideas of Alexander Hamilton to approving nods from John Marshall. But the Court's greatest applause went to William Pinkney, a former attorney general who shared the podium with Webster for the national bank. "I never, in my whole life, heard a greater speech," Justice Story later gushed in praise.

Webster and Pinkney both relied heavily on Hamilton's written opinion to President Washington in 1791, arguing that Congress had more extensive powers than those enumerated in Article I of the Constitution. Hamilton had pointed to the clause that empowers Congress to "make all laws which shall be necessary and proper" to execute the enumerated powers. Defending the first national bank charter, he read into this clause "a more or less direct" relationship "to the powers of collecting taxes, borrowing money, regulating trade between the states, and raising and maintaining fleets and navies." The relation became more remote as Hamilton recited his list of congressional powers that supposedly authorized creation of a national bank.

In his countering argument to Washington, Jefferson had replied that the national bank would not collect taxes, borrow money, regulate commerce, or finance the nation's army and navy. Creating a national bank would not come within any of the enumerated powers of Congress. Hamilton's reliance on the "necessary and proper" clause struck Jefferson as overreaching. The enumerated powers of Congress, he wrote, "can all be carried into execution without a bank. A bank therefore is not necessary, and consequently not authorized by this phrase."

Between them, Jefferson and Madison had appointed five of the seven justices who heard the *McCulloch* arguments. All five were nominally Republicans and presumably receptive to claims of states' rights against the federal government. But the arguments of Maryland's lawyers fell on deaf ears. Luther Martin, the state's attorney general—who had reportedly argued the *Fletcher* case ten years earlier in a drunken state—was "rumored" to be inebriated during his *McCulloch* argument as well.

Drunk or sober, Martin was a skilled orator, and he quoted extensively from Jefferson's arguments against the national bank as exceeding congressional powers under the Constitution. He concluded with a flourish, looking directly at the Chief Justice and reciting the speech Marshall had delivered in 1788 to the Virginia convention that ratified the Constitution. Responding to Patrick Henry, Marshall had posed several rhetorical questions. "Has the government of the United States power to make laws on every subject?" Marshall denied that the Constitution gave Congress such powers. "Can they go beyond the delegated powers?" He again answered no. "If they were to make a law not warranted by any of the powers enumerated," Marshall concluded, "it would be considered by the judges as an infringement of the Constitution which they are to guard." Reminding the Chief Justice of words he spoke thirty years earlier did not help Martin; changes in conditions had changed Marshall's positions on these questions.

Luther Martin rested his case on the "express" powers of Congress, while Daniel Webster and William Pinkney relied on the doctrine of "implied" powers. Which view of the Constitution would prevail in the *McCulloch* case? Marshall had shown in earlier opinions that he would adopt the approach that best matched his goals. His *Marbury* opinion had looked to the "express" limitations the Constitution imposed on Congress in defining the Court's jurisdiction. Marshall's goal in *McCulloch* was to uphold the power of Congress to charter a national bank; he found the means to that end in the powers "implied" to Congress in the "necessary and proper" clause of Article I, which he pushed to its limits.

Marshall's opinion for a unanimous Court in *McCulloch* read much like an essay in *The Federalist Papers*. Almost two decades into his tenure as Chief Justice, he wrote at the peak of his judicial power, and clearly savored his role as chief arbiter of the Constitution. Marshall barely mentioned the national bank, but he wrote expansively of congressional powers. His lengthy opinion, issued just two weeks after Daniel Webster concluded his argument, posed and answered two questions. Did Congress possess the power to charter a national bank? If it did, could a state impose a tax on its operations?

As he often did, Marshall began with a truism. "The government is acknowledged by all to be one of enumerated powers," he wrote. He then made a concession, as he also did in many opinions. "Among the enumerated powers, we do not find that of establishing a bank." But this was a tactical concession. Requiring the Constitution to list all the powers granted to Congress, Marshall continued, "would partake of a prolixity of a legal code, and could scarcely be embraced by the human mind." The nature of a constitution required only that "its great outlines should be marked" in its provisions and "its important objects designated" for congressional action. Such "minor ingredients" of legislative policy as chartering a national bank could be "deduced" from the "great powers" entrusted to Congress by the Constitution, he reasoned. Marshall "deduced" the power to charter a national bank from the enumerated powers of collecting taxes, borrowing money, regulating commerce, and supporting armies and navies. This part of his opinion repeated—in almost verbatim form—Daniel Webster's argument to the Court. Marshall rarely stated anything original in his important opinions; he simply placed his judicial imprimatur on the arguments of the side he favored.

Before moving to the question of whether Maryland could tax the national bank, Marshall paused to make a magisterial statement. Why, he asked, had the Framers not employed "any restrictive term" that limited the enumerated powers of Congress? "In considering this question," he wrote, "we must never forget that it is a constitution we are expounding."

What, if anything, did Marshall mean by this sentence? Later generations of judges and scholars have treated this pronouncement as if it were the Eleventh Commandment of the Mosaic tablets. In truth, Marshall's statement was not scripture, but a self-evident fact. The Framers did not limit the enumerated powers of Congress because they did not intend to limit them. That was the reason for the Necessary and Proper Clause, which Marshall construed to authorize a national bank. He could, of course, have construed that clause to justify any federal law he deemed "necessary" to promote "the general welfare of the United States," a power delegated to Congress by the Constitution.

Marshall put the principle of the Necessary and Proper Clause into words that have often been quoted and rarely been subjected to critical analysis. "Let the end be legitimate, let it be within the scope of the constitution, and all means which are appropriate, which are plainly adapted to that end, which are not prohibited, but consist with the letter and spirit of the constitution, are constitutional." This statement is not self-evident fact, but contains six phrases that beg for interpretation. Deciding what is a "legitimate end" of governmental power, how far the Constitution's "scope" extends, what are "appropriate means" of achieving governmental aims and how those means are "adapted" to legitimate ends, and—above all—how to match laws with the "letter and spirit" of the Constitution: these are not simple tasks for judges to perform. It was broad statements like these in his *McCulloch* opinion, rather than his analysis of the legal questions in the case, that gave his opinion the patina of authority it later acquired.

Marshall addressed the question of Maryland's power to tax the national bank almost as an afterthought. Again, he spoke in sweeping terms. The "great principle" of the Constitution, he wrote, was that it controlled the "laws of the respective states, and cannot be controlled by them." From this "axiom" of constitutional law, Marshall concluded that states could not tax the national bank. States could not "destroy" through taxation the powers of Congress. "That the power to tax involves the power to destroy," he wrote, was a proposition "not to be denied."

The Chief Justice would not be denied in the *McCulloch* case. His opinion rang with certitude. He literally handed Congress a blank check, to be filled in with any "necessary and proper" purpose and amount. Far more than Marshall's opinion in *Marbury*, an easy case for the Court, his *McCulloch* decision offered simple answers to hard questions. Does the Constitution place *any* limits on the power of Congress to legislate for the "general welfare" of the people? If it does, how should the Court define those limitations? Most of the "good and wise" people in 1819 supported the *McCulloch* decision, because it suited their economic interests. The national bank that Marshall protected from state regulation, now known as the Federal Reserve System, has fastened such a grip on banking and finance that a mere twitch by its chairman can produce tremors in the stock market.

For almost two centuries, constitutional scholars have lauded *McCulloch* as Marshall's greatest judicial triumph, even more important than his *Marbury* opinion. If *Marbury* exemplified the "sophistical" judicial reasoning that Thomas Jefferson had deplored, it reached a conclusion about judicial review of legislation that most of the Framers clearly anticipated. In contrast, *McCulloch* read into the Constitution words the Framers never employed, and intentions they never stated. In this regard, Marshall moved from sophistry to sleight-of-hand. He "deduced" in *McCulloch* a congressional power over banking that not a single delegate had addressed in the Constitutional Convention of 1787. Marshall conjured up—almost from thin air—a federal power that crushed state resistance to a national bank.

Whatever the constitutional shortcomings in the *McCulloch* opinion, it has proved impervious to change. The Constitution stands as the "supreme law of the land," as Marshall reminded his readers, and the Court's interpretation of its broad provisions cannot confine the Congress to the "narrow limits" of its enumerated powers. Marshall looked ahead in *McCulloch* to even greater national growth and power. The Constitution, he wrote, was "intended to endure for ages to come" and "to be adapted to the various crises of human affairs."

Writing for the Court in *Fletcher v. Peck* in 1810, Marshall posed a rhetorical question: "What is a contract?" His answer was short and simple: "A contract is a compact between two parties." If law were that simple, courts would not have to decide thousands of disputes between the parties to contracts. Like most general statements, Marshall's left many questions unanswered. Two of them came before the Court in 1819. Is a corporate charter a contract? And can a state alter the terms of such charters? The Supreme Court addressed these questions in another landmark case, *Trustees of Dartmouth College v. Woodward.*

The conflicts that gave rise to this case were largely political, although religious and financial interests were also at stake. In 1754, the Rev. Eleazar Wheelock had founded an "Indian charity school" in New Hampshire for the purpose of "spreading the knowledge of the great Redeemer, among their savage tribes," as King George III stated in the corporate charter he had granted to Wheelock in 1769. The royal charter established a board of twelve trustees who could perpetuate themselves "forever" through the selection of successors. Over time, Dartmouth College broadened its student body, educating the sons of many of New Hampshire's leading families. One of its graduates, in 1801, was Daniel Webster.

The royal charter also permitted the college's president to designate his successor, and when he retired, Eleazer Wheelock chose his son John. The younger Wheelock lacked his father's religious fervor and became a convert to Republican politics. The elder Wheelock's handpicked trustees voted in 1815 to remove his son as president. The conflict then became partisan, as New Hampshire's Republican governor, William Plumer, urged the state legislature to revise Dartmouth's charter to provide some public control over the college. The governor also hoped to save John Wheelock's job and thus reward a political ally. Thomas Jefferson, writing to Plumer from Monticello, supported his move; the notion "that institutions, established for the use of the nation, cannot be touched nor modified" struck Jefferson as "most absurd." He rejected the idea "that the earth belongs to the dead, and not to the living."

The New Hampshire legislature passed a law in 1815 that increased the Dartmouth board of trustees to twenty-one, and also set up a board of overseers, who rescinded the firing of John Wheelock. The original twelve trustees then sued the new board's secretary, William Woodward, in state court, seeking the return of the college charter and records. They claimed that the charter from King George was a contract—first with England and, following the Revolution, with the state—that the legislature had violated. After the state court ruled against the college, Daniel Webster agreed—for a fee of $1,000—to represent his alma mater in the Supreme Court. His arguments in *McCulloch v. Maryland* had taken up several days, but he spoke for just four hours in the *Dartmouth College* case. Webster's justly renowned eloquence reached new heights and he larded his remarks with Latin phrases, none of which Chief Justice Marshall could understand, since he lacked Webster's classical education at Dartmouth.

But the highly political and partisan Chief Justice understood the main thrust of Webster's argument, which took an unusual tack. Speaking as one Federalist to another, Webster placed less emphasis on principles of contract law and judicial precedent than on the political factors in the case. Every college in the country was then nominally private, although they all operated under state charters. "They have a common principle of existence," Webster said, which was "the inviolability of their charters. It will be a dangerous, a most dangerous, experiment, to hold these institutions subject to the rise of popular parties, and the fluctuations of political opinions." He told the Court what would happen if Dartmouth lost its case. "Colleges and halls will be deserted by all better spirits, and become a theater for the contention of politics; party and faction will be cherished in the places consecrated to piety and learning."

The account of Webster's argument in the Court's official report is close to verbatim, and ends with several sentences in Latin, to the effect that only the justices could save Dartmouth. But in 1853, after Webster's death, one of his eulogists, Rufus Choate, gave a secondhand report of his argument. Dartmouth professor Chauncey Goodrich had attended the Supreme Court session and told Choate that after Webster had apparently concluded, he "stood for some moments silent before the Court, while every eye was fixed intently upon him." Looking directly at Chief Justice Marshall, Webster then said, "Sir, you may destroy this little institution; it is weak, it is in your hands!" Webster's voice choked as he went on: "It is, Sir, as I have said, a small college. And yet, there are those who love it." With that, Webster's eyes flooded with tears. Goodrich added that Marshall's "tall and gaunt figure bent over as if to catch the slightest whisper, the deep furrows of his cheeks expanded with emotion, and his eyes suffused with tears."

Marshall's leading biographer, Albert Beveridge, noted that we have only the account of "two men of vivid and creative imaginations" for this story. But there is no doubt that whether or not Webster ended his argument in Latin or with these lachrymose words, the lawyer for New Hampshire could not best him in eloquence or influence. John Holmes, a Massachusetts congressman, was "notoriously unfitted to argue a legal question of any weight in any court," Beveridge sniffed. The "new" Dartmouth trustees had hired him because John Woodward—the defendant in the case—considered him a "good lawyer, inferior to [Webster] only in point of oratory."

However lacking in eloquence, Holmes nonetheless made a respectable argument. He claimed that the Contract Clause "did not extend to grants of political power; to contracts concerning the internal government and police of a sovereign state." Holmes used the term "police" in the common-law meaning of state power to promote the "health, safety, welfare, and morals" of the people. He added that the clause did not "extend to contracts which relate merely to matters of civil institution, even of a private nature." Holmes pointed to marriage as one institution whose "contracts" could be impaired or even canceled by the state through divorce proceedings. Charters to "charitable" institutions fell within this category, he asserted. There was some legal substance to this argument, and little precedent to support Webster's claim that corporate charters were contracts between the state and the grantees of such charters. In fact, Marshall had written in 1804 in *Head & Amory v. Providence Insurance Company* that a corporation "is a mere creature of the act to which it owes its existence; its powers are only those which the legislature granted to it." Presumably, the legislature could modify the terms of corporate charters at will.

Marshall said nothing in this early opinion about the Contract Clause. But now, fifteen years later, Marshall had changed his mind. His *Dartmouth College* opinion made up in certitude what it lacked in substance. "It can require no argument to prove," he wrote, "that the circumstances of this case constitute a contract." Marshall ignored, in fact, a very strong argument that the Dartmouth College charter lacked the most basic element of any valid contract, expressed in legal terminology as "consideration." In simple words, this means that each party to a contract must give something of value to the other party in exchange for their mutual promises to perform the terms of the contract. (Even a "peppercorn" would do, an English common-law judge once ruled.) What had King George and the Rev. Eleazar Wheelock given each other? Nothing of any monetary value, or anything that would be a "detriment" to either party.

Marshall brushed aside this fundamental principle of contract law. He noted that Wheelock's application to King George stated that "large contributions" had been promised to his school, once it received a royal charter. "The charter is granted, and on its faith the property is conveyed," Marshall wrote. "Surely, in this transaction every ingredient of a complete and legitimate contract is to be found." But the benefactors who promised money to Dartmouth College offered nothing of value to the king in exchange for the charter. Marshall's ignorance of basic contract law—willful or not—so concerned Justice Joseph Story that he wrote a lengthy concurring opinion, in which he construed the charter as conferring "vested rights" on the original trustees that the New Hampshire legislature could not alter. The legal doctrine of "vested rights" stems from English common law and was designed to protect individuals against governmental actions that would upset private bargains. In applying this doctrine to the *Dartmouth College* case, Story relied on notions of "natural law" which allowed him to ignore constitutional provisions and the legal terms on whose meaning their interpretation rested.

Marshall did not object in principle to "natural law" arguments; his earlier opinion in *Fletcher v. Peck* rested on the "vested rights" doctrine and adverted to the "nature of society" as prescribing limits on legislative power. But in the *Dartmouth College* case, Marshall decided to confer "immortality" upon those who held corporate charters with charitable goals. This was the term he used to describe charters which allowed the "perpetual succession" of trustees or officers, who became in effect "one immortal being," in Marshall's words. By definition, immortality confers protection against death, legal or natural. Under this presumption, no legislature could kill this "artificial person" by revising its charter any more than it could murder a "natural person" to whom the government had entrusted charitable works. However strained this reasoning may seem, this is precisely what Marshall decided in the *Dartmouth College* case.

By ruling that corporate charters were "contracts" and thus protected against "impairment" by state legislatures, Marshall protected those who provided capital for America's expanding corporations from political meddling in their business. Justice Story, who differed with Marshall in legal reasoning but agreed with the outcome of the *Dartmouth College* case, expressed his hope that the Court's decision "will check any undue encroachments upon civil rights, which the passions or the popular doctrines of the day may stimulate our State Legislatures to adopt." This equation of "civil rights" with corporate power speaks volumes about the Court's priorities during this period: the protection of property far outweighed the rights of people like blacks or women.

Another part of "the people" to whose rights the Marshall Court gave little weight was the growing debtor class, whose ranks expanded rapidly during the years that culminated in the Panic of 1819. A case the Court decided that year provided a judicial test of the powers of state legislatures to protect debtors from financial disaster. Construing the meaning of the Contract Clause in *Sturges v. Crowninshield*, the Court shaped constitutional doctrine from the kind of debt collection dispute that would be handled today in small-claims courts.

The case began when Richard Crowninshield borrowed $1,544 from Josiah Sturges in March 1811. Both men then lived in New York, where promissory notes were executed for payment the following August. Crowninshield suffered a business failure and did not pay Sturges at the scheduled time. In November 1811, Crowninshield filed for bankruptcy under an act of the New York legislature, passed in April of that year "for the benefit of insolvent debtors and their creditors." A state court discharged Crowninshield from his debt to Sturges in February 1812. He then returned to his original home state of Massachusetts, where he prospered in the textile business. Sturges waited until 1816 to file suit against Crowninshield in federal court in Boston, claiming that the New York law "impaired the obligation of contract" and violated the Constitution.

Two Supreme Court justices, Bushrod Washington and Brockholst Livingston, ruling as circuit judges in 1814 and 1817, had reached different conclusions in deciding similar "insolvency" cases. Washington ruled that state laws could not apply to contracts made before the laws were passed, and were only valid in "prospective" effect, while Livingston held that insolvency laws could have "retrospective" application to debts contracted before their passage. Justice Joseph Story, sitting on circuit court in Boston, heard arguments in *Sturges v. Crowninshield* and persuaded the district judge who sat with him to decide the case without an opinion. Under the Supreme Court's rules, this action would allow the Court to resolve the conflicts between the earlier opinions of Justices Washington and Livingston. Story believed the New York bankruptcy law violated the Contract Clause, and he lobbied his fellow justices to support his position.

By any measure, the conflict between Sturges and Crowninshield was small potatoes. But from such trivial disputes as theirs, hundreds of Supreme Court cases have arisen over the past two centuries. Several of these penny-ante cases have changed the course of constitutional history. Chief Justice Marshall grabbed the *Sturges* case to strike down state laws relieving debtors from contracts entered into before the insolvency laws were passed. Writing for a unanimous Court, Marshall first held that the Constitution's grant to Congress in Article I of power to establish "uniform laws on the subject of bankruptcies throughout the United States" did not invalidate existing state laws, since Congress had not yet enacted a "uniform" bankruptcy law.

Having cleared this easy hurdle, Marshall proceeded to "the great question" before the Court. "Does the law of New York," he asked, "impair the obligation of contracts" entered into before the law was passed? Marshall held that New York could not impair the contract Sturges and Crowninshield had made the month before the state legislature passed its insolvency act. "In the case at bar," Marshall wrote, "the defendant has given his promissory note to pay the plaintiff a sum of money, on or before a certain day." This obligation could not be changed by subsequent legislation. "Any law which releases a part of this obligation," he concluded, "must, in the literal sense of the word, impair it."

Much like his twentieth-century successor Earl Warren, John Marshall was pragmatic and flexible in reading the Constitution. When the "plain meaning" of its provisions suited his purpose, Marshall cited them with Bible-thumping certitude. But when they were vague or imprecise, he retreated to "general principles" of law—drawn from English common law—to justify his opinions. Marshall relied on the "literal" words of the Constitution in the *Sturges* case, while he cited the common law for support in *Fletcher v. Peck*. In both cases, Marshall was less concerned with means than ends. His goal in both was to protect those who owned property from state lawmakers who listened to the victims of land speculators and debt collectors.

A second clause in the Constitution offered Marshall another tool with which to construct a nationalist bulwark against "popular" control of the economy. The Framers had given Congress the power to "regulate commerce . . . among the several states" in Article I. The Court's first major decision involving this clause, *Gibbons v. Ogden* in 1824, blocked state interference with the commercial "intercourse" on which the expanding capitalist system depended. (This case was not related, we should note, to the later *Ogden v. Saunders* decision.)

The *Gibbons* case began in 1798 when the New York legislature granted Robert Livingston a charter that gave him a monopoly over steamboat navigation in New York Harbor and the Hudson River. Livingston's company had no real competition; at that time, steamboats were slow and costly to operate. But with Robert Fulton's improvements of steamboat design, the New York monopoly became highly profitable, and Fulton joined in a partnership with Livingston. Their company later granted the right to operate steamboats between New York and New Jersey to the partnership of Aaron Ogden, a former New Jersey governor, and Thomas Gibbons, a wealthy Georgia lawyer. Like many business partners, the two men had a falling-out and fought for control of their company. Ogden held title to the New York monopoly under state law, while Gibbons had acquired a federal permit under the Coastal Licensing Act of 1793. After his break with Ogden, Gibbons joined forces with Cornelius Vanderbilt—the leading capitalist of his time—and challenged Ogden's monopoly by operating ferries across the Hudson. Ogden then sued Gibbons in state court to enforce his monopoly; not surprisingly, the New York judges ruled in his favor. Gibbons then appealed to the Supreme Court, arguing that his federal permit was superior to Ogden's state charter.

A great deal of money rested on the outcome of *Gibbons v. Ogden*. Before the construction of bridges that spanned rivers like the Hudson, ferries that held state charters could charge high fares for carrying passengers and goods. Monopolies, by definition, had no competitors to keep prices down. During this period of rapid economic growth, those who looked ahead to an expanding national economy viewed monopolies as drags upon commerce. John Marshall shared this vision, and held no sympathy for claims of state power over interstate commerce.

For an initial retainer of $500, Cornelius Vanderbilt hired Daniel Webster to argue for Thomas Gibbons before the Supreme Court. This proved a shrewd investment, as Chief Justice Marshall repeated Webster's argument almost verbatim in his opinion for a unanimous Court. Marshall began by stating that since the Constitution gave Congress the power to regulate "commerce" among the states, "it becomes necessary to settle the meaning of the word." Ogden's lawyer had argued that "commerce" meant only the "buying and selling" of goods and not their movement between states. Marshall rejected this definition. "All America understands," he wrote, that the word "commerce" includes navigation. The Framers of the Constitution "must have used the word in that sense," Marshall added, because "the power over commerce, including navigation, was one of the primary objects for which the people of America adopted their government, and must have been contemplated in forming it."

What the Framers "must have" meant was clear to Marshall but did not appear in the Constitution. Not a word in Madison's notes of the Constitutional Convention refers to navigation between the states as an object of the Commerce Clause. While Marshall probably was correct in concluding that the Framers had "contemplated" the powers of Congress over interstate commerce to include all forms of "commercial intercourse" between the states, including the navigation of rivers and bays, his reading of the term "commerce" allowed the states no powers of regulation. The power of Congress "to prescribe the rule by which commerce is to be governed," he wrote, "is complete in itself, may be exercised to its utmost extent, and acknowledges no limitations, other than are prescribed in the Constitution." And he found no limits on this power in the Constitution.

Marshall's opinion in *Gibbons v. Ogden* marked the last victory of the Federalists over the Republicans on the economic battlefield. By this time, in the mid-1820s, the parties of Hamilton and Jefferson had changed their names and split into quarreling factions. In fact, the electors in the presidential contest in 1824 split their votes between four candidates who all claimed to be Democratic-Republicans. The Federalist Party had vanished, but John Marshall still waved its banner. His opinion in *Gibbons* suited the temper of the times; the federal government had become the engine of expansion, and the states were now seen as brakes on the road to prosperity. For the first—and only—time in his long judicial career, Marshall issued an opinion that gained popular acclaim. Almost everyone opposed monopolies and high prices, and very few people looked closely at Marshall's reasoning in the steamboat case. Those who wanted to cross the Hudson did not care how the Framers defined the word "commerce" in the Constitution; they simply wanted the cheapest fares across the river.

Three years after the cheering ended for his *Gibbons* opinion, Marshall found himself in bitter dissent from another Supreme Court decision the public greeted with applause. The Court's ruling in the 1827 case of *Ogden v. Saunders* illustrates the impact of shifting political tides on judicial doctrine. In his *Sturges* opinion in 1819, Marshall had built the "impairment of contracts" clause into a rigid barrier against state bankruptcy laws. Eight years later, the majority he commanded in that case had eroded. The presidential elections of 1820 and 1824 resulted in the addition of two justices who displayed more independence than Marshall appreciated. President James Monroe, who buried John Quincy Adams by 231 electoral votes to one in 1820, nominated only one justice to the Supreme Court. Smith Thompson of New York, a former state judge and Monroe's navy secretary, replaced Brockholst Livingston in 1824 and served until his death in 1843. Although he resembled William Johnson in voting as a states' rights advocate in cases that tested federal powers, Thompson hardly ever spoke for himself, writing just eighty-five opinions during twenty years on the Court. Like his New York predecessor Chief Justice John Jay, he preferred dabbling in state politics to judicial service. Unlike Jay, who finally won election as New York's governor, Thompson failed in his only campaign for that office in 1828.

John Quincy Adams ran second to Andrew Jackson in the 1824 presidential election, winning only eighty-four electoral votes to Jackson's ninety-nine, with the remaining seventy-eight split between two other Democratic-Republican candidates. Since no candidate had a majority, the House of Representatives—with each state having one vote—placed Adams in the White House. The northern states prevailed over the southern, while the growing western region split its votes between Jackson of Tennessee and Henry Clay of Kentucky. Adams made only one appointment to the Supreme Court, choosing Robert Trimble in 1826 to replace Thomas Todd in the "Kentucky seat." Adams was a mediocre president and Trimble—who died in 1828—an equally mediocre justice.

Although the Court did not decide the case of *Ogden v. Saunders* until 1827, this lawsuit began in 1808 with the bankruptcy of George Ogden, a New York merchant whose many creditors pursued him for years in federal courts. New York had passed a bankruptcy law in 1806 that differed from the "retrospective" law that Marshall struck down in the *Sturges* case because it altered the terms of contracts made before the law's passage. In contrast, the law challenged in *Ogden* applied "prospectively" to contracts made after its enactment; one of its provisions discharged New York debtors from obligations to out-of-state creditors.

Because the Court had already ruled in *Sturges* that states could pass bankruptcy laws, the outcome in *Ogden v. Saunders* should not have caused much judicial dissension. It seemed to be such a simple case that Daniel Webster, who argued for the creditors who sued George Ogden, was forced to rely on fanciful legal doctrine in attacking the New York law. Webster argued that states could not pass *any* bankruptcy laws, and went further to claim that contract terms were governed by principles of "universal law" and not by "the particular law of the place" where the contract was made. Surprisingly, three justices—led by Chief Justice Marshall—agreed with Webster's rejection of well-established legal doctrine and precedent, an indication of their hostility to any legislative relief for debtors. But a majority of four spared the bankruptcy laws of all the states from judicial invalidation. Justices Thompson and Trimble, who had joined the Court after the *Sturges* decision, voted to uphold the New York bankruptcy law. Justice William Johnson stated the majority view in arguing that states shared "concurrent" power with Congress in this field. Unlike Marshall, he looked at states as more than "counties" with few powers. "The rights of all must be held and enjoyed in subserviency to the good of the whole," Johnson wrote. "The state construes them, the state applies them, the state controls them, and the state decides how far the social exercise of the rights they give us over each other can be justly asserted." It seemed obvious to Johnson and the Court's majority that the provisions of existing bankruptcy laws are incorporated into contracts made after their enactment. James Wilson, who had been instrumental in placing the Contract Clause in the Constitution, told the Framers in 1787 that "retrospective interferences only are to be prohibited" by the clause. In other words, lawmakers cannot revoke or alter contracts after the parties agreed on their terms. There could be no clearer expression of the Framers' "original intent" on this question. But Marshall believed so firmly in the sanctity of contract that he exploded in dissent. The Court's decision in *Ogden v. Saunders*, he wrote, would make "inanimate, inoperative and unmeaning" a constitutional provision "on which the good and the wise reposed confidently." These provident and prudent citizens, of course, were those who always paid their debts on time. Reading the Contract Clause as a means to promote "the good of the whole" over the interests of "the good and the wise" struck Marshall as pandering to the improvident and imprudent.

Chief Justice Marshall cared more deeply about constitutional doctrine than about whether his opinions drew cheers or catcalls from the public. One final opinion illustrates Marshall's consistent vision of a Supreme Court empowered "to say what the law is" in every case raising claims under the Constitution, with little concern for the impact of the Court's decisions on the rights of ordinary Americans. In *Barron v. Baltimore*, decided in 1833, the justices faced the question of whether the Constitution prohibits the states as well as Congress from depriving "any person" of their "life, liberty, or property, without due process of law," as provided by the Fifth Amendment. The *Barron* case required the Court to decide, for the first time, whether the Bill of Rights applied to the states or just to the federal government. As has often happened in American constitutional history, a question of great significance was presented in a run-of-the-mill case.

The suit between John Barron and the city of Baltimore began with a road-building project in 1815. Barron's family operated a shipping wharf in Baltimore's harbor, and the largest vessels could dock at the wharf. But the soil dumped into the harbor as roads were graded and washed into it by rains gradually blocked access to the wharf for the large ships that had previously loaded and unloaded goods into nearby warehouses. Barron sued the city in state court in 1822, claiming that its actions violated the Fifth Amendment provision barring the taking of "private property . . . for public use without just compensation." A jury awarded Barron $4,500 in damages, but the state's highest court reversed this judgment, holding that the city was not subject to the provisions of the Bill of Rights.

Chief Justice Marshall disposed of this case in one of his shortest opinions. He stated Barron's claim to the protection of the Fifth Amendment in these words: "He insists that this amendment, being in favor of the liberty of the citizen, ought to be so construed as to restrain the legislative power of a state, as well as that of the United States." Marshall brushed aside Barron's argument: "The question thus presented is, we think, of great importance, but not of much difficulty." The Constitution was "established by the people of the United States for themselves, for their own government, and not for the government of the individual states," he wrote. But the question was not as simple, nor the answer as clear, as Marshall presumed. For one thing, the Framers had placed in the Constitution, in Section 10 of Article I, several express limitations on state powers. One of them—as we have seen—barred states from passing laws "impairing the obligation of contracts," a provision Marshall had used to strike down many state laws. But he attempted to turn the provisions of Section 10 to his advantage. "It is worthy of remark," he wrote, "that these inhibitions generally restrain state legislation on subjects entrusted to the general government, or in which the people of all the states feel an interest." Legislation regarding contracts, however, was not solely entrusted to Congress, and the people of all the states had an interest in protecting their property from "taking" without just compensation. Why could they not turn to federal courts for protection of rights granted in the Constitution?

Marshall answered this question by asserting that the express limitations on state power in Section 10 were the only ones intended by the Framers. He required some "strong reason" for departing from this "safe and judicious" reading of their intent. "We search in vain for that reason," Marshall wrote. He noted that the Constitution was ratified over the "immense opposition" of those who demanded a bill of rights to restrain the powers of Congress.

Marshall, of course, had voted in the Virginia ratification convention against Anti-federalist demands for a bill of rights. But with the Fifth Amendment before him for interpretation, he took the "safe and judicious" course of deciding that it "is not applicable to the legislation of the states." Marshall ruled in John Barron's lawsuit that the Supreme Court "has no jurisdiction of the cause; and it is dismissed."

The Court's unanimous decision in *Barron v. Baltimore* came near the end of Marshall's long tenure as Chief Justice. His opinion attracted little notice in 1833, and little discussion since then; one recent history of the Supreme Court relegated the *Barron* case to a footnote. Most constitutional scholars have simply assumed that Marshall reached the right conclusion in this case, and that those who framed the Bill of Rights had not intended to protect the people against oppression by the states, as they did from Congress. But Marshall was a fervent nationalist and almost always gave an expansive reading to the Constitution. It would have been more in character for him to force the states into compliance with federal standards. However, he had little respect for the rights of "the people" against the government—state or federal. Forced to choose between these countering principles, he did not find "much difficulty" in rejecting the argument based on individual rights.

Today, we look to the Due Process and Equal Protection Clauses of the Fourteenth Amendment—ratified after the Civil War in 1868—for protection against state laws that violate the provisions of the Bill of Rights. But why not look to those first ten amendments themselves? Marshall's answer to this important question in *Barron* effectively barred "the people" for another century from relying on the Bill of Rights to shield them against oppressive state laws, until the Supreme Court began to "incorporate" its provisions into the Fourteenth Amendment, a judicial journey that started in 1925 and has not yet been completed. One reason this doctrinal change took so long to develop was that the Court remained faithful—well into the twentieth century—to Marshall's view of the Constitution. He succeeded in limiting state powers under the Contract and Commerce Clauses, but he refused to apply the Bill of Rights to the states. In deciding these cases, he may have read the Constitution as the Framers intended. Marshall was certainly closer to them in time, and in shared experiences, than those who view him from the perspective of two centuries of momentous change in America's size, population, and technology. But Marshall also read the Constitution through the eyes of a committed and partisan Federalist, and as a fervent advocate of judicial supremacy. His was not the only possible reading of the Constitution, but it was—for more than three decades—the one that counted.

12

"Great, Good, and Excellent Man!"

Speaking for the Supreme Court in 1819, Chief Justice Marshall wrote in *McCulloch v. Maryland* that the Constitution was "intended to endure for ages to come, and, consequently, to be adapted to the various crises of human affairs." Even at that time, the nation faced a serious crisis in the conflict over slavery. Increases in population and the westward march for new territory had intensified the battles that raged between slavery's opponents and defenders. While the justices listened to Daniel Webster's arguments in the *McCulloch* and *Dartmouth College* cases, the halls of Congress in the same Capitol building rang with debate over the extension of slavery into the western territories.

The political battle over slavery began when residents of Missouri petitioned Congress for statehood early in 1819. The House first approved the proposal, but with an amendment, offered by Representative James Tallmadge of New York, that would prohibit the further importation of slaves into the state and free all slave children at the age of twenty-five. The Senate refused to accept the Tallmadge amendment, and the Missouri statehood bill languished until Congress met for its next session in December 1819. By that time, residents of Maine (then a part of Massachusetts) had also asked for statehood. With the admission of two states at issue, House speaker Henry Clay forged a compromise: both states would be admitted to the Union, with Maine as a free state and with slavery allowed in Missouri but "forever forbidden" in that part of the Louisiana Purchase above Missouri's southern border.

Congressional passage of the Missouri Compromise did not end debate on the slavery issue. In fact, it provoked the more extreme partisans on both sides to intensify their efforts. Northern abolitionists and southern defenders of slavery began talking of "disunion" and "secession." James Tallmadge, whose amendment to end slavery in Missouri had failed, spoke to the House with heated words: "If a dissolution of the Union must take place, let it be so! If civil war . . . must come, I can only say, let it come!" On the southern side, Representative Thomas Cobb of Georgia replied: "We have kindled a fire which . . . seas of blood can only extinguish." With heated rhetoric like this, the slavery issue became impossible to resolve peacefully. Over the next four decades, the warring sides moved closer and closer to real bloodshed.

During this period, and throughout the remainder of John Marshall's tenure as Chief Justice, the Supreme Court remained virtually silent on the question of slavery. This did not reflect the Court's refusal to face the issue as much as the reluctance of state and federal officials to enforce the Fugitive Slave Act of 1793, which did not come before the Court until 1842, seven years after Marshall's death. How he would have ruled on a direct challenge to slavery cannot be answered, but we do have evidence of Marshall's ambivalence on the issue. He owned slaves, but opposed the institution of slavery. He believed that slavery violated the "natural law," but believed even more strongly that the Constitution gave it sanction. He considered slaves as "property" but admitted their humanity. Caught in these contradictions, he avoided committing himself to either side in the slavery dispute. Six years after passage of the Missouri Compromise, Marshall lamented to a friend that "nothing portends more calamity & mischief to the Southern States than their slave population. Yet they seem to cherish the evil and to view with immovable prejudice & dislike every thing which may tend to diminish it." He did not "wonder that they should resist any attempt, should one be made, to interfere with the rights of property, but they have a feverish jealousy of measures which may do good without the hazard of harm that is, I think, very unwise."

The measure that Marshall thought would do the most good was repatriation of free blacks to Africa. He eagerly joined the American Colonization Society in 1829, and served as president of the Virginia branch until his death, with James Madison as one of the vice presidents. Writing to the society's secretary in 1831, Marshall supported the "removal of our colored population" to Africa. "The whole Union would be strengthened by it, and relieved from a danger, whose extent can scarcely be estimated." The colonization movement raised enough funds to return several thousand free blacks to the west coast of Africa, where they founded the nation of Liberia. But that left almost two million slaves in bondage in the United States.

Marshall addressed the slavery issue just once as Chief Justice, in a strange case known as *The Antelope*, decided in 1825. This was the name of a Spanish vessel involved in the slave trade off the coast of Africa. According to the Supreme Court report in the case, a "privateer" ship called the *Columbia* sailed from Baltimore in 1819, and then "hoisted the Artegan flag, assuming the name of the Arraganta." (Geography books make no mention of any nation called Artega, but the Court may have meant Antigua in the Caribbean.) The *Arraganta* then rampaged along the African coast, stopping and boarding American, Spanish, and Portuguese slave ships and stealing their human cargoes. After the *Arraganta* was wrecked on the coast of Brazil, about 280 Africans were transferred to *The Antelope*, which sailed for the United States. Her captain, John Smith, evidently hoped to smuggle the Africans into the country and sell them into slavery. Since Congress had barred the further importation of slaves, this would have been illegal. An American revenue cutter, under the command of Captain Jackson, intercepted *The Antelope* off the Georgia coast and brought her into the port at Savannah.

Five separate parties claimed ownership of—or rights to—the hapless Africans. The claimants included Spain and Portugal, from whose ships some of the captives had been stolen; Captain John Smith, who claimed them as *jure belli*, or the fruits of war; Captain Jackson, who claimed the Africans as either bounty or salvage, depending on which party won the case; and the United States government, which argued that they "were entitled to their freedom" under American law "and by the law of nations."

John Marshall assumed the task of sorting out these conflicting claims. He approached this question of "momentous importance" with full recognition that the case involved "claims in which the sacred rights of liberty and property come into conflict with each other." But he sternly admonished that "this court must not yield to feelings which might seduce it from the path of duty, and must obey the mandate of the law."

Marshall did his duty, as he saw it under the law of nations. "However abhorrent this traffic may be," he wrote of the slave trade, "it has been sanctioned, in modern times, by the laws of all nations who possess distant colonies" and who profit from it. Marshall spoke disapprovingly of slavery. "That it is contrary to the law of nature, will scarcely be denied," he wrote. But "feelings of humanity" must yield to "the law of nations." The Africans held on *The Antelope* were captured, wrote Marshall, from an "immense continent" which still adhered to the ancient law that "prisoners are slaves." But he still faced the question of whether his country, having "renounced this law," could allow others to enslave "the beings who are its victims." Should the Court order the government to deliver the Africans to the Spanish and Portuguese claimants, who would return them to slavery? "Whatever might be the answer of a moralist to this question," Marshall wrote, "a jurist must search for its legal solution" in the law of nations.

Acknowledging "the perfect equality of nations," the Chief Justice wrote of slavery that "this traffic remains lawful to those whose governments have not forbidden it." Marshall's final order smacked of Solomon's decision to cut the disputed baby in half. The lower court had found—by very rough calculation—that sixteen of the Africans had been stolen from an American ship, and could not be held in slavery under American law. Consequently, sixteen were chosen "by lot" and freed. The unlucky losers in this human lottery were turned over to their Spanish and Portuguese claimants and left the United States as slaves.

Very few historians have even mentioned Marshall's opinion in *The Antelope* case, and none have discussed it at any length. Why is it important in understanding his role in constitutional history? The answer reflects the conflicting aspects of Marshall's personal and professional lives. On one hand, Marshall has been celebrated as a man of humane sentiments. He was not pretentious or ostentatious; he was a "plain, unpretending" man, generous to both friends and enemies. Despite the lifelong hostility between Marshall and Jefferson, he "never spoke a personally offensive word" about his rival. Only once, responding to Jefferson's attack on his conduct in the XYZ affair, did Marshall reply publicly, to avoid—as he wrote to a friend—"the appearance of crouching under the lash, and admitting the justice of its infliction." But in *The Antelope* case, Marshall subordinated his feelings of humanity to the "lash" of the law, as he read its dictates. He did not—indeed, he could not—look at the captured Africans as fellow human beings, but only as the "property" of their Spanish and Portuguese owners. This was the harsh consequence of Marshall's adherence to a higher principle than human rights. He was born into a family that owned slaves and raised in a society that depended on slavery for its good life, and he chose a profession that was devoted—as it still is for most lawyers—to the protection of property. It is no surprise that faced with a choice between "the sacred rights of liberty and of property," Marshall decided in favor of the latter.

During most of his long life, Marshall enjoyed remarkably good health. But he spent his last five years in considerable pain, suffering from stones in his bladder and liver disease. Marshall remained at the Court's helm until the very end. His closest friend and ally, Justice Joseph Story, expressed his feelings in March of 1835: "What a gloom will spread over the nation when he is gone! His place will not, nay, it cannot be supplied." Three months later, Marshall left for treatment in Philadelphia and Story knew the end was near. "Great, good and excellent man!" he wrote to a friend. "I shall never see his like again! His gentleness, his affectionateness, his glorious virtues, his unblemished life, his exalted talents, leave him without a rival or a peer."

Two months short of his eightieth birthday, Marshall died on July 6, 1835, in "the city through which, a patriot soldier, he had marched from Valley Forge to Monmouth nearly sixty years before," Beveridge wrote of his judicial hero. He "met his fate with the fortitude of a Philosopher, and the resignation of a Christian," said one of the doctors who witnessed his death. His body was sent by boat to his home in Richmond, Virginia, where he was buried next to his beloved wife in an Episcopal service. The encomiums poured in, from old friends and enemies alike. The *Richmond Enquirer*, a Republican paper that had often criticized Marshall, praised his "brilliant talents" and offered this portrait: "There was something irresistibly winning about him." One of Marshall's most unrelenting critics, Hezekiah Niles, editor of the widely read political journal *Niles' Weekly Register*, lamented his death and wrote: "Next to Washington only, did he possess the reverence and homage of the American people."

There were still those who could not praise Marshall, even in death. William Leggett, an editor of the *New York Evening Post* and founder of the Equal Rights Party, wrote that Marshall "distrusted the virtue and intelligence of the people, and was in favor of a strong and vigorous General Government, at the expense of the rights of the states and of the people." Deploring the "fawning, hypocritical and unqualified lamentations" of others who opposed Marshall's policies and opinions, Leggett added that "we cannot but experience joy" that in his death "the cause of aristocracy has lost one of its chief supports."

For almost two centuries, praise for Marshall as a judicial statesman has far outweighed criticism of his role as Chief Justice. But the historical scale requires some balance. Marshall was plain and humble in person, yet he was an aristocrat in outlook. He came from a state that vigorously insisted on its "sovereign" rights within the Union, but he favored the "General Government" in almost every case he decided. He read the Constitution broadly to protect the rights of property, but narrowly when he addressed individual rights. Most important, Marshall disregarded his "feelings of humanity" and looked at blacks as property, not as persons. This last weight on the historical scale strips the mantle of "statesman" from Marshall's shoulders.

Marshall was, to be sure, a man of his times. But not every man—or woman—of those times shared his beliefs on "the sacred rights of liberty and of property." Men like Nat Turner and Frederick Douglass, and women like Harriet Tubman and Sojourner Truth, suffered as slaves under laws that Marshall considered "abhorrent" but felt bound by "duty" to uphold. Men of Marshall's race and class, like Horace Mann and Charles Sumner, considered it their "duty" to fight against slavery. Even with the hindsight of two centuries, we must remember that a person with Marshall's status and influence had choices that were laid out in clear and unambiguous terms. Marshall made his choices after listening to lengthy arguments on both sides. The choices he made, and the opinions he wrote, tell us much about the man who served as Chief Justice for more than thirty years.

John Marshall's death placed the choice of his successor in the hands of President Andrew Jackson, then in his second and final term. Fifteen associate justices had served with Marshall during his long tenure, but seven held their seats for periods ranging from fifteen to thirty years, and this group constituted the solid core of the Marshall Court. Only one, Bushrod Washington, came to the Court before Marshall, and the two Federalists agreed in virtually every case until Washington's death in 1829. The other six "old-timers" had all been chosen by three Democratic-Republican presidents: Jefferson, Madison, and Monroe.

But, as we have seen, Marshall dominated the Court so completely that he rarely found himself in dissent. Only his death would give the incumbent president a chance to reshape the Court.

That president, first elected in 1828, was Andrew Jackson, the Tennessee politician and war hero known as "Old Hickory" by friends and foes alike. Jackson was the first real "populist" to occupy the White House. He was, in fact, the first president to invite "the people" to visit his new home; the throngs of visitors to Jackson's inauguration reportedly stole china and silverware, broke chairs, and trampled the grass. Justice Joseph Story, who witnessed the scene, wrinkled his Yankee nose and sniffed, "The reign of King 'Mob' seems complete."

Jackson had already begun reshaping the Supreme Court before Marshall's death in 1835, midway through Jackson's second term. His first nomination—two days after his inauguration in 1829—was an unintended gift from his predecessor, John Quincy Adams. Justice Robert Trimble died in August 1828, shortly before the presidential election. Adams, by then a very lame duck, could not persuade the Senate to confirm former senator John Crittendon of Kentucky to replace Trimble, despite the endorsement of Chief Justice Marshall. Jackson's supporters controlled the Senate and wanted to present the incoming president with this judicial plum. The new president gave the post to John McLean of Ohio. Although McLean had served for six years on the Ohio supreme court, his real passion was not law but politics. A major factor in McLean's appointment, in fact, was that putting him on the Court, on a pledge not to pursue his presidential ambitions, would remove a potential obstacle to Jackson's second term in the White House. McLean broke his pledge not once but six times between 1832 and 1860, seeking the presidential nominations of six different parties during those years. McLean saw no impropriety in campaigning from the bench, assuring one critic that he would not be subject to "any improper influence" that might "tend to corrupt the Bench." During his thirty-two years on the Court, McLean wrote majority opinions in 247 cases, but he plowed old furrows and broke little new legal ground. One biographer summarized his long career in one sentence: "Few justices have worked so hard, for so long, with such little impact."

President Jackson's second chance to reshape the Marshall Court came in 1829 when Bushrod Washington died after thirty years of devoted service to the Chief Justice and their shared Federalist cause. Jackson chose Henry Baldwin of Pennsylvania for the post. Like McLean, Baldwin was a career politician; he campaigned for "Old Hickory" in the 1828 election and had earlier supported Jackson's military suppression of the Seminole Indians in Florida. Baldwin sat on the Supreme Court bench for fourteen years, during which time he wrote no major opinions and teetered on the brink of mental illness, veering between amiable agreement and vituperative outbursts against his colleagues. The death of Justice William Johnson in 1834 gave Jackson a third opportunity to place a states' rights advocate on the Marshall Court. His nominee, James

Wayne of Georgia, was a former Representative and one of Jackson's leaders in the House. Wayne, who served on the Court for thirty-two years, left the bench, as one Supreme Court historian noted, "without making any conspicuous contribution" to constitutional doctrine.

Justice Gabriel Duvall retired from the Court in January 1835 at the age of eighty-two, having far outlived his ability to contribute to the Court's work. Jackson promptly nominated a close friend and political supporter, Roger Brooke Taney of Maryland, to replace Duvall. An experienced and eminent lawyer, Taney seemed to have every qualification for the post. Born in 1777, he graduated from Dickinson College in Pennsylvania at eighteen, "read law" with a Maryland judge, and began his practice in 1799, the year he first gained election to the Maryland legislature. The aspiring politician built a flourishing law practice in Baltimore and was elected as the state's attorney general in 1827. Taney campaigned vigorously for Jackson in 1828 and was rewarded with appointment in 1831 as attorney general of the United States. In this post, he issued an opinion that upheld the power of southern states to prohibit free blacks (from other states or the British Empire) from entering their borders. Taney wrote that "the African race in the United States even when free, are everywhere a degraded class, and exercise no political influence. The privileges they are allowed to enjoy, are accorded to them as a matter of kindness and benevolence rather than right. . . . They are not looked upon as citizens by the contracting parties who formed the Constitution."

This legal opinion did not damage Taney's position, but he later joined Jackson's war against the Bank of the United States and drafted the president's veto message against rechartering the bank in 1834. After two treasury secretaries refused presidential orders to withdraw federal deposits from the bank, Jackson fired them and gave Taney a recess appointment to the cabinet post. Taney loyally carried out the president's directives and withdrew the funds from the bank. In retaliation, the bank's supporters in Congress blocked his nomination as treasury secretary, whereupon Taney resigned and returned to private law practice in Maryland. President Jackson wrote him that "I owe you a debt of gratitude and regard which I have not the power to discharge."

Determined to place Taney on the Court, Jackson decided to bide his time. Reports of Chief Justice Marshall's declining health affected this decision; his death in July 1835 gave Jackson the chance to fill two seats at once. James Madison's "twin" appointments of Gabriel Duvall and Joseph Story in 1812 had placed one mediocre and one distinguished justice on the Supreme Court. Jackson's "twin" nominations of Philip Barbour to replace Duvall and Roger Taney to succeed Marshall as Chief Justice did the same in 1836. Barbour, a Virginian and former speaker of the House of Representatives, was a staunch defender of slavery in Congress and a close ally of the president. He served for only five years before his death in 1841, and dissented in only two of the 155 cases decided during his brief judicial tenure.

Barbour's nomination sparked considerable Senate opposition, largely from northern Whigs who objected to his "strident" states' rights views, but his confirmation battle produced little of the partisan combat that greeted Jackson's choice of Roger Taney to replace John Marshall. Influential senators like Henry Clay, John Calhoun, and Daniel Webster argued strenuously against Taney's confirmation, fearing that he would lead a new Supreme Court majority in a frontal assault on Marshall's judicial nationalism. Despite these attacks, Taney survived a three-month struggle in the Senate. President Jackson twisted enough arms to prevail by a vote of twenty-nine to fifteen, and Taney took his seat as Chief Justice on March 15, 1836. John Marshall's dwindling band of loyalists expressed their dismay in private. "Judge Story thinks the Supreme Court is gone, and I think so, too," lamented Webster to a friend.

Webster had ample cause for lamentation, as a case he first argued before the Marshall Court in 1831—and confidently expected to win—dragged on without decision until 1837. The case of *Charles River Bridge v. Warren Bridge* has won renown (at least among constitutional scholars) not from its impact on the parties—although thousands of dollars were at stake—but from Taney's focus on "the happiness and prosperity of the community" as the Constitution's first principle. The sacred rights of property, secured through the Contract Clause, lost their primacy in the *Charles River Bridge* case to the interests of "the people," in whose name Taney wrote his opinion.

Like most Contract Clause cases decided by the Court during its first five decades, the dispute between the owners of two competing bridges in Boston stemmed from political conflicts between Federalists (later Whigs) and Republicans (later Democrats). Back in 1785, the Massachusetts legislature granted an "exclusive" charter to the Charles River Bridge Company for the construction of a toll bridge between Boston and Charlestown (which provided the fastest travel between Harvard College in Cambridge and Boston's financial and legal district). Many of the bridge's shareholders, in fact, had Harvard connections. The charter provided that after seventy years, in 1855, the bridge would become state property. But in 1828, Jacksonian Democrats won control of the Massachusetts legislature and chartered another group, the Warren Bridge Company, to build another toll bridge, just one hundred yards away. This company was authorized to collect tolls for six years, or until the costs of construction were met, after which it would revert to public ownership.

The owners of the first Charles River bridge, who had profited handsomely from their monopoly over four decades, sought an injunction in state court to block their upstart competitors. The state judges upheld the legislature's power to "revise" the first charter, and the losers appealed to the Supreme Court. Not surprisingly, they hired Daniel Webster to argue their case. Webster had argued and won the *Dartmouth College* case in 1819, and he relied on Marshall's opinion—which largely repeated his own words—when he first argued the bridge case in 1831. But Marshall could not muster a majority of the Court to strike down the second charter, with two of the seven justices absent, one prepared to dissent, and another who felt the Court had no jurisdiction over the case. Marshall put off a decision and ordered reargument in 1833. Once again, he could not fashion a majority and the case languished on the Court's docket.

When the case returned for a third time in 1837, Taney had replaced Marshall as Chief Justice and Webster no longer felt confident of victory. Those who attended the final argument reported that Webster seemed resigned to defeat and merely went through the motions of arguing that granting a competing charter "would destroy the security of all property and all rights derived under it." But the days of state-chartered monopolies were ending, and competition had became the watchword of American economic expansion. Three weeks after this argument, which pitted Webster against Professor Simon Greenleaf of Harvard's law school, the Supreme Court upheld the state court judgment for the Warren Bridge Company.

Webster's defeat had actually been foreshadowed by Justice Story's concurring opinion in the *Dartmouth College* case, in which he hinted to state legislators that they could "reserve" the power to change the terms of corporate charters. Greenleaf argued that the Massachusetts legislature had "reserved" this power to act for the public welfare. John Marshall would have emphatically rejected Greenleaf's argument, but it fit perfectly into Roger Taney's goal of freeing the states from the constitutional shackles of the Contract Clause that John Marshall had forged.

Taney's opinion in *Charles River Bridge* patched together Jefferson's political ideals and the economic expansionism of the new Democrats, led first by Jackson and then by Martin Van Buren, who became president in 1837. "The object and end of all government is to promote the happiness and prosperity of the community by which it is established," Taney wrote. "And in a country like ours, free, active, and enterprising, continually advancing in numbers and wealth; new channels of communication are daily found necessary, both for travel and trade; and are essential to the comfort, convenience, and prosperity of the people."

At the time Taney wrote these words, the economy was booming, fueled by another frenzy of land speculation. Bank loans had grown by more than 500 percent since 1830; nearly forty million acres of public land were sold between 1835 and 1837; and Congress distributed a federal surplus of some $40 million to the states in 1836 for the construction of highways, railroads, and canals. Taney's opinion fit perfectly into this optimistic scenario. When Andrew Jackson left office in 1837, he reminded the public in his farewell address that "the planter, the farmer, the mechanic, and the laborer, all know that their success depends on their own industry and economy."

However solicitous of "the people," Taney and his fellow Democrats harbored no animosity toward the "capitalists" who were busily constructing factories to manufacture goods and building railroads to ship them to markets. "While the rights of private property are sacredly guarded," Taney continued in his *Charles River Bridge* opinion, "we must not forget that the community also have rights, and that the happiness and well being of every citizen depends on their faithful preservation." He looked closely at the original bridge charter and found no grant of an "exclusive privilege" against future competition. And he found no such privilege "by implication" in the charter. The Contract Clause could not invade "the rights reserved to the states" to protect the interests of "privileged corporations." Taney reminded those who sought to protect monopolies for bridges, turnpikes, and canals that "newer and better modes of transportation" such as railroads would make their charters "not worth preserving." The power of states to promote "internal improvement" through free competition could not be blocked by the Contract Clause.

Justice Joseph Story, the last of Marshall's loyalists on the Court, wrote a bitter dissent. He claimed that "the state, impliedly, contracts" in every charter not to "destroy or essentially to impair the franchise" granted for a monopoly. Story could not, however, point to any provision in the charter granted by the Massachusetts legislature to the Charles River Bridge proprietors that promised any protection against future competition. Lacking any express language to support his claim, Story used the words "implied" and "implication" more than a dozen times to patch the holes in his opinion. The English common-law judges whom Story venerated had often assumed the power to read "implied" terms into contracts in the absense of express provisions. But in relying on legal principles he called "as old as the very rudiments of the common law," Story unwittingly exposed the crumbling foundation of doctrines that had outlived their usefulness. At the same time, and also unwittingly, Story's opinion exposed the perils of economic competition that makes every contract subject to revision by the voters.

The rampant speculation of the 1830s came to a crashing halt in the Panic of 1837. Hundreds of banks closed, thousands of businesses failed, unemployment rose to record levels, and "bread riots" broke out in several cities as the poor and hungry fought over food that was offered by charitable groups. The resulting depression, the worst the American people had yet experienced, lasted for five years. The Taney Court's decision in the *Charles River Bridge* case cannot be blamed for the Panic of 1837 any more than the Marshall Court bore responsibility for the Panic of 1819 in its *McCulloch* and *Sturges* rulings. But in one sense, the Court's decisions in both years affected national politics and contributed to the partisan battles that ultimately shaped a Supreme Court that viewed the nation's greatest crisis—the conflict over slavery—through southern eyes, with a constitutional vision distorted by racism, controlled by men who could not hear what Jefferson had called the "fire-bell in the night" ringing louder and louder as the United States raced toward disunion and disaster.

Writing for the Supreme Court in the *Charles River Bridge* case in 1837, Chief Justice Roger Taney proclaimed that "the community" had "rights" under the Constitution, and that "the happiness and well being of every citizen depends on their faithful preservation." Taney's glowing testament to the democratic ideal left unanswered three very important questions. First, which "community" did he have in mind—the United States as a nation or the individual states? Second, who were the "citizens" of this community, whichever one he meant? And third, what "rights" were granted by this concept of citizenship? One conclusion from Taney's earlier and later opinions is perfectly clear: he never intended to include African Americans—free or slave—as citizens who belonged to the political communities of the nation or the states, and he denied that they had any rights protected by the Constitution. In short, Taney was a racist who looked at blacks as items of "property" and not as "persons" who shared with whites the "privileges and immunities of citizens of the several states." He was not the only racist or defender of slavery to sit on the Supreme Court; most of the men who served with him shared his views, and many who succeeded Taney—well into the twentieth century—upheld the doctrines of white supremacy and racial segregation.

Two factors make Taney's racist views especially relevant to American constitutional history. First, he *was* the Chief Justice, holding a position of great influence and visibility. John Marshall had rescued the Court from weakness and obscurity, and Taney inherited his mantle of leadership. And second, Taney became Chief Justice at a time of bitter political conflict over slavery, with disputes that wound up on the Court's docket and proved the truth of Alexis de Tocqueville's comment written in the 1830s: "Scarcely any political question arises in the United States that is not resolved, sooner or later, into a judicial question."

Slavery was the most divisive political question confronting the nation between the framing of the Constitution and the Civil War. And it became the most divisive judicial question during Taney's tenure as Chief Justice, from 1836 to 1864. Of the dozen or so Supreme Court decisions in slavery cases during these years, three deserve special discussion. The first, which decided the fate of the Africans who rebelled against their captors on the slave ship *Amistad*, did not raise constitutional issues but captured the nation's attention. The second, which stemmed from the Fugitive Slave Clause in the Constitution, tested the powers of Congress to force its provisions onto the states. And the third, by far the most famous (and infamous) of the Court's slavery decisions, focused on whether a black man named Dred Scott, held in slavery in Missouri, was a citizen of the United States and thus capable of suing for his freedom in federal court.

The background to these cases lies in the Great Compromise over slavery in the Constitutional Convention of 1787. In addition to placing clauses in the Constitution that counted slaves as "three fifths" of a person in apportioning House seats and allowing the slave trade to continue until 1808, the Framers also provided in Article IV that "No person held to service or labor in one State under the laws thereof, escaping into another, shall, in consequence of any law or regulation therein, be discharged from such service or labor, but shall be delivered upon claim of the party to whom such service or labor may be due." Stripped of verbiage, this meant that every state was bound to return escaped slaves to their owners.

In 1793, Congress had also passed a Fugitive Slave Act that authorized slave owners or their agents to cross state lines, seize escaped slaves, take their captives before any federal judge or local magistrate, offer proof of ownership, and obtain a certificate allowing the captor to return his quarry to slavery. The Fugitive Slave Act remained on the books for almost fifty years before the Supreme Court faced a challenge to its constitutionality in 1842. But it had provoked great conflict long before that year. Did the Fugitive Slave Clause and the other slavery provisions in the Constitution authorize Congress to pass laws on this issue that would bind the states? Or did they simply express policies that did not expand the powers delegated to Congress in Section 8 of Article I?

As the nation's westward expansion continued, many of the settlers who surged into the new territories brought slaves with them, raising the question of whether Congress had power to prohibit slavery in federal territories. Northern "abolitionists" claimed that it did, while southern defenders of slavery denied that Congress had any power to legislate on the issue. As the residents of the western territories pressed for statehood, the conflicting sides—almost evenly balanced in Congress—initially resolved their differences in the Missouri Compromise of 1820. But that political compromise, brokered by House speaker Henry Clay of Kentucky, enraged the militant abolitionists, who responded first with magazines like *The Emancipator* and later with the "Underground Railroad" that guided slaves to freedom in the North and to Canada. By 1827, more than 130 antislavery groups had spread across the country, even into the South.

The emergence in the 1830s of William Lloyd Garrison as the uncompromising leader of the "immediatist" abolitionists sent shudders of fear throughout the South. Garrison published the first issue of his newspaper, *The Liberator*, on New Year's Day of 1831. He denounced slavery as a "monstrous evil" and vowed a campaign against it that did not exclude lawbreaking and violence. Later that year, the South's leading defender of slavery, John C. Calhoun, who then served as vice president under Andrew Jackson, proclaimed, "Abolition and the Union cannot coexist." The extremists on both sides were headed on a collision course. Several of the southern states, led by Virginia, passed laws making the advocacy of abolition a felony with severe penalties. Vigilante groups hunted out abolitionists and punished them with whippings. By 1837, not one antislavery group remained in the South. North of the Mason-Dixon line, abolitionists "rescued" fugitive slaves and on occasion assaulted and even murdered slave-catchers. The battle lines were drawn, and both sides were prepared to use force to accomplish their goals.

The first case that raised the slavery issue before the Supreme Court had all the drama of a Hollywood movie, which it later became (with scant regard for historical accuracy, particularly in its lengthy courtroom scenes). In June 1839 the Spanish schooner *Amistad* set sail from Havana, bound for the Cuban port of Principe. Its cargo included fifty-four Africans, captured in their native land of Mende by Portuguese slavers and taken to Cuba to be sold into slavery. But the *Amistad* never reached Principe. Led by a Mende headman named Cinque, the Africans revolted, killing the ship's captain and one of the crew (two others escaped). Cinque spared the lives of two crewmen, Pedro Montez and José Ruiz, on their promise to sail the ship back to Africa. For the next two months, Montez and Ruiz played a stealthy game, steering the *Amistad* to the east during daylight and then shifting course to the west and north under cover of darkness. The Spaniards hoped to reach a slave state in America, where they could seek official protection and return their cargo to Cuba. But the winds did not cooperate, and the *Amistad* finally reached land off Montauk Point in Long Island Sound, between New York and Connecticut. By this time, the *Amistad* was out of food and water and fifteen of the Africans had died of starvation and exposure.

Lieutenant Thomas Gedney of the navy brig *Washington*, which was surveying the sound, boarded the ship and was greeted by Montez and Ruiz, relieved to be rescued from Cinque and his mutinous tribesmen. Lieutenant Gedney towed the *Amistad* into the port of New London, Connecticut, where the ship and its human cargo soon became pawns in a four-way contest over their fate. After the Spaniards told their story to local officials, the Africans were jailed and charged with murder, mutiny, and piracy. None of the Africans spoke either Spanish or English, and no one in New London could communicate with them. Montez and Ruiz promptly filed claims in federal court for the return of the *Amistad* and the Africans, who they said were lawfully enslaved under Spanish law. Lieutenant Gedney filed a salvage claim, as did two American ship captains who had met some of the Africans on shore, where they pleaded for food and water with sign language. The administration of President Martin Van Buren tried its best to appease the Spanish government, despite the lack of evidence— except the claims of Montez and Ruiz—that the Africans on the *Amistad* had been lawfully enslaved and were therefore "property" of the Spaniards. Spanish law, in fact, prohibited the slave trade in its possessions. Nonetheless, the federal government also filed a claim, asking the court to return the *Amistad* and the Africans to Ruiz and Montez "in pursuance of the treaty between the United States and Spain."

With the Africans held in prison for trial on murder charges, abolitionists mounted a campaign for their release. Roger Baldwin, a New Haven lawyer and later Connecticut's governor and senator, undertook their legal defense, while Lewis Tappan, a wealthy New Yorker, raised funds and organized public support for the "Amistads," as they became known. The various claims finally came before a federal district judge, Andrew Judson, who ruled that because slavery did not exist in Connecticut, the Amistads were free men. He also dismissed the criminal charges, since none of the alleged crimes had taken place within American waters. But Judson nonetheless ordered the Amistads held in custody until a later hearing on the federal government's claim. By this time, a British sailor and former slave who spoke the Mende language had been found, and the Africans' story of their kidnapping and desperate measures to liberate themselves was widely reported.

The *Amistad* case became a national and international issue. Many northerners, previously lukewarm toward the abolitionist movement, agitated for the release of the Amistads. The Spanish government insisted on the return of the Africans to Cuba, and the Van Buren administration supported their claim. After hearing argument from all the claimants, Judge Judson finally ruled in 1840 that they should be returned by the Federal government to their homeland. Referring to Cinque and his fellows, Judson wrote that they "shall not sigh for Africa in vain. Bloody as may be their hands, they shall embrace their kindred."

The federal government appealed Judson's ruling to the Supreme Court, where the case was argued for eight days in February 1841. The legal issues related primarily to international law, but the arguments in the *Amistad* case provided abolitionists a chance to expose the horrors of the African slave trade and to denounce the complicity of the Van Buren administration. Roger Baldwin was joined in the Supreme Court by John Quincy Adams, who had returned to public office after his presidential term ended in 1829, serving in Congress as a representative from Massachusetts until his death in 1848.

Baldwin focused on issues of international law, while Adams spent three days at the podium, bitterly denouncing slavery and the government's refusal to abide by Judson's ruling. Adams had a notoriously bad temper, and before the argument he wrote in his diary, "I implore the mercy of God so to control my temper, and to give me utterance, that I may prove myself in every respect equal to the task." But his plea was not answered. Justice Joseph Story later wrote that Adams's argument was "extraordinary . . . for its power and its bitter sarcasm, and its dealing with topics far beyond the record and points of discussion." Adams voiced his contempt for President Van Buren, who he said would "turn himself into a jailer" for the Spanish government. Attorney General Gilpin responded that Van Buren was bound by a treaty with Spain to return all ships and property seized by "pirates or robbers" on the high seas. Adams replied with scorn, asking "who were the pirates and robbers? Were they the Africans?"

Cinque and his fellows had been kidnapped by the Spaniards, Adams said, and were entitled to free themselves by any means, including force.

To the surprise of many, the Supreme Court upheld Judson's ruling in 1841. Only one justice, the irascible and unpredictable Henry Baldwin, dissented from Justice Joseph Story's opinion, although Baldwin did not explain his grounds. Story picked a careful path through the thickets of international law. He wrote that if the Amistads had been lawfully held in slavery, they would be "items of merchandise" and property of the Spaniards, returnable under the treaty with Spain. But, he concluded, "They are natives of Africa, and were kidnapped there, and were unlawfully transported to Cuba, in violation of the laws and treaties of Spain." Story ruled that the Amistads "are entitled to their freedom," and they were eventually returned to their homeland, educated in English and converted to Christianity.

Abolitionists celebrated the Court's decision in the *Amistad* case, but its ruling that the Africans had never been enslaved did not help the campaign against slavery in the United States. The next year, Justice Story again displayed his skill at navigating through shifting legal currents in a case that tested the Fugitive Slave Act of 1793. Although less dramatic than the mutiny of the Amistads, the plight of Margaret Morgan also captured public attention. She had escaped from slavery in Maryland, fleeing with her children to Pennsylvania. In 1837, a professional slave-catcher named Edward Prigg tracked her down, seized her and the children, and brought them before a state judge, seeking the certificate required by federal law to return his captives to slavery.

But the Pennsylvania legislature had also passed a "personal liberty" statute in 1826, which imposed greater burdens of proof on slave-catchers and gave fugitives the right to challenge their captivity. The state judge refused to issue Prigg the removal certificate, but he took Margaret Morgan and her children back to Maryland anyway, returning them to Margaret Ashmore, who paid him for returning her human "property." Prigg was later indicted in Pennsylvania for kidnapping, tried and convicted in state court, and released pending his appeal to the Supreme Court. The record suggests that officials of the two states colluded in this case, hoping to resolve the growing conflicts over enforcement of the Fugitive Slave Act. The abolitionist movement had lost support in Pennsylvania, and state officials did not defend their "personal liberty" law with much enthusiasm.

During the Supreme Court arguments in *Prigg v. Pennsylvania*, Maryland's lawyers pointed to the Great Compromise in the Constitutional Convention to support their claim that the Framers intended Congress to have exclusive jurisdiction over the "rendition" of fugitive slaves to their masters. During the period of confederation, they argued, many northern states allowed no aid "to the owners of fugitive slaves; and sometimes, indeed, they met with open resistance." Faced with this situation, the Framers—and later the Congress—turned the whole issue over to federal authority.

On their part, Pennsylvania's lawyers put up a feeble defense. Responding to Maryland's arguments that "slaves are not parties to the Constitution" and that " 'we, the people,' does not embrace them," they "admitted" these claims. Pennsylvania wanted only to protect its "freemen" from unlawful capture. The state's lawyers spoke directly to Maryland. "Pennsylvania says: Instead of preventing you from taking your slaves, we are anxious that you should have them; they are a population we do not covet; and all our legislation tends toward giving you every facility to get them; but we do claim the right of legislating upon this subject so as to bring you under legal restraint, which will prevent you from taking a freeman." Pennsylvania did not claim that Margaret Morgan was free on her soil, only that Edward Prigg had not followed the rules for her capture under state law. If he had, the state would not have objected to her return to slavery in Maryland.

As he had in the *Amistad* case, Justice Story wrote for the Court in *Prigg v. Pennsylvania*. But he looked at Margaret Morgan through different lenses than he had at Cinque and his fellows. The Africans on the *Amistad* were not slaves, but Margaret and her children—the youngest born in a free state—were, he ruled. That fact really disposed of the case for Story. The Framers had recognized the lawfulness of slavery in the Constitution, and Congress thus had power to adopt the Fugitive Slave Act in 1793. Story praised the "courteous and friendly spirit" in which the neighboring states had brought the case before the Court, and hoped that "the agitation on this subject, in both states, would subside, and the conflict of opinion be put at rest." But this was a vain hope, as the conflict over slavery that gripped the nation was mirrored in the Court. Seven justices wrote separate opinions, and Story's caused the most conflict. Although he struck down Pennsylvania's "personal liberty" law, his opinion hinted that states were under no duty to aid the enforcement of the federal Fugitive Slave Act. This suggestion, which Story may not have intended, encouraged abolitionists and upset Chief Justice Taney, who argued in concurrence that states could— and should—pass laws that made it easier for slave-catchers to return their captives to slavery. Story had ruled that all state laws relating to fugitive slaves violated the Constitution, while Taney argued that only those that hindered the return of "property" to its owner stepped on federal toes.

Whether intended or not, Story's hint encouraged several northern states to pass laws that prohibited their officials from aiding slave-catchers in any way. Shortly after the Supreme Court decided the *Prigg* case, a fugitive slave named George Latimer was seized by police in Boston, acting for his Virginia owner, James Gray. Abolitionists filed a habeas corpus petition in state court to free Latimer, but the state's chief judge, Lemuel Shaw, ruled that he was bound by the *Prigg* decision and ordered Latimer returned to Gray, who paid the Boston city jailer to keep him in custody. Crowds of abolitionists and free blacks tried and failed to "rescue" Latimer from jail, and the public uproar convinced Gray to give up; he "sold" Latimer to a group of abolitionists for $400, and they promptly freed him from both jail and slavery. Prompted by a petition with 65,000 signatures, the Massachusetts legislature passed the "Latimer Law," prohibiting state judges and local police from taking any part in the rendition of fugitive slaves.

Contrary to Story's hopes, his *Prigg* decision did not end the sectional conflict over slavery. In fact, passage of the Latimer Law and similar state laws enraged southern defenders of slavery, who pressed Congress to enact a more stringent fugitive slave law. They succeeded in 1850, when Henry Clay—thirty years after he pushed the Missouri Compromise through Congress—traded the admission of California to the Union as a free state for a new and tougher fugitive slave law. The Compromise of 1850, as it became known, was as doomed to failure as its predecessor. The nation moved closer to disunion as partisans on both sides moved from rhetoric to direct action. The election of Franklin Pierce in 1852 returned the Democrats to the White House and gave the proslavery faction a political boost.

The Pierce administration enforced the fugitive slave laws with a vengeance. The arrest of Anthony Burns in Boston in May 1854 prompted a massive abolitionist protest. Burns had escaped from slavery in Virginia and was seized by a federal marshal, who held him for his owner. When Burns was taken before a state judge for a rendition hearing, his owner's lawyers argued that state courts were required to comply with the Fugitive Slave Act. After the judge ruled that the Latimer Law was in conflict with the federal statute, and ordered Burns's rendition to Virginia, federal troops and the state militia trained a cannon on a crowd of twenty thousand who gathered on Boston Common to protest the decision. William Lloyd Garrison seized the moment with a dramatic gesture. Holding up a copy of the Constitution, he denounced it as "a covenant with death and an agreement with hell." With those words, he put a torch to the Constitution and burned it to ashes. "So perish all compromises with tyranny!" he cried, echoed by the shouts of the assembled crowd.

Neither side had any desire for compromise after 1850. Congressional passage of the Kansas-Nebraska Act in 1854, introduced by Democratic senator Stephen Douglas of Illinois, moved the conflict from fiery words to real flames. Douglas proposed and Congress adopted a law that put the slavery issue before the voters in the neighboring territories of Kansas and Nebraska. This proved a fatal decision, as "free-state" and proslavery groups took up arms and turned "Bleeding Kansas" into the first battleground of the Civil War. After a proslavery posse sacked and burned the town of Lawrence in 1855, killing several "free-staters" during the attack, a fanatical abolitionist named John Brown gathered his followers and murdered five proslavery settlers in Pottawatomie in retaliation. The "Pottawatomie Massacre" foreshadowed Brown's doomed assault on the Harpers Ferry arsenal in West Virginia in 1859, his tragic response to the Supreme Court's decision two years earlier in the *Dred Scott* case, the third of the slavery disputes that created increasing dissension among the justices and across the nation.

Fifteen years before *Dred Scott*, the *Prigg* decision provoked a fierce battle over the Constitution. The Court's divisions in the case gave both sides ammunition against their foes. Abolitionists took heart from Story's hints that states could refuse to aid slave-catchers, while southern legislators relied on Taney's opinion in pressing for more stringent federal laws. There is much irony in this reversal of roles: northerners adopted a states' rights position and southerners asked for more federal power. Don Fehrenbacher, the leading historian of the *Dred Scott* case, wrote in the 1970s that the *Prigg* decision "rivals *Dred Scott* . . . in historical importance." A century earlier, Frederick Brightly, a noted lawyer who edited and annotated the Supreme Court's opinions, wrote in 1885 that the *Prigg* decision "resulted in the passage of the fugitive slave law of 1850, the repeal of the Missouri compromise, and ultimately, the civil war and the entire abolition of slavery" in the United States. These historical judgments may give the *Prigg* case more influence than it deserves. But the capture of Margaret Morgan by Edward Prigg in 1837 and the Supreme Court's decision in 1842 certainly contributed to the battles over slavery that ended in a bloody civil war.

SECTION III

"Justly and Lawfully
Be Reduced to Slavery"

13

"A Small,

Pleasant-Looking Negro"

No individual litigant in American constitutional history has equaled the fame of Dred Scott, whose suit for freedom brought the slavery issue to a boil in the political cauldron of the 1850s. Every student of constitutional history knows Dred Scott by name, but hardly anyone knows anything about him beyond his name. Just who *was* the man whose Supreme Court case pushed the nation over the brink of sectional conflict and into the Civil War? This is not a trivial question. Every Supreme Court case that involves a claim of individual rights is brought by a real person, who has sought legal redress for some kind of oppression. American constitutional history is the history of real people with real grievances. Judges—who are also real people—do not always uphold these claims, but their decisions affect many lives: first, of the individuals who brought the case, and second, of those whose rights are determined by the Court's ruling. We often learn more from the personal stories of these real people than from the impersonal pages of Supreme Court decisions.

One thing we learn about Dred Scott is that, like most slaves, his identity and history are riddled with historical gaps. This fact tells us a great deal about an institution that robbed its victims not only of rights but often of their names. This was true of Dred Scott, who may have been known simply as "Sam" for most of his life, and acquired the name "Dred Scott" after his sale in 1833 to Dr. John Emerson in St. Louis, Missouri. His previous owner, Peter Blow, arrived in St. Louis from Alabama in 1830 with six slaves, five male and one female. He set up a boardinghouse but died in 1832, a year after his wife's death. After Blow's death, his executor sold two male slaves to settle claims against the estate, one named Sam and the other with no recorded name. No one knows which of these two slaves was purchased by Dr. Emerson, whether Sam became Dred Scott, or whether the unnamed slave was in fact named Dred Scott.

No one even knows for sure when or where Dred Scott was born. He was literally a man without a past, or at least one known to white people.

We do know that the Blow family remained close to their former slave and supported Dred Scott during his long struggle for freedom. Three months after the Supreme Court ruled in March 1857 that Scott was still a slave, Peter Blow's son Taylor regained title to him and promptly freed him. But Dred lived only fifteen months as a free man, working as a hotel porter in St. Louis; he died of "consumption" in September 1858. He never sought the limelight, although he did talk with several newspaper reporters about his case. One report, published in 1857, described Dred Scott as "illiterate but not ignorant" and as a person with a "strong common sense." An article in 1858 called him "a small, pleasant-looking negro" with an "imperial" beard, wearing a "seedy" black suit and looking "somewhat the worse for wear and tear."

Life imposed a great deal of "wear and tear" on Dred Scott, particularly after Dr. Emerson purchased him from the Blows. By all accounts, Emerson was a poor doctor and a chronic malcontent. He finagled a position in 1832 as an army medical officer and was posted in 1834 to Fort Armstrong in the "free" state of Illinois. Dred Scott—then in his early thirties—accompanied his new owner, who disliked life on the frontier and asked to return to St. Louis for treatment of a "syphiloid disease." After several rebuffs by the army brass, Dr. Emerson finally secured a new post in 1836 when Fort Armstrong was closed. He and Dred moved to Fort Snelling, located in Wisconsin Territory (later renamed Iowa Territory and now part of Minnesota).

These chapters in Dred Scott's life have great significance. Fort Armstrong and Fort Snelling both lay in "free" territory, north of the line drawn by the Missouri Compromise in 1820. Slavery was illegal in both Illinois and Wisconsin Territory, and Dred could not lawfully be held as a slave by Dr. Emerson in either place. While he lived at Fort Snelling, Dred met Harriet Robinson, a teenage girl, also held as a slave by the resident Indian agent, Major Taliaferro. He either sold Harriet to Emerson or gave her to Dred as a wife, and they were married by the major as a local justice of the peace. The Scotts had four children; two sons died in infancy, but two girls—Eliza and Lizzie—grew up and joined their parents' suit for freedom.

Dr. Emerson complained about the cold weather in the North (the weather never suited him) and secured a transfer back to St. Louis in 1837, only to find orders when he arrived that he report to Fort Jesup in Louisiana. The weather was too damp in the South for his taste, and he wangled a return to Fort Snelling in 1838. But during his stay in Louisiana, Emerson got married and Dred and Harriet Scott—who had remained at Fort Snelling—traveled down the Mississippi by steamboat to join them. The Emersons and the Scotts journeyed back to Fort Snelling by boat; Eliza Scott was born on this trip, north of the Missouri Compromise line in "free" territory.

Emerson got into violent quarrels with the personnel at Fort Snelling, and he was ordered in 1840 to Florida, where the army was engaged in the Seminole War against the Indians. Emerson's wife returned from Fort Snelling to St. Louis with the Scotts. Dr. Emerson's complaints became too much for the army, and he was dismissed from service in 1842. He returned to St. Louis but could not build a private practice there. He moved to Davenport, Iowa, in 1843, and died there—most likely of syphilis—at the end of that year. The Scotts remained in Missouri, although where they lived at the time of Emerson's death is unclear.

The sad story of Dr. Emerson bears recounting largely because it shows that Dred Scott and his family lived at least twice in "free" territory where slavery was illegal. Did their residence on free soil in Illinois and Wisconsin Territory remove the chains of slavery? Surprisingly, this question had a fairly clear answer in 1846, when Dred and Harriet Scott filed identical suits for their freedom in Missouri state court in St. Louis.

Their suits did, however, raise two puzzling questions. First, who actually owned the Scotts, or claimed ownership? Second, who encouraged them to file suit and put up the money to hire lawyers? In his exhaustive account of the *Dred Scott* case, Don Fehrenbacher concluded that the answer to both "remains a mystery." John Sanford, the brother of Emerson's wife, Eliza, claimed ownership during the lawsuits, but there are no records to support his claim. It is possible that Dred Scott himself decided to sue for his freedom, with help from his former owners, the Blow family. Fehrenbacher notes that Dred Scott possessed "some measure of self-reliance, as well as a fund of practical knowledge, and suits for freedom occurred often enough to be common talk among St. Louis slaves."

Missouri law was on the Scotts' side, at least when they filed their suits. The state's highest court had repeatedly held that masters who took slaves into "free" territory thereby emancipated them, and that slavery did not reattach when they returned to Missouri. The legal doctrine of that time was "once free, always free." But Dred and Harriet Scott had the misfortune to find their suits caught in the shifting currents of Missouri (and national) politics. That misfortune stemmed from the snail's pace at which their cases proceeded through the state courts. More than a year passed between the time the Scotts filed their suits in 1846 and their first trial in June 1847. Dred's complaint alleged that Dr. Emerson's widow, Irene, had "beat, bruised, and ill-treated him" and then "imprisoned" him for twelve hours on April 4, 1846, two days before he filed suit against her for assault and false imprisonment, asking for damages of $10. Dred also claimed to be a "free person" in his complaint. His claims that Irene Emerson beat and imprisoned him may or may not have been true; she was apparently not a cruel or violent person, and may not even have seen Dred on April 4. But charges like these were necessary in suits for freedom. If the defendant had beaten or imprisoned a slave, those acts constituted lawful "chastisement", and slaves could receive no damages. But a "free person" could not be lawfully beaten or imprisoned, and juries could award them damages. So the jurors in Dred's case had to determine, before they reached the damage issue, whether he was a free man or a slave.

Whoever put up the funds for the Scotts' lawsuit picked a prominent lawyer in Samuel Bay, Missouri's former attorney general. But prominent lawyers make mistakes just like obscure ones, and Bay made a serious error. Before he could argue that the Scotts' residence in Illinois and Wisconsin Territory had freed them from slavery, he needed to show that Irene Emerson claimed their ownership and controlled them. Unfortunately, Bay's witnesses failed to produce satisfactory evidence on this issue. A man named Samuel Russell testified that he "hired out" the Scotts from Mrs. Emerson and paid her father, Alexander Sanford, for their labor. But Russell had no personal knowledge that Mrs. Emerson owned the Scotts; he testified that his wife made all the arrangements. Without evidence on the important—and disputed—issue of whether Irene Emerson "owned" Dred Scott, the jury returned a verdict in her favor.

Hoping to correct his legal error, Samuel Bay filed a motion for a new trial, which the state judge granted after some delay. But Irene Emerson had a prominent lawyer as well, George Goode, a Virginian who held strong proslavery views. He opposed the judge's order for a new trial, and the dispute came before the Missouri supreme court in April 1848. Although that court dismissed Mrs. Emerson's claim two months later and sent the case back for a second trial, proceedings did not begin until January 1850. By this time, the Scotts' cases were almost four years old, and the sectional battles over slavery in Congress—which produced the Compromise of 1850—had affected Missouri politics as well.

The second time around, Dred Scott's case went to the jury with testimony from Mrs. Russell that Irene Emerson had hired out the Scotts to the Russells, claiming "ownership" of her slaves. This testimony, along with evidence that the Scotts had lived in "free" territory, convinced the jurors that Dred Scott was a free man under Missouri law. But the law allows for appeals from jury verdicts, and appeals take time. And Mrs. Emerson and her lawyers—hired by her brother, John Sanford—were determined to carry the issue to higher courts. They filed an appeal with the Missouri supreme court in March 1850, but that court did not decide the case until 1852. By that time, Missouri voters had placed two new judges on the state's supreme court. One of them, William Scott, was a fervent proslavery Democrat, and he persuaded the court to reverse the trial jury's decision that Dred Scott was a free man.

The Missouri judges ruled that they were bound by an 1851 decision of the United States Supreme Court in a case called *Strader v. Graham*. This case began when two black musicians—both of them slaves—traveled from Kentucky to Ohio to perform in minstrel shows. They had been to Ohio many times and had always returned to Kentucky. But on this last trip they kept on traveling to Canada, where they reached freedom. Kentucky was a slave state and Ohio a free state, and the musicians' owner in Kentucky brought a suit for damages against several Ohio residents who allegedly helped them escape from slavery. The defendants relied on the Northwest Ordinance of 1787, in which Congress banned slavery in the territories of the United States. Kentucky's highest court rejected this argument, on the ground that Ohio was now a state, and no longer part of the Northwest Territory. Consequently, the Northwest Ordinance no longer governed the case and the dispute became purely a matter of state law. Not surprisingly, the Kentucky judges ruled that their state's laws prevailed over those of Ohio. Because the escaped minstrels, had they been apprehended and returned to Kentucky, would have been slaves—and thus the "property" of their master—in that state, the master was entitled to damages against the Ohioans who helped them escape. The Kentucky judges, of course, dismissed the "once free, always free" doctrine in their ruling.

When the *Strader* case reached the Supreme Court, the "states' rights" decision of the Kentucky judges found a receptive audience. Chief Justice Roger Taney wrote for a unanimous Court, dismissing the case for lack of federal jurisdiction. However, he took sides in the dispute, writing that if the slave musicians had returned to Kentucky—willingly or not—their status would have "depended altogether upon the laws of that State and could not be influenced by the laws of Ohio." Since they never returned to Kentucky, Taney's opinion on this issue was the rankest form of dictum, the Latin term for judicial statements that go beyond—in this case, far beyond—the questions presented in the case. But the Chief Justice seemed determined in *Strader* to instruct state judges that the doctrine of "once free, always free" no longer applied in suits for freedom.

The Missouri judges followed Taney's instructions in Dred Scott's case, which they finally decided in March 1852. Judge Scott—certainly no relation to Dred—echoed Taney in writing that Missouri was not "bound to carry into effect enactments conceived in a spirit hostile to that which pervades her own laws." And what enactment of hostile spirit did Judge Scott have in mind? The Missouri Compromise of 1820, which banned slavery in the northern territories. Just as Chief Justice Taney ruled that the Northwest Ordinance no longer had effect, Judge Scott ruled that the Missouri Compromise had no effect in his state. And just as Taney wrote his racial views into the *Strader* opinion, Judge Scott added his to the *Dred Scott* decision. He rejected his court's earlier rulings on the grounds that "circumstances" had changed. "Times are not now as they were when the former decisions on this subject were made," Scott wrote. "Since then not only individuals but States have been possessed with a dark and fell spirit in relation to slavery, whose gratification is sought in the pursuit of measures, whose inevitable consequences must be in the overthrow and destruction of our government." After these ominous words, Scott offered praise to God for instituting slavery to raise men like Dred Scott above the level of "miserable" Africans. He was convinced "that the introduction of slavery amongst us was, in the providence of God, who makes the evil passions of men subservient to His own glory, a means of placing that unhappy race within the pale of civilized nations."

Five years passed between this ruling in 1852 and the final decision of the United States Supreme Court in 1857. During these years, Dred Scott's case moved from state to federal court, new lawyers appeared on both sides, the legal issues changed, and national politics once again affected judicial opinions. Irene Emerson's brother, John Sanford, still claimed ownership of the Scott family, although he had supposedly moved to New York. After their defeat in state court, Dred's lawyers filed suit against Sanford in federal court in St. Louis, claiming jurisdiction under the "Diversity of Citizenship" Clause of the Constitution, which gave federal courts jurisdiction over suits between citizens of different states. There is much doubt that Sanford actually resided in New York, and much speculation that the suit was contrived by lawyers on both sides to reach the Supreme Court. Nonetheless, the federal judge who presided at the trial in May 1854, Robert Wells, ruled that he was bound by the Supreme Court's decision in *Strader v. Graham* and instructed the jury to return a verdict in Sanford's favor.

In his opinion, Judge Wells overlooked a crucial question. The Diversity Clause of the Constitution allows only "citizens" of one state to bring suit against those of another state in federal court. Wells did not decide this critical issue. He merely ruled that Dred Scott was a "resident" of Missouri, and allowed his suit to go before the jurors. But in ruling that Dred had always been a slave, Wells left open the question of whether Dred was a "citizen" of Missouri, a requirement for bringing suit in federal court. The judge's failure—deliberate or not—to decide this issue made Dred's "citizenship" the central question when the case reached the Supreme Court.

After their defeat in federal district court, Dred's lawyers filed an appeal with the Supreme Court in December 1854. They had little money, and little chance of success. What they needed, most of all, was a lawyer of national renown to argue the case. John Sanford had already recruited a former United States attorney general, Reverdy Johnson of Maryland. Johnson was an old friend of Chief Justice Taney and a formidable lawyer. Dred's supporters appealed for help in a twelve-page pamphlet he supposedly wrote, despite his illiteracy. Whether it was written by Dred or not, the pamphlet spoke volumes about his plight. "I have no money to pay anybody at Washington to speak for me," he said. "My fellow-men, can any of you help me in my day of trial? Will nobody speak for me at Washington, even without hope of other reward than the blessings of a poor black man and his family?" On Christmas Eve of 1854, Dred Scott's appeal for help reached Montgomery Blair, a prominent lawyer and former West Point cadet. After years of practice in St. Louis, Blair had moved to Washington (where he lived in Blair House, now the official guest house of the president) and established a legal practice before the Supreme Court. Blair gave Dred Scott the Christmas present of his services without fee.

The case of *Dred Scott v. Sandford* (a clerk had misspelled John Sanford's name, and the Court never corrected its error) reached the Supreme Court clerk's office on December 30, 1854. And there it languished for more than a year, until oral arguments were scheduled in February 1856. Because the Court's rules then required the justices to hear appeals in any case from lower federal courts, its docket was crowded and cases moved slowly. The justices who took the bench to hear arguments in the *Dred Scott* case reflected the appointments of six presidents, from Andrew Jackson in 1829 to Franklin Pierce in 1853. This was a period in which the slavery issue dominated national politics, and during which not one president spoke out forcefully against the existence of slavery in the South, or its extension into the western territories. Just as both major parties— the Democrats and Whigs—became hostage to their southern wings, presidents made Supreme Court nominations with an eye on the Senate, aware that powerful southerners like John C. Calhoun of South Carolina could derail the confirmation of anyone suspected of "abolitionist" sentiments.

Four of the nine justices who voted in the *Dred Scott* case owed their seats to Andrew Jackson. John McLean of Ohio and James Wayne of Georgia had joined the Court before the death of Chief Justice John Marshall, and they remained on the bench under Roger Taney for more than two decades. Given the sectional nature of the slavery conflict, geography played an important role in Supreme Court selections during this period. Wayne and Taney were southerners, and both came from slave-owning families. Jackson's nomination of John Catron of Tennessee (who was confirmed by the Senate four days after Martin Van Buren replaced Jackson as president in 1837) gave the South a third seat on the Court. Like his colleague Wayne, Catron supported the institution of slavery but remained on the Court during the Civil War as a staunch Unionist. He also left the Court after twenty-eight years without leaving any visible mark on constitutional law. Justice Peter V. Daniel of Virginia, nominated by President Van Buren, took his seat in 1842 and shifted the Court's balance further to the South. A slaveholder and former federal judge, Daniel served for eighteen years and had "little lasting influence on the Supreme Court," one biographer concluded.

With four southerners on the Taney Court, the North got its due in the next three appointments. President John Tyler, himself a Virginian, shored up the Democratic Party's shaky northern wing by nominating Samuel Nelson of New York to the Court in 1845. Nelson had extensive judicial experience, serving in state judicial office for more than two decades before he joined the Supreme

Court. Like his colleague Justice Wayne, Nelson was a judicial workhorse, grinding out 347 opinions during his twenty-seven years on the Court. Sitting on New York's courts, Nelson had never expressed his opinions on slavery, but on the Supreme Court he turned out to be a southerner in sheep's clothing. As a fervent states' rights advocate, he refused to acknowledge any federal power to ban slavery in the nation's territories.

President James Polk of Tennessee, a Democrat who took office in 1845, added to the Taney Court another northerner who voted with the southerners on the slavery issue. Robert Grier, a Pennsylvania state judge, took his seat in 1846 and served for twenty-six years without distinction. Defending his party's stand on states' rights, Grier upheld in 1852 an Illinois fugitive slave law, writing for the Court that states had the power to "repel from their soil a population likely to become burdensome and injurious, either as paupers or criminals."

After the Whigs evicted the Democrats from the White House in 1849, President Millard Fillmore (who replaced Zachary Taylor after his sudden death in 1850) nominated Benjamin Curtis of Massachusetts to fill the "New England seat" on the Supreme Court. Curtis, who came to the bench from private practice in Boston, specialized in commercial law and had been highly recommended by Daniel Webster. Before he joined the Court, Curtis had supported the constitutionality of the Fugitive Slave Act of 1850, and abolitionists in the Senate briefly held up his confirmation. Curtis served on the Court for only six years, but with greater distinction than any other member of the Taney Court.

President Franklin Pierce of New Hampshire took office in 1853 as a Democrat. This obscure politician (who gained his party's nomination on the forty-ninth ballot) won election by a narrow margin, only because the slavery issue had divided the Whigs and provoked its abolitionist wing to support the Free-Soil Party. During his one term in office, Pierce nominated just one man to the Supreme Court. But his choice of John Campbell of Alabama, designed to placate the southerners who dominated the Democrats, gave the South a crucial fifth seat on the Court. Campbell had practiced law since the age of eighteen and had argued six cases before the Supreme Court before his nomination. The New York Tribune, edited by the fervently abolitionist Horace Greeley, described Campbell as "a gentleman of shining and profound talents," but on the slavery issue "a fire-eater of the blazing school." Unlike his southern colleagues, Wayne and Catron, Campbell supported the South during the Civil War and resigned his Supreme Court seat in 1861 to serve the Confederate government as assistant secretary of war.

The arithmetic of the Supreme Court is simple: five is a majority of nine. To win his freedom—and that of his wife and daughters—Dred Scott needed the votes of five justices. Judicial politics is not always simple, but five of the nine justices who decided his case were southerners, whose personal views and sectional ties made it virtually certain that Dred Scott would remain a slave. Hardly anyone—including Scott's lawyers and his abolitionist supporters—doubted that the Court would decide that Dred Scott was not a "citizen" of Missouri, and was thus unable to bring suit for his freedom in federal court. Beyond this likely outcome, some crucial questions remained, and it was hard to predict whether the justices would address them. If the Court ruled against Scott and ordered that his suit be dismissed on jurisdictional grounds, would the proslavery majority decide issues that were not raised in the case? Most important, would the Court rule, as urged by southern "fire-eaters" in Congress, that the national government had no constitutional power to outlaw slavery in the western territories? This was the burning issue in national politics, one the justices could either face directly or evade in the *Dred Scott* case. Whatever decision it made, the Court would endure heated criticism from the partisans on both sides of the slavery issue.

In retrospect, it seems odd that the case attracted little attention before the Court first heard arguments in February 1856. Even the *Missouri Republican* of St. Louis, a newspaper that opposed slavery, did not mention it in listing the cases the Court would hear during the term. Not surprisingly, the heated debates over slavery in Congress aroused more public interest than an obscure case that had dragged on for ten years in state and federal courts. Montgomery Blair, the prominent Washington lawyer who agreed to represent Dred Scott before the Supreme Court without fee, submitted a legal brief to the Court— quite brief at ten pages—that made no mention of the territorial issue or the claim that Dred Scott's residence in Wisconsin Territory had freed him from slavery. Blair put all his chips on the argument that Scott had been "emancipated by his master's having taken him to reside in the State of Illinois." This was a risky strategy, since the federal court in St. Louis—agreeing with the Missouri supreme court—had ruled that Missouri law prevailed over that of Illinois in the case.

The two lawyers who opposed Montgomery Blair matched him in eminence and experience. Henry S. Geyer represented Missouri in the Senate and was highly regarded as a Supreme Court advocate. Reverdy Johnson of Maryland, an old friend of Chief Justice Taney, was himself a former senator and attorney general under President Zachary Taylor. It is unlikely that John Sanford—the nominal defendant in the case—possessed the funds or even the mental capacity to hire Geyer and Johnson. Sanford would shortly be confined to a mental asylum, and Johnson later said that an unidentified "southern gentleman" had recruited him to the case.

The Supreme Court record does not contain any brief filed by Geyer and Johnson. Based on fragmentary newspaper accounts, we know that the oral arguments in February 1856 began with Blair's claim that Dred Scott had been emancipated by his residence in Illinois. Blair rested his case on the dissenting opinion in the Missouri supreme court decision that had rejected Dred's suit for freedom. Relying on dissenting opinions by lower-court judges is a risky strategy, but Blair had nowhere else to turn for legal authority on this point. On their part, Geyer and Johnson argued that the Supreme Court should uphold the "plea in abatement" that Sanford had filed in the lower federal court. This legal term—no longer in use—meant that Sanford objected to Dred Scott's suit on the ground that it had been improperly filed in federal court. In effect, Sanford had asked the court to dismiss the case for lack of jurisdiction, on the ground that Scott, as a slave, was not a "citizen" of Missouri. Therefore, he lacked standing under the Diversity Clause of the Constitution to bring suit in federal court against a resident of New York. Scott had filed a "demurrer" to this plea, a reply that disputed the legal grounds of Sanford's objection to his suit; the lower federal court had upheld Scott's demurrer and had ruled that his "residence" in Missouri gave him enough standing to bring suit against Sanford. But this ruling did not address the question of whether Scott was a "citizen" of Missouri, or of the United States. Arguing that the lower court had erroneously rejected Sanford's plea in abatement, Geyer and Johnson urged the Supreme Court to reverse the lower court on this issue. Pushing their argument beyond the narrow issue of state law decided by the lower courts, Geyer and Johnson also attacked the constitutionality of the Missouri Compromise, hoping to slam every legal door in Dred Scott's face.

After the arguments in February 1856, the justices met at least five times to discuss the case. But their lengthy discussions over the next three months failed to produce a decision. The justices were apparently divided, four to four, on the crucial question of whether the Court could review Sanford's plea in abatement. Montgomery Blair had argued that Sanford's lawyers had "waived" this claim by "pleading over to the merits" in the lower court, which meant they had proceeded with the trial after the federal judge rejected their plea. Consequently, Blair added, they could not revive the plea in higher courts. On this important issue, Justice Samuel Nelson was unwilling to cast the deciding vote. On the more political question raised in the case, Justice Benjamin Curtis confided to a friend that the Court "will not decide the question of the Missouri Compromise" in the case. Most likely, the justices were hesitant to rule on this politically charged issue just before the nation became embroiled in a divisive presidential campaign. Whatever their real opinions or motivations, the justices agreed without dissent on May 12 to set the case for reargument in December, after the electoral votes had been counted.

The presidential election of 1856 was the seventh in a row that gave voters a choice between three or more candidates. The Democrats met in June and dumped President Franklin Pierce, who had proved incapable of healing his party's divisions over slavery. They replaced him with James Buchanan of Pennsylvania, who had stayed away from the controversy while serving as minister to England. The Democratic platform sidestepped the issue of congressional power over slavery in the territories. The Whig Party, under the new banner of the Republicans, turned down the presidential bid of Justice John McLean and nominated John Frémont, who had little political experience but was widely admired for his frontier explorations. The Republican platform backed the power of Congress to ban slavery in the territories, but Frémont was not a "fire-eater" on the issue and left most voters lukewarm toward him. The third major candidate, former president Millard Fillmore, represented the American Party, which waffled on the slavery issue and largely represented diehard Whigs who could not support either Buchanan or Frémont. All three candidates avoided the slavery issue, and the election did not become the national referendum that might have settled—or inflamed—this festering issue. When the ballots were counted, Fillmore proved to be a spoiler, draining enough votes from Frémont to elect Buchanan, who received a plurality of the popular vote but won a solid majority in the electoral college. Buchanan's election placed in the White House a "timid and indecisive" man who proved "a disaster for the nation," as a leading historian of the period wrote.

14

"Beings of an Inferior Order"

The equivocal outcome of the 1856 presidential election raised the stakes in the *Dred Scott* case, forcing the Supreme Court to face the slavery issue the candidates had evaded in their campaigns. The second round of arguments began on December 15, 1856. By this time, the case had attracted considerable attention, and the press noted that the Court's chamber was crowded with "many distinguished jurists and members of Congress." Once again, the Court did not record the arguments. "The reporter regrets that want of room will not allow him to give the arguments of counsel," he lamented in the official report, "but he regrets it the less, because the subject is thoroughly examined" in the 234 pages of opinions the justices produced in this momentous case.

All three lawyers who had argued the case previously returned for the second round. Montgomery Blair led off, once again, with the claim that John Sanford had waived his jurisdictional objections to the suit by "pleading over to the merits" in the lower federal court. This was a shaky argument, because appellate courts had long asserted their power to correct the jurisdictional mistakes of lower courts. Blair spoke with more authority in arguing that Dred Scott had been a "citizen" of Missouri when he filed his suit for freedom. He pointed to federal and state laws that made no distinction between "citizens" and "free inhabitants." This argument assumed, of course, that Scott's residence in Illinois and Wisconsin Territory had emancipated him from slavery. Given this assumption, Blair continued, Scott was a citizen of Missouri and thus had standing to bring suit in federal court. Significantly, Blair made no effort to claim that slaves were citizens, either of the states in which they resided or of the United States. His argument stood or fell on the Court's decision as to whether Dred Scott was a free black or a slave.

The issue of the constitutionality of the Missouri Compromise had not been raised before any of the courts, state and federal, that had already ruled in the case, nor had the Supreme Court asked for argument on the question. Sanford's lawyers, Henry Geyer and Reverdy Johnson, however, devoted much of their time before the Court to attacking the Missouri Compromise. Their motivation was partly legal and largely political. A simple ruling on Scott's status as a citizen would end the case without further inflaming the sectional debate that raged directly above the Court's chamber, in both wings of the Capitol. But Sanford's lawyers—and the southern "gentlemen" who supported them—wanted to enlist the Court in their campaign to, in effect, nationalize slavery by ruling that Congress could not prohibit slavery in any state or territory. A ruling that the Missouri Compromise was unconstitutional would pave the way for later cases that raised this issue.

The lawyers on both sides devoted much argument to Section 3 of Article IV in the Constitution, which provided that "Congress shall have power to dispose of and make all needful rules and regulations respecting the territory" of the United States. Sanford's lawyers urged a narrow construction of this clause. Conceding that Congress did have power to institute temporary governments in the territories, pending their admission as states, they argued that prohibition of slavery was not the kind of "needful" legislation required to govern a territory. Montgomery Blair had recruited George Curtis, a prominent Boston lawyer and brother of Justice Benjamin Curtis, to address this issue before the Court. Curtis replied to Sanford's lawyers by arguing that deciding what legislation was "needful" was a political question, to be answered by Congress and not the Court. Congress and the states had both legislated many times on the slavery issue, and prohibiting slavery was as much within legislative power as allowing or regulating it. Curtis noted that even staunchly proslavery lawmakers like John Calhoun had voted for the Missouri Compromise and thus accepted congressional power to prohibit slavery. In their rebuttal to Curtis, Sanford's advocates replied that Calhoun and other southerners in Congress had made a "compromise of principle necessary to the existence of the Union" without abandoning their constitutional objections to the Missouri Compromise. They added that the statements of congressmen did not decide the constitutionality of legislation; that was the Court's job.

Seated at the center of the Court's mahogany bench, Chief Justice Taney listened to the arguments with his mind already made up. As the nation's attorney general, he had earlier stated his opinion that blacks, "even if free," had not been "looked upon as citizens by the contracting parties who formed the Constitution." The question that remained, as the lawyers left the podium and the justices trooped out behind Taney, was not how the Court would rule on Dred Scott's suit for freedom, but whether its decision would further inflame the slavery dispute that divided the nation.

———

Dred Scott and his family—and the entire country—waited almost three months for a decision by the Supreme Court, while the justices conferred behind closed doors and labored over drafts of opinions on both sides of the case. During these months, very few outside the Court were aware that voting alignments on the various issues in the case shifted more than once, and that no single resolution commanded a clear majority. Initially, only the five southern justices were willing to hold the Missouri Compromise unconstitutional. Two justices, McLean and Curtis, disagreed and were prepared to dissent. The remaining northerners, Nelson and Grier, did not want to deal with the territorial issue and urged their colleagues to issue a narrow ruling that upheld the lower-court decision and avoided the questions of the Missouri Compromise and whether blacks, free or slave, were citizens. Nelson and Grier feared that if the Court split on sectional lines over these divisive issues, the public would conclude that the justices were swayed more by personal and political sentiments than by legal arguments.

Initially, the seven justices who wanted to keep Dred Scott in slavery agreed that Nelson would write a narrow opinion, upholding the lower-court ruling that Scott had "reverted" to slavery under Missouri law. Nelson quickly drafted a relatively brief opinion of about five thousand words (the final opinions, on both sides, consumed more than 100,000 words). But the shaky coalition for which Nelson wrote soon fell apart; at least three of the southern justices decided that the Court should rule on the Missouri Compromise. Don Fehrenbacher attributes this shift to the "bitter sectionalism" of Chief Justice Taney, and to pressure from President-elect Buchanan, who wanted to point approvingly to the Court's opinion in his forthcoming inaugural address, scheduled for March 4, 1857. Buchanan wrote in early February to Justice Catron, an old friend, asking when the Court would issue its decision. Buchanan was obviously hoping for inside information of the scope of the Court's ruling as well as its timing. Catron replied that the Court would dispose of the case before the inauguration, but without a ruling on the Missouri Compromise, the issue that most concerned Buchanan.

During the two weeks that followed Catron's first letter to Buchanan, Chief Justice Taney decided to throw moderation to the winds and write a "fire-eating" opinion that would serve as a proslavery manifesto. Taney recognized, however, that his position would be stronger if at least one northern justice joined the five southerners on the territorial issue. The most likely candidate was Robert Grier, from Buchanan's state and party. Justice Catron sent a second letter to Buchanan, urging him to exert his influence on Grier. Buchanan wrote to Grier, who conferred with Taney and Justice James Wayne, who matched and perhaps exceeded the Chief Justice in defending slavery. The deal was sealed in Grier's reply to Buchanan: "I am anxious that it should not appear that the line of latitude should mark the line of division in the court." Grier deferred to Taney: "On conversation with the chief justice, I have decided to concur with him" on the Missouri Compromise issue.

Having capitulated on this question, Grier was reluctant to let Buchanan read from the *Dred Scott* opinion in his inaugural address and point approvingly at the justices, who would sit behind him on the podium. "I fear some rather extreme views may be thrown out by some of our southern brethren," Grier added in his letter to Buchanan. And he made sure that the Court's opinions would not be issued before March 6, two days after the inauguration. Consequently, the new president told his audience—and the nation—that the question of whether slavery could be lawful in the territories "is a judicial question, which legitimately belongs to the Supreme Court, before whom it is now pending and will, it is understood, be speedily and finally settled. To their decision, in common with all good citizens, I shall cheerfully submit, whatever this may be."

Hardly anyone who attended the inauguration could have believed that Buchanan remained in the dark on the *Dred Scott* decision. Chief Justice Taney administered the presidential oath of office, and briefly conferred with Buchanan during the ceremony. Their conversation was not overheard, but it was certainly noticed, and tongues wagged all over Washington after the Court issued its ruling on March 6, 1857. On that day, Taney read from his lengthy "opinion of the Court" for more than two hours, speaking in a low voice to a crowded chamber. Justices Nelson and Catron followed with their concurring opinions. The next day, Justices McLean and Curtis read from their dissents for some five hours. The four remaining justices simply filed their opinions with the Court's clerk and did not read them from the bench. Although the Court had much earlier abandoned the practice of *seriatim* opinions, with each member expressing his views in print, all nine justices wrote something in the case, ranging from a few paragraphs to fifty-five pages of small print. They split into several factions on the various issues the Court addressed. But the bottom line, decided by a vote of seven to two, was that Dred Scott was still a slave.

What *did* the Court decide in the *Dred Scott* case, aside from its final judgment? This question is complicated by the plethora of opinions, some of which stated no position on one or more of the four major questions before the Court. First, was the "plea in abatement" subject to appellate review? Second, could a "Negro of the African race" be a citizen of the United States? Third, did Congress have power to enact the Missouri Compromise and prohibit slavery in the territories? And fourth, did the laws of Missouri allow Dred Scott's "reversion" to slavery after his residence in Illinois? If the Court lacked a majority on any of these questions, could the final judgment stand? These were important, even momentous, questions.

Historians who have puzzled over the nine separate opinions have reached differing verdicts, much like reading Tarot cards. Some have concluded that any justice's failure to object to various parts of Chief Justice Taney's "opinion of the Court" implied consent with his conclusions. Others have argued that Taney's opinion had no force of authority, aside from its narrow ruling that

Dred Scott remained a slave under the laws of Missouri, because Taney lacked a majority on the crucial issue of black citizenship. Because only two justices, Wayne and Daniel, clearly stated their agreement with Taney on this question, his conclusion that blacks were not United States citizens was *obiter dictum,* a judicial statement with no binding force as precedent. One noted scholar, in fact, omitted Taney's opinion from his *Cases on Constitutional Law* in 1895, substituting Justice Nelson's narrow opinion because it was limited "to grounds agreed upon by a majority of the court." But these differing historical judgments overlook one basic fact: Taney *did* speak for the Court, and his opinion was considered at the time—even by its fiercest critics—to represent the judgment of the majority. Taney's opinion was clearly a political tract, even with its judicial trappings, but the slavery issue was political, and the Court's decision instantly shaped the terms of that long-standing debate.

Taney addressed the four major questions in the case over the course of fifty-five pages, but the first and last questions received scant discussion. He devoted just three pages to the plea in abatement, holding that the Court had power to review—and reverse—the decision of the lower court. This was a crucial issue, because Judge Wells had decided that Dred Scott had standing to bring suit under the "diverse citizenship" provision of the Constitution. Unless the Supreme Court could review that decision, Scott (and other blacks who sued for their freedom) would stand on equal footing with whites in federal court. Taney concluded that John Sanford had not "waived" his objection to Scott's citizenship by "pleading over" to the merits of the case. Consequently, the Supreme Court had power to review "the whole record of the proceedings in the court below."

Having decided this key jurisdictional issue, Taney devoted the next twenty-four pages to the question of black citizenship. He began, as judges often do, by posing the question before the Court in broader terms than necessary. "The question is simply this: Can a negro, whose ancestors were imported into this country, and sold as slaves, become a member of the political community formed and brought into existence by the Constitution of the United States, and as such become entitled to all the rights, and privileges, and immunities, guarantied by that instrument to the citizen?" In these words, Taney placed on the advocates of black citizenship the task of proving that the Framers meant to include blacks as citizens. Given the decision of Judge Wells that Dred Scott had standing to sue under the Diversity of Citizenship Clause, it would seem incumbent on Taney to demonstrate that the Framers clearly meant to exclude all blacks—even "free Negroes"—from citizenship.

Taney simply bypassed his first major obstacle, by posing the question in terms of "national" rather than state citizenship. The Constitution provided that federal courts could decide suits "between citizens of different States," with no requirement of national citizenship. But the Chief Justice wanted to avoid two damaging facts: first, that the Constitution did not exclude free blacks from either state or national citizenship; second, that several states—before and after the Constitution was ratified—allowed free blacks to vote and exercise other political rights. In providing for the apportionment of House seats in Article I, the Framers distinguished between "free persons" and "all other persons," their euphemism for slaves in the "three fifths" clause. The term "free persons" clearly included free blacks, who were counted equally with whites in apportioning House seats.

Every state had free blacks in 1787, even though most imposed some legal disabilities on them. Taney seized on this latter fact to argue that the Framers did not mean to confer national citizenship on any blacks. He reached this conclusion through the back door. Taney first claimed that the Framers did not consider blacks—free or slave—as "persons," let alone as citizens. His asserted evidence for this dubious claim rested on a highly distorted reading of European and colonial history. Taney first conceded that "every person" who was considered a state citizen by the Framers "became also citizens of this new political body," the United States. "It becomes necessary," he continued, "to determine who were citizens of the several States when the Constitution was adopted."

On this question, Taney looked for guidance not to the states that adopted the Articles of Confederation but to "every European nation" of the colonial era. His shift of geographic focus reflected the fact that Taney found little support for his argument in the laws of the confederated states, several of which conferred political rights on free blacks. So he looked instead to "the state of public opinion" in the European nations "when the Constitution of the United States was framed and adopted." Taney could not point to any concrete evidence on this issue. He simply reflected the racial attitudes of his time. Speaking of the century that preceded the Declaration of Independence and the Constitution, he wrote that blacks were "regarded as beings of an inferior order, and altogether unfit to associate with the white race, either in social or political relations; and so far inferior, that they had no rights that the white man was bound to respect; and that the negro might justly and lawfully be reduced to slavery for his own benefit."

Taney depicted the treatment of blacks under slavery in cold, hard words. "He was bought and sold, and treated as an ordinary article of merchandise and traffic, whenever a profit could be made by it," he wrote of slaves during the colonial period. "This opinion was at that time fixed and universal in the civilized portion of the white race," he added. Taney accurately conveyed the racist attitude most influential Europeans (he had England primarily in mind) held toward blacks, but the opinion that they were nothing more than property was by no means "fixed and universal" in England, let alone in the American colonies. In his influential *Commentaries on the Laws of England*, which the Supreme Court had often cited with respect, Sir William Blackstone wrote that "a slave or negro, the instant he lands in England, becomes a freeman," with all the rights of English citizenship. Long before the *Dred Scott* opinion, Blackstone had refuted every claim Taney made about the citizenship status of blacks in England, where slavery had been outlawed by Parliament.

Taney faced a problem in dealing with the affirmation in the Declaration of Independence that "all men are created equal" and were "endowed by their Creator with certain inalienable rights" that government could not limit or destroy. Included in these rights was the "liberty" to be free of legal or physical restraints. Under the English law that Taney ignored, law that was rooted in the Magna Carta and recognized by the Framers, this "liberty" did not distinguish between whites and blacks. The Declaration of Independence made no reference to skin color. Taney, however, found it "too clear for dispute, that the enslaved African race were not intended" by the men who signed the Declaration in 1776 to be included as citizens of the nation they sought to establish. In concluding that all blacks were "never thought of or spoken of except as property" and were thus "doomed to slavery," Taney argued that "public opinion had undergone no change" between 1776 and 1787. But his evidence for this claim was thin and tendentious. Free blacks could vote in many states and enjoyed other rights of citizenship as early as 1776. So how did they lose these rights—which Taney refused to acknowledge—after the Constitution was framed and ratified? Because, he claimed once again, they were considered by the Framers as "property" and not as "persons" with all the "rights, privileges, and immunities" they shared with whites. This argument had no historical basis, but Taney was determined to strip all blacks—free or slave—of their status as "persons" with constitutional rights. His stated his conclusion with certitude: not only slaves but free blacks were "identified in the public mind with the race to which they belonged . . . and regarded as a part of the slave population rather than the free." This was an audacious, and totally false, conclusion from dubious historical facts, but only two justices dissented from his "opinion of the court" on this crucial question.

After removing all blacks—free or slave—from the category of "persons," it would seem that Chief Justice Taney had no further legal issues to decide in the *Dred Scott* case. If Scott was nothing more than an "article of merchandise," with no more right than a horse to bring suit in federal court, why should the Supreme Court decide the constitutionality of the Missouri Compromise? The obvious answer is that it had no legitimate reason for doing so. Taney, however, was determined to provide a legal basis for extending slavery into the territories. To accomplish this goal, he devoted twenty-one pages to an argument he could have made in one or two. He offered an exceedingly narrow—and historically wrong—reading of the "territory" clause in Article I of the Constitution, authorizing Congress "to dispose of and make all needful rules and regulations respecting the territory or other property belonging to the United States."

Taney first echoed the claim of John Sanford's lawyers that this clause did not confer any power on Congress to provide for governing the territories, but simply to dispose of land. This claim was patently false; otherwise, the "rules and regulations" part of the clause would be superfluous and meaningless. Having adopted this absurd position, Taney narrowed the clause even further, arguing that it referred solely to land already owned by the federal government in 1798, and not to territory later acquired by treaty or purchase, such as the Louisiana Purchase in 1803. "It was a special provision for a known and particular territory," Taney wrote, with the purpose of transferring "to the new Government the property then held in common by the States" under the Articles of Confederation. This was an equally groundless claim, for which Taney provided no evidence. In fact, the Framers had discussed the acquisition of new territories at length, and James Madison had proposed at the Constitutional Convention that Congress be granted power to "institute temporary governments for new States arising therein."

Taney then claimed that the words "needful rules and regulations" did not give Congress any power to legislate for the government of territories. "They are not the words usually employed by statesmen," he wrote, "when they mean to give the powers of sovereignty, or to establish a Government, or to authorize its establishment." This was semantic nonsense. The grants to Congress in Article I of powers to "establish a uniform rule of naturalization" and to "make rules for the government" of the armed forces both contemplated that Congress would pass "necessary and proper" laws for these purposes. On this issue, Taney faced the unequivocal ruling of Chief Justice Marshall in an 1828 opinion, *American Insurance Company v. Canter*, a case that dealt with congressional power to legislate for the Florida Territory (which was acquired after the Constitution was ratified, a fact Taney ignored). "In legislating for them," Marshall had written of the territories, "Congress exercises the combined powers of the general, and of a state government." States clearly had the power to prohibit slavery within their borders, and Marshall had extended to Congress the same power over the territories. Taney construed Marshall's opinion, however, as limited to congressional power to regulate territorial judiciaries, the issue before the Court in the 1828 case. Lawyers learn to "distinguish" cases that hold against them ("that case dealt with a green car, and this car is red"), but Taney offered an absurd distinction, since Marshall's words applied generally to congressional power over the territories. Most likely, Taney dragged out this section of his opinion to cover with wordiness the weakness of his argument. For him, the real issue was not Dred Scott, but the extension of slavery into the territories. Striking down the Missouri Compromise would open the door for the "nationalization" of slavery, as Taney's critics—including Abraham Lincoln—soon claimed. If Congress could not prohibit slavery, territorial legislatures were equally barred from doing so.

When Taney turned to the fourth and final question he had posed, that of Dred Scott's alleged "reversion" to slavery, the Chief Justice first addressed—at great length—the issue of his residence in Wisconsin Territory, even though Scott's two years in Illinois came earlier in time. The reason for this chronological reversal explains why Taney devoted just one page of his opinion to this question. "Our notice of this part of the case will be very brief," Taney explained, because Scott had not asked the Supreme Court to review the decision of the Missouri court. Even if he had, Taney wrote, "it is too plain for argument that the writ must have been dismissed for want of jurisdiction in this court." And why did the Supreme Court lack jurisdiction? Because it had ruled, in deciding that the Missouri Compromise was unconstitutional and that consequently Scott's residence in Wisconsin Territory did not free him from slavery, that Scott was not a "citizen" of the United States. And how did that ruling affect his claim that residence in Illinois granted him freedom in Missouri? Because it established that Scott was not a "citizen" and thus could not raise such a claim in any court, state or federal. If this sounds like a classic "Catch-22" situation, it is. By ruling first on the territorial question, Taney closed the door on Scott's claim under state law, which had arisen first in time. Because the lower federal court had allowed Scott to proceed under the "diversity of citizenship" clause, it became necessary for Taney to reverse this holding before he dealt with the state-law claim. Had he dealt with the issues in chronological order, Taney would have faced a more difficult task in arguing that Scott lacked standing to bring suit in state court.

If this all sounds confusing, which it surely does, much of the blame lies with Taney. He misread history, twisted legal precedent, and bent the Constitution out of shape, all to achieve his predetermined goal of promoting the extension of slavery into the territories. Historians have uniformly agreed with Don Fehrenbacher that Taney presented "an argument weak in its law, logic, history, and factual accuracy." To be more blunt, Taney's opinion was a travesty of the judicial craft, riddled with obvious errors and outright lies.

Hardly anyone today has the fortitude to plow through all 234 pages of the nine opinions in the *Dred Scott* case, let alone to check all their citations against the historial record. Those who read the dissenting opinions of Justices McLean and Curtis, which together matched Taney's in length, will appreciate (and most likely agree with) their detailed, point-by-point rebuttal to each of his contentions and conclusions. But they will not be reviewed or quoted here, because the fierce political debate that followed the Court's decision in March 1857 focused almost entirely on Taney's opinion. The Chief Justice had spoken for the Court on the slavery issue, and those on both sides—in Congress and the press—looked to his opinion for ammunition to fire against their opponents. The rhetorical battle that followed the *Dred Scott* decision, as we know, later erupted into the gunfire and bloodshed of the Civil War. Whether or not Roger Taney expected—or welcomed—this result, he could hardly have been unaware of the explosive force of his words.

In retrospect, it seems clear that the proslavery extremism of Chief Justice Taney doomed his cause to ultimate defeat. Most important, his assertion in *Dred Scott* that states which prohibited slavery nonetheless had to recognize the right of slave owners to bring their "property" into those states came close—some thought all the way—to ruling that slavery was lawful wherever slaves resided. In that case, the charge that Taney intended to "nationalize" slavery had force, and his opinion touched off an explosive reaction on both sides of the slavery issue.

Republicans in the press and Congress denounced the ruling in heated terms: Horace Greeley's newspaper, the *New York Tribune*, hurled invective at Taney's "mean and skulking cowardice" and the "detestable hypocrisy" of his opinion. On the other side, defenders of slavery exulted: "Southern opinion on the subject of southern slavery," trumpeted the *Constitutionalist* of Augusta, Georgia, "is now the supreme law of the land . . . and opposition to southern opinion on this subject is now opposition to the Constitution, and morally treason against the Government." Men of the cloth joined the fray, speaking from their pulpits and in the press. The Rev. George Cheever of the Church of the Puritans in New York sounded like his Puritan forebear Cotton Mather: "If the people obey this decision," he warned, "they disobey God." The Providence Conference of the Methodist Episcopal Church denounced Taney's opinion as the first step toward "nationalizing slavery," a charge soon taken up by Abraham Lincoln.

These responses to the *Dred Scott* ruling, culled from a voluminous record, illustrate the extent to which Taney's opinion dominated public attention and shaped the debate over slavery as the nation plunged into the most serious constitutional crisis in its history. The initial battles in the growing sectional conflict were fought in the halls of Congress, just above the Supreme Court chamber in which Taney struck down the congressional effort to forge a compromise on the slavery issue. The debate over slavery in the territories, of course, began more than three decades before the Court decided the *Dred Scott* case. But it threatened to dissolve the Union after that decision, as Congress debated the "Lecompton Constitution" for Kansas in early 1858.

Settlers in Kansas had already fought bloody skirmishes over slavery, with deaths on both sides. Shortly after the *Dred Scott* decision in 1857, proslavery settlers gathered in the territorial capital of Lecompton and drafted a constitution that drew inspiration from Taney's opinion. "The right of property is before and higher than any constitutional sanction," it proclaimed, "and the right of the owner of a slave . . . is as inviolable as the right of the owner of any property whatever." Taney had not based his opinion on "higher law" principles, but he clearly reflected the views of those who traced the "right of property" to a higher law than the Constitution.

Congress became embroiled in debate over the Lecompton Constitution during much of 1858, with both the Republican and Democratic Parties seeking to curry support as elections approached in November. It was predictable that politicians, who had fought over the slavery issue for years, would pound their fists on the congressional podium. Republican senator John Hale of New Hampshire accused proslavery Democrats of attempting "to carry out this Dred Scott decision" by forcing slavery on Kansas. "I hope the men of Kansas will fight," Hale thundered. "I hope they will resist to blood and to death." Senator William Seward of New York, who coveted the Republican presidential nomination, spoke during the same debate. Recalling the "whisperings" between Taney and President Buchanan at the 1857 inauguration, Seward insinuated that the two men had conspired to hang "the millstone of slavery" on the people of Kansas.

Southern defenders of slavery responded to this oratory with outrage. Senator Judah Benjamin of Mississippi, who had earlier declined a Supreme Court nomination and later served the Confederacy as secretary of war, defended Taney against his northern critics and praised his opinion for holding that slaves were property, a position Benjamin said reflected the "principles of eternal justice." Taney's old friend Reverdy Johnson, who argued and won *Dred Scott* before the Supreme Court, denounced Seward's "mad and reckless" assault on the Chief Justice, accusing him of subjecting the Court to "as calumnious an attack as ever dishonored human lips." Taney later told his biographer that he would have refused to administer the oath of office if Seward had been elected president in 1860.

Democrats controlled both houses of Congress in 1858, but their party was split over the Kansas question. Southern Democrats, supported by President Buchanan, tried to push the proslavery constitution through Congress. But the party's northern wing, led by Senator Stephen Douglas of Illinois, feared that Republicans would brand them as pawns of the slave owners. Not only would Douglas face the Illinois voters that fall in seeking reelection to his Senate seat, but he also coveted his party's presidential nomination in 1860. Douglas knew that most Illinois voters opposed the admission of Kansas as a slave state. Torn between party loyalty and personal interest, he decided to lead a revolt against Buchanan.

Faced with Douglas's defection, President Buchanan reached into his patronage bag and handed out enough federal jobs to force another compromise through Congress. He prevailed on Representative William English of Indiana to sponsor a "compromise" bill that would admit Kansas to statehood with the proslavery Lecompton Constitution, conditioned on approval by Kansas voters of a federal "land grant" from Congress, which offered the carrot of cheap farmland to settlers. Pressured by Buchanan, most northern Democrats supported the English bill, and it became law. Breaking with his party, Senator Douglas voted with the Republican minority, a stand that gained him votes in Illinois and cost him support in the South. Presented with a congressional "compromise" that would allow slavery in their state, voters in Kansas buried the Lecompton Constitution in August 1858 by an overwhelming margin.

15

"Another Explosion
Will Soon Come"

The most dramatic consequence of Taney's ruling in *Dred Scott*, and the one most Americans recall from history lessons, came in the face-to-face debates between Abraham Lincoln and Stephen Douglas in 1858, when the two men campaigned across Illinois for the Senate seat Douglas then held. Douglas tried to distance himself from Taney's effort to "nationalize" slavery by advocating "popular sovereignty" on slavery in the territories—letting the voters in each territory decide the question. Ironically, six months before the *Dred Scott* ruling, Abraham Lincoln had spoken for Republicans in telling Democrats that the Supreme Court was the body charged with deciding the issue of slavery in the territories and that "we will submit to its decisions; and if you do also, there will be an end to the matter." Shortly after the ruling, Lincoln changed his tune and claimed that "the *Dred Scott* decision is erroneous. We know the court that made it has often overruled its own decisions, and we shall do what we can to have it overrule this. We offer no resistance to it."

During the twenty months between the *Dred Scott* decision and the 1858 elections, Lincoln and Douglas spoke to hundreds of audiences in Illinois and around the country, and they discussed the case in almost every speech. The seven formal—and now famous—debates between the two senatorial candidates focused largely on the Court's ruling and its consequences for national unity, as talk of secession grew louder in the South. The Constitution had become the topic of stump speeches, barroom debate, and dinner-table conversation across the nation. During the Lincoln–Douglas debates, each man charged his opponent with hostility to the Constitution. Douglas accused Lincoln of conducting "warfare on the Supreme Court," while Lincoln shot back that Douglas was complicit in a "conspiracy to perpetuate and nationalize slavery."

As the Senate election neared, the campaign rhetoric became more heated.

Douglas insinuated that Lincoln favored the "amalgamation" of the races, which drew an indignant denial. He had no desire to "set the niggers and white people to marry together," Lincoln assured his listeners in Ottawa, Illinois. During their debate in Charleston, Lincoln declared that "I am not, nor ever have been, in favor of bringing about the social and political equality of the white and black races." In their last debate in Alton, Lincoln spoke for more than two hours on *Dred Scott*, tearing apart the ruling on the Missouri Compromise. But he pointedly denied any difference with Taney on the issue of black citizenship. "I am not in favor of Negro citizenship," Lincoln stated firmly.

Douglas narrowly bested Lincoln in this crucial electoral test of public sentiment on the slavery issue. Shortly after his defeat, Lincoln wrote to a friend that "Douglas had the ingenuity to be supported in the late contest both as the best means to break down and to uphold the slave interest. No ingenuity can keep these antagonistic elements in harmony long. Another explosion will soon come." Lincoln was prophetic in more than one way. Douglas continued to support "popular sovereignty" in voting on slavery, which prompted the southern Democrats in the Senate to depose him as chairman of the Committee on Territories after eleven years in that post. As the presidential campaign of 1860 neared, the Democrats fought bitterly over southern demands for federal legislation to protect slavery in the territories. Douglas opposed the bill sponsored by Senator Jefferson Davis of Mississippi, and the Republicans exulted at the internecine warfare among their opponents. "The *Dred Scott* decision," one Republican stated, "is the only Democratic platform that now exists."

The Democratic convention in 1860, which met in the proslavery stronghold of Charleston, South Carolina, turned conflict into chaos. Party rules required a two-thirds majority to nominate a candidate, but only a simple majority to adopt a platform. Delegates who favored Douglas outnumbered those who supported other candidates, but southerners had enough votes to block Douglas. The platform committee, with one delegate from each state, adopted by a one-vote margin a proslavery document that rejected Douglas's "popular sovereignty" position and called for support of the Jefferson Davis bill to protect slavery. The Douglas forces on the convention floor rejected the proposed platform, which prompted the delegates from eight southern states to walk out.

The convention promptly adjourned in confusion, and the delegates assembled two months later in Baltimore. After a bitter wrangle over seating rival delegations, the southerners again walked out, leaving Douglas with the nomination but without half of his party. Those who bolted in Baltimore later nominated Vice President John Breckinridge as the second Democratic candidate, running on a platform that endorsed the *Dred Scott* decision. Meanwhile, the Republicans surprised many, including Abraham Lincoln, by nominating him for president over Senator William Seward, a party stalwart with more national prominence than Lincoln. A fourth candidate, John Bell of Tennessee, represented diehard Whigs who now called themselves the Constitutional Union Party. The presidential campaign of 1860 had none of the drama or suspense of the Senate contest between Douglas and Lincoln. With the Democrats fatally split, Lincoln won easily; although he received less than 40 percent of the popular vote, he garnered 60 percent of the electoral votes.

Lincoln had predicted the "explosion" in the Democratic Party, which blew apart over the *Dred Scott* decision. But a much greater explosion shook the nation soon after Lincoln's inauguration on March 4, 1861. The new president, the first Republican in the White House, spoke to a throng at the Capitol for an hour about the Constitution and the Supreme Court in measured, sober words. Lincoln appealed to the Constitution more than twenty times, as the foundation of the Union and protector of minorities, alluding to southern defenders of slavery and not to the slaves. "All the vital rights of minorities," he said, "are so plainly assured . . . in the Constitution, that controversies never arise concerning them." But the Constitution cannot "express provisions for all possible questions."

Lincoln turned to the burning questions of the time. "May Congress prohibit slavery in the Territories? The Constitution does not expressly say. Must Congress protect slavery in the Territories? The Constitution does not expressly say. From questions of this class spring all our constitutional controversies, and we divide upon them into majorities and minorities. If the minority will not acquiesce, the majority must, or the government must cease." Lincoln had discussed *Dred Scott* in hundreds of speeches over the past four years, deploring the Court's decision, but he spoke in general terms in his inaugural address. He agreed that "constitutional questions are to be decided by the Supreme Court" and that its decisions were binding "upon the parties to a suit, as to the object of that suit," but Lincoln did not show much deference to the Court. Its decisions were "entitled to very high respect and consideration" by the other branches of government, a far cry from the position of judicial supremacy that Marshall had fashioned and that Taney had shaped to his own uses.

With the Chief Justice sitting uncomfortably behind him, Lincoln spoke critically of the Court, asserting that "if the policy of the government, upon vital questions affecting the whole people, is to be irrevocably fixed by decisions of the Supreme Court, the instant they are made, in ordinary litigation between parties in personal actions, the people will have ceased to be their own rulers, having to that extent practically resigned their government into the hands of that eminent tribunal." In this lengthy sentence, and without mention of the *Dred Scott* decision, Lincoln delivered a forceful rebuke to Taney and those who had voted with him, although he disclaimed "any assault upon the court or the judges." The justices were not to blame "if others seek to turn their decisions to political purposes." But the president *did* blame Taney for writing a political tract in his opinion, and for handing ammunition to his fellow proslavery extremists.

Many presidents have criticized the Supreme Court, before and since Lincoln, from Jefferson's campaign to impeach Justice Samuel Chase to Franklin Roosevelt's attack on the "Nine Old Men" who blocked his New Deal program. But never has a president spoken at such length of the Constitution and its role in national life. Lincoln, of course, came to office during the greatest constitutional crisis the nation ever faced, and he brought to his speech—delivered as the country slid ever more quickly into civil war—a profound respect for the Constitution, tempered with an appreciation of the Court's role as a political body.

Just five weeks after Lincoln's inaugural address, on April 12, Confederate forces fired on Fort Sumter in South Carolina, and its beleaguered defenders waved the white flag of surrender on April 14. That same day, Lincoln called the Congress into special session, citing "the power in me vested by the Constitution" to call out the state militias and "to cause the laws to be duly executed." The Civil War had begun. Before it ended in 1865, some 600,000 Americans—most of them young men in blue or gray uniforms—lost their lives in battles whose first shots were fired by the Supreme Court in 1857.

The Civil War changed American society in profound and lasting ways, and the Supreme Court changed as well before that bloody conflict ended. The most significant change came with the death of Chief Justice Taney in October 1864, but the Taney Court was almost dead before its leader was buried, after the resignations of two justices and the deaths of two others. Both of the *Dred Scott* dissenters were gone: Benjamin Curtis resigned in disgust, six months after the decision; and John McLean died in April 1861, days before the Confederates fired on Fort Sumter. Two justices in the *Dred Scott* majority also left the Court: Peter Daniel died in 1860, and John Campbell resigned just days after Fort Sumter fell, to serve the Confederacy as assistant war secretary.

The abrupt departure of Justice Curtis gave James Buchanan, a thoroughly undistinguished president, his only chance to influence the Court. He filled the "New England seat" in 1858 with a fellow Democrat, Nathan Clifford of Maine, who was a close friend of Chief Justice Taney and had expressed southern sympathies. Antislavery forces opposed his confirmation, and Clifford barely survived a Senate battle, winning his seat by three votes. After that shaky start, he served for twenty-three years and wrote some four hundred opinions, none of them still remembered. His judicial record was as undistinguished as Buchanan's in the White House.

The death of Justice Daniel in 1860 actually gave Buchanan a second Court seat to fill. But he took too long to choose between several candidates, and his final choice, Jeremiah Black of Pennsylvania, fell victim to election-year politics. Buchanan's party rival, Senator Stephen Douglas, opposed Black, and his confirmation lost by one vote. Douglas had reluctantly handed Abraham Lincoln a judicial plum, which the new president gave to Noah Swayne, an Ohio lawyer with strong abolitionist views but southern roots. His nomination sailed through the Senate in 1862 with just one dissent, and Swayne served for nineteen years, voting consistently to uphold civil rights laws and federal power over the states.

Lincoln's five Court nominations were tightly bunched together in the two years between 1862 and 1864. Samuel Miller of Iowa, who replaced Peter Daniel, and David Davis of Illinois, who took the seat abandoned by John Campbell, both joined the Court in 1862. Lincoln hardly knew Miller, while Davis was a home-state friend and political ally, but both men were loyal Republicans and noted lawyers. Miller served on the Court for twenty-eight years and Davis for fifteen, and both left indelible marks on constitutional law, although their opinions in landmark cases rejected both presidential and federal power and would likely have pained Lincoln, had he lived through his second term.

Congress handed Lincoln a judicial "bonus" in 1863, when it increased the Court's membership to ten. This move reflected the growing population and influence of the western states, which gained a new judicial circuit that year. It also ensured, with Chief Justice Taney still alive, that he would be unable to frustrate the Union's war powers. (Congress reduced the number of seats to seven in 1866, and returned it to nine in 1869, both moves dictated by political factors.) Lincoln's choice for this extra seat won quick approval and widespread approbation. Stephen Field of California, although a nominal Democrat, staunchly backed the Union and had distinguished himself as California's chief justice. Field served until 1897, almost to the century's end, and followed his own admonition that judges must speak with "absolute fearlessness" of the consequences. During thirty-four years on the Court, he wrote 640 opinions, dissented in 220 cases, and became the leading judicial advocate of laissez-faire economics during a period of intense conflict over governmental regulation of business and industry.

Roger Taney remained on the Court until his death in 1864, increasingly feeble but dependent on his salary to support two daughters. Few mourned his passing. One critic wrote that Taney "has earned the gratitude of his country by dying at last. Better late than never." Professing charity in its judgment, the *New York Times* concluded that Taney's *Dred Scott* opinion had been "an act of supreme folly, and its shadow will ever rest on his memory."

Before we leave the Taney Court and move into the Reconstruction period, we should consider one last question about the man who served as Chief Justice for almost thirty years, during a period of explosive growth and explosive conflict in American history. What made Roger Taney not only a racist but a man who could not divorce his personal views from his judicial duty? He was born into a slave-owning family, but so were many men who rejected and fought against slavery. Unlike them, Taney was infected with racism, unwilling to look at men like Dred Scott as fellow humans, let alone as fellow citizens. In his hands, the Constitution was rewritten as a proslavery charter. It is true that the Framers recognized slavery in the Constitution, as the price for the "Great

Compromise" that created the Union, but they did not intend that the federal government must protect slavery and allow its expansion across the continent.

Lincoln correctly charged Taney with trying to "nationalize slavery" by his twisted and tortured reading of the Constitution in *Dred Scott*. That his opinion was ultimately reversed by constitutional amendment is no consolation to the hundreds of thousands of young men who died after the Supreme Court shot holes through the Constitution. It is fitting to speak ill of the dead when they committed acts of infamy. Taney wrote an infamous opinion in *Dred Scott*, and no later judgments of his judicial "greatness" can remove that stain from the Court's history.

But those who write history often close their eyes to the human cost of infamous decisions by famous men. "It is a pity that Taney is so often remembered by that case rather than by his supreme accomplishments in achieving governmental concord and constitutional understanding," wrote an academic apologist who viewed *Dred Scott* as "an attempt to stem the oncoming tide of civil war," an astounding and appalling judgment. Without a moral compass, historians risk becoming lost in an intellectual desert, beguiled by the mirage of "objectivity" that recedes as one treks through "facts" that pile up like grains of sand. The carnage of the Civil War is an objective fact, and to absolve Taney of blame for his role in firing a judicial cannon at the Constitution is an affront to the sacrifice of those who died to save the Union he tried to sunder. The Supreme Court has never fully healed from the "self-inflicted wound" that Taney caused in *Dred Scott*, to use the apt term of a later Chief Justice, Charles Evans Hughes.

Taney's death offered Lincoln the chance to replace his judicial nemesis with a staunch opponent of slavery, one who supported the president's bold assertion of war powers and his program for postwar "reconstruction" of the South. The obvious choice was Salmon P. Chase of Ohio, former senator, governor, and treasury secretary in Lincoln's cabinet before his abrupt resignation in 1864. His antislavery credentials were impeccable; during the 1840s his legal defense of fugitive slaves gained him fame (or infamy, depending on one's views) as "Attorney General for Runaway Negroes." However, Chase had one serious disability: his intense political ambition placed him at odds with Lincoln. Chase had been a candidate for the Republican presidential nomination in 1860 and considered another contest against Lincoln in 1864, although he finally withdrew from contention. The president still doubted that Chase would refrain from campaigning for office from the Supreme Court bench.

Given this problem, Lincoln considered at least ten other men, including three sitting justices and three cabinet members. His personal choice was Montgomery Blair, a close friend and counsel for Dred Scott before the Supreme Court. However, Blair had feuded with Chase, who enjoyed the backing of the growing "Radical Republican" bloc in Congress, those who pressed for harsh measures against the South as the Union neared final victory in the bloody war. Lincoln also recognized that Chase—unlike Blair—had the political stature and personal magnetism to effectively lead a Court whose prestige and power had eroded under Chief Justice Taney. Despite his misgivings about Chase, Lincoln nominated his political rival to the nation's highest judicial office on December 6, 1864. The Senate confirmed its former member the same day, without even the formality of committee hearings.

The Civil War ended when General Robert E. Lee surrendered his sword—and his failed cause—to General Ulysses S. Grant at Appomattox Court House in Virginia on April 9, 1865. What the Union gained in victory the divided nation lost in blood. Just one month earlier, on March 4, Abraham Lincoln delivered his second inaugural address. The previous November, he had defeated the Democratic candidate, George McClellan, who headed the Union armies until Lincoln dismissed him in 1862 after the disastrous defeat at Antietam Creek in Virginia. In his first inaugural speech, Lincoln had discussed the Constitution for more than an hour; now he delivered a brief homily that drew its inspiration and text from the Bible. With military victory in sight, he spoke to the South in words of reconciliation. "With malice toward none, with charity for all," Lincoln said, let us "bind up the nation's wounds" and fashion "a just and lasting peace" between the warring sections. But he spoke also of the slaves whose "every drop of blood drawn by the lash" had been their only payment for "two hundred and fifty years of unrequited toil" in the service of their owners.

One month later, on April 11, 1865, Lincoln made his last public reference to the Constitution, in his last public address. Speaking from a White House window to a crowd that had gathered to celebrate the Union victory, he briefly thanked General Grant and his troops, but moved quickly to his plans for "reconstruction" of the Union. Lincoln spoke at length of "the constitutional amendment recently passed by Congress, abolishing slavery throughout the nation." He praised the former Confederate state of Louisiana for being the first to ratify the Thirteenth Amendment and for "giving the benefit of public schools equally to black and white, and empowering the legislature to confer the elective franchise upon the colored man."

These words in support of the Thirteenth Amendment cost Lincoln his life. Among the crowd on the White House lawn was an actor named John Wilkes Booth, who became so enraged at Lincoln's support of voting by former slaves that he vowed the president would never make another speech. Three nights later, on April 14, Lincoln and his wife attended a play at Ford's Theatre in Washington. Booth entered the president's box, which was not guarded, and shot him in the head with a pistol. Leaping from the box onto the stage, Booth shouted, "Sic semper tyrannis!" and fled from the theater. His cry, "Thus always to tyrants," voiced the sentiments of the diehard Confederates who refused to surrender their support for white supremacy, even after the Thirteenth Amendment abolished slavery.

Lincoln died the next day, a martyr to the Constitution whose protections he had worked to extend to all Americans, white and black. While the nation struggled to recover from this shock, Booth—who broke a leg in his escape—took refuge on a Maryland farm. He was tracked down by Union troops on April 26 and shot to death in a blazing barn. Eight men charged as fellow conspirators with Booth were later convicted, and four went to the gallows for their parts in the plot to kill the president.

Lincoln's death, so soon after the Union victory, badly damaged the Reconstruction program he had labored to fashion over the preceding months. His successor, Vice President Andrew Johnson of Tennessee, was a former Democrat and slave owner who had served in both houses of Congress and as his state's governor. Despite his electoral success and his prowess as a forceful stump speaker, Johnson had little of Lincoln's political skills or forensic talents. He was crude and intemperate in speech and habits, prone to losing his temper when confronted by hecklers. He owed his place on the Republican ticket largely to his residence in one of the border states in which Lincoln was unpopular.

The Radical Republicans who controlled Congress initially welcomed Johnson, believing his proclamations of support for black suffrage in the South, which they considered the foundation of Reconstruction. "Johnson, we have faith in you," declared Senator Benjamin Wade of Ohio, a fire-breathing Radical. But Wade and his fellow Radicals soon lost their faith, as Johnson waffled on black suffrage and pardoned many former Confederate officials—including governors, generals, and even the rebel vice president—for their "treason" against the Union, allowing them to take seats in Congress.

By 1868, Johnson's reluctance to implement the congressional Reconstruction program led to his impeachment by the House and trial in the Senate, over which Chief Justice Chase presided with strict adherence to rules of evidence. The "high crimes and misdemeanors" of which Johnson stood accused stemmed largely from his dismissal of Secretary of War Edwin Stanton, who sided with the Radicals in debates over Reconstruction. Senator Wade (who stood to become president if Johnson was convicted) voted to remove the man he had earlier praised, but seven Republican senators refused to convict Johnson for what were clearly political offenses, and he survived by a one-vote margin.

The unsuccessful effort by Radical Republicans to remove President Johnson had a twofold effect on the Constitution. First, his continued refusal to provide federal protection of black suffrage in the South and his unwillingness to implement the "ironclad" loyalty oath that Congress had imposed on Confederate supporters as a condition for voting and holding public office emboldened white southerners to stiffen their resistance to Reconstruction programs and laws. Second, his reluctance to fulfill his constitutional obligation to "take care that the laws be faithfully executed" spurred the Radical Republicans to provide "ironclad" guaranties of black citizenship and voting rights in the Constitution. The Fourteenth and Fifteenth Amendments, ratified in 1868 and 1870, both provided that Congress had power "by appropriate legislation" to enforce their protections of civil rights for the former slaves. Resistance to their legislative enforcement confronted the Supreme Court with its most difficult task since the *Dred Scott* case. Once again, the Court failed to perform its constitutional duty.

Before the Court dealt with laws that affected the rights of newly freed slaves, it grappled with presidential orders designed to punish those who gave "aid and support" to the Confederacy. The case of Lambdin P. Milligan, which began during the war in 1864, tested the powers of all three branches of government in dealing with civilians during wartime. The facts of the case were alarming to the Union. Milligan was a lawyer and a fervent Democrat who lived in southern Indiana, a stronghold of Confederate sympathy. He attracted the attention of Union officials by organizing groups that openly espoused the southern cause, with names like the Order of American Knights and the Sons of Liberty. Milligan also participated in efforts to persuade draft-age men to refuse military service in the Union army. Known as "Copperheads," after the poisonous snake whose brown-and-copper skin provided camouflage among fallen leaves, men like Milligan posed a threat to Union forces in midwestern states from Ohio to Missouri.

Faced with demands from Union generals to allow them to arrest and punish these disloyal civilians, President Lincoln gave military commanders broad powers to establish military courts that could try accused Copperheads; he also issued orders suspending the right of habeas corpus in certain areas, including southern Indiana. These orders prevented anyone arrested by the military from asking civilian judges to rule on the legality of their detention. Lincoln's actions posed a serious constitutional question: Section 9 of Article I provides that "The privilege of the writ of habeas corpus shall not be suspended, unless when in cases of rebellion or invasion the public safety may require it." The Civil War obviously constituted a rebellion, but Article I grants legislative powers to Congress, not to the president. And if civilian courts were operating in areas free of armed conflict, was the "public safety" sufficiently threatened to displace their jurisdiction over those accused of violating federal law?

Not only did Milligan and the Copperheads who worked with him agitate against the war, but military officials suspected them of hatching plots to steal Union munitions and then raid prisoner of war camps in Ohio, Indiana, and Illinois. The Confederate soldiers freed and armed by the conspirators could then take control of the three states. Alarmed by reports of this plot, military agents followed Milligan and compiled records of his movements and meetings. On October 5, 1864, General Alvin Hovey authorized Milligan's arrest; he was seized at his home and tried before a military tribunal in Indianapolis later that month, along with four men charged with conspiring with him. The military court, whose members were all army officers, convicted Milligan and sentenced him to hang, but they set his execution for May 1865. It is unclear why the sentence was deferred for seven months after trial, but the delay gave Milligan time to challenge his conviction in federal court. Just after Lee surrendered at Appomattox, Milligan filed a habeas corpus petition, arguing that he had been illegally arrested and tried.

Milligan's case—under the caption *Ex parte Milligan*—reached the Supreme Court after Lincoln's assassination, which reduced the pressure to support the president during wartime. In addition to this advantage, the convicted Copperhead had three more on his side. First, a federal grand jury had met in January 1865, after his military trial, and had declined to indict Milligan for any crime. Second, his legal team before the Supreme Court included David Dudley Field, a noted New York lawyer and brother of Justice Stephen Field. And third, the Constitution was clear—in the Sixth Amendment—on the right of criminal defendants to a jury trial. The question that remained was whether the president had power to establish military tribunals and suspend habeas corpus while civilian courts were open and functioning.

The Court had no difficulty in reaching a unanimous decision in December 1866 that Milligan had been unlawfully tried and convicted. Writing for the Court, Justice David Davis acknowledged that the "late wicked Rebellion" had roiled passions and prevented "that calmness in deliberation and discussion so necessary to a correct conclusion of a purely judicial question." He posed the question in these words: "Had this tribunal the legal power and authority to try and punish this man?" The answer was simple: no. Davis put his conclusion in these words: "Martial law cannot arise from a threatened invasion. The necessity must be actual and present; the invasion real, such as effectually closes the courts and deposes the civil administration." Indiana had not been invaded by Confederate forces, and the civilian courts remained open during the war.

The Court's decision freed Milligan and saved his life. But Justice Davis did not stop with a narrow ruling: he felt compelled to lecture Congress and the president on their constitutional responsibilities. "The Constitution of the United States is a law for rulers and people, equally in war and peace, and covers with the shield of its protection all classes of men, at all times, and under all circumstances," Davis wrote. "No doctrine, involving more pernicious consequences, was ever invented by the wit of man than that any of its provisions can be suspended during any of the great exigencies of government. Such a doctrine leads directly to anarchy or despotism, but the theory of necessity on which it is based is false; for the government, within the Constitution, has all the powers granted to it, which are necessary to preserve its existence; as has happily been proved by the result of the great effort to throw off its just authority."

Even those who sought to subvert the Union, Davis ruled, were as much entitled to the Constitution's protection as those who fought to maintain it. The *Milligan* doctrine of "one law in war and peace" would later be tested—and rejected—by the Supreme Court in several wartime cases. During World War I, Justice Oliver Wendell Holmes upheld a "sedition" conviction for obstructing the draft. "When a nation is at war many things that might be said in times of peace are such a hindrance to its effort," Holmes wrote, "that no court could regard them as protected by any constitutional right." And during World War II, the justices upheld military orders that forced all Americans of Japanese ancestry into concentration camps, without charges or trial. These later cases show how the "great exigencies of government" can blind the Court to the clear text of the Constitution.

16

"A Higher Law Than

the Constitution"

The Thirteenth Amendment to the Constitution is short and simple: "Neither slavery nor involuntary servitude, except as a punishment for crime whereof the party shall have been duly convicted, shall exist within the United States, or any place subject to their jurisdiction." Section II provides that "Congress shall have power to enforce this article by appropriate legislation."

But the political struggle to abolish slavery through constitutional amendment was neither short simple. In fact, after the Senate approved this article in 1864, President Lincoln and Republican leaders could not secure the necessary two-thirds vote for adoption in the House. Not until Lincoln won his second term and Radical Republicans picked up congressional seats in 1864 did the House narrowly approve the amendment, 119 to 56. The switch of three votes would have blocked the abolition of slavery once more. The final House tally on January 31, 1865, ignited wild cheering in the galleries, while congressmen "joined in the shouting" and wept openly with relief and joy.

However simple in wording, the Thirteenth Amendment reflected a complex mixture of legal doctrine and political discord. Many of the Radical Republicans who pressed for its adoption based their support on "higher law" principles. They did not view the Constitution—which they recognized as the charter of American laws and liberties—as paramount in legal authority, but as subordinate to a "higher law" rooted in "the laws of nature and of nature's God," as Senator William Seward put it. In a famous speech, Seward spoke in biblical terms. "The Constitution regulates our stewardship," he said of Congress, and "devotes the domain to union, to justice, to defense, to welfare, and to liberty. But there is a higher law than the Constitution, which regulates our authority over the domain, and devotes it to the same noble purposes."

Most political leaders who appealed to "higher law" principles also recognized the "positive law" enactments of legislatures, and counseled obedience to them. Lincoln, for example, agreed in 1858 that "the people of the Southern states are entitled to a fugitive-slave law" and vowed that he would not obstruct its enforcement. But others preached resistance to all laws they saw as violating the "higher law" that rejected slavery on moral grounds. "Let no man tell you that there is no higher law" than fugitive slave laws, proclaimed Joshua Giddings, a former congressman and fervent abolitionist. Benjamin Wade won election to the Senate from Ohio with a pledge to disobey all slavery laws. And Senator Hannibal Hamlin of Maine, Lincoln's first vice president, warned southerners that they "must answer to a higher power for the wrongs they perpetrate" against slaves.

These fire-and-brimstone fulminations illustrate the moralistic fervor of those who vowed to abolish every vestige of slavery. They expected the Thirteenth Amendment to accomplish this goal, assuming that all the southern laws that enforced slavery were struck down by this constitutional provision. Radical Republicans soon learned that many former Confederate leaders had no intention of treating the freedmen as political equals, or even as fellow humans. Their resistance to Reconstruction—even President Johnson's modest and conciliatory program—encouraged widespread violence against blacks who dared to seek the ballot or challenge "the established usages, customs and traditions" of white southerners, the racial practices which the Supreme Court later cited in *Plessy v. Ferguson* as grounds for upholding Jim Crow laws.

For blacks across the South, 1865 and 1866 were years of terror. Stung by their military defeat, unrepentant Confederates responded to Reconstruction and the Thirteenth Amendment with a wave of violence. A few examples from the bloodstained list will show the carnage. Henry Adams, a former slave, testified before Congress that after the Confederate surrender in 1865, "over two thousand colored people were murdered" in the area around Shreveport, Louisiana. The following year, after disputes with freedmen over land, whites near Pine Bluff, Arkansas, set fire to a black settlement and rounded up its residents. A white man who visited the scene the next morning described "a sight that apaled me 24 Negro men women and children were hanging to trees all round the Cabbins." White mobs massacred hundreds of blacks during 1866. In Memphis, Tennessee, a collision between two horse-drawn cabs—one driven by a white and the other by a black—led to three days of violence in which forty-six died and hundreds of black homes, schools, and churches were pillaged or burned. Later that year, Louisiana's Reconstruction governor called a state convention to enfranchise blacks and bar former "rebels" from voting. Blacks who gathered to support the convention were attacked by New Orleans police, most of them former Confederate soldiers. Before federal troops arrived, thirty-four blacks had been shot dead and more than one hundred others injured. One Union army veteran who witnessed the scene wrote that "the wholesale slaughter" on the streets of New Orleans rivaled anything he had experienced on Civil War battlefields.

Reports of violence against blacks and restrictions on voting enraged Radicals in Congress and prompted them to support the Civil Rights Act of 1866. Sponsored by Senator Lyman Trumbull of Illinois, a moderate Republican who chaired the Judiciary Committee, this bill granted national citizenship to all persons born in the United States (except Indians) and provided that every citizen enjoyed "full and equal benefit of all laws and proceedings for the security of person and property." Trumbull's bill also authorized federal attorneys to file suits in federal courts against local and state officials who deprived "any person" of rights guaranteed by the law, subject to fine and imprisonment.

Supporters of Trumbull's bill viewed it as a means to enforce the Thirteenth Amendment. If southern states could deprive blacks of rights to own land and vote, one Republican asked, "then I demand to know, of what practical value is the amendment abolishing slavery?" Opponents of the Civil Rights Act charged that it violated the Tenth Amendment, which "reserved to the states" those powers not granted to Congress. Even its advocates recognized the bill's replacement of state with federal authority. "I admit," Senator Lot Morrill of Maine said, "that this species of legislation is absolutely revolutionary. But are we not in the midst of a revolution?"

Determined to appease the South, President Johnson rejected Trumbull's bill and vetoed it after congressional passage. Sounding like the Dixiecrats of the next century, he denounced it as a "stride toward centralization, and the concentration of all legislative powers in the national Government." Johnson also displayed his racism in claiming that the bill—which provided equal rights for both races—was "made to operate in favor of the colored and against the white race." In the end, Johnson dug his own political grave by vetoing the Civil Rights Act of 1866. Although both houses of Congress overrode Johnson's veto by more than the required two-thirds majority, enacting Trumbull's bill into federal law, Radical Republicans decided to protect the freedmen from any future congressional revision or judicial invalidation of its provisions by adding them to the Constitution through the amendment process. Even before passage of the Trumbull bill over Johnson's veto, members of Congress had introduced more than seventy proposed amendments. One of them, sponsored by Representative John A. Bingham of Ohio, provided that "Congress shall have power to make all laws which shall be necessary and proper to secure to the citizens of each State all privileges and immunities of citizens in the several States, and to all persons in the several States equal protection in the rights of life, liberty, and property."

Speaking to the House, Bingham stated that he had designed his proposed amendment "for the enforcement of these essential provisions of our Constitution, divine in their justice, sublime in their humanity, which declare that all men are equal in the rights of life and liberty before the majesty of American law." Bingham rested his argument on "higher law" principles that he derived from the Declaration of Independence. But he wanted to give Congress the power to enact these principles into "positive law" that would allow federal enforcement of "rights of life and liberty" against southern obstruction.

With Senator Trumbull's bill on the floor, Bingham agreed to postpone consideration of his proposed amendment, but after the Civil Rights Act became law over Johnson's veto, Bingham renewed his campaign to place its provisions in the Constitution. His first proposal was designed to enlarge congressional powers in the field of civil rights. The southern resistance to Reconstruction spurred Bingham to recast his proposal as a limitation on state powers. He revised the amendment to provide that "No state shall make or enforce any law which shall abridge the privileges or immunities of citizens of the United States; nor shall any state deprive any person of life, liberty, or property without due process of law, nor deny to any person within its jurisdiction the equal protection of the laws."

Bingham's words survived lengthy congressional debate without change and became the heart of the Fourteenth Amendment. During that debate, he declared his intention to extend "protection by national law from unconstitutional State enactments" to "citizen and stranger" alike. This last phrase expressed Bingham's desire to extend the Constitution's protection to immigrants who had not yet become citizens. His amendment would shelter "any person" under the Constitution's wide umbrella. A century later, Justice William O. Douglas wrote of the "penumbras" of the Bill of Rights—the shadow cast by this metaphorical umbrella—as creating "zones of privacy" that protect "the people" from governmental invasion of public and private spaces. Bingham had no such expansive purpose; he simply wanted to protect the freed slaves from state oppression.

The amendment that Congress finally adopted contained five sections; the first included the protections of individual rights that Bingham had drafted. Before its final passage, Congress added a sentence at the beginning of Section I: "All persons born or naturalized in the United States and subject to the jurisdiction thereof, are citizens of the United States and of the State wherein they reside." These twenty-eight words reversed the twenty thousand words of Chief Justice Taney's *Dred Scott* opinion. The Constitution now recognized the former slaves—and free blacks as well—as citizens with legal rights equal to those of whites. The significance of this sentence must not be overlooked as we examine the Constitution's long and troubled history. Six hundred thousand Americans died in the Civil War that followed Taney's ruling that blacks were not citizens, but the "property" of their owners.

The grant of citizenship to "all persons" born in the United States has continued to provoke debate. In recent years, politicians in California and other states have pressed for legislation and constitutional amendments to deny citizenship to children born in the United States of parents who illegally crossed the border. During the nineteenth century, however, there were no "illegal immigrants." The nation welcomed "all persons" who left their native lands to seek a better life in the United States. Many states allowed immigrants to vote even before they became naturalized citizens, and their children did not fear deportation or denial of constitutional rights.

Congressional debate on the Fourteenth Amendment focused less on Bingham's wording of Section I than on provisions aimed at the former Confederate states. Section II erased from the Constitution the clause that counted slaves as "three fifths" of a person in allocating House seats. The new provision based apportionment on "all persons" rather than "free persons," and punished states that denied voting rights to any "male inhabitants" by reducing their representation in the House. Section III barred from Congress or federal office any former Confederate who had previously held federal or state office, had taken an oath "to support the Constitution of the United States," and had "engaged in insurrection or rebellion" against the Union. Some congressional Radicals wanted to deny federal office to any former Confederate, but they finally agreed to this watered-down version, which affected only state and federal officials among those who had waged war against the Union.

Section IV of the proposed amendment barred federal payment of "any debt or obligation incurred in aid of insurrection or rebellion against the United States, or any claim for the loss or emancipation of any slave," and held such debts and claims to be "illegal and void." This slap at the Confederate states was aimed at slave owners and wealthy merchants who had financed the Confederacy, but Congress had no sympathy for those who hoped to "profit from treason," as some Radicals put it. Finally, Section V authorized Congress "to enforce, by appropriate legislation, the provisions of this article." This section, like the similar provision in the Thirteenth Amendment, gave Congress sweeping powers to protect the former slaves against southern hostility.

Congressional passage of the Fourteenth Amendment in June 1866 did not guarantee that it would become part of the Constitution. Ratification by three fourths of the state legislatures was still necessary. The question was, which states? Could the former Confederate states block the amendment? Could their readmission to the Union be conditioned on ratification? At the time Congress adopted the amendment, the Union included thirty-six states, with Nevada the most recent addition in 1864. The refusal of ten states to ratify the Fourteenth Amendment would create another political crisis.

Sentiment in the white South was "very unanimous against adopting the Amendment," observed an Alabama editor. To make matters worse, President Johnson openly campaigned against ratification. His position cost him what little Republican support he had inherited from Lincoln, especially after he suggested that Providence had removed Lincoln to elevate Johnson to the presidency. One former supporter wrote that Johnson had "sacrificed the moral power of his position, and done great damage to the cause of Constitutional reorganization."

Among the former Confederate states, only Tennessee ratified the Fourteenth Amendment, although it required strongarm tactics to gain a House quorum. One recalcitrant member was arrested and brought to the chamber after a "wild night-chase by mule and on foot through the hills," and two who refused to take their seats were forcibly detained and marked "present" for the session. After the vote, Tennessee's governor sent a telegram to Congressman Bingham: "Battle fought and won," he wrote. "Two of Johnson's tools refused to vote. Give my compliments to the dead dog in the White House." All ten remaining Confederate states refused to ratify by huge margins. A few southerners saw the inevitable retribution from Radical Republicans, who vowed to punish the rebellious states. "Are we not," one South Carolinian asked, "actually inviting our own destruction?"

The Radicals turned the 1866 congressional elections into a referendum on the Fourteenth Amendment. Public sentiment in the North became almost as unanimous in support as the opposition in the South. Rarely in American politics, observed the *New York Times*, had elections been fought "with so exclusive reference to a single issue." Even moderate Republicans scrambled on the bandwagon. "If I was ever Conservative, I am Radical now," vowed one California congressman. The Congress that convened in December 1866 had more than enough Radicals to override any presidential veto of its Reconstruction measures.

Radicals in Congress quickly moved to depose the state governments that President Johnson had installed, replacing them with military rule. The Reconstruction Act of 1867 divided the former Confederate states—except Tennessee—into five military districts, each governed by a Union general. As conditions for readmission to the Union, southern states were required to hold conventions and write new constitutions. Each state had to provide the ballot to all males—white and black—and ratify the Fourteenth Amendment before electing members of Congress. Since Congress had denied voting rights to most Confederate army veterans and officials, black voters formed a substantial majority in several states. The law provided that military commanders would register voters and conduct elections. This was, pure and simple, government at gunpoint. But the southern states had, in fact, invited their own destruction by refusing to ratify the Fourteenth Amendment. After the "reconstructed" southern legislatures voted for ratification, the amendment finally became part of the Constitution on July 9, 1868.

Protected by federal troops, blacks voted in large numbers during the early years of Military Reconstruction. Turnouts ranged from 70 to 90 percent of eligible black voters in the southern states. In elections to state conventions, blacks not only voted but gained seats in all ten states, including a majority in South Carolina and Louisiana and nearly 40 percent in Florida. More than half of the 265 black delegates to state conventions later gained election to state legislatures, and nine served in Congress. Despite their voting strength, however, blacks did not receive their fair share of state and federal offices. Only one black, P. B. S. Pinchback of Louisiana, served as a state governor during Reconstruction, and his tenure lasted just one month. Blacks did hold statewide office in five states, but in the other states under military rule they were shut out from political office or real influence. Sixteen blacks gained election to Congress during Reconstruction, including two senators from Mississippi, Hiram Revels and Blanche Bruce. But no more than five served during any congressional session. The reasons for this decided shortfall in electoral offices are complex: blacks often deferred to white Republicans; many felt themselves unqualified by education or experience; and many others feared the violence unleashed on "upstart" blacks by the Ku Klux Klan and other vigilante groups.

It is difficult in retrospect to measure the full extent of Klan violence during Reconstruction, or its impact on the black population. Founded in 1866 as a social club in Memphis, by 1870 the Klan had spread across the South and imposed a reign of terror on blacks and their white supporters. A few examples, selected from congressional testimony on Klan violence, will illustrate this bloody record: Jack Dupree, a black leader in Monroe County, Mississippi, known as a man who "would speak his mind," was disemboweled in front of his wife, who had just given birth to twins. In October 1870, armed whites attacked a Republican rally in Greene County, Alabama, killing four blacks and wounding fifty-four. That same month, after a Republican election victory in Laurens County, South Carolina, Klansmen held a "Negro chase" that ended with thirteen murders.

Confronted with wholesale slaughter across the South, federal officials did virtually nothing. Republicans in Congress tried to legislate against the intimidation of black voters. They first patched a gaping hole in the Fourteenth Amendment, which had not provided blacks with a federal guarantee of voting rights. Black suffrage had been the rallying cry of Radical Republicans, and Congress adopted the Fifteenth Amendment in February 1869. Like the Thirteenth Amendment abolishing slavery, this addition to the Constitution was short and simple in wording: "The right of citizens of the United States to vote shall not be denied or abridged by the United States or by any state on account of race, color, or previous condition of servitude." Like the two earlier Reconstruction amendments, the Fifteenth provided that "Congress shall have power to enforce this article by appropriate legislation." Final ratification came on February 3, 1870, a year marked by escalating violence against blacks who dared to exercise their new electoral rights.

Congress utilized the powers granted by the Reconstruction amendments with three Enforcement Acts, passed in 1870 and 1871. The first, known as the Ku Klux Klan Act, was aimed at the hooded marauders who terrorized blacks across the South. The law provided that "if two or more persons shall band or conspire together, or go in disguise upon the public highway" with an intent to "injure, oppress, threaten, or intimidate any citizen" or to "hinder his free exercise of any right or privilege granted or secured to him by the constitution or laws of the United States," violators could be prosecuted in federal court and imprisoned for ten years. The second law strengthened federal enforcement of election laws in large cities and was directed primarily at Democrats in northern cities who stuffed ballot boxes (an issue that returned in the 1960 presidential election of John F. Kennedy over Richard Nixon). The third act imposed criminal penalties on any person acting "under color of law" to deprive another person of constitutional rights. Congress intended with this law to give federal judges the power to punish local and state officials in the South—many of whom belonged to or collaborated with the Klan—who prevented blacks from voting or exercising other civil rights.

These laws are still on the books, with minor amendments over the years, and were dusted off by federal officials in the 1960s to prosecute Klansmen and southern sheriffs who terrorized and arrested Freedom Riders, sit-in demonstrators, and organizers of voting drives in the Deep South. Even today, these laws form the backbone of federal enforcement of civil rights. During the Reconstruction era, however, the Supreme Court stripped the Enforcement Acts of any force and turned the clear intent of Congress into legislative impotence. The Court's rejection of federal power to protect the former slaves reflected the nation's growing lack of concern for their plight, from the president down to local officials charged with enforcing Reconstruction laws.

The stream of indifference flowed directly from the White House. In 1868, Ulysses S. Grant ran for president on the Republican ticket and won a bare majority of the popular vote over Horatio Seymour, a former New York governor whose fellow Democrats saddled him with a platform that opposed Reconstruction. Grant, the hugely popular commander of the Union army, had wrested the Republican nomination from President Andrew Johnson, whose appeasement of the South turned Grant's military victory into political surrender. Grant's battlefield prowess, however, did not shield him from the crossfire on Capital Hill over Reconstruction. Johnson had failed to heed Lincoln's call to "bind up the nation's wounds," and Grant proved equally lacking in leadership, presiding over an administration tarnished by scandal and corruption. Despite the constant drumbeat of criticism, Grant marched to a second term and spent eight years in the Oval Office.

Grant could point to few accomplishments, but he did place four men on the Supreme Court, one short of a majority. His nominees, all of them corporation lawyers, looked like peas in a pod. Grant's first chance to shape the Court came in 1870, a year after Congress restored the ninth seat it had removed in 1866. For this "bonus" seat, Grant first nominated his attorney general, Ebenezer Hoar, whose legal ability was unquestioned. But his opposition to Andrew Johnson's impeachment, and other political stands, had created enemies, and the Senate rejected Hoar by a substantial margin. The Senate was still debating Hoar's nomination when Justice Robert Grier announced his retirement in 1870, after twenty-four years on the Court. Four days after Hoar's defeat, Grant sent two names to the Senate: William Strong of Pennsylvania and Joseph Bradley of New Jersey. Strong was a prominent railroad lawyer who had earlier been considered by President Lincoln for the post of Chief Justice. His nomination sailed through the Senate, and he then spent ten years in "relative obscurity" on the Court, voting to uphold the constitutional rights of corporations and to deny those of blacks.

Bradley, like Strong a railroad lawyer, came to the Court with a record of hostility toward equal rights for blacks. After Congress passed the strong Civil Rights Act of 1875, giving blacks access to "public accommodations" like restaurants and theaters, Bradley wrote in his journal that depriving "white people of the right of choosing their own company would be to introduce another kind of slavery." Unable to distinguish human bondage from restaurant discrimination, Bradley had no trouble in reading the Constitution to protect corporations from legislative regulation. He sat on the Court for almost twenty-two years and voted in almost every case against the claims of blacks, women, and criminal defendants. For Bradley, the Constitution was a charter for white men like him.

The retirement of Justice Samuel Nelson in 1872, after almost three decades on the Court, gave President Grant a third nomination, which he offered to Ward Hunt of New York, a former corporation lawyer who served as chief judge of his state's highest court. Like Strong and Bradley, Hunt displayed little concern for the rights of blacks, voting on the Court against the federal Reconstruction Enforcement Acts and state laws that prohibited racial segregation in public accommodations. Hunt served on the Court for nine years, but during the last four—after a paralytic stroke—he did not participate in any proceedings. He remained on the Court to collect his salary and resigned only when Congress passed a special pension bill for him. His tenure, one biographer wrote, was "generally undistinguished," a description that fits all the justices Grant placed on the Court.

These undistinguished men first confronted the Reconstruction amendments in 1873, deciding a case that had nothing to do with the rights of blacks. The Supreme Court's decision in what were called the *Slaughterhouse Cases*, however, had a devastating impact on federal enforcement of civil rights. This case (which combined several suits for decision) dealt with a statute passed by the

Louisiana legislature in 1869. In creating the Crescent City Livestock Landing & Slaughterhouse Company, the state established a monopoly that required all livestock dealers and butchers in the New Orleans area to conduct their business at the company's facilities. The ostensible reason for this law was to protect the public's health by reducing the stench and pollution from dumping animal waste into the Mississippi River. However genuine this motive, the monopoly's backers had secured their charter through wholesale bribery. The Louisiana supreme court later ruled that its sponsors had doled out thousands of dollars "for the purpose of corrupting and improperly influencing members of the Legislature."

After the legislature paid its political debts, butchers who objected to the monopoly filed suit in federal court. Their claim relied on three clauses of the Fourteenth Amendment: first, that the state had abridged their "privileges and immunities" as United States citizens; second, that the Due Process Clause protected their "property" right to engage in their occupation without state hindrance; and third, that the monopoly favored some butchers over others and thus deprived them of the "equal protection of the laws." The butchers also threw into their suit a claim that the monopoly violated the Thirteenth Amendment by forcing them into "involuntary servitude." It was ironic that an all-white business group—the Butchers' Benevolent Association—brought the first claim before the Supreme Court under an amendment designed to remove the shackles of slavery from blacks. The irony was compounded by the butchers' choice of former justice John A. Campbell to argue their case. Campbell had resigned from the Supreme Court in 1861 to join the Confederate government; he returned to its chamber as a prominent corporation lawyer. The Confederate states had loudly opposed the Fourteenth Amendment; Campbell now waved it like a battle flag for the butchers. Like his rebel compatriots, Campbell lost this contest with the Union forces that controlled the Supreme Court. But he came close to victory, just one vote shy of success.

As they had in 1810, when they ignored evidence of corruption in the Yazoo land grants, the justices shut their noses to the stench of bribery in the *Slaughterhouse Cases*. The Court's majority, led by Justice Samuel Miller, upheld the New Orleans monopoly with reasoning that rejected the clear wording and intent of the Fourteenth Amendment. Its first clause, designed to reverse the *Dred Scott* decision and confer citizenship on blacks, stated that "all persons born or naturalized" in the United States "are citizens of the United States and of the state wherein they reside." This clause raised a serious constitutional question: Did Congress intend to eliminate the distinction between national and state citizenship on which Chief Justice Taney had based his *Dred Scott* opinion? Congressional debate on the Fourteenth Amendment in 1866 had focused largely on the "privileges and immunities" clause; the citizenship provision had been inserted near the end of debate, with little discussion. The whole context of the issue, however, indicated that Congress wanted to wipe out Taney's ruling and create one form of citizenship, and to provide citizens with rights protected against state infringement.

Justice Miller, however, ignored the debates of 1866 and turned the clock back to 1857. Restating Taney's position in *Dred Scott*, Miller stated that "the distinction between citizenship of the United States and citizenship of a state is clearly recognized and established" in the Fourteenth Amendment's first clause. He added that the two forms of citizenship provide each person with different sets of rights, one conferred by the state and the other by the Constitution. Miller based this dubious proposition on the Fourteenth Amendment's provision that states could not "abridge the privileges or immunities of citizens of the United States." This wording seemingly defined those rights in terms of national citizenship and limited them to constitutional guarantees. But the two clauses that followed this provision applied the guarantees of due process and equal protection to "any person," without distinction of citizenship.

With this semantic twist, Congress had unwittingly given Miller a tiny loophole, through which he wriggled with ease. "It is too clear for argument," he wrote, that states were not bound to provide their citizens with the same "privileges and immunities" they enjoyed as national citizens. Miller went on, in a significant paragraph, to list "the very few express limitations" imposed by the Constitution on the states. In fact, he found just three: "the prohibition against ex post facto laws, bills of attainder, and laws impairing the obligation of contracts." Even with the enforcement powers granted by Section 5 of the Fourteenth Amendment, Miller concluded, Congress could not go beyond these limitations to interfere with state "powers for domestic and local government, including the regulation of civil rights, the rights of person and of property," and all other powers not delegated to Congress. The Louisiana legislature, not Congress, had the power to regulate the livestock business and create a slaughterhouse company with monopoly control.

The Court's majority brushed aside the due process and equal protection claims that Campbell had raised for the butchers. Given the later importance of these clauses in constitutional law, this seems odd. But the Court had not yet embarked on its later search for the "substantive" content of these clauses, despite the claim of the *Slaughterhouse* dissenters that "following a lawful employment" was a "liberty" right protected by the Fourteenth Amendment against state deprivation. Justices Stephen Field and Joseph Bradley led the judicial charge against Miller's opinion. Although they both dissented, Field and Bradley wrote separately and stressed different points. Taking a close look at the citizenship clauses of the Fourteenth Amendment, Field could not see any distinction between national and state citizenship. "A citizen of a state is now only a citizen of the United States residing in that state," he wrote. Consequently, the "privileges and immunities" of any person "are not dependent upon his citizenship of any state." Field did not list all the federal rights he would protect from state regulation, but he singled out protection from legislative "grants of exclusive privileges" to corporate monopolies.

Justice Bradley, even more hostile than Field to governmental regulation of business and industry, looked at the Due Process and Equal Protection Clauses of the Fourteenth Amendment. "In my view, a law which prohibits a large class of citizens from adopting a lawful employment," he wrote, deprives them "of liberty as well as property, without due process of law." The right of citizens to choose an occupation "is a portion of their liberty; their occupation is their property." Under this double-barreled approach, members of the Butchers' Benevolent Association were shielded from both state and federal regulation.

Significantly, the four *Slaughterhouse* dissenters raised no objections to the paragraphs that Justice Miller added to his opinion on the powers of Congress, granted by Section V of the Fourteenth Amendment, to enforce its provisions "by appropriate legislation." This clause had no relevance to the Louisiana law before the Court, but Miller wanted to warn Congress to stay away from the business of civil rights enforcement. He chose his words carefully, looking ahead to cases that raised claims of discrimination by blacks, not by white butchers. "We doubt very much whether any action of a state not directed by way of discrimination against the negroes as a class, or on account of their race, will ever be held to come within the purview of this provision," Miller wrote. At first glance, this sentence allowed Congress to legislate against racial discrimination. A closer look, however, reveals its limitation to acts "of a state" that are "directed" against blacks. Discrimination that is "private" in nature did not fall within Miller's narrow reading of the Fourteenth Amendment. The Supreme Court still employs the "state action" doctrine that Miller proclaimed in his *Slaughterhouse* opinion to shield "private" acts of racial discrimination from federal prohibition or prosecution.

The Supreme Court decided the *Slaughterhouse Cases* just three weeks before Chief Justice Salmon Chase died on May 7, 1873. Although weakened by illness, Chase had joined the dissenters in this momentous case. His death gave President Grant a fourth opportunity to shape the Court during a period of political and economic turmoil. Southern resistance to Reconstruction was growing increasingly vocal and violent. And, once again, land speculation and bank failures led to economic disaster; the Panic of 1873 produced a four-year depression that cost three million workers their jobs and thousands of farmers their land. The Supreme Court would deal with these issues in dozens of cases, under the leadership of Morrison R. Waite of Ohio, an undistinguished lawyer who specialized in real estate law and had no judicial experience. Waite was actually Grant's seventh choice for Chief Justice; the prior six either declined nomination or withdrew in the face of Senate opposition. Ebenezer Hoar, Grant's first attorney general, wrote sardonically that Waite was "that luckiest of all individuals known to the law, an innocent third party without notice." Justice Stephen Field, who served under four Chief Justices, thought the least of Waite, whom he dismissed as "an experiment which no President has a right to make with our Court."

Salmon Chase and Morrison Waite had much in common: both were born in New England (New Hampshire and Connecticut); attended Ivy League colleges (Dartmouth and Yale); moved to Ohio as young lawyers and set up commercial and corporate practices; were Republican in politics; and were far down the lists of potential Chief Justices of the presidents who appointed them. Behind these similarities, which suggest common views on constitutional issues, the two men differed on the great issue of their time: the power of the federal government to enforce Reconstruction laws. Chase voted to uphold the Civil Rights Act of 1866 and the broad grant of enforcement power to Congress in the Thirteenth Amendment, and he dissented in 1867 from two decisions that struck down state and federal laws requiring former Confederates to swear loyalty to the Union as a condition of practicing law and other professions. Chief Justice Waite, however, showed little sympathy during his fourteen years in office for federal efforts to enforce voting rights and protect blacks from violence. Probably the worst opinion of the 967 he wrote for the Court was handed down in March 1876. Waite's opinion in *United States v. Cruickshank*, striking down the Enforcement Acts that were based on the Reconstruction amendments, illustrates his deliberate blindness to the murders of hundreds of black voters.

This case began in 1873 (ironically, the day before the Court issued its *Slaughterhouse* decision) with a real slaughter in Colfax, Louisiana, the county seat of Grant Parish. An election dispute between white Democrats and black Republicans escalated into violence and turned into "the bloodiest single instance of racial carnage in the Reconstruction era," wrote Eric Foner, that period's leading historian. Black voters who feared that whites planned to seize the county government gathered at the courthouse, digging trenches and drilling with shotguns. They were assembled by the local sheriff, a Republican, and deputized as a posse to protect county offices in Colfax. On Easter Sunday, after three weeks of sporadic gunfire, a band of whites armed with rifles and a cannon blasted the courthouse, set it ablaze, and massacred the blacks who poured out, waving a white flag of surrender. The death toll remains in dispute; Foner wrote that "some fifty blacks" died, while a black Louisiana legislator stated at the time that "when the sun went down that night, it went down on the corpses of two hundred and eighty negroes." Whatever the true number, there is no dispute that white racists had turned the Colfax courthouse into a human slaughterhouse.

The gunfire from the Colfax Massacre reverberated across the nation. In its wake, Foner reported, "an avalanche of heart-rending pleas for protection descended upon the South's Republican governors." But local officials did nothing to prosecute the attackers. Federal investigators, however, identified ninety-six men, who were indicted for violating the Ku Klux Klan Act of 1870. Of this group, only nine stood trial, and six were acquitted by jurors who heard conflicting testimony about their presence at the massacre. Presented with clear evidence of the participation of three men—William Cruikshank, John Hadnot, and William Irwin—the jurors convicted them of conspiring to prevent two black men—Levi Nelson and Alexander Tillman—from "the free exercise and enjoyment of the right to peaceably assemble" and depriving them of "life and liberty without due process of law," rights guaranteed by "the Constitution and laws of the United States." Nelson and Tillman had been killed at the Colfax courthouse, but federal officials could not prosecute Cruikshank and his fellow marauders for murder, because that was a state crime. Charging them with depriving Nelson and Tillman of their lives may seem to us like the same offense as murder, but not to the Supreme Court in 1876.

Chief Justice Waite wrote for a unanimous Court in reversing the convictions of Cruikshank and his fellow Colfax killers. In many ways, Waite's opinion rivaled that of Chief Justice Taney in *Dred Scott* in its deliberate misreading of law and history. The Reconstruction amendments had been adopted to reverse *Dred Scott*, but Waite seemed oblivious to this fact. In his *Cruikshank* opinion, Waite repeated Justice Miller's reliance in the *Slaughterhouse Cases* on Taney's distinction between national and state citizenship. And he reached back to Chief Justice Marshall's opinion in *Barron v. Baltimore*, decided in 1833, for the proposition that the Bill of Rights did not bind the states to their enforcement.

Waite began his opinion by searching the Ku Klux Klan Act for legal defects. Under the law, the rights "enjoyed" by Levi Nelson and Alexander Tillman and "hindered" by the Colfax conspirators must be among those "granted or secured by the constitution or laws of the United States." The Chief Justice never mentioned that the two black men had been murdered and could not "enjoy" any rights, or that Cruikshank had "hindered" them by joining in the massacre. He simply shut his eyes to these bloody facts. Waite cited *Slaughterhouse* for the dubious proposition that "the same person may be at the same time a citizen of the United States and a citizen of a State, but his rights of citizenship under one of these governments will be different from those he has under the other." Among the rights that Cruikshank had denied to Nelson and Tillman was that of peaceable assembly at the Colfax courthouse, a right guaranteed by the First Amendment. Waite saw two problems with this "right" as a basis for enforcing the Constitution. First, he read the amendment to require that those who "assemble" must gather "for the purpose of petitioning Congress for a redress of grievances." The First Amendment makes no such requirement; the rights of assembly and petition are distinct, and the amendment speaks broadly of "the Government," not just Congress. However, the last clause of the First Amendment is not a model of clarity, and Waite may have correctly parsed its meaning.

He was certainly incorrect, however, in reading its words to require that the blacks who assembled at the Colfax courthouse did not enjoy the protection of federal law unless they had gathered "for consultation in respect to public affairs." This was clearly one purpose of their assembly, considering the election dispute that brought them together. Waite simply ignored this obvious fact. "Such, however, is not the case," he stated with no reference to law or facts. This deliberate blindness allowed him to conclude that Nelson and Tillman had not gathered with other blacks to exercise any right guaranteed by the Constitution. Consequently, the Colfax conspirators had not "hindered" their "enjoyment" of the First Amendment. Waite's reading of the Constitution may strike us as tortured or even absurd, but he wrote for a Court that seemed determined to end Reconstruction by judicial fiat.

The second defect Waite found in the Ku Klux Klan Act was that federal law, as he read the Constitution, could not protect blacks in exercising their right to vote. He reached this conclusion by walking around the Fifteenth Amendment, which prohibits "any State" from denying "citizens of the United States" their right to vote "on account of race, color, or previous condition of servitude." It would be hard to deny that Nelson and Tillman, after their murders, were denied their right to vote "thereafter" in Louisiana elections, as Cruikshank's indictment charged. But the Chief Justice argued that "the right of suffrage is not a necessary attribute of national citizenship," and that states were only bound by the Fifteenth Amendment to protect voters against racial discrimination. Waite looked closely at the indictment and found that "it is nowhere alleged in these counts that the wrong contemplated against the rights of these citizens was on account of their race or color." The indictment did, in fact, charge that Cruikshank and his fellow conspirators had deprived persons "of African descent" of their constitutional rights. Were not Nelson and Tillman murdered "on account of" their race? The Chief Justice simply ignored this obvious fact.

Having denied that the Constitution protected the blacks who assembled in Colfax to defend their courthouse, Waite also denied that federal law could protect their "lives and liberty" from murderous conspiracies. He found this charge in the indictment "even more objectionable" than those based on rights to assemble and vote, on two grounds. First, he claimed, the power to bring prosecutions for murder "rests alone with the States." Waite ignored the fact that Congress had passed the Enforcement Acts because the southern states refused to protect blacks from terrorists like Cruikshank. His opinion reached previously unscaled heights of hypocrisy in quoting the Declaration of Independence for the proposition that the "very highest duty of the States" was to "protect all persons" in their enjoyment of the "unalienable rights with which they were endowed by their Creator." Louisiana had refused to protect Levi Nelson and Alexander Tillman, or to prosecute their killers. But it was "no more the duty or within the power of the United States" to step in when the states failed in their duty, Waite piously stated.

Waite's second ground for denying federal power to protect the "lives and liberty" of blacks rested on the Fourteenth Amendment's provision that prohibits "any State" from depriving "any person" of life or liberty without due process of law. This provision "adds nothing to the rights of one citizen as against another," Waite wrote. He applied the same reasoning to the charge that Nelson and Tillman had been denied the "equal protection of the laws" of Louisiana. Again, this provision of the Fourteenth Amendment added nothing "to the rights which one citizen has under the Constitution against another." Under this logic, the only legal remedy that Nelson or Tillman—actually, their families—had against Cruikshank was a private suit for damages for causing their "wrongful death." In recent years, the families of blacks murdered by white racists have sued the killers in state courts and won substantial damages. But in 1876, this form of legal recourse could not have prevailed in the climate of hostility toward blacks.

Chief Justice Waite's opinion in the *Cruikshank* case slammed every legal door in the face of federal officials who tried—and ultimately failed—to protect southern blacks against intimidation and violence. Not a single justice dissented from this ruling. By 1876, the Supreme Court—and most northern whites—had tired of Reconstruction battles and were ready to surrender to the former Confederates. The reaction of southern whites to Waite's opinion reflected their sense of impending victory. One prominent lawyer expressed his jubilation: "When the decision was reached and the prisoners released, there was the utmost joy in Louisiana, and with it a return of confidence which gave best hopes for the future." Needless to say, blacks across the South looked to the future with fear and foreboding.

17

"An Evil Eye and an

Unequal Hand"

The Union's military forces won the Civil War in 1865, but its political leaders surrendered that hard-won victory to the former Confederates over the next twelve years. The two men who succeeded Abraham Lincoln as president— Andrew Johnson and Ulysses Grant—followed appeasement policies that encouraged violent resistance to Reconstruction and weakened Republican resolve to protect the civil rights of the former slaves. Despite the presence of federal troops in southern states, the Ku Klux Klan and other groups that vowed to "redeem" the South were able to terrorize and murder blacks with virtual impunity. The Supreme Court's decision in *United States v. Cruikshank*, handed down in 1876, simply underscored the fact that no branch of the federal government would offer southern blacks any protection from the reign of terror that swept the region.

Well before the *Cruikshank* decision, southern "Redeemers" had backed up their fiery political rhetoric with guns and ropes. Intimidation and violence escalated as the 1874 elections neared. Blacks appealed vainly for protection from bands of armed whites, many of them former Confederate soldiers. "They are going around the streets at night dressed in soldiers clothes and making colored people run for their lives," black residents of Vicksburg, Mississippi, wrote to the Reconstruction governor. "We are intimidated by the whites. We will not vote at all, unless there are troops to protect us." A group of Mississippi whites attacked a gathering of black voters in Coahoma County and killed six. The black sheriff, who had been addressing the crowd, fled the area and never returned.

The tactics of terror succeeded. Blacks—and the dwindling number of southern white Republicans—stayed away from the polls in 1874 and Democrats won two thirds of the region's congressional seats, giving them control of the House, although Republicans still controlled the Senate. Before the new members took office, however, Republicans pushed the Civil Rights Act of 1875 through Congress, a law declaring "that all persons within the jurisdiction of the United States shall be entitled to the full and equal enjoyment of the accommodations" in restaurants, theaters, hotels, and railroads. Based on the enforcement clauses of the Thirteenth and Fourteenth Amendments, early drafts of this law would have required integration of public schools and provided federal enforcement of its provisions.

Before its final passage, the Civil Rights Act was weakened by compromises. Congress eliminated the school integration and federal enforcement provisions, turning the enforcement burden over to individual litigants. Since few blacks had the money to file suits under the law or the fortitude to pursue them in the courts, the new law proved virtually toothless. Even the bill's supporters expressed weariness and resignation. "Is it possible that you can find power in the Constitution to declare war . . . and pass laws upon all conceivable subjects," one House Republican challenged his reluctant colleagues, "but can find no power to protect American citizens . . . in the enjoyment and exercise of their constitutional rights?"

The Civil Rights Act of 1875 proved to be the last gasp of the exhausted and embittered remnant of Radical Republicans in Congress. By then, many had deserted their positions and waved the white flag of surrender. Just before House Republicans turned their chamber over to the Democrats, who thirsted for more power and vowed to end Reconstruction, Joseph Hawley of Connecticut spoke in words of resignation. "I have been a radical abolitionist from my earliest days," he said, but he now felt that "social, and educational, and moral reconstruction" in the South could "never come from any legislative halls."

Like sharks who smelled blood, Democrats looked forward to an election contest with President Grant, whose two administrations had suffered the cuts of many scandals. Grant longed to run for a third term, but most Republicans considered him a liability. The party's most popular leader, former House speaker James Blaine of Maine, lost his luster after press reports of his role in an Arkansas land scandal (long before the Whitewater problems of President Bill Clinton). The Republican convention in 1876 turned to Rutherford B. Hayes of Ohio, a man described by Henry Adams as a "third-rate nonentity." A graduate of Harvard Law School and a three-term governor, Hayes won the nomination and campaigned on a platform of civil service reform, an important issue but one that failed to excite the electorate. The party's platform completely ignored the issue of Reconstruction. Frederick Douglass, the former slave who feared a new enslavement of his people, challenged the Republican delegates: "Do you mean to make good to us the promises in your constitution?" The answer was silence.

Sensing victory, the Democrats united behind New York governor Samuel J. Tilden, one of the nation's richest men in a period that rewarded the "Captains of Industry" with enormous wealth. Tilden gained his fortune as legal counsel to railroad and banking magnates like Jim Fiske and Jay Gould, who rewarded him with stock for steering them around the shoals of bankruptcy. "He is connected with the moneyed men of the country," one supporter wrote. "That is exactly what we want."

Once again, southern Democrats did not shrink from violence in their search for votes. "Armed bands disrupted Republican meetings, whipped freedmen, and murdered local officials," wrote Eric Foner. To cite one bloody example, a white mob in Hamburg, South Carolina, attacked a Fourth of July gathering of black militiamen, capturing twenty-five as they fled. Matthew Butler, a former Confederate general and the area's Democratic leader, reportedly singled out five blacks for summary execution. After the Democrats won control of South Carolina's legislature, white legislators rewarded Butler with election to the United States Senate.

Considering the violence against black voters, the rift among Republicans, and the Wall Street money behind the Democrats, it was not surprising that Tilden won a majority of the popular vote, by some 300,000 over Hayes. In addition to the "solid South," Tilden carried the northern states of New York, New Jersey, Connecticut, and Indiana. But the embattled Republicans claimed victory in South Carolina, Florida, and Louisiana, states controlled by blacks and their white supporters. If the nineteen electoral votes from these states (plus one disputed vote from Oregon) went to Hayes, he would prevail in the electoral college by one vote. Without these votes, Hayes would lose to Tilden. The resolution of a great national issue rode on the outcome of this dispute.

Truthfully, the 1876 elections were a mess. Rival governments in the contested southern states presented Congress with rival slates of electors. For the first time since 1800—when the electors were evenly split between Thomas Jefferson and Aaron Burr—Congress faced a real dilemma. Ironically, the Constitution had been amended in 1804 to prevent just this problem. The Twelfth Amendment gave the House the power to choose a president if no candidate gained a majority in the electoral college. But this amendment did not address the question of disputed electors. It simply provided that the Senate's president shall "open all the certificates" and count the votes. "The person having the greatest number of votes for President," the amendment read, "shall be the President, if such number be a majority of the whole number of electors appointed."

Which candidate had the greatest number of electoral votes in 1876, Tilden or Hayes? Unable to decide the disputed claims, Congress turned the problem over to a blue-ribbon panel of fifteen members: five representatives, five senators, and five Supreme Court justices. The congressmen were divided equally by party, and the bill named four justices, two from each party. The final—and potentially decisive—vote would be cast by a fifth justice, chosen by the other four on the panel. Since only two Democrats sat on the Court at that time, it was certain that the fifth justice would be a Republican. But the expected choice, Justice David Davis, was considered by many to favor Tilden. Democrats in Illinois, however, damaged their party's cause before Davis was appointed by support-ing his election to the Senate, a choice made by the state legislature after the presidential election. Shortly after the Illinois lawmakers named Davis to the Senate, he resigned from the Court.

With Davis no longer available, the four justices on the election panel chose Justice Joseph Bradley, a highly partisan Republican, to join them. Predictably, Bradley voted with his party colleagues to award every disputed elector to Rutherford Hayes. Behind the scenes, Hayes had assured southern Democrats that he would look with "kind consideration" on their demands that Recon-struction end. Tilden's backers suspected that Illinois Republicans had made deals with "slow-witted" Democrats to remove Davis from the electoral com-mission. "We have been cheated, shamefully cheated," complained one Demo-crat. Those Republicans who supported Reconstruction knew they had lost. "I think the policy of the new administration will be to conciliate the white men of the South," one lamented. "Carpetbaggers to the rear, and niggers take care of yourself."

The outcome of the "Stolen Election of 1876" bears directly on the Supreme Court's reading of the Constitution over the next three decades. In a nutshell, the Court turned its back on the claims of blacks and opened its arms to those of corporations. In large measure, this was a direct result of judicial appoint-ments over the decade that followed the "election" of Rutherford Hayes. The new president had a seat to fill as soon as he took office in 1877, following the resignation of Justice Davis to join the Senate. Hayes paid an enormous politi-cal debt in nominating John Marshall Harlan of Kentucky. Born in 1833, Har-lan was named for the former Chief Justice, whom his father, a prominent lawyer, greatly admired. Like his namesake, Harlan came from a slave-owning family, had just a year of formal legal education, very little judicial experience, and great political ambition. He was admitted to the bar at the age of twenty, joined the Whig Party, and served as a county judge for one year, his only judi-cial post before his Supreme Court service. Harlan made an unsuccessful bid for Congress in 1859, served as Kentucky's attorney general from 1863 to 1867, and lost two races for governor on the Republican ticket in 1871 and 1875. During the 1876 presidential campaign, he played a key role at the Republican convention, swinging his state's delegates behind Hayes. Harlan's nomination to the Supreme Court was largely a political reward, but he was also an experi-enced and widely respected lawyer.

Before the Civil War, Harlan had voiced no opposition to slavery, but he supported the Union, organizing and leading a regiment until he resigned his commission in 1863 to take over the family law practice after his father died.

Harlan opposed ratification of the Thirteenth Amendment in 1865 as a violation of the property rights of slave owners. Harlan's views on race take on added significance in light of his solitary dissenting opinions in the *Civil Rights Cases* in 1883 and *Plessy v. Ferguson* in 1896, in which he supported the rights of blacks to enjoy public accommodations on an equal basis with whites. But these prophetic opinions, for which Harlan has been justly praised by historians, should be viewed in the context of his own history.

What is not widely recalled is that Harlan's firm belief in political equality for blacks was tempered by his equally firm rejection of their social equality with whites. On this issue, Harlan echoed the views and the words of Abraham Lincoln, whom he resembled in many ways. Both men agreed, as Harlan wrote, that "even upon grounds of race, no legal right of a citizen is violated by the refusal of others to maintain merely social relations with him." Harlan and Lincoln did not consider blacks to be their social equals. In this regard, they shared the views of most whites, even the most educated and enlightened. But their commitment to the legal and political equality of both races put Harlan and Lincoln at odds with those who considered blacks inferior in every respect. This was the contested ground on which Harlan and his colleagues fought their postwar battles.

President Hayes, who had pledged to serve just one term, made two more nominations to the Supreme Court. To replace the undistinguished Justice William Strong, who resigned in December 1880, Hayes nominated William B. Woods, an Ohio native who had moved to Alabama after the Civil War to serve as a "carpetbagger" on the federal circuit court. Like John Harlan, Woods served in the Union army and belonged to the Republican Party. Aside from those facts, the two men had nothing in common. During his six years on the Court, Woods voted consistently against the rights of blacks, and is justly considered a "forgotten justice," the epitaph bestowed by one biographer.

Before he left office in 1881, President Hayes nominated his Kenyon College classmate, Stanley Matthews of Ohio, to fill the seat of Justice Noah Swayne, who retired after nineteen years of undistinguished service. As a federal attorney, Matthews had prosecuted violators of the fugitive slave laws, but he later fought in the Union army. Elected to the Senate as a Republican, he served on the commission that placed Hayes in the White House. The Senate hardly ever rejected one of its own members for the Supreme Court, but Matthews was closely tied to railroad interests as chief counsel to Jay Gould, whose financial deals had ruined many investors. The Senate Judiciary Committee refused to act on the nomination, and Matthews was left to hang after Hayes left the White House.

President James Garfield, who replaced Hayes in 1881, surprised many by renominating Matthews. Garfield owed his debts to Jay Gould and the railroad lobby, and this was a small price to pay for political favors. After two months of heated debate, Matthews squeaked through the Senate by one vote. During his seven years on the Supreme Court, Matthews wrote only two significant opinions; one denied the protections of the Bill of Rights to criminal defendants, and one extended those protections to members of racial minorities. This legal ambivalence, which reflected his personal struggles, turned Matthews into the classic "man in the middle."

Garfield spent just six months in the White House before his death from a bullet fired by a disappointed office seeker. His unexpected and unprepared successor, Vice President Chester A. Arthur of New York, assumed his office with a reputation as a "spoilsman" who handed out political offices for the benefit of party coffers. To the surprise of many, President Arthur supported civil service reform in the federal government and added two respected lawyers—both with substantial judicial experience—to the Supreme Court. Arthur's first nomination, to replace Justice Nathan Clifford, whose death in 1881 came after several years of senility, gave the Court's "New England seat" to Horace Gray of Massachusetts. Gray had served for almost two decades on his state's highest court, including eight years as chief justice. An economic and social conservative, Gray served on the Supreme Court for twenty years and wrote only ten dissents; he flowed with the tide of his time, supporting corporate powers over human rights. President Arthur bestowed his second nomination on Samuel Blatchford to succeed his fellow New Yorker Ward Hunt, who retired in 1882. Blatchford was a loyal Republican and had served on federal courts for fifteen years; during his eleven years on the Supreme Court, he specialized in admiralty and patent law. He died in 1893, leaving no visible imprint on constitutional law.

Five Republican presidents left their marks on the Supreme Court during the two decades between Lincoln's nomination of Noah Swayne in 1862 and Arthur's choice of Samuel Blatchford in 1882. The fourteen men who joined the Court over this period include one—John Harlan—who was ranked with the "great" justices in a 1970 survey of legal scholars, and four—Samuel Miller, Stephen Field, Joseph Bradley, and Morrison Waite—ranked in the "near great" category. (Waite's ranking owed more to his longevity and position as Chief Justice than to his legal abilities or judicial leadership.) But with the exception of Harlan, none of these five (or the other nine) displayed much sympathy for the constitutional claims of blacks. As Reconstruction faltered and finally died, one southern editor boasted that the Fourteenth and Fifteenth Amendments "may stand forever; but we intend . . . to make them dead letters on the statute-book." The Supreme Court did the job for the unrepentant South.

The Court imposed a judicial death sentence on the Civil Rights Act of 1875 eight years after its passage. Under the caption *Civil Rights Cases*, the justices decided four cases from Kansas, California, Tennessee, and Missouri. The dry legal wording of the federal indictments in these disparate cases illustrates the humiliation that black citizens endured every day, north and south and across the continent; these musty records put human faces on cases decided without names.

In Topeka, Kansas (the home of Linda Brown of the celebrated *Brown* case in 1954), "on the tenth day of October, in the year of our Lord one thousand eight hundred and seventy-five, one Murray Stanley, having management and control of a certain inn, did unlawfully deny to one Bird Gee the full enjoyment of the accommodations of said inn by denying to said Bird Gee the privilege of partaking of a meal, to wit, of a supper, at the table of said inn, for the reason that he, the said Bird Gee, was a person of color and of the African race, and for no other reason whatever, contrary to the act of Congress, and against the peace and dignity of the United States of America."

The California indictment charged that "on the 4th day of January, A.D. 1876, Michael Ryan did unlawfully deny to George M. Tyler, the full enjoyment of accommodations of Maguire's Theatre in the city of San Francisco, as follows, that the said George M. Tyler did purchase a ticket of admission, for the sum of one dollar, to the orchestra seats, and said orchestra seats did possess superior advantages to any other portion of said theatre, and that the said Michael Ryan, who was the ticket-taker of said theatre, did then and there, by force and arms, deny to said George M. Tyler, admission to said theatre, solely for the reason that said George M. Tyler was and is of the African or negro race, being what is commonly called a colored man, and not a white man."

The third indictment charged the Memphis & Charleston Railroad Company with discriminating against Sallie J. Robinson, stating that "on the 22nd of May, 1879, Mrs. Robinson, wishing to be carried from Grand Junction, Tennessee, to Lynchburg, Virginia, purchased tickets entitling her to be carried as a first-class passenger over the defendant's railway, and that being so entitled Mrs. Robinson got upon defendant's train of cars at Grand Junction, Tennessee, and attempted to go into the ladies' car, being the car provided for ladies and first-class passengers, when the conductor of the train refused to admit her into the car, and that in so refusing her admission the conductor took Mrs. Robinson by the arm and jerked her roughly around, wherefore she was damaged $500, and therefore the plaintiff sues."

The final indictment, printed without dates, alleged that in St. Louis, Missouri, "one Samuel Nichols was the proprietor of a certain common inn called the Nichols House, for the accommodation of travelers and the general public, that one W. H. R. Agee, was an applicant to the said Samuel Nichols for the accommodations of said inn as a guest therein, but the said Samuel Nichols did deny to the said W. H. R. Agee admission as a guest in said inn, for the sole reason that the said W. H. R. Agee, was a person of color and one of the Negro race."

The Supreme Court decided the *Civil Rights Cases* on October 15, 1883, with an opinion by Justice Joseph Bradley (whose deciding vote had elected Rutherford Hayes as president in 1877). During the intervening six years, Bradley had compiled a mixed record in cases that dealt with the rights of blacks. In 1880, he voted to nullify a West Virginia law that restricted jury duty to whites: the Court declared that the Fourteenth Amendment's Equal Protection Clause was designed "to protect an emancipated race and to strike down all possible legal discriminations" against blacks. The same year, Bradley joined a decision that rejected a habeas corpus petition by a Virginia judge who had been indicted and held in federal custody for excluding blacks from jury duty. These cases involved what the Court called "political rights," those which stemmed from the essential duties of citizenship, as distinguished from "civil rights," defined as those which protect equal access to public facilities. But only in the jury cases did Bradley vote to strike down state laws or practices that singled out blacks for discrimination. In a case decided in 1883, before the *Civil Rights Cases* reached the Court, Bradley voted to invalidate the section of the Ku Klux Klan Act of 1870 that the Court had read so narrowly in its *Cruikshank* decision in 1876. The Court's decision in the Klan case, *United States v. Harris*, slammed the door on federal protection of blacks against terrorist attacks.

Justice Bradley's opinion in the *Civil Rights Cases* slammed more doors in black faces, those of restaurants, hotels, theaters, and railroads. Congressional sponsors of the Civil Rights Act had relied on the enforcement clauses of both the Thirteenth and Fourteenth Amendments; Bradley knocked down both of the law's constitutional supports. In dealing with the Thirteenth Amendment, he offered two statements of its purpose. The amendment, he first wrote, "has only to do with slavery and its incidents." Bradley then posed a rhetorical question. Did the refusal of proprietors of "public accommodations" to admit or serve blacks, he asked, "inflict upon such persons any manner of servitude, or form of slavery, as those terms are understood in this country?" This question had an easy answer. "The Thirteenth Amendment," Bradley responded, "has respect, not to distinctions of race, or class, or color, but to slavery."

The answer to Bradley's question was not as simple as it seemed to him. His first statement of the amendment's purpose included not only the prohibition of slavery but also of "its incidents." Bradley did not invent this term; it came from the speeches of the amendment's congressional sponsors, who defined the "incidents" of slavery as laws or practices designed to keep blacks in subjugation to whites. Racial discrimination in public accommodations could well be considered an "incident" of slavery. Almost a century later, in 1968, the Supreme Court ruled that Congress had power under the Thirteenth Amendment to outlaw housing discrimination as an "incident" of slavery. But in 1886, Justice Bradley ignored this qualifying term in his strictly literal reading of the Thirteenth Amendment.

Bradley treated the Fourteenth Amendment in a similar manner. He first conceded that, unlike the Thirteenth Amendment, the Fourteenth "extends its protections to races and classes, and prohibits any State legislation which has the effect of denying to any race or class, or to any individual, the equal protection of the laws." Bradley then posed another rhetorical question. "Can the act of a mere individual, the owner of the inn, the public conveyance or place of amusement," he asked, be regulated by Congress unless "the denial of the right has some State sanction or authority?" Once again, Bradley had framed a question to provide an easy answer. Although "the laws of all the states, so far as we are aware," he wrote, required the proprietors of public accommodations to serve "all unobjectionable persons who in good faith apply for them," unless "the laws themselves make any unjust discrimination" on racial grounds, the Fourteenth Amendment provided no power to prohibit such discrimination. In other words, Congress could only deal with "state action" that denied blacks the equal protection of the laws.

Having dismissed the claims of Bird Gee, George Tyler, Sallie Robinson, and W. H. R. Agee, Justice Bradley concluded his opinion with a patronizing lecture to them and all other black citizens. "When a man has emerged from slavery," he wrote, "and with the aid of beneficent legislation has shaken off the inseparable concomitants of that state, there must be some stage in the progress of his elevation when he takes the rank of a mere citizen, and ceases to be a special favorite of the laws, and when his rights as a citizen, or a man, are to be protected in the ordinary modes by which other men's rights are protected." This one sentence summed up the racial attitudes of "enlightened" whites—like Bradley—who paid no heed to the hooded night riders whose whips and ropes had become the "ordinary modes" of enforcing the Jim Crow laws that southern lawmakers passed after the Supreme Court struck down the federal Civil Rights Act.

Only one justice took issue with Bradley's constitutional literalism and condescending tone. "The opinion in these cases proceeds," wrote John Marshall Harlan, "upon grounds entirely too narrow and artificial." He devoted most of his thirty-five-page dissent to Bradley's dismissal, in just four pages, of the Fourteenth Amendment claims in the *Civil Rights Cases*. Congress had intended, Harlan noted, to wipe out all discrimination against blacks and "to secure and protect rights belonging to them as freemen and citizens; nothing more." He took aim at Bradley's formalistic distinction between "state action" and private discrimination. "In every material sense applicable to the practical enforcement of the Fourteenth Amendment," he wrote, "railroad corporations, keepers of inns, and managers of places of public amusement are agents or instrumentalities of the State, because they are charged with duties to the public, and are amenable, in respect of their duties and functions, to governmental regulation."

On that issue, Harlan relied on the common-law principle that "when private property is devoted to a public use, it is subject to public regulation," as the Court had stated in an 1877 opinion by Chief Justice Waite, upholding state regulation of fees charged by owners of grain elevators. Harlan saw no legal difference between grain elevators, railroads, and restaurants. All served the public and all were subject to regulation. Bradley had conceded that owners of "public accommodations" were required to serve "all unobjectionable persons who in good faith apply for them." How, then, could those owners refuse service on the basis of race or color? Bradley's invocation of the "state action" doctrine to answer this question seemed "artificial" to Harlan.

One paragraph in Harlan's dissent drew little notice at the time, but proved an accurate prophecy of the Court's later ruling on the "public accommodations" provisions of the Civil Rights Act of 1964, in which Congress used language virtually identical to the statute the Court struck down in 1883. Addressing the case of Sallie Robinson against the Memphis & Charleston Railroad, Harlan raised "the question whether Congress, in the exercise of its power to regulate commerce amongst the several states," could prohibit discrimination "in public conveyances passing from one State to another." He suggested that the Court could have upheld the 1875 law, at least in Mrs. Robinson's case, under the Commerce Clause of the Constitution. His fellow justices did not heed Harlan's suggestion, but in 1964 the Court relied on the Commerce Clause in *Heart of Atlanta Motel v. United States*, upholding the power of Congress to outlaw discrimination in hotels and motels that attracted guests from other states. The Court later expanded this ruling to cover every kind of "public accommodation," even those as small and local as barber shops.

Harlan concluded with a swipe at Bradley's patronizing lecture to blacks. "It is," he wrote, "scarcely just to say that the colored race has been the special favorite of the laws. The statute of 1875, now adjudged to be unconstitutional, is for the benefit of citizens of every race and color." He reminded his colleagues—and the nation—that "class tyranny" could be imposed by any group that controlled power. "Today, it is the colored race which is denied, by corporations and individuals wielding public authority, rights fundamental in their freedom and citizenship," Harlan wrote. "At some future time, it may be that some other race will fall under the ban of race discrimination."

Harlan's warning fell on deaf ears. Editorial reaction to the *Civil Rights Cases* lauded the ruling. *The Independent*, a leading journal, stated that "the Court is clearly right. The question as to the class of rights involved belongs exclusively to the States." *Harper's Weekly* called the decision "another illustration of the singular wisdom of our constitutional system." The *New York Times* was equally pleased. "The Court has been serving a useful purpose in thus undoing the work of Congress," its editors wrote.

Justice Harlan was right; another race did "fall under the ban of race discrimination" and appealed to the Court for protection. This time, the race was Oriental, and the discrimination fell on Chinese laundrymen in San Francisco. And this time, in 1886, the Court struck down a law because it violated the Equal Protection Clause of the Fourteenth Amendment. Perhaps his colleagues had read Harlan's dissent in the *Civil Rights Cases* and found it convincing. A more likely explanation for the Court's ruling in *Yick Wo v. Hopkins* is that there was clearly "state action" behind the discrimination, and no good reason for treating Chinese laundrymen differently from their Caucasian competitors.

Who *was* Yick Wo, and how did his case wind up in the Supreme Court? The record is sparse, because most documents in the case were burned in the fires that followed the San Francisco earthquake of 1906. We do know that Yick Wo was born in China, came to California in 1861, and operated a laundry in downtown San Francisco until the city's fire marshal (a man named Hopkins) denied his application to renew his license in 1885. Five years earlier, the city's board of supervisors had passed an ordinance making it unlawful to operate a laundry "without having first obtained the consent of the board of supervisors," unless the laundry "be located in a building constructed either of brick or stone." Of some 320 laundries in San Francisco, only ten were housed in brick or stone structures. The rest were in wooden buildings, subject to the licensing power of Fire Marshal Hopkins.

More than two hundred Chinese laundrymen, including Yick Wo, applied to Hopkins for licenses, which required a prior safety inspection. Hopkins turned down every Chinese applicant, but he granted licenses to all but one of eighty Caucasians; the sole exception was Mary Meagles. (Because almost every non-Chinese laundry operator was either French or Belgian, we can speculate that Mrs. Meagles was handicapped by either her gender or her Irish name). At any rate, Yick Wo and another Chinese laundryman, Wo Lee, refused to obey the order to close down their laundries and wound up in jail, unwilling to pay their fines after being convicted of violating the city ordinance.

Justice Stanley Matthews, who attracted little notice during his eight-year tenure, wrote for a unanimous Court in the *Yick Wo* case. Reviewing the record, Matthews found that "the ordinances in actual operation" showed their application to Chinese laundrymen "with a mind so unequal and oppressive as to amount to a practical denial" of the "broad and benign provisions" of the Fourteenth Amendment. "Though the law itself be fair on its face and impartial in appearance," he continued, "if it is applied and administered by public authority with an evil eye and an unequal hand, so as practically to make unjust and illegal discriminations between persons in similar circumstances, material to their rights, the denial of equal justice is still within the prohibition of the Constitution."

Unlike the *Civil Rights Cases*, the *Yick Wo* decision passed almost without notice; the Court's most noted historian, Charles Warren of Harvard, relegated the case to a footnote in his two-volume tome. The facts of the case suggest some reasons for its obscurity. Unlike blacks, who numbered some five million at the time, fewer than 100,000 Chinese lived in the United States, the vast majority in California. The institution of slavery had provoked a bloody Civil War, while the Chinese—although feared and hated by many Californians—were ignored by most people outside the West Coast. And the Supreme Court disposed of the case without dissent, slapping the hands of San Francisco officials but not striking down any federal statutes.

The *Yick Wo* decision stands out as an exception to the Court's narrow reading of the Fourteenth Amendment in the last decades of the nineteenth century. It could have—and should have—served as "controlling" precedent in later discrimination cases, such as *Plessy v. Ferguson*, second only to *Dred Scott* in Supreme Court infamy. But *Yick Wo* flashed for a moment, like a shooting star, and quickly disappeared from sight.

As the Civil War faded from memory, and with the demise of Reconstruction in 1877, the white population outside the South turned its attention from the plight of blacks to the delights of prosperity, fueled by the rapid growth of industry. John D. Rockefeller, who started as a bookkeeper in Cleveland, formed the Standard Oil Company of Ohio in 1870; by the century's end, his fortune exceeded $200 million. Andrew Carnegie, a telegraph clerk at seventeen, built his first steel plant in 1872 and sold the U.S. Steel Corporation to J. P. Morgan in 1900 for $492 million. The first railroad to link the East and West was completed in 1869; by the 1890s, a vast network of railroads—largely controlled by J. P. Morgan—shipped goods and carried passengers to every state. More than a million immigrants streamed through American ports every year and spread across the country, filling jobs in factories, mines, forests, and farms. This rapid growth exacted a heavy toll from the workers who labored for long hours and little pay; in 1889, 22,000 railroad workers were killed or injured. Other workers— whose language or color stirred up prejudice—paid for their jobs with their lives; in 1885 a mob of whites attacked five hundred Chinese miners in Rock Springs, Wyoming, killing twenty-eight and chasing the rest out of town.

Beginning with the election of Grover Cleveland in 1884, Democrats and Republicans traded the presidency every four years until the nineteenth century ended. The issue of race faded from national politics—although it dominated political campaigns in the South—and presidential elections turned on economic issues. Not surprisingly, Supreme Court nominations during the "Gilded Age" in American history went to men, regardless of party, whose legal experience and judicial philosophy favored the interests of business and industry. Cleveland, the first Democrat in the White House since the Civil War, named two justices during his first presidential term, which began in 1885. His first appointment, after the death of Justice William Woods in 1887, went to Lucius Q. C. Lamar of Mississippi, a Confederate colonel who later served in the federal Congress and in Cleveland's cabinet as interior secretary. Lamar served on the

Court for just five years after his narrow confirmation in 1888; although John F. Kennedy included Lamar in his book, *Profiles in Courage*, he displayed little courage on the bench, voting consistently against the rights of blacks.

Two months after Lamar's confirmation, Chief Justice Morrison Waite died after fourteen years of service. Cleveland considered several candidates, and finally chose a lawyer described by one newspaper as "the most obscure man ever nominated as Chief Justice." Melville Fuller, whose formal legal education consisted of six months at Harvard Law School, had been an active Democrat in Illinois; he supported Stephen Douglas over Abraham Lincoln for senator and president, he backed a state constitutional amendment to deny voting rights to blacks, and he denounced President Lincoln's Emancipation Proclamation. His busy and lucrative practice in Chicago served business clients, and he was a close friend of President Cleveland. The Senate confirmed Fuller in 1888 by a vote of forty-one to twenty, over the objections of Republicans who questioned his Civil War loyalties. During his twenty-two years as Chief Justice, the longest tenure after Marshall and Taney, Fuller's loyalty to corporate interests was never questioned. As one biographer noted, "the Fuller Court would go down in history as the incarnation of free enterprise, of the equation of laissez-faire with constitutionally protected rights."

Grover Cleveland won election in 1884 by the razor-thin margin of 23,000 votes; four years later he defeated Republican Benjamin Harrison by 100,000 votes (out of eleven million ballots), but lost the presidency by sixty-five electoral votes. An Indiana lawyer, Union army general, and former congressman, Harrison served one undistinguished term before Cleveland wrested his job back in 1892. Cautious and conservative, Harrison added four men to the Supreme Court, all conservative corporate lawyers. His first nomination, to replace Justice Stanley Matthews in 1889, went to David Brewer of Kansas, who represented railroad and banking clients before serving on state and federal courts for nineteen years. Brewer joined his uncle, Stephen Field, on the bench and "became the leader of the ultraconservative economic laissez-faire advocates on the Court," wrote one biographer. He told the Yale graduates of 1891 that the principles of "absolute and eternal justice forbid that any private property" could be "destroyed in the interests of public health, morals, or welfare." Brewer was saying that the "police powers" of government to protect the people were subservient to the powers of those who controlled property. He assured his privileged audience that "the love of acquirement, mingled with the joy of possession, is the real stimulus to human activity." No justice ever penned a greater ode to economic avarice.

Justice Samuel Miller died in 1890, after twenty-eight years on the Court, and President Harrison replaced him with Henry B. Brown, a prominent corporate lawyer in Detroit who then served on the federal district bench. Although he proved to be slightly less supportive of laissez-faire doctrine than Brewer,

Brown's fifteen years of service were marked by many "routine" opinions and one, in *Plessy v. Ferguson*, that was anything but routine. One friendly biographer described Brown as "intelligent, expertly trained, hardworking, and pleasant," words that could equally describe many of the men who owned slaves before the Civil War and enacted Jim Crow laws after Reconstruction ended. A more critical scholar noted that Brown's *Plessy* decision "reflected the era's racial, social, and legal assumptions" that blacks were inferior to whites. He was, in sum, a typical lawyer of his time.

When another longtime justice, Joseph Bradley, died in 1892 after twenty-two years on the Court, Harrison replaced him with George Shiras, Jr., a Pennsylvania lawyer who represented coal, oil, railroad, iron and steel, and banking interests. Andrew Carnegie urged Harrison to appoint Shiras, who served for eleven years and "could normally be counted aboard the laissez-faire bandwagon of the times." Harrison's final nomination placed Howell Jackson of Tennessee in the Court's "Southern seat," vacated by Lucius Q. C. Lamar, who died in 1892 after five years on the bench. A former Confederate official and corporate lawyer, Jackson died of tuberculosis in 1895, after less than three years on the Court. During his brief service, Jackson broke with his conservative brethren in just one major case, voting three months before his death to uphold a federal income tax; the majority opinion in this case was overturned in 1913 by the Sixteenth Amendment.

The roster of corporate lawyers on the Court continued to grow after Grover Cleveland returned to the White House in 1893 for a second term. Four months after his inauguration, Justice Samuel Blatchford died, and Cleveland twice attempted to fill the Court's "New York seat" with conservative New Yorkers. However, the state's senior senator was feuding with the president over patronage jobs and blocked both nominees. Cleveland responded by depriving New York of its traditional seat and choosing Senator Edward D. White of Louisiana, a Confederate veteran and the first Roman Catholic on the Court since Roger Taney. A successful business lawyer in New Orleans, and briefly a state supreme court judge before his Senate election, White served on the Court for twenty-seven years, the last ten as Chief Justice. White's tenure on the Court spanned three decades of vocal and often violent conflict—over Jim Crow laws, union organizing, child labor, antitrust regulation, and wartime protest. In virtually every case, he voted for states' rights over federal power, business over workers, economic concentration over competition, and repression of dissent over free expression. Any "assessment of the rightness or wrongness of his opinions," one scholar observed, "will probably depend on the views of the observer." But those who assess White's opinions can easily see where he stood on the great issues of his time.

With the death of Howell Jackson in 1895, President Cleveland got the chance to choose one more justice. Twice rebuffed in filling the "New York seat," he turned to that state once more and selected Rufus Peckham, a corporate lawyer who advised such tycoons as Cornelius Vanderbilt, John D. Rockefeller, and Pierpont Morgan. Peckham "would not disappoint them during the fourteen years he served on the Supreme Court," said one biographer. He wrote his most noted (and notorious) opinion in 1905 in *Lochner v. New York*, a case testing a state law that limited the working hours of bakers to ten each day and sixty for a week. Peckham fit in perfectly with the Court's laissez-faire majority; during his fourteen-year tenure, he wrote 303 opinions and dissented in only nine cases.

Presidents Cleveland and Harrison each placed four men on the Supreme Court; most left no mark on constitutional law, and one—Henry Brown—left an enduring stain in the *Plessy* case. Scholars later ranked seven of this group as "average" justices and one—Edward White—as "near great." White came that close to the judicial pantheon more because of his lengthy tenure than the quality of his opinions. These justices were not thoroughbreds; they were draft horses, turning out some two hundred opinions every year, most of which dealt with disputes over money. But money was more important to most people, during this period of growing prosperity, than "parchment" rights the Court did not even recognize.

18

"Our Constitution Is

Color-Blind"

As the nineteenth century neared its end, the "Gilded Age" became tarnished by labor strife and economic depression. The virtual identity of the two major parties on most issues vanished, as Republicans embraced corporate values and Democrats absorbed the "populist" movement that railed against the bankers and railroad tycoons who controlled the economy. American politics became more and more divisive as the elections of 1896 approached. Grover Cleveland and Benjamin Harrison, who fought their election campaigns with kid gloves, both retired from politics and turned their parties over to more combative candidates.

The Republican candidate in 1896, William McKinley of Ohio, campaigned on a platform of "hard money" at home and hard talk abroad. Insurgent movements against Spanish rule in Cuba and the Philippines spurred demands for military intervention to expand the "American empire" around the globe. "We want a foreign market for our surplus products," McKinley stated. His Democratic opponent, William Jennings Bryan of Nebraska, also ran on the Populist Party ticket; he accused Republicans of nailing workers and farmers to a "cross of gold" and advocated the use of silver to back the currency. Bryan also opposed American "imperialism" and annexation campaigns. Aided by the highest voter turnout of the century (and massive corporate donations), McKinley defeated Bryan and began sixteen years of Republican rule. With Congress, the White House, and the Supreme Court under firm corporate control, groups like blacks, workers, and women had little voice in government. As hardship mounted, grassroots protest movements turned from electoral politics to direct action. Strikes, marches, and even bombs rattled the nerves of those with power and property. Amid this growing strife, the Court remained a bastion of conservatism, earning this banquet toast from a New York banker in 1895: "I give you, gentlemen, the Supreme Court of the United States—guardian of the dollar, defender of private property, enemy of spoliation, sheet anchor of the Republic." The Court was eager to strike down—as violations of the Fourteenth Amendment—laws that interfered with the "liberty" of businessmen to dictate the wages, hours, and working conditions of their employees. But the justices were not eager to provide the same "liberty" rights to ordinary people, especially blacks.

Confronted with mounting legal challenges to the "Jim Crow" laws that southern lawmakers had passed in the 1890s to enforce racial segregation, the Supreme Court decided the most important of these cases in *Plessy v. Ferguson*, which arrived in Washington after a four-year journey from Louisiana. The case began on June 7, 1892, when Homer Adolph Plessy entered the New Orleans station of the East Louisiana Railway and bought a first-class ticket to Covington, Louisiana, a trip of about fifty miles around Lake Pontchartrain. Most passengers wanted to arrive at their destination for pleasure or business. Plessy, however, took no pleasure in his trip and had no particular business in Covington. What he wanted—and expected—was to be arrested for violating the 1890 state law requiring that "no person or persons shall be permitted to occupy seats in coaches, other than the ones assigned to them on account of the race they belong to." The law required that railroads provide "equal but separate" facilities for those of different races; however, it did not define "race" and left to conductors the job of assigning passengers to the proper cars.

Plessy had almost certainly arranged his arrest before he bought his ticket, although perhaps not the way it was carried out. According to the Supreme Court's later statement of facts, Plessy "entered a passenger train, and took possession of a vacant seat in a coach where passengers of the white race were accommodated." The conductor then ordered him "to vacate said coach" and move to one "for persons not of the white race." When Plessy refused to move, "he was, with the aid of a police officer, forcibly ejected from said coach and hurried off to and imprisoned in the parish jail of New Orleans." His stay in jail was brief, and Plessy was released after arraignment in the local recorder's court.

We can gain much insight into America's racial history by bridging the gap between Homer Plessy and a later civil rights pioneer, Rosa Parks. On December 1, 1955, she boarded a city bus in Montgomery, Alabama, and took a seat in the row just behind one occupied by white passengers. Every seat on the bus was full when a white man boarded and stood in the aisle. The driver then ordered the blacks in the first row behind the whites to stand up and move back. Three black passengers complied, but Rosa Parks remained seated and refused to move. A seamstress by trade, she later explained why she refused the driver's order to move: "I was quite tired after spending a full day working. I handle and work on clothing that white people wear. It just happened that the driver made a demand and I just didn't feel like obeying his demand. He called a policeman and I was arrested and placed in jail." Her arrest sparked the Montgomery bus boycott and thrust its young leader, the Rev. Martin Luther King, Jr., into national prominence. A year later, the Supreme Court struck down bus segregation in Montgomery.

Separated by more than six decades, Homer Plessy and Rosa Parks shared an important connection. Whatever their personal motives for refusing to change seats, both had affiliations with civil rights groups that supported challenges to Jim Crow laws. Plessy was a friend of Rodolphe Desdunes, a leader of the American Citizens' Equal Rights Association in New Orleans and a prominent figure in the city's Creole community. Desdunes also helped to organize a "Citizens' Committee to Test the Constitutionality of the Separate Car Law," and most likely he recruited Plessy to challenge the law. Rosa Parks had been an active member and secretary of the Montgomery chapter of the National Association for the Advancement of Colored People; in fact, she sent King the letter appointing him to the chapter's executive board. It is likely that Rosa Parks understood—or even welcomed—the probable reaction to her act. She later said that "this is what I wanted to know: when and how could we ever determine our rights as human beings?"

We know a great deal about Rosa Parks, who has been honored many times since her act of defiance, but we know very little about Homer Plessy, not even his occupation. He made no statements and gave no interviews to reporters. He died in 1925 at the age of sixty-three; his cemetery headstone makes no reference to his place in history. Despite his personal obscurity, Plessy deserves recognition because his case represented one of the first examples of "interest group" litigation, in which organizations like the New Orleans citizens' committee bring "test cases" to expand—or defend—the constitutional rights of their members and constituents. Since the *Plessy* case, the NAACP, founded in 1909 by blacks and sympathetic whites, and another important organization, the American Civil Liberties Union, formed in 1920, have brought more Bill of Rights cases before the Supreme Court than all other groups combined. Many of these cases are carefully planned and prepared; others result from impulsive acts, like refusing to move from a bus seat or burning an American flag. Some clients are sympathetic and others are just pathetic. One famous ACLU client, Ernesto Miranda, was a rapist and kidnapper whose Supreme Court case, *Miranda v. Arizona* in 1966, established the "right to remain silent" under police interrogation. But whether saints or sinners, these "test case" clients allow their sponsors to bring constitutional issues before the courts; it takes real people with an actual "case or controversy" to begin the legal journey to the Supreme Court.

Similar in many ways, Homer Plessy and Rosa Parks differed in one visible characteristic. The bus driver in Montgomery ordered Parks to move because she was clearly black. Plessy, in contrast, had to arrange his arrest because he looked white and "passed" the color line in the racial gumbo of New Orleans. He was an "octoroon," the word then used to describe people with seven white great-grandparents and one (most often a female slave) who was black. His name suggests that Plessy was a Creole of French ancestry; most of the men who founded the citizens' committee in New Orleans—like Rodolphe Desdunes—had "roots" going back to French control of Louisiana. The legal papers filed in Plessy's case noted that "the mixture of colored blood was not discernible in him." If he could "pass" for white, why did Plessy court arrest to challenge the Jim Crow law? The answer is not certain, but it might reflect the "marginal" status of Creoles in New Orleans. They were "almost" white, but under state law they had no more rights than the darkest black. Even in the same family, some could pass and others could not. Those with darker skin certainly resented their segregation from whites, but people like Plessy must have felt more anxious when they boarded a "white" railroad car and came under the conductor's gaze.

Louis Martinet, a prominent Creole physician and lawyer, joined Rodolphe Desdunes as the guiding force behind the *Plessy* case. Shortly after the Louisiana legislature passed the "separate cars" law in 1890, Martinet launched a campaign in his column in the *New Orleans Crusader*. "We'll make a case," he wrote, "a test case, and bring it before the Federal Court on the ground of the invasion of the right of a person to travel through the States unmolested." It took Martinet almost two years to find a good test case; one problem was that most Louisiana railroads did not support the Jim Crow law, which cost them money for separate cars. Officials of two railroads told Martinet that "the law was a bad and mean one; they would like us to get rid of it."

Even before Desdunes recruited Homer Plessy for the test case and arranged with the East Louisiana Railway to have him arrested, Martinet had recruited the nation's leading civil rights lawyer to handle the court battle. Albion W. Tourgee of New York was a former Union army officer who moved to North Carolina during Reconstruction; he helped to write its radical constitution and served as a state judge for six years. After the white "Redeemers" took control in 1877, Tourgee returned to New York and became—in his biographer's words—"the most vocal, militant, persistent, and widely heard advocate of racial equality in the United States, black or white." He agreed to represent Plessy without fee (what we now call "pro bono" work). Because Tourgee did not belong to the Louisiana bar, Martinet hired a local white attorney, James C. Walker, to assist him for a fee of $1,000.

The case of *State v. Plessy* began slowly on its journey through the lower courts. Louis Martinet had first planned to ask a federal judge to rule that the "separate cars" law interfered with interstate travel and violated the Commerce Clause of the Constitution. But a federal court had recently held that Louisiana railroads could not segregate passengers who held tickets for travel across state lines. That decision, although favorable to blacks, forced the *Plessy* case into state court. In July 1892, Assistant District Attorney Lionel Adams formally charged Plessy with violating the Jim Crow law, and in October he appeared before Judge John H. Ferguson in the criminal district court of New Orleans.

Normally, judges ask criminal defendants at arraignments to enter pleas of "guilty" or "not guilty" and set trial dates for those in the latter group. Homer Plessy, however, did not make a plea. His lawyers filed a lengthy document with Judge Ferguson, asking him to dismiss the charges on the grounds that the state law violated the Thirteenth and Fourteenth Amendments. Ferguson heard several hours of oral argument on October 28, 1892. Albion Tourgee and James Walker claimed that the law imposed a "badge of servitude" on Plessy and deprived him of the "privileges and immunities" of citizenship. Lionel Adams defended the law as a "reasonable" exercise of the state's "police powers" to protect the public health, safety, welfare, and morals. Just which of these four powers he relied on is unclear, but Adams did claim that "the foul odors of blacks in close quarters" made the law reasonable. The record does not show that he presented any evidence for this claim, or mentioned that most blacks lived in homes without bathtubs (or even running water) and labored for long hours in hot, humid weather.

Judge Ferguson issued his ruling on November 18, 1892. Not surprisingly, he denied Plessy's constitutional challenge, citing the Supreme Court decisions in the *Slaughterhouse Cases* of 1873 and the *Civil Rights Cases* of 1883. Tourgee and Walker had originally planned to appeal Ferguson's decision—which they fully expected—to the federal court in New Orleans, but they abruptly shifted course and took the case to the Louisiana supreme court. Most likely, they decided that waiting for decisions in two lower federal courts would delay their case longer than one stop in state court. Chief Justice Francis T. Nicholls, despite the fact that he had signed the Jim Crow law as governor in 1890, promptly issued a "writ of prohibition" that ordered Judge Ferguson to "show cause" why his ruling should not be reversed. But after hearing oral argument, the Louisiana supreme court upheld Ferguson's ruling on January 2, 1893. Three days later, Plessy's lawyers asked Justice Nicholls to issue a "writ of error" to the United States Supreme Court. He granted this request the same day, and the legal documents in *Plessy v. Ferguson* arrived in Washington by mail train before the end of February.

The *Plessy* case completed its journey through the Louisiana courts in less than eight months, but it then sat on a siding in the Supreme Court clerk's office for another three years. One reason for this lengthy delay stemmed from the Court's swollen docket; appeals from state and federal courts flooded the justices with hundreds of cases each year (the Court decided 392 in the 1895 term). The justices did not then have the bevy of law clerks they now employ, or computers on which to draft and polish opinions. (Not until Congress passed the Judiciary Act of 1925 did the Court gain its long-sought "discretion" to decide which cases deserve argument and decision.)

Another factor slowed down the *Plessy* case: Albion Tourgee looked at the justices and did not like what he saw. The Court's rules allowed for expedited hearings in criminal cases, but Tourgee decided to wait his turn on the regular docket. "Of the whole number of Justices there is but one who is known to favor the view we must stand upon," he wrote to James Walker in October 1893, obviously counting Justice John Marshall Harlan on his side. Tourgee saw four certain votes against Plessy; these justices—he did not name them—would "probably stay where they are until Gabriel blows his horn," he lamented. The remaining four would probably uphold the Jim Crow law, but shifts in public sentiment might affect their votes. "The Court has always been the foe of liberty," Tourgee wrote, "until forced to move on by public opinion."

Public opinion *did* shift before the Court ruled in 1896, but it became even more hostile toward blacks. Southern states passed more Jim Crow laws and began to purge blacks from voting rolls; in 1894 Congress repealed almost every Reconstruction law that remained on the books. Faced with this gloomy outlook, Tourgee's brief to the Supreme Court reflected his refusal to temporize; he threw caution to the wind and challenged the justices to look racism in the face. "Suppose a member of this court, nay, suppose every member of it," he wrote, "should wake tomorrow with black skin and curly hair—the two obvious and controlling indications of race—and in traveling through that portion of the country where the 'Jim Crow Car' abounds, should be ordered into it by the conductor. It is easy to imagine what would be the result, the indignation, the protests, the assertion of pure Caucasian ancestry. But the conductor, the autocrat of Caste, armed with the power of the State conferred by this statute, will listen neither to denial or protest."

Tourgee continued his philippic: "What humiliation, what rage would then fill the judicial mind! How would the resources of language not be taxed in objurgation! Why would this sentiment prevail in your minds? Simply because you would then feel and know that such assortment of citizens on the line of race was a discrimination intended to humiliate and degrade the former subject and dependent class—an attempt to perpetuate the caste distinctions on which slavery rested."

Although his brief included more lawyerly argument on the Thirteenth and Fourteenth Amendments, Tourgee also asked the justices to imagine the possible consequences of upholding Jim Crow laws. "Why not require all colored people to walk on one side of the street and whites on the other? Why not require every white man's house to be painted white and every colored man's black?" (The Court's majority opinion considered these hypotheticals—as lawyers call them—and dismissed them as not being "reasonable" exercises of the state's police powers.) Tourgee added a sentence that wound up, slightly changed, in the solitary dissent: "Justice is pictured blind and her daughter, the Law, ought at least to be color-blind," he wrote.

The Supreme Court heard oral argument in *Plessy v. Ferguson* on April 13, 1896; no record or accounts have survived, but the lawyers on both sides probably restated the points in their extensive briefs. Five weeks later, on May 18, the Court handed down its decision. Seven justices voted to uphold the Jim Crow law, while only John Harlan dissented (Justice David Brewer had been absent during argument and did not vote). Justice Henry B. Brown wrote for the majority; his only major opinion in fifteen years on the Court was certainly his worst. The list of Brown's deficiencies is long: he virtually ignored the constitutional issues raised by Plessy's lawyers; he relied heavily on cases that had little or no authority as precedent; and he based his decision on thinly veiled racism, dressed up in polite language.

Brown first addressed the Thirteenth Amendment claim that the Jim Crow law imposed a "badge of servitude" on Homer Plessy and all blacks. In just three paragraphs, he brushed aside this claim as "too clear for argument." That amendment abolished "the ownership of mankind as a chattel" and did nothing more, Brown asserted. He cited for precedent the *Civil Rights Cases* of 1883, ignoring the fact that all those cases involved "private" discrimination and not the kind of "state action" clearly present in the *Plessy* case.

Turning to the Fourteenth Amendment, Brown admitted its intent to prohibit state-imposed racial discrimination and laws "imposing upon the colored race onerous disabilities and burdens," which was precisely what Louisiana did to Homer Plessy. Brown used an old lawyer's trick to escape this dilemma: semantic evasion. The Jim Crow law did not "discriminate" on racial grounds, he claimed; it simply recognized a "distinction" between the races "which must always exist so long as white men are distinguished from the other race by color." But in separating the races in railroad cars, had Louisiana deprived Plessy of any of the "privileges and immunities" he enjoyed as a citizen? Brown answered this question with more wordplay, drawing a distinction between "political" and "social" equality. Conceding that states could not deprive blacks of political rights, he looked at the Court's earlier cases and found just one right protected by the Fourteenth Amendment. Brown cited the 1880 decision in *Strauder v. West Virginia*, striking down a law that limited jury duty to whites. This law imposed "a discrimination which implied a legal inferiority" of blacks, he wrote.

Brown would go no further than admitting blacks to jury boxes. "The distinction between laws interfering with the political equality of the negro and those requiring the separation of the two races in schools, theatres and railway carriages has been frequently drawn by this court," he claimed. The discussion that followed this forceful statement exposed the legal quicksand on which

Brown's opinion rested, since none of the cases he cited as precedent for this proposition were Supreme Court decisions that involved laws requiring—rather than permitting or forbidding—racial segregation. Brown first cited an 1849 Massachusetts supreme court ruling that upheld school segregation in Boston. In *Roberts v. City of Boston*, Chief Justice Lemuel Shaw—the most respected state judge of his time—deferred to pubic sentiment, writing that racial prejudice "is not created by law, and cannot be changed by law." Justice Brown liked Shaw's statement so much that he inserted it—slightly altered in wording—into his own opinion. However, *Roberts* had been decided by a state court, two decades before ratification of the Fourteenth Amendment, and lacked any authority as precedent.

Brown's citation of the *Civil Rights Cases*, decided in 1883, also lacked precedential authority. The Civil Rights Act of 1875 did not "require" separation of the races; it prohibited such conduct. In fact, Brown's quotation from Justice Joseph Bradley in the *Civil Rights Cases* undermined his *Plessy* opinion. Bradley made clear in that decision that the Fourteenth Amendment offered "relief against state legislation, or state action" that violated "the fundamental rights specified in the amendment." Bradley did not list all such rights, nor did Brown, but neither justice excluded the right of equal access to public accommodations from Fourteenth Amendment protection.

Brown's third citation was to a Mississippi supreme court decision, holding that railroads could not refuse to provide Jim Crow cars on their trains. The Supreme Court—with Justice Harlan dissenting—had sustained this ruling in 1889, but rested its decision on the Commerce Clause, with no reference to the Fourteenth Amendment. The majority reasoned that railroads, even those that crossed state lines, must abide by state laws that did not "burden" their passage. None of the cases Brown cited offered much authority for his *Plessy* opinion, but he nonetheless concluded that "the enforced separation of the races" by state law did not violate the Fourteenth Amendment.

The contradictions in Brown's opinion were compounded by his discussion of the *Yick Wo* case, which offered real "authority" for striking down the Louisiana law. Ruling in 1886, the Court held that San Francisco officials—by denying business licenses to all Chinese laundrymen—had made "an arbitrary and unjust discrimination against the Chinese race," as Brown summarized that unanimous decision. A better precedent for the *Plessy* case would be hard to imagine. However, after Brown accurately stated the *Yick Wo* holding, he simply dropped the case and said nothing more about state laws that required or allowed racial discrimination.

Having dismissed arguments against the Jim Crow law based on the Constitution, Brown looked outside its pages for doctrine and precedent to support his opinion. He found his doctrine in the "police powers" of government and precedent in one state court decision. As noted earlier, states possess implied "police powers" to protect the public's health, safety, welfare, and morals. In the absence of constitutional limitations, which Brown had already denied in *Plessy*, laws based on these powers need only demonstrate a "reasonable" basis to pass judicial scrutiny. Brown did not specify which of Louisiana's police powers the Jim Crow law furthered. And he did not elaborate on the "reasonable" basis for the law. He simply granted a "large discretion" to the state legislature. "In determining the question of reasonableness," he wrote, lawmakers were "at liberty to act with reference to the established usages, customs and traditions of the people, and with a view to the promotion of their comfort, and the preservation of the public peace and good order."

The "people" Brown had in mind, to whose "customs and traditions" he deferred, and whose "comfort" he wished to protect, were those white people in Louisiana who did not want to share railway cars with blacks. In other words, the racists of Louisiana. To support his position, Brown cited a New York supreme court decision of 1883, upholding racial segregation in Brooklyn's schools. A twelve-year-old black girl, Theresa King, had sued James Gallagher, principal of Public School No. 5, after she was turned away from the white school, the closest to her home. Justice Brown borrowed liberally from the opinion in *King v. Gallagher*, including its statement that racial harmony cannot be achieved "by laws which conflict with the general sentiment of the community upon whom they are designed to operate." This meant, of course, the "sentiment" of the white community. It is ironic that both cases Brown cited on the issue of school segregation came from northern states, Massachusetts and New York; Jim Crow did not perch only in southern trees.

Justice Bradley had told blacks in the *Civil Rights Cases* that they were no longer "the special favorite of the laws." Justice Brown delivered his own patronizing lecture to Homer Plessy. "We consider the underlying fallacy of the plaintiff's argument," he wrote, "to consist in the assumption that the enforced separation of the two races stamps the colored race with a badge of inferiority. If this be so, it is not by reason of anything found in the act, but solely because the colored race chooses to put that construction upon it."

Albion Tourgee's challenge that the justices imagine themselves with black skin and envision their reaction to discrimination obviously failed with Justice Brown. He wore a black robe, but his white skin protected him from "social" inferiority. Brown's last words in *Plessy* signaled the judicial capitulation to racism. "If one race be inferior to the other socially, the Constitution of the United States cannot put them upon the same plane."

Justice Brown's majority opinion covered twelve pages in the Court's reports; Justice Harlan's dissent matched it precisely in length. Point by point, case by case, Harlan answered with a devastating rebuttal. He turned first, as had Brown, to the Thirteenth Amendment. "It not only struck down the institution of slavery," he wrote, "but it prevents the imposition of any burdens or disabilities that constitute badges of slavery or servitude. It decreed universal civil freedom in this country. This Court has so adjudged." Despite the intent of those who framed that amendment, Harlan recognized that it proved "inadequate to the protection of the rights of those who had been held in slavery," which led to adoption of the Fourteenth and Fifteenth Amendments. Between them, the Civil War amendments "removed the race line from our governmental systems." It was no longer allowed for "any public authority to know the race of those entitled to be protected in the enjoyment" of constitutional rights.

Harlan turned for precedent on this point to his own words, quoting from an opinion handed down the same day *Plessy* was argued. Referring to the Court's prior decisions in jury discrimination cases, he had written in *Gibson v. Mississippi* that "underlying all of those decisions is the principle that the Constitution" forbids official discrimination "against any citizen because of his race. All citizens are equal before the law." Harlan did not mention, however, that his *Gibson* opinion had upheld a death sentence against a black defendant, convicted by an all-white jury in a county where blacks far outnumbered whites but never served on juries. Like most judges, Harlan looked for legal principles wherever he could find them.

A major thrust of Harlan's dissent was that Brown had erred in distinguishing between "political" and "social" rights, limiting the former to jury duty and removing the latter from constitutional protection. Harlan used the broader term of "civil rights" to include protection from discrimination in all places subject to state regulation, reaching back almost five decades in citing a Supreme Court ruling that a railroad company held "a sort of public office, and has public duties to perform," which must be done without discrimination. But Harlan did not rest his dissent on precedent; he cited just ten cases, against more than forty in Brown's opinion. He relied on one simple point: the Civil War amendments were designed to prohibit states from discriminating against blacks in their enjoyment of the "civil rights" that all citizens held. Borrowing from Albion Tourgee's brief, Harlan put this point into a sentence that has become famous, perhaps the most quoted in Supreme Court history: "Our Constitution is color-blind, and neither knows nor tolerates classes among citizens." Harlan's next sentence borrowed his own words from the *Gibson* opinion: "In respect of civil rights, all citizens are equal before the law."

The notion of a "color-blind" Constitution has enormous appeal as a guiding principle. But there are dangers in substituting slogans for hard, realistic analysis. Harlan's famous sentence has been ripped from its context by those— including Supreme Court justices—who have wielded it in recent years as a weapon against affirmative action and other "race-conscious" remedial laws and programs. Those who quote the "color-blind" sentence invariably fail to quote the sentences that preceded it in Harlan's opinion. "The white race deems itself to be the dominant race in this country," he wrote. "And so it is, in prestige, in achievements, in education, in wealth and in power. So, I doubt not, it will continue to be for all time, if it remains true to its great heritage and holds fast to the principles of constitutional liberty."

Harlan stated in these sentences the reality of race in 1896. Whites held the reins of power, which they used to whip blacks into submission. Harlan does not deserve scorn for acknowledging this reality, however much it reflected the "pride of race" that he celebrated. He had no more desire for "social equality" with blacks than Justice Brown. He was, after all, a man of his times, the son of slave owners and a man of superior prestige, education, wealth, and power. But he was not a racist like Chief Justice Taney. "In my opinion," Harlan wrote in his *Plessy* dissent, "the judgment this day rendered will, in time, prove to be quite as pernicious as the decision made by this tribunal in the Dred Scott case." He was right. But hardly anyone agreed at the time. The Court handed down decisions in fifty-two other cases the day it ruled against Homer Plessy. Three of these—dealing with the laws of contract, inheritance, and copyright—were reported on the front page of the *New York Times*. The editors relegated the *Plessy* decision to a third-page column on railroad news, between cases on train routes and improvement bonds. And the Court's leading historian, Charles Warren, did not even mention *Plessy* in his massive work, published three decades later.

The immediate impact of the Court's decision fell on Homer Plessy. On January 11, 1897, he entered a "guilty" plea in criminal district court to the charges brought against him in 1892 and paid a fine of $25. The citizens' committee that supported his challenge had raised almost $3,000; it spent the last $60 to inscribe a "flattering testimonial" to Albion Tourgee. Plessy's lawyer did not flatter the Supreme Court, lamenting that its decision had "virtually nullified the fourteenth amendment . . . and emasculated the thirteenth."

The later impact of *Plessy* and the "separate but equal" doctrine fell upon all black Americans and other racial minorities as well. Even Justice Harlan bowed to its "authority" as precedent. Writing for the Court in 1899, he upheld the power of Richmond County in Georgia to provide a high school for white students but none for blacks. Harlan held in *Cumming v. Board of Education* that "the education of the people in schools maintained by state taxation is a matter belonging to the respective States" and was immune from federal judicial scrutiny "except in the case of a clear and unmistakable disregard of rights secured by the supreme law of the land." Regardless of his own view of these rights, *Plessy* left Harlan with no choice in this case.

Almost three decades later, ruling in 1927, the Supreme Court relied on Harlan's statement in *Cumming* to keep Martha Lum out of the white high school in Bolivar County, Mississippi. School officials assigned Martha, who was Chinese, to the "colored" school; her father, Gong Lum, sued the state education superintendent. His lawyers argued to the Supreme Court that " 'Colored' describes only one race, and that is the negro." Whites maintained separate schools to protect their children from the "danger" of "the infusion of the blood" from blacks. "The white race may not legally expose the yellow race to a danger that the dominant race recognizes and . . . guards itself against," Gong Lum's lawyers argued. Upholding Martha's exclusion from the white school, Chief Justice William Howard Taft quoted both Henry Brown in *Plessy* and John Harlan in *Cumming* to support his conclusion that no "different result can be reached, assuming the cases above cited to be rightly decided." Years after they died, the judicial antagonists of 1896 had become partners in providing judicial support for the Jim Crow system that survived both Harlan and Brown.

The *Plessy* decision did not, of course, end the legal conflicts over Jim Crow laws, nor did it dampen the smoldering anger of blacks against their denial of the "equal protection of the laws" promised them in the Constitution. Justice Harlan added a prophetic warning to his *Plessy* dissent. "The destinies of the two races, in this country, are indissolubly linked together," he wrote, "and the interests of both require that the common government of all shall not permit the seeds of race hate to be planted under the sanction of law." The *Plessy* decision, of course, watered the seeds of Jim Crow laws that sprouted across the country and flourished for another six decades. Another warning came in 1903 from W. E. B. Du Bois, the leading black thinker of his time, in his book *The Souls of Black Folk*. "The problem of the Twentieth Century," Du Bois wrote at its beginning, "is the problem of the color-line." As we enter a new century, that problem remains unsolved in a country whose founders proclaimed long ago that "all men are created equal."

SECTION IV

"Liberty in a Social Organization"

19

"The Spectre of Socialism"

No country on earth grew faster than the United States during the last four decades of the nineteenth century. Between 1860 and 1900 the nation's population swelled from 31 to 75 million, with 20 million people living west of the Mississippi. The number of farms grew from two million to six million, and the development of machines like combines, reapers, and harvesters turned barren land into "amber waves of grain" that spread across hundreds of miles in the Midwest. It took three hours of labor in 1830 to produce a bushel of wheat; by 1900 the time had decreased to ten minutes. American farmers produced more than their counterparts in any other country, but they did not receive their fair share of the bounty they reaped from the land.

Blacks were not the only group of Americans that lived in virtual peonage after the Civil War. Farm equipment was expensive, and farmers borrowed heavily from banks to purchase machines and supplies. Especially in the South, black and white farmers alike became victims of the "crop-lien" system: the merchants who sold them supplies would demand a lien—in effect, a mortgage on the crop—and charge up to 25 percent interest. Lawrence Goodwyn, a leading historian of farmers' protest movements, wrote that "the crop lien system became for millions of Southerners, white and black, little more than a modified form of slavery."

In the Midwest, bankers and railroads squeezed farmers with high interest rates and even higher tolls for shipping their goods to markets. Railroads brought millions of bushels of wheat to cities like Kansas City and Chicago, where farmers paid exorbitant prices to store their produce in grain elevators, the giant storage bins into which grain was "elevated" before its sale to millers. In most cases, those who owned railroads and grain elevators enjoyed—and exploited—monopolies granted by compliant state legislators, many of them bribed for their votes. Beginning in 1870, a movement called the Grange—also known as the Patrons of Husbandry—spread across the Midwest like a grass fire, enlisting thousands of angry farmers in a crusade against price gouging. The Grangers railed most loudly against the railroads: "The State must either absorb the railroads or the railroads will absorb the State," they cried.

Grangers flexed their political muscles and persuaded lawmakers in several midwestern states to pass laws that set maximum rates for railroads and grain elevators. The Panic of 1873 forced many railroads into bankruptcy, and their owners could no longer bankroll the widespread bribery that had protected them from rate regulation. But they still complained about the Granger movement. "That it has effectually destroyed all future railroad enterprises, no one who is acquainted with its effect in money centers will for a moment doubt," one railroad president wrote in 1874.

Rebuffed by state lawmakers, the midwestern monopolists turned to federal judges for protection, hoping they would employ the emerging doctrine of "substantive due process" to strike down the Granger laws. Corporate lawyers filed dozens of suits against these laws, claiming they violated the Fourteenth Amendment by depriving their clients of liberty and property without "due process of law." In making this claim, the corporate bar urged judges to review the "substance" of laws and decide whether they infringed a protected right. Prior to the 1870s, most judges considered themselves limited to examining the "process" by which a law was enacted. If legislators had followed the rules, and the law was a "reasonable" exercise of the state's "police powers," or of an express constitutional power, judges would uphold the law. This was the doctrine known as "procedural due process," a seemingly redundant term that was devised in this period of legal innovation to distinguish it from "substantive due process," under which laws that obeyed all the procedural rules could still be struck down.

Debates over judicial power to examine the "substance" of legislation took place largely in the pages of law reviews and legal treatises; the general public had little idea of the stakes until judges began striking down hundreds of state laws in the 1880s and 1890s. One of the earliest and most influential proponents of substantive due process doctrine was Thomas M. Cooley, a Michigan judge and law professor whose *Treatise on Constitutional Limitations*, published in 1868, argued that a "legislative enactment is not necessarily the law of the land." Laws that met all the "procedural" tests of due process would nonetheless fail if they represented "arbitrary interference" by the state with rights of private property. Cooley elevated "liberty of contract" to the constitutional pantheon; if a law interfered with the right of any person—including corporations—to make any lawful contract, he wrote, "it can scarcely be doubted that the act would transcend the due bounds of legislative power, even if it did not come into conflict with express constitutional provisions."

Cooley's treatise offered legal support for laissez-faire economics and the

Social Darwinism of Herbert Spencer, the most influential nineteenth-century advocate of limited government. Spencer, an Englishman, transformed Charles Darwin's flexible concept of "natural selection" in the evolution of species into an inflexible law, based on "the survival of the fittest." His major book, *Social Statics*, was first published in England in 1851 and found a receptive audience for the American edition in 1865. Spencer preached a stern doctrine, much like the Puritans who preceded him by two centuries. "The poverty of the incapable, the distresses that come upon the imprudent, the starvation of the idle, and those shoulderings aside of the weak by the strong," he wrote, "are the decrees of a large, far-seeing benevolence."

"It would be difficult to overestimate Spencer's popularity in the United States during the quarter-century after the Civil War," historian Sidney Fine wrote in *Laissez Faire and the General-Welfare State*. Spencer's American publisher sold almost a half million copies of his books, and his most zealous supporter, Edward Youmans, founded the *Popular Science Monthly* in 1872 to spread the gospel of Social Darwinism. Articles like "Law as a Disturber of Social Order" and "Encroachments of the State" denounced every legislative effort to improve the lot of working people. One author complained that the people had "found a new toy—the power of legislative action—and were playing with it with a kind of greedy zest."

Lawyers and judges embraced Spencer's ideas with special passion. "It was in the courts that the idea of laissez faire won its greatest victory," wrote Sidney Fine, although judicial endorsement of Social Darwinism had its critics and temporary setbacks. The most important regulation case of the 1870s, *Munn v. Illinois*, posed a "due process" challenge to an Illinois law that set maximum charges for grain storage in Chicago, into which grain poured in railroad cars and left in flour bags. Of the city's fourteen grain storage companies, Munn & Scott dominated the business with a capacity of 2,700,000 bushels. Its principal owner, Ira Munn, drew the wrath of farmers for his shady dealings and exorbitant charges. Munn mixed superior grain with inferior grades and conspired with his "competitors" to fix prices. The exposure of Munn's corrupt practices led farmers to press city officials to curb his abuses, but he had powerful friends in City Hall and farmers did not vote in Chicago. They did, however, vote in "downstate" districts, and the Grangers persuaded the state legislature to curb Munn's price-fixing deals with prices fixed by a public board he did not control. The 1871 law required the owners of storage companies in Chicago to secure a licence from the Cook County court and set a maximum charge of two cents per bushel for the first thirty days of storage.

Ira Munn refused to apply for a license to operate his business and continued to charge more for grain storage than the law allowed. The state's attorney general brought charges in 1872, and Munn's company was fined $100 in county court after a brief trial in which both sides agreed on the facts. The Illinois supreme court upheld Munn's conviction, and his appeal joined several other "Granger cases" that were pending in the Supreme Court. Before the Court decided these cases, corporate lawyers expressed optimism that it would strike down "this assault upon private property," as one wrote in the prestigious *American Law Review*. He added that the Granger movement "was really directed, not against abuses, but against the rights of property." This lawyer found it "perfectly clear that the Granger movement was rank communism." The first Red Scare in America had begun, although midwestern farmers hardly resembled the industrial proletariat that Karl Marx called upon in his *Communist Manifesto* to overthrow the capitalist system.

Ira Munn declared bankruptcy before his case reached the Supreme Court, but lawyers for the successor to Munn & Scott pursued the appeal of the company's conviction. Their brief first argued that the grain storage business was part of the "stream" of interstate commerce and could only be regulated by Congress. Although the brief cited eleven Supreme Court decisions as precedent, the cases offered little support on this issue and the Court brushed the claim aside. The company's lawyers placed more reliance on the Due Process Clause, claiming that the Illinois law deprived its owners of their "liberty" to engage in business free of "arbitrary" state regulation. Lacking any Supreme Court precedent, this section cited just three state court cases, but it pointed the justices to Judge Cooley's *Treatise on Constitutional Limitations* for legal authority.

Ruling in March 1877, the Court turned down the invitation to read Cooley's treatise into the Constitution, with seven justices voting to uphold the Illinois law as a "reasonable" regulation of a "virtual monopoly" of the grain storage business. Chief Justice Morrison Waite, a former corporate and railroad lawyer, wrote for the Court and turned against his former clients. He reached back more than two centuries for support from Lord Matthew Hale, an eminent English jurist whose decisions, one American judge wrote, had so much force that judges looking for precedent "do not trouble themselves to search any further." Waite cited Hale for the proposition that "when private property is affected with a public interest it ceases to be *juris privati* only" and becomes subject to "reasonable" state regulation. He translated Hale's Latin phrase into simple English: "When private property is devoted to a public use, it is subject to public regulation." The Illinois law came "within the meaning of the doctrine which Lord Hale has so forcibly stated," Waite continued. The Chief Justice had one last word for the advocates of substantive due process: "For protection against abuses by legislatures, the people must resort to the polls, not to the Courts."

The first—and most vehement—response to Waite came from Justice Stephen Field. The majority opinion was "subversive of the rights of private property, heretofore believed to be protected by constitutional guaranties against legislative interference," Field complained. His dissenting opinion, joined by Justice William Strong, denied Waite's claim that "private property held for a public use" became subject to state regulation. "If this be sound law," Field wrote, "all property and all business in the State are held at the mercy of a majority of its legislature." The doctrine Field denounced was, in fact, "sound law" that went back, as Waite had noted, "as long ago as the third year of the reign of William and Mary." American judges had followed Lord Hale's lead in hundreds of cases over the century before the Court decided *Munn v. Illinois.*

Waite's opinion in the *Munn* case alarmed the advocates of substantive due process. One leading corporate lawyer, John N. Pomeroy, could barely contain his anger. "No other decision has ever been made in the course of our judicial history—not even excepting the notorious Dred Scott Case—which threatens such disastrous consequences for the future welfare and prosperity of the country," Pomeroy wrote in the *American Law Review.* He predicted that Waite's opinion would be seized upon by "the demagogues who are conducting the agitation now going on throughout the country" and who pressed for "yet more communistic and destructive legislation" to restrain corporate monopolists.

Pomeroy's alarmed prediction of renewed "agitation" for legislation to protect farmers and working people came true within months of the *Munn* decision. "In the year 1877," Howard Zinn wrote in *A People's History of the United States,* "the country was in the depths of the Depression" that began with the Panic of 1873. Hunger and disease struck the urban poor with deadly force. The *New York Times* reported that "already the cry of dying children begins to be heard. . . . Soon, to judge from the past, there will be a thousand deaths of infants per week in the city." During the summer of 1877, "there came a series of tumultuous strikes by railroad workers in a dozen cities; they shook the nation as no labor conflict in its history had done," wrote Zinn. Deep cuts into already low wages ($1.75 per day for brakemen who worked twelve hours) prompted workers to bring the nation's railroads to a screeching halt.

President Rutherford Hayes, heeding appeals from J. P. Morgan, August Belmont, and other railroad magnates and bankers, sent federal troops to Baltimore, St. Louis, Chicago, and Pittsburgh. Pitched battles erupted between strikers and soldiers, with deadly results. In Pittsburgh, twenty-four people (including four soldiers) died in fighting around Union Depot; the day after police in Chicago shot and killed three strikers, Zinn recounts, "an armed crowd of five thousand fought the police. The police fired again and again, and when it was over, and the dead were counted, they were, as usual, workingmen and boys, eighteen of them, their skulls smashed by clubs, their vital organs pierced by gunfire."

News of the railroad strikes reached Europe and impressed Karl Marx, who wrote to Friedrich Engels: "What do you think of the workers of the United States? This first explosion against the associated oligarchy of capital which has occurred since the Civil War will naturally again be suppressed, but can very well form the point of origin of an earnest workers' party." The Workingmen's Party, formed in Chicago on July 4, 1876—the centennial of the Declaration of

Independence—gained recruits from the strikers. "When the great railroad strikes of 1877 were over," Zinn wrote, "a hundred people were dead, a thousand people had gone to jail, 100,000 workers had gone on strike, and the strikes had roused into action countless unemployed in the cities."

The combined forces of federal troops, state militias, and local police finally beat down the railroad strikers. But their struggle continued through propaganda and insurgent politics. Henry George, a workingman and self-educated economist, published a book called *Progress and Poverty* in 1879, which argued that landownership was the basis of all wealth. His book sold millions of copies, and his proposal of a "single tax" on land gained millions of adherents. The Independent Labor Party drafted George to run for mayor of New York City in 1886. That year was marked by a wave of railroad strikes across the nation, which erupted into violence in Chicago's Haymarket Square.

What became known as the Haymarket Affair grew out of labor's campaign for laws to establish an eight-hour workday and was sparked by a strike by workers at the McCormick Harvester works in Chicago. On May 3, 1886, Chicago police fired into a crowd of strikers at the McCormick plant, wounding dozens and killing four. The next day, a detachment of 180 police tried to break up a protest rally in Haymarket Square; someone threw a bomb into the police ranks, wounding sixty-six officers, seven of whom later died. The bomb-thrower was never identified, but eight members of anarchist groups that organized the rally were charged with murder and sentenced to death; seven of them had not been in Haymarket Square and the eighth was speaking from the podium when the bomb exploded. The Supreme Court refused to hear appeals from the convictions, and four of the anarchists were hung; a fifth blew his head off with dynamite in his cell, and the remaining three were later pardoned by Illinois governor Peter Altgeld after a storm of protest over the unfair trials.

The Haymarket Affair shook the nation and polarized the political system. Democrats and Republicans closed ranks behind calls for "law and order," while labor candidates exploited public outrage over the executions and gained votes in local elections. The New York City campaign of Henry George caught national attention; in an election marked by fraud and bribery, he placed second behind the Tammany Hall Democrat and ran far ahead of the Wall Street Republican, Theodore Roosevelt. Although he lost the election, George won converts to his cause and sparked campaigns that persuaded legislators in several states to pass laws that limited working hours and regulated safety and health conditions in mines, factories, and the "sweatshops" in which workers toiled long hours for little pay.

It is no exaggeration to describe the battles of workers and employers of the 1870s and 1880s as class warfare, a struggle waged both in the streets and voting booths. Faced with assaults on their power and privilege, business leaders found a welcome haven in state and federal courtrooms, in which judges—most of whom came to the bench from corporate practice—became increasingly receptive to "substantive due process" claims. Beginning in 1885, a series of state court decisions struck down regulatory laws and elevated "liberty of contract" to constitutional primacy over the "police powers" of government.

One of the first state court rulings, and the most widely cited as precedent in later cases, struck down one of the "sweatshop" laws passed by the New York legislature in 1884. This statute prohibited the manufacture of cigars in tenement houses that contained living quarters. Its stated purpose was to protect the health and safety of cigar rollers who worked in their cramped apartments, most of which lacked adequate ventilation and fire escapes. A challenge to this law, in a case called *In re Jacobs*, confronted New York's highest court with choosing between the state's assertion of "police powers" and the "due process" claims of business owners. The state judges eagerly adopted the laissez-faire arguments of William Evarts, a disciple of Herbert Spencer and former United States attorney general who represented the cigar industry in the *Jacobs* case. In his opinion, Judge Robert Earl conceded the state's power to protect its citizens' health and safety, but he placed in judicial hands the power to examine the statute to "see whether it really relates to . . . the public health." Without venturing from his Albany courtroom into Manhattan's tenements, Earl could not see "how the cigarmaker is to be improved in his health or his morals by forcing him from his home and its hallowed associations and beneficent influences, to ply his trade elsewhere." Without any mention of the evidence in the state's brief, documenting the health and safety hazards of cigar rolling in tenements, Earl echoed the words of Herbert Spencer in writing of "the fierce competition of trade and the inexorable laws of supply and demand" and "the unceasing struggle for success and existence which pervades all societies of men." Social Darwinism gained a judicial foothold in the *Jacobs* decision.

One legal historian looked at hundreds of later cases and found the *Jacobs* opinion cited "in practically every case where state power over individual liberty and property rights was challenged." Its influence spread through the publication in 1886 of *A Treatise on the Limitations of Police Power*, written by Christopher G. Tiedeman, a law professor at the University of Missouri. His book was more a political tract than a legal treatise. "Socialism, Communism, and Anarchism are rampant throughout the civilized world," Tiedeman warned. "The State is called on to protect the weak against the shrewdness of the stronger, to determine what wages a workman shall receive for his labor, and how many hours daily he shall labor." Deploring the "extraordinary demands of the great army of discontents," Tiedeman declared that "the conservative classes stand in constant fear of the advent of an absolutism more tyrannical and more unreasoning than any before experienced by man, the absolutism of a democratic majority." Even more extreme than Judge Cooley in his attack on the police powers doctrine, Tiedeman found a receptive audience in the bench and bar.

When the second edition of his treatise appeared in 1900, he boasted that the first edition had been favorably cited in hundreds of cases decided in the fourteen years since its publication.

Despite the growing number of state-court decisions based on substantive due process claims, the Supreme Court refused to scrap the police powers doctrine. Ruling in 1887, ten years after its *Munn* decision, the Court upheld a Kansas law providing that "the manufacture and sale of intoxicating liquors shall be forever prohibited in this State." Kansas was an early target of the "temperance" crusade led by Carrie Nation, a native Kansan, and the state legislature passed the prohibition law in 1881. The Saline County district attorney promptly charged Peter Mugler with violating the law by selling beer. Mugler was born in Germany and operated a brewery that quenched the thirst of the county's German farmers and factory workers.

Justice John Marshall Harlan, who wrote for the Court in *Mugler v. Kansas*, rejected claims that the prohibition law deprived Peter Mugler of both "liberty" and "property" in violation of the Fourteenth Amendment. Harlan cited *Munn* to support the proposition that "society has the power to protect itself, by legislation, against the injurious consequences" of the liquor trade. Kansas could exercise its police powers in this area, and the Court would not second-guess the state's lawmakers. But Harlan, perhaps without looking through it, opened the door to substantive due process just a crack. He first stated that the power to determine what laws are necessary to protect the public "is lodged with the legislative branch of the government." Judges should defer to legislators in most cases, as the Court did in *Mugler*. Harlan was not willing, however, to hand a blank check to the states. "It does not at all follow," he wrote, that every law "is to be accepted as a legitimate exertion of the police powers of the State. There are, of necessity, limits beyond which legislation cannot rightfully go." Marking these constitutional limits was a job for judges. "They are at liberty—indeed, are under a solemn duty—to look at the substance of things, whenever they enter upon the inquiry whether the legislature has transcended the limits of its authority." If a law purported to exercise a state's police powers, Harlan wrote, but made "a palpable invasion of rights secured by the fundamental law, it is the duty of the courts to so adjudge, and thereby give effect to the Constitution."

Three years later, Harlan's colleagues accepted his invitation in *Mugler* to "look at the substance" of laws in a railroad regulation case, *Chicago, Milwaukee & St. Paul Railway Company v. Minnesota*. (It is worth nothing that railroad cases dominated the Court's docket during the last third of the nineteenth century, reflecting conflicts over the industry's enormous power, both economic and political.) Ruling in 1890, the Court struck down a Minnesota law that established a commission to set "reasonable" rates for freight traffic. The law made the commission's decisions final, with no recourse to judicial review. The majority opinion of Justice Samuel Blatchford in the *Chicago, Milwaukee* case pushed wide open the door Harlan had held ajar in *Mugler*. Deciding the "reasonableness" of rate charges, Blatchford wrote, "is eminently a question for judicial investigation, requiring due process of law for its determination." The Minnesota railroad commission had conducted extensive hearings before setting "reasonable" rates, but the Supreme Court threw out its findings with no reference to the record.

Justice Joseph Bradley, a former railroad lawyer, wrote for the three dissenters in the *Chicago, Milwaukee* case. Joined by Justices Horace Gray and Lucius Lamar, Bradley complained that the Court's decision "practically overrules *Munn v. Illinois*," in which he had joined the opinion of Chief Justice Morrison Waite. Referring to the railroad cases decided along with *Munn*, Bradley reminded his colleagues that the "governing principle of those cases was that the regulation" of fares and rates "is a legislative prerogative and not a judicial one."

Responding to the *Chicago, Milwaukee* decision, Governor William Larrabee of Iowa warned that "further changes in the personnel of the Court" would increase the "danger of its deviating from the sound principles of law laid down" in the *Munn* case. His fears were confirmed after the deaths of justices Samuel Miller in 1890 and Joseph Bradley in 1892. President Benjamin Harrison, a pro-business Republican, picked their successors, Henry B. Brown and George Shiras, Jr., from the ranks of corporate practice. Like most lawyers of that era, these new justices had been schooled by Judge Cooley and Professor Tiedeman in the doctrines of laissez-faire economics and substantive due process.

The same year the Court handed down the *Chicago, Milwaukee* decision, Congress passed the Sherman Antitrust Act, which reflected "populist" pressure to break up the giant monopolies that dominated the American economy. The Sherman Act made it illegal to form a "combination or conspiracy" to restrain trade in interstate or foreign commerce. Senator John Sherman, the act's sponsor, warned his colleagues that failing to curb the monopolies would give ammunition to those who railed against their power. "You must heed their appeal or be ready for the socialist, the communist, the nihilist," he said. "Society is now disturbed by forces never felt before." The Sherman Act would play a role in two of the three major cases decided by the Court in 1895, cases whose outcomes illustrated just how well the justices had learned from Cooley and Tiedeman.

One of the first Sherman Act cases brought by the Justice Department sought to dissolve the American Sugar Refining Company and its subsidiaries, which between them controlled 98 percent of the industry. The federal government filed suit against one subsidiary, the E. C. Knight Company, which pleased the families—and voters—who resented the high prices they paid for sugar. The Supreme Court, however, preferred to drink its coffee unsweetened. Every justice but John Harlan voted to limit the reach of the Sherman Act in *United States v. E. C. Knight Company*, holding that the Commerce Clause did not allow

Congress to regulate the "manufacture" of products that were later shipped from one state to another.

Chief Justice Melville Fuller's opinion for the Court took semantics to hair-splitting extremes. "Commerce succeeds to manufacture, and is not a part of it," he wrote. Fuller conceded that sugar produced at the Knight Company's refinery in Philadelphia was "undoubtedly" shipped into other states, and that the monopoly's aim was "manifestly private gain" from its control over sugar refining. But he stubbornly refused to admit that the sugar monopoly had "any intention to put a restraint upon trade or commerce" between the states, despite the mountain of evidence presented by the Justice Department. The fact that sugar prices might be "indirectly affected" by monopoly power did not budge Fuller from his narrow reading of the Commerce Clause. The American people lost this case, and paid for the Court's decision every time they opened a sugar bowl.

The second important case decided in 1895 involved another federal statute, enacted the previous year, that Congress also passed in response to populist pressures. The first national income tax imposed a 2 percent levy on corporate profits and personal incomes. Those with incomes under $4,000 were exempt from the tax; most working people earned less than this amount, and the law's burden fell largely on the wealthy class. One member of this class, Charles Pollock of New York, filed a suit on behalf of fellow shareholders in the Farmers' Loan and Trust Company, seeking to block the bank from paying the tax. This was clearly a "collusive" lawsuit, since both Pollock and the company wanted to avoid taxation. The bank's lawyers argued that the law violated the Constitution's provision, in Section 9 of Article II, that no "direct" tax could be imposed "unless in proportion to the census" of the population. In other words, federal taxes must apply the same rate to every citizen, without any exemptions based on income.

The case of *Pollock v. Farmers' Loan & Trust Company*, which the justices accepted for argument within a few months of the law's passage, split the Court down the middle. In fact, the justices divided four to four after the case was first argued, since Justice Howell Jackson was bedridden with tuberculosis and could not vote. After Jackson returned to the bench—just three months before his death—the Court heard further argument from leaders of the corporate bar. Joseph Choate, the most eminent Wall Street lawyer of the time, denounced the tax law as "communistic in its purposes and tendencies" and predicted that no justice "will live long enough to hear a case which will involve a question of more importance than this, the preservation of the fundamental rights of private property" from "populistic" attacks.

Five justices heeded Choate's warning and voted to strike down the law. Chief Justice Fuller again wrote for the majority, holding that an income tax was "unconstitutional and void because not apportioned according to representation" under the provision of Article II of the Constitution. Fuller's opinion distorted history and twisted precedent, dismissing the Court's rulings in cases that went back to 1796 as "a century of error" on this question. Justice Henry Brown, certainly not a communist, issued the most pointed of the four dissents. "The decision involves nothing less than a surrender of the taxing power to the moneyed class," he wrote. "Even the spectre of socialism is conjured up to frighten Congress from laying taxes upon the people in proportion to their ability to pay them."

The *Pollock* decision provoked denunciation from labor and "progressive" groups, but they had little influence until pressure mounted for more equitable ways to finance the expanding federal government. The "spectre of socialism" did not frighten Congress from voting in 1912 to submit for state ratification a constitutional amendment to reverse the *Pollock* decision. Only twice before, first in 1795 with the Eleventh Amendment and then in 1868 with the Fourteenth, had Congress and the states responded to unpopular Supreme Court decisions by amending the Constitution. The Sixteenth Amendment, the first addition to the Constitution since Reconstruction, gave Congress the "power to lay and collect taxes on incomes, from whatever source derived" and "without regard to any census or enumeration." The Senate adopted the amendment without a single dissent, the House approved it by a margin of 318 to 14, and it sailed through the state legislatures with little opposition, winning final ratification in 1913.

The last of the Court's 1895 decisions provoked another storm of protest, and calls for judicial impeachment. The *Debs* case began the year before with another railroad strike, even larger and more violent than the bitter conflict of 1877. Again, the economy was crippled by depression and working people felt the sting of poverty and privation. Railroad workers fared better than most; engineers were the "aristocrats of the rails" and earned an average of $957 in 1890, but railroads had their caste system and brakemen took home only $212 that year for the most dangerous job on the trains. More than two thousand railroad workers died in accidents each year, and thirty thousand suffered injuries. The Panic of 1893 prompted a small band of workers to form the American Railway Union, under the leadership of Eugene Debs of Indiana, who began working on the roads at fifteen and joined the Brotherhood of Locomotive Firemen. Each job category had its own union, which allowed managers to pit workers against each other. After a friend was crushed to death under a locomotive, Debs left the roads and later took a job as a railway billing clerk. The union Debs helped to found hoped to unite all railroad workers, from engineers to laborers. "It has been my life's desire to unify railroad employees and to eliminate the aristocracy of labor," he stated.

The railway strike of 1894 began in June when workers at the Pullman Palace Car Company near Chicago walked off their jobs, to protest five successive wage cuts, the most recent of almost 30 percent. These workers made the Pullman cars in which passengers ate and slept on long trips. The American

Railway Union, whose ranks had swelled to 150,000 members, supported the Pullman strikers and asked its members not to handle Pullman cars, which brought passenger trains across the nation to a shuddering halt. The strike quickly spread to freight lines, and the General Managers Association—which spoke for twenty-four railroads—vowed to break the strike and crush the union that Debs headed. The managers called on Attorney General Richard Olney for help, and the former railroad lawyer responded with federal warrants for the arrest of anyone who "obstructed" the U.S. mails. Since most letters and packages were shipped by rail, Olney's warrants could be served on any striking worker.

At Olney's direction, the federal attorney in Chicago persuaded federal judges to issue a sweeping injunction against the use of "threats, intimidation, persuasion, force, or violence" to block trains moving in interstate commerce. Ironically, the judges based the "Debs injunction" on the Sherman Antitrust Act, which the Supreme Court had refused to apply to business monopolies in the *Knight* case. The judicial prohibition on "persuasion" by strikers or sympathizers, which effectively banned all picketing and distribution of handbills, was unprecedented, and it outlawed the only peaceful means of reaching other workers and the public. Debs vowed to defy the injunction and called on his members to refrain from violence. Many strikers, however, vented their anger by derailing freight cars, blocking tracks, and dragging engineers from their cabs if they refused to quit work. President Grover Cleveland, taking the advice of Attorney General Olney, sent federal troops to Illinois. On July 6, 1894, hundreds of soldiers battled a crowd of five thousand strikers and their supporters in Chicago. When the gunfire ended, thirteen people lay dead, fifty-seven were seriously injured, and seven hundred went to jail. Four days later, federal marshals arrested Debs and he was charged with "contempt of court" for violating the injunction. The strike was broken, the union was wrecked, and the victorious railroad managers placed thousands of strikers on a "blacklist" that barred them from any railway job in the country.

Labor suffered a crushing defeat, and the Supreme Court upheld "government by injunction" when it unanimously affirmed Debs's contempt conviction and his two-year prison sentence. Justice David Brewer spoke for a Court that included several former railroad lawyers, including himself. "The strong arm of the National Government may be put forth to brush away all obstructions to the freedom of interstate commerce or the transportation of the mails," he wrote. "If the emergency arises, the army of the Nation, and all its militia, are at the service of the Nation to compel obedience to its laws."

Reaction to the Court's decision split along political lines. One conservative lawyer wrote that "all must applaud the promptness and vigor with which the Federal power acted, saving the country perhaps from a reign of anarchy and bloodshed." On the other side, Governor Sylvester Pennoyer of Oregon, elected on the combined Democratic-Populist ticket, denounced the *Debs* ruling and the decisions in the *Knight* and *Pollock* cases: "Our constitutional government has been supplanted by a judicial oligarchy," he wrote in the *American Law Review*. He called on Congress to "impeach the nullifying Judges for the usurpation of legislative power" and suggested that its members assume the power to reserve the Court's decisions. During the presidential election campaign of 1896, the Democrats adopted a platform that deplored "government by injunction as a new and highly dangerous form of oppression" by federal judges. But the Republicans won that election, and the next three, and named ten Supreme Court justices over the next sixteen years.

The Court's ruling in the *Debs* case made a lasting impact on American politics. Eugene Debs entered prison as a Democrat and emerged as a Socialist. "I was to be baptized in Socialism in the roar of conflict," he later wrote; "in the gleam of every bayonet and the flash of every rifle the class struggle was revealed." Debs became the Socialist Party's charismatic leader and four-time presidential candidate, winning close to a million votes in both 1912 and 1920. He crossed the country dozens of times, speaking in hundreds of cities and towns; perhaps a million Americans heard Debs speak, before the time of radio and television. His appeals to working people did not lead the country to socialism, but they forced other politicians to borrow from his party's platform to keep their own voters from defecting to Debs.

"The Work Was Light

and Healthful"

The claim that the Due Process Clause of the Fourteenth Amendment protected "liberty of contract" as a substantive right won converts among conservative legal writers and state judges well before the Supreme Court confronted this issue in 1897. The case of *Allgeyer v. Louisiana* dealt with a state law that barred Louisiana citizens and corporations from purchasing property insurance from any out-of-state company not licensed to conduct business within the state. The state prosecuted the E. Allgeyer Company in New Orleans for notifying a New York marine insurance firm—not licensed in Louisiana—that it was shipping goods under a policy written by the "foreign" firm. The company challenged its conviction, arguing that the state law infringed its "liberty" under the Due Process Clause to enter contracts that did not violate laws regulating "domestic" insurance firms. Since it discriminated between insurance firms within and outside the state, the law could also have been challenged on equal protection grounds, but the Allgeyer Company staked its case on the "liberty of contract" doctrine.

The company's gamble paid off in spades. Every justice joined the opinion of Rufus Peckham, who defined "liberty" in broad terms that embraced "the right of the citizen to be free in the enjoyment of all his faculties; to be free to use them in all lawful ways; to live and work where he will; to earn his livelihood by any lawful calling; to pursue any livelihood or avocation, and for that purpose to enter into all contracts which may be proper, necessary and essential to his carrying out" these rights. Peckham made a slight bow to the "police powers" doctrine, writing that states could limit the right to contract when it conflicted with "the policy of the State as contained in its statutes," but he warned state lawmakers "not to infringe upon those other rights of the citizen which are protected by the Federal Constitution." Peckham's opinion did not specify these "other rights," but his wording suggested—without invoking its provisions—that the Ninth Amendment's mention of rights "retained by the people" limited state power to the bare minimum of protecting the public against clear dangers to its health and safety. Barring its citizens from contracting with out-of-state firms for insurance coverage was certainly not a legitimate exercise of Louisiana's police powers.

Having inserted "liberty of contract" into the Constitution, the Court was not quite ready to scrap the police powers doctrine. Ruling in 1898, the year after the *Allgeyer* decision, seven of the justices who had joined Peckham's opinion voted in *Holden v. Hardy* to uphold a Utah law that set an eight-hour working day for "hard-rock" miners, primarily those who tunneled for coal, lead, and copper. The Utah constitution required its legislature to "pass laws to provide for the health and safety" of miners, and state judges had found that working long hours in hard-rock tunnels posed a serious threat to miners, whose death rate from accidents far exceeded that in any other industry. Confronted with hard figures and gruesome accounts of rock falls and explosions, the Court rejected the argument of company lawyers that miners were "perfectly competent to contract" on an equal basis with their bosses and to assume the risk of disability or death without any protection from state law. The "liberty of contract" doctrine rested on the notion that workers and employers held "equal bargaining power" in negotiating the terms of wages, hours, and working conditions. Only the most dogmatic judge could actually believe that John D. Rockefeller and the immigrant and illiterate workers in his hard-rock mines sat around the bargaining table on equal terms and hammered out fair contract terms.

Writing for the majority in *Holden v. Hardy*, Justice Henry Brown dismissed the company's "right of contract" argument. This implied right, he wrote, was "subject to certain limitations which the State may lawfully impose in the exercise of its police powers." While Brown found this power "inherent in all governments," he concluded that "it has doubtless been greatly expanded in its application during the past century, owing to an enormous increase in the number of occupations which are dangerous" to workers or "detrimental" to their health. Brown did not, however, hand the states a blank check in passing "health and safety" laws; he reserved for judges the power to decide whether a legislature acted "in exercise of a reasonable discretion or whether its actions be a mere excuse for an unjust discrimination." Perhaps because of this assurance, Justices Peckham and Brewer, the Court's laissez-faire stalwarts, filed their dissents in the *Holden* case without writing opinions.

Justices Peckham and Brewer might well have written a strong dissent in the *Holden* case had they not suffered the loss, just months before that decision, of their strongest ally with the retirement of Justice Stephen Field, the Court's most effective and eloquent defender of laissez-faire doctrine. After thirty-four years on the bench, spanning the terms of nine presidents, Field was determined to break John Marshall's record of service, even though he could barely lift his pen during his last two years. His colleagues persuaded Justice John Harlan to visit Field and suggest that he resign. Years later, Chief Justice Charles Evans Hughes recounted the scene, relying on the memories of justices who had served with Field. Hughes wrote that Harlan approached Field in the Court's robing room, where he sat alone, "apparently oblivious of his surroundings." Harlan diplomatically reminded Field of the time he had been delegated, thirty years earlier, to make the same request of Justice Robert Grier. "The old man listened, gradually became alert and finally, with his eyes blazing with the old fire of youth, he burst out: 'Yes! And a dirtier day's work I never did in my life!' " True or not, this story reflects Field's dogged persistence and fierce will. Hanging on until he broke Marshall's record by one month, Field finally submitted his resignation to President William McKinley. He wrote his own judicial epitaph during his last year on the Court. "Timidity, hesitation and cowardice," he said, were traits that "deserve only contempt" in a judge. Setting his own standard, Field never yielded to "the clamor of the crowd" in voicing his conservative views.

McKinley made his only Supreme Court appointment in filling the "California seat" that Field had vacated with a member of his cabinet, Joseph McKenna. Turning to a political crony, as many other presidents did, McKinley replaced a brilliant conservative with an incompetent one. McKenna had served with McKinley in Congress and later joined his administration as attorney general. "He was a poor lawyer and knew it," one biographer wrote. After McKenna had served twenty-seven lackluster years on the bench, his colleagues suggested that he retire; like Field, he first refused and later stepped down, after learning that the other justices had agreed not to decide any cases in which his vote would determine the outcome.

McKinley's second presidential term was cut short in 1901 by a bullet fired by a self-proclaimed anarchist. His successor, Theodore Roosevelt, had placed a distant third in running for mayor of New York City in 1886 but persevered in politics. Hoping to placate the "progressive" wing of the Republican Party, McKinley had picked Roosevelt to replace his first vice president, the totally forgotten Garret A. Hobart. Roosevelt appealed to progressives because he had broken his Wall Street ties and now posed as a "trust-busting" crusader. In reality, his rhetoric was designed more to attract voters than to attack the corporations that financed the Republican Party. Roosevelt did, however, look for Supreme Court nominees who rejected the doctrine of "substantive due process" and its hostility to economic regulation. His first chance to swing the judicial pendulum back to acceptance of the "police powers" doctrine came in 1902, with the death of Justice Horace Gray after twenty years of dutiful service to corporate interests.

Teddy Roosevelt valued courage and vigor and disclaimed any intellectual pretensions, but he admired those whose lives combined action and reflection. His first choice for the Supreme Court seemed a perfect fit with these attributes. He filled the Court's "Massachusetts seat" with Oliver Wendell Holmes, Jr., and the Senate confirmed him without dissent. Holmes was born in 1841 into an illustrious Boston family (his father was a physician and essayist, famous as the "Autocrat of the Breakfast Table"). He left Harvard in his senior year to enlist in the Union army; during three years on the front lines, he was wounded three times and almost died on the battlefield.

After his wartime service, Holmes entered Harvard Law School in 1864, and he combined law practice with teaching at Harvard until he joined the Massachusetts supreme court in 1882, serving for twenty years, the last ten as chief justice. Holmes also became the most prolific and illustrious legal scholar on the bench since Joseph Story, also the son of a Massachusetts physician and a former Harvard law professor. He wrote essays on legal history and jurisprudence for the *American Law Review*, edited a volume of Chancellor Kent's *Commentaries on American Law*, and produced in 1881 an influential book, *The Common Law*. In this work, based on his essays and lectures at Harvard, Holmes deplored the rigid formalism of legal doctrine. "The life of the law," he wrote, "has not been logic; it has been experience." He acknowledged that "the prejudices which judges share with their fellow-men have had a great deal more to do than the syllogism in determining the rules by which men should be governed." He looked to the "felt necessities of the times" for guidance in deciding cases, rather than political or economic dogma.

Presidents do not always choose justices whose decisions please them, and Holmes soon displeased Roosevelt. After Holmes voted in 1904 against the president's position in a major antitrust case, Roosevelt wrote of his "bitter disappointment" in placing him on the Supreme Court. On his part, Holmes dismissed the president as a "shallow intellect." Although he joined the Court at the age of sixty-one, Holmes served for almost thirty years before he retired in 1932, just shy of ninety-one and just a year before Franklin Roosevelt moved into the White House. He died in March 1935, two days short of his ninety-fourth birthday.

Although he would probably have responded to the "felt necessities" of the Great Depression by voting to uphold FDR's New Deal programs, Holmes did not share his sympathy for the "common man." His outlook on life, shaped in the cauldron of the Civil War, reflected a deep-seated cynicism about politics and law. Holmes looked down on "the people" from his aristocratic vantage and considered them poorly suited to make wise decisions. But he equally distrusted his judicial colleagues, locked into legal formalism and laissez-faire doctrine. Like Winston Churchill, whom he matched as master of the pithy phrase, Holmes considered democracy the worst of all systems, except for the rest. A convinced Social Darwinist in his personal views, Holmes disclaimed any desire to rescue the people from their ignorance and prejudice. He once told Justice

Harlan Fiske Stone that "when the people . . . want to do something that I can't find anything in the Constitution expressly forbidding them to do, I say, whether I like it or not, 'Goddamit, let 'em do it.' "

Some of Holmes's rulings carried his deferential philosophy to extremes; the best (or worst) example was his 1927 opinion in *Buck v. Bell,* upholding Virginia's "eugenic sterilization" law, under which several thousand "feeble-minded" and "morally delinquent" women had their Fallopian tubes cut by court order. Holmes endorsed the forced sterilization of Carrie Buck, the eighteen-year-old "daughter of a feeble minded mother" and herself "the mother of an illegitimate feeble minded child," as he stated the facts from the case record. His opinion reeked of the arrogance of aristocracy, and could easily have been written by Herbert Spencer. "It is better for all the world," Holmes pontificated, "if instead of waiting to execute degenerate offspring for crime, or to let them starve for their imbecility, society can prevent those who are manifestly unfit from continuing their kind." Comparing forced sterilization with compulsory vaccination, Holmes had a last, callous word for Carrie Buck and her family: "Three generations of imbeciles are enough."

Five decades later, a journalist who tracked down Carrie Buck and dug into old records discovered that she had been committed to Virginia's "State Colony for Epileptics and Feeble Minded" only because she had been raped by the eminent doctor who employed her as a housekeeper. Her daughter, Emma, was a perfectly normal child, and the "eugenic expert" who recommended her sterilization was later honored by the German Nazi regime for helping draft its "Race Hygiene" law, which laid the tracks that ended in the gas chambers of Auschwitz and other death camps. Holmes knew nothing about the scientific fallacies of the "eugenic" movement; more important, he did not feel any duty to look behind the fabricated record in the *Buck* case. His philosophy of "judicial restraint" allowed state officials to exercise their "police powers" without any effective oversight.

Legal scholars later voted Holmes into the ranks of "great" justices by acclamation; his literary upbringing and interests made him perhaps the best writer who ever sat on the bench. But Theodore Roosevelt's other two choices placed well down the list of "average" justices. Both had better political than judicial credentials, and both had worked closely with Roosevelt during his stint as assistant navy secretary during McKinley's first term. The retirement of Justice George Shiras in 1903 gave Roosevelt the chance to give Holmes a colleague who shared his support for governmental regulation of business and industry. The president first offered the seat to William Howard Taft, a prominent Ohio Republican who then served as governor of the Philippine Islands, but Taft had presidential ambitions and declined to leave the political arena. Ironically, Taft succeeded Roosevelt as president and later became Chief Justice, the only man who ever held both offices.

After Taft spurned his offer, Roosevelt turned to William R. Day, a less prominent Ohio Republican who had built a thriving corporate practice and then served the McKinley administration in several positions, including a brief stint as secretary of state. McKinley rewarded Day for party loyalty with a post as federal circuit judge, where he sat for three years with Taft. Roosevelt knew Day as a fellow enthusiast of the Spanish-American War, which Day fought from his State Department office. Confirmed by the Senate without dissent, Day served on the court for nineteen years and compiled a divided voting record; he deferred to state "police powers" in business regulation cases and opposed federal laws in the same area. Day voted with Holmes in dissenting from a decision that invalidated a New York law setting a ten-hour workday for bakers, but he split with Holmes in striking down a federal law that prevented children under twelve from working in textile miles. Day was not alone in espousing the "dual sovereignty" doctrine that set different standards for state and federal laws, but he carried it to extremes that even Holmes could not follow.

Theodore Roosevelt conferred his third and final Supreme Court nomination on William Moody of Massachusetts to replace Justice Henry Brown in 1907. Moody resembled Day in several respects: both were loyal Republicans who served in Congress during the McKinley years; both held cabinet posts and met Roosevelt in dealing with naval policy; and both took a Supreme Court seat that William Howard Taft had declined to fill. Unlike Day, however, Moody served a short term; crippled by rheumatism, he resigned in 1910 after less than three years on the bench. His only significant constitutional opinion, *Twining v. New Jersey* in 1908, held that the right against self-incrimination in criminal trials "is not fundamental in due process of law," a ruling that was finally overruled by the Court in 1964.

Americans entered the twentieth century full of optimism and energy; jobs were plentiful, and living standards improved rapidly. The spreading use of inventions like vacuum canning, electric refrigeration, and telephones helped to make daily life easier and more pleasant. Drawn by visions of prosperity— and often lured by free steamship tickets—more than a million immigrants swarmed each year through Ellis Island and other ports of entry. Between 1900 and 1912, three Republican presidents—William McKinley, Theodore Roosevelt, and William Howard Taft—presided over a nation whose most influential citizen was the banker and industrialist J. P. Morgan. Described by historians Thomas Cochran and William Miller as the "imperial leader of the new oligarchy," Morgan headed a financial empire with holdings in 1912 of $22 billion, more than the assessed value of all property west of the Mississippi River. Presidents listened carefully to Morgan, and several of their Supreme Court nominees had represented Morgan's interests in corporate practice.

But the nation's prosperity did not trickle down to the men who labored in factories controlled by the "House of Morgan," the women who operated sewing machines in urban "sweatshops," the children who tended looms in textile mills, and the families who followed the seasons to pick crops from Florida's oranges to Washington's apples. Many of these workers heeded calls to join the Industrial Workers of the World, formed in 1905, or the International Ladies Garment Workers Union, the Western Federation of Miners, and a growing band of radical unions and political groups. Workers died and were injured by the thousands; the government's Commission on Industrial Relations reported 35,000 deaths and 700,000 accidents in 1914. Employers shouldered none of the costs of death, injury, or disease.

America's working people enjoyed few legal rights during the years after the Supreme Court adopted the "liberty of contract" doctrine in *Allgeyer*, a case that dealt with legislative restrictions on business contracts. But they drew hope from the Court's return to the "police powers" doctrine in *Holden*, which involved state regulation of employment contracts. The justices seemingly had enough concern for the well-being of workers in 1898 to overcome their commitment to laissez-faire principles. Over the next several years, however, the Court became more conservative and the labor and progressive movements grew in political influence. These factors combined to produce a judicial showdown in 1905 between the competing doctrines.

The case of *Lochner v. New York* began with the campaigns of populist and socialist movements in the 1890s for legislation to protect working people against low wages, long hours, and unsafe and unhealthy "sweatshop" conditions. These movements pressed for change with a wide range of tactics. They ran candidates for public office, most often to spread "propaganda" but sometimes with real chances to win; at one time, Socialists held 1,200 offices in 340 towns and cities, including mayoralties in Milwaukee and Cleveland. They organized workers into unions, from the "bread-and-butter" approach of the American Federation of Labor to the "class war" appeals of the Industrial Workers of the World, the "Wobblies" who preached the gospel of "One Big Union." And they engaged in lobbying, matching the financial clout of their corporate foes with voting strength and ideological fervor. With shades on the political spectrum from pink to red, from "progressive" to "revolutionary," these loosely connected movements won enough elections and passed enough laws to thoroughly frighten their "conservative" and "reactionary" enemies.

One lobbying effort paid off in 1897 when the New York legislature passed a statute limiting the working hours of bakers to ten per day and sixty per week. The driving force behind the law was Henry Weismann, secretary of the Journeymen Bakers' Union. He enlisted the support of the Church Association for the Advancement of Labor and other "social gospel" groups, whose members sent letters, signed petitions, and visited their representatives in Albany. Weismann also presented legislators with medical reports on the serious health problems of bakers; one noted the effects of working long hours in hot, dusty workshops: "The constant inhaling of flour dust causes inflammation of the lungs and of the bronchial tubes. The long hours of toil to which all bakers are subjected produce rheumatism, cramps, and swollen legs." Impressed by this medical testimony, New York lawmakers stated in the law's preamble that it was enacted as a "health" measure. The statute was inserted, however, in the "labor law" section of the state code, a bureaucrat's decision that later provided ammunition to its opponents.

Joseph Lochner owned Lochner's Home Bakery in Utica, a small city in upstate New York. This was not a big commercial bread factory, but a neighborhood bakeshop that specialized in cakes and pies. The Journeymen Bakers' Union, which represented the workers at many large bakeries, could not win a majority of Lochner's bakers to their cause. But some disgruntled employees complained to state inspectors that Lochner required them to work more than sixty hours each week. He was convicted in 1899 of violating the "bakers law" and paid a $25 fine. Two years later, he was charged with forcing Aman Schmitter to work longer than sixty hours and was fined $50 for a second offense; this time Lochner challenged his conviction on due process grounds.

After New York's highest court upheld the law, Lochner took his case to the Supreme Court, represented by a battery of Wall Street lawyers. Ironically, one member of his legal team was Henry Weismann, who had lobbied for the law as a union official and now argued against it as counsel for the State Association of Master Bakers, which funded Lochner's appeal. Weismann later explained his change of clients: "When I was young," he told a *New York Times* reporter, "I was fiery and full of ideals. Later I became a master baker, and, undergoing an intellectual revolution, saw where the law which I had succeeded as a journeyman baker in having passed was unfair to the employers." Weismann's experienced baker's hands could be seen in the brief he helped write for the Supreme Court. He argued that the ten-hour day unreasonably limited an industry with "busy seasons" like holidays, when employers found it "absolutely necessary to keep their bakers until the business of the day or the night is finished." He also disputed the law's stated purpose as a "health" measure. "The average bakery of the present day is well ventilated, comfortable both summer and winter, and always sweet smelling," Weismann wrote. Limits on working hours had no relation to legitimate health concerns. "Insofar as the baker works under unsanitary conditions, in small and poorly ventilated bakeshops, his interests are protected by the other sections of this law."

Weismann also appealed to the "liberty of contract" doctrine. "Each new attempt by the States to interfere with the contract and property rights, and freedom to exercise a trade or calling by the citizen, should be most closely and jealously scrutinized by this court," he argued. He deplored "a government so paternal in its character that the treasured freedom of the individual and his right to the pursuit of life, liberty, and happiness, should be swept away under the guise of the police power of the State." The former baker put the frosting on his brief with a flourish: "Then there is the American housewife. Here is the real artist in biscuits, cake, and bread, not to mention the American pie. The housewife cannot bound her daily and weekly hours of labor. She must toil on, sometimes far into the night, to satisfy the wants of her growing family. It seems never to have occurred to these ungallant legislators to include within the purview of the statute these most important of all artists in this most indispensable of trades."

Few brief-writers have ever topped Weismann's appeal to apple pie and motherhood. New York's attorney general, Julius Mayer, did not even try; his skimpy brief was flat and stale. Mayer defended his state's law by claiming, with no elaboration, that "it was a proper exercise of the police power of the State." He also paternally suggested that bakers were deficient in brains: "The State, in undertaking this regulation, has a right to safeguard the citizen against his own lack of knowledge." Weismann presented the Court with a rhetorical pie, Mayer with a day-old bagel.

Justice Rufus Peckham could hardly wait to sink his teeth into the *Lochner* case. He was born into a political family in New York's capital city of Albany; his father was a prominent lawyer who served in Congress as a conservative Democrat before his election to the New York Court of Appeals, the state's highest court. Peckham followed his father into both law and politics, building a thriving corporate practice before winning election, like his father, to the court of appeals. He knew many of the lawmakers and lobbyists who dined and cut deals in the restaurants around Albany's capitol building. Conservative in politics, Peckham was equally conservative as a state judge; dissenting in 1889 from a decision that upheld the state's power to regulate grain elevator rates, Peckham deplored legislation that set "class against class" and denounced the law as "vicious in its nature, communistic in its tendency."

With this political background and legal ideology, it is hardly surprising that Peckham seized the chance in the *Lochner* case to strike down a law that offended his laissez-faire principles. He wrote for a bare majority of five justices, but his opinion made few concessions to the dissenters. He began on an uncompromising note: "The statute necessarily interferes with the right of contract between the employer and employees" in New York's bakeries. Peckham cited his own *Allgeyer* opinion for authority that the right to make contracts "is part of the liberty of the individual protected by the Fourteenth Amendment of the Federal Constitution." He noted in disparaging words that the Court had relied on what are "somewhat vaguely termed police powers" in cases such as *Holden v. Hardy*, but added that the Utah law regulating the working hours of underground miners had included an "emergency clause" that allowed longer hours "where life or property is in imminent danger." New York's law had no such provision. "There is nothing in *Holden v. Hardy* which covers the case now before us," Peckham concluded. Why the emergency clause made a difference he left for conjecture.

Peckham rejected the state's "police powers" arguments in his *Lochner* opinion. Claims that the law protected bakers from the unilateral power of employers to set labor terms "may be dismissed in a few words," he wrote. Peckham responded to Mayer's ill-advised suggestion that bakers needed protection from their own ignorance with ill-concealed disdain. "There is no contention that bakers as a class are not equal in intelligence and capacity to men in other trades," he wrote. "They are in no sense wards of the State." Peckham used a few more words in dismissing the state's "health" claim, but he made no reference to medical evidence, since Mayer had offered none in his brief. This did not deter Peckham from taking off his black robe and donning a doctor's white coat. "To the common understanding the trade of a baker has never been regarded as an unhealthy one," he stated, adding with obvious sarcasm that doctors would probably not prescribe working in bakeries "as a remedy for ill health." Peckham professed no doubt that "the limit of the police power has been reached and passed in this case."

The majority opinion could have ended with these words. But the conservative justices felt the need to conjure up the specter of socialism. "It is impossible for us to shut our eyes to the fact that many of the laws of this character, while passed under what is claimed to be the police power for the purpose of protecting the public health or welfare, are, in reality, passed from other motives," Peckham wrote. He looked beyond the "proclaimed purpose" of the New York law and found it was "not really a health law" at all but one designed to interfere with "the freedom of master and employee to contract with each other" on equal terms. Courts must uphold "the right of free contract and the right to purchase and sell labor" without state regulation, Peckham concluded.

Four justices found this expression of laissez-faire principles too extreme, and Peckham's opinion drew separate dissents by John Marshall Harlan and Oliver Wendell Holmes. Joined by Edward White and William Day, Harlan wrote a lengthy rebuttal that cited more than a dozen earlier decisions for precedent. The "police powers" arguments that Peckham had "dismissed in a few words" provided Harlan ample grounds for upholding the New York law. He found "no room for dispute" that no law could "be disregarded or held invalid unless it be, beyond question, plainly and palpably in excess of legislative power." The justices should presume that laws are constitutional and "keep their hands off, leaving the legislature to meet the responsibility for unwise legislation." Harlan considered it "plain" that the law was designed to "protect the physical well-being" of bakers, who were "not upon an equal footing" with their employers and were "often compelled" to work long hours that "unduly taxed their strength." Harlan sounded the call of judicial restraint: "Whether or not this be wise legislation it is not the province of the court to inquire."

Harlan made his case in dry legal prose, looking to precedent and grounding his arguments on well-established principles. His opinion bested Peckham's in craft and consistency. But it lacked the rhetorical polish of Holmes's two-page dissent, which stated the case for judicial restraint with literary flair. "This case is decided upon an economic theory which a large part of the country does not entertain," Holmes wrote of laissez-faire doctrine. "But a constitution is not intended to embody a particular economic theory, whether of paternalism and the organic relation of the citizen to the State or of laissez-faire. It is made for people of fundamentally differing views, and the accident of our finding certain opinions natural and familiar or novel and even shocking ought not to conclude our judgment upon the question whether statutes embodying them conflict with the Constitution of the United States."

Holmes sprinkled his *Lochner* dissent with the pithy aphorisms he delighted in crafting. "Every opinion tends to become a law," he wrote. "General propositions do not decide concrete cases," he added. These two brief sentences compressed the ideas that Harlan had developed over ten pages. New York's lawmakers had put their opinions on bakers' working hours into law, and laissez-faire doctrines should not displace their considered judgment, whether judges concurred or not. "I strongly believe," Holmes asserted, "that my agreement or disagreement has nothing to do with the right of a majority to embody their opinion in law." He skewered Peckham with one pointed sentence: "The Fourteenth Amendment does not enact Mr. Herbert Spencer's *Social Statics.*"

However persuasive his dissent now appears, Holmes was on the losing side in the *Lochner* case. But the seeming victory for "liberty of contract" did not dissuade state and federal lawmakers from passing laws to protect women and children from economic exploitation. One such law came before the Court in 1908, in a case that challenged an Oregon statute that limited the working hours of women in laundries to ten per day. Curt Muller, who owned the Lace House Laundry in Portland, Oregon, had been charged by the county attorney with "the crime of requiring a female to work in a laundry more than ten hours" on September 4, 1905, "against the peace and dignity of the State of Oregon." On its face, the law seemed vulnerable to legal challenge, since it clearly interfered with the freedom "to purchase and sell labor" that Justice Peckham had proclaimed in his *Lochner* opinion.

The case of *Muller v. Oregon* became famous (at least among legal scholars) because of the unusual brief filed by Louis Brandeis, the Boston lawyer who argued for Oregon in the Supreme Court. Widely known as "the people's lawyer" for challenging the power of railroads, banks, and insurance companies, Brandeis joined the *Muller* case at the invitation of the National Consumers League, which lobbied for legislation to protect working women. Oregon's attorney general turned his case over to Brandeis, who buried himself in the Boston Public Library and emerged with a brief that included just two pages of legal argument, followed by 113 pages of excerpts from medical and sociological reports that documented the damaging effect of long hours on the health of women workers. This was the famous "Brandeis brief," emulated by lawyers in many later cases to seek "judicial notice" of social and statistical data that did not appear in the case record.

Confronted with the hard data of the "Brandeis brief" in Curt Muller's appeal to the Supreme Court, his lawyers fell back on appeals to the spirit of Sir Walter Raleigh. "For reasons of chivalry," they argued, "we may regret that all women may not be sheltered in happy homes, free from the exacting demands upon them" to support their families. But those women who ventured from their homes into the workplace, argued Muller's lawyers, should not be sheltered from the hard bargaining over hours and wages that men hammered out with their bosses.

The Court's unanimous opinion in the *Muller* case reflected the marriage of sociology and chivalry. Justice David Brewer, who had joined the *Lochner* majority three years earlier, first noted the "very copious" brief filed by Louis Brandeis. Brewer was impressed by "extracts from over ninety reports" which agreed that "long hours of labor are dangerous to women, primarily because of their special physical organization." Although he cited *Lochner* for the "right to contract" over working hours, Brewer turned to biology on this issue. The "burdens of motherhood," he wrote, have "injurious effects upon the body, and as healthy mothers are essential to vigorous offspring, the physical well-being of woman becomes an object of public interest and care in order to preserve the strength and vigor of the race." Justice Peckham had written in *Lochner* that the five justices in the majority would not "shut our eyes" to the political motives behind New York's ten-hour law for bakers. Writing for every justice in his *Muller* opinion, Justice Brewer found it "impossible to close one's eyes to the fact" that "woman has always been dependent upon man" and that her "physical structure and a proper discharge of her maternal functions—having in view not merely her own health, but the well-being of the race—justify legislation to protect her from the greed as well as the passion of man."

Although women workers scored a victory in *Muller*, the Court threw up judicial barricades against the organizing efforts of labor unions in two other cases decided in 1908. The Court ruled in *Loewe v. Lawlor* that union boycotts of nonunion products—in this case, felt hats—constituted "restraints of trade" and violated the Sherman Antitrust Act. A second decision in *Adair v. United States* struck down a federal law prohibiting railroads from imposing "yellow-dog" contracts on their workers, subjecting them to dismissal if they joined a union (supposedly, a railroad boss told a worker, "I'd rather hire a yellow dog than a union member").

Labor not only lost in the Court in 1908, it lost at the polls as well. William Howard Taft of Ohio led the Republicans to victory over William Jennings Bryan, who suffered his third and final presidential defeat. Taft's election did more than place a pro-business conservative in the White House; it also allowed the new president to solidify conservative control of the Supreme Court. During his single term in office, Taft named six justices, more than any president since Washington. His first nominee, Horace Lurton of Tennessee, replaced Rufus Peckham—author of the *Lochner* opinion—in 1909; a former Confederate soldier and Democrat, Lurton served just four years and left no mark on constitutional law. The following year, Taft chose two justices, replacing David Brewer and Chief Justice Melville Fuller, who died just three months apart in 1910. Taft selected Charles Evans Hughes of New York for Brewer's seat. Born in 1862—his life spanned the period from the Civil War to World War II—Hughes gained wealth and power as a Wall Street lawyer and served as Republican governor of New York before Taft offered him a Supreme Court nomination. Political factors clearly influenced this choice, since Taft viewed Hughes as a potential rival for a second term in 1912; Taft won the nomination but lost the election to Woodrow Wilson. During his service on the Court, over a period of thirty-one years, Hughes shifted his judicial position from conservative to liberal, following public opinion on the bench as he had courted voters at the polls. He was pragmatic above all, balancing his devotion to property rights with recognition of public needs. "The Constitution," Hughes once said, "is what the judges say it is," echoing the view of Oliver Wendell Holmes that judicial interpretation of constitutional provisions reflects "the felt necessities of the times," as the courts respond to social change.

The death of Chief Justice Fuller gave President Taft a third seat to fill. He followed the pragmatic Hughes with a dogmatic conservative, elevating Justice Edward D. White to the Court's leadership. One biographer suggested that Taft, with a burning ambition to become Chief Justice, chose the sixty-five-year-old White in hopes of a brief tenure, with himself as successor. That is, in fact, what happened in 1921, although no evidence of such Machiavellian plotting exists. At any rate, White's eleven years as Chief were marked by his consistent support of corporate power; his invention of the "rule of reason" to undermine the government's antitrust powers led Holmes to lament: "How could you be against that without being for a rule of unreason?"

Taft's selection of White as Chief Justice opened another seat, which he filled with Willis Van Devanter of Wyoming, who then served as a federal circuit judge after heading his state's high court. A brief stint in the Interior Department, handling public lands and Indian affairs, had gained him a reputation as a pro-government progressive and impressed Theodore Roosevelt, who placed Van Devanter on the federal bench. Taft chose him largely to fill a "western seat" on the Court and to satisfy Republicans who grumbled that two of the president's three nominees—Lurton and White—were Democrats. (House speaker Joseph Cannon joked: "If Taft were Pope, he'd want to appoint some Protestants to the College of Cardinals.") Van Devanter's supposed progressivism quickly vanished; during twenty-seven years on the Court, he voted so consistently against governmental power that Justice Harlan Fiske Stone dubbed him "Commander in Chief of Judicial Reaction."

The resignation of Justice William Moody in 1910 gave Taft his fourth nomination in one year; perhaps to spite Speaker Cannon (with whom he often feuded), he chose another southern Democrat, Joseph R. Lamar. A former Georgia legislator and judge, Lamar served for just five years before his death in 1916, consistently voting with the conservative majority and writing no opinions of any importance. Taft filled one last seat when John Marshall Harlan died in 1911 after thirty-four years of distinguished service. His replacement, Mahlon Pitney of New Jersey, was a former state judge and two-term congressman whose service over ten years proved thoroughly undistinguished and reactionary. Taft regretted this appointment; after he became Chief Justice, he publicly called Pitney a "weak member" of the Court and said he would "not assign cases" to him.

It seems odd that four of Taft's six Court nominees were lackluster justices; scholars have ranked Hughes as "great" and White as "near great," the latter a judgment more on his role as Chief Justice than on his jurisprudence. Perhaps Taft looked for men he could dominate as Chief Justice, a job he wanted much more than the presidency and expected to achieve. Perhaps he simply could not assess judicial quality; Louis Brandeis said that Taft had "a first-rate second-rate mind." It also seems odd that Taft, a partisan Republican, chose three Democrats. But they were all conservative southerners, and Taft had better relations with southern Democrats in Congress than with his own party's "progressives." All in all, few presidents used their power to shape the Court as poorly as Taft.

Woodrow Wilson took office in 1913 as the first Democratic president in sixteen years, after serving as New Jersey's governor and president of Princeton University. He won election with just 42 percent of the popular vote, the lowest margin since Lincoln's first victory in 1860. Wilson benefited from a split in Republican ranks, with Theodore Roosevelt taking his "Bull Moose" faction into the Progressive Party and William Howard Taft leading the GOP's conservative loyalists to a third-place finish; Eugene Debs won almost a million votes for the Socialists, whose party elected a Milwaukee congressman, ten New York legislators, and seventy-three mayors that year. The conservative press warned of "the rising tide of socialism," while the Wilson administration moved to placate business leaders with promises to relax antitrust enforcement.

Although he served two presidential terms, Wilson had only three chances to affect the Supreme Court, largely because Taft had recently filled six seats. His first nomination, to replace Horace Lurton in 1914, went to James C. McReynolds of Tennessee, who served Wilson as attorney general and—like Willis Van Devanter—had gained a "progressive" reputation as a Justice

Department "trust-buster" under Theodore Roosevelt. Wilson made a serious mistake; McReynolds turned out to be a judicial reactionary, with a violent temper and a vicious streak of anti-Semitism. He refused for several years to speak with Justice Louis Brandeis and pointedly read a newspaper when Justice Benjamin Cardozo took the oath of office in 1932. As a member of the "Four Horsemen of Reaction" during the New Deal years, McReynolds became "their loudest, most cantankerous, sarcastic, aggressive, intemperate, and reactionary representative," one biographer wrote before running out of adjectives.

Wilson redeemed himself in 1916 with the nomination of Louis Brandeis to replace Joseph Lamar, following his selection of a reactionary anti-Semite with a Jewish progressive. Brandeis was never faulted for his legal skills, which dazzled both friends and foes, but his fame as "the people's lawyer" prompted some critics to call him a dangerous radical. This was a label that did not fit; Brandeis wanted to reform capitalism, not abolish it, and he opposed "bigness" in both industry and government. Nonetheless, his nomination set off a loud and lengthy partisan battle that lasted more than four months. Leading the opposition to the slight, soft-spoken Brandeis was William Howard Taft, gargantuan in bulk (more than three hundred pounds) and bombastic in speech. Taft wanted the post for himself, but he would accept any seat, hoping for later elevation. Wilson would never have chosen his political foe, but the nomination of Brandeis inflicted "one of the deepest wounds" he suffered "as an American and a lover of the Constitution," Taft lamented to a friend. He urged Republican senators to reject Brandeis, telling Henry Cabot Lodge his nomination "is an evil and a disgrace that ought to be avoided."

Taft was one of six former American Bar Association presidents who signed a letter to the Senate: "The undersigned feel under the painful duty to say to you in their opinion, taking into view the reputation, character and professional career of Mr. Louis D. Brandeis, he is not a fit person to be a member of the Supreme Court of the United States." (However, eleven former ABA presidents did not sign this letter.) When the Senate debate ended on June 1, 1916, Brandeis won confirmation by a vote of forty-seven to twenty-two; just three Republicans and one Democrat crossed party lines. Brandeis joined his old friend Oliver Wendell Holmes on the bench. The two men differed greatly in temperament and sentiment: the Boston Brahmin distrusted the people but let them have their way; the Jewish reformer placed his trust in the people and let them have their way. Traveling different paths, they met at the same point and voted together—often in dissent—in most cases during the sixteen years they served together.

Almost overlooked by historians, John H. Clarke of Ohio joined the Court four months after Brandeis, replacing Charles Evans Hughes, who resigned in June 1916 to seek the Republican presidential nomination. The Senate confirmed Clarke, a former corporate lawyer and federal judge, without dissent (over the objection of the still-smarting William Howard Taft). During six years of service, Clarke compiled a more "progressive" record than Brandeis, who recommended him to Wilson. He was a firm supporter of labor and women, and his votes prompted Taft (after he finally became Chief Justice) to complain that Clarke approached cases "as he would vote on it in the Senate or the House, rather than to decide as a judge." Coming from Taft, this comment smacked of hypocrisy. Clarke became disillusioned with the Court—Taft undoubtedly contributed to this feeling—and resigned in 1922; he lived until 1945 and devoted the rest of his life to the cause of world peace.

The justices named by Presidents Taft and Wilson constituted a majority when the Court confronted in 1923 a choice between the "freedom of contract" rule established in the *Lochner* decision and the "chivalrous" exception for women workers in the *Muller* case. Members of the "weaker sex" had flexed their political muscles and won the right to vote in 1920, with ratification of the Nineteenth Amendment. Would the justices continue to lay their robes before women? The answer came in a case that involved the minimum wage board of the District of Columbia, over which Congress exercised legislative control. The board set a minimum wage for women of $71.50 per month, based on detailed studies of prices for food, housing, clothing, and a dozen other budget items, including "religion" and entertainment.

The board's findings and figures were challenged in two suits, one filed by the Children's Hospital and the other by Willie Lyons; the defendant in both cases was Jesse Adkins, chairman of the minimum wage board. The Children's Hospital claimed it could not afford to pay its female housekeepers the wage set by the board. Willie Lyons, employed by the Congress Hall Hotel as an elevator operator for $35 per month and two meals a day, alleged in her suit that "the work was light and healthful, the hours short, with surroundings clean and moral, and that she was anxious to continue it for the compensation she was receiving and that she did not earn more." One might wonder why Willie Lyons would challenge a law that would more than double her meager wage. Her lawyers denied the board's claim that she had been "induced to bring this action against her own interest." They argued that women "want, and they deserve, equal rights with men. They believe in self-reliance, independence and character. And they believe that the right to make their own bargains will result ultimately in better pay, a finer sense of self-respect and a higher quality of citizenship." One might wonder if Willie Lyons ever read these words in her lawyers' brief. But her name did not appear in the *Washington Post* or any other publication, and she became one of the many "forgotten" litigants whose names are now relegated to footnotes in history books.

The National Consumers League, which in 1908 enlisted a future Supreme Court justice, Louis Brandeis, to brief the successful *Muller* case, turned to another future justice, Harvard law professor Felix Frankfurter, to brief the case of *Adkins v. Children's Hospital.* Frankfurter produced another "Brandeis brief," which offered the Court voluminous data on the economic plight of working women. Five justices voted to strike down the minimum wage law. (Brandeis, who joined the Court in 1916, did not vote in *Adkins* because of his former ties to the Consumers League.) Justice George Sutherland, named to the Supreme Court in 1922 by President Warren Harding, wrote for the court in *Adkins.* He dismissed the *Muller* decision as precedent and returned to *Lochner* for authority. Sutherland made no reference in his opinion to the burdens of "motherhood" on women workers, arguing instead that legal and political differences between the sexes "have now come almost, if not quite, to the vanishing point." He pointed for support to the Nineteenth Amendment, ratified three years earlier in 1920, which extended voting rights to women. This "revolutionary" change in women's legal status convinced Sutherland they held the same rights to "liberty of contract" enjoyed by men. The "liberty" women enjoyed on an equal basis with men included, of course, freedom from minimum wage laws.

Sutherland's opinion was so reactionary that even Chief Justice William Howard Taft felt compelled to dissent. Echoing the appeals of Holmes and Harlan for judicial restraint, Taft argued that "it is not the function of the Court to hold congressional acts invalid simply because they are passed to carry out economic views which the Court believes to be unwise or unsound." Holmes also replied to Sutherland with thinly veiled scorn in a brief dissent. He first traced the path of judicial interpretation of "liberty" under the Fourteenth Amendment from "an unpretentious assertion of the liberty to follow the ordinary callings . . . into the dogma, Liberty of Contract." The former Harvard law professor gave Sutherland a lesson in first-year law. "Contract is not specially mentioned in the text that we have to construe," he wrote. "It is merely an example of doing what you want to do, embodied in the word liberty. But pretty much all law consists in forbidding men to do some things that they want to do, and contract is no more exempt from law than other acts." Holmes pointed Sutherland to some fifteen cases upholding economic regulations, from insurance rates to the "size of a loaf of bread." He could not understand why the majority did not follow the *Muller* decision, which he called "as good law today as it was in 1908." The obvious reason, which Holmes left unstated, was that only he and Justice McKenna (who had joined the unanimous opinion in *Muller* but switched sides in the *Adkins* case) remained from the Court that decided *Muller* in 1908. Four of the new justices—George Sutherland, Pierce Butler, Willis Van Devanter, and James McReynolds—who voted against the minimum wage law in *Adkins* were fiercely committed to laissez-faire doctrine. These four judicial reactionaries were later dubbed the "Four Horsemen of Reaction" for voting as a bloc in the 1930s against state and federal laws designed to rescue the American people from the ravages of the Great Depression. But the Four Horsemen first joined ranks to battle progressive legislation in the *Adkins* case, a decade before they led the charge on New Deal programs.

21

"Falsely Shouting Fire

in a Theatre"

The overriding issue during the presidential election of 1916—in which Woodrow Wilson sought a second term—was the war in Europe, which began in 1914 and quickly spread across the continent. Campaigning on a dual platform of diplomatic "neutrality" and military "preparedness," Wilson won reelection by just twenty-three electoral votes (and 3 percent of the popular vote) over Charles Evans Hughes, who found it hard to attack the president. When German submarines attacked American shipping in the Atlantic, Congress declared war on Germany in April 1917. No shocking event like the Japanese bombing of Pearl Harbor in 1941 precipitated this momentous decision; historian Richard Hofstadter called Wilson's appeal to Congress "rationalization of the flimsiest sort." But when the roll was called, six senators and fifty representatives stood up and voted against war.

Most Americans have forgotten—or never learned—that World War I was not a popular war, as the second clearly was. Few Americans had any desire to "pull England's chestnuts" out of the fire that raged in Europe. The bloody warfare between British and French soldiers on one side and Germans on the other—opponents whose trenches were often just yards apart—cost the lives of several million young men. Each side suffered 500,000 casualties in the First Battle of the Marne; almost 600,000 British and French soldiers were killed or wounded in the Battle of Verdun; and the Third Battle of Ypres cost the British 250,000 lives. In terms of battlefield deaths, this was the bloodiest war in history. Before the mortars and machine guns fell silent, ten million men had died on the battlefield and another twenty million people, many of them women and children, had perished from hunger and disease.

The Supreme Court heeded the call of patriotism and enlisted in the "War to End All Wars." In a symbolic but very real sense, the justices hung up their black robes and donned the khaki uniforms of American soldiers. Only two justices—Oliver Wendell Holmes and Chief Justice Edward White—had served during wartime, on opposite sides in the Civil War. All but one justice was over sixty in 1917, but they displayed as much martial spirit as the most eager young volunteer. Unable to face German troops in combat, they fought the Kaiser from the Court's bench.

Many in the United States had good reason to resist appeals to support the king of England in his territorial squabbles with the German Kaiser. Some based their reluctance on ethnic ties. Among three million Americans of German ancestry, many supported their country of origin; an equal number of Irish descent held even more hostility to the king as their countrymen struggled for independence and staged the abortive "Easter uprising" in 1916. Others based their objections to warfare on religious grounds; members of "peace churches" such as the Quakers, Mennonites, and Brethren refused military service as pacifists. Another large group, led by the Socialist Party, denounced the war as a conflict between rival capitalist nations whose leaders considered working people "cannon fodder" for their "imperialist" designs. Between these disparate groups, resistance to American involvement in the European war (hard to measure before the time of opinion polls) approached and perhaps exceeded the heights—or depths—of the Vietnam War period.

One fact about the government's policy toward the "Great War" is clear: once the Wilson administration decided to enter the conflict, it viewed all opposition as "seditious" and even treasonous. Early in 1917, one of Wilson's closest advisers, Elihu Root—a former war secretary and Wall Street lawyer—laid down the law: "We must have no criticism now." A few months later, upset that his words had not been heeded, Root warned that "there are men walking around the streets . . . tonight who ought to be taken out at sunrise tomorrow and shot for treason."

The Wilson administration initiated a "private" campaign against its critics that encouraged Americans to spy on their neighbors and fellow workers. The Justice Department sponsored the American Protective League, which by June 1917 had units in six hundred cities and towns and claimed a membership of almost 100,000 "patriotic" citizens. Ignoring the constraints of the Constitution, league members rifled through the mail of suspected "disloyals," infiltrated private meetings, and recorded speeches at public gatherings. The government's volunteer spies viewed any criticism of the war effort as a criminal offense. The APA claimed to have uncovered three million cases of disloyalty; the evidence for this dramatic claim, needless to say, was never offered for the public record.

Links between private vigilantes and public officials grew stronger: the popular magazine *Literary Digest* urged its readers to scan other periodicals and "send to us any editorial utterances which seem to them seditious or treasonable." The government's official propaganda agency, the Committee on Public

Information, asked the public to "report the man who spreads pessimistic sto-ries. Report him to the Department of Justice." Attorney General A. Mitchell Palmer (who escaped a bomb that blew up his home in 1919) said: "It is safe to say that never in its history has this country been so thoroughly policed."

The government backed up the private and official "policing" of wartime critics with an espionage law, passed by Congress in June 1917, shortly after Congress adopted a draft law that subjected all men between eighteen and thirty-five to military service. The Espionage Act was not directed against spy-ing for the enemy, but imposed maximum terms of twenty years in prison for anyone "who shall wilfully cause or attempt to cause insubordination, disloyalty, mutiny, or refusal of duty in the military or naval forces of the United States, or shall wilfully obstruct the recruiting or enlistment service of the United States." The law's sponsors—and government prosecutors—argued that any criticism of the government's wartime policies might induce draft-age men to refuse military service. There was good reason for this concern. Men of draft age did not flock to recruiting centers, and many sought exemptions from service or simply ignored draft notices. The *New York Herald* reported in August 1917 that ninety of the first hundred draftees in New York City claimed exemptions. Headlines in the *Journal* of Minneapolis, Minnesota, a state with many Germans and Socialists, read "DRAFT OPPOSITION FAST SPREADING IN STATE" and "CON-SCRIPTS GIVE FALSE ADDRESSES." Senator Thomas Hardwick of Georgia re-ported "general and widespread opposition on the part of many thousands" of young men, with "largely attended mass meetings held in every part of the State" to protest the draft. Before the war ended in November 1918, over 330,000 men were officially classified as draft evaders, more than 10 percent of those who reported for duty.

The government's draft machinery was slow and cumbersome, and most "evaders" escaped prosecution, although several thousand—those who regis-tered but refused to take the physical examination—wound up in jail. Men in this group were tried in civilian courts and faced a maximum one-year term. Those who refused to register—most often for religious or political reasons— were subject to military court-martial and the death penalty; 450 of these "ab-solutists" were convicted and twenty sentenced to die, although none reached the Fort Leavenworth gallows before the war ended. Ironically, the War Depart-ment's judge advocate general, who supervised military court-martials, was a Harvard law professor on leave, Felix Frankfurter, who later served on the Supreme Court and expressed his fervent patriotism in the flag-salute cases of the 1940s.

Justice Department lawyers brought two thousand prosecutions under the Espionage Act and sent more than nine hundred people to prison. The most ironic case in this group was *United States v. Spirit of '76*, brought against Robert Goldstein, producer of a film about the American Revolution; his depiction of

British atrocities against the colonists tended "to question the good faith of our ally, Great Britain," said the judge, who imposed a ten-year sentence on Goldstein. However, prosecutors ran into unexpected problems in securing Espionage Act convictions: jurors in some areas, especially the Midwest—home to many "isolationists" and German Americans—refused to expose war critics to twenty-year sentences; many of those prosecuted, like the Nebraska woman who knitted socks for soldiers and voiced doubt they would reach them, clearly posed no threat to military recruitment, and several federal judges threw out indictments or refused to send those convicted to prison. Judge George Borquin directed a Montana jury to acquit a sharp-tongued rancher named Ves Hall, who declared in a saloon that "the United States was only fighting for Wall Street millionaires" and who also used a barnyard expletive (deleted in the judicial opinion) to describe President Wilson. Judge Borquin ruled that a person's "beliefs, opinions, and hopes" were protected from prosecution, and that Hall's statements did not reflect a "specific intent to commit specific crimes," required by the terms of the Espionage Act.

Prompted by Montana's two senators, Congress responded to Judge Borquin's ruling in 1918 by adding a "sedition" clause to the Espionage Act, outlawing "any disloyal, . . . scurrilous, or abusive language about the form of government of the United States . . . or any language intended to bring the form of government of the United States . . . into contempt, scorn, contumely, or disrepute." This new Sedition Act recalled the notorious Alien and Sedition Act of 1798, down to its wording. The Supreme Court never ruled on the first law, which expired in 1801 before any challenge reached the justices. But challenges to the Espionage and Sedition Acts of World War I did reach the Court, putting the justices on a collision course with the First Amendment. For the first time since ratification of the Bill of Rights in 1791, the Court was asked to rule that Congress had violated the constitutional ban on laws that abridged "freedom of speech, or of the press."

The first case to test the First Amendment began in Philadelphia, not far from the Constitution's birthplace at Independence Hall. On August 13, 1917, members of the city's Socialist Party executive committee gathered for their monthly meeting. After discussing the party's campaign against the recently enacted draft law, the assembled comrades directed their general secretary, Charles J. Schenck, to prepare a leaflet for mailing to men whose names were listed in the newspapers as having passed their army physical examinations.

Schenck already had copies of a leaflet the party had been distributing in its antidraft campaign. It was headed "LONG LIVE THE CONSTITUTION OF THE UNITED STATES" and reprinted the words of the Thirteenth Amendment, which abolished slavery and "involuntary servitude." The leaflet employed what Justice Oliver Wendell Holmes later called "impassioned language" against the draft. "A conscript is little better than a convict," it read. "He is deprived of his liberty and of his right to think and act as a free man." The leaflet urged readers to join the party's campaign to repeal the draft law. "Do not submit to intimidation," it implored. "Exercise your rights of free speech, peaceful assemblage and petitioning the government for a redress of grievances. Come to the headquarters of the Socialist Party, 1326 Arch Street, and sign a petition to Congress for the repeal of the Conscription Act."

The first side of the leaflet simply asked readers to sign a petition. Schenck drafted language for the other side, which he headed, "ASSERT YOUR RIGHTS!" Justice Holmes later summarized its text: "It stated reasons for alleging that any one violated the Constitution when he refused to recognize 'your right to assert your opposition to the draft,' and went on, 'If you do not assert and support your rights, you are helping to deny or disparage rights which it is the solemn duty of all citizens and residents of the United States to retain.'" Holmes continued: "It denied the power to send our citizens away to foreign shores to shoot up the people of other lands, and added that words could not express the condemnation such cold-blooded ruthlessness deserves, &c., &c., winding up, 'You must do your share to maintain, support and uphold the rights of the people of this country.'" Schenck's language did not ask readers to take any other action than voicing their objections to the draft law.

On August 20, Schenck picked up fifteen thousand copies from the printer and set to work addressing them; some copies—the record never stated how many—were actually mailed to draftees. Federal officials soon learned of the leaflets, secured a search warrant for the party headquarters, seized papers about the leaflets, and arrested Schenck and four executive committee members. They were charged under the Espionage Act with conspiring to "obstruct the recruiting and enlistment services of the United States." After a four-day trial in December 1917, the federal judge who presided directed the jury to acquit three defendants for lack of evidence. Schenck and Dr. Elizabeth Baer, the executive committee secretary, were convicted; he received a six-month sentence and the judge gave her a ninety-day term. Both were released on bail pending their appeals, which went directly to the Supreme Court under rules allowing cases that challenged federal laws on constitutional grounds to bypass the circuit courts.

More than a year passed between the trial of Schenck and Baer and their Supreme Court hearing in January 1919. By then, the "Great War" had ended with the Armistice in November 1918. The draft had also ended, but not the government's campaign to punish its opponents. The Socialist Party's lawyers in the case, Henry Nelson and Henry Gibbons, filled their brief with excerpts from lower-court rulings against the Espionage Act. The most persuasive and influential was written by Judge Augustus N. Hand, who belonged to an eminent judicial family and served on the federal district court in New York City. Justice Department lawyers had charged editors of *The Masses*, a "literary" radical magazine, with violating the Espionage Act for criticizing the war in its pages. Judge Hand instructed the jurors to acquit the editors—who included such noted writers as Max Eastman and John Reed—for lack of proof they intended to obstruct military recruiting. "It is the constitutional right of every citizen to express his opinion about the war" and "the merits and demerits of the system of conscription," Hand wrote, "even though the expression of such opinion may unintentionally or indirectly discourage recruiting and enlistment."

Judge Hand and Justice Holmes were old friends, but the two men differed greatly on the First Amendment. The Civil War veteran had only contempt for pacifists and radicals, expressing his views in letters to friends. He told one that "man's destiny is to fight," and asked another, "doesn't this squashy sentimentality of a big minority of our people about human life make you puke?" Holmes was equally dismissive of free speech claims. Society had as much right to protect itself against dangerous opinions as against contagious diseases. "Free speech stands no differently than freedom from vaccination," he wrote to Judge Learned Hand, who sat on the federal appeals court in New York and was the cousin of Augustus. Expanding on this view to another friend, Harold Laski, Holmes wrote that "we should deal with the act of speech as we deal with any other overt act that we don't like."

Holmes did not like what Charles Schenck had written about the draft law. Neither did any other justice; they all joined his opinion in *Schenck v. United States*, issued on March 3, 1919. After briefly recounting the facts and brushing aside objections to the government's search warrant, Holmes addressed the First Amendment claims in just two paragraphs. But they abounded in memorable phrases. "We admit that in many places and in ordinary times the defendants in saying all that was said in the circular would have been within their constitutional rights," Holmes began. "But the character of every act depends upon the circumstances in which it is done." In these two sentences, Holmes set a trap for Schenck and Baer. He obviously felt that August 1917 was not an "ordinary time" and that the "circumstances" of their acts deprived them of constitutional protection. Holmes sprang the trap with an example of unprotected speech. "The most stringent protection of free speech would not protect a man in falsely shouting fire in a theatre and causing a panic."

Perhaps no other sentence in any Supreme Court opinion has been as widely—and as inaccurately—remembered and repeated. Those who cite the "shouting fire" phrase, however, most often forget to include the "falsely" qualifier. No one disputes that falsely shouting fire in any crowded place would not be protected speech. But was Schenck falsely shouting fire in his leaflet? What, if anything, in the circular was false? More important, what relevance did Holmes's example have to Schenck's appeal to "assert your rights"? Holmes employed an arresting illustration of unprotected speech, but his sentence only served to inflame the reader against Schenck and to view him as inciting panic.

Holmes continued with another well-remembered sentence: "The question in every case is whether the words used are used in such circumstances and are of such a nature as to create a clear and present danger that they will bring about the substantive evils that Congress has a right to prevent." Holmes did not invent the "clear and present danger" test in First Amendment law, but his *Schenck* opinion made it a catchword, repeated and employed by later judges in dozens of cases. Like any legal phrase, its words require definition. How "clear" must the danger be, and who judges its clarity? How "present," and who judges its imminence? Holmes offered some guidance—presumably to lower-court judges—in applying his test to the facts of a case: "It is a question of proximity and degree." He may have adapted these terms from Judge George Borquin, who ordered the acquittal of Ves Hall in Montana and used the terms "magnitude and proximity" in his opinion as tests of criminal intent. But the two judges reached opposite conclusions in the two cases; Borquin found no intent by Hall to commit "specific crimes," while Holmes concluded that Schenck intended to induce draft-law violations.

Holmes returned to the First Amendment question: "When a nation is at war many things that might be said in time of peace are such a hindrance to its effort that their utterance will not be endured so long as men fight and that no Court could regard them as protected by any constitutional right." But did the Constitution allow this distinction between peacetime and wartime speech? Holmes made no reference to the Court's 1866 opinion in *Ex parte Milligan*: "The Constitution of the United States is a law for rulers and people, equally in war and in peace, and covers with the shield of its protection all classes of men, at all times, and under all circumstances," the justices had ruled unanimously. "No doctrine, involving more pernicious consequences," they added, "was ever invented by the wit of man than that any of its provisions can be suspended during any of the great exigencies of government." If the government cannot suspend Fifth Amendment protections during wartime, can it suspend—or limit—First Amendment rights? Holmes clearly thought so, but his brief opinion did not expand on this crucial question.

Holmes concluded by noting that the government was not required to prove that Schenck's leaflet had induced any draftee to refuse induction. Simply showing "the tendency and the intent" of the leaflet to accomplish this aim was enough; "we perceive no ground for saying that success alone warrants making the act a crime."

Far more people recognize the "clear and present danger" phrase than remember the *Schenck* case or have any familiarity with its facts. Charles Schenck clearly hoped that some potential draftees would heed his appeal, not just to sign petitions against the draft law but to refuse induction as well. But he only counseled the first act, not the second. Holmes conceded that the Socialist leaflet, on its face, "confined itself to peaceful measures such as a petition for the repeal of the act." However, "it would not have been sent unless it had been intended to have some effect," he continued, "and we do not see what effect it could be expected to have upon persons subject to the draft except to influence them to obstruct" military recruitment. Holmes did not address the fact that every criticism of government policy might have the "tendency" to influence someone to obstruct its operation.

"The life of the law," Holmes wrote in 1881, "has not been logic, it has been experience." His *Schenck* opinion, glittering with memorable phrases, lacked any logical consistency; but it reflected Holmes's wartime experience and his contempt for those who refused to acknowledge that "man's destiny is to fight."

One week after the Court issued its *Schenck* decision, the justices unanimously upheld a ten-year sentence imposed on Eugene Debs for violating the Espionage Act. The charismatic Socialist leader had been prosecuted for making a two-hour speech at Nimasilla Park in Canton, Ohio, on June 16, 1918. Speaking on a Sunday afternoon at an outdoor picnic and rally, Debs larded his speech with indignation, humor, bombast, and passion. Among the crowd of several thousand was E. R. Sterling, who scribbled out Debs's words in shorthand for the Justice Department, whose agents had shadowed Debs on a national tour to protest the imprisonment of other Socialists.

Pointing to the county jail across the street from the park, Debs told the crowd, "I have just returned from a visit over yonder, where three of our most loyal comrades are paying the penalty for their devotion to the cause of the working class." He had visited three young men serving sentences for obstructing military recruitment. "They have come to realize," Debs said of his imprisoned followers, "that it is extremely dangerous to exercise the constitutional right of free speech in a country fighting to make Democracy safe in the world." (Sterling noted "applause" at these words; the crowd applauded, cheered, and laughed more than three hundred times during the speech.)

Debs was well aware that government agents were recording his words. "I realize that, in speaking to you this afternoon," he said, "there are certain limitations placed upon the right of free speech. I must be exceedingly careful, prudent, as to what I say, and even more careful and more prudent as to how I say it." The crowd laughed. "I may not be able to say all that I think (laughter and applause); but I am not going to say anything that I do not think (applause). But, I would rather a thousand times be a free soul in jail than to be a sycophant and coward on the streets (applause and shouts)."

The Socialist leader turned his oratorical guns on the judges who had sentenced his comrades to prison. "Who appoints the federal judges? The people? In all the history of the country, the working class have never named a Federal judge. There are 121, and every solitary one of them holds his position, his tenure, through the interests and power of corporate capital. The corporations and trusts dictate their appointment. And when they go to the bench, they go, not to serve the people, but to serve the interests that placed them where they are." The crowd cheered these words.

Debs denounced the judges who had sentenced two Socialist women, Kate Richards O'Hare and Rose Pastor Stokes, to prison for making antiwar speeches. Both were tireless organizers and effective speakers for the party. O'Hare received a five-year term for telling a crowd in Bowman, North Dakota, that the government said, "We need your boy to protect the profits of the Capitalist class, and your child is a slave, cannon fodder." Imposing sentence on O'Hare, federal judge Martin Wade warned: "Every day she is at liberty she is a menace to the government." Debs rebuked Wade for refusing to allow testimony that government agents had attributed remarks to O'Hare that she had not made. "This would seem incredible to me," Debs said, "if I had not had some experience of my own with a Federal court."

Stokes received a ten-year sentence for declaring, "I am for the people and the government is for the profiteers." Debs voiced his outrage at these convictions. "The United States, under the rule of the plutocracy," he thundered, "is the only country that would send a woman to the penitentiary for ten years for exercising her constitutional right of free speech (applause). If this be treason let them make the most of it (applause)."

Debs paid a price for these remarks. Justice Holmes took offense at the aspersions Debs cast on his fellow judges. In his opinion, Holmes recounted what Debs had said about "false testimony" at O'Hare's trial and how Stokes had been convicted at a "mock trial" and sentenced by "a corporation tool on the bench." The indictment against Debs included two counts based on these comments, and the trial judge had allowed prosecutors to read them to the jury and to note that O'Hare and Stokes had been sentenced for obstructing military recruitment. Jurors would presumably conclude—and probably did—that Debs shared his comrades' views and was equally guilty. Debs's lawyers had objected to this testimony, but Holmes found it relevant. "The defendant purported to understand the grounds on which these persons were imprisoned," he wrote, and prosecutors could introduce evidence of "his expression of sympathy" with O'Hare and Stokes "to throw light on the intent" of his speech.

During his Canton speech, Debs cast blame for the war on both sides, denouncing both the Allies and Germany for seeking "profits" at home and "plunder" abroad. "The master class has always declared the war," he declaimed; "the subject class has always fought the battles; the master class has all to gain, nothing to lose, and the subject class has had nothing to gain and all to lose including their lives (applause). They have always taught you that it is your patriotic duty to go to war and to have yourselves slaughtered at a command." This was as close as Debs came to mentioning the draft, perhaps from the "prudence" of knowing his words were being recorded.

The fact that Debs had not urged draft resistance failed to sway Justice

Holmes. The Socialist Party had adopted a resolution calling for "continuous, active, and public opposition to the war, through demonstrations, mass petitions, and all other means within our power." Holmes read this statement, and Debs's speech, as "evidence that if in that speech he used words tending to obstruct the recruiting service he meant that they should have that effect."

Debs made clear in Canton his opposition to the "junkers" who ruled Germany. "I hate, I loath, I despise junkerdom," he told the crowd. "I have no earthly use for the junkers of Germany, and not one particle more use for the junkers in the United States (thunderous applause and cheers)." His listeners had no trouble understanding Debs, but Justice Holmes professed to hear sympathy for the Germans. Addressing these words, Holmes abandoned his usual clarity for the murky statement that Debs had "expressed opposition to Prussian militarism in a way that naturally might be thought to be intended to include that mode of proceeding in the United States." Holmes did not explain how anyone could interpret Debs's denunciation of German "junkerdom" as advocating "that mode of proceeding" in America.

Holmes made only a passing reference to the First Amendment in his *Debs v. United States* opinion. All he said, in fact, was that objections to the conviction "based upon the First Amendment to the Constitution" had been "disposed of in *Schenck v. United States*." Holmes did not repeat, or rely on, the "clear and present danger" test in *Debs*, perhaps because he thought its application was implied in his opinion. More likely, he realized it would be more difficult to find a "clear and present danger" to the draft in Debs's words than in Schenck's leaflet. It was enough for Holmes that the "natural tendency" of the Canton speech was to "obstruct the recruiting service." What legal scholars later called the "bad tendency" test, which cast a much wider net over speech, owes its genesis to the *Debs* opinion, much less remembered than *Schenck* but more dangerous to dissenters.

Speaking to the judge who sentenced him, Debs put his politics into a few words: "Your honor, years ago I recognized my kinship with all living beings, and I made up my mind that I was not one bit better than the meanest on earth. I said then, and I say now, that while there is a lower class, I am in it; while there is a criminal element, I am of it; while there is a soul in prison, I am not free." The opinion Holmes wrote sent Debs to prison, and President Woodrow Wilson refused all appeals to release his political opponent. Debs campaigned for the presidency in 1920 from his cell in Atlanta Penitentiary against Republican Warren Harding and Democrat James Cox, and again garnered almost a million votes. Harding won by the largest margin in American history, and set Debs free in 1921 after three years in prison. By this time, the Socialist firebrand was tired and ill at sixty-six, and the party he had built into a real force in American politics never regained its electoral strength.

Justice Holmes issued his *Schenck* and *Debs* opinions in March 1919. Something happened to him during the next eight months. The man who found that

Charles Schenck's leaflet posed a "clear and present danger" to the draft and that the "natural tendency" of Eugene Debs's speech would obstruct military recruiting changed his mind about the First Amendment by November 1919. The story of his move from certitude to skepticism is not entirely clear, but Holmes obviously listened to his critics and heeded their words. One of the first to suggest that he had erred was Judge Learned Hand, who exchanged letters with Holmes after the two men shared a train ride and began a dialogue on free speech issues. Shortly after Holmes issued his *Debs* opinion, Hand wrote to argue that speech only violated the Espionage Act "when the words were directly an incitement" to break the law. Hand questioned whether the evidence met this test. Holmes replied that "I don't quite get your point," adding that he saw little difference between a "direct incitement" test and his own standard of "clear and present danger."

Holmes received more pointed, and more public, criticism from Ernst Freund of the University of Chicago Law School. Writing in *The New Republic* on "The Debs Case and Freedom of Speech," Freund attacked the notion of "implied provocation" to violate laws and argued that only "direct provocation" could satisfy the First Amendment. Freund also dismissed the example Holmes offered in *Schenck* to support the "clear and present danger" test. "Justice Holmes would make us believe that the relation of the speech to obstruction is like that of the shout of Fire! in a crowded theatre to the resulting panic! Surely implied provocation in connection with political offenses is an unsafe doctrine if it has to be made plausible by a parallel so manifestly inappropriate." Holmes composed a reply to Freund that stood by his opinions but admitted some doubts. "I hated to have to write the Debs case," he confessed. "I could not see the wisdom of pressing the cases, especially when the fighting was over and I think it quite possible that if I had been on the jury I should have been for acquittal," he added. Holmes had second thoughts about debating his opinions in public and did not send his letter to *The New Republic*.

A more persuasive—and more tactfully phrased—response to the *Schenck* and *Debs* opinions came from Zechariah Chafee of Harvard Law School. In his *Harvard Law Review* article "Freedom of Speech in War Time," Chafee admitted the difficulty of deciding "where the line runs" between lawful and unlawful speech. He suggested that Holmes had missed a "magnificent opportunity'" to draw such a line by comparing Schenck's leaflet with a false shout of "Fire!" Chafee offered a better example: "How about the man who gets up in a theater between the acts and informs the audience honestly but perhaps mistakenly that the fire exits are too few or locked. He is a much closer parallel to Schenck or Debs." He supported the "direct incitement" test that Learned Hand had proposed to Holmes, adding that "absolutely unlimited discussion" of public issues—even during wartime—was necessary for "the discovery and spread of truth on subjects of general concern." Holmes read Chafee's article and met with him over tea during the summer of 1919. Perhaps he read the leaves in his cup with an eye toward First Amendment cases on the Court's docket for argument that fall.

The case that led Holmes to revise his First Amendment views began on a Thursday evening, August 22, 1918, on Second Avenue near Eighth Street in New York City. The Lower East Side in Manhattan was home to thousands of Russian Jews, most of them refugees over the past decade from the anti-Semitic "pogroms" of the czarist government, which had fallen to the Communist Bolsheviks in the October Revolution of 1917. Passersby noticed dozens of leaflets falling onto the sidewalks from a rooftop. Those who picked up copies discovered that some were printed in English, others in Yiddish. A storekeeper picked up one in English and was incensed by its contents, printed under the heading "The Hypocrisy of the United States and Her Allies." He rushed up the stairs to the rooftop but could not find the culprit. He then brought copies of both the English and Yiddish leaflets to the police, who conducted a house-to-house search without locating the perpetrator. Newspaper headlines the next day alerted New Yorkers: "Seditious Circulars Scattered in Streets" and "Wilson Attacked in Circulars from Roofs of East Side."

On the morning of August 23, four men brought more copies to the police and said they saw the leaflets floating from a window at 610 Broadway. Two detectives from the army's Military Intelligence Division visited the building, checked the time cards of workers at the American Hat Company on the third floor, and found that Hyman Rosansky had punched in earlier than usual. They approached Rosansky and asked to see his draft card; he pulled it out of his coat pocket with other papers, including copies of both the English and Yiddish leaflets. Rosansky claimed he had found them on the fire escape, but no one had seen him near it that morning. The detectives took him to his apartment in East Harlem, where they found more leaflets and a loaded .32 caliber revolver.

Grilled at police headquarters, Rosansky said he was born in Russia and had entered the United States in 1910. He admitted being an anarchist but claimed he had nothing to do with producing the leaflets. He had been approached the night before by some men he knew from anarchist circles. "I know the fellows but don't know exactly the names," he said. "Lachowsky I know by name." The men gave Rosansky leaflets to distribute. "I says, 'What kind of leaflets?' 'It is all right, you don't have to know what kind of leaflets.' 'What I got to do with this?' He says, 'You have got to throw them from the window.' " Thoroughly frightened, Rosansky told the detectives he had arranged to meet Lachowsky and other members of his shadowy "Group" that evening on East 104th Street to receive more leaflets. Military agents staked out the block while Rosansky nervously waited for his contacts to appear. By ones and twos, several people approached Rosansky; one handed him a bundle of leaflets. Detectives followed them into apartments and restaurants and arrested four young men and one woman: Jacob Abrams, Hyman Lachowsky, Samuel Lipman, Jacob Schwartz, and Mollie Steimer. They were all held in the city jail, charged with violating the Sedition Act of 1918, arraigned the next morning, and held on $10,000 bail. The *New York World* reported that all five belonged to "the Blast Group and all are long-haired anarchists who came here from Russia."

What had so alarmed the shopkeeper who picked up a leaflet on Second Avenue that he took it to the police? The English-language circular denounced American military intervention in Russia and efforts "to crush the russian revolution." The previous month, President Wilson had approved sending 7,500 American troops to eastern Russia, purportedly to divert German forces from the European front. The Wilson administration had yielded to pressure from its wartime allies for military action against the Bolsheviks, who had signed a separate peace treaty with the Germans in March 1918. Many Americans paid little attention to this faraway military adventure, but most Russian immigrants opposed the Allied intervention. The leaflets that Abrams and his fellow Blast Group members had tossed from rooftops and windows denounced Wilson for failing to inform the American public about his real purpose in sending troops to Siberia, to support the "White" soldiers who battled the "Red" forces of the Bolshevik regime. "His shameful, cowardly silence about the intervention in Russia reveals the hypocrisy of the plutocratic gang in Washington," read the English version. The Blast Group took pains to distance themselves from German sympathizers. "It is absurd to call us pro-German," they wrote. "We hate and despise German militarism more than do your hypocritical tyrants."

The English leaflet did no more than exhort "workers of America, workers of Germany" to be "AWAKE!" to their governments' efforts to destroy the Russian Revolution. However, the Yiddish version—headed "Workers, Wake Up!"—appealed to workers in munitions factories who "are producing bullets, bayonets, cannon, to murder not only the Germans, but also your dearest, best, who are in Russia and are fighting for freedom." The Blast Group urged direct action: "Workers, our reply to the barbaric intervention has to be a general strike!" Taking its heated rhetoric at face value, this leaflet was hardly likely to foment a "general strike" or any disruption of war production. The "sweatshops" of the Lower East Side produced clothing and buttons, not cannons and bullets. Even if workers in munitions factories read the Yiddish leaflet, few if any would risk their jobs by striking for any reason. But these facts did not dissuade government prosecutors from charging the Blast Group members with violating the Sedition Act by publishing "disloyal, scurrilous and abusive language about the form of Government of the United States" and with inciting "curtailment of production of things and products, to wit, ordnance and ammunition, necessary and essential to the prosecution of the war."

The trial of the Russian anarchists took place in October 1918 while

German and Allied diplomats were negotiating the Armistice that ended the bloody carnage of World War I the next month. But the assault on the First Amendment continued in the courtroom of Judge Henry D. Clayton, Jr., who came from Alabama to help shoulder the burden of wartime prosecutions in New York City. The son of a Confederate officer, Clayton faced the Russian defendants not only across his judicial bench, but across a cultural and political chasm. He belittled their broken English and openly disparaged their beliefs. When the jury returned with its inevitable "guilty" verdicts, Clayton sentenced Jacob Abrams, Samuel Lipman, and Hyman Lachowsky—Jacob Schwartz, who suffered numerous police beatings, died in jail the night before the trial began— to maximum terms of twenty years. In a gesture of southern chivalry, Clayton cut five years from the maximum for Mollie Steimer.

The Supreme Court heard the appeals of the convicted anarchists in October 1919, a year after their trial and sentences. Their lawyer, Harry Weinberger, submitted a brief that took an uncompromising view of First Amendment rights. Not only did he reject the "clear and present danger" test of Justice Holmes, he went beyond the "direct incitement" standard of Judge Learned Hand to argue that only "overt acts" could be punished; speech itself must be "perfectly unrestrained" by government. Weinberger asserted that "absolute freedom of speech is the only basis upon which the Government can stand and remain free." The government's brief took an equally extreme position, claiming that the First Amendment's framers did not intend to protect "the unlimited right to publish a seditious libel." This effort to revive the doctrine that any criticism of government could be punished had little historical support, but it reflected the hard-line position of Justice Department officials. The brief also claimed that the Yiddish leaflet calling for a general strike was intended "to stop the production of munitions, and to overthrow by force the form of government of the United States by law established."

Jacob Abrams's name went first in alphabetical order on the appeal, and the Supreme Court decided *Abrams v. United States* on November 10, 1919. Seven justices lined up with the government; only Oliver Wendell Holmes and Louis Brandeis stood behind the First Amendment. Justice John H. Clarke, a "progressive" on most issues, wrote for the majority. His opinion dismissed in one sentence Harry Weinberger's argument that the Sedition Act violated the First Amendment. "This contention is sufficiently discussed and is definitely negatived in *Schenck v. United States*" is all Clarke wrote on this issue. But he devoted six pages to answering Weinberger's claim that "there is no substantial evidence in the record to support the judgment" that the anarchists intended to disrupt war production with their call for a general strike. Clarke conceded that their primary motivation was "resentment" against American military intervention in Russia, but nonetheless concluded that "the plain purpose of their propaganda was to excite, at the supreme crisis of the war, disaffection, sedition, riots, and, as they hoped, revolution, in this country for the purpose of embarrassing and if possible defeating the military plans of the Government in Europe." Perhaps a general strike that spread from the Lower East Side of Manhattan across the country might have led to riots and revolution, but Clarke read more into the Yiddish leaflet than its authors—who directed their appeal to Yiddish-speaking Russians—had intended or even hoped for. Clarke concluded that "the language of these circulars was obviously intended to provoke and encourage resistance to the United States in the war" and ruled that "the judgment of the District Court must be Affirmed."

Clarke's opinion stretched the First Amendment too far for Justice Holmes, who had first pulled its words out of shape in his *Schenck* and *Debs* opinions. He tried now, writing in dissent, to repair the damage he had caused. But Holmes was unwilling—whether from pride or conviction is unclear—to disavow his earlier opinions. "I have never seen any reason to doubt that the questions of law that alone were before this Court" in *Schenck* and *Debs* "were rightly decided," he wrote. This carefully worded sentence left open the question of whether the facts in those cases supported the convictions. Holmes made no effort to argue that they did. His seven-page opinion, joined by Louis Brandeis, made clear his belief that the facts in *Abrams* did not justify the convictions. He disparaged and belittled the Russian anarchists and their "silly" leaflets. Even if "enough can be squeezed from these poor and puny anonymities to turn the color of legal litmus paper," he wrote, only "the most nominal punishment" would be justified. The anarchists were really being punished "for the creed that they avow—a creed that I believe to be the creed of ignorance and immaturity," Holmes declared.

Holmes did not shrink, however, from confronting in *Abrams* the First Amendment issues he had ducked in *Schenck* and *Debs*. He put into words, eloquent in phrasing and resonant in meaning, the thoughts that had germinated in his mind over the past eight months. Without mentioning Learned Hand, Ernst Freund, or Zechariah Chafee by name, he drew upon their critiques of his earlier opinions to refashion his First Amendment views. Holmes did not fully embrace the "libertarian" position on free speech, but he came close. He first adopted the "direct incitement" test that Hand and Freund had proposed. Nothing in the English leaflet advocated any law violation or obstruction of war production; only the Yiddish leaflet "affords even a foundation for the charge," Holmes wrote, but "it is evident from the beginning to the end that the only object of the paper is to help Russia and stop American intervention there against the popular government—not to impede the United States in the war that it was carrying on."

In his *Schenck* opinion, Holmes viewed the First Amendment through two lenses, one for wartime and one for peacetime. "When a nation is at war many things that might be said in time of peace," he argued, were so dangerous that "no Court could regard them as protected by any constitutional right." Eight months later in his *Abrams* dissent, Holmes brought free speech into clearer focus, although the line between lawful and unlawful speech remained blurred. The government's power to punish speech "undoubtedly is greater in time of war than in time of peace," he wrote, "because war opens dangers that do not exist at other times." But "the principle of the right to free speech is always the same," he asserted. "It is only the present danger of immediate evil or an intent to bring it about that warrants Congress in setting a limit to the expression of opinion" on public issues. Holmes was not simply restating the "clear and present danger" test. His new test required that speech "so imminently threaten immediate interference" with government's lawful purposes or programs "that an immediate check is required to save the country." Words like "imminent" and "immediate" carry more urgency than "present." None of the speech punished in any of the wartime Sedition Act cases could possibly have met the stringent test that Holmes proposed in his *Abrams* dissent. The Court adopted this test exactly fifty years later in 1969, ruling in *Brandenburg v. Ohio* that only speech "directed to inciting or producing imminent lawless action" could be punished.

Holmes concluded his *Abrams* dissent with words that express, perhaps better than any before or since, the values that animate the First Amendment. He adapted them from his own letters and from the writings of others, especially Zechariah Chafee, but they ring with a resonance that only Holmes could produce. "Persecution for the expression of opinions seems to me perfectly logical," he began. "If you have no doubt of your premises or your power and want a certain result with all your heart you naturally express your wishes in law and sweep away all opposition," Holmes continued. "But when men have realized that time has upset many fighting faiths, they may come to believe even more than they believe the very foundations of their own conduct that the ultimate good desired is better reached by the free trade in ideas—that the best test of truth is the power of the thought to get itself accepted in the competition of the market, and that truth is the only ground upon which their wishes safely can be carried out. That at any rate is the theory of our Constitution."

These lofty sentiments echoed the arguments of John Stuart Mill in his essay "On Liberty," which Holmes had recently reread, but even Mill had agreed that words "lost their immunity" from punishment when they became "a positive instigation to some mischievous act." Holmes in both *Schenck* and *Debs* had found an instigation to violate the draft law, and the Court's majority in *Abrams* found a similar instigation to obstruct war production. The test of "immediate interference" with government's lawful purposes and programs would bring most speech within the First Amendment's protective arms, but Holmes wrote only for himself and Justice Brandeis in *Abrams*.

The Court's majority sent the four Russian anarchists from the New York jails where they had been held since their arrests to state and federal prisons in November 1919. Mollie Steimer, just twenty years old, was sent to the Missouri state penitentiary; the three young men—Jacob Abrams, Hyman Lachowsky, and Samuel Lipman—went to the Atlanta federal penitentiary, where they joined Eugene Debs, who was serving his ten-year sentence. All the anarchists endured "hard time" behind bars, forced to work at exhausting prison jobs and punished with solitary confinement for any violation of prison rules. Harry Weinberger, who defended them in court, mounted a campaign for an "amnesty" that would allow their deportation to Soviet Russia. Friends and supporters of President Wilson urged that he commute the sentences of all those imprisoned for Espionage Act violations, but he adamantly refused. "I do not think the men you refer to are in any proper sense political prisoners," he replied to Norman Hapgood, a prominent journalist. Rather, all those in prison had "violated criminal statutes." Not until Wilson relinquished the White House to Warren Harding did amnesty appeals finally succeed.

On November 23, 1921, the four young anarchists boarded a ship in New York that took them to Latvia, from where they traveled by train to Moscow. Having endured prison in the United States for supporting the Soviet revolution, they encountered persecution by the Bolshevik government. Vladimir Lenin ordered a crackdown on anarchists after a mutiny at the Kronstadt naval base in March 1921 in which they played leading roles. Bolshevik troops killed six hundred insurgents and marched several thousand to prisons, while thousands more fled to neighboring Finland. "The time has come," Lenin warned, "to put an end to opposition, to put a lid on it; we have had enough opposition." The Bolsheviks put an end to Russian anarchism, and the four young people who chose deportation over prison all met sad ends. Samuel Lipman—who was more of a Marxist than an anarchist—joined the Communist Party but could not escape his past and was murdered in the Stalinist purges of the 1930s. Hyman Lachowsky moved from Moscow to Minsk in 1922 and most likely died when German troops overran the city in 1941 and systematically murdered all Jews who remained. Quickly disillusioned, Jacob Abrams and Mollie Steimer left Russia and found exile in Mexico by different paths. Abrams died in 1953 and Steimer in 1980. Mollie Steimer, the most uncompromising of the group, wrote in 1960 what could serve as an epitaph for them all: "We fought injustice in our humble way as best we could; and if the result was prison, hard labour, deportations and lots of suffering, well, this was something that every human being who fights for a better humanity has to expect."

"Every Idea Is an

Incitement"

The guns fell silent across Europe in November 1918, and most Americans breathed a sigh of relief. The Socialist Party no longer scared the public, and the anarchist movement—never more than a few thousand in numbers—had been decimated by Sedition Act prosecutions and had dwindled to an impotent handful. But a new and far more frightening enemy soon appeared, in the form of the Communist Party, first organized in 1919. Members of the Socialist Party's "left-wing" faction, which opposed participation in "capitalist" elections and supported the Soviet Revolution of 1917, broke away in June 1919 and formed the Communist Labor Party; internal disputes within this group later produced a competing Communist Party made up largely of Russian immigrants.

Most factories had operated at full speed during the war, and peacetime brought falling wages and rising unemployment. Workers responded in 1919 with the greatest strike wave in American history; Seattle was paralyzed by a general strike, and even the Boston police walked off their beats and marched in picket lines. A wave of terrorist bombings created fear and panic; Seattle mayor Ole Hanson received a bomb in the mail and another exploded at the home of former Georgia senator Thomas Hardwick, injuring his maid. A New York postal clerk read the news, remembered some suspicious packages, and discovered thirty-four bombs addressed to such prominent people as John D. Rockefeller, J. P. Morgan, Justice Oliver Wendell Holmes, and Attorney General A. Mitchell Palmer. The person or group that sent these bombs escaped detection, which turned every "radical" into a potential suspect. On June 2, 1919, someone placed another bomb on Palmer's doorstep; it exploded prematurely and blew the bomber into such tiny pieces that he was never identified.

During the war, an ambitious young clerk in the Justice Department's Bureau of Investigation named J. Edgar Hoover began compiling lists of actual and alleged "Reds" and soon had files on 200,000 people; federal agents stole membership lists of radical groups and other names came from volunteer spies who reported "subversives" to federal officials. In the wake of the 1919 bombings, a wave of fear gripped the nation and unleashed a campaign of repression against radicals. With Hoover supplying names and addresses, federal agents began the "Palmer raids" in November 1919, arresting hundreds of members of the Union of Russian Workers; on December 21, some 249 Russian aliens— who did not enjoy the legal rights of citizens—were hustled aboard a ship dubbed the "Red Ark" by the press and deported to the Soviet Union.

Cheered on by the press, federal agents conducted a second round of Palmer raids on January 2, 1920, rounding up more than four thousand suspected radicals in thirty-three cities. J. Edgar Hoover directed the operation, dispensing with arrest warrants and encouraging his agents to grab any documents they could find, especially lists of members and contributors. The raiders made quite a few mistakes; many of those arrested were citizens, others were simply curious observers at public meetings, and some were innocent bystanders, nabbed on sidewalks outside buildings that housed "radical" groups.

The press again cheered the raids. "There is no time to waste on hairsplitting over infringement of liberty," proclaimed the *Washington Post*. But the government's actions stirred a small band of "civil libertarians" to protest. The newly formed American Civil Liberties Union, which grew out of groups that defended war protesters and draft resisters, joined the National Popular Government League in publishing a scathing *Report upon the Illegal Practices of the United States Department of Justice*, documenting many examples of police brutality during the raids, prolonged detention of those arrested without access to counsel or families, and due process violations in the courts. Twelve prominent lawyers, including Zechariah Chafee and Felix Frankfurter of Harvard Law School, signed the report and condemned the "utterly illegal acts which have been committed by those charged with the highest duty of enforcing the laws." The ACLU report stung Attorney General Palmer, who insinuated that his critics were "soft" on communism.

Palmer left office in 1921 after Warren Harding reclaimed the White House for the Republicans. The next attorney general, Harry Daugherty, was forced from office by the Teapot Dome scandal, which broke after Harding's death in August 1923. Had he lived much longer, Harding would almost certainly have faced impeachment for the widespread corruption he tolerated by his cronies. Vice President Calvin Coolidge, who remained untouched by scandal, moved quickly as Harding's successor to clean house in Washington. He appointed Harlan Fiske Stone, former dean of Columbia Law School (and future Chief Justice), as attorney general. Sweeping his own broom in the Justice Department, Stone fired the head of the Federal Bureau of Investigation and replaced him with J. Edgar Hoover, not yet thirty years old. Stone ordered Hoover to end all political surveillance, and the young bureaucrat complied. But Stone spent just one year as Hoover's boss; as soon as President Coolidge named Stone to the Supreme Court in 1925, Hoover moved his "radical" files out of storage and put hundreds of FBI agents to work on creating more. The former file clerk turned "Red hunter" outlasted seven presidents and more than twenty attorney generals before his death in 1972. The contents of Hoover's files sent hundreds of real and suspected radicals—from Communists to Black Panthers—to prison over some fifty years, and the Supreme Court decided more than a dozen First Amendment cases that began inside the covers of FBI files.

Most of the political cases that reached the Court during the two decades between the world wars involved state and not federal laws. The Sedition Act of 1918 expired in 1921 and was not replaced until 1940, when Congress made it a crime to "advocate" the overthrow of government "by force or violence." During the intervening years, however, state lawmakers filled the gap with dozens of laws to punish "criminal anarchy" and "criminal syndicalism," terms that most people would have trouble defining. These laws actually stemmed from two prewar campaigns: first, to keep Russian anarchists who slipped past immigration inspectors from spreading their view that organized government should be abolished; and second, to prosecute the IWW "Wobblies" who advocated a "syndicalist" government based on workplace elections in which "bosses" could not vote. Ironically, the Communists who later became the prime targets of these laws rejected both anarchism and syndicalism; they advocated a strong central government based on the "dictatorship of the proletariat."

By 1921, thirty-five states had enacted criminal anarchy or criminal syndicalism laws. New York's law, the first to be passed in 1902, defined criminal anarchy as "the doctrine that organized government should be overthrown by force or violence ... or by any unlawful means." Anyone who advocated this doctrine "by word of mouth or writing" faced a ten-year prison term. California adopted its criminal syndicalism law in 1919, defining the term as "any doctrine or precept advocating ... the commission of crime, sabotage ... or unlawful methods of terrorism as a means of accomplishing a change in industrial ownership or control, or effecting any political change." Directed against the Wobblies who preached and sometimes practiced workplace sabotage during strikes—like the French workers who threw their *sabots* or wooden shoes into machines—the California law provided a maximum fourteen-year sentence.

Challenges to the New York and California laws reached the Supreme Court in cases that both began in November 1919. Police in New York City arrested Benjamin Gitlow, a Russian immigrant and business manager of *The Revolutionary Age*, the organ of the Left Wing Section of the Socialist Party. He was charged with "criminal anarchy" for printing and distributing sixteen thousand copies of the "Left Wing Manifesto" that dissident Socialists had adopted in June 1919. (By the time of his arrest, Gitlow had joined other members of the left-wing faction in forming the Communist Party.) The manifesto called on workers to reject electoral "parliamentarism" and to fight against "the bourgeois state and Capitalism" with action that "starts with strikes of protest, developing into mass political strikes and then into revolutionary mass action that will conquer the power of the state." The goal of "mass action" was to establish "a revolutionary dictatorship of the proletariat." The manifesto that Gitlow printed disavowed any call for "immediate revolution" and stated that "the final struggle against Capitalism may last for years and tens of years." It ended with this exhortation: "The Communist International calls the proletariat of the world to the final struggle!" The Communist International linked revolutionary parties around the world and had its headquarters in Moscow. The manifesto's fiery rhetoric and Gitlow's allegiance to Moscow convinced a jury that he belonged behind bars, and a New York judge sentenced him to five years in state prison.

Charlotte Whitney and Benjamin Gitlow lived on opposite sides of the country and came from opposite sides of the class line; they also wound up in opposing Communist parties. Born into a prominent California family in 1867, Whitney was a niece of Justice Stephen Field, a Wellesley graduate, and a "charity" worker in the Oakland slums. She moved from "philanthropic work" into the Socialist Party in 1914, and moved again from its left-wing faction into the Communist Labor Party in 1919. Unlike Gitlow, she supported electoral politics as a tactic in the class struggle; at a convention to organize the party's California branch, she supported a resolution urging workers "to cast their votes for the party which represents their immediate and final interest—the CLP—at all elections." The resolution failed, but Whitney remained in the party, which called on members to "put in practice the principles of revolutionary industrial unionism and Communism." Whitney's party also proclaimed its allegiance to "the Communist International of Moscow," whose leaders forced their squabbling American followers to join ranks in 1920 behind the United Communist Party. Despite her eminent relative and her relative moderation, Whitney was convicted of "criminal syndicalism" for her involvement in the Communist Labor Party and sentenced to a one-to-fourteen-year prison term.

Benjamin Gitlow and Charlotte Whitney both appealed their convictions, and their cases bounced up and down the court system for years before final decisions. Gitlow's conviction was affirmed by three New York courts, and was argued twice before the Supreme Court before the justices ruled in June 1925. Only four members remained from the bench that decided the *Abrams* case in 1919: Willis Van Devanter and James McReynolds from the majority, and the two dissenters, Oliver Wendell Holmes and Louis Brandeis. President Warren Harding fulfilled the lifelong dream of William Howard Taft in 1921 by naming the former president to replace Edward White as Chief Justice. The two men were equally hostile to governmental power in economic regulation and civil rights, and Taft's record before his death in 1930 extended conservative control of the Chief's post to almost sixty years.

Few historians quarrel with the consensus that Harding was the most inept president the country ever had; he privately confessed, "I am not fit for this office and should never have been here." After placing Taft in charge of the Court, Harding looked to him for guidance in naming three more justices. Taft told friends that his goal was "to prevent the Bolsheviki from getting control" of the Court and giving the "dangerous twosome" of Holmes and Brandeis any more votes. The men he recommended were all conservative—perhaps "reactionary" is more accurate—but they varied widely in background and ability. John Clarke's resignation in 1922 removed a liberal from the Court and allowed Harding to place his close friend and political ally George Sutherland of Utah on the Court. Born in England in 1862 to parents who converted to Mormonism, moved to Utah, and then left the church, Sutherland studied law at the University of Michigan under Judge Thomas Cooley, absorbing his gospel of laissez-faire economics and Social Darwinism. Sutherland had practiced law and Republican politics in Utah; he served in both the House and Senate between 1901 and 1917, leaving office for private practice and a term as president of the American Bar Association. On the Court, Sutherland quickly became the intellectual leader of the conservative faction, emerging as the dominant figure among the "Four Horsemen of Reaction" who bedeviled President Franklin Roosevelt.

Two months after Clarke resigned his seat, Justice William R. Day retired after two decades as a moderate liberal. Harding gave Taft another conservative vote with his nomination of Pierce Butler of Minnesota, who earned millions as a railroad lawyer and befriended both Taft and Harding. Born in 1866 to Irish Catholic parents who left for America during the 1848 potato famine, Butler displayed no sympathy for the poor during his legal and judicial career. On the bench, he approached cases with a stern moralism and a rigid commitment to laissez-faire doctrine. The last justice to join the Four Horsemen of Reaction became the group's most avid defender of the "sanctity" of contract. Butler did, however, ride off alone to dissent—often without an opinion—in cases that offended his Catholic morality; he was the sole dissenter in *Buck v. Bell*, in which Justice Holmes upheld a forced sterilization law in 1927. Holmes told another justice that Butler was "afraid of the Church" on that issue. And in *Palko v. Connecticut*, which upheld in 1937 a death penalty imposed on a murder defendant who gained a new trial after being first sentenced to life imprisonment, Butler lashed out at the state's attorney during oral argument: "What do you want? Blood?"

The retirement of Justice Mahlon Pitney in December 1922 gave Harding his third nomination in four months. Taft felt the Court needed someone with considerable judicial experience, since Sutherland and Butler had none, and he recommended Edward T. Sanford, a Tennessee native and Harvard Law School graduate who prosecuted antitrust cases in the Justice Department before President Theodore Roosevelt placed him on the federal district court in his home state. Confirmed by the Senate without dissent, Sanford took his seat in February 1923 and, as Taft had hoped, became the Court's expert in technical fields like bankruptcy and jurisdiction. Sanford generally sided with the Chief in constitutional cases, and the two men died on the same day in March 1930.

Harding's death in August 1923 made Calvin Coolidge president, and the dour Yankee won election the next year on his own, riding a wave of prosperity that created a growing middle class that gobbled up cars, radios, refrigerators, and other consumer goods. Most of these satisfied customers rewarded the Republicans with their votes, nodding their heads to Coolidge's boast that "the business of America is business." But the booming economy did not spread its benefits evenly; in 1929—the year the stock market crashed—families with incomes in the top tenth of 1 percent earned as much as all those in the bottom 40 percent. The "Roaring Twenties" were also years of racism and nativism. A revived Ku Klux Klan recruited more than four million members by 1924 and spread into the North, gaining political influence in states like Pennsylvania, Indiana, and Oregon. Congress responded in 1924 to pressure from the Klan and other groups—including conservative trade unions—by cutting further immigration to a trickle and setting national quotas that favored "Anglo-Saxons" and turned away Italians, Russians, Asians, and Africans.

During his five years in office, Coolidge named just one Supreme Court justice. But he chose wisely in selecting Harlan Fiske Stone to replace Joseph McKenna in 1925. Born in New Hampshire in 1872 and educated at Amherst College (where Coolidge was a classmate and friend), Stone went to Columbia Law School and taught there after graduation in 1899, becoming dean in 1910. He did not enjoy what he called "administrivia" and resigned in 1923 to join a prestigious Wall Street firm, but left after one year to join his college friend's cabinet as attorney general. Once again, Stone found himself bored with office work, and he welcomed Coolidge's offer to join the Court. Chief Justice Taft drew on his skills in tax and patent law, but Stone slowly moved away from Taft on issues of civil rights and liberties and joined the "dangerous twosome" of Holmes and Brandeis, most often in dissent.

The Supreme Court decided *Gitlow v. New York* on June 8, 1925, four months after Stone took his seat. In voting to uphold New York's criminal anarchy law, the newest justice stuck with Taft and did not join Holmes and Brandeis in dissent. The majority spoke through the next-most-junior member, Edward Sanford, who first noted that Gitlow's lawyers attacked New York's criminal anarchy law as "repugnant to the due process clause of the Fourteenth Amendment." There was nothing remarkable about this; the Court had ruled in many cases that state laws denied persons—or corporations—various forms of "liberty" protected by this clause. The Court had invented the doctrine of "substantive due process" to strike down these laws. However, in no previous case had the "liberty" at stake been that of free speech. Almost a century earlier in 1833, Chief Justice John Marshall had ruled in *Barron v. Baltimore* that the Bill of Rights did not apply to the states. The First Amendment restrained only Congress from "abridging the freedom of speech," and states presumably could regulate speech as they saw fit, subject only to limitations in their own constitutions.

Arguments that the Fourteenth Amendment's Due Process Clause "incorporated" all or parts of the Bill of Rights and applied their protections to the states had been made before 1925. But the Court had steadfastly rejected this notion until Justice Sanford stated without fanfare that "we may and do assume that freedom of speech and of the press—which are protected from abridgement by Congress—are among the fundamental personal rights and 'liberties' protected by the due process clause of the Fourteenth Amendment against impairment by the States." This was a constitutional breakthrough, worthy of headlines in newspapers across the nation, or at least in the *New York Times*. But Sanford's bland sentence passed without notice at the time. And it did not help Benjamin Gitlow.

Having brought the New York law within the First Amendment's reach, Sanford looked at Gitlow's case as if the free speech clause had no relevance. He treated the *Schenck* and *Debs* cases very oddly, and in highly opaque language. The "clear and present danger" and "natural tendency" tests of those cases did not apply to the criminal anarchy law, Sanford wrote, since the federal Espionage Act punished "certain acts involving the danger of substantive evil, without any reference to language itself" as an essential part of those criminal acts. This was nonsense, since the "acts" for which Schenck and Debs went to prison necessarily involved the content of their speech; they would not have faced prosecution for speech that supported the war effort. Sanford clearly engaged in such obfuscation because the record in Gitlow's case, as he conceded, showed "no evidence of any effect resulting from the publication and circulation of the Manifesto." But this did not matter, since the New York legislature had "determined the danger of a substantive evil arising from utterances of a specified character." In other words, given the legislative finding that the state would be imperiled by advocacy of "the doctrine that organized government should be overthrown by force or violence," there was no need to show a "clear and present danger" from the "Left Wing Manifesto" or that its "natural tendency" would be to incite revolutionary acts. Simply advocating that doctrine would violate the law, with no protection from the First Amendment.

Sanford's badly and broadly written opinion did much greater harm to the principle of free speech than any of Holmes's efforts to link the "circumstances" of speech with the "evils" it might produce. Sanford held that states could exercise their "police powers" to punish "utterances" that lawmakers decide "by their very nature, involve danger to the public peace and to the security of the state." He cited earlier cases upholding state regulation of liquor and rail-road rates for support, because citation of *Schenck* or *Debs* would have required some showing—however tenuous or speculative—that the "Left Wing Mani-festo" posed a danger to New York that was not remote or negligible. The state did not even attempt such a showing, forcing Sanford to set the First Amend-ment aside and base his ruling on the "police powers" doctrine. But the First Amendment was designed as a check on those powers, which—if unrestrained—could make any unpopular "utterance" a criminal offense.

Something about incendiary political rhetoric inspires justices to use "fire" analogies in their opinions. Sanford replied to Holmes's "falsely shouting fire" example of unprotected speech with his own metaphor. "A single revolutionary spark may kindle a fire that, smouldering for a time, may burst into a sweeping and destructive conflagration," he wrote. "It cannot be said that the State is act-ing arbitrarily when in the exercise of its judgment as to the measures necessary to protect the public peace and safety, it seeks to extinguish the spark without waiting until it has enkindled the flame or blazed into the conflagration." How long might a rhetorical fire "smoulder" before it burst into revolution? Sanford did not say, or even hazard an estimate. His "smouldering" test was not tied to the "circumstances" of speech; New York could "extinguish" any revolutionary "utterance" at any time, because it might someday prompt someone to burn down the capitol in Albany.

Justice Holmes could not resist the impulse to reply to Sanford in kind. He responded to twenty pages of opinion with less than two, scolding his junior colleague as a parent would scold a child playing with matches. Embracing with renewed fervor the "clear and present danger" test he devised in *Schenck*, Holmes wrote that applying the "correct test" to *Gitlow* would have revealed "no present danger" to New York from the "Left Wing Manifesto." He matched Sanford's "smouldering" metaphor with his own. "Every idea is an incitement," Holmes wrote. "Eloquence may set fire to reason." But the "redundant dis-course" of the manifesto "had no chance of starting a present conflagration." It was the job of judges, not lawmakers, to look at "circumstances" and assess "whether there was any danger the publication could produce any result" that might harm the state. "But the indictment alleges the publication and nothing more," he complained. That was not enough to satisfy Holmes, or the First Amendment.

Charlotte Whitney waited two more years for a ruling on her appeal. One rea-son the Court delayed its decision until May 1927 was that her wealthy family had retained two prominent corporate lawyers to defend her in the California courts. They did not raise any First Amendment challenge to California's crimi-nal syndicalism law in 1920, which is not surprising, since *Barron v. Baltimore* had blocked that path since 1833. The justices could have declined to hear Whitney's appeal, because her lawyers had not raised a "federal question" at trial, which normally would foreclose Supreme Court review of a decision based on state law. In fact, the Court dismissed her first petition for review in 1925, shortly after its *Gitlow* decision. But a new set of lawyers from the American Civil Liberties Union stepped in and took Whitney's case back to California; they persuaded state judges to consider a claim that the law was "repugnant" to the Fourteenth Amendment's Due Process Clause. The ACLU team was headed by Walter Pollak, a prominent New York corporate lawyer who plunged into free speech cases and had argued—and lost—the *Gitlow* case in the Supreme Court.

The California judges denied Pollak's new claim without opinion, but they placed it on the record, and he persuaded the Supreme Court to reconsider *Whitney v. California* in 1927. Writing again for the Court, Justice Sanford reviewed the case's tangled procedural history and sniffed that Pollak's move "is not to be commended" as a tactic for gaining a rehearing. Sanford did not explain why the justices bent their rules in this case; most likely, the conservative majority wanted to warn political radicals that not only could publishing calls for revolution be punished—as *Gitlow* had ruled—but that simply joining a "revolutionary" group could lead to prison.

Sanford devoted less than two pages to the First Amendment issue in his *Whitney* opinion. He quoted his own words in *Gitlow* for the proposition that revolutionary "utterances" could be punished. But he needed to go another step, since Whitney had not been prosecuted for "utterances" of any kind, but simply for joining the Communist Labor Party. Sanford returned to *Gitlow* and cited the liquor and railroad regulation cases from that opinion to establish state "police powers" over the advocacy of revolutionary doctrine. The act of "joining and furthering an organization" with revolutionary goals, Sanford concluded, was a form of advocacy that made Whitney part of a "criminal conspiracy" whose "united and joint action involves even greater danger to the public peace and security than the isolated utterances and acts" of individuals. Charlotte Whitney was an active organizer, but Sanford's opinion could be stretched by zealous prosecutors and compliant judges to expose every member of radical groups to criminal charges.

Justice Holmes, having already scolded Sanford in his *Gitlow* dissent, held his tongue in *Whitney*. However, Justice Louis Brandeis felt compelled to respond and to voice his own First Amendment views. But he faced two problems. First, he did not think the Court should have heard the case at all, because Walter Pollak's belated due process challenge "was not taken in the trial court." Second, Whitney's trial lawyers had not made any effort to counter the state's claim that her party posed a "clear and present danger" to California. Charlotte Whitney paid a price for their mistakes. Brandeis, whose trial skills were unmatched, looked at the record and found "evidence on which the court or jury might have found that such danger existed." He reluctantly concluded that "the judg-ment of the state court cannot be disturbed."

Given this position, Brandeis could hardly dissent from the Court's ruling. But he also felt strongly about the free speech issues, so he wrote a lengthy con-curring opinion—which read like a dissent—in which Holmes joined. Brandeis spoke with eloquence and passion about the values of an earlier generation of revolutionaries. "Those who won our independence believed that the final end of the State was to make men free to develop their faculties," he wrote, "and that in its government the deliberative forces should prevail over the arbitrary." He spoke of the men who framed the First Amendment: "Recognizing the oc-casional tyrannies of governing majorities, they amended the Constitution so that free speech and assembly should be guaranteed."

Brandeis matched Holmes in the power of his prose. "Fear of serious injury cannot alone justify suppression of free speech and assembly," he wrote. "Men feared witches and burnt women. It is the function of speech to free men from the bondage of irrational fears." Brandeis refined Holmes's "clear and present danger" test in words that underscored the state's burden in proving that "im-mediate serious violence" would occur if speech was not suppressed. "If there be time to expose through discussion the falsehood and fallacies" of revolu-tionary speech, he added, "the remedy to be applied is more speech, not en-forced silence. Only an emergency can justify repression. Such must be the rule if authority is to be reconciled with freedom. Such, in my opinion, is the com-mand of the Constitution."

The *Gitlow* and *Whitney* cases grew out of the "Red Scare" that gripped the country in the wake of World War I and the Bolshevik Revolution in Russia. Once the national hysteria faded, calmer voices prevailed. Governor Al Smith of New York pardoned Benjamin Gitlow in 1925, and Governor Charles Young of California spared Charlotte Whitney a prison term in 1927. Even when the Communist Party grew in strength and numbers during the Great De-pression of the 1930s, the Supreme Court reversed convictions of party orga-nizers under laws identical to those upheld in Gitlow and Whitney. Two cases decided in 1937 showed the Court's reluctance to stifle revolutionary speech. Dirk De Jonge was arrested for speaking in 1934 at a Communist Party meeting in Portland, Oregon, that was broken up by police. "Someone hollered 'Cops' and disorder broke out immediately, some making a run for fire escapes, stair-ways and windows," a state's witness testified at De Jonge's trial. He was sen-tenced to seven years for violating Oregon's criminal syndicalism law, which was identical in wording to the California law upheld in *Whitney*. But in reversing De Jonge's conviction, the Court did not overrule that case, despite the virtual iden-tity of the facts and laws in both cases. Chief Justice Charles Evans Hughes avoided the constitutional issue by faulting the Oregon court for upholding De

Jonge's conviction simply for speaking at the Communist meeting, "regardless of what was said or done at the meeting." Hughes ruled that "peaceable assembly for lawful discussion cannot be made a crime."

Every justice voted with Hughes in *De Jonge v. Oregon* except Stone, who did not participate because of illness but certainly agreed with the outcome. Why, then, did the Court decide not to overrule *Gitlow* and *Whitney*, which could hardly be squared with Hughes's opinion? It was not because of any reluctance to overturn earlier decisions; two weeks before *De Jonge* was decided, the justices had voted in *West Coast Hotel v. Parrish*—a ruling that upheld a state minimum wage law—to overrule the *Adkins* decision of 1923, although Stone's illness held up the opinions until March 1937. Most likely, Chief Justice Hughes—who also wrote for the Court in *West Coast Hotel* over the heated dissent of the "Four Horsemen of Reaction"—knew he could not persuade them in *De Jonge* to further limit the government's power to punish "dangerous" speech.

Although the Four Horsemen joined the *De Jonge* majority, they all dissented in April 1937 from a decision that reversed the conviction of Angelo Herndon, a black Communist organizer convicted in 1932 of inciting fellow blacks to "insurrection" in Georgia. The state law exposed anyone who attempted "to induce others to join in any combined resistance to the lawful authority of the State" to a death penalty; Herndon's all-white jury had recommended "mercy" and the judge sentenced him to eighteen years in prison. Justice Owen Roberts followed Hughes's lead in *De Jonge* and wrote a narrow opinion in *Herndon v. Lowry*. Roberts stressed the fact that Herndon's organizing efforts consisted of holding three meetings for "discussion of relief for the unemployed." It was clear that Angelo Herndon, like Dirk De Jonge, was arrested solely for being a Communist organizer. Making "membership in a party and solicitation of members for that party a criminal offense, punishable by death," Roberts wrote, "is an unwarranted invasion of the right of freedom of speech." But he did not base his opinion on that point, ruling instead that Georgia's "insurrection" law set no "reasonably ascertainable standard of guilt" and was so "vague and indeterminate" that it violated the Fourteenth Amendment's Due Process Clause.

Justice Willis Van Devanter wrote for the Four Horsemen in the *Herndon* case. His dissent reeked of racism. "It should not be overlooked that Herndon was a negro member and organizer in the Communist Party and was engaged actively in inducing others, chiefly southern negroes, to become members of the party," he wrote. Van Devanter pointed to literature found in Herndon's room advocating "self-determination for the Black Belt," the party's slogan for an independent black nation in the Deep South. The "past and present circumstances" of blacks, he added, "would lead them to give unusual credence" to the "inflaming and inciting features" of this proposal. Georgia's lawyers presented no evidence that Herndon had given anyone—black or white—this literature; Van Devanter nonetheless concluded that "distribution by him reasonably could be inferred" and that its contents were "nothing short of advising a resort to force and violence, for all know that such measures could not be effected otherwise."

The decisions in *De Jonge* and *Herndon* marked a retreat from the Court's hostility toward radical speech in the *Gitlow* and *Whitney* cases. Reversing the criminal convictions of Dirk De Jonge and Angelo Herndon reflected two facts: first, that during the Great Depression, the Communist Party had gained recruits and political influence; and second, that both party organizers were fairly small fish and posed no threat to Oregon or Georgia. But these decisions also showed the Court's reluctance to deprive state prosecutors of their legislative weapons against Communists and other revolutionaries, should the danger of left-wing insurrection ever become real. Unwilling to break ranks with the Four Horsemen, the Court's majority left *Gitlow* and *Whitney* on the books, available as precedent in later cases that raised issues of "revolutionary" speech and organizing.

"The General Welfare of the

United States"

The Great Depression began with a loud crash in October 1929. When the rubble from the stock market collapse had settled, millions of Americans had lost their jobs, homes, businesses, farms, and hopes for the future. Factory managers locked their gates and store owners shuttered their windows; sheriff's deputies served eviction notices on families that failed to make their mortgage payments; farmers slaughtered pigs, dumped milk, and burned wheat as prices sank below the cost of production. Dry statistics cannot fully convey the human toll: the stock market lost almost 90 percent of its value between 1929 and 1933; industrial production fell more than 50 percent during this period; some fifteen million workers—almost a third of the workforce—lost their jobs; farm income continued its postwar slide from $17 billion in 1919 to $5 billion in 1932.

Once again, the national economy had fallen victim to rampant speculation, with financial gamblers shifting their bets from land to stocks. The paper prosperity of the 1920s had created a new class of the nouveau riche, whose extravagant lives were chronicled by F. Scott Fitzgerald in *The Great Gatsby*. Sinclair Lewis portrayed the complacent middle class in *Main Street* and *Babbitt*, while the gaunt faces of the rural poor stared blankly from the photographs in James Agee's book *Let Us Now Praise Famous Men*. There was, in truth, little to praise in the words and acts of famous men. Shortly before the Crash, President Herbert Hoover—who replaced Calvin Coolidge as president in 1929—spoke with assurance: "We in America today are nearer to the final triumph over poverty than ever before in the history of any land." A few months later he urged the jobless to turn for relief to private charity; Hoover's "self-reliant" view of government included no role in relieving poverty. Henry Ford, the nation's leading employer, spoke of hiring more workers in March 1931: "There is plenty of work to do if people would do it." A few weeks later his managers handed out 75,000 pink slips to laid-off autoworkers.

Many who became casualties of the Crash spent their days scrabbling for survival. Social critic Edmund Wilson described their privation: "There is not a garbage-dump in Chicago which is not diligently haunted by the hungry. Last summer in hot weather when the smell was sickening and the flies were thick, there were a hundred people a day coming to one of the dumps, falling on the heap of refuse as soon as the truck had pulled out and digging it in with sticks and hands." Others took to the streets in protest; newspapers carried daily reports like this: "Indiana Harbor, Indiana, August 5, 1931: Fifteen hundred jobless men stormed the plant of the Fruit Growers Express Company here, demanding that they be given jobs to keep from starving. The company's answer was to call the city police, who routed the jobless with menacing clubs." Another story: "Chicago, April 1, 1932: Five hundred school children, most with haggard faces and tattered clothes, paraded through Chicago's downtown section to the Board of Education offices to demand that the school system provide them with food."

Not even the Depression shook President Hoover's belief that "poor relief" should come from private charity and not from public funds. He did support the Reconstruction Finance Corporation, which made loans to banks and businesses, and near his term's end he finally heeded calls for federal grants to local governments for relief programs. But this was all too little and too late to stave off widespread poverty. After beating one New York governor, Al Smith, during the boom year of 1928, Hoover lost badly to another, Franklin D. Roosevelt, after the defection of six million Republican voters in 1932. Roosevelt brought a patrician's touch and tone to politics, but his appeal to the "common man" rose above class and party. "The country needs," he declared in 1932, "and, unless I mistake its temper, the country demands bold, persistent experimentation."

Before he turned the government over to Roosevelt and the "New Dealers" who rode his coattails to Congress, Hoover added three members to the Supreme Court that would decide if their legislative experiments would blow up the Constitution. The resignation of Chief Justice William Howard Taft in February 1930, a month before he died, gave Hoover a chance to shift the Court's direction from the right to the center. Hoover had formed a close friendship with Justice Harlan Stone, and many observers thought he would elevate Stone to the Chief's position. But Taft literally whispered from his deathbed into Hoover's ear, urging the president to appoint Charles Evans Hughes as his successor. Taft had placed Hughes on the Court in 1910 and, despite their later political rivalry, considered him more "solid" than Stone in defending business interests. After resigning from the Court in 1916 to make an unsuccessful run for the White House, Hughes had joined a powerful Wall Street firm, which exposed him to criticism from "progressive" senators in both parties. "No man in public life," declared Senator George Norris of Nebraska, "so exemplifies the influence of powerful combinations in the political and financial world as does Mr. Hughes." But the Senate confirmed Hughes by fifty-two to twenty-six, in contrast to the unanimous vote for his first term.

Two weeks after Hughes took the Court's center seat, Justice Edward Sanford died. Hoover's first choice to replace him was John J. Parker of North Carolina, a federal appellate judge who had carried the Republican banner in state politics. One remark he made as the party's candidate for governor in 1920 returned to doom his nomination. Black voters had long backed the party of Lincoln, but Parker rejected their support: "The participation of the Negro in politics is a source of evil and danger to both races," he stated. Parker had also followed Supreme Court precedent as a judge in upholding "yellow dog" employment contracts. The combined opposition of the NAACP and organized labor kept him off the Court by the narrow margin of two votes. Forced to choose a less controversial nominee, Hoover turned to Owen J. Roberts of Pennsylvania, a wealthy and well-connected corporate lawyer who had garnered praise for serving as special prosecutor in the Teapot Dome scandals that rocked Washington in the 1920s. Roberts had no judicial experience, but senators were tired and bruised from the Parker battle and confirmed him without dissent. He came to the bench with no exposure to constitutional law, and he sailed without a compass through the New Deal storms that soon battered the Court.

An era in American law ended on January 12, 1932, with the resignation of Justice Oliver Wendell Holmes. Still alert at ninety, he stepped down after twenty-nine years, bequeathing not only the funds to underwrite a multivolume history of the Supreme Court, but also a major part of that history in his many opinions. Holmes once wrote that he wanted "to put as many new ideas into the law as I can, to show how particular solutions involve general theory, and to do it with style." His constitutional theory may have lacked rigor and consistency, but he certainly put forth new ideas with inimitable style.

Holmes could hardly be replaced, but President Hoover satisfied his many admirers by selecting Benjamin N. Cardozo of New York to succeed him. Like Holmes, Cardozo had gained renown as a legal scholar and as chief judge of his state's highest court. His 1921 book *The Nature of the Judicial Process* recognized the human element in judging and the changing social and economic forces that influence legal rules. Unlike Holmes, who harked back to the "common law" for guidance, Cardozo looked ahead to statutory law and administrative regulations as signposts for the future. Hoover first hesitated in making his choice, fearing that adding another Jew to the Court—to join Louis Brandeis—would have "religious or sectarian repercussions," but the outpouring of support for Cardozo overcame this caution. The Senate confirmed him unanimously, and the *New York Times* approvingly commented that "seldom, if ever, in the history of the Court has an appointment been so universally commended."

After Franklin Roosevelt took office, Cardozo joined Brandeis and Stone in the Court's "liberal" wing, generally voting to uphold federal and state laws designed to aid workers or consumers. Justices McReynolds, Van Devanter, Sutherland, and Butler had already formed a solid wall of resistance to such laws. This split left Chief Justice Hughes and Justice Roberts in the middle as swing votes. Either one could join the conservatives to strike down laws, but it took the votes of both to uphold them. This judicial arithmetic put the fate of New Deal legislation in the hands of two former corporate lawyers and staunch Republicans.

Eager to carry out Roosevelt's electoral mandate, Congress plunged into the "Hundred Days" session in March 1933, determined to revive both industry and agriculture. Scores of young lawyers—derided as "boys with their hair ablaze" by one critic—worked around the clock to draft the National Industrial Recovery Act and the Agricultural Adjustment Act, the twin pillars of the New Deal program. Congress wrapped up work on the NIRA and AAA bills by June 1933 and sent them to the White House for Roosevelt's signature These laws certainly fit Roosevelt's prescription of "bold experimentation" in treating a sick economy, but they rested on shaky constitutional ground. Both laws faced challenges in federal courts within days, but these suits—dozens were filed against each statute—had to climb several rungs on the judicial ladder and did not reach the Supreme Court until 1935. However, many states passed their own "Little New Deal" laws in early 1933, and challenges moved rapidly through state courts. Two important cases—from Minnesota and New York—were ready for Supreme Court argument in late 1933 and were closely watched for signs of how the justices might rule on the "big" New Deal cases. The state cases were, in fact, "big" in the sense that they affected millions of homeowners and consumers, not only in Minnesota and New York but in states with similar laws.

The first case began when the Minnesota legislature passed a "mortgage moratorium" law in April 1933. It extended for up to two years the period in which homeowners could "redeem" property foreclosed by mortgage holders by making payments set by a judge. The law's preamble declared that "the severe financial and economic depression existing for several years" had created "an emergency of such nature" that justified use of the state's "police powers" to protect homeowners who could not "meet all payments as they come due" on mortgages. The Supreme Court confronted a challenge to the Minnesota law in a case that stemmed from one of thousands of foreclosures during the Depression. John H. Blaisdell obtained a $15,000 mortgage for a house in Minneapolis from the Home Building & Loan Association; he and his family lived in three rooms and rented the others. Blaisdell fell behind on payments the next year when his tenants lost their jobs. Home Building foreclosed and purchased the house and lot at auction for $3,700. Two weeks before his "redemption" period expired, the moratorium law took effect; Blaisdell ran to state court and got an extension for two years, conditioned on mortgage payments of $40 each month.

Home Building's lawyers objected at the state court hearing that the moratorium law violated the "impairment of contract" clause of the federal Constitution and did not fall within the state's police powers. The company won this round, and Blaisdell sued to reclaim his property. After the state's highest court ruled for Blaisdell and upheld the law, Home Building appealed to the Supreme Court, which issued its ruling in January 1934. In this closely watched case, Chief Justice Hughes and Owen Roberts sided with the Blaisdell family and upheld the Minnesota law over the dissent of the Four Horsemen of Reaction.

Conscious of the case's impact, Hughes took the opinion in *Home Building & Loan Assn. v. Blaisdell* for himself. "The Constitution was adopted in a period of grave emergency," he reminded his readers. "While emergency does not create power, emergency may furnish the occasion for the exercise of power," he continued. Conceding that the Minnesota law did "impair" Home Building's contract with John Blaisdell, Hughes stated that "where constitutional grants and limitations of power are set forth in general clauses, which afford a broad outline, the process of construction is essentially to fill in the details. That is true of the contract clause." Hughes did not explain how the Minnesota law filled in any "details" of the Contract Clause. He met another problem by distinguishing the "insolvency" cases decided a century earlier, noting that Blaisdell's debt to Home Building was not wiped out, but merely extended for two years.

In effect, Hughes had filled in the Contract Clause with compassion for people like John Blaisdell. The Four Horsemen responded in a scornful dissent by Justice George Sutherland. "The Minnesota statute either impairs the obligation of contracts or it does not," he wrote. Even Hughes conceded that it did. Sutherland did not find an "emergency" exit in the Contract Clause. States could not impair contract rights "no matter what may be the occasion," he declared. Looking ahead with foreboding, Sutherland warned that Hughes had opened the door for "gradual but ever-advancing encroachments upon the sanctity of public and private contracts."

Two months after the *Home Building* decision, the Court upheld another state law, this one designed to save New York's dairy farmers from what lawmakers called their "desperate" situation. The problem was not too little milk for the state's consumers but too much. Swelling production and shrinking consumption had reduced the price that farmers received far below cost. The state legislature held extensive hearings on the problem and passed a law in April 1933 that established a state milk control board with the power to fix minimum and maximum prices for milk sold in retail stores. The board fixed the price of a quart at nine cents. However, dealers who delivered milk to homes were not covered by the law and generally sold a quart for eight cents; their customers got better service and lower prices. Leo Nebbia, who ran a grocery store in up-state Rochester, fought back by selling a five-cent loaf of bread with two quarts of milk for eighteen cents; in effect, he gave the bread away to lure customers into his store. Nebbia volunteered to bring a "test case" on behalf of fellow grocers, and the county attorney arranged a quick trial at which Nebbia was convicted and fined $25. The state's highest court rejected Nebbia's claim of a "liberty" right to set his own prices and upheld the law on "police powers" grounds, and he appealed to the Supreme Court.

The stakes in *Nebbia v. New York* were much greater than a nickel loaf of bread. Price-fixing was an essential part of the New Deal program; the National Industrial Recovery Act set up "codes of fair competition" for a thousand different industries that restricted competition with fixed prices. The Court's ruling on a state law might forecast its decision when the NIRA came up for review. The justices lined up in *Nebbia* as they had in the *Home Building* case. This time, however, Owen Roberts wrote for the Court and James McReynolds for the Four Horsemen. Roberts did not need an "emergency" exit in this case; he cited the 1877 ruling in *Munn v. Illinois* for the proposition that property rights are not absolute. "Equally fundamental with the private right is that of the public to regulate it in the common interest," Roberts wrote. So long as laws were not "arbitrary in their operation and effect," he continued, "the state may regulate a business in any of its aspects, including the prices to be charged" to consumers.

McReynolds saw clearly the majority's implicit overruling of the *Lochner* and *Adkins* cases, although Roberts had not cited either decision. Laissez-faire doctrine was in such grave peril that McReynolds signaled his alarm with exclamation points. He pictured a mother who did not have nine cents for a quart of milk although the grocer "is anxious to accept what you can pay and the demands of your household are urgent!" The Court's "facile disregard of the Constitution as long interpreted and respected will inevitably lead to its destruction," McReynolds warned. "Then, all rights will be subject to the caprice of the hour; government by stable laws will pass."

Defeated in these skirmishes over state legislation, the Four Horsemen refused to surrender to the New Dealers and regrouped for the looming battles over the "Blue Eagle" and "Triple A" laws, as the National Industrial Recovery Act and Agricultural Adjustment Act were dubbed by the press. These "emergency" laws, which Congress enacted by huge margins during the "Hundred Days" session in 1933, handed the government over to business groups in both industry and agriculture. It would be hard to imagine any laws that more directly challenged the laissez-faire ideals of freedom of contract and free-market competition. It would be equally hard to imagine laws that more clearly rested on expansive notions of constitutional powers.

The National Industrial Recovery Act closely resembled Benito Mussolini's "corporate state" regime in fascist Italy. Hugh Johnson, the former army general who ran the National Recovery Administration, made no secret of his admiration for Mussolini, whose "shining name" he invoked in exhorting the NRA staff to emulate the Italian model. This does not mean that fascist "Black Shirts" took over the Blue Eagle program, but the parallels were close enough to alarm critics, who warned that giant "cartels" would swallow up their smaller competitors and turn government regulators into corporate clerks. The NIRA, in fact, suspended operation of the antitrust laws and delegated to business groups the power to frame "codes of fair competition" that allowed price-fixing and production controls.

The law's drafters, drawn from the academic "Brains Trust" that Franklin Roosevelt recruited to translate his campaign slogans into law, gave the president final authority to approve, revise, or reject proposed codes. But the statute offered no precise standards for drafting more than a thousand codes that governed products from iron and steel to powder puffs. Charles Wyzanski, the young Brains Truster from Harvard Law School who put the finishing touches on the Recovery Act, confessed to his law-school mentor Felix Frankfurter that the code-making powers delegated by Congress to Roosevelt "go so far beyond the bounds of constitutionality that it would be useless" to expose the law to judicial scrutiny. But its chief backer, New York senator Robert Wagner, expressed confidence the Supreme Court would uphold the law. "It is true that legislative power cannot be delegated," he admitted during Senate debate on the bill. "But in order that the wheels of government may continue to turn, the Court has always sanctioned the use of administrative agencies to fill gaps in those statutes which set up reasonable guides to action."

Chief Justice Hughes had allowed the Court to "fill in the details" of the Contract Clause in his *Home Building* opinion. Would he and Justice Roberts permit General Johnson and President Roosevelt to "fill gaps" in the Recovery Act? Their votes in the *Home Building* and *Nebbia* cases encouraged the New Deal's supporters when the long-anticipated "big" case reached the Court in May 1935. But there were dark clouds on the judicial horizon. Ruling four months earlier in January, the Court had struck down—over the solitary dissent of Justice Cardozo—one section of the Recovery Act that Congress had tacked on with hardly any debate. Known as the "hot-oil" law, this section dealt with gushing oil wells and falling prices by barring the interstate shipment of petroleum that was produced in excess of quotas set by states. Congress authorized President Roosevelt to police the hot-oil section; he delegated this power to his interior secretary, Harold Ickes, who in turn set up an agency to monitor oil shipments and enforce state production quotas.

Lawyers for the Panama Refining Company in Texas, a small producer in the biggest oil state, challenged the hot-oil law in federal court. A district judge who did not conceal his hostility to the New Deal issued an injunction against the law's enforcement, but federal circuit judges reversed his decision and the company appealed to the Supreme Court. During arguments in *Panama Refining v. Ryan*, the company's lawyers invoked the Constitution's "separation of powers" and asserted that Congress had improperly delegated its responsibility for setting legislative standards to the executive branch. Writing for the Court, Chief Justice Hughes agreed. Congress had declared "no policy as to the transportation of excess production" of oil, he stated, and set "no criterion to govern the President's course" in setting regulations. The hot-oil law ran into the judicial doctrine that bars the delegation of legislative powers to administrative officials and came up dry.

The government's loss in *Panama Refining* was clearly a setback, but the Court's decision did not necessarily doom the rest of the Recovery Act. The hot-oil law basically required federal officials to rubber-stamp the production quotas set by states, with no power to examine or revise them. In contrast, Congress had declared the policy of "fair competition" in the Recovery Act and authorized the president to revise or reject any industry codes that he felt did not meet this standard. In truth, however, this was a slim reed on which to rest the entire New Deal recovery program. And the case that tested the strength of the "fair competition" reed, as Charles Wyzanski had feared, showed that it could not bear the weight of judicial scrutiny.

The four Schechter brothers—Joseph, Martin, Aaron, and Alex—ran a wholesale business in Brooklyn that slaughtered and dressed kosher poultry for retail shops that catered to New York's large Jewish population. Every day, trucks from the Schechter Poultry Company would cross the Brooklyn Bridge to the West Manhattan terminal of the New York Central Railroad; strong men would load dozens of "coops" that contained about one hundred chickens from train cars onto their trucks and return with their squawking cargo to the Schechters' slaughterhouse. Retail dealers and butchers arrived before dawn and gave their orders to one of the brothers, who would pick chickens from coops and hand them to the *shochtim*, who worked under rabbinical supervision. The *shochtim* would slit the chickens' throats and drain the blood according to Jewish law. After plucking and dressing, the birds went to retail shops and wound up in ovens and soup pots across the city.

New York's kosher poultry business was a $90 million industry with some sixteen hundred workers, and the Schechter brothers operated one of the biggest wholesale outlets. They also cut corners to lure customers in this highly competitive business. Even before the National Recovery Administration set up an industry board to draft a live poultry code for the New York region, government lawyers called the brothers as reluctant witnesses in a case against the corrupt union that represented poultry workers. Their testimony exposed payoffs from favored customers who wanted the best chickens, sales of thousands of pounds of diseased birds, and widespread cheating of workers in their pay envelopes. Under the NRA code, the Schechters were required to follow the practice of "straight killing," which prohibited any picking and choosing to get "better" birds from coops; they could only sell chickens that had been inspected for disease; and they had to pay their workers fifty cents an hour for a forty-hour week.

But the Schechters could not resist temptation. "It didn't take Joe Schechter and his brothers long to see the advantages of breaking the code," wrote journalist Drew Pearson. "And it didn't take enforcement officers long to catch them." Government agents compiled a massive file on the Schechters, and in July 1934 all four brothers and their company were indicted on sixty criminal charges. One typical count alleged that "on or about June 24, 1934," the Schechters "knowingly, wilfully and unlawfully sold for human consumption an unfit chicken to Harry Stauber." It was this aspect that gave the case its lasting label, the "sick chicken" case. After a three-week trial, a jury convicted the Schechters on nineteen counts and Judge Marcus Campbell handed down jail terms of one to three months, with the oldest brother, Joe, getting the stiffest sentence. Federal circuit judges upheld the convictions on seventeen counts, but reversed two charges of violating the live poultry code's wage-and-hour provisions, ruling that these labor regulations "cannot be said to affect interstate commerce."

The Schechters' appeal reached the Supreme Court in May 1935. Solicitor General Stanley Reed argued for the government, and things went badly from his opening words. The case record showed that 96 percent of chickens sold in New York were shipped from other states, and Reed defended the Recovery Act as a permissible exercise of congressional power to regulate "commerce among the several states." But his effort to portray an unbroken "flow of commerce" from chicken farms to consumers was snapped by a question from the Four Horsemen's leader, Justice Sutherland: "Is everything that the defendants do which affects the poultry done after it is passed to them?" Reed conceded that the chickens "came to rest" in the Schechters' shop before they were slaughtered and sold. Justice Stone, one of the liberals known as the Three Musketeers, posed another tough question; in approving NRA codes, he asked Reed, "what is the standard which the President has to follow?" Reed weakly replied that "there is no primary standard in the statute other than that of fair competition."

With those exchanges, the fate of the Recovery Act was sealed even before Reed sat down. But the Schechters' lawyer, Joseph Heller, added a note of levity in his strong Brooklyn accent. Asked by Justice McReynolds to explain the "straight killing" requirement, Heller replied that "you have got to put your hand in the coop and take out whatever chicken comes to you." Justice Sutherland broke in: "What if the chickens are all at one end?" Heller's answer was lost in the gale of laughter that swept the courtroom.

The justices restrained their chuckles in the Court's sober opinion, which Chief Justice Hughes again took for himself to underscore its importance. Even Justice Cardozo, who dissented in the *Panama Refining* case, joined the unanimous ruling in *Schechter Poultry Corp. v. United States*. Hughes ruled that the Schechters were not engaged in interstate commerce and that Congress had no authority to regulate their business. He looked at the chickens and concluded that they came to roost in Brooklyn. "So far as the poultry here in question is concerned," he wrote, "the flow in interstate commerce had ceased. The poultry had come to a permanent rest within the State."

Hughes turned to his own opinion in *Panama Refining* for precedent on the "delegation" issue raised by the Schechters' lawyers. He found little in the congressional policy of "fair competition" to guide the president in judging the provisions of a thousand separate industrial codes. The business groups that drafted codes "may roam at will and the President may approve or disapprove their proposals as he may see fit," Hughes wrote disapprovingly. He compared the "virtually unfettered" discretion given the president by the Recovery Act with the detailed "code of laws" in the Interstate Commerce Act, in which Congress established an "expert body" to make "findings of fact which in turn are sustained by evidence." The "sweeping delegation" of power to the president in the Recovery Act imposed no restraints on his discretion. "We think that the code-making authority thus conferred is an unconstitutional delegation of legislative power," Hughes concluded.

The Court's decision in the "sick chicken" case produced a major bout of presidential indigestion. Two days after the ruling, Roosevelt invited reporters to the Oval Office for an "off-the-record" chat. Waving a sheaf of telegrams urging that he ask Congress to "fix" the Recovery Act, he spoke of "what is happening as a result of the Supreme Court decision in every industry and in every community in the United States." He read a telegram from the Cotton Textile Industry Committee, exhorting its members to continue voluntary adherence to the textile code. "What are we going to do," Roosevelt asked, "if some mill starts lengthening out its hours and cutting its minimum wages?" He imagined a garment shop owner in New York telling his workers to stay at their machines until nine at night. "What are the girls going to do? Are they going to walk out at five o'clock and lose their jobs?" Roosevelt complained that the court had thrown the Recovery Act "straight in our faces and we have been relegated to the horse-and-buggy definition of interstate commerce."

The reporters in his office begged to put the "horse-and-buggy" quote in headlines, but Roosevelt deflected their pleas. Two days later, after several thousand more telegrams and letters flooded the White House, he called a formal press conference and spoke to two hundred reporters for ninety minutes. After reading more than twenty messages from the public and businessmen, he held up a copy of the Court's opinion. "The implications of this decision," he said gravely, "are much more important than almost certainly any decision of my lifetime or yours, more important than any decision probably since the Dred Scott case." The reporters were delighted when Roosevelt repeated his "horse-and-buggy" quote, and they galloped to their typewriters. Although the president had deftly avoided any comment on plans to limit the Court's powers or reform its structure, the press was not deterred from speculation. His speech, concluded *Time* magazine, "was obviously a trial balloon to see whether the U.S. would rally to a constitutional amendment giving the Federal Government centralized powers which it has never had."

Having launched his trial balloon, Roosevelt let it ride the currents of public opinion while he waited for the Court's ruling on the Agricultural Adjustment Act, the second pillar of his New Deal recovery program. One reason the president deferred any showdown with the Court was that his political and legal advisers could not agree on the best response: some advocated a constitutional amendment requiring a "super-majority" of six or seven justices to invalidate a federal law, while others felt Congress should exercise its power under Article III of the Constitution to make "exceptions" to the Court's jurisdiction and limit its power to decide cases based on "emergency" proclamations. Roosevelt decided to bide his time, and the lawyers who began drafting plans for any later assault on the Court were sworn to secrecy.

More than seven months passed between the *Schechter* decision in May 1935 and the Court's ruling on the "Triple A" program in January 1936. During this time, government lawyers struggled to frame a constitutional defense of a program that Congress had planted on rocky legal ground. The Agricultural Adjustment Act was designed to remedy a basic problem—farmers produced too much and received too little for their goods, from cattle to corn. The law's drafters fashioned a two-pronged scheme to cut agricultural production and raise farm income. One section authorized the agriculture secretary, Henry A. Wallace, to set "voluntary" quotas for each farm product: farmers who grew crops like corn or cotton would cut back the acres they planted; those who raised animals like cows or chickens would limit their stock. The inducement for signing these "marketing agreements" would be payments to farmers from "processing taxes" collected from those who turned agricultural products into consumer goods, like meatpackers and textile manufacturers. These "taxes" would pass through the national treasury directly from processors to producers. In effect, the Triple A program would pay farmers not to farm and pass the cost to the public in higher prices.

Despite many snags in working out quotas and policing the agreements, the program achieved its purpose of raising farm income. However, some processors—especially those who shipped goods abroad—complained that the "taxes" imposed on their products put them at a competitive disadvantage in foreign markets. The meatpacking industry in particular, which competed with countries like Argentina in selling canned meat in Europe, raised loud objections to the processing tax. On the surface, the case that tested the Triple A in the Supreme Court did not involve an industrial giant, but a bankrupt textile firm in Massachusetts. Federal officials had filed a claim against the receivers of the Hoosac Cotton Mills for the collection of $81,694.28 in overdue processing taxes. Prew Savoy, the government lawyer sent to discuss this debt with the company's lawyers, discovered that Hoosac Mills was controlled by the board chairman of Armour & Company, a meatpacking giant, and that he had picked the bankrupt mill as a legal Trojan horse to shield his company from scrutiny. Savoy reported that Hoosac Mills' lawyers were "convinced the tax was unconstitutional" and wanted "to make it a test case" of the entire Triple A program. After the government pressed its claim for overdue taxes, one of the Hoosac receivers, William A. Butler, filed suit in federal court to block their collection. The Triple A won the first judicial round, but lost in the court of appeals and asked the Supreme Court to decide the case.

The lawyers who drafted the government's brief in *United States v. Butler* faced two major obstacles. First, the powers granted Congress by Article I of the Constitution did not include regulation of agriculture. Second, the "taxes" collected from processors did not go into the national treasury's general funds but were earmarked for payment directly to farmers. The only path the government's lawyers could find around these roadblocks went through the unmapped land of the clause in Article I that gave Congress "power to lay and collect taxes" for the "general welfare of the United States." The Supreme Court had never before construed the General Welfare Clause, but no other provision offered a smooth road to victory. "It is our position," the Triple A lawyers boldly stated, that the court should construe the General Welfare Clause "to include anything conducive to the national welfare" and that "the question of what is for the general welfare" was solely for Congress to decide. They appealed to the Court not to "substitute its judgment for the judgment of the legislature" on the reach of this broad power.

Pressed in his *Schechter* argument to point the Court to a congressional standard for industrial codes, Solicitor General Stanley Reed came up blank. Seven months later, he faced more questions in *Butler* about standards for computing processing taxes. Justice McReynolds began the grilling: "How is the tax fixed?" Reed answered that "the tax shall be equal to the difference between the farm value of the commodity and its purchasing power, or fair exchange value." This vague answer did not satisfy McReynolds. "Farmers buy all sorts of articles, silk stockings, woolen coats, and so on," he retorted. "With which are you going to compare it?" Reed finally conceded that the agriculture secretary was "at liberty" to set processing tax levels. He also backed away from the expansive reading of the General Welfare Clause in his brief. Reed asked the Court to construe the clause "not as a general power, but as a special power in Congress to expend this money" for a public purpose, that of reviving American agriculture. However, the Court had ruled in 1872 that states could not appropriate tax revenues to aid a private business, regardless of any "public purpose" it served. Try as he might, Reed could not push this precedential boulder from his path.

The Court issued its *Butler* ruling on January 6, 1936. Chief Justice Hughes and Justice Roberts joined the Four Horsemen in chopping down the Triple A program like an overgrown weed. Roberts wrote for the Court and returned to his conservative roost. The processing tax was really "an exaction laid upon processors" with "an aim foreign to the procurement of revenue for the government," he declared. The term "taxation," he continued, "has never been thought to connote the expropriation of money from one group for the benefit of another." Roberts conceded that the General Welfare Clause did not limit Congress in legislating beyond its "enumerated" powers, but he restricted its reach to "matters of national, as distinguished from local, welfare." In his view, the welfare of each farmer was a local matter and that of agriculture as a whole not one of national concern.

This last statement prompted the Three Musketeers to unsheath their rhetorical swords in dissent. Speaking for Brandeis and Cardozo, Justice Stone excoriated Roberts's opinion as a "tortured construction of the Constitution" that substituted "judicial fiat" for the judgment of Congress. "Courts are not the only agency of government that must be assumed to have capacity to govern," Stone reminded the majority. Roberts had written that the Court's only duty was "to lay the article of the Constitution which is invoked beside the statute which is challenged and to decide whether the latter squares with the former." This mechanistic formula, relegating the judge to the role of a carpenter with a T-square, provoked Stone to reply that judges must recognize "that language, even of a constitution, may mean what it says: that the power to tax and spend includes the power to relieve a nation-wide economic maladjustment by conditional gifts of money" to those who are distressed.

Mindful that every remark he made during an election year would be seen as political, President Roosevelt heeded the advice of his press secretary, Steve Early, to resist pressure from reporters to comment on the *Butler* decision. "Please resist all—say nothing," Early begged his boss. Roosevelt said nothing, but the lawyers he put to work on plans to "reform" the Supreme Court continued their labors behind closed doors.

24

"To Save the Constitution

from the Court"

The president's resolve to avoid public criticism of the Court was sorely tested by two decisions handed down four months after *Butler* ended the Triple A program. On May 18, 1936, the Court struck down the Bituminous Coal Conservation Act, which Congress had designed to bring labor peace to the bloody coal industry, wracked for years by open warfare between union miners and gun-toting company guards. Known as the Guffey Act after its chief sponsor, Senator Joseph Guffey of Pennsylvania, the law was passed in August 1935, after the Court ruled against the National Industrial Recovery Act in the *Schechter* case. But the Guffey Act included, word for word, the same labor provisions the justices had invalidated in the "sick chicken" case. Even Roosevelt, urging Congress to pass the law, expressed doubt "that the proposed act will withstand constitutional tests."

The same day Roosevelt signed the Guffey bill, three directors of the Carter Coal Company, one of the industry's largest producers, met in Washington. James W. Carter, the company's young president, was a bitter foe of the United Mine Workers and was determined to keep its members out of his mines. Two directors, Carter's father and a company employee, voted at this meeting to sign a coal industry code that protected miners' rights to join unions. The next morning, Frederick Wood, a prominent Wall Street lawyer, appeared in federal court in Washington and filed suit for James Carter against his own company, claiming that Carter's father and employee had signed an unconstitutional code. Wood had recently argued the *Schechter* case in the Supreme Court along with Joseph Heller; he focused on the constitutional issues while Heller educated the justices about the kosher poultry business. Returning to the Court in the *Carter* case, Wood relied on *Schechter* in arguing that labor relations were local in nature and subject only to state regulation.

Wood persuaded the Court that Congress had no power to regulate either kosher chickens or bituminous coal. Writing for the *Carter* majority, Justice Sutherland deplored federal meddling in "local" disputes between miners and their bosses. "Every journey to a forbidden end begins with the first step," he warned. Sutherland feared that federal regulation of labor relations in the mining industry was the first step toward reducing states "to little more than geographical subdivisions of the national domain." His journey to this conclusion stopped at the mineshaft, before the coal was loaded into railroad cars for shipment to other states. Coal production, Sutherland ruled, "is a purely local activity." Congress had declared in the Guffey Act that strikes over wages or union recognition disrupted interstate commerce in coal. Sutherland answered that "the evils are all local evils over which the federal government has no legislative control. The relation of employer to employee is a local relation."

Writing for the Three Musketeers in dissent, Justice Cardozo disputed Sutherland's claim that strikes in the mining industry did not affect interstate commerce. Cardozo agreed that coal production itself might be distinguished from commerce, but he cited the voluminous evidence in the government's brief of labor conflict in the coalfields. "Commerce had been choked and burdened" by the "violence and bloodshed and misery and bitter feeling" on both sides, he wrote. Noting that 97 percent of the coal produced by Carter's company was shipped out of state, Cardozo linked the industry's labor relations with its coal shipments and argued that their relation to interstate commerce "may be such that for the protection of the one there is need to regulate the other." But again, the Four Horsemen had corralled the votes of Hughes and Roberts to strike down another New Deal law.

The *Carter* decision removed Congress from the battlefield of labor relations as workers formed ranks on picket lines and employers stockpiled tear gas. In early 1936, workers at the Firestone rubber plant in Akron, Ohio, devised a new tactic to protest the firing of several union members: they sat down in the tire factory and refused to move. Workers at the nearby Goodyear plant soon joined the "sit-down" strikers, who ignored a court injunction to leave the plants. After some ten thousand striking workers brought the tire industry to a complete stop, they won recognition for their union. And their new tactic spread across the country, as workers in other industries waged forty-eight sit-down strikes during 1936. With labor conflict growing, and with elections approaching, the Supreme Court faced the issue of state power to regulate wages and working conditions in a challenge to a New York law that set minimum wages for women. The question in *Morehead v. Tipaldo* became more significant in the wake of the *Carter* decision. If Congress lacked power under the Commerce Clause to regulate labor conditions, did the "police powers" of the states allow them to occupy this field?

The ostensible parties in the New York case were Joseph Tipaldo and Frederick Morehead. Tipaldo, a Brooklyn laundry owner, had been arrested and jailed for violating the minimum wage law and filed a habeas corpus petition against Morehead, warden of the Kings County jail. Concealed behind the petition's caption, *Morehead v. Tipaldo* really pitted the state's New Deal politicians against business leaders who saw the "specter of socialism" in minimum wage laws. New York's highest court upheld Tipaldo's challenge to the wage law on March 3, 1936, and the state filed its appeal with the Supreme Court two weeks later. The case's timing raises an intriguing—but unanswerable—question about judicial politics. The Court rarely accepts cases for decision this late in its yearly term, which normally ends in June, but the *Morehead* case was briefed, argued, and decided in less than ninety days. Not only did the lawyers on both sides write briefs and prepare arguments, but the Court received amicus curiae briefs supporting the New York law from six other states, and briefs opposing it from the New York Hotel Association and the National Women's Party. Another relevant fact is that only the Four Horsemen voted to hear the *Morehead* appeal; the Court's unwritten "rule of four" permits any four justices to put a case on the docket. These facts suggest—but do not prove—that the Four Horsemen wanted to mount one last charge against the New Dealers before the 1936 elections. If they succeeded, Franklin Roosevelt—the New Deal's commanding general—would have suffered another defeat as he rallied his troops for the decisive battle in November. And if they failed, Roosevelt's complaint about the "horse-and-buggy" Court would lose appeal as a potential campaign slogan.

Despite their string of judicial losses, New Deal partisans held out some hope for a narrow victory in the *Morehead* case. After all, the Court had upheld state powers in two important 1934 decisions, sustaining Minnesota's "mortgage moratorium" statue in the *Home Building* case and New York's milk-pricing scheme in the *Nebbia* case. But these were "emergency" laws, and the worst days of the Great Depression had given way to recovery, however slow and uneven. New York's appeal in *Morehead* faced another obstacle, because the New York law had great similarities to the District of Columbia statute the Court had ruled unconstitutional in its *Adkins v. Children's Hospital* decision of 1923. The only significant difference in the two cases was that the same minimum wage applied to all female workers in the District, regardless of occupation, while New York set wages for each industry based on "the reasonable value of services rendered" by women. Grasping this weak straw, New York's solicitor general, Henry Epstein, argued to the Supreme Court that differences in the two laws "make the rule of the *Adkins* case inapplicable to this case." Epstein could have urged the Court to overrule *Adkins*, but he claimed instead that his case was "distinguishable" from this troubling precedent.

Epstein's opponents dismissed as "fanciful" his effort to distinguish the cases. "We have had a depression," they conceded, but this fact did not justify a minimum wage law; on the contrary, "a depression makes such a law the more harmful and oppressive by increasing the difficulty of the least efficient in securing employment." Tipaldo's lawyers warmly embraced the *Adkins* decision. "A social philosophy in conflict with the fundamental principles of the American Constitution has doubtless gained many adherents since that case was decided," they granted, "but every argument that can be presented in favor of minimum wage legislation was heard and considered then."

The Four Horsemen did not need argument to decide the *Morehead* case. They did, however, need one additional vote to strike down the New York law, and Justice Owen Roberts gave them the crucial vote; the ruling came on June 1, 1936, two weeks after the *Carter* decision. Between these two cases, the Court effectively created a constitutional no-man's-land from which both Congress and the states were barred. The Commerce Clause blocked federal regulation of labor relations, and the Due Process Clause of the Fourteenth Amendment erected a barrier against state laws.

Justice Pierce Butler spoke for the *Morehead* majority in the laissez-faire words of the *Lochner* era. "The right to make contracts about one's affairs is a part of the liberty protected by the due process clause," he wrote. Butler gave an economics lecture to New York's women workers: "In making contracts of employment, generally speaking, the parties have equal right to obtain from each other the best terms they can by private bargaining. Legislative abridgment of that freedom can only be justified by the existence of exceptional circumstances. Freedom of contract is the general rule and restraint the exception." The Great Depression did not impress Butler as grounds for breaking this rule.

Butler's reaffirmation of *Lochner* and *Adkins* provoked a stinging dissent from the Three Musketeers. Harlan Fiske Stone, joined by Brandeis and Cardozo, professed disbelief that Justice Butler could ignore economic reality. "There is a grim irony in speaking of the freedom of contract of those who, because of their economic necessities, give their service for less than is needful to keep body and soul together," he wrote. "In the years which have intervened since the *Adkins* case we have had opportunity to learn that a wage is not always the resultant of free bargaining between employers and employees," Stone reminded the Court's majority.

The public did not need any reminder of the Depression. More than any other decision of the New Deal period, the *Morehead* ruling unleashed a barrage of criticism against the Court. Conservatives joined liberals in denouncing the decision. Irving Brant, the respected *St. Louis Star-Times* editorialist, responded caustically: "Because five is a larger number than four, and for no other reason, the law is unconstitutional." With the presidential election just five months away, President Roosevelt once again held his tongue. Turning the Supreme Court into a campaign issue had both advantages and risks that were hard to calculate. Attacking the "horse-and-buggy" Court would please his partisans, but many voters still venerated this august institution. Besides, Irving Brant and other widely read columnists were blasting the Court in harsher terms than Roosevelt had ever employed. The president decided to issue his dissent to the Court's decisions after the polls. The almost universal condemnation of the Supreme Court's decision in the *Morehead* case, and President Roosevelt's refusal to join the chorus of critics, placed Republicans in a dilemma as they gathered in June 1936 to choose a candidate to oppose the popular incumbent. Should the GOP nominee warn the voters that Roosevelt could not be trusted to respect the Supreme Court as an independent branch of government? Claims that he wanted to tamper with the Court might appeal to those who viewed it as a counterweight to the elected branches. On the other hand, many voters saw the Court as a logjam that blocked the flow of laws and programs they had launched at the ballot box. The fact that Roosevelt had not criticized the Court since his "horse-and-buggy" remark in May 1935, and had not suggested or endorsed any plans to limit its powers or reshape its structure, made it harder to convince voters that the Court faced an imminent assault from the White House.

The Republican delegates to the party's convention in Cleveland, Ohio, first cheered a rousing speech by former president Herbert Hoover, who warned that a second term for Roosevelt might give him enough Supreme Court nominations to turn Americans into a "regimented people." But when the cheers died down, the delegates turned to Alf Landon of Kansas, the only Republican governor returned to office in 1934, as their candidate. Landon supported federal aid to agriculture, welfare benefits, and social security. The party's platform also signaled the decision to offer voters a "moderate" alternative to the New Deal. The delegates inserted a plank committing the party to seek "the adoption of state laws ... to protect women and children with respect to maximum hours, minimum wages, and working conditions. We believe that this can be done within the Constitution as it now stands."

Landon's campaign speeches avoided direct attacks on Roosevelt, and he fired his rhetorical guns at anonymous New Deal bureaucrats with accusations of waste and mismanagement. Only in the closing days of his lagging campaign did Landon make an issue of the Supreme Court. Speaking to a throng at Madison Square Garden in New York, and to a national radio audience, he charged that Roosevelt "has been responsible for nine acts declared unconstitutional by the Supreme Court." The president "has publicly belittled" the Court and "has publicly suggested that the Constitution is an outworn document," Landon charged.

But these charges lost their sting as Landon continued. "Our Constitution is not a lifeless piece of paper," he said. "But if changes in our civilization make amendment to the Constitution desirable it should be amended." Landon told his audience, "I am on record that, if proper working conditions cannot be regulated by the States, I shall favor a constitutional amendment giving the States the necessary power." He questioned Roosevelt's intentions toward the

Constitution. "Does he believe changes are required? If so, will an amendment be submitted to the people, or will he attempt to get around the Constitution by tampering with the Supreme Court?" But Roosevelt had given his opponent no answers. "No one can be sure," is all that Landon could say about the questions he had posed. This was hardly a ringing conclusion to a speech that asked millions of voters to turn an incumbent president out of office.

Roosevelt buried Landon at the polls in 1936 with more than a landslide, winning every state but Maine and Vermont. New Deal candidates rode the president's coattails to victory across the country as Republicans were left with only eighty-nine House seats and sixteen in the Senate. With the campaign over, the president tucked his electoral mandate in his pocket and left Washington for a South American tour. Before departing, Roosevelt held a cabinet meeting to discuss plans for his second term. Interior Secretary Harold Ickes noted in his diary that "there was a good deal of discussion about the Supreme Court. I think that the President is getting ready to move on that issue and I hope that he will do so." Before his trip, Roosevelt also told publisher Joseph Patterson, whose New York *Daily News* supported his reelection, that the Court problem "is a mighty difficult one to solve but one way or another I think it must be faced."

Which way would the president move? The fact is that only one trusted adviser, Attorney General Homer Cummings, knew what Roosevelt intended to do. For more than a year, since the *Schechter* decision in May 1935, Cummings had sent young lawyers to the library with research tasks: How much had the Supreme Court docket grown over the years? What was the age distribution of all federal judges? What were the retirement benefits of Supreme Court justices? What arguments had been made for giving Congress the power to override Court decisions? None of these lawyers knew why Cummings asked for this material, or what he did with their reports. Those who may have guessed the purpose did not reveal their thoughts.

Most of Roosevelt's advisers, formal and informal, leaned toward constitutional amendment as the best solution to the "Court problem." They could not agree, however, on whether to pursue "procedural" or "substantive" amendments, to borrow language from judicial doctrine. One example of the first approach would require a "supermajority" of six or seven justices to strike down federal laws. Similar proposals had been made—but never adopted—by many politicians over the years. Another procedural approach would allow Congress to override Supreme Court decisions by two-thirds vote of each chamber, after an intervening congressional election. The competing "substantive" approach would limit the Court's power to decide certain kinds of cases, or grant additional powers to Congress in fields such as agriculture or labor relations. None of these proposals was new; similar efforts to "curb the Court" went back some fifty years, and all had failed. Other problems faced those who pressed for amendments: the process took time and ratification could be blocked by the legislatures of thirteen states. With important New Deal cases on the Court's docket, Roosevelt had little patience for a process that might take years.

The president wanted a quick solution, and Attorney General Cummings handed him one from an unlikely source. Back in 1914, an earlier attorney general had proposed adding one judge to lower federal courts for every sitting judge who reached the age of seventy. "This will insure at all times," the proposal's author wrote, "the presence of a judge sufficiently active to discharge promptly and adequately all the duties of the court." That proposal came from James McReynolds, now seventy-two and the most dogmatic of the Four Horsemen of Reaction on the Supreme Court. McReynolds was not the first "court-packing" advocate; as Roosevelt later noted, the House had approved a similar plan in 1869, although that bill never became law. Cummings learned of the McReynolds plan shortly before Christmas in December 1936, and he offered it to Roosevelt like a gift-wrapped present. A legislative solution to the Court problem had two great advantages over the amendment approach. First, it could be enacted quickly, before the Court inflicted further damage on the New Deal program. Second, with 331 Democrats in the House and 76 in the Senate, the president could absorb the defections of 113 representatives and 25 senators from his own party and still win majorities in both chambers. Considering that most congressional Democrats had just ridden Roosevelt's electoral bandwagon into Washington, the prospect of substantial defections on this issue was virtually unthinkable.

The "judicial reorganization bill," as Roosevelt dubbed his court-packing plan, was hammered out and polished during January 1937. The final version authorized the president to nominate up to fifty new federal judges, one for each sitting judge who failed to resign or retire within six months of his seventieth birthday. No more than two judges could be added to each circuit court, or six justices to the Supreme Court. The number six had not been picked from a hat; there were currently six justices over the age of seventy. Attorney General Cummings supervised the bill's drafting and secured the President's approval on January 30.

Roosevelt hosted his annual White House dinner for the federal judiciary on February 3. All the Supreme Court justices attended except Brandeis, who rarely ventured from his apartment, and Stone, who had been ill with amebic dysentery since October. The other guests included Senator William Borah of Idaho, who had warned the president the day before in a Senate speech to keep his hands off the Court. But at this festive dinner, Roosevelt chatted warmly with Borah and even with Justice Van Devanter.

Two days later, on the morning of February 5, the president summoned the Democratic leaders of Congress, including the men who chaired the House and Senate Judiciary Committees, to a White House meeting. Briskly and without introduction, Roosevelt began reading the message he would send to Congress at noon. It took him an hour to complete his reading, after which he made just one request of the powerful men who sat around the cabinet table. "If we can pass the legislation," he said of his bill, "the whole country will move forward." With that, Roosevelt returned to his office to meet with reporters who had been told only that the president had a "confidential" message for the press. When they gathered around his desk, Roosevelt read his message again and then answered a few questions. One reporter asked about the reaction from congressional leaders at the earlier meeting. "As soon as I finished I came in here," Roosevelt responded. "There was no discussion."

There was plenty of discussion after Roosevelt's message reached Congress and reporters had digested it for the public. The presidential message itself did not even mention the potential increase in Supreme Court membership; that was buried in the accompanying bill prepared by Homer Cummings. Roosevelt clothed his message in concern for the judicial workload: "The simple fact is that today a new need for legislative action arises because the personnel of the Federal judiciary is insufficient to meet the business before them." The president noted that in the past year the Supreme Court had declined to hear 695 of 803 cases presented for review by nongovernmental parties. "Many of the refusals were doubtless warranted," he conceded. "But can it be said that full justice is achieved when a court is forced by the sheer necessity of keeping up with its business to decline, without even an explanation, to hear 87 percent of the cases presented to it by private litigants?"

Roosevelt made another argument that sounded more like a doctor's report. "The modern tasks of judges call for the use of full energies. Modern complexities call also for a constant infusion of new blood in the courts." He continued his diagnosis. "A lowered mental or physical vigor leads men to avoid an examination of complicated and changed conditions. Little by little, new facts become blurred through old glasses fitted, as it were, for the needs of another generation; older men, assuming that the scene is the same as it was in the past, cease to explore or inquire into the present or the future."

The president made a serious blunder in portraying the justices as doddering graybeards who needed help to shoulder their load. His two premises were demonstrably false. First, there was no evidence that the Supreme Court docket was clogged with a backlog of cases. When Chief Justice Hughes finally shed his reluctance to embroil the Court in the controversy, he sent a letter to the Senate Judiciary Committee citing statistics to show that the Court "is fully abreast of its work," with "no congestion of cases upon our calendar." Second, Roosevelt's equation of age with incompetence deeply wounded Hughes, who was vigorous at seventy-four, and Brandeis, at eighty still one of the Court's most productive members.

Roosevelt made another blunder in not allowing discussion of his court-packing plan by the Democratic leaders who had to shepherd it through Congress. Had he asked for comment before February 5, or even at the meeting that morning, he might have avoided the debacle that followed. Hatton Sumners of Texas, who chaired the House Judiciary Committee, refused to introduce the bill. "Boys, here's where I cash in my chips," he told friends. The Senate Judiciary Committee chairman, Henry Ashurst of Arizona, gave the plan lip-service backing in public but worked behind the scenes to sabotage it. Senator Burton Wheeler of Montana, a New Deal stalwart, broke with Roosevelt and headed the opposition. The list of Democratic defectors swelled in the month after the President dropped his plan on Congress like a bombshell. There were not enough to defeat the bill, should it come to a vote, but the congressional opponents were prominent and powerful.

The growing realization that his legislative bombshell was a dud prompted Roosevelt to look beyond Congress for support. The first—and perhaps greatest—political master of the airwaves held a lengthy Fireside Chat with the American people on March 9, 1937. Dropping all pretence about judicial overwork and senility, the president revealed his real complaint about the Court: he disliked its decisions. He charged that the Court "has improperly set itself up as a third House of the Congress—a super-legislature, as one of the Justices has called it—reading into the Constitution words and implications which are not there, and which were never intended to be there." One by one, Roosevelt ticked off decisions that struck down federal and state laws, quoting with approval from the dissents of Chief Justice Hughes and Justice Stone. He omitted, of course, the *Schechter* case, in which the Court unanimously voided the Industrial Recovery Act.

Roosevelt struck a messianic note in his appeal. "We have," he argued, "reached the point as a Nation where we must take action to save the Constitution from the Court and the Court from itself." He made clear his intention to create a "liberal-minded Judiciary" of "younger men" who were not "fearful of the future" but who understood the "modern facts and circumstances under which average men have to live and work." Embracing the slogan of his critics, the President said that "if the appointment of such Justices can be called 'packing the Courts,' then I say that I and with me the vast majority of the American people favor doing just that thing—now."

The public majority behind Roosevelt's plan was hardly vast, but his Fireside Chat did shift opinion to his side, although most of those polled indicated a preference for constitutional amendment rather than legislative court-packing. But the calculations of politicians who counted votes on Capitol Hill, on both sides of the issue, were abruptly revised when the Supreme Court issued its decision on March 29, 1937, in *West Coast Hotel v. Parrish*, a case that challenged Washington State's minimum wage law for women. This case reflected, in Elsie Parrish's suit for back wages, the struggles of many workers to "keep body and soul together" during the Depression, as Justice Stone wrote in his *Morehead* dissent. Parrish worked at the Cascadian Hotel in Wenatchee, Washington, the center of the state's apple-growing region. The Cascadian, which was owned by the West Coast Hotel Company, paid her twenty-two cents an hour for cleaning toilets and making beds. When the manager discharged her in 1935, Elsie Parrish discovered she had been paid less than the weekly minimum wage of $14.30, set by state law. She demanded $216.19 in back wages, and the manager offered to settle for $17. She turned him down and found a local lawyer who took her case for a small fee. The Supreme Court agreed to resolve this $200 dispute after Washington's high court thumbed its nose at the *Adkins* decision and ruled for Elsie Parrish.

The Supreme Court's ruling on the Washington law surprised many people. Justice Owen Roberts, who had voted with the Four Horsemen to strike down New York's virtually identical law in the *Morehead* case, switched sides in *West Coast Hotel v. Parrish* to join Chief Justice Hughes and the Three Musketeers. What historians have called the "Constitutional Revolution" of 1937 had begun, with a most unlikely revolutionary on the judicial ramparts. In his majority opinion, Chief Justice Hughes laid out three reasons for his "reexamination of the Adkins Case." He first noted the "importance of the question" to the many states with minimum wage laws similar to Washington's. The "close division" of the Court in *Adkins* provided a second reason. Hughes finally cited "the economic conditions which have supervened" since *Adkins* was decided in 1923. This last factor was clearly the most important in his mind. "We may take judicial notice of the unparalleled demands for relief which arose during the recent period of depression and still continue to an alarming extent despite the degree of economic recovery which has been achieved," Hughes wrote. He did not need statistics to show the extent of suffering that was "common knowledge through the length and breadth of the land." Hughes sounded more like a Socialist than a Republican in calling the "exploitation of a class of workers" like Elsie Parrish a "compelling" reason to protect them from "unconscionable employers" like the West Coast Hotel Company.

Hughes turned his guns on the crumbling fortress of laissez-faire doctrine. Those who challenged minimum wage laws, he noted, always claimed they deprived workers of their "freedom of contract." Hughes posed a rhetorical question and answered for the new majority. "What is this freedom? The Constitution does not speak of freedom of contract. It speaks of liberty and prohibits the deprivation of liberty without due process of law. In prohibiting that deprivation the Constitution does not recognize an absolute and uncontrollable liberty." The Chief Justice fashioned a modern definition of "liberty" from ancient terms. "Liberty in each of its phases has its history and connotation. But the liberty safeguarded is liberty in a social organization which requires the protection of law against the evils which menace the health, safety, morals and welfare of the people. Liberty under the Constitution is thus necessarily subject to the restraints of due process, and regulation which is reasonable in relation to its subject and is adopted in the interests of the community is due process." Hughes stated the obvious when he concluded that "the case of *Adkins v. Children's Hospital* should be, and it is, overruled."

Chief Justice Hughes spoke for "the people" and their "community" in his *West Coast Hotel* opinion, but his words were not new. Exactly a century earlier, in 1837, Chief Justice Roger Taney proclaimed in *Charles River Bridge* that "the community" had "rights" under the Constitution and that "the happiness and well being of every citizen depends on their faithful preservation." But Taney spoke for a "community" that denied slaves and women and working people most of the "rights" enjoyed by white men with property. A century later, the Constitution had been amended to abolish slavery and give blacks and women the vote, and the Court had upheld state power to require minimum wages for workers. These rights of a broader community were not always respected, particularly those of blacks in the South, but the Supreme Court had finally defined "the people" without distinctions of race, sex, or wealth. How the Court would rule in cases seeking vindication of those rights by people who had long been denied them remained to be seen.

The Four Horsemen—all over seventy, and with eighty years on the Court between them—knew they had fought and lost their final judicial battle. Justice Sutherland, who spoke for the Court in *Adkins*, wrote its epitaph in his *West Coast Hotel* dissent. But he was truculent in defeat. He found no power in the Constitution to protect "exploited" workers against "unscrupulous" employers. "The remedy in that situation—and the only true remedy—is to amend the Constitution," Sutherland wrote. In a real sense, the new majority had done just that. Hughes had written that legislation "adopted in the interests of the community is due process." Those words transformed the Due Process Clause from a negative restraint on state power into a positive force to promote the "public interest."

"Hughes Thundered Out

the Decision"

The Court's decision in *West Coast Hotel v. Parrish* on March 29 was simply the opening salvo in the "Constitutional Revolution" of 1937. Two weeks later, the justices handed down another ruling of equal constitutional significance, in a case that tested congressional power to protect the right of workers to organize unions and bargain with their employers over contract terms. This case, *National Labor Relations Board v. Jones & Laughlin Steel Company*, grew out of legislation first passed by Congress during the "Hundred Days" session in 1933. Responding to pressure from union leaders who had supported President Roosevelt's election, Congress provided in Section 7(a) of the National Industrial Recovery Act that "employees shall have the right to organize and bargain collectively through representatives of their own choosing, and shall be free from the interference, restraint, or coercion" of employers. Union organizers promptly swarmed to factory gates with leaflets telling workers, "The President Wants You to Join the Union!" Roosevelt, in fact, only grudgingly accepted Section 7(a) as a concession to union leaders who backed Senator Hugo Black's proposal to increase employment through a thirty-hour work week. The president had both economic and constitutional objections to Black's bill, and adding "Labor's Bill of Rights" to the Recovery Act paid his campaign debts to organized labor.

But unions did not organize many workers under the Recovery Act, largely because the National Labor Board, set up to enforce Section 7(a), could not force anti-union employers to obey its orders. The board ruled that unions chosen by majority vote had "exclusive" rights to represent all workers in a bargaining unit. Employers insisted that members of "minority" unions—most often "company unions" they funded and controlled—be allowed to bargain for separate contracts. Roosevelt himself undercut the board's powers when he intervened in March 1934 to settle disputes between striking autoworkers and industry leaders over union election rules. Without consulting the board, Roosevelt forced union leaders to make room at the bargaining table for the company union.

The president's endorsement of the "minority rule" made the National Labor Board totally impotent. His support of industry's position had two other effects. Angry workers responded in April to Roosevelt's "sellout" with a strike wave that began in Toledo with auto parts workers and quickly spread to truck drivers in Minneapolis, longshoremen in San Francisco, and textile workers throughout the South. The country was engulfed in virtual class warfare, as strikers battled police and the death toll mounted. Faced with a threatened national strike by steelworkers, Roosevelt persuaded Congress to create a new body, the National Labor Relations Board, with power to order and supervise union elections. The new board, however, relied on Justice Department lawyers for enforcement, and they did not support the "majority rule" policy on union representation. The vice president for industrial relations of U.S. Steel told the press that the new board "is not going to bother us very much."

But the president's move greatly bothered Senator Robert Wagner of New York, a New Deal loyalist and labor's chief ally in Congress. Wagner challenged Roosevelt by introducing the National Labor Relations Act in February 1935. This bill retained Section 7(a) of the Recovery Act, but added a list of "unfair labor practices" that prohibited employers from supporting company unions, firing workers for union activities, and refusing to bargain with unions. The Wagner Act also codified the majority rule policy by granting "exclusive representation" to unions that won elections and placing enforcement powers with the Labor Board's lawyers. Roosevelt first adopted a hands-off position that encouraged Wagner's opponents, including Labor Secretary Frances Perkins and Attorney General Homer Cummings, whose departments shared enforcement duties under the Recovery Act and stood to lose ground in this political turf war. Several factors, however, pushed Roosevelt off the fence. The 1934 elections added to labor's clout in Congress, some two million workers joined industrial unions, and the Supreme Court struck down the Recovery Act in the *Schechter* case. Roosevelt finally gave his blessing to Wagner's bill, and the former antagonists smiled for the cameras when the president signed the National Labor Relations Act at the White House on July 5, 1935.

Having cleared the hurdles of Congress and the White House, the Wagner Act faced its greatest obstacle in the Supreme Court. The bill's preamble declared that denying workers the rights to organize and bargain collectively led to "strikes and other forms of industrial strife and unrest," which in turn constricted the flow of goods into the "channels of commerce" and adversely affected levels of employment and wages. The preamble also stated that the "inequality of bargaining power" between employers and workers deprived the latter of "actual liberty of contract," and that this deprivation "substantially burdens and affects the flow of commerce" between states. Given the twin pillars of Due Process and Commerce Clause precedent blocking their path, the bill's drafters hoped that pushing one against the other would topple both.

The Labor Board's general counsel, Charles Fahy, came from the Interior Department, where he had drafted the "hot-oil" regulations the Supreme Court struck down in the *Panama Refining* decision. Fahy was determined not to lose another case, and he directed the young lawyers on his staff—as one later recalled—to "search out good test cases" that fit into his "master plan for testing the constitutionality" of the Wagner Act. Fahy wanted to present the Court with a package of cases that reflected the range of industries—both large and small—covered by the Wagner Act. He also directed his lawyers to carefully prepare records with strong evidence of "unfair labor practices" by employers who fired union members or refused to bargain with them.

Armed with these marching orders, Fahy's legal platoon fanned out across the country and conducted dozens of "unfair labor practice" hearings. They returned to Washington with bulging files of testimony and affidavits, which they presented to the Labor Board for decision and enforcement orders. They went back to federal circuit courts for judicial enforcement of orders that employers had refused to obey. After consulting Fahy's "master plan" for guidance, they offered him five cases that fit his criteria for presentation to the Supreme Court. All they had in common was records of "unfair labor practices" by employers and their refusal to obey the Labor Board's orders.

Fahy wanted one case against an industrial giant with interstate activities and a record of labor strife. He found a good candidate in the Jones & Laughlin Steel Company in Pennsylvania, the nation's fourth-largest steel producer and an anti-union bulwark since 1897. With some 22,000 employees, Jones & Laughlin owned iron ore, coal, and limestone properties in several states, and railroad and barge subsidiaries for shipping raw materials into Pennsylvania and finished products out of the state. The Labor Board filed charges after the company fired some twenty union supporters before an election scheduled for June 1935. "There is an exceedingly vicious history of terrorism in this community," the board's regional director reported of the company's anti-union campaign at its main plant in Aliquippa, Pennsylvania.

Fahy hoped the Supreme Court would uphold the Labor Board's power to force Jones & Laughlin to rehire its fired workers and recognize their union. But he also wanted the Court to recognize the board's jurisdiction over smaller companies with less direct impact on interstate commerce. Fahy picked other cases to give the Court a full menu for its five-course dinner. The second case involved the Freuhauf Trailer Company, a leading truck-trailer manufacturer. Company foremen had fired six union members and threatened others with discharge if they did not quit the union. Another advantage of the Freuhauf case was that the company had infiltrated the union with spies from the Pinkerton

Detective Agency; this was the kind of "interference" with unions the Wagner Act prohibited.

Fahy picked a third case from the garment industry, a battleground of labor conflict. The Friedman–Harry Marks Company produced men's clothing in Virginia and was an organizing target of the Amalgamated Clothing Workers Union. The company's president, Morton Marks, had been caught spying on a union meeting at a church; the next day, his plant manager fired four workers who attended the meeting. Fahy also wanted cases involving companies that did not manufacture goods but provided services on an interstate basis. He found one in the Associated Press, which provided hundreds of newspapers with articles by its reporters. The company was locked in a bitter dispute with the American Newspaper Guild over the transfer of union activists to night-shift jobs. The news agency fired the guild's vice president, Morris Watson, after he protested the moves. "He is an agitator and disturbs morale of staff," wrote the company's executive editor the day he fired Watson. Fahy's final case was a last-minute substitution for one against the Greyhound Bus Lines, which became stalled in a hostile federal court in Philadelphia. Searching his docket for bus cases, Fahy found one against the Washington, Virginia, and Maryland Coach Company, which carried passengers in the capital area and had fired eighteen employees for union activities.

The Supreme Court arguments in the Wagner Act cases began on February 9, 1937, and spanned three days, with eager crowds packing the chamber for hints of the Court's reaction to President Roosevelt's court-packing proposal. Eleven lawyers addressed the justices in the five cases, devoting a torrent of legal oratory to the government's claim that labor strife diverted the "stream of commerce" between states and thus provided Congress with power to smooth its currents with the Wagner Act. The most noted lawyer on the corporate side was John W. Davis, a former solicitor general who now headed a prominent Wall Street firm. Arguing for the Associated Press, Davis assured the justices that he did not dispute the merits of trade unionism or collective bargaining, but he did challenge "the power of the Federal Government to make collective bargaining compulsory in all the industries of this country." Davis aimed his fire at the government's "stream of commerce" theory, which relied for precedent on Supreme Court decisions that upheld federal regulation of grain elevators and stockyards. "There is no current here," Davis said of the news-reporting business. "We do not sit like the stockyards, abreast a current of commerce which other men are trying to conduct." Charles Fahy responded for the government that strikes in one state blocked the shipment of goods to other states. He urged the Court to uphold "the right of self-organization" by workers. "Unless that right may be protected by law there is only recourse to strike in order that it may be protected by combat," Fahy warned.

More than a thousand people lined up outside the Supreme Court on April 12,

1937, hoping to find places among the 220 seats in the red-curtained court-room. They wanted to witness the next act in the constitutional drama that had begun two weeks earlier with the *West Coast Hotel* decision. Those who crowded the chamber were treated to a bravura show by Chief Justice Hughes. Without a glance at the audience, he began reading his majority opinion in the *Jones & Laughlin* case, the first of the five Wagner Act decisions. "It was an amazing per-formance," recalled a Labor Board lawyer, Tom Emerson. "Hughes thundered out the decision with his beard wagging. You would have thought that he was deciding the most run of the mill case, that the law had always been this way, that there had never been any real dispute about it, and that he was just applying hundreds of years of decisions to a slightly new kind of situation," Emerson said. "And he did it with an air of absolute confidence, as if the Constitution had always been construed this way."

At this turning point in constitutional history, Hughes barely looked back at the *Schechter* and *Carter Coal* decisions of 1935, noting only that the distinction between interstate and intrastate commerce remained "vital to the maintenance of our federal system." But the heart of his opinion was judicial recognition of the reality of a national economic system. "We are asked to shut our eyes to the plainest facts of our national life and to deal with the question of direct and in-direct effects in an intellectual vacuum," Hughes wrote of those who read the Commerce Clause through nineteenth-century lenses. "When industries orga-nize themselves on a national scale, making their relation to interstate com-merce the dominant factor in their activities," he asked, "how can it be maintained that their industrial labor relations constitute a forbidden field into which Congress may not enter when it is necessary to protect interstate com-merce from the paralyzing consequences of industrial war?"

With that question and the Court's answer, Hughes cleared the constitu-tional no-man's-land of all barriers to state and federal regulation of labor relations, from hiring to firing. The Court had finally opened its eyes to the twentieth century. Charles Fahy's careful preparation of test cases brought vic-tory in all five. Amazingly, the Court unanimously sustained the Labor Board's powers in the *Coach Company* case; even the Four Horsemen were unwilling, as their constitutional fortress collapsed about them, to deny federal jurisdiction over interstate transportation. But they remained defiant in defeat. Justice James McReynolds, the most crusty of the conservatives, read their dissent in the three manufacturing cases. A reporter described the scene: "Old McReynolds was sore as hell," he wrote, "poking his pencil angrily at the crowd as he shouted his opinion" to the audience. His opinion cited two of the old "yellow dog" contract cases on the due process question and *Schechter* on the commerce issue, although none of these cases remained alive as precedent; McReynolds was attending their judicial funeral. But he wrote as if Jones & Laughlin's plant man-agers were inviting guests to a garden party. "The right to contract is fundamen-tal and includes the privilege of selecting those with whom one is willing to assume contractual relations," he stated. "This right is unduly abridged by the Act now upheld. A private owner is deprived of power to manage his own property by freely selecting those to whom his manufacturing operations are to be entrusted." But the court's ruling meant that company managers could no longer evict union members from their premises.

When McReynolds put down his pencil and stopped shouting, the Four Horsemen of Reaction left the bench in silence. The "industrial war" that raged outside the court had inflicted casualties within its chambers. Like the Articles of Confederation in 1787, the laissez-faire Constitution of the *Lochner* era was replaced in 1937 by a charter that "the people" ratified at the ballot box. The "plainest facts of our national life" were finally acknowledged in the new Constitution, unchanged in wording but profoundly altered in meaning.

The Supreme Court truly launched a "Constitutional Revolution" with its *West Coast Hotel* and *Jones & Laughlin* decisions, which demolished the laissez-faire doctrine of the *Lochner* era. But the enormous constitutional significance of these two rulings has been overshadowed by debate over their relation to President Roosevelt's court-packing proposal. In particular, historians have scrutinized the about-face by Justice Roberts between the *Morehead* and *West Coast Hotel* decisions, which prompted quips at the time about "the switch in time that saved nine." Many historians have repeated this quip, and have assumed that Roberts switched positions in response to Roosevelt's court-packing plan. But a closer look at events between the *Morehead* decision in June 1936 and *West Coast Hotel* in March 1937 will dispel the "switch in time" myth.

The significant date in this chronology is actually December 19, 1936, when the justices voted on the *West Coast Hotel* case at their closed-door conference, two days after arguments concluded. Justice Roberts joined Chief Justice Hughes and Justices Brandeis and Cardozo in voting to uphold Washington's minimum wage law. However, Justice Stone was seriously ill and did not attend the conference. Under the Court's rule, the four-to-four tie vote left the lower-court decision standing and would have sustained the Washington law. Everyone knew that Stone would repeat his *Morehead* vote, so Roberts had really decided the *West Coast Hotel* case in December, before Roosevelt finally settled on the court-packing plan and two months before he sent his proposal to Congress.

Chief Justice Hughes, however, had agreed to hold up decisions in close cases until Stone returned to the bench. Another reason for delay was that the Court does not issue opinions in cases decided by tie votes. Hughes wanted to write for the Court in *West Coast Hotel*, and he wanted Stone to read his opinion before it was issued, in case Stone had revisions to suggest or decided to write a concurrence of his own. Stone's recuperation took longer than expected, and he did not return to the Court until February 1, 1937. According to

Roberts, Stone cast his vote at the conference on February 6, the day after Roosevelt dropped his court-packing bombshell on Congress. Hughes had probably drafted his *West Coast Hotel* opinion by this time, but he very likely held up the decision until the justices had circulated their opinions in *Jones & Laughlin* and the other Wagner Act cases. Arguments in these cases had begun on February 9, and Hughes was writing the majority opinion in *Jones & Laughlin*, the most important Wagner Act case. It is also likely that Hughes delayed the *West Coast Hotel* decision until the Senate Judiciary Committee released its response to the court-packing plan on March 22.

The combination of Stone's illness, the uproar over Roosevelt's proposal, and the Court's work on the Wagner Act cases explains the long delay in the *West Coast Hotel* case. This chronology of events also shows that Roberts's switch was not influenced by announcement of the court-packing plan in February 1937. But it does not explain *why* he switched. His own later explanation—given after he retired in 1945—is unconvincing. During the conference on March 30, 1936, to consider New York's appeal in the *Morehead* case, Roberts wrote, "I said I saw no reason to grant the writ unless the Court was prepared to reexamine and overrule the *Adkins* case. To this remark, there was no response around the table." None was needed, in fact, because four justices had already voted to hear the case. During the argument on April 29, New York's lawyers tried to "distinguish" the *Adkins* decision and did not press for its reversal. "The argument seemed to me to be disingenuous and born of timidity," Roberts wrote. "I could find nothing in the record to substantiate the alleged distinction. At conference, I so stated, and stated further that I was taking the state of New York at its word" and would vote against its law.

It is more likely that Roberts was being disingenuous. If he wanted to reverse *Adkins*, nothing prevented him from joining a majority to do that. No canon of constitutional law requires that justices wait until lawyers ask them to overrule a precedent. In their *Morehead* dissent, the Three Musketeers argued that the *Nebbia* decision of 1934 had effectively reversed *Adkins* and that the Court became "free of its restriction as a precedent" in later cases. What Roberts did not say, however, was that—despite later denials—he still harbored presidential ambitions while *Morehead* was before the Court. The *New York Times* reported predictions of a "substantial 'favorite son' vote" for Roberts by Pennsylvania delegates to the GOP convention in June 1936. Lacking any consistent judicial philosophy, Roberts might well have decided that voting to uphold a law backed by New Dealers would not please the upper-crust Republicans who urged him to seek his party's nomination. This is speculation, but it makes more sense than Roberts's claim that he was waiting for an invitation to overrule *Adkins*, but did not receive one until *West Coast Hotel* reached the Court in October 1936.

Most historians now agree that Roberts switched positions in December 1936, two months before the unveiling of Roosevelt's court-packing plan. They conclude from this fact that Roberts's vote in *West Coast Hotel* was not influenced by the plan and the ensuing uproar. But it is nonetheless possible that reports of such a plan did affect Roberts. On October 8, 1936, the *New York Times* reported a speech by former senator James Reed of Missouri, charging that President Roosevelt had "threatened to 'pack' the Supreme Court by increasing its membership." Reed said that if FDR denied this claim, "I'll prove it by documentary evidence." The press reported no presidential denial or evidence from Reed, and the issue did not resurface during the final weeks of the presidential campaign. But the question had been raised, and Roberts was certainly aware that Congress had several times increased the Court's membership and that Roosevelt might consider this an option.

Four days after this court-packing story, Roberts voted to hear the *West Coast Hotel* case. This coincidence proves nothing, but its place in the sequence of events may help us understand why Roberts switched his votes in the minimum wage cases. The answer clearly lies closer to politics than to jurisprudence. Roberts was hardly the first presidential aspirant on the Supreme Court, nor the last. He did not campaign from the bench, but neither did he publicly disavow his "favorite son" supporters in Pennsylvania. Roberts cast his *Morehead* vote at a time when a "conservative" position might increase his political appeal to Republican delegates. By October 1936, however, no doubt remained that Roosevelt would win the election. And his crushing victory in November must have impressed Roberts, who did not share the ideological fervor of the Four Horsemen. Roberts had voted in the *Home Building* and *Nebbia* cases to uphold state laws, and we might better consider his *Morehead* vote an aberration and *West Coast Hotel* a return to this judicial path.

So there was, after all, a "switch in time that saved nine." The fact that it happened close on the heels of Roosevelt's election victory and not after his blunder in sending the court-packing plan to Congress underscores the truth of Mr. Dooley's aphorism that "the Supreme Court reads th' iliction returns." Political events outside the Court affect decisions within its chambers, often slowly but sometimes quickly. And things moved quickly as the Court finally responded to the "felt necessities" of the American people in 1937.

The "Constitutional Revolution" inflicted its first judicial casualty on May 18, with the announcement by Justice Willis Van Devanter of his retirement at the term's end in June, after twenty-six years on the Court. Ironically, the Senate Judiciary Committee retired President Roosevelt's court-packing plan the same day, with a formal report of disapproval. Despite his legislative defeat, Roosevelt gained what he really wanted with Van Devanter's departure, a chance to begin shaping a "liberal-minded" Court. Before his second term ended in 1941, the president had placed seven New Dealers on the bench and elevated an honorary New Dealer—Harlan Fiske Stone—to the post of Chief Justice. With these nominations, Roosevelt fulfilled his pledge to pump "younger blood" into the Court's hardened arteries; the new justices averaged fifty-two years in age when they joined the Court, replacing men who averaged seventy-seven when they left. This quarter-century difference in age reflected a century's difference in outlook. The older justices all began their legal practices in the nineteenth century, their successors in the twentieth.

The man Roosevelt named to replace Justice Van Devanter, Senator Hugo Black of Alabama, perfectly fit the president's judicial mold as a fifty-one-year-old Democratic loyalist with a liberal record. The eighth child of a small-town merchant, Black grew up in rural Alabama and befriended the sharecroppers, both white and black, who patronized his father's store. He never finished high school, but completed both liberal arts and law degrees in three years at the University of Alabama. Black practiced law in Birmingham, also serving as police court judge. During three years as the city's prosecuting attorney, he brought charges against several police officers for abusing black defendants. Elected to the Senate in 1927, Black staked out a liberal position well before he joined the New Deal majority in 1933. Many considered him a "radical" for championing the causes of poor people, and his nomination drew opposition from the conservative press. The *Washington Post* faulted him for "lack of training on the one hand and extreme partisanship on the other," and the *Chicago Tribune* declared that Roosevelt had picked "the worst he could find" for the Court.

The worst thing about Hugo Black was his membership in the Ku Klux Klan as a young Alabama politician. The press reported his Klan affiliation before the Senate confirmed Black in August 1937 by sixty-three to sixteen, with all the negative votes cast by conservative Republicans. This issue did not cost him votes; Black's colleagues accepted his claim that he thought he was joining a social club and resigned in 1925 when he discovered the Klan's true nature. However, shortly after Black took his Supreme Court oath on August 17, reports surfaced that in 1926 he had secretly been sworn to life membership in the Klan. Black remained silent for six weeks, but the growing press storm finally bent his resolve not to respond. He stepped before radio microphones on October 1 and spoke to a national audience. "I did join the Klan," Black admitted. "I later resigned. I never rejoined." He did not consider the "unsolicited" life membership card he received in 1926 "as a membership of any kind in the Ku Klux Klan," Black explained. "I never used it. I did not even keep it." He urged his listeners to consider instead his membership in "that group of liberal Senators who have consistently fought for civil, economic and religious rights of all Americans, without regard to race or creed." Black's forceful and forthright words satisfied most critics, and during thirty-four years on the Court he consistently fought for the rights of the poor people and blacks he grew up with in Alabama. Only in his eighties, increasingly crotchety and conservative, did Black chastise young people who protested Jim Crow laws and the Vietnam War for "running loose" and rejecting the "parental discipline" of their elders.

Like a drum major, Black led a parade of New Dealers to the Court. Next in line was Stanley Reed, replacing George Sutherland, the Four Horsemen's advocate general, who retired in January 1938 after being wounded by the Court's reversal of his *Adkins* decision. Born in 1884 in Kentucky, Reed held undergraduate degrees from Kentucky Wesleyan College and Yale and studied law at the Sorbonne in Paris. He later attended Columbia and the University of Virginia and completed his legal education by "reading law" with a Kentucky lawyer. Reed built a thriving corporate practice and served a term in the state legislature as a Wilsonian progressive. But he was more attracted to public service than to politics and joined the Hoover administration in 1929 as counsel to the Federal Farm Board. Reed moved to the Reconstruction Finance Corporation in 1932 and remained in that post after Franklin Roosevelt took office.

The new president heard good things about the hardworking lawyer and named Reed as solicitor general in 1935. Hard as he tried, Reed could not rescue the *Schechter* and *Butler* cases from Supreme Court rejection. Some lawyers faulted his performance in oral argument as too cautious and plodding, but Reed kept working and finally prevailed in the *Jones & Laughlin* case. Relatively young at fifty-three and a loyal New Dealer, he neatly fit Roosevelt's goal of adding "younger" blood to a "liberal-minded" Court. But as a justice, Reed moved slowly to the right and hardly ever galloped with his spirited colleagues down new constitutional paths. Much like a draft horse, Reed found himself tugged one way and then another by the forces of change and continuity.

The death of Benjamin Cardozo in July 1938 offered Roosevelt his third chance to reshape the Court. Six months passed before the president asked the Senate to confirm his successor. Part of the delay stemmed from indecision; Justice Sutherland's retirement had left the Court without a westerner, and FDR felt pressure to look beyond the Mississippi. He asked his old friend and trusted adviser, Felix Frankfurter, to prepare dossiers on prospective candidates. The peppery Harvard Law School professor had already salted New Deal agencies with dozens of former students, who became known as "Felix's Happy Hot Dogs." Born in Vienna in 1882, Frankfurter emigrated with his parents to New York City's Lower East Side at the age of twelve. Entering public school as a German-speaking foreigner, he emerged as a fully assimilated American, able to recite the Gettysburg Address in perfect English. Jewish in heritage but secular in outlook, insecure in personal relations but cocksure of his opinions, Frankfurter was an "outsider" who curried favor with "insiders" like Franklin Roosevelt.

After reviewing Frankfurter's files on prospective candidates for Cardozo's seat, Roosevelt concluded that "there isn't anybody in the West . . . of sufficient stature." Solicitor General Robert Jackson urged the President to choose someone "with scholarship and with sufficient assurance to face Chief Justice Hughes in conference and hold his own in discussion." Frankfurter fit Jackson's model to a T. The author of *The Business of the Supreme Court* had no rivals in knowledge of its history and decisions. And he had no rivals in assurance that struck many as arrogance. Roosevelt took Jackson's advice and sent Frankfurter's nomination to the Senate, which confirmed him without dissent. This was probably the last time he received the unanimous approval of any group. Once he joined the Court, Frankfurter treated his colleagues like first-year law students; his endless lectures annoyed even those who agreed with him. "All Frankfurter does is talk, talk, talk," one fellow justice complained. "He drives you crazy."

Frankfurter certainly drove Hugo Black crazy. Their judicial disputes flared into personal animosity. "I thought Felix was going to hit me today, he got so mad," Black told his son after one conference battle. The former Harvard professor and the former police court judge differed profoundly in constitutional philosophy. Frankfurter preached the gospel of judicial "self-restraint" and seldom voted to invalidate a legislative decision. His few exceptions to this deferential rule included racial discrimination and bias against aliens. But political and religious dissenters found little sympathy in Frankfurter. Justice Black, on the other hand, read the Bill of Rights literally and had no sympathy for lawmakers who muzzled dissenters of any kind. Frankfurter construed the Due Process Clause broadly and the First Amendment narrowly, while Black took the opposite view. However revealing of their combative natures, the conflict of these two New Dealers also shows that political agreement does not always produce judicial accord. Placed on the Court by a president whose vision they shared, Frankfurter and Black read the Constitution through very different lenses.

Two weeks after Frankfurter took his seat on the Court's bench, Louis Brandeis stepped down at the age of eighty-two. His retirement in February 1939 gave Roosevelt a fourth nomination; having found no lawyers of "sufficient stature" in the West, he picked a former westerner who still rode horses after twenty years in New York, New Haven, and Washington. Born in Minnesota in 1898 and raised in Washington state, William O. Douglas went east as a young man to Columbia Law School, where he taught after graduating at the top of his class. He moved to Yale's law faculty in 1928, joining the "legal realists" who looked behind judicial doctrine to explore the social, political, and economic forces that shaped the law. Douglas staked a claim in the growing field of public and corporate finance, and Roosevelt picked the young professor to head the Securities and Exchange Commission. Word got around that Douglas was a card shark, and he soon became one of the president's "poker buddies" and a New Deal insider. Ironically, the only four senators who voted against his confirmation opposed Douglas as a "reactionary tool of Wall Street."

William Douglas joined the Court at forty, the youngest justice since Joseph Story. He stayed for thirty-six years, the longest tenure of any justice. Douglas came to the bench without a well-defined judicial philosophy, and left as he came. Much like the woodsman he was, Douglas avoided the beaten path and blazed his own trail. Raised in poverty and struck by polio as a child, he developed a visceral sympathy for society's "outcasts," including Communists and criminals. He shared Frankfurter's expansive view of due process and Black's "absolutist" devotion to the Bill of Rights. Douglas was often criticized for failing to articulate a coherent judicial philosophy. Certainly he never followed the narrow—but divergent—paths from which Frankfurter and Black rarely strayed. But there was an animating principle behind the twelve hundred opinions Douglas wrote over more than three decades. "Our starting point has always been the individual, not the state," he wrote in 1958. However far he wandered from the beaten path, Douglas never lost sight of his judicial lodestar.

No president before or since Franklin Roosevelt appointed three justices with the longevity and legacies of Hugo Black, Felix Frankfurter, and William Douglas. They served for ninety-three years between them and wrote close to three thousand opinions, almost one of every ten in the Court's history. And their opinions had great impact on American law and society: Black's "absolutist" defense of First Amendment rights, Frankfurter's "compendious" vision of due process, and the "privacy" that Douglas sought for himself and protected for all. But these men of very different backgrounds—an urban immigrant Jew, a rural southern Baptist, and a wide-open-spaces agnostic—ascribed very different meanings to the Constitution's narrow words and broad phrases. We see reflected in their differing judicial approaches the lights and shadows of personality and principles.

Roosevelt added one more justice before his second term ended. Pierce Butler's death in November 1939 left James McReynolds as the lone horseman on the Court's right flank. In naming Frank Murphy of Michigan to Butler's seat, the president replaced one Irish Catholic midwesterner with another. But he also replaced one of the Court's most reactionary justices with perhaps the most liberal in its history. Born in 1890, Murphy absorbed his father's radical politics and his mother's devout Catholicism. The British hanged his Irish great-grandfather for insurrection and jailed his father as a youth for Fenian sympathies. His mother's influence, Murphy later wrote, would not allow him to "remain silent in the face of wrong."

Frank Murphy viewed law and politics as inseparable, and he pursued an ambitious political career, with the White House as the ultimate goal. First elected as a Detroit criminal judge in 1923, he treated black defendants with respect and fairness, and the black vote helped him win election as Detroit's mayor in 1930. Murphy helped swing Michigan to Roosevelt in 1932 and was named governor of the Philippines in reward. He became popular by supporting the independence movement and bringing money from Washington for jobs and welfare. The political bug lured Murphy back to Michigan in 1936; his term as governor began with the crisis of sit-down strikes by autoworkers. He called out National

Guard troops to maintain peace while laboring behind the scene to head off industrial warfare. The irony of his success was that both sides accused him of favoring the other, and Murphy lost his reelection bid in 1938.

President Roosevelt paid his political debts by appointing Murphy as attorney general in 1939. His major achievement in this post was creation of the Civil Liberties Unit, whose lawyers dusted off unused federal laws to prosecute local officials who abused—and even murdered—blacks and union organizers. Murphy's crusading zeal made enemies—including the FBI's imperious director, J. Edgar Hoover—and Roosevelt appeased Hoover and unhappy southern Democrats by shifting Murphy to the Supreme Court. With the 1940 election looming, Roosevelt also removed a potential contender for the presidential nomination. During nine years on the Court, Murphy never abandoned the sympathy he absorbed from his parents for those who "have been burned at the stake, imprisoned, and driven into exile in countless numbers for their political and religious beliefs," as he wrote in one opinion. Murphy gave less deference to lawmakers than Frankfurter, more sympathy to underdogs than Douglas, and greater latitude to the Bill of Rights than Black. Refusing to bind himself to the Constitution's text, Murphy wrote in 1947 that "fundamental" rights deserved judicial protection "despite the absence of specific provisions in the Bill of Rights." He summed up his constitutional philosophy in one sentence: "Only by zealously guarding the rights of the most humble, the most unorthodox and the most despised among us can freedom flourish and endure in our land." No justice ever rivaled Murphy in devotion to the rights of the most despised; even Japanese war criminals, Nazi saboteurs, and Soviet spies received fair hearings from the keeper of the Court's conscience.

SECTION V

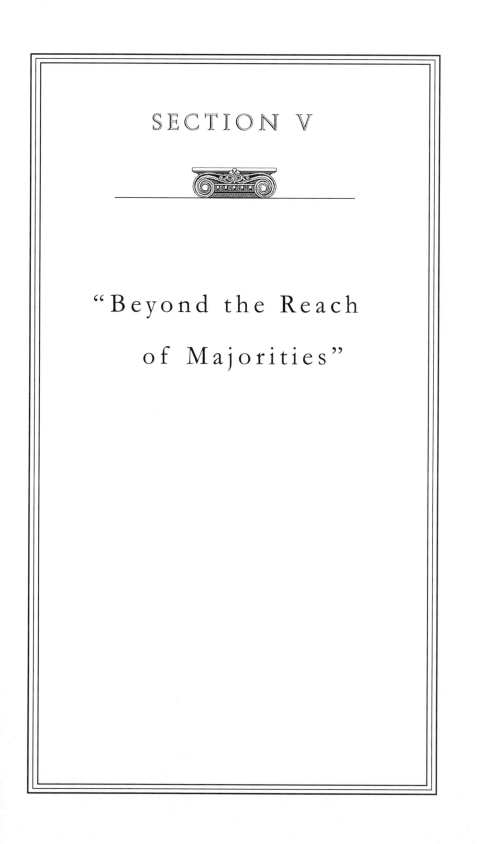

"Beyond the Reach of Majorities"

26

"We Live by Symbols"

The New Deal justices that Franklin Roosevelt added to the Supreme Court continued the "Constitutional Revolution" their predecessors had begun in 1937 by shifting their agenda from property rights to human rights. They were led in this judicial crusade by Harlan Fiske Stone, who had served on the Court since 1925 and was a nominal Republican. But his Yankee conscience was affronted by intolerance and bigotry, and Stone read the newspapers in 1937 and 1938 with growing concern. Stone expressed his concerns in an unusual way, by adding an important footnote to an opinion in an otherwise unimportant case. Almost unnoticed when it appeared in 1938, Footnote Four in *United States v. Carolene Products* soon became the deadliest weapon in the judicial war against those who deny minorities their rights.

The story of Footnote Four deserves far more space than it occupies in Stone's opinion. It really began in 1933 with the rise to power of two men, Franklin Roosevelt and Adolf Hitler. One courted the votes of blacks and Jews; the other vowed to maintain "Aryan" racial purity and to purge his country of Jewish influence. Despite their political differences, both men headed parties with powerful factions that employed violence against the minorities they despised. Roosevelt could not control the white-hooded Klansmen, many of them loyal Democrats, who waved the Confederate flag, while Hitler totally controlled the brown-shirted thugs who marched under the Nazi swastika in Germany. But the Great Depression, which swept both men into office, also fueled racial and religious violence in both countries. During the 1930s, American blacks and German Jews became victims of lawless mobs. More than a hundred blacks, most accused of raping white women, were lynched in the South, while Nazi mobs beat hundreds of Jews and murdered dozens suspected of Communist sympathies.

Justice Stone viewed these atrocities with disgust and growing alarm. Early in 1938, he decided to offer the Supreme Court as a refuge for persecuted minorities. The *West Coast Hotel* and *Jones & Laughlin* decisions had effectively cleared the Court's docket of economic regulation cases, but several remained for argument and decision. Searching the list, Stone picked an unlikely podium for his announcement of a new judicial agenda. The case of *United States v. Carolene Products Company* involved the Filled Milk Act of 1923, in which Congress prohibited the shipment in interstate commerce of "skimmed milk compounded with any fat or oil other than milk fat." The Carolene Products company made something called Milnut, a compound of condensed milk and coconut oil. During the Depression, many families could not afford whole milk for their children and turned to products like Milnut, cheaper than whole milk but lacking its nutritional value. After the company's indictment for selling "an adulterated article of food, injurious to the public health," its lawyers challenged the law as violating both the Commerce and Due Process Clauses. They won the first round in federal court and the government appealed to the Supreme Court.

The *Carolene Products* case was argued on April 6, 1938. Justice Stone read in that morning's *New York Times* that under Nazi rule in Austria, "2,000 Jewish lawyers in Vienna will be excluded from the bar" and that "Jewish physicians and surgeons have been removed from all hospitals." That week's *Time* magazine reported a speech by Hitler's propaganda minister, Joseph Goebbels: "Our racial theory is the sole basis for the correct solution of the Jewish problem." Stone had earlier read in the *New York Times* that Roosevelt Townes, accused of murder in Duck Hill, Mississippi, was tied to a tree, his "eyes were gouged out with an ice pick," and he was "tortured slowly to death with flames from a blow-torch." The week before the *Carolene Products* argument, Stone read about the death of the federal antilynching law at the hands of southern Democrats. Mississippi senator Theodore Bilbo, whose racist diatribes rivaled those of Goebbels, railed against "the Ethiopian who has inspired this proposed legislation" and "the lust and lasciviousness of the rape fiend in his diabolical effort to despoil the womanhood of the Caucasian race."

Justice Stone expressed his reaction to these reports in a letter to Irving Lehman, a New York judge: "I have been deeply concerned about the increasing racial and religious intolerance which seems to bedevil the world, and which I greatly fear may be augmented in this country." With the aid of his Jewish law clerk, Louis Lusky, Stone drafted a footnote for his *Carolene Products* opinion, which reversed the district judge and upheld the Filled Milk Act as "an appropriate means of preventing injury to the public." Stone emphasized that the Court would presume the constitutionality of regulatory laws "affecting ordinary commercial transactions" if they rested upon "some rational basis within the knowledge and experience of the legislators." He did not invent the "rational basis" test, but applied it to *Carolene Products* like a schoolmaster.

Stone could have ended the lesson on that note, but he continued his lecture in Footnote Four. "There may be narrower scope for operation of the presumption of constitutionality," he wrote, "when legislation appears on its face to be within a specific prohibition of the Constitution, such as those of the first ten amendments, which are deemed equally specific when held to be embraced within the Fourteenth." Boiled down, this lengthy sentence expressed the doctrine that the Fourteenth Amendment "incorporated" at least some provisions of the Bill of Rights and applied them to the states. Stone warned that "legislation which restricts those political processes which can ordinarily be expected to bring about repeal of undesirable legislation" would in the future "be subjected to more exacting judicial scrutiny" than regulatory laws such as the Filled Milk Act. Stone devised in this sentence what soon became known as the "strict scrutiny" test for laws that were challenged as violations of the Bill of Rights. Under the "rational basis" test, regulatory laws enjoyed a presumption of constitutionality; Stone's new test reversed that presumption for laws that restricted political rights.

Stone continued with another warning to lawmakers who might be swayed by "popular passions" against religious, national, or racial minorities. Laws directed at members of these groups would also lose their presumption of constitutionality and trigger "more searching judicial inquiry" of the motives behind their passage. Stone provided examples by citing prior cases that dealt with Catholics, people of German or Japanese origin, and blacks. He added that laws reflecting "prejudice against discrete and insular minorities" of other kinds would also be subjected to the "strict scrutiny" test. Stone left this category open, but his wording suggested that members of groups "set apart" from the majority by some characteristic other than religion, nationality, or race would be equally protected from official prejudice.

Footnote Four handed engraved invitations to lawyers for groups like the NAACP and American Civil Liberties Union, assuring them of admission to the Court's docket. But the people who knocked most loudly and insistently on the Court's massive doors, insisting that the justices listen to Scripture, were Jehovah's Witnesses. Their door-to-door proselytizing and street-corner preaching offended many and prompted scores of laws designed to muzzle their apocalyptic message, which predicted a bloody war of Armageddon between the forces of Christ and Satan that only a remnant of believers would survive to enter heaven. Catholics felt insulted by the Witnesses' attacks on the Pope, and Southern Baptists resented the appropriation of their fire-and-brimstone fulminations. Lawmakers in communities with Catholic or Baptist majorities eagerly passed ordinances directed at the Witnesses, often without debate or legal advice. Some laws imposed licensing fees on "solicitors," while others restricted leafleting, canvassing, and literature sales. Between 1938 and 1955, usually assisted by ACLU lawyers, the Witnesses took forty-five cases to the Supreme

Court and won thirty-six; not even the NAACP—victorious in twenty-nine of thirty-two cases during these years—matched this record. And in most cases, the Witnesses added Footnote Four to their Scripture lessons for the Court.

The Witnesses began their winning streak with victories over officials in Georgia, New Jersey, and Connecticut. In *Lovell v. City of Griffin*, the Court ruled in 1938 that towns could not require permits to distribute pamphlets; the justices agreed without dissent that streets and parks were open to all for expressing their views. The Court struck down "antilittering" laws enforced only against Witnesses in *Schneider v. Town of Irvington*, decided in 1939. And in *Cantwell v. Connecticut*, the Court in 1940 "incorporated" the "free exercise of religion" clause of the First Amendment into the Fourteenth. In this case, Newton Cantwell and his two sons had been arrested for playing a recording and distributing pamphlets attacking the Pope in a heavily Catholic area of New Haven, Connecticut. The Cantwells requested donations from those who took their pamphlets, but did not insist on payment. Responding to complaints by outraged Catholics, police arrested the Witnesses for violating a state law barring the solicitation of money "for any cause" without a "certificate of approval" from the Public Welfare Council, whose secretary was required to determine whether "the cause is a religious one" or a "bona fide object of charity." Giving a public official the power to decide which causes are "religious" violates the First Amendment, the Court ruled unanimously in striking down the Connecticut law.

The victory streak ended in 1940 with a resounding eight-to-one loss in a case that pitted two young Witnesses against a heavily Catholic town in Pennsylvania's anthracite coal region. The five thousand residents of Minersville came from Lithuania, the Ukraine, Poland, Russia, Greece, Italy, Germany, and Wales. The town's eight Catholic churches held services in eight different languages, but the parishioners shared a common reverence for the American flag. And the town's school superintendent from 1915 to 1942, Charles Roudabush, was a strict disciplinarian who tolerated no challenge to his authority. Students in Minersville's public schools had saluted the flag and recited the Pledge of Allegiance each morning since World War I. None had ever objected or refused to participate until one day in October 1935.

The flag-salute controversy actually began in Germany, where Nazi officials banned the Witnesses in 1933 on Hitler's orders, for refusing to join the raised-palm salute to Nazi flags in schools and at public events. Ultimately, more than ten thousand German Witnesses were imprisoned in concentration camps. In response to this persecution, the leader of American Witnesses, Joseph Rutherford, denounced compulsory flag-salute laws. Witnesses "do not 'Heil Hitler' nor any other creature," he told his followers. In a radio speech, Rutherford praised Carleton Nicholls, a third-grade student in Massachusetts who was arrested after refusing to salute the flag in his classroom. Carleton made a "wise choice" and other Witnesses "who act wisely will do the same thing," Rutherford advised his listeners.

Among the Witnesses who listened intently to Rutherford's speech were Walter Gobitas and his family in Minersville. Walter's parents had come from Lithuania, and he attended St. Francis Lithuanian Catholic Church and the Minersville schools, where he saluted the flag every day. He took over his mother's grocery store and did well until the Depression hit Minersville like a rockfall in the coal shafts. Walter and his family became Witnesses in 1931, but their new religion did not cause any problems until Joseph Rutherford urged Witnesses to stop saluting the American flag. The two oldest Gobitas children, Lillian and William, were in seventh and fifth grades in October 1935.

Lillian later described what happened after she listened to Rutherford's radio speech: "I loved school, and I was actually kind of popular. I was class president in the seventh grade, and I had good grades. And I felt that, Oh, if I stop saluting the flag, I will blow all this! And I did. This wasn't something my parents forced on us. They were very firm about that, that what you do is your decision, and you should understand what you're doing. And I did. I did a lot of reading and checking in the Bible and I really took my own stand. I went first to my teacher, so I couldn't chicken out of it. She listened to my explanation and surprisingly, she just hugged me and said she thought it was very nice, to have courage like that. But the students were awful. I really should have explained to the whole class but I was fearful. I didn't know whether it was right to stand up or sit down. So I sat down and the whole room was aghast. After that, when I'd come to school they would throw a hail of pebbles and yell things like, Here comes Jehovah!"

Superintendent Roudabush threw a fit when he learned that Lillian and William refused to salute the flag and recite the Pledge of Allegiance. After an angry confrontation with Walter Gobitas, who refused to pledge that his children would end their defiance, Roudabush marched to the Minersville school board, which promptly adopted a resolution requiring all students "to salute the flag of our Country as a part of the daily exercises" and providing that refusal to participate "shall be regarded as an act of insubordination and shall be dealt with accordingly." Roudabush immediately told the board he was expelling Lillian and William from school "for this act of insubordination." Walter Gobitas left the meeting with a parting shot at the board members: "I'm going to take you to court for this!"

Walter Gobitas was a man of his word. His suit against the Minersville school board, brought as "next friend" of his children, first came before federal judge Albert Maris in Philadelphia. Placed on the bench by President Roosevelt, Maris was a Quaker and sympathized with members of another religious minority. The board's lawyers argued that the flag-salute requirement was a "secular regulation" of the curriculum, adopted for the "reasonable" purpose of "inculcating patriotism" in the classroom. The board had simply exercised its "police powers" to protect the "health, safety, welfare, and morals" of Minersville students. After listening to Lillian and William explain their religious beliefs and objections to the flag-salute ceremony, Judge Maris ruled that it was "clear from the evidence that the refusal of these two earnest Christian children to salute the flag cannot even remotely prejudice or imperil the safety, health, morals, property or personal rights of their fellows."

A federal appellate panel upheld Maris in an opinion that bristled with scorn for compulsory flag-salute laws, which had spread across the country since the Minersville school board expelled the Gobitas children. "Eighteen big states have seen fit to exert their power over a small number of little children," wrote Judge William S. Clark for the panel in December 1939. The compulsory salute "happens to be abhorrent to the particular love of God of the little girl and boy now seeking our protection."

After two judicial defeats, the Minersville board first decided against an appeal to the Supreme Court. But promises of financial support from the American Legion and other "patriotic" groups overcame the board's initial reluctance. Asking the Court to hear the case did not guarantee a ruling; five times in recent years the justices had declined to review flag-salute cases decided by lower courts. All those cases, however, had upheld state or local laws. Declining to hear an appeal from Judge Clark's opinion, on the other hand, would leave his decision in place and strike down the Minersville regulation. Along with this factor, it seems likely that the justices looked at the looming war clouds over Europe in deciding to hear a case that raised issues of patriotism and loyalty.

Joseph W. Henderson, the Philadelphia lawyer hired by the Minersville board, repeated the arguments he had made without success in the lower courts when he appeared before the Supreme Court on April 25, 1940. (A clerk misspelled "Gobitas" as "Gobitis" on the Court papers and the case went into the lawbooks as *Minersville School Board v. Gobitis*.) The core of Henderson's argument was that the flag-salute ceremony "is not a religious rite" and was intended simply to inculcate "loyalty to the state and national government." Two lawyers divided the time alloted to Walter Gobitas and his children. George K. Gardner, a Harvard law professor, presented the position of the American Civil Liberties Union, stressing the primacy of the First Amendment over the "police powers" of state and local governments. Joseph Rutherford, who practiced law before he took over leading the Witnesses, restated the theological objections of his followers to flag-salute laws. The Gobitas family traveled to Washington to witness the arguments. Lillian recalled Rutherford's words: "He did it a lot from a Biblical standpoint, like with Shadrach, Meshach, and Abednego, when they took a stand and wouldn't bow down to the image of Nebuchadnezzar. And of course he discussed legal things too. It was extremely arresting. You could really hear a pin drop! The justices listened attentively."

The justices actually paid little attention to Rutherford's argument. When they met in their conference room to debate and decide the *Gobitis* case, the first to speak was Chief Justice Charles Evans Hughes, who assured his colleagues that the case had "nothing to do with religion" and involved only "a question of state power" to foster patriotism in the classroom. The only other justice to speak at length was Felix Frankfurter, an immigrant who had polished his English skills in high school by reciting Abraham Lincoln's wartime appeals to patriotism and national unity. Impressed by Frankfurter's "moving statement at conference on the role of the public school in installing love of country" in the children of immigrants, Hughes asked him to write the Court's opinion. Because none of the justices had objected at the conference, Hughes assumed that Frankfurter would write for a unanimous Court.

Frankfurter's opinion began with a bow to the "grave responsibility" the Court faced in balancing "the conflicting claims of liberty and authority." The *Gobitis* case, he noted, forced the Court "to reconcile two rights in order to prevent either from destroying the other." America's historic role as a haven for religious dissenters required that "every possible leeway should be given to the claims of religious faith." Despite these disclaimers, Frankfurter rejected claims that First Amendment rights deserved special protection against abridgment by legislative bodies. Religious belief, he wrote, "does not relieve the citizen from the discharge of political responsibilities." Frankfurter venerated the flag as a symbol that fostered "the binding tie of cohesive sentiment" among the citizenry. "We live by symbols," he quoted from his judicial mentor, Oliver Wendell Holmes, adding that the flag "is the symbol of our national unity, transcending all internal differences" over religion or politics. "National unity is the basis of national security," Frankfurter added, sounding like a recruiting poster in linking the flag-salute ceremony to growing concerns that war clouds might reach American shores.

Exempting Lillian and William Gobitas from the salute, Frankfurter warned, "might cast doubts in the minds of the other children" in Minersville and weaken their American loyalty. Claims that "exceptional immunity must be given to dissidents" like the Gobitas children would hinder schools in "competing with the parent's authority" in the contest for the "child's mind," he wrote. In Frankfurter's school, teachers could force "dissident" children to express beliefs "contrary to those implanted by the parent." Those who objected could find another classroom, as Lillian and William did in a makeshift "Kingdom School" thirty miles from their home, set up in a farmhouse for young Witnesses expelled from public schools. After Frankfurter's ruling, they never returned to public school.

Frankfurter's opinion displayed the "judicial restraint" he counseled in responding to laws that might seem "harsh" or "foolish" to judges. Even if his colleagues were convinced of "the folly of such a measure" as the flag-salute regulation, Frankfurter urged deference to the judgments of elected officials. Striking down the Minersville rule "would in effect make us the school board for the country," he wrote. "But the courtroom is not the arena for debating issues of educational policy." Perhaps unaware that Witnesses do not vote, Frankfurter concluded with a civics lecture to Walter Gobitas. "Where all the effective means of inducing political changes are left free from interference," he wrote, "education in the abandonment of foolish legislation is itself a training in liberty." Frankfurter advised Gobitas to speak out at school board meetings and stay out of courtrooms. "To fight out the wise use of legislative authority in the forum of public opinion and before legislative assemblies rather than to transfer such a contest to the judicial arena," he pontificated, "serves to vindicate the self-confidence of a free people." Frankfurter had obviously not attended many small-town meetings and witnessed the treatment of dissidents like Walter Gobitas.

Justice Harlan Fiske Stone was raised in the small town of Chesterfield, New Hampshire, and taught in a high school before he began law school. He had instructed students like Lillian Gobitas and knew that pressures toward conformity were hard to resist at her age. Like her, Stone had been expelled from school, not for remaining silent but for an angry outburst at teachers. Perhaps with these memories in mind, he surprised and angered Frankfurter by circulating a pointed dissent in *Gobitis*. Frankfurter's suggestion that Witnesses employ "the remedial channels of the democratic process" to protect their children from expulsion struck Stone as "no less than the surrender of the constitutional protection of the liberty of small minorities to the popular will."

Stone cited his own Footnote Four in *Carolene Products* to remind Frankfurter that the Court had "previously pointed to the importance of a searching judicial inquiry into the legislative judgment in situations where prejudice against discrete and insular minorities may tend to curtail the operation of those political processes ordinarily to be relied on to protect minorities." He would open courtroom doors to "politically helpless minorities" who found "little toleration or concern" from hostile lawmakers and officials. Frankfurter pleaded with Stone to withdraw his dissent, arguing in a private letter that the Court should not hold "too tight a rein" on state and local officials as the nation saddled up for battle. Patriotic observances like the flag-salute ceremony were "surely not irrelevant" to wartime preparations, Frankfurter wrote. But Stone would not carry the flag for the Court. He rode alone in dissent, unwilling to join the roundup of stragglers and strays into the "national unity" corral.

Lillian Gobitas recalled the morning of June 3, 1940, when the Court handed down its decision: "We were in the kitchen with the radio on and it was time for the news, and they said, In Washington today, the Supreme Court decided the flag case. It was against us, eight to one. Talk about a cold feeling! We absolutely did not expect that. That just set off a wave of persecution. It was like open season on Jehovah's Witnesses."

Supreme Court rulings are often criticized, and some are disobeyed, but few have ever provoked as violent a reaction as the *Gobitis* decision. Frankfurter's opinion unleashed a wave of attacks on Witnesses across the country. Within two weeks of the Court's decision, two federal officials later wrote, "hundreds of attacks upon the Witnesses were reported to the Department of Justice." The Justice Department officials listed several of the most violent incidents. "At Kennebunk, Maine, the Kingdom Hall was burned. At Rockville, Maryland, the police assisted a mob in dispersing a Bible meeting. At Litchfield, Illinois, practically the entire town mobbed a company of some sixty Witnesses who were canvassing it, and it was necessary to call on the state troopers to protect members of the sect." The federal officials reported that the "chief of police and deputy sheriff had forced a group of Witnesses to drink large doses of castor oil and had paraded the victims through the streets of Richwood, West Virginia, tied together with police department rope." Equally horrifying, a Nebraska Witness was kidnapped, beaten, and castrated by vigilantes. The officials traced these terrorist acts directly to the Supreme Court's decision in the *Gobitis* case. "In the two years following the decision," they wrote, "the files of the Department of Justice reflect an uninterrupted record of violence and persecution of the Witnesses. Almost without exception, the flag and the flag salute can be found as the percussion cap that sets off these acts."

Eighteen months after Frankfurter's opinion, much deadlier explosions rocked the American naval base in Hawaii on the quiet Sunday morning of December 7, 1941. The "sneak attack" of Japanese planes on Pearl Harbor sent more than two thousand Americans to watery graves, and shock waves through the American people. As the nation entered a second world war, newly mobilized soldiers and sailors joined schoolchildren in saluting the flag, while jittery residents of the West Coast feared another Pearl Harbor and viewed their Japanese neighbors with suspicion. Anyone who refused to salute the flag, voiced sympathy for the Axis cause, or looked like the Japanese enemy became the target of newly enacted laws designed to protect "national security" from the disloyal and disobedient.

American participation in World War I had provoked widespread dissent, and White House and Justice Department officials had refused to restrain the vigilantes who whipped up wartime hysteria or to protect their victims. But officials had little dissent to suppress in World War II, which most Americans supported without reservation. Eight days after the Pearl Harbor attack, Roosevelt promised to respect the Constitution. "We will not, under any threat, or in the face of any danger, surrender the guarantees of liberty our forefathers framed for us in our Bill of Rights," he assured the American people. Wendell Willkie, the Wall Street lawyer whose Republican bid to block Roosevelt's third-term election in 1940 had failed by five million votes, echoed the president. "We must preserve civil liberties for all or else our sacrifices in winning this war may be in vain," he stated. Roosevelt's attorney general, Francis Biddle, told the country it was "essential at such a time as this that we keep our heads, keep our tempers,— above all, that we keep clearly in mind what we are defending."

Not all Americans kept these admonitions clearly in mind. Shortly after the smoke cleared over Pearl Harbor, the West Virginia board of education adopted a resolution that borrowed liberally from Justice Frankfurter's *Gobitis* opinion. Proclaiming that "national unity is the basis of national security" and that "conscientious scruples" do not excuse students from "obedience to the general law," the board made the flag-salute ceremony mandatory in all schools. The resolution also borrowed wording from the Minersville school board in Pennsylvania and provided that "refusal to salute the flag be regarded as an act of insubordination, and shall be dealt with accordingly."

Enforcement of the new regulation varied in West Virginia's schools, but local boards in several communities around Charleston expelled dozens of Jehovah's Witnesses for refusing to salute the flag. Their parents could not heed Frankfurter's advice to Walter Gobitas. With the "forums of public opinion" closed by majority vote and the "judicial arena" shut by the *Gobitis* decision, Witnesses had nowhere to turn. Their lawyer, Horace Meldahl of Charleston, filed three suits in state court asking for a "writ of prohibition" against the board's resolution, and each was denied without hearing. But the gloomy legal weather suddenly cleared on June 8, 1942. On that sunny day in Washington, three justices who had joined Frankfurter in *Gobitis* repented their votes. Justices Black, Douglas, and Murphy lined up at the confessional and asked for absolution. They took this unusual step in dissenting from Justice Reed's opinion in another Jehovah's Witnesses licensing case from Georgia, *Jones v. Opelika*, decided with similar cases from Arkansas and Arizona. Five justices voted to uphold the licensing laws, which imposed modest fees on "peddlers" of literature. Witnesses refused to pay the fees, claiming First Amendment protection for soliciting donations for their religious pamphlets. "We see nothing in the collection of a nondiscriminatory license fee," Reed wrote, "which abridges the freedoms of worship, speech, or press." Chief Justice Stone, recently elevated to that post by President Roosevelt, argued in dissent that Opelika's fee burdened "itinerant" preachers like the Witnesses while the town's "accepted clergymen" could distribute literature in their churches without any license.

The three judicial penitents joined Stone's dissent, but they added a statement calling Reed's opinion "a logical extension of the principles" on which *Gobitis* rested. "Since we joined in the opinion in the *Gobitis* case, we think this is an appropriate occasion to state that we now believe that it also was wrongly decided." Clearly, news reports and photographs of handcuffed Witnesses and burned churches had seared their consciences. Frankfurter, who derided the judicial trio as "the Axis" to friends, scornfully asked Douglas if Black had been reading the Constitution. "No, but he has read the papers," Douglas replied.

Stone and his "Axis" allies still lacked one vote to reverse *Gobitis*, but that vote was likely to arrive soon. Two members of the *Gobitis* majority, James McReynolds and Charles Evans Hughes, had already departed through retirement in 1941. Hardly anyone missed the bigoted and belligerent McReynolds, but the Chief Justice had been widely respected; his *West Coast Hotel* and *Jones & Laughlin* opinions had finally moved the Court into the twentieth century. Roosevelt replaced McReynolds with Senator James Byrnes of South Carolina, who won his Court seat as a consolation prize for losing the vice-presidential nomination to Henry Wallace in 1940. Byrnes spent just one unhappy term on the Court, and eagerly accepted Roosevelt's offer to become "assistant president for economic affairs." He later served as South Carolina's governor and staunchly defended racial segregation; his long life—he died at ninety-two—made his brief judicial tenure fortunate.

Roosevelt's first choice to replace Hughes as Chief was his attorney general, Robert H. Jackson, who badly wanted the post. Jackson had spent just one year in law school, but he built a thriving practice in upstate New York and became a trusted adviser to Roosevelt during his term as governor. He followed FDR to Washington in 1933 and moved quickly up the legal ranks to serve as solicitor general and attorney general. Jackson had pressed Roosevelt to place Frankfurter on the Court, and expected Frankfurter to return the favor. But the politically savvy justice told the president that although "I'd prefer Bob" on personal grounds, he backed Stone's elevation for political reasons. Stone was a Republican, and with war looming, FDR would win plaudits "as a national and not a partisan President" by choosing him. Jackson did not get the job he wanted, but he took Stone's place as associate justice. His resentment at being passed over for Chief soured his relations with Stone, and his personal feud with Hugo Black spilled into public sniping in 1945 and embarrassed the Court.

The last of Roosevelt's nominees, Wiley Rutledge, filled the seat that James Byrnes had barely warmed. Born in Kentucky in 1894, the oldest child of a Baptist minister, Rutledge had a peripatetic education and career, attending school in North Carolina, Tennessee, and Wisconsin and teaching high school and then law in Colorado, Indiana, New Mexico, Missouri, and Iowa. An ardent liberal and loyal New Dealer, he spent four years on the District of Columbia appellate bench before Roosevelt picked him at the urging of Francis Biddle and Justices Douglas and Murphy, whose *Opelika* dissent read almost like a want ad for Rutledge. After chatting about his background, Roosevelt quipped, "Wiley, you have geography!" He also had the courage to dissent from opinions by Stone and Black that he considered betrayals of the Bill of Rights. Rutledge served only six years before his sudden death at fifty-five, but he earned in that short time the "near great" ranking that scholars later bestowed on him.

Even before Rutledge joined the Court, the *Opelika* dissents and rumors of Byrnes's impending departure had encouraged the Witnesses' lawyers to prepare new challenges to flag-salute laws. They found a large group of expelled students in West Virginia and brought suit in their parents' names in federal court. Walter Barnette, whose two daughters had been expelled from Slip Hill Grade School, came first in alphabetical order. Filed in August 1942, the case moved quickly from the district court in Charleston to the Supreme Court, arriving for argument in March 1943. It came with a ruling against the state's flag-salute law; a panel of lower-court judges rejected any "blind following" of *Gobitis* as precedent, because the *Opelika* dissenters "have given public expression to the view that it is unsound," and because forcing children to salute the flag against their beliefs was "petty tyranny" and violated the spirit of the Constitution. The judges virtually invited the Supreme Court to overrule *Gobitis*. With Rutledge on the bench, their invitation was eagerly accepted.

The only surprise was that Robert Jackson, Frankfurter's close friend and judicial ally, joined the "Axis" in *West Virginia Board of Education v. Barnette*. Even more surprising was that Jackson agreed to write an opinion that would surely infuriate Frankfurter. Most amazing of all, Jackson tore Frankfurter's *Gobitis* opinion to shreds; the justice with one year of law school handed the Harvard professor a failing grade in front of the whole class. This hardly rivaled Justice Roberts's "switch in time" that derailed Roosevelt's court-packing plan, but it raised questions about Jackson's switch from Frankfurter's side to the "Axis" position during the same judicial conference session. What made flag-salute laws so different from licensing fees? And what prompted Jackson to break with his friend so publicly? Unfortunately, Jackson never discussed his reasons, and Frankfurter's letters and diary shed no light. Whatever the reasons, Jackson wrote his *Barnette* opinion with passion and power.

Like a table, Frankfurter's *Gobitis* opinion rested on four legs. One held up the flag as a symbol of "national unity." A second found the flag-salute ceremony an "appropriate means" of fostering the "cohesive sentiment" on which that unity depended. A third held that compelling students to join the ceremony on pain of expulsion was an allowable means of fostering that sentiment. Lastly, matters of "school discipline" were better entrusted to local officials than to federal judges. These legs supported Frankfurter's conclusion that giving "exceptional immunity" to children with "conscientious scruples" against saluting the flag would hinder "the promotion of national cohesion."

One by one, Justice Jackson knocked out each leg of Frankfurter's table. He did not question the flag's symbolic potency. "Symbolism is a primitive but effective way of communicating ideas," Jackson wrote. But not everyone agrees on a symbol's message. "A person gets from a symbol the meaning he puts into it, and what is one man's comfort and inspiration is another's jest and scorn," he wrote. Jackson noted that officials who wield symbols often demand "a salute, a bowed or bared head, a bended knee" as gestures of deference. He pointed to William Penn and other Quakers who "suffered punishment rather than uncover their heads in deference to any civil authority" in colonial America.

Jackson denied Frankfurter's assertion that compulsory flag-salute ceremonies would foster the "cohesive sentiment" on which "national unity" supposedly depended. Demanding that children "simulate assent by words without belief and by a gesture barren of meaning" to them, he argued, would more likely produce conflict than cohesion. Jackson looked both to ancient history and recent headlines for support. He cited "the Roman drive to stamp out Christianity," the Spanish Inquisition of Jews, the Siberian exile of Soviet dissidents, and "the fast failing efforts of our present totalitarian enemies" as evidence of the "ultimate futility" of efforts to "coerce uniformity of sentiment" behind religions or regimes. "Those who begin coercive elimination of dissent soon find themselves exterminating dissenters," he warned. "Compulsory unification of opinion achieves only the unanimity of the graveyard."

Frankfurter had mentioned the Bill of Rights in *Gobitis* only to deny that it excused "obedience to a general law not aimed" directly at religious dissenters. He advised them to "fight out" their battles with local officials at the ballot box. Jackson answered in words that matched the best of Holmes and Brandeis: "The very purpose of a Bill of Rights was to withdraw certain subjects from the vicissitudes of political controversy, to place them beyond the reach of majorities and officials and to establish them as legal principles to be applied by the courts. One's right to life, liberty, and property, to free speech, a free press, freedom of worship and assembly, and other fundamental rights may not be submitted to vote; they depend on the outcome of no elections."

Frankfurter had entrusted to elected officials "the guardianship of deeply cherished liberties" and praised the local school board as "one of our most cherished democratic institutions." Jackson did not trust local officials to guard the Bill of Rights against voters who demanded that religious minorities defer to majority sentiment. He knew from his small-town experience that "village tyrants" could exert more power in their communities than far-off politicians or even presidents. Jackson concluded with these words of admonition: "If there is any fixed star in our constitutional constellation, it is that no official, high or petty, can prescribe what shall be orthodox in politics, nationalism, religion, or other matters of opinion or force citizens to confess by word or act their faith therein."

The final sentence in Jackson's opinion sent the *Gobitis* opinion to the judicial graveyard. The opinion that eight justices had joined, only three years earlier, was now overruled by a majority of six. The *Barnette* decision, in effect, offered the Court's apology to Jehovah's Witnesses for their children's suffering.

Justices Roberts and Reed dissented in silence, perhaps abashed by the consequences of their earlier votes. But Frankfurter remained unabashed and unrepentant; his angry dissent made no effort to hide his wounded feelings. Two colleagues, Owen Roberts and Frank Murphy, counseled him to strike its first sentences as "too personal," but Frankfurter took the overruling of his *Gobitis* opinion as a personal rebuff, and rejected their advice.

"One who belongs to the most vilified and persecuted minority in history is not likely to be insensible to the freedoms guaranteed by our Constitution," Frankfurter began. It was this reference to his Jewish roots that Roberts and Murphy considered out of place. But as Frankfurter confided in his diary, "I was literally flooded with letters" after his *Gobitis* opinion "by people who said that I, as a Jew, ought particularly to protect minorities" from public hostility. He decided to answer those letters in his *Barnette* dissent. "Were my purely personal attitude relevant," he explained, "I should wholeheartedly associate myself with the generally libertarian views in the Court's opinion, representing as they do the thought and action of a lifetime. But as judges we are neither Jew nor Gentile, neither Catholic nor agnostic."

Having spoken as a Jew, Frankfurter now spoke as a judge. "As a member of this Court I am not justified in writing my private notions of policy into the Constitution, no matter how deeply I may cherish them or how mischievous I may deem their disregard," he continued. "It can never be emphasized too much that one's own opinion about the wisdom or evil of a law should be excluded altogether when one is doing one's duty on the bench. The only opinion of our own even looking in that direction that is material is our opinion whether legislators could in reason have enacted such a law." Frankfurter emphasized his "duty of deference to those who have the responsibility for making the laws," a duty relieved only when he could find no "rational justification for the legislation." These sentences expressed the "rational basis" test that Justice Stone had limited to "ordinary commercial transactions" in *Carolene Products*. But in Footnote Four of that opinion, Stone had urged "more exacting judicial scrutiny" of laws infringing religious or political rights. Frankfurter, however, rejected Stone's test, reasserting his belief that no constitutional provision occupied a "preferred position" over any other.

What angered Frankfurter even more than Jackson's *Barnette* opinion was the apostasy of the "Axis" justices who joined it. Without naming them, he noted that every justice but Rutledge "has at one or more times found no constitutional infirmity in what is now condemned." Frankfurter was outraged that flag-salute laws the Court had upheld in five prior cases were "now outlawed by the deciding shift of opinion" of the justices who changed their minds. Unlike Hugo Black, who read the papers, Frankfurter was not moved by news reports of violence against Witnesses or editorials condemning the vigilantes. "The Court has no reason for existence if it merely reflects the pressures of the day," he complained. He asked with unconcealed sarcasm whether a Constitution designed "to endure for all times" had now capsized under "the shifting winds of doctrine."

In a symbolic gesture, the Court handed down its *Barnette* decision on June 14, 1943, celebrated as "Flag Day" across the nation. Jehovah's Witnesses could now return to the schools that had expelled them for disloyalty. But the Gobitas and Barnette children, and other young Witnesses who stood up to "village tyrants" like Superintendent Roudabush, had a higher loyalty to their deeply held religious beliefs. Even today, other young people—not all of them Witnesses—face pressures to salute the flag under pain of suspension. In 1998, MaryKait Durkee decided to remain seated during the flag-salute ceremony in her eleventh-grade class at Fallbrook High School in southern California. She took her stand—by refusing to stand—because "I don't believe there is 'justice for all' in this country all the time," as she told a reporter after being suspended from school. It took a lawsuit filed by the American Civil Liberties Union to remind school officials that the Supreme Court had decided this issue more than fifty years earlier. Even after MaryKait's legal victory, she received an editorial paddling by the *San Diego Union-Tribune* for "her lack of respect for the country she lives in." MaryKait remained seated as her senior year began at Fallbrook High, but she started classes with "a more positive outlook," because "I have learned that justice is possible through a process."

27

"A Jap's a Jap"

The justices who decided the *Barnette* case on Flag Day in 1943 were bitterly divided over the expulsion of young Witnesses from their schools for disloyalty. Just a week later, however, they agreed without dissent in a case that involved more than 100,000 Americans who were expelled from their communities for disloyalty. The mass evacuation of Japanese Americans from the West Coast during World War II and their confinement for three years in tar-paper barracks—fenced by barbed wire and guarded by armed soldiers—confronted the justices with their own test of loyalty. Does the Constitution protect "all classes of men, at all times, and under all circumstances, equally in war and in peace," as the justices stated without dissent in 1866? Or can "the clamor of an excited people" and the government's claims of "military necessity" allow the suspension of constitutional rights during wartime? The justices faced these momentous questions in deciding the challenges of three young Japanese Americans—Gordon Hirabayashi, Minoru Yasui, and Fred Korematsu—to the army's evacuation and exclusion orders.

Taking a closer look at events we "know" through history books can be surprising. One surprise about the wartime treatment of Japanese Americans is that the initial reaction in the area most stricken with "Pearl Harbor panic" was one of tolerance and understanding. Most of the "thousands of Japanese here and in other coast cities," the *Los Angeles Times* editorialized on December 8, 1941, were "good Americans, born and educated as such." Published in the city with the largest number of Japanese Americans, this influential paper urged its readers that "there be no precipitation, no riots, no mob law." The *Times* editors tried to calm fears of a follow-up Japanese attack on West Coast targets. "Let's Not Get Rattled," they cautioned on December 10. It would be virtually impossible for Japanese aircraft carriers to "sneak up on this Coast undetected by our now aroused sky scouters," they assured a jittery public. Echoed by other prominent West Coast papers, such assurances helped to calm public fears and protected Japanese Americans from retaliation.

Some six weeks after Pearl Harbor, however, the tide of public opinion abruptly shifted. Both the press and public officials demanded the removal of all Japanese Americans from the West Coast. On January 16, 1942, Los Angeles congressman Leland Ford urged that "all Japanese, whether citizens or not, be placed in inland concentration camps." Two weeks later the *Los Angeles Times* reversed its editorial stance and argued that "the rigors of war demand proper detention of Japanese and their immediate removal from the most acute danger spots" along the coast. Walter Lippmann, the nation's most respected columnist, deplored "the unwillingness of Washington to adopt a policy of mass evacuation and mass internment" of Japanese Americans. "Nobody's constitutional rights include the right to reside and do business on a battlefield," he wrote like a judge. Westbrook Pegler issued another ruling in his widely read column: "The Japanese in California should be under armed guard to the last man and woman right now—and to hell with habeas corpus until the danger is over."

The growing force of demands like these hit Washington like a tidal wave. Officials in the War and Justice Departments ended their squabbling over legal niceties and sent a two-page document to the White House. On February 19, 1942, President Franklin Roosevelt signed Executive Order 9066, authorizing Secretary of War Henry L. Stimson and his subordinates to designate military zones "from which any or all persons may be excluded." General John L. DeWitt, the West Coast army commander, first imposed a nighttime curfew on "all persons of Japanese ancestry" and then issued "exclusion orders" that were backed by Congress with criminal penalties. By the end of 1942, all but a handful of the Japanese Americans who lived between Seattle and San Diego had been herded into ten "relocation centers," the government's euphemism for America's wartime concentration camps. Scattered from the California desert to Arkansas swamps, these camps imprisoned more than 110,000 people—most of them native-born American citizens—who were never charged with crimes or given a hearing.

Behind the initial appeals for tolerance after Pearl Harbor lay decades of intolerance toward Orientals of any nationality. The arrival of Chinese laborers in the 1850s to lay railroad track and pick vegetables produced resentment among Caucasian workers, many of them also recent immigrants. With congressional passage in 1882 of the Chinese Exclusion Act, nativist groups turned their demagoguery against the Japanese, who numbered only two thousand in 1890, almost all in California. But the flow increased until Congress shut off all further Japanese immigration in 1924, by which time more than 100,000 lived on the West Coast. Japanese natives were excluded from citizenship and barred in California from owning or leasing land.

Despite these legal barriers, Japanese Americans worked hard and prospered. Many found ways around the Alien Land Law and operated farms owned by friendly whites, or bought land in the names of their native-born children, granted citizenship at birth by the Fourteenth Amendment. By 1940, Japanese farmers produced close to half of California's vegetables. Leaders of the Grower-Shipper Vegetable Association, a powerful lobby of white farmers, took advantage of "Pearl Harbor panic" to cut down their competitors. "We're charged with wanting to get rid of the Japs for selfish reasons," the group's manager said. "We might as well be honest. We do."

Another group was less honest in its campaign to rid the coast of Japanese Americans. Military officials made claims of widespread "sabotage and espionage" in arguing for mass internment. But they had no evidence that any Japanese American had committed such crimes. They were not deterred by this fact. In the "Final Recommendation" he sent to Secretary Stimson, urging mass internment, General DeWitt blamed this lack of evidence against Japanese Americans on their sneaky nature: "The very fact that no sabotage has taken place to date is a disturbing and confirming indication that such action will be taken," he claimed. DeWitt's support for internment was really based on unvarnished racism. "The Japanese race is an enemy race," he stated, "and while many second and third generation Japanese born on United States soil, possessed of United States citizenship, have become 'Americanized,' the racial strains are undiluted." DeWitt used blunter language before a congressional panel: "A Jap's a Jap," he said; "it makes no difference whether he is an American citizen or not. I have no confidence in their loyalty whatsoever."

General Dewitt was hardly alone in basing his wartime decisions about Japanese Americans on racial stereotypes. DeWitt had no legal training, but many military and civilian officials who attended prestigious law schools showed little respect for the Constitution they had sworn to uphold as lawyers. One of the first and most influential advocates of mass internment was Colonel Karl Bendetsen, a Stanford Law School graduate who drafted General DeWitt's "Final Recommendation" for the evacuation of Japanese Americans. Admitting in February 1942 the army's inability to justify "the sheer military necessity for such action," Bendetsen nonetheless argued that "a substantial majority" of Japanese Americans "bear allegiance to Japan, are well controlled and disciplined by the enemy, and at the proper time will engage in organized sabotage" to aid the Japanese cause. He presented no evidence for this claim, simply asserting that the "racial affinities" of Japanese Americans predisposed them to disloyalty.

Even those officials with qualms about the constitutional basis for mass internment fell prey to racial stereotypes. During the internal debate that preceded President Roosevelt's executive order, even General DeWitt acknowledged the legal barriers to the military orders he later signed. "An American citizen, after all, is an American citizen," he reminded the army's chief lawyer. At the War Department's very top, Secretary Henry Stimson—a Harvard lawyer—knew the Constitution stood in Dewitt's way. "We cannot discriminate against our citizens on the ground of racial origin," he admitted before De-Witt's "Final Recommendation" reached his desk. But after reading its racist claims, Stimson agreed that "their racial characteristics are such that we cannot understand or trust even the citizen Japanese." He backed mass internment even though "it will make a tremendous hole in our constitutional system." Perhaps the most revealing—and cynical—remark came from John J. McCloy, another Harvard lawyer who served as Stimson's chief deputy. "To a Wall Street lawyer," he told an army official, "the Constitution is just a piece of paper."

Many civilian officials shared the racial views of their military counterparts. Attorney General Francis Biddle asked three young government lawyers to advise him on the internment question. All three—Benjamin Cohen, Oscar Cox, and Joseph Rauh—were trained at Harvard Law School. None had any training in anthropology, but this did not deter them. "Since the Occidental eye cannot readily distinguish one Japanese resident from another," they told Biddle, "effective surveillance of the movement of particular Japanese residents suspected of disloyalty is extremely difficult if not impossible." As Caucasians, Biddle's legal advisers considered it unnecessary "to bar the millions of persons of German or Italian stock from either seacoast area," since "the normal Caucasian countenances of such persons enable the average American to recognize particular individuals by distinguishing minor facial characteristics." None of these lawyers had ever met Gordon Hirabayashi, Min Yasui, or Fred Korematsu, whose faces were easily distinguishable to anyone with normal vision. Biddle's legal adviser recommended setting aside "special reservations" where Japanese Americans could "live under special restrictions."

Perhaps the most extreme version of the "racial characteristics" argument was presented in a brief submitted to a federal district judge by Charles Burdell, a special assistant to Attorney General Biddle. Urging the judge to dismiss a constitutional challenge to the army's internment orders, Burdell wrote that "Jap citizens are inevitably bound, by intangible ties, to the people of the Empire of Japan. They are alike, physically and psychologically." Burdell elaborated his genetic theory of loyalty. "Even now, though we have been separated from the English people for over 100 years, we still take pride in the exploits of the RAF over Berlin, and the courageous fighting of the Aussies in Northern Africa. Why? Because they are people like us. They are Anglo-Saxons." Burdell's theory equally fit the Japanese Americans. "Who can doubt that these Japs in this country, citizens as well as aliens, feel a sense of pride in the feats of the Jap Army—this feeling of pride is strong in some, weak in others, but the germ of it must be present in the mind of every one of them."

What feelings *did* go through the minds of the three young men whose challenges to General DeWitt's military orders reached the Supreme Court? Much like Dred Scott and Homer Plessy before them, these young Americans were viewed by the Supreme Court solely on the basis of their shared race and ancestry. But their stories, even briefly told, show us how members of the same group—supposedly identical in their physical and psychological characteristics—can differ in many ways.

Gordon Hirabayashi was born in 1918 in Auburn, a rural town near Seattle, where his father ran a roadside fruit market. His parents belonged to a Japanese pacifist sect, similar to the Society of Friends, better known as Quakers; both groups worshiped without ministers and rejected military service. During high school, Gordon became an Eagle Scout and served as president of the Auburn Christian Fellowship. When he entered the University of Washington in Seattle in 1937, he joined the University Quaker Meeting and registered with his local draft board as a conscientious objector. When General DeWitt imposed a nighttime curfew order on all Japanese Americans in March 1942, Gordon was living in the campus YMCA dormitory. He obeyed the curfew for more than a month, often running back to his dorm to beat the clock. He later recalled thinking, "Why the hell am I running back? Am I an American or not? Why am I running back and nobody else is?"

On the night of May 4, Gordon stopped running and stayed out past the curfew hour. He recorded his feeling in his diary: "Peculiar, but I received a lift—perhaps it is a release—when I consciously break the silly old curfew." The army's evacuation orders gave Japanese Americans one week to dispose of their property and report to "assembly centers" at racetracks and fairgrounds. Before the orders reached Seattle, Gordon worked with the Quakers in helping families store their household goods and move with suitcases to the Puyallup Fairgrounds near Seattle. "Gosh!—something seems wrong there; helping people to go behind barbed wires and flimsy shacks," he wrote. "What a mixed-up life this is—the American way."

When the evacuation orders reached Seattle on May 16, Gordon became a conscientious objector to internment. He went to the downtown FBI office and told Special Agent Francis Manion that he would not report to Puyallup. Manion recorded Gordon's statement that "it was the principle of the Society of Friends that each person should follow the will of God according to his own convictions and that he could not reconcile the will of God, a part of which was expressed in the Bill of Rights and the United States Constitution, with the order discriminating against Japanese aliens and American citizens of Japanese ancestry." Agent Manion arrested Gordon for violating both the curfew and evacuation orders and placed him in the county jail to await trial.

Minoru Yasui did not share Gordon Hirabayashi's pacifism. Born in 1916 in the apple-growing region of Hood River, Oregon, he entered the University of Oregon in 1933 and volunteered for the army's reserve officer training program. After receiving a second lieutenant's commission in 1937, Min attended the university's law school, graduating in 1939. His law dean later wrote that he held a "relatively high opinion" of Yasui as a student, "but on many occasions I detected a streak of blind stubbornness in him." Unable to find legal work in Oregon, Min landed a job with the Japanese consulate in Chicago. His work was mostly clerical, but he also gave speeches defending Japanese policies in Asia before Rotary Clubs and similar groups. As an American citizen, he duly registered with the State Department as a foreign agent.

The day after Pearl Harbor, Min received a telegram from his father: "Now that this country is at war and needs you, and since you are trained as an officer, I as your father urge you to enlist immediately." Responding to this patriotic appeal, he resigned his consular post and returned to Oregon. Min then received an army order to report for duty at Fort Vancouver, near Portland. But when he arrived in uniform, army officers told him he was unacceptable for service and ordered him off the base. This rebuff on racial grounds triggered a stubborn reaction; Min returned eight times to Fort Vancouver and was turned away each time.

Even before the evacuation orders reached Portland, Min decided to challenge the curfew, imposed by General DeWitt through Military Order Number 3 of the army's Western Defense Command. Min had no quarrel with a curfew applied to aliens. "But Military Order Number 3 applied to all persons of Japanese ancestry," he later said. "I said, 'There the general is wrong, because it makes distinctions between citizens on the basis of ancestry.' That order infringed my rights as a citizen." The night of March 28, 1942, Min approached a policeman in downtown Portland. "I pulled out this order that said all persons of Japanese ancestry must be in their place of abode, and I pulled out my birth certificate and said, 'Look, I'm a person of Japanese ancestry, arrest me.' And the policeman said, 'Run along home, you'll get in trouble.'" Min stubbornly persisted, finally convincing a sergeant at police headquarters to arrest him for curfew violation. He spent nine months in solitary confinement before his trial.

Fred Korematsu did not challenge the internment from religious conviction or legal training. Unlike Gordon Hirabayashi and Min Yasui, he did not court arrest. In fact, Fred tried to evade the evacuation orders by changing his name, altering his draft card, and undergoing plastic surgery on his eyelids and nose. But his effort to escape detection as a Japanese American failed. On the afternoon of May 30, 1942, police officers in San Leandro, California, got a tip and picked up a young man walking down the street with his girlfriend. The suspect claimed to be Clyde Sarah, of Spanish-Hawaiian origin. But his story quickly fell apart; he spoke no Spanish, and his draft card had been crudely altered with ink eradicator. The officers took him to police headquarters. "One of the girls who worked in the office seemed to recognize me," Fred recalled, "and so I finally said who I was."

Born in 1919 in Oakland, California, Korematsu finished high school in 1938 and dropped out of college after one month for financial reasons. He then attended welding school in Oakland and worked as a shipyard welder following this training. The navy turned him away in June 1941 because of gastric ulcers, and his union expelled its Japanese American members after Pearl Harbor. Fred took piano lessons from an Italian woman and fell in love with her daughter. After his arrest, he told an FBI agent what he did after his family reported to the Tanforan Racetrack for evacuation: "I stayed in Oakland to earn enough money to take my girl with me to the Middle West. Her name is Miss Ida Boitano. She is a different nationality—Italian. The operation was for the purpose of changing my appearance so that I would not be subjected to ostracism when my girl and I went East." Fred never saw Ida again; FBI agents reported that she answered Fred's letters from jail by "telling him not to write her anymore."

Fred Korematsu did not volunteer to challenge the evacuation orders, but he eagerly accepted legal help from Ernest Besig, the ACLU director in San Francisco. The city's newspapers had reported Fred's arrest, and Besig visited him in jail. He was pleased to find a willing client for a test case. Behind his personal reasons for evading the evacuation, Fred shared with Gordon Hirabayashi and Min Yasui an awareness of his constitutional rights. During a jailhouse visit, he gave Ernest Besig a handwritten statement arguing that Japanese Americans "should have been given a fair trial in order that they may defend their loyalty at court in a democratic way, but they were placed in imprisonment without a fair trial!" He posed this quesiton to the government: "Is this a racial issue?" And he suggested a way to find the answer: "Fred Korematsu's Test Case may help."

Despite the differing motivations of the "test case" defendants, their criminal trials in federal district courts were uniformly brief and perfunctory. Judge Lloyd Black, who presided at Gordon Hirabayashi's trial in Seattle, rejected his lawyers' claims that General DeWitt's curfew and evacuation orders violated the Due Process Clause of the Fifth Amendment by singling out a racial group for "special restrictions" not imposed on others. Noting the proximity of aircraft plants and naval bases to Seattle, Black pointed to "the fact that the parachutists and saboteurs, as well as the soldiers, of Japan make diabolically clever use of infiltration tactics. They are shrewd masters of tricky concealment among any who resemble them. With the aid of any artifice or treachery they seek such human camouflage and with uncanny skill discover and take advantage of any disloyalty among their kind." Judge Black directed the jurors to convict Gordon, which they did after just ten minutes of deliberation.

Min Yasui's trial in Portland took a bit longer, largely because Judge Alger Fee took over the questioning from the government's lawyer, Charles Burdell, who had pressed the "genetic disloyalty" claim in his pretrial brief. Fee surprised Min, who had never been to Japan, with questions about Japanese customs and beliefs. "What is Shinto?" he abruptly asked. Min was clearly puzzled by the question. "Shinto? As I understand, Shinto is the national religion of Japan," he answered. "Do you give adherence to its precepts?" Fee asked. "My mother and father were Methodists in Japan," Min replied, "and I myself have been a Methodist in this country and I don't know the precepts of the Shinto religion." Fee pressed on doggedly: "Was not Shinto practiced in your household?" Min tried to conceal his irritation. "Both my mother and father are good, devout Methodists," he assured Fee. "They are really Christians." Fee heard the case without a jury, and pronounced Min guilty for his admitted curfew violation. Before passing sentence, Fee ruled in a written opinion that despite Min's American birth and citizenship, he considered him "a citizen of Japan and subject to the Emperor of Japan," a finding the judge based on "the nativity of his parents and the subtle nuances of traditional mores engrained in his race by centuries of social discipline." After linking Min to "the treacherous attack by the armed forces of Japan" on Pearl Harbor, Judge Fee imposed the maximum penalty of one year in prison and a $5,000 fine.

Fred Korematsu came to trial in San Francisco before Judge Adolphus St. Sure, who differed from his Seattle and Portland colleagues in treating the defendant with respect. After an FBI agent testified about Fred's draft-card forgery and plastic surgery, the soft-spoken defendant took the stand to explain his actions. His description of Dr. Bennett Masten's bargain-rate surgery drew smiles in the courtroom. "I don't think he made any change in my appearance," he said, "for when I went to the Tanforan Assembly Center everyone knew me and my folks didn't know the difference." Fred told the judge that he had applied for military service before Pearl Harbor, but had been rejected on medical grounds. "As a citizen of the United States I am ready, willing, and able to bear arms for this country," he affirmed. This forthrightness impressed Judge St. Sure, but he nonetheless found Fred guilty and sentenced him to a five-year probationary sentence. When Fred's lawyer announced his intention to appeal the conviction, St. Sure obligingly set bail at $2,500. Fred was legally free to remain at liberty, but when he stepped outside the courthouse he was grabbed by a waiting military policeman, who pulled a pistol and took his prisoner to the army jail at General DeWitt's headquarters, from which Fred was shipped to the Tanforan Racetrack, where his parents were confined in horse stalls, awaiting transfer to an internment camp in the Utah desert.

All three test-case defendants appealed to the Supreme Court after circuit court judges upheld their convictions, but the Justices sent Fred Korematsu's case back to the circuit court for a ruling on Judge St. Sure's sentencing decision. Before it returned, the Court heard argument in the *Hirabayashi* and *Yasui* cases in April 1943. The briefs on both sides stuck closely to legal issues and included no evidence on the government's claim that Japanese Americans posed a danger of "espionage and sabotage" to West Coast defense facilities. There was, in fact, no evidence that *any* member of this racial group had committed these treasonous acts.

The government's brief in *Hirabayashi v. United States* asserted that "an unknown number of the Japanese may lack to some extent a feeling of loyalty toward the United States" because of resentment against legal discrimination. Largely drafted by Arnold Raum, a Harvard Law School graduate in the solicitor general's office, the brief cited laws barring Japanese immigrants from American citizenship and landownership. This discrimination supposedly produced "a consequent tie to Japan" and a "compensatory feeling of racial pride" in Japan's achievements. Asserting without any supporting evidence "the virtually impossible task of promptly segregating the potentially disloyal from the loyal" among Japanese Americans, Raum argued that "the only certain way" of removing the disloyal "was to remove the group as a whole."

Solicitor General Charles Fahy, who commanded the legal battalion that won the Wagner Act cases in 1937, defended General DeWitt's orders in arguing the *Hirabayashi* case in 1943. Claiming that Japanese Americans "had never become assimilated" into American society, he called it "not unreasonable" to fear that members of this group "might assist the enemy." The fear he attributed to DeWitt "was not based on race but on these other factors," Fahy assured the justices. Harold Evans, who argued for Gordon Hirabayashi, relied on the Supreme Court's 1866 ruling in *Ex parte Milligan* for the proposition that "legislative authority over civilians may not be delegated to the military when the area in question is not a strictly military area." The *Milligan* decision, holding that Confederate sympathizers could not be tried by military tribunals while civilian courts remained open, did not impress Justice Felix Frankfurter, an army prosecutor during World War I. "There's a lot in Milligan," he told Evans, "that will not stand scrutiny in 1943, a lot of talk that is purely political." Frankfurter did not elaborate on his cryptic statement, leaving Evans without a question to answer. "That's for this Court to decide," he weakly replied.

The Court issued its *Hirabayashi* decision on June 21, 1943, along with a short opinion in the *Yasui* case. Chief Justice Stone wrote for a unanimous Court in upholding Gordon Hirabayashi's conviction for curfew violation. He sidestepped the conviction for violating the evacuation order, on the ground that Judge Black had imposed concurrent sentences on both counts and that Hirabayashi consequently faced no additional penalty for the evacuation violation. Stone most likely dodged the more difficult issue of evacauation in hopes that government officials might end the internment program before Fred Korematsu's case, which directly challenged the evacuation orders, returned from the circuit court. In that event, of course, the case—and the internment issue—would become moot and the Court would be off the hook.

The Chief Justice also dodged the statement in Footnote Four of his *Carolene Products* opinion that laws directed against racial minorities should be subjected to "more searching judicial inquiry" than statutes involving economic regulations. The author of the "strict scrutiny" doctrine proved highly lenient in judging the government's "military necessity" claims. "Distinctions between citizens solely because of their ancestry," he conceded, "are by their very nature odious to a free people whose institutions are founded upon the doctrine of equality." But "the danger of espionage and sabotage" by Japanese Americans overrode the Constitution's promise of "the equal protection of the laws" to every American, regardless of ancestry. Stone proclaimed that "those facts and circumstances which are relevant to measures for our national defense" provided military officials with reason to "place citizens of one ancestry in a different category from others." And what *were* the facts and circumstances that justified General DeWitt's military orders? On this crucial issue, Stone accepted Solicitor General Fahy's "racial characteristics" argument without questioning its veracity.

"At a time of threatened Japanese attack upon this country," Stone wrote, "the nature of our inhabitants' attachments to the Japanese enemy was consequently a matter of grave concern." Citing the references in Arnold Raum's brief to laws directed against Japanese immigrants, Stone concluded that such discrimination had "intensified their solidarity" and "prevented their assimilation as an integral part of the white population." Raum's brief also contained data on the number of children who attended Japanese language classes and those who returned to Japan for schooling. Stone concluded from this data that Japanese Americans sought "relatively little social intercourse between them and the white population." It was thus "reasonable" for military authorities to consider Japanese Americans "a menace to the national defense and safety" and to restrict their movements. All these factors gave President Roosevelt and War Department officials "a rational basis for the decision" to "set these citizens apart from others who have no particular association with Japan."

One week before the Court issued its *Hirabayashi* decision, Justice Felix Frankfurter had referred to his Jewish ancestry in angry response to the overruling of his *Gobitis* opinion in the *Barnette* decision. Frankfurter had rejected Justice Frank Murphy's appeal to avoid "catapulting a personal issue into the arena." But Frankfurter made his own appeal when Murphy circulated a blistering dissent in *Hirabayashi*, finding a "melancholy resemblance" between the restrictions on Japanese Americans and "the treatment accorded to members of the Jewish race" in Germany. Frankfurter asked Murphy to consider whether his statement might be read as accusing his colleagues of "playing into the hands of the enemy." This appeal to wartime unity convinced Murphy to change his dissent to a concurrence, but he retained the comparison of Japanese Americans to German Jews and his conclusion that the military orders approached "the very brink of constitutional power."

Stone's wish that government officials would end the internment program and thereby moot the *Korematsu* case was not granted before the Court heard arguments in October 1944. The decision to keep Japanese Americans behind barbed wire, long after Japanese forces posed any threat to the West Coast, reveals the dominance of politics over law. Dillon Myer, who headed the Interior Department agency that ran the internment camps, appealed to Assistant Secretary of War John J. McCloy in October 1943 for "the return of evacuees to the West Coast" because "the military necessity for total exclusion from this area no longer exists." McCloy replied that "active and powerful groups in California" opposed the return of Japanese Americans. "This means that considerations other than of mere military necessity enter into any proposal" for ending the internment program, McCloy added. Attorney General Francis Biddle appealed directly to President Roosevelt in December 1943. "The present practice of keeping loyal American citizens in concentration camps on the basis of race for longer than is absolutely necessary is dangerous and repugnant to the principles of our Government," Biddle argued. Roosevelt simply ignored his letter.

The real reason for delay became apparent as the 1944 elections approached. Secretary of War Stimson raised the internment question at a cabinet meeting in May of that year. Biddle recorded Stimson's admission that internment could be ended "without danger to defense considerations but doubted the wisdom of doing it at this time before the election." President Roosevelt agreed with Stimson. Interior Secretary Harold Ickes made another appeal to Roosevelt in June 1944, arguing that the detention of Japanese Americans "is clearly unconstitutional in the present circumstances." He predicted that "the continued retention of these innocent people in the relocation centers would be a blot upon the history of this country." Roosevelt again raised his electoral concerns. "I think the whole problem, for the sake of internal quiet, should be handled gradually," he told Ickes. Later in June, John McCloy attended a White House meeting to present the army's plan for returning a "substantial number" of Japanese Americans to the West Coast. Roosevelt "put thumbs down on this scheme," McCloy reported to army officials. "He was surrounded at the moment by his political advisors," McCloy added, "and they were harping hard that this would stir up the boys in California and California, I guess, is an important state." McCloy told the army officials that internment could not end before "a date somewhat later than November 6." The elections, as McCloy well knew, would be held on November 6. On that date, the voters gave Roosevelt a fourth presidential term and the Democrats picked up four House seats in California. Japanese Americans, who had been deprived of their right to vote, remained behind barbed-wire fences while Roosevelt celebrated his victory in the White House.

Argument in *Korematsu v. United States* began on October 11, 1944. The justices also heard argument in *Ex parte Endo*, which involved a habeas corpus petition filed by Mitsuye Endo, a young Japanese American woman who had volunteered to test the government's power to detain citizens the army had conceded were loyal. Her case had languished in the lower courts for more than two years before the Supreme Court agreed to hear Endo's appeal from a district court ruling that dismissed her petition. Since the government made no effort in its *Endo* brief to defend the continued detention of loyal Japanese Americans, the central issue before the justices was the question, raised in the *Korematsu* case, of the power to order their evacuation in the first place. Once again, the government's *Korematsu* brief made the "racial characteristics" argument that had convinced the Court in *Hirabayashi*. But this time, the brief turned the argument completely around. Government lawyers now claimed that mass internment was necessary to protect Japanese Americans against racial hostility, rather than to protect military installations against their hostile reaction to discrimination. No longer were DeWitt's orders a "reasonable" response to the dangers posed by disloyal Japanese Americans. They had in fact been designed to "prevent incidents involving violence between Japanese migrants" and Caucasians who blamed them for Pearl Harbor. "The belief of the military authorities in the danger of violence has not been shown to be unreasonable," the government's brief weakly claimed. Fred Korematsu had not met "the burden which rested upon him" to disprove the evidence "of hostility to the evacuees, which lay at the basis of the decision to impose detention" on them. This about-face in the government's position reflected the fact that Japanese forces posed no threat to the West Coast after 1943, eroding arguments based on the danger of espionage and sabaotage by Japanese Americans.

The obvious absurdity of forcing Korematsu to prove that whites were not hostile toward Japanese Americans did not faze Justice Hugo Black, who wrote for six justices in upholding Korematsu's criminal conviction. Determined to rescue the government from an untenable position, Black returned to *Hirabayashi* for support, quoting Stone's claim that the danger posed by "disloyal" Japanese Americans justified the curfew imposed on them. Black brushed aside complaints that removing people from their homes imposed greater hardships than curfews. "But hardships are part of war," he replied, "and war is an aggregation of hardships."

Solicitor General Fahy had argued that racial hostility against Fred Korematsu justified his internment. Justice Black denied that racial hostility had anything to do with the case. "Korematsu was not excluded from the Military Area because of hostility to him or his race," Black asserted. "He was excluded because we are at war with the Japanese Empire" and because "the military urgency of the situation demanded that all citizens of Japanese ancestry be segregated from the West Coast" until the danger passed. The internment camps protected West Coat residents from people like Fred Korematsu, not the other way around. Years later, Black exposed the racial stereotypes on which his opinion rested. "People were rightly fearful of the Japanese," he told an interviewer, because "they all look alike to a person not a Jap."

Justice Murphy stood with the Court at "the very brink of constitutional power" in the *Hirabayashi* case. But he would not stand with Black in *Korematsu*. The exclusion of Japanese Americans from their homes, he wrote in dissent, went over that brink "and falls into the ugly abyss of racism." Murphy attacked the racial stereotypes on which both Stone's and Black's opinions rested. He called the government's justifications of internment "largely an accumulation of much of the misinformation, half-truths and insinuations that for years have been directed against Japanese Americans by people with racial and economic prejudices—the same people who have been among the foremost advocates of the evacuation." Murphy repeated the word that must have stung his colleagues: "I dissent, therefore, from this legalization of racism."

Murphy had withdrawn his *Hirabayashi* dissent because he did not want to stand alone on the constitutional battlefield. But two colleagues stood with him in *Korematsu*. Justices Owen Roberts and Robert Jackson wrote separate dissents with different objections to Black's opinion. Black denied that Fred Korematsu faced detention if he violated the evacuation order, asserting that he could have left California before the order became effective. This struck Roberts as a denial of reality, because an earlier order forbid Korematsu from leaving the state. He called the two orders "a cleverly devised trap to accomplish the real purpose of the military authorities, which was to lock him up in a concentration camp." Jackson accused the majority of validating "the principle of racial discrimination" under the guise of military necessity. "The principle then lies about like a loaded weapon ready for the hand of any authority that can bring forward a plausible claim of an urgent need," he warned.

The Court announced its *Korematsu* decision on December 18, 1944, a Monday, along with a unanimous ruling that reversed the dismissal of Mitsuye Endo's habeas corpus petition. Justice Douglas wrote the *Endo* opinion for the court, declining to reach "the underlying constitutional issues which have been argued." He simply held that military authorities had "no authority to subject citizens who are concededly loyal" to continued detention. Douglas wrote an equivocal opinion in *Endo* to avoid a head-on collision with Justice Black's claim in *Korematsu* that the Constitution did not block General DeWitt's power to order the evacuation of all Japanese Americans. Justices Murphy and Roberts needled Douglas in separate concurrences; Roberts assailed his colleague for encouraging "the evasion of law and the violation of constitutional rights" by government officials.

The timing of the *Korematsu* and *Endo* decisions was no accident. The Court had waited to issue the opinions while government officials—most likely alerted by Justice Frankfurter—prepared for the Court's ruling that loyal Japanese Americans could no longer be detained. One day earlier, in an unusual Sunday statement, the War Department had issued a press release. "Those persons of Japanese ancestry whose records have stood the test of Army scrutiny during the past two years," the release stated, would be released from internment camps and "permitted the same freedom of movement throughout the United States as other loyal citizens and law-abiding aliens." The decision to close the internment camps met with a mixed reaction on the West Coast. Press reports of the new policy played up the threat of vigilante action: "Outbreak of

Violence Seen by Nips' Return," headlined the *Los Angeles Times*. Public officials, however, did their best to protect the returning Japanese Americans. California governor Earl Warren, an original advocate of mass evacuation, proclaimed his belief that "all Americans will join in protecting constitutional rights, and will maintain an attitude that will discourage friction and prevent civil disorder." Only a few scattered incidents of violence and harassment marred the peaceful return of Japanese Americans to their homes, farms, and businesses along the West Coast.

The impact of Supreme Court decisions is often immediately apparent; the *Gobitis* ruling in 1940 provoked a wave of persecution against Jehovah's Witnesses. But that decision was reversed just three years later, after the Court realized the destructive consequences of its action. The impact on Japanese Americans of the *Hirabayashi* and *Korematsu* decisions, however, was not evident to many people for more than three decades after the Court upheld their exclusion from the West Coast. The former internees returned to their communities after the war and rebuilt their lives as hardworking, law-abiding citizens. But underneath their image as a "model minority" was pent-up anger at the injustice they endured for no reason but their race. Some of them, and many of their children, marched for civil rights and against the Vietnam War. During the 1970s, several groups of Japanese Americans began a grassroots lobbying campaign, asking Congress to make symbolic payments to Japanese Americans who had been forced into internment camps.

The first victory of the "redress movement" came in 1980 when Congress established a blue-ribbon Commission on Wartime Relocation and Internment of Civilians, charged with reviewing the mass internment and making recommendations for methods of redress. This nine-member body—which included former Supreme Court justice Arthur Goldberg—conducted hearings around the country at which more than 750 people testified, many speaking tearfully about their wartime hardships and lingering pain. In a 467-page report in 1983, the commissioners agreed unanimously that Japanese Americans had suffered a "grave injustice" that was produced by "race prejudice, war hysteria, and a failure of political leadership." All but one commissioner—Republican congressman Daniel Lungren of Caliornia—recommended that Congress provide compensation of $20,000 for each survivor of the internment camps.

The redress campaign included a legal effort to reverse the wartime convictions of Gordon Hirabayashi, Min Yasui, and Fred Korematsu. Normally, criminal defendants cannot ask judges to reopen their cases after appeals have been exhausted and sentences completed. The only exception to the "finality" rule stems from one of the "ancient writs" of English law, called the writ of error coram nobis. This term is legal Latin for "error before us," referring to the trial judges. This application for judicial relief is related to the better-known writ of habeas corpus, an order to "bring the body" of the defendant into court for a hearing on the legality of the detention. In coram nobis cases, the former defendant must show that "prosecutorial misconduct" during the original trial deprived him or her of a fair trial. There are two grounds for coram nobis relief: one requires proof that government lawyers deliberately withheld "exculpatory" evidence that would show the defendant's innocence; the other involves the government's introduction at trial of false evidence of the defendant's guilt. The burden of proof on defendants is high, and coram nobis relief is rarely sought and even more rarely granted.

The coram nobis effort in the wartime internment cases began in 1981, when Peter Irons (this book's author and also a lawyer) was conducting research for a book on the cases, hoping to explain why the Supreme Court—with so many "liberal" members—made decisions in these cases that scholars have agreed were judicial "disasters," as Yale law professor Eugene Rostow wrote in 1945. Using the Freedom of Information Act, Irons obtained the Justice Department's files in the *Hirabayashi*, *Yasui*, and *Korematsu* cases, and he discovered several astounding documents. The "loaded weapons" that Justice Jackson warned about in his *Korematsu* dissent were really "smoking guns" of legal misconduct.

Two memoranda by Edward Ennis, who headed the Justice Department's Alien Enemy Control Unit, shot out of these files. He sent the first to Solicitor General Fahy in April 1943, shortly before Fahy's Supreme Court argument in the *Hirabayashi* case. Ennis had obtained military intelligence reports to General DeWitt, informing him that no evidence existed to support claims of Japanese American disloyalty. Ennis reminded Fahy of his "duty to advise the Court of the existence" of these crucial reports. Failing to perform this duty "might approximate the suppression of evidence," he warned. But Fahy ignored the warning and assured the Court that DeWitt had evidence of disloyalty among Japanese Americans before he signed the internment orders in 1942. Chief Justice Stone based his *Hirabayashi* opinion in large part on Fahy's assurances, citing "the judgment of the military authorities" that "there were disloyal members" of the Japanese American community who constituted "a menace to the national defense and safety" on the West Coast.

Ennis sent another memorandum to Fahy in September 1944, during his preparation for the *Korematsu* argument. Suspicious of General Dewitt's claims to have evidence of "espionage and sabotage" by Japanese Americans, Ennis had found more intelligence reports that refuted the charges DeWitt made in his "Final Report" on the internment program. Excerpts of DeWitt's report were included in the *Korematsu* brief that Fahy was about to file with the Court. Ennis urged Fahy to disavow the report's claims that "overt acts of treason were being committed" by Japanese Americans. "Since this is not so," Ennis wrote, "it is highly unfair to this racial minority that these lies, put out in an official publication, go uncorrected." Again, Fahy ignored Ennis and assured the justices that he vouched for "every sentence, every line, and every word" in De-Witt's report. Again, the Court accepted Fahy's assurances in upholding Fred Korematsu's conviction; Justice Hugo Black cited DeWitt's report as providing sufficient "evidence of disloyalty" among Japanese Americans to justify their mass evacuation from the West Coast.

Armed with these "smoking guns"and other records of legal misconduct, Irons tracked down Gordon Hirabayashi, Min Yasui, and Fred Korematsu and showed them his findings. All three men, then in their sixties, agreed to join an effort to erase their criminal records. Irons then recruited a team of committed young lawyers, most of them the children of internment camp survivors, headed by San Francisco attorney Dale Minami. The coram nobis team prepared a 150-page petition, which was submitted in 1983 to federal district judges in San Francisco, Portland, and Seattle, the courts in which the "test case" defendants had been tried and convicted in 1942. Based entirely on evidence from government files, the petition urged the judges "to carefully weigh the complete record of governmental abuses" in the wartime cases and "do justice where it was denied forty years ago."

Fred Korematsu's petition came before federal judge Marilyn Hall Patel in November 1983, at a hearing crowded with internment survivors. After Dale Minami reviewed the evidence of legal misconduct, Fred made a brief statement to Judge Patel. "Your Honor, I still remember 40 years ago when I was handcuffed and arrested as a criminal," he began. Fred recalled his family's living quarters at the Tanforan Racetrack: "The horse stalls that we stayed in were made for horses, not human beings." Speaking for "all Japanese Americans who were escorted to concentration camps," he asked the government to "admit that they were wrong and do something about it so this will never happen again to any American citizen of any race, creed, or color." The government's lawyer, Victor Stone, denied that the Supreme Court's *Korematsu* decision still "lies around like a loaded gun" and asked Judge Patel to dismiss Korematsu's petition. Ruling from the bench, she found "substantial support" in the petition that "the government deliberately omitted relevant information and provided misleading information" to the Supreme Court in 1944. Judge Patel passed a posthumous verdict on Solicitor General Fahy. "The judicial process is seriously impaired when the government's law enforcement officers violate their ethical obligations to the court," she concluded. Patel ended by reminding her audience— which needed no reminder—that the *Korematsu* decision "remains on the pages of our legal and political history" as a "constant caution that in times of war or declared military necessity our institutions must be vigilant in protecting constitutional guarantees."

Federal judges in Portland and Seattle later vacated the wartime convictions of Min Yasui and Gordon Hirabayashi. Justice Department lawyers had with-

drawn an earlier appeal of Judge Patel's ruling to the Ninth Circuit Court of
Appeals, but they pursued an appeal in 1987 of the ruling of Judge Donald
Voorhees that granted Hirabayashi's petition. Government lawyers never revealed their reasons, but members of the coram nobis legal team suspected that
pressure from veterans' groups on the Reagan administration lay behind this legal about-face. During argument before the Ninth Circuit panel, Judge Mary
Schroeder asked Victor Stone why the government had not acted on its own to
vacate the convictions. "We didn't think there was anyone out there who cared,"
Stone replied, bringing gasps from the courtroom audience. Writing for the appellate panel, which unanimously reversed both of Hirabayashi's wartime convictions, Judge Schroeder showed that she cared: "A United States citizen who
is convicted of a crime on account of race is lastingly aggrieved." Government
lawyers did not appeal Schroeder's ruling, and the coram nobis campaign ended
with total victory: all three wartime defendants had their records cleared after
more than forty years. Gordon Hirabayashi spoke the last words on the steps of
the Seattle courthouse in which he received final vindication of his wartime
stand: "Ancestry is not a crime."

The nation finally showed that it cared as well. At a White House ceremony
in January 1998, President Bill Clinton placed the Presidential Medal of Freedom around Fred Korematsu's neck. "A man of quiet bravery," the president
said, "Fred Korematsu deserves our respect and thanks for his patient pursuit
to preserve the civil liberties we hold dear." Fred pursued his constitutional
rights for almost half a century, never losing his faith in American justice. But
other Japanese Americans had lost faith, and more than sixty thousand camp
survivors had died before Congress finally enacted a redress bill in 1988 and
President Ronald Reagan signed the national apology that accompanied the redress checks of $20,000 to those who remained. For three years of their lives,
imprisoned without charges in desolate camps and denied their rights and dignity, this was small compensation.

28

"My Little Soul Is

Overjoyed"

World War II, which began for the United States with the explosion of Japanese bombs at Pearl Harbor, ended with the deadliest explosion in history, the atomic blast that killed 100,000 Japanese in Hiroshima on August 6, 1945. Three days later, a second atomic bomb killed 50,000 Japanese in Nagasaki. The war that began on a "day of infamy" in Hawaii ended four years later with Japan's unconditional surrender on September 2, 1945.

Around the world, some twenty million people—including six million Jews in Europe—perished in the global battle between the Allies and the Axis. It would be wrong to call the war a contest between democracy and dictatorship, since America's allies included the Soviet Union, which denied its people the "fundamental rights" our Constitution protected, and countries like England and France, whose colonial subjects lacked the "inalienable rights" that Americans had won through revolution.

The war's end did not stop the fighting, as revolutionary fervor swept around the world with campaigns for independence in Africa and Asia. Many of those who led movements against colonialism echoed the sentiments—and often the words—of earlier American revolutionaries. Ho Chi Minh, the Communist leader of Vietnamese resistance to French colonial rule, quoted from our Declaration of Independence in the one he drafted in 1945. "All men are created equal," it began. "They are endowed by their Creator with certain inalienable rights; among these are Life, Liberty, and the Pursuit of Happiness."

Most of the postwar revolutionaries belonged to "colored" races, and some were Communists. They fought in their native lands against racism and political repression, with the moral support of many Americans. Had they been American citizens they would have been forced to obey Jim Crow segregation laws from Delaware to Texas, and been subject to prosecution for revolutionary speech under state and federal "sedition" laws. This irony struck many Americans as evidence that our Constitution did not "secure the blessings of liberty" to those whose race or politics differed from the majority. At the war's end, people who were black in color or "Red" in politics found little protection in courtrooms from the "prejudice against discrete and insular minorities" that Justice Harlan Fiske Stone had condemned in Footnote Four of the *Carolene Products* decision in 1938, before the war began.

On April 22, 1946, ten days past the first anniversary of Franklin Roosevelt's death, Stone died after five years at the Court's helm. Fittingly, he was presiding as Chief Justice over the Court whose human rights agenda he helped to shape when a fatal stroke ended his life. Neither successor of these two men even approached their stature in American politics and law. Harry Truman had served as vice president for just three months, picked for that job to replace Henry Wallace, who had become a political liability for Roosevelt. A product of the Democratic machine in Kansas City, Missouri, Truman became a New Deal stalwart in the Senate and gained headlines by chairing a wartime committee that exposed profiteering in military contacts. More comfortable in smoke-filled rooms than at fancy-dress dinners, Truman reacted to his sudden accession to power with winning modesty: "Did you ever have a load of hay fall on you?"

The choice of a new Chief Justice fell to Truman, who looked no further than his poker-table cronies. The new president had already added one Justice, naming Republican senator Harold Burton of Ohio to replace Justice Owen Roberts, who resigned in July 1945 out of frustration with his dwindling influence. Under pressure from Republicans to keep their party represented on the Court, Truman picked Burton as a reward for supporting Roosevelt's wartime policies. A former Cleveland mayor who joined the Senate in 1940, Burton had no judicial experience and no discernible judicial philosophy. He strongly backed the government in "Red" cases and usually supported the rights of blacks. Burton helped maintain the "wall of separation" between church and state and took a hard line in criminal cases. Over thirteen years on the Court, he wrote no opinions of lasting impact. The first of Truman's four Court nominees was among the three later ranked as judicial "failures" by scholars.

Truman's choice of Fred Vinson of Kentucky to replace Stone as Chief Justice looked good on the surface. Vinson had experience in all three branches of government, in local, state, and federal posts. He moved upward in public office from city attorney to congressman to federal judge to treasury secretary. In naming Vinson, Truman lauded him as "capable of unifying the Supreme Court and thereby improving its public image." During seven years as Chief Justice, Vinson accomplished neither goal. Affable and modest, he resembled Truman in many ways. And like the president who gained his post through another's sudden death, he came unprepared for the highest post in his life. Vinson's talent for political compromise was sorely tested by the personal and ideological feuds that divided the justices like the Hatfields and McCoys of his native Kentucky. But he stayed out of the conference-room arguments between Felix Frankfurter and Hugo Black and remained silent during the ugly public fight that erupted when Robert Jackson accused Black of blocking his nomination as Chief Justice after Stone's death.

Truman's crony almost always supported the positions of his administration, most notably in a 1952 case that challenged the president's power to forestall a nationwide strike by seizing the country's steel mills during the Korean War. Frankfurter and Black buried their differences in *Youngstown Sheet & Tube Co. v. Sawyer*, joining a majority of six that returned the mills to their owners. Black wrote for the Court in ruling that Truman acted without constitutional or congressional sanction; Vinson replied in dissent that those who would deny the president "extraordinary powers should be mindful that these are extraordinary times." Vinson would not deny Truman *any* powers, making his vote as predictable as the sunrise. The few opinions he wrote lacked both substance and style; Vinson turned this job over to his clerks and "did all his 'writing' with his hands in his pockets," one biographer noted. The weakest Chief Justice of the twentieth century died suddenly in September 1953, shortly after the Court heard argument in the historic school segregation cases. Vinson would most likely have failed to persuade his colleagues to join a unanimous opinion in *Brown v. Board of Education*, a task his successor, Earl Warren, performed brilliantly. In this respect, Vinson's death came at a providential moment in American history.

Franklin Roosevelt had placed his attorney general on the Court when he named Frank Murphy in 1940. Murphy's death in July 1949 gave Harry Truman a third appointment, and he also turned to his attorney general, Tom C. Clark, who became the first Texan on the Court. Born into a family of lawyers in 1899, Clark attended the University of Texas Law School and joined his father's Dallas firm in 1922. He spent most of his career in government service, with ten years in the Justice Department. As head of the War Frauds Unit, he worked closely with Senator Truman; as an active Texas Democrat, Clark helped Truman win the vice-presidential nomination in 1944 and was promoted to head the Justice Department in reward.

Under Clark's direction, the Justice Department took an active role in civil rights enforcement and an equally active role in searching for subversives. He pressed a reluctant J. Edgar Hoover to assign FBI agents to lynching cases and authorized the prosecution of Communist Party leaders for sedition. During eighteen years on the Court, Clark remained consistent, voting for civil rights plaintiffs and against Communist defendants. His opinions were dull but competent, and he spent much time working to improve judicial administration. Clark retired in 1967 when President Lyndon Johnson named his son, Ramsey Clark, as attorney general. He devoted the years before his death in 1977 to improving the quality of justice, concerned more with nuts and bolts than grand designs, much as he had approached cases on the Court.

Truman's final judicial appointment was also his worst. Justice Wiley Rutledge died in September 1949, two months after Frank Murphy; the president quickly named another former Senate crony, Sherman Minton of Indiana, to succeed Rutledge. Elected to the Senate in 1934, the tobacco-chewing Hoosier had befriended Truman and vocally supported President Roosevelt's court-packing plan. When Indiana's Republicans swept back to power in 1940, Minton lost his Senate seat. President Roosevelt rewarded him for political loyalty with a federal appellate judgeship; he served for eight years without distinction before Truman promoted him to the Supreme Court. He joined the "Truman Bloc" in most cases, although he dissented in several cases that struck down Jim Crow laws. Forced by illness to resign in 1956, Minton returned to Indiana without leaving any mark in Washington. He well deserved the failing grade that scholars placed beside his name.

No president added more illustrious names to the Court's history than Franklin Roosevelt. And none placed more failures on the bench than Harry Truman. We could aptly call his nominees the "Four Horsemen of Mediocrity," the term applied by Justice William O. Douglas to all but Tom Clark, whose mediocre opinions were balanced with devoted service to judicial reform. Ironically, scholars have consistently ranked Truman among the "top ten" presidents, and he certainly grew in the job after the "load of hay" fell on him in 1945. But he never recovered from his bad case of "cronyism" in making appointments. Fortunately, the Supreme Court survived the bout of mediocrity it caught from Truman.

During the war, more than 900,000 black soldiers risked their lives to defend a Constitution whose protections they did not enjoy in a segregated army and navy. One expressed his resentment in angry words: "The Army jim-crows us. The Navy lets us serve only as messmen. The Red Cross refuses our blood. Employers and unions shut us out. Lynchings continue. We are disenfranchised, jim-crowed, spat upon. What more could Hitler do than that?" Many of these soldiers returned home determined to do something about segregation. They joined the NAACP, boosting its membership and energizing local chapters that had been dormant for years. In communities across the South, black veterans tried to register to vote, pressed local officials to improve their children's schools, and protested discrimination in jobs and housing.

The southern reaction to black demands for full citizenship was often hostile and sometimes violent. The case of Isaac Woodward was just one of dozens reported in 1946. After combat duty in the Philippines and New Guinea, Woodward reported to Camp Gordon, Georgia, for his army mustering-out. Carrying his honorable discharge papers, he headed for home in North Carolina on a Greyhound bus on February 12. The white driver cursed the black veteran for taking too long at a "comfort stop" and summoned police in Batesburg, South

Carolina. They dragged Woodward into the local jail and beat him senseless. During this assault, Chief L. I. Shaw gouged Woodward's eyes with a billy club and left him blind. State officials refused to prosecute Shaw, and an all-white federal jury acquitted him of charges that he had violated Woodward's civil rights. The federal attorney who prosecuted Shaw failed to produce any witnesses other than the bus driver who had Woodward arrested. White spectators cheered the jury's verdict.

On July 25, a band of twenty white men dragged two black farmhands and their wives from a car in Monroe, Georgia. One of the black men had recently been charged with stabbing his white employer. Led by a "dignified looking white man," the vigilantes lined up their victims, counted "one, two, three," and fired more than sixty bullets into them. "The upper parts of the bodies were scarcely recognizable from the mass of bullet holes," the *New York Times* reported. One of the murdered blacks, George Dorsey, had just returned from army service in North Africa and Australia. Georgia governor Eugene Talmadge told the press that "things like that are to be regretted," adding that "nothing can be gained by giving equal rights to someone with an artificial civilization." Sheriff E. S. Gordon said that because a white farmer who witnessed the massacre "could not identify any member of the band he had gone as far as he could with his investigation." Attorney General Tom Clark ordered "a complete investigation" of the murders, but no prosecutions resulted.

"Mob acts of violence against Negroes are assuming alarming proportions," the NAACP charged in September 1946. Two months later, President Truman appointed a blue-ribbon President's Committee on Civil Rights to determine whether new federal laws were needed "to safeguard the civil rights of the people." The committee's 1947 report, *To Secure These Rights*, urged "the elimination of segregation" in housing, education, employment, public facilities, and transportation. The president endorsed the report and urged Congress to enforce its recommendations with legislation.

One witness before the president's committee spoke from years of experience in civil rights litigation. Thurgood Marshall, counsel for the NAACP Legal Defense and Education Fund, was the nation's leading black lawyer. Born in Baltimore in 1908, he applied to the University of Maryland's all-white law school after graduating from an all-black college. Turned down because of his race, Marshall studied law at Howard University, the "black Harvard" in Washington, D.C. He won his first civil rights case in 1936, forcing Maryland to admit Donald Murray to its law school. Because the state did not appeal to the Supreme Court, the *Murray* case did not establish any precedent on racial segregation outside Maryland.

Thurgood Marshall commanded a dedicated platoon of lawyers who fought segregation with a battle plan drafted in 1931 by Nathan Margold, a young Jewish lawyer and protégé of Felix Frankfurter, then a Harvard law professor. Hired by the NAACP to research Jim Crow laws and recommend a long-range litigation strategy against segregation in public education, Margold produced a 218-page document that became the "master plan" for Marshall's legal troops. Margold took the Supreme Court's "separate but equal" ruling in *Plessy v. Ferguson* as his starting point. After documenting the obvious fact that schools for blacks were rarely equal to those for whites, Margold considered two legal strategies. One would focus on lawsuits designed to force southern officials to make black and white schools truly equal in quality. This approach had two advantages: it would avoid a frontal attack on *Plessy*, which stood firmly in the 1930s as precedent; and judicial rulings that ordered equal facilities would impose heavy financial burdens on local school boards. The second legal strategy would assert that separate schools could never be equal because segregation imposed a "badge of servitude" on black children. This approach had many risks, but one virtue: judges could not evade the Equal Protection Clause of the Fourteenth Amendment. Margold urged NAACP lawyers to rely for precedent on *Yick Wo v. Hopkins*, in which the Supreme Court ruled in 1888 that laws that public officials applied to racial minorities "with an evil eye and an unequal hand" violated the Constitution.

Margold advised NAACP leaders that "it would be a great mistake to fritter away our limited funds on sporadic attempts to force the making of equal divisions of school funds in the few instances where such attempts might be expected to succeed." This approach would force civil rights lawyers to file separate lawsuits in each southern school district, to recruit plaintiffs in each district who had the courage and fortitude to face hostility from whites and delays in court, and to perform the laborious task of digging out the facts of school funding disparities in each case. Even if they succeeded, lawsuits to equalize facilities would require judges to act as school superintendents, checking the quality of textbooks, playgrounds, and lavatories. "And we should be leaving untouched the very essence of the existing evils" of segregation, Margold warned. "On the other hand," he wrote, "if we boldly challenge the constitutional validity of segregation if and when accompanied irremediably by discrimination, we can strike directly at the most prolific sources of discrimination."

The "Margold Report" became a bible for Thurgood Marshall and his legal staff. But they did not read it literally as commanding a frontal attack on elementary and secondary school segregation in the Deep South. Such an approach would have sent Marshall's troops on a suicide mission. The notion of little black boys rubbing knees with little white girls was unthinkable in the 1930s. Marshall decided instead to mount a flanking attack on the Old Confederacy, beginning with graduate education in border states. This campaign, if successful, would establish legal precedent for a final assault on the citadel of segregation, grade schools in the Deep South.

Marshall's strategy of encirclement won its first major victory in 1938 over the University of Missouri, which excluded blacks from its law school. Lloyd Gaines was denied admission because he was black, just as Thurgood Marshall had been turned away in Maryland. University officials agreed to pay his tuition if Gaines attended law school in another state, but he demanded admission in Missouri. The NAACP filed suit in state court against the university's registrar, whose last name was Canada; the Missouri supreme court ruled against Gaines, and the Supreme Court accepted his appeal.

Chief Justice Hughes wrote for the Court in *Gaines v. Canada*, holding that Missouri could not give whites a legal education in the state and deny blacks that right. Hughes cited *Yick Wo* for support on this issue, calling that decision "the pivot upon which the case turns." But he then let Missouri off the hook. Hughes cited *Plessy* in holding that states could provide black and white law students with "equal facilities in separate schools" without violating the Constitution. Missouri promptly established a black law school, but Lloyd Gaines never showed up for classes and his case ended with a Pyrrhic victory for NAACP lawyers.

World War II interrupted the NAACP campaign against segregated education, and ten years separated the *Gaines* decision from the next graduate school case. Ada Lois Sipuel graduated with honors from Oklahoma's State College for Negroes and applied in 1946 to the state's all-white law school. She was denied admission and promised that a black law school with "substantially equal" facilities would soon be established. Thurgood Marshall argued for Ada Sipuel in the Supreme Court on January 8, 1948. This was an easy case for the justices. Four days later, they unanimously ordered Oklahoma to provide her a legal education "as soon as it does for applicants of any other group." The Court's brief and unsigned opinion cited the *Gaines* decision as precedent. Missouri had opened a real law school for blacks, although it was certainly not equal to the all-white school. Oklahoma took a different tack, roping off a section of the state capitol and calling it a law school. This pretend school had no library and no faculty, and Ada Sipuel refused to be a pretend student.

Thurgood Marshall returned to the Supreme Court in *Sipuel v. Oklahoma Board of Regents* and argued, for the first time, that segregation was flatly unconstitutional. Even if states provided blacks with better schools than whites, he said, separating them by race imposed a "badge of inferiority" on blacks. But 1948 was a presidential election year and the Court shied away from this divisive issue. Over the dissents of Justices Frank Murphy and Wiley Rutledge, the Court sent the *Sipuel* case back to state court for hearings on whether Oklahoma's pretend law school was equal to its real, all-white school. Marshall called Dean Erwin Griswold of Harvard Law School as a witness, but the state judges covered their ears and ruled against Ada Sipuel. By 1949, after Harry Truman returned to the White House with a surprising upset of Thomas Dewey, Oklahoma officials wearied of legal battle and admitted Ada Sipuel to its real law school.

The NAACP victories in the *Gaines* and *Sipuel* cases did nothing to end public school segregation in the Deep South. They did not topple *Plessy* or destroy the "separate but equal" doctrine. They did not even force the admission of blacks into all-white schools; Oklahoma legislators, not the state's judges, ended segregation at the university level. But these cases gave civil rights lawyers a powerful weapon for the battles that lay head. The *Gaines* decision established, and *Sipuel* echoed, the principle that states must furnish blacks with educational facilities "substantially equal" in quality to those afforded whites. Given the vast disparity in funding between black and white schools, virtually no chance existed that separate schools would ever approach equality. In 1940, the average yearly expenditure in southern states for black children was $21.40, less than half the $50.14 spent on whites. Bridging this gap would cost each state millions of dollars, and white lawmakers were not willing to spend that much on black children.

Between 1948 and 1950, civil rights lawyers and leaders debated their options in challenging segregation at the elementary and secondary level: they could file suits to equalize school expenditures, or mount an attack on segregation itself. During this time, two more graduate school cases—from Texas and Oklahoma—moved slowly through the lower courts. Thurgood Marshall viewed these cases as the last skirmishes before the final assault on public school segregation in the Deep South. He offered lawmakers in Texas and Oklahoma a last chance to make separate university facilities equal in every respect. This alternative to integration would impose a crushing financial burden on southern states. In Texas, for example, the physical plant of the state's white universities was valued at $72 million, those for blacks at $4 million. Whites could choose from 106 fields of study, blacks from only forty-nine (including carpeting and mattress making). The white libraries owned 750,000 volumes, the black schools just 82,000. Complying with *Plessy* would cost the Jim Crow states hundreds of millions of dollars at the university level, and billions more for elementary and secondary schools. Hoping to evade the equally unpleasant choices of integration or bankruptcy, university officials in Texas and Oklahoma tried different approaches in the *Sweatt* and *McLaurin* cases.

Heman Marion Sweatt, a black postal worker, had applied to the University of Texas Law School in 1946 and was rejected on racial grounds. After NAACP lawyers filed suit against state officials, Texas judges gave the university six months to offer Sweatt a legal education "substantially equivalent" to that provided whites. Charles T. McCormick, dean of the all-white law school, quickly offered plans for an all-black school. It would occupy four basement rooms in an Austin office building, it would have no library, and it would employ three part-time instructors. McCormick would also serve as the new school's dean. Marshall promptly challenged these plans, and state judges ordered a second hearing, at which McCormick testified under oath that the two law schools were equal in quality. The Texas judges agreed that four rooms for blacks equaled the massive building in which 850 white students took classes. Marshall filed an appeal with the Supreme Court that invited the justices—including Tom Clark, an alumnus of the Austin law school—to look for themselves at the two schools and decide whether Dean McCormick had testified truthfully.

George McLaurin applied in 1948 to the University of Oklahoma's graduate education school. Then in his sixties, McLaurin had taught for decades in black public schools; he held a master's degree and now sought a doctorate. The Supreme Court had ruled in January 1948 that Oklahoma must offer Ada Sipuel a legal education "as soon at it does" for any white applicant. Rather than build a new school for blacks, officials in the Sooner State admitted her to the white law school. They also admitted George McLaurin to the white graduate school. But his "equal" education came with conditions. University officials decided to teach the longtime teacher a lesson. He could not sit in classrooms, but could listen to lectures from a hallway seat, next to a sign that read "Reserved for Colored." He could study at a "colored" desk on the library's mezzanine, but not in the reading room. He could eat at a "colored" table in the cafeteria, but only after white students finished their meals. NAACP lawyers challenged these demeaning conditions as "badges of slavery" imposed on McLaurin, but they lost the first two rounds in lower federal courts.

While the *Sweatt* and *McLaurin* cases moved slowly through courts in Texas and Oklahoma, another trio of cases reached the Supreme Court in record time. These cases all raised challenges to restrictive covenants in housing, a method of enforcing residential segregation in many cities, north and south. These covenants, part of the property deed, typically barred the sale or leasing of housing to blacks, Jews, or Asians, depending on the property owner's prejudices. Restrictive covenants were supposedly "private contracts" between buyers and sellers, binding subsequent purchasers to their terms. Entire neighborhoods in some cities were covered by covenants signed by most or all property owners.

Two white neighbors in the District of Columbia, who had both signed covenants barring sales to blacks, got into a legal squabble in 1924 when one sold her home to a black woman. Ruling in 1926, the Supreme Court held in *Corrigan v. Buckley* that the Constitution did not prevent "private individuals from entering into contracts respecting the control and disposition of their own property." The Court disclaimed any opinion on whether such covenants violated the Fifth or Fourteenth Amendment, holding only that judicial enforcement of the covenants did not constitute "state action" in such private suits.

Two decades later, civil rights lawyers decided to launch another attack on restrictive covenants. The growing black migration to northern cities had created a demand for decent housing, but covenants excluded blacks from many neighborhoods. The Supreme Court, now dominated by "liberal" justices, seemed receptive to arguments based on Fifth and Fourteenth Amendment claims. Thurgood Marshall convened a meeting in July 1945 of lawyers interested in housing issues. He proposed bringing suits in several states, forcing the Supreme Court to accept one or more cases for decision. One lawyer at the conference, George L. Vaughn of St. Louis, predicted success in his city because "the Negro vote played such an important part in the election of judges" sympathetic to civil rights.

Shortly after Vaughn returned to St. Louis, he learned that J. D. Shelley had been served with an eviction notice by Louis Kraemer. Shelley, a Mississippi native who had joined the black migration to northern cities in the 1930s, worked in a munitions factory in St. Louis during World War II. He and his wife, Ethel, put aside a little money each month, hoping to move with their six children from a crowded apartment in the city's black ghetto into their own home. Their pastor, Robert Bishop, was also a real-estate agent and a friend of George Vaughn's. Bishop found the Shelleys a yellow-brick house on Labadie Avenue, a tree-shaded street in the Grande Prairie neighborhood. Most of the neighbors were white, but the Shelley kids made friends and people were friendly. However, Louis and Fern Kraemer, who lived ten blocks away, were not friendly to J. D. and Ethel Shelley. The Kraemers sent a process server to their doorstep with a court summons, which informed the Shelleys that their property deed included a covenant, recorded in 1911, barring ownership or occupancy of any house on their block "by people of the Negro or Mongolian Race."

Reverend Bishop related the Shelleys' legal plight to George Vaughn, who was delighted to find a client and took the case without fee. Judge William Koerner presided at the trial in October 1945 and asked Ethel Shelley, when she took the stand, if she knew "why you have been sued and why you are here." She certainly did know. "Well, I understand the white people didn't want me back." Vaughn claimed the covenant had never been enforceable because nine of the thirty-nine owners on the block in 1911 had not signed the document; he also noted that five houses on the block had been occupied by blacks, going back to 1882. The covenant's purpose, to keep *any* blacks from living on the block, had never been met. Vaughn also argued that judicial enforcement of the covenant would violate the federal Civil Rights Act of 1866, which extended to newly emancipated blacks the same right to buy and sell real property "as is enjoyed by white citizens."

Judge Koerner's ruling justified Vaughn's prediction of judicial sympathy in St. Louis. He based his decision on a single point. The covenant was intended to bind property owners on Labadie Avenue only if "all the landowners should sign." Because nine had not signed in 1911, and black families had lived on the block for many years, Koerner refused to enforce the covenant against the Shelleys. But the Missouri supreme court reversed his judgment in December 1946. Judge James Douglas held that the covenant was intended "to cover only the property of those owners who signed it." The original signatories knew that blacks lived on the block and "it must have been their intention to prevent greatly increased occupancy by negroes." Judge Douglas also cited the *Corrigan* case in ruling that judicial enforcement of restrictive covenants did not constitute "state action" under the Fourteenth Amendment.

During 1946, judges in Michigan and the District of Columbia also rejected attacks on restrictive covenants in cases brought by NAACP lawyers. Thurgood Marshall still wanted to bring appeals to the Supreme Court, but he also wanted to present the justices with evidence on "the economic and social aspects of race restrictive covenants," which was lacking in the three cases already decided. He called another meeting in January 1947 and urged civil rights lawyers to begin another case, with testimony by prominent social scientists. George Vaughn, who did not attend this meeting, upset Marshall's cautious strategy by filing a Supreme Court appeal in *Shelley v. Kraemer* in April 1947. This move upset Marshall, who quickly rushed the Michigan and District of Columbia cases along; the Court agreed to hear all the appeals in January 1948.

Marshall did manage to prepare a brief with material on the impact of restrictive covenants on housing segregation; he also enlisted fifteen amicus groups, including Jewish, Protestant, Japanese American, Native American, labor, and fraternal organizations. The Truman administration also filed a brief arguing that federal efforts to "clear and replace slum areas" were hindered by racial covenants, which deprived "minority racial groups" of access to decent housing. Marshall hoped to impress the Court with the broad coalition against racial and religious covenants.

The Court was impressed. George Vaughn gave a powerful oration in the *Shelley* case, telling the justices that his father had been born into slavery and that Congress had passed the Civil Rights Act in 1866 to give blacks like his father the right to own property on an equal basis with whites. Vaughn ended with a shout that startled the justices. "The Negro knocks at America's door," he thundered, "and cries out: 'Let me come in and sit by the fire. I helped build the house.'" Thurgood Marshall and Solicitor General Philip Perlman spoke in quieter words for the NAACP and the federal government.

Only six justices heard the arguments and voted in *Shelley* and its companion cases, decided on May 3, 1948. The Court's official report stated blandly that Stanley Reed, Robert Jackson, and Wiley Rutledge "took no part in the consideration or decision of these cases." They most likely held property covered by restrictive covenants and felt that voting would pose a conflict of interests. Chief Justice Fred Vinson wrote for the remaining justices. Property owners had the right to adopt restrictive covenants, he said, but they could not ask the courts to enforce them. "The Constitution confers on no individual the right to demand action by the State which results in the denial of equal protection of the laws to other individuals," Vinson asserted. In effect, the Court created in *Shelley* an exception to the old legal maxim that there exists "no right without a remedy." The Kraemers had no legal remedy for their right to dislike the Shelleys.

The Supreme Court decided the *Shelley* case just after the Democratic national convention, at which most delegates from the former Confederate states bolted from their party over its strong civil rights plank. The defecting Dixiecrats formed the States' Rights Party and chose Senator Strom Thurmond of South Carolina to carry the segregationist banner against Harry Truman in 1948; Thurmond won close to a million votes and almost cost Truman his narrow victory over Republican Thomas Dewey. One of Thurmond's supporters, Mississippi congressman John Rankin, thundered on the House floor that "there must have been a celebration in Moscow" when the Court struck down racial covenants. There was certainly a celebration at 4600 Labadie Avenue in St. Louis. Ethel Shelley expressed her reaction to news that her family could keep their new home: "My little soul is overjoyed. I'll tell the Lord of my thankfulness."

The graduate school cases of Heman Sweatt and George McLaurin finally reached the Supreme Court for argument in April 1950. The NAACP's briefs in both cases offered the justices a choice: they could order states to equalize school funding, or they could overrule *Plessy* and rule that racial segregation violated the Constitution. The Court's decisions would help NAACP lawyers determine their strategy in school cases from the Deep South. Perhaps the time was near for the final assault on segregation.

Thurgood Marshall argued for Heman Sweatt, and his young NAACP assistant counsel, Robert L. Carter, for George McLaurin. Both lawyers urged the Court to overrule the *Plessy* decision. Marshall pointed out the physical inequality of the separate Texas law schools, but he focused on the issue of racial segregation. "They can build an exact duplicate but if it is segregated, it is unequal," he said. The attorneys general of the eleven former Confederate states filed an amicus brief that dropped any pretense of legal argument. Southern whites, they warned the justices, do not "want their women folk in intimate social contact with Negro men." Enforcing this taboo required segregation at every educational level, from kindergarten to graduate school.

The justices declined Marshall's appeal to overrule *Plessy*, and they ignored the southern appeal to sexual fears. Chief Justice Vinson wrote for a unanimous Court in both cases. His opinion in *Sweatt v. Painter* accepted Marshall's invitation to look closely at the Texas law schools, white and black. After comparing their facilities, Vinson found it "difficult to believe that one who had a free choice between these law schools would consider the question close." The answer depended not only on factors like books and buildings, he added, but also on "those qualities which are incapable of measurement but which make for greatness in a law school." The black school could not match the "reputation of the faculty" and "influence of the alumni" that added to the "rich traditions and prestige" of the white school. The Court ordered that Heman Sweatt "be admitted to the University of Texas Law School" without delay.

George McLaurin had already been admitted to the University of Oklahoma graduate education school. The only question in his case, Vinson wrote in *McLaurin v. Oklahoma State Regents*, stemmed from his separation from other students in the classroom, library, and cafeteria. "Such restrictions impair and inhibit his ability to study, to engage in discussions and exchange views with other students, and, in general, to learn his profession," Vinson concluded. McLaurin "must receive the same treatment at the hands of the state as students of other races," the Court instructed his instructors. The "colored" signs came down, and McLaurin finally taught the university a lesson.

The Supreme Court handed down its *Sweatt* and *McLaurin* decisions on June 5, 1950. Twenty days later, North Korean soldiers crossed the 38th parallel to invade South Korea. The Cold War suddenly turned hot. American troops joined the United Nations "police action" in Korea and pushed the North Koreans back into their own territory, almost to the Yalu River border with Communist China. General Douglas MacArthur, who commanded the American military forces, promised they would be home for Christmas. But he could not keep that promise, as Chinese "volunteers" poured across the Yalu River and forced MacArthur's troops down the bloody peninsula in disordered retreat.

The rout of American forces in Korea took place as the Supreme Court heard arguments in a case that threatened a retreat from First Amendment values. This case, *Dennis v. United States*, began in July 1948 with the federal indictment of twelve Communist Party leaders for conspiring to "teach and advocate the overthrow and destruction of the government of the United States by force and violence." Eugene Dennis, the party's general secretary, headed the list of defendants, which included most of the party's national committee. They were charged with violating the Alien Registration Act of 1940, better known as the Smith Act after its House sponsor, Howard Smith of Virginia. Congress decided to punish American Communists for backing the Hitler-Stalin pact of 1939, which created the "unholy alliance" of German Nazis and Soviet Communists while France and England fought for their lives against Hitler's forces. The Smith Act made it unlawful to advocate "the propriety of overthrowing or destroying any government in the United States by force and violence." The law also punished those who organized any group that advocated revolution or circulated literature with such advocacy.

Ironically, after Germany invaded Russia in June 1941, American Communists had dropped their red banners and loyally waved the Stars and Stripes. They did not even field a candidate against President Roosevelt in 1944, and they vocally supported the "people's war" against fascism. In fact, the Communist Party disbanded in 1944, becoming the "Communist Political Association" with a platform of peaceful social change. The former revolutionaries now sounded like a left-wing American Legion. But in 1945, as the Soviets began pulling an "Iron Curtain" across Europe, American Communists heeded orders from Moscow and brought their party and its red flags out of mothballs. The party's newspaper, the *Daily Worker*, now bristled with denunciations of President Truman and his "saber-rattling" foreign policies. With the 1948 elections approaching, Truman actually welcomed the party's hostility; Democrats had lost control of Congress in 1946 and wanted to deflect Republican charges they were "soft on communism." Attorney General Tom Clark privately doubted that American Communists posed a "clear and present danger" of revolution, but he approved their prosecution after Truman launched his reelection campaign.

The case against Eugene Dennis and his fellow Communists resembled the earlier prosecution of left-wing propagandist Benjamin Gitlow, whose conviction for violating New York's "criminal anarchy" law was based solely on his distribution of literature calling for "proletarian revolution" against the "capitalist state." No evidence connected Gitlow to any concrete plans to instigate an insurrection at any time, but the Supreme Court ruled in 1925 that his "utterances" endangered "the security of the State" and threatened "ultimate revolution." Very few of the "utterances" for which the government prosecuted Eugene Dennis and his comrades came from their mouths or pens; Justice Department lawyers based their case largely on the words of foreign revolutionaries who had never set foot in the United States. The bulk of the government's evidence, in fact, came from the writings of Karl Marx, Vladimir Lenin, and Joseph Stalin, published between 1848 and 1929.

The trial of the American Communists began in March 1949 at the federal courthouse in New York City. Outside the Foley Square judicial fortress, pickets chanted, "Hey judge, we won't budge, until the twelve are free." Inside the courtroom, Judge Harold Medina presided over his first criminal trial; his short temper and obvious sympathy for the prosecution sparked outbursts from defense lawyers and prompted reporters to call the trial "the Battle of Foley Square." Prosecutors asked the jurors, carefully screened by FBI agents for loyalty, to connect the Communist Party leaders with the Soviet government. Given the American party's membership in the Communist International, which was headquartered in Moscow, this proved an easy task.

Prosecutors had a harder time showing that the defendants themselves advocated "force and violence" against the American government. Judge Medina helped out by ruling that because Lenin and Stalin had advocated "the violent shattering of the capitalist states," circulating their writings showed that American Communists were "basically committed to the overthrow of the Government of the United States" by violent means. But the writings of Lenin and

Stalin conflicted with the American party's 1945 constitution, subjecting any member who conspired or acted to overthrow "the institutions of American democracy" to immediate expulsion. Medina allowed Louis Budenz, a former *Daily Worker* editor and now the government's prize witness, to tell jurors that such "Aesopian" language was merely "window dressing asserted for protective purposes" against Smith Act prosecutions. Medina's ruling placed the defendants in a Catch-22 dilemma: their disavowal of revolutionary acts proved their intention to commit them. The judge virtually instructed jurors to disregard the protestations of defense witnesses that the party's constitution meant exactly what it said.

When the Foley Square trial concluded in October 1949, Medina instructed jurors that all they needed to convict the defendants was "language" in Communist literature showing the party's intention to overthrow the government "as speedily as circumstances would permit." They could infer that intention from the words of Marx, Lenin, and Stalin, even though the defendants had denied endorsing their calls for violent revolution. The jurors worked speedily as well; after hearing eight months of testimony, they deliberated just eight hours before returning guilty verdicts against eleven Communist leaders (William Z. Foster, the party's elderly chairman, had his case severed for health reasons). Judge Medina imposed five-year sentences on all but one defendant, who had won the Distinguished Service Cross for heroism in the South Pacific and received a three-year term in reward. For good measure, Medina sentenced five party lawyers to jail terms for contempt of court, getting the last word in his courtroom arguments.

Eugene Dennis and his fellow Communists, now branded as felons by Judge Medina, asked a federal appellate panel to reverse their convictions on First Amendment grounds. Three judges of the Second Circuit Court of Appeals, all elderly Republicans appointed by President Calvin Coolidge, heard the case in June 1950. Even before argument began, Judges Harrie Chase and Thomas Swan made clear their hostility toward the defendants, refusing them permission to travel outside New York to make speeches and raise funds for their appeal. Chase denounced the "shocking" idea of letting the Communists "try their cause in public." Swan commented sourly that he was prepared to "have all the oral argument we can stomach." In a highly unusual move, armed guards were stationed outside the courthouse and inside the courtroom.

With two votes almost certainly against them, lawyers for the Communists—themselves under sentence for contempt—viewed the hearing as a trial run for the Supreme Court. But they hoped for a dissent by Judge Learned Hand, who had ruled in 1917 that governments could only punish direct incitement to criminal acts. Hand had argued with Justice Holmes over this issue in 1919, and lost when Holmes devised the "clear and present danger" test in his *Schenck* opinion. Hand did not agree with Holmes that leaflets against the World War I draft posed much danger to military recruitment, but the prospect of nuclear war in 1950 was a real danger in his mind. Hand expressed his fears in writing for the Second Circuit panel in the *Dennis* case. "We must not close our eyes to our position in the world," he cautioned. Citing the Berlin airlift of 1949, Hand warned that any border flare-up or diplomatic incident might spark warfare. "We do not understand how one could ask for a more probable danger," he concluded.

Still uneasy about the "clear and present danger" test, Hand devised his own First Amendment formula. Judges must ask, he wrote, "whether the gravity of the 'evil,' discounted by its improbability, justifies such invasion of free speech as is necessary to avoid the danger." Like an algebraic equation, the answer in each case depended upon the value assigned to each factor. The danger in *Schenck* was disruption of military recruitment in Philadelphia, while the danger in *Dennis* was violent overthrow of the national government. Totting up his mental calculations, Hand concluded that the "gravity" of revolution far outweighed the "improbability" that American Communists might overthrow the government.

The *Dennis* appeal reached the Supreme Court at a bad time for the defendants. Arguments began on December 4, 1950; that morning's headlines read, "Enemy Is Closing on Pyongyang" and "Scorched Earth Aids Chinese Korean Drive." Against this backdrop of grim news, First Amendment appeals seemed unlikely to sway justices who read the newspapers. Conceding their clients' sympathy for the Soviet Union, lawyers for the American Communists defended their right to voice their political views. Upholding the Second Circuit decision "would merely be a confession of our unwillingness to take the risk of permitting political dissent to be heard," they wrote. "This is a suppression of the democratic process itself."

Government lawyers replied that Soviet-sponsored "aggression and disruption" around the world created a clear and present danger from domestic Communists. "Recent events in Korea" provided evidence of this danger, as did Communist participation in "such overt activities as sabotage and espionage" carried out "to assist the Soviet Union and its policies." But the government's brief offered no evidence of such acts; requiring proof that Communists were plotting insurrection, its authors stated, "would mean that the First Amendment protects their preparations until they are ready to attempt a seizure of power, or to act as a fifth column in time of crisis."

The oral arguments on both sides offered the justices more rhetoric than reflection. Speaking for the defendants, Abraham Isserman warned that upholding the Smith Act might prompt the government to prosecute "the 500,000 Americans who, according to J. Edgar Hoover, do the bidding of the Communist party." He pointed to Senator Joseph McCarthy, the Red-hunting Wisconsin Republican whose charges that Communists "were shaping the policy of the

State Department" sent tremors around the country. "Already men in high places have suffered from McCarthyism," Isserman told the Court. He might have looked at Justice Frankfurter, whose former law clerk, Dean Acheson, was now secretary of state and McCarthy's prime target. Solicitor General Philip Perlman, who had supported the NAACP in the *Shelley* and *Sweatt* cases, spoke for the government in *Dennis*. "When Justices Holmes and Brandeis talked about 'clear and present danger,' " he said, "they were thinking about isolated agitators, not about these tightly organized, rigidly disciplined people, operating under orders from a foreign country."

The Supreme Court decided the *Dennis* case on June 4, 1951. Six justices voted to uphold the convictions and the Smith Act. President Roosevelt's three most conservative judicial nominees—Felix Frankfurter, Stanley Reed, and Robert Jackson—joined three of Truman's four conservatives—Fred Vinson, Harold Burton, and Sherman Minton. Justice Tom Clark, who had reluctantly approved the prosecutions as attorney general, took no part in the decision. Hugo Black and William Douglas, the Court's First Amendment absolutists, wrote separate but equally pointed dissents.

Chief Justice Vinson spoke for only three other justices in writing for the Court; Frankfurter and Jackson each wrote concurrences that avoided Vinson's warm embrace of the "clear and present danger" test. Vinson had been reading the newspapers, and reports of "world crisis after crisis" alarmed him. Borrowing the "fire" metaphor that Justice Holmes first kindled in *Schenck* and Justice Sanford adopted in *Gitlow*, Vinson considered "the inflammable nature of world conditions" ample grounds for upholding the convictions. He conceded that it was "impossible to measure" the probability of revolution, or "the immediacy of a successful attempt," but this did not trouble Vinson. He endorsed Judge Medina's ruling that American Communists would attempt revolution "as speedily as circumstances would permit." Party leaders would order an armed insurrection "when they thought the time was ripe."

Vinson gave a broad definition to the terms in the "clear and present danger" test. "Obviously, the words cannot mean that before the Government may act, it must wait until the putsch is about to be executed, the plans have been laid and the signal is awaited." Vinson's thinly veiled reference to the failed Nazi uprising against the German government in 1923, which started in a Munich beer hall, was intended to support his claim that "an attempt to overthrow the Government by force, even though doomed from the outset because of inadequate numbers or power of revolutionists, is a sufficient evil for Congress to prevent." Presumably, Communists who gathered in beer halls near the party's New York headquarters were plotting to storm City Hall. The Communist leaders were "properly and constitutionally convicted for violation of the Smith Act," Vinson concluded.

Justice Frankfurter, however, expected more from Vinson than uncritical endorsement of the Smith Act, making clear in concurrence his distaste for the law. Nonetheless, as in the earlier flag-salute cases, Frankfurter performed his judicial "duty" and deferred to the "reasonable" judgment of Congress. "It is not for us to decide how we would adjust the clash of interests which this case presents," he wrote. The question marks that punctuated Frankfurter's opinion underscored his doubts that the Communists had been "properly" convicted.

Hugo Black had no doubts in the *Dennis* case. The Smith Act "is a virulent form of prior censorship of speech and press, which I believe the First Amendment forbids," he replied. Black stressed that the Communist leaders "were not charged with any overt acts of any kind designed to overthrow the Government," but had been convicted solely for their speech. Black rejected both the "clear and present danger" test and Frankfurter's "reasonableness" test of legislation challenged on First Amendment grounds. "Public opinion being what it is now," Black lamented, "few will protest the conviction of these Communist petitioners." But he expressed hope that "in calmer times, when present pressures, passions, and fears subside, this or some later Court will restore the First Amendment liberties to the high preferred place where they belong in a free society."

The passions and fears of the Cold War period subsided very slowly. Senator Joseph McCarthy made the fatal mistake of shifting his target from the State Department to the Pentagon. His charges of Red cells on army bases evaporated on national television, and the Senate censured him in December 1954 for his abusive conduct. McCarthy faded from view and died of alcoholism in 1957, but "McCarthyism" survived in the House Committee on Un-American Activities and the Senate Internal Security Subcommittee, until Congress finally abolished these Cold War relics in the 1970s.

The Supreme Court has never overruled *Dennis*, but later decisions have robbed it of any vitality. One month after Joe McCarthy died, the Court reversed the convictions of twelve "second-rank" Communist leaders. Justice John Marshall Harlan, grandson of the sole *Plessy* dissenter, wrote in *Yates v. United States* that the Smith Act was directed at "the advocacy of action, not ideas." The government offered no evidence the *Yates* defendants had advocated revolutionary action. Even Justice Frankfurter joined Harlan's opinion, confessing to friends that Senator McCarthy's bully-boy tactics had sickened him. But the Smith Act remains on the books and "lies about like a loaded weapon," to borrow the words of Justice Robert Jackson in his *Korematsu* dissent. Congress has not yet mustered the courage to finally disarm this dangerous law.

29

"Give Me the

Colored Doll"

The long road to the Supreme Court for black children began in Clarendon County, South Carolina, on July 28, 1947. Their journey ended on May 17, 1954, with the momentous ruling in *Brown v. Board of Education of Topeka, Kansas*. During this seven-year period, five cases that challenged racial segregation in public schools moved through the courts in four states and the District of Columbia. Oliver Brown, acting as "next friend" of his eight-year-old daughter Linda, was the first of twelve plaintiffs in the Topeka lawsuit that made his last name the best known in American constitutional history. But the *Brown* case was not the first that Thurgood Marshall and his staff of NAACP lawyers filed against school segregation. That distinction went to a suit against school officials in rural South Carolina; Harry Briggs, Sr., the "next friend" of his nine-year-old son Harry Jr., was the first of twenty plaintiffs in *Briggs v. Elliott*.

Only a handful of Americans recognize the name of Harry Briggs, Jr., yet students in every American school read about Linda Brown and the landmark case brought on her behalf. A quirk of court scheduling put the *Brown* case before *Briggs* on the Supreme Court docket when the five school cases were combined for argument and decision. This historical accident has no real significance, but it reminds us that history reflects many accidents of time and place. The deeper forces of social change, however, move with little regard to names and dates. It does not really matter which name—Oliver Brown or Harry Briggs—appears in the caption of the school cases. What matters is that both men challenged their children's segregation at a time when the Court was finally ready to confront the "separate but equal" doctrine of the *Plessy* decision.

Thurgood Marshall had several good reasons for picking Clarendon County as the first target in his final assault on school segregation. First, segregation in the Deep South was deeply rooted in the region's laws and customs; it stemmed from three centuries of slavery and Jim Crow discrimination. Second, NAACP lawyers could easily document the enormous disparities between Clarendon County's black and white schools to point up the utter hypocrisy of "separate but equal" and its defenders. Third, Marshall wanted to acknowledge the courage of black parents who stood up for their children in a citadel of segregation like South Carolina, where politicians like Governor Strom Thurmond pandered to racial bigots. These are also good reasons for looking more closely at Clarendon County than at Topeka in following the school cases to the Supreme Court.

Located on the flat plain between the swampy lowlands along the Atlantic coast and the rolling Piedmont hills in the west, Clarendon County in 1947 had some 32,000 residents, more than 70 percent of them black. All but a few black families lived on farms, but few owned their land. They raised cotton and worked as sharecroppers for white owners. More than two thirds of the black families earned less than a thousand dollars each year; more than a third of all blacks over ten could not read or write. Black children attended sixty-one ramshackle schools, most without plumbing or electricity. The county spent $179 for each white child in public school, but only $43 for each black child.

On the surface, blacks and whites got along well in Clarendon County. "We got a good bunch of nigras here," said David McClary, who owned the biggest feed and livestock business in the county. "Colored have made wonderful progress down here," echoed H. C. Carrigan, the twelve-term mayor of Summerton, a town of one thousand. "I have several farms, and they all have Negroes on them. I sharecrop with them, and they are all as happy as can be." But not all the county's blacks were happy. "Oh, there was a lot goin' on that we didn't like," said Joseph Richburg, a black teacher, "but everything was fine on the face of it, so long as we kept saying, 'Yes, sir' and 'No, sir' and tipping our hat."

One black man in Clarendon county did not tip his hat to whites. The Rev. J. A. DeLaine, pastor of the African Methodist Episcopal church in Summerton, also taught in a rural black school. His students walked to school along dirt roads, their clothes spattered with dust or mud by school buses that carried white children past them. The lack of buses for black children bothered DeLaine. During the summer of 1947, he attended a speech in Columbia, the state capital, by the Rev. James Hinton, president of the state's NAACP chapters. Hinton told his listeners that South Carolina's black schools were a disgrace, and would improve only if they forced whites to make them better. Hinton suggested they start with buses. And he challenged his audience. "No teacher or preacher in South Carolina has the courage," he charged, "to find a plaintiff to challenge the legality of the discriminatory bus-transportation practices of this state."

J. A. DeLaine took the challenge. The first Sunday after returning to Summerton, he visited Levi Pearson, a black farmer with three children at the Scott's

Branch high school, nine miles from their home. Pearson owned his farm and was known for standing up to whites. He listened to DeLaine and agreed to stand up for his kids. DeLaine then drove back to Columbia and visited Harold Boulware, the state's only black civil rights lawyer. He returned to Summerton with a two-page petition, which Levi Pearson signed. DeLaine then visited another preacher, the Rev. L. B. McCord, a Presbyterian pastor and the county's school superintendent. The two men knew each other well. "I was one of McCord's good niggers," DeLaine said. But not after their meeting on July 28. The black teacher handed the white superintendent Pearson's petition, demanding bus transportation "for use of the said children of your Petitioner and other Negro school children similarly situated." McCord read it and told DeLaine the county had no money for buses for black children.

After this rebuff, Harold Boulware wrote the school board that Levi Pearson had retained his legal services and asked for a hearing on his petition. He got no answer to this or subsequent letters. Finally, on March 16, 1948, Boulware filed suit in federal court, seeking an injunction to bar Clarendon County officials from making any "distinction on account of race or color" in busing children to school. But the case was dismissed in June 1948 because Pearson's farm straddled the line between two school districts; he paid property taxes in one and his children attended school in another.

Levi Pearson paid for his stand; every white-owned bank and store cut off his credit and no white farmer would rent him a harvester. His crops rotted in the field that fall. Whites told him to forget about buses, and finally gave him credit for next year's crops. But he could not forget his children's inferior schools. The next spring, in March 1949, Harold Boulware summoned Pearson and DeLaine to Columbia to meet another civil rights lawyer. Thurgood Marshall had come from New York to South Carolina, looking for plaintiffs willing to ask for more than buses. Marshall proposed a new lawsuit, demanding equal treatment in every area: buildings, teachers, books, and buses. The NAACP lawyer told Pearson and DeLaine that he wanted at least twenty plaintiffs, to spread the risk of retaliation. And he wanted Clarendon County, to expose the myth of "separate but equal" in South Carolina's most unequal county.

It took Pearson and DeLaine eight months to find twenty black parents willing to challenge the county's white power structure. They got the last signature on November 11, 1949, and took the list to Boulware. He drafted a complaint and put names on the caption in alphabetical order. The first was Harry Briggs, a navy veteran with five children; his oldest boy was Harry Jr., whose name appeared first among the black children. Harry Sr. pumped gas and fixed cars at Mayor Carrigan's Sinclair station in Summerton, and his wife, Liza, worked as a motel chambermaid. The same day he got the twenty names, Boulware drove to the federal courthouse in Charleston and filed the complaint—listing himself and Thurgood Marshall as counsel—in *Briggs v. Elliott*; the first defendant was Roderick Elliott, the county school board chairman.

Word spread quickly in Clarendon County that "nigras" had sued the school board. Virtually every plaintiff paid a heavy price for joining the suit. Mayor Carrigan fired Harry Briggs, and the motel fired his wife. Bo Stukes lost his garage job; James Brown was fired by a trucking company; John McDonald, a combat veteran of Iwo Jima and Okinawa, lost his credit for farm equipment; and Lee Richardson had his farm mortgage foreclosed. Even Harry Briggs's cow got arrested for stepping on a headstone in a white cemetery. Whites laughed at that little comedy, but blacks in Clarendon County found no humor in the spiteful response to their lawsuit.

May 24, 1951, is one of those unremembered dates that marks a significant event. On that hot spring day in Clarendon County, Kenneth B. Clark visited the Scott's Branch school near Summerton and met with sixteen black children between six and nine years old. He came with a box of four dolls, each about a foot high and dressed in diapers. Two dolls were boys and two were girls. They differed in one other way: two were pink and two were brown. One by one, Clark sat down with the youngsters and gave them instructions: "Give me the white doll." "Give me the colored doll." "Give me the Negro doll." Clark then said, "Give me the doll you like to play with." "Give me the doll that is the nice doll." "Give me the doll that looks bad." "Give me the doll that is a nice color."

Clark made notes of each child's responses. When he tallied them, the results closely matched his findings in similar tests he had conducted in New York City, Philadelphia, Boston, and several Arkansas communities. All sixteen of the Clarendon County black children correctly identified both the white and brown dolls. But ten chose the white doll as the one they wanted to play with; eleven said the brown doll looked "bad" to them; and nine picked the white doll as the "nice" one.

What brought Kenneth Clark from New York to Scott's Branch? Thurgood Marshall had decided to use the *Briggs* case to attack school segregation at its roots: what made the enforced separation of black children from whites most damaging, he felt, was not tattered books and untrained teachers, but the stigma of inferiority that segregation inflicted on black children. School officials could buy newer books and hire better teachers for black children, but they could not erase feelings of inferiority from their minds. Marshall enlisted Clark as an expert witness, hoping that his testimony would make this point. His credentials were impressive. A social psychologist who taught at City College in New York, Clark and his wife, Mamie, also a psychologist, had devised the doll test to study the development of self-images in black children. "We were really disturbed by our findings," Clark later said of his initial studies. "What was surprising was the degree to which the children suffered from self-rejection. I don't think we had quite realized the extent of the cruelty of racism and how hard it hit." The Clarks published an article in 1940 titled "Segregation as a Factor in the Racial

Identification of Negro Pre-School Children" and reported on a decade of follow-up studies at a White House conference in 1950. Thurgood Marshall hoped that federal judges would listen carefully to this eminent scholar.

The *Briggs* case was assigned to federal district judge J. Waties Waring, a scion of Charleston society. Marshall had tailored the case for Judge Waring, certain that he would get a favorable ruling. Born in 1880 into a family that had owned slaves, Waring had slowly turned against segregation. He joined the federal bench in 1941 and shocked fellow members of the upper-crust Charleston Light Dragoons with his judicial rulings. He jailed a white farmer for holding a black man in "peonage" against his will and ruled in 1945 that South Carolina must equalize the salaries of black and white teachers. He also presided in 1946 over the trial of the white police chief who had blinded Isaac Woodward, a black army veteran, with his billy club. "I was shocked by the hypocrisy of my government," Waring later said of the federal prosecutor's failure to call witnesses against the chief. And in 1948, Thurgood Marshall argued before Waring that South Carolina could not exclude blacks from its primary elections. "It is time for South Carolina to rejoin the Union," Waring wrote in ruling for Marshall. For this opinion, he endured burning crosses on his lawn, gunshots at his house, and a large chunk of concrete through his front window. "Unfortunately, the judge was not hit," a rural newspaper lamented.

Unfortunately for Marshall, Waring shared the bench at the *Briggs* trial with two other federal judges. Putting the case before a three-judge panel had been Waring's decision. Marshall had originally sought only equal spending on Clarendon County's schools, but Waring had urged him to amend his complaint and attack South Carolina's segregation laws directly. Federal law then provided that constitutional challenges to state laws would come before three-judge panels. Marshall complied with Waring's initiative, although the outcome of the *Briggs* case was now doubtful. Judge George Timmerman, who sat with Waring on the South Carolina federal bench, was a rabid defender of white supremacy and a sure vote for segregation. The third judge, John Parker of the Fourth Circuit Court of Appeals, had been nominated to the Supreme Court in 1930 by President Hoover, but was rejected by the Senate, largely because he had spoken against black voting. However, Parker had gained the respect of blacks after his defeat and upheld their claims in two important cases Thurgood Marshall had argued before him. Everyone knew the *Briggs* case rested on Parker's vote.

The trial began on May 28, 1951, and opened with a surprise. The school board's lawyer, Robert Figg, admitted to the judges that "inequalities in the facilities, opportunities and curricula in the schools of this district do exist." Figg hoped his concession would "eliminate the necessity of taking a great deal of testimony." He also hoped, quite obviously, that his ploy would keep Marshall's expert witnesses off the stand. Marshall looked stunned, but quickly replied that since his complaint attacked segregation on constitutional grounds, "we must be able to show the inequalities as they actually exist." Fortunately, Judge Parker, who presided, allowed Marshall to continue. He first called L. B. McCord, Clarendon's school superintendent. Marshall asked why the county separated the white and black children. "You would have to ask the children why," McCord replied. "None of them have ever asked me to go to one school or the other." He had trouble with other questions as well, refusing to admit that the county spent less on black children than whites. Roderick Elliott, the first defendant and school board chairman for twenty-five years, could not even identify the district's boundaries or name any schools.

Marshall turned the podium over to Robert Carter, his young but experienced associate. He first called Matthew Whitehead, professor of education at Howard University, who had inspected both white and black schools in Clarendon, armed with Judge Waring's order. Whitehead's report had prompted Robert Figg to concede the obvious inequalities. The white schools all had lunchrooms; none of the black schools did. In one black school "there was not a single desk" for students; "there was a desk for every child" in the white schools. The white schools had indoor toilets; the black schools had outhouses.

Kenneth Clark spent just one hour on the witness stand in the *Briggs* trial. He had never before testified as an expert, but he spoke calmly and confidently. "I was just stating what I had learned over the years," he later recalled. Robert Carter led him through his background and credentials, and Clark outlined his prior research on the self-images of black children. The cumulative effects of discrimination, prejudice, and segregation "have definitely detrimental effects on the personality development of the Negro child," Clark stated. "The essence of this detrimental effect is a confusion in the child's concept of his own self-esteem—basic feelings of inferiority, conflict, confusion in his self-image, resentment, hostility towards himself, hostility towards whites," he continued.

Clark then described his "doll studies" at the Scott's Branch school. "The conclusion which I was forced to reach was that these children in Clarendon County, like other human beings who are subjected to an obviously inferior status in the society in which they live, have been definitely harmed in the development of their personalities," he concluded. Robert Figg hardly bothered with cross-examination; he expressed surprise that Clark had conducted his tests alone with each child. Once the judges knew "that his testimony was based on very few children, that there was no witnesses to the tests," Figg later said, "I didn't press the matter." His final comment showed how badly Figg misjudged Clark's testimony: "Nobody took it seriously."

Three years would pass before the American people learned how seriously the Supreme Court took Kenneth Clark's testimony. Meanwhile, the three judges who heard it met to decide the case. Robert Figg had conceded the inequality of Clarendon County's schools at the trial. Judge Parker had asked him what decree the court should issue "in the light of your admissions." Figg asked in return for "a reasonable time" to draw up plans to equalize the black and white schools. Judge Parker issued the panel's decision on June 23, 1951. Writing for himself and Judge Timmerman, Parker gave the defendants six months to report back on progress toward that goal. He also denied the plaintiff's motion to declare school segregation unconstitutional. Parker did not consider the *Sweatt* and *McLaurin* decisions relevant to public schools, where "the thought of establishing professional contacts does not enter into the picture." He deferred to *Plessy* in declining to find that "segregation is violative of fundamental constitutional rights." Parker ended with an echo of Oliver Wendell Holmes's dissent in the *Lochner* case: "The members of the judiciary have no more right to read their ideas of sociology into the Constitution than their ideas of economics."

Judge Waring filed a lengthy dissent that focused on the connections of racial prejudice and segregation. "There is absolutely no reasonable explanation for racial prejudice," he wrote. "It is all caused by unreasoning emotional reactions and these are gained in early childhood." Waring considered *Sweatt* and *McLaurin* even more reason to rule for the *Briggs* plaintiffs: "If segregation is wrong, then the place to stop it is in the first grade and not in graduate colleges." He put his last words into italics: *"Segregation is per se inequality."*

Much like Harry Briggs and the other Clarendon County plaintiffs, Judge Waring paid a price for his *Briggs* dissent. Social ostracism and death threats finally drove Waring from his ancestral home in Charleston. He resigned his judicial post and moved to New York, where he died in 1968 at eighty-eight. He returned in death to Charleston; only a handful of white people attended the services at Magnolia Cemetery, but two hundred black mourners came, many from Clarendon County. "He's dead," one black farmer said, "but living in the minds of the people here still."

Two days after Judge Parker ruled against the *Briggs* plaintiffs in South Carolina, Robert Carter and Jack Greenberg traveled to Topeka, Kansas, to represent the plaintiffs in *Brown v. Board of Education*, a case that had been filed in federal district court on February 28, 1951. The two young NAACP lawyers, one black and one white, could not both stay in white hotels in this Jim Crow city. They actually hoped to win this case, with three sympathetic federal judges on the bench. The relative equality of black and white schools in Topeka worked in their favor; the only real issue was segregation. Kenneth Clark did not come to Topeka, but Carter and Greenberg called another social psychologist with impressive credentials. Louisa Holt held a doctorate from Radcliffe, was a University of Kansas professor, and also taught in the school of psychiatry at the prestigious Menninger Clinic in Topeka. It did not hurt that Judge Walter Huxman, who presided at the *Brown* trial, greatly admired the clinic's founder and director, Dr. Karl Menninger.

Robert Carter asked Louisa Holt to assume that Topeka's separate schools were equal in quality. Considering "the segregated factor alone," he continued, "in your opinion does enforced legal separation have any adverse effect upon the personality development of the Negro child?" She answered in a lengthy sentence. "The fact that it is enforced, that it is legal, I think, has more importance than the mere fact of segregation by itself does because this gives legal and official sanction to a policy which inevitably is interpreted both by white people and by Negroes as denoting the inferiority of the Negro group."

Despite Holt's forceful testimony, Robert Carter and Jack Greenberg lost their case in Kansas. Ruling on August 3, 1951, all three judges upheld Topeka's right to keep Linda Brown out of the white school near her home. Writing for the panel, Judge Huxman considered himself bound by *Plessy* as controlling precedent. Nonetheless, he cited Louisa Holt's testimony in holding that enforced segregation injured black children. "Segregation of white and colored children in public schools has a detrimental effect upon the colored children," he wrote. "The impact is greater when it has the sanction of law; for the policy of separating the races is usually interpreted as denoting the inferiority of the negro group." Huxman's opinion also included findings that Topeka's separate schools were virtually equal in quality, a holding that he hoped would force the Supreme Court to confront *Plessy* head-on when the *Brown* case reached the justices on appeal. "I tried to wrap it up in such a way that they could not duck it," Huxman later boasted.

Along with the *Briggs* and *Brown* cases, three more challenges to school segregation reached the Supreme Court in 1952. One came from Delaware, tucked just under the Mason–Dixon line and southern in sympathy if not geography. The lower-court decision in this case, *Gebhart v. Belton*, marked the only NAACP victory among the five school cases. The state's highest judicial officer, Chancellor Collins J. Seitz, had earlier ordered the all-white University of Delaware to admit black undergraduates, the first such ruling in the nation. In the *Gebhart* case, after visiting several black and white schools around the state, Seitz ordered the immediate admission of black students to white schools in April 1952. "This is the first real victory in our campaign to destroy segregation of American pupils in elementary and high schools," Thurgood Marshall crowed to the press.

The Virginia case, *Davis v. Prince Edward County*, came before three judges who differed greatly from Chancellor Seitz. Circuit judge Armistead Mason Dobie presided at the June 1952 trial along with district judges Sterling Hutcheson and Albert Bryan. Native sons of Virginia, they honored its traditions and mores, including racial segregation. The judges allowed the state's lawyer, Justin Moore, to demean black plaintiffs and insult Jewish witnesses. Isador Chein, a prominent psychologist, endured Moore's anti-Semitism with stoic restraint. Moore asked Chein "what sort of racial background" he had. "I think what you want to know is am I Jewish," Chein replied. "Are you 100 percent Jewish?" pressed Moore. "How do I answer that?" Chein inquired. "I don't know—you know," Moore demanded. Chein replied that "all of my ancestors, as far back as I know, were Jewish." Moore looked triumphant. "That answers my question," he said knowingly.

Judge Bryan wrote for all three judges in ruling for their native state. Racial separation in Virginia's schools, they held, rested "neither upon prejudice nor caprice" but had "for generations been a part of the mores of her people. To have separate schools has been their use and wont." This use of the archaic term for "custom" reflected the judges' attachment to Virginia's past, and their exclusion of blacks from "her people" spoke volumes. They dismissed all evidence that enforced segregation inflicted emotional wounds on black children. "We have found no hurt or harm to either race," they concluded. Sitting in the Confederacy's last capital, the defiant judges refused to follow General Lee in surrendering their lost cause.

The NAACP played no formal role in the final school case, *Bolling v. Sharpe*, which was filed in the District of Columbia by James Nabrit III, who taught many NAACP lawyers at Howard Law School. Nabrit had worked for years with Thurgood Marshall, but he chafed at Marshall's cautious approach. When a group of black parents approached him in 1950, Nabrit decided to file a suit that made no mention of unequal school facilities. He put all his chips on the number five. Because the Fourteenth Amendment applied only to states, Nabrit could not raise an equal protection challenge to Washington's segregated schools. He relied instead on the Fifth Amendment's protection of "liberty" against governmental abridgment. "The educational rights which petitioners assert are fundamental rights protected by the due-process clause of the Fifth Amendment from unreasonable and arbitrary restrictions," Nabrit claimed. But he lost his bet when federal judge Walter Bastian ruled that Nabrit had failed to show any evidence of school inequality. Therefore, *Plessy* governed the case and barred any relief for the plaintiffs. Ironically, the *Plessy* majority in 1896 had approvingly cited Washington's segregated schools to justify Louisiana's segregated railroads. Fifty-five years later, Judge Bastian returned the favor.

The first round of Supreme Court argument in the five school cases began on Monday, December 8, 1952. Promptly at noon, Chief Justice Fred Vinson led his colleagues from behind a velvet curtain to the bench. Every seat in the Supreme Court chamber was occupied, more than half by blacks who came to hear Thurgood Marshall and other lawyers give voice to their grievance against segregation. If anyone expected verbal fireworks, there were few pops. Jack Greenberg, who succeeded Thurgood Marshall as NAACP director-counsel in 1961, argued briefly in the Delaware case. "Any description of the oral arguments," he later wrote, "must make clear how dull" they were. More than a dozen lawyers, on both sides, stood up and sat down without making a single memorable statement.

Contrary to widespread belief, Marshall did not argue the leadoff *Brown* case. Robert Carter spoke for Linda Brown and other black children in Topeka. He wanted to talk about school inequalities, but the justices wanted to know how he felt about *Plessy*. After all, if the cases raised no greater issue than which schools had better facilities, people would not be crowding the courtroom and hallways to hear the arguments. Carter finally offered his opinion that *Plessy* "should squarely be overruled." The lawyer for Kansas used less than half of his allotted time and said nothing of importance. Thurgood Marshall then rose to speak for the *Briggs* plaintiffs in South Carolina. He had appeared many times before the Court, but never in a case of this significance. "He hovered imposingly over the lectern as he addressed the justices familiarly, but respectfully," Jack Greenberg recalled. Unlike Carter, who conceded the relative equality of Topeka's separate schools, Marshall hammered on the glaring disparities in Clarendon County's schools. He also tried to deflect questions on *Plessy*, but agreed with Carter that it should be overruled. Just before he sat down, Marshall brought laughter from the audience by declining Justice Jackson's facetious invitation to file suits for American Indians who were segregated in reservation schools. "I have a full load now, Mr. Justice," Marshall smilingly replied.

The lawyer who opposed Marshall did not smile, or produce chuckles in the chamber. But he brought far more experience to the podium. John W. Davis had been the Democratic presidential candidate in 1924, had served as solicitor general of the United States, and was now a senior partner in a powerful Wall Street law firm. Still tall and imposing at seventy-nine, he had appeared before the Court in more cases than any lawyer except the legendary Daniel Webster. Davis had welcomed South Carolina's invitation to argue in *Briggs* because he firmly believed in the state's right to require racial segregation. He also firmly believed he would win the case. But he made a mistake that would have gotten a junior lawyer fired at his own firm. Justice Burton asked Davis if changing social conditions might affect judicial construction of terms like "equal protection." After claiming that social changes "cannot broaden the terminology of the Constitution," Davis volunteered that definitions of "interstate commerce" had shifted over time.

Justice Frankfurter jumped into the exchange, treating the legendary advocate like a first-year law student. "Mr. Davis, do you think that 'equal' is a less fluid term than 'commerce between the states'?" Davis demurred: "I have not compared the two on the point of fluidity." Frankfurter pressed him: "Suppose you do it now." Davis asked if Frankfurter meant that "what is unequal today may be equal tomorrow, or vice versa." That was his question, Frankfurter replied. "That might be," Davis cautiously answered. He had just conceded his case, but he would not concede that many things had changed since *Plessy* was decided. Pointing out that Congress in 1862 had provided for segregated schools in the District of Columbia, Davis concluded that he saw no reason "why this Court or any other should reverse the findings of 90 years." Ninety years earlier, of course, the nation had been convulsed in a bloody war over slavery. Davis did not mention that the segregation he defended was slavery's legacy to the black children of Clarendon County.

John W. Davis did not think he would return to the Court's podium. "I think we've got it won," he assured a colleague. But neither side won the first round of arguments, and Davis and Marshall both returned a year later for a second round before the justices. Setting the cases for reargument had been Justice Frankfurter's solution to a serious problem. He firmly believed the Court must reverse *Plessy* without dissent. However, the initial discussions in the conference room showed that at least Justice Reed, and possibly Chief Justice Vinson and Justices Clark and Jackson, were not prepared to overturn *Plessy*. To avoid dissension in these momentous cases, Frankfurter proposed ordering the lawyers to answer several questions. The former Harvard professor drafted a test with five questions and eight subparts. Boiled down, they raised two issues: had the framers of the Fourteenth Amendment intended to outlaw school segregation; and if not, did the Court have the power to do that?

The Court sent out Frankfurter's questions on June 8, 1953, with answers due on October 12. Lawyers on both sides struggled with his examination over the summer. Radio bulletins interrupted their labors on September 8, with news that Chief Justice Vinson had died suddenly of a heart attack. Frankfurter had proposed reargument largely because he despaired that Vinson could shape a unanimous Court in the school cases. His private reaction to Vinson's death was vintage Frankfurter: "This is the first indication I have ever had that there is a God." His prayers for judicial leadership were quickly answered by President Dwight Eisenhower, who had swept into office in 1952 with the largest margin in history over his Democratic opponent, Adlai Stevenson. With his wide grin and disarming manner, "Ike" stayed above the political fray while GOP partisans lambasted the Democrats, who were saddled with the Korean War. During his election campaign and eight months in office, the new president avoided taking sides on school segregation or the Supreme Court cases. Privately, Eisenhower confessed that he could see why white parents objected to having a "big black buck" sit next to their daughter in school.

In choosing Earl Warren to replace Vinson as Chief Justice, Eisenhower paid a large political debt to the California governor, who had swung his state's delegates behind Ike at a crucial point in the 1952 GOP convention. Warren's move scuttled the candidacy of Ohio senator Robert Taft, the party's right-wing favorite and Eisenhower's leading opponent for the presidential nomination (ironically, Taft was far more supportive of civil rights than Eisenhower). Born in 1891 to Norwegian parents, Warren had received two law degrees from the University of California at Berkeley and practiced briefly before joining the army in World War I, leaving infantry service as a captain. He then spent twenty years in government legal service, rising from deputy district attorney to become California's attorney general in 1939. Warren was a tough prosecutor, sometimes accused of targeting his political enemies. With his eye on the governor's post, he supported the wartime internment of Japanese Americans, along with every other California politician. As governor in 1943, Warren echoed General John DeWitt in warning that "if the Japs are released, no one will be able to tell a saboteur from any other Jap." The most popular official in California history, Warren was elected governor three times, the last two on both the Republican and Democratic tickets. His only defeat came in 1948 as Thomas Dewey's vice-presidential running mate, but that narrow loss did not tarnish his political luster.

Several months before Vinson's death, Eisenhower had told Warren he was "definitely inclined" to offer him the next Supreme Court seat. Although he later said this offer did not include the Chief's post, Ike kept his word and named Warren on September 30, 1953, just five days before the Court's term began. Because the Senate was in recess, Warren did not need formal confirmation, which came the next March. The initial reaction to the new Chief Justice was not uniformly warm. Felix Frankfurter groused privately that Warren was just a political hack, and several critics noted his lack of prior judicial experience, a deficiency he shared with John Marshall, Charles Evans Hughes, and Harlan Fiske Stone. But within a few weeks, the hearty and solicitous Warren won over the justices; he sought Frankfurter's counsel, soothed Jackson's hurt feelings, asked Black to preside at the first conference, and brightened the Court's dimmer lights—Burton, Clark, and Minton—with his glow.

30

"War on the

Constitution"

The second round of arguments in the school cases began on December 7, 1953. Two months after he replaced Fred Vinson as Chief Justice, Earl Warren led his colleagues through the red velvet curtain to the bench. Stacked before each justice were briefs that reflected six months of hard labor by dozens of lawyers and historians who struggled to answer the basic question Justice Frankfurter had posed: Did the Fourteenth Amendment's framers intend to outlaw school segregation? Each side put its best gloss on the reports of debates in Congress and state legislatures, but they reached similar conclusions: the evidence was equivocal at best. In the end, more than a thousand pages of briefs had no impact on the Court's final decision.

The arguments stretched over three days and largely rehashed points made a year earlier. Warren had shuffled the docket and the Virginia case led off. Jack Greenberg later described the argument of Spottswood Robinson III, the NAACP's southern regional counsel, as "a meticulous, dull, historical presentation" that went on for forty minutes before the first question. Greenberg found Thurgood Marshall "equally uninspiring" in his *Briggs* argument; Richard Kluger, who masterfully chronicled the school cases in *Simple Justice*, called it "one of his least creditable performances before the Court." Marshall got stuck in the nineteenth-century cases and stumbled over the *McLaurin* case, decided just three years earlier. He sat down without making the obvious point that if Oklahoma could not rope off George McLaurin from his white classmates, how could South Carolina rope off all its white schools from black children?

Now eighty, John W. Davis took the podium after Marshall to speak once again for South Carolina. No other lawyer that day "came near matching him for bite, eloquence, or wit," Kluger wrote. Davis first summarized the answers to the Court's historical quiz; the lawyers on both sides differed, he noted, and the attorney general, as amicus for the United States, "says he does not know which is correct." Davis paused for effect. "So your honors are afforded a reasonable field for selection," he said dryly, as the justices chuckled. After the laughter, Davis turned serious. Proclaiming South Carolina's "good faith and intention to produce equality for all of its children of whatever race or color," he choked up as he concluded, "Here is equal education, not promised, not prophesied, but present. Shall it be thrown away on some fancied question of racial prestige?" Tears flowed down his cheeks as Davis left the podium for the last time, after 140 appearances that stretched over four decades. Even Thurgood Marshall was moved by his opponent's emotion. But one lawyer whispered to another, "That sonofabitch cries in every case he argues."

Marshall had reserved some time to answer Davis, and he spoke the next morning. Greenberg recalled that "Thurgood's rebuttal was his best argument ever." Marshall opened with a bow to his adversary. "As Mr. Davis said yesterday, the only thing the Negroes are trying to get is prestige," he began. "Exactly correct. Ever since the Emancipation Proclamation, the Negro has been trying to get . . . the same status as anybody else regardless of race." Marshall told the justices about watching the black and white children of Clarendon County: "They play in the streets together, they play on their farms together, they go down the road together, they separate to go to school, they come out of school and play ball together. They have to be separated in school." Marshall deplored South Carolina's "determination that the people who were formerly in slavery, regardless of anything else, shall be kept as near that stage as possible, and now is the time, we submit, that this Court should make clear that is not what our Constitution stands for."

The arguments concluded on December 10, 1953, but five months passed before Chief Justice Warren announced the Court's decision. During that time, the Court's marble walls concealed from outsiders the politicking that swirled inside. Earl Warren made no pretensions of legal scholarship, but no other justice ever matched his political skills. Even more than Frankfurter, the Chief was determined to forge a unanimous Court around a brief and forceful opinion. Only if the justices spoke with one voice, in words the American people could understand, would the Court be able to help the nation heal its racial wounds.

Warren set himself an ambitious task, and spent months cajoling his colleagues. Three justices required the full Warren treatment. Felix Frankfurter wanted an unequivocal ruling that school segregation violated the Fourteenth Amendment, but he also wanted to give southern districts time to comply with the Court's mandate; he proposed a decree allowing them to proceed "with all deliberate speed." Robert Jackson wanted the Court to admit frankly that ending segregation had no constitutional warrant; he drafted a concurrence that read like the fable about the emperor with no clothes. Stanley Reed posed the greatest challenge to Warren's unrelenting charm; the courtly Kentuckian had drafted a dissent arguing that the Fourteenth Amendment only provided blacks "an opportunity to obtain facilities substantially equal to his neighbors for himself."

Warren won over Frankfurter by suggesting that the Court issue the opinion he wanted and also order a third round of argument on methods of compliance. If the southern states balked at dismantling their dual-school systems, the Court would frame a flexible decree ordering compliance "with all deliberate speed," as Frankfurter proposed. Warren's tactic worked like a charm. "What a pleasure to do business with him," Frankfurter gushed to Justice Jackson, who never got back to his concurrence after suffering a heart attack in March 1954. Warren visited Jackson's hospital room and left his draft opinion. The ailing justice asked his law clerk, Barrett Prettyman, to read it. Prettyman scanned Warren's opinion and offered Jackson his own: "I said that I wished that it had more law in it but I didn't find anything glaringly unacceptable in it." Jackson called Warren and joined his opinion. Stanley Reed finally succumbed to Warren after more than twenty lunchtime discussions. After Frankfurter and Jackson climbed aboard his bandwagon, Warren offered Reed the last seat: "Stan, you're all by yourself in this now. You've got to decide whether it's really the best thing for the country." Reed decided that holding out was not the best thing for the country.

The Supreme Court's chamber was not crowded on May 17, 1954. Thurgood Marshall got a tip from a friend and took a train to Washington that Monday morning. He entered the chamber as Chief Justice Warren presided over the admission of lawyers to the Court's bar. Justice Clark then read an opinion in an antitrust case, followed by Justice Douglas, who read two opinions in cases dealing with corporate negligence and labor picketing. Most of the news reporters present that day were lounging in their basement quarters when the Court's press officer stuck his head in the door. "Reading of the segregation decisions is about to begin in the courtroom," he informed them. The reporters dashed up the stairs to witness an historic moment. "I have for announcement," Warren began, "the judgment and opinion of the Court in No. 1,—*Oliver Brown et al. v. Board of Education of Topeka*." As Warren read through his opinion, reporters could not tell who won. "The Court's ruling could not be determined immediately," the Associated Press flashed in its first bulletin.

Reading in "a firm, clear, unemotional voice," Warren reviewed the procedural history of the school cases and the grounds of their challenges to school segregation. He then reviewed the briefs submitted on the Fourteenth Amendment's purpose and reach, stating that "although these sources cast some light, it is not enough to resolve the problem with which we are faced." Warren also found no illumination from precedent, dismissing *Plessy* in one sentence as a case "involving not education but transportation." Decades of arguments, millions of words, and mountains of briefs on *Plessy* had no impact on Warren. In deciding the school cases, he wrote, "we cannot turn the clock back" to the nineteenth century, when *Plessy* was decided. Warren was equally unmoved by evidence on "the tangible factors in the Negro and white schools involved in each of the cases." Lower courts had found that school facilities "have been equalized, or are being equalized" in each case. In the end, the school cases had nothing to do with the schools themselves.

What the cases really involved was the psychological impact of enforced separation on black children. Warren stressed "the importance of education to our democratic society." Surprisingly, he said nothing about reading, writing, or arithmetic. The primary role of public education lies in fostering "cultural values" and "good citizenship" among children, he stated. Warren asked whether children could absorb these values and become good citizens in segregated schools. He found the answer in the social science data that John W. Davis had dismissed as irrelevant, and that even some NAACP lawyers had doubted. Warren quoted a long paragraph from Judge Huxman's opinion in the *Brown* case, which itself quoted the testimony of Louisa Holt at the Topeka trial. Separation by race denotes "the inferiority of the negro group," she had said, and feelings of inferiority diminish "the motivation of a child to learn." Warren cited in a footnote the studies of Kenneth Clark and other social scientists, including Isador Chein, to support Holt's findings. The vice of segregation was not bad schools for black children, but the bad lesson it taught them. "To separate them from others of similar age and qualifications solely because of their race," Warren concluded, "generates a feeling of inferiority as to their status in the community that may affect their hearts and minds in a way unlikely ever to be undone."

Warren finally read the words the reporters had waited for. "We conclude unanimously that in the field of public education the doctrine of 'separate but equal' has no place. Separate educational facilities are inherently unequal." The word "unanimously" was not in the Court's printed opinion, but Warren inserted it during his reading for emphasis. Those who listened, including Thurgood Marshall, were unaware that Warren had worked hard for five months to use this word. He paid the cost of unanimity in the final paragraph. Citing "the great variety of local conditions" in southern states, Warren ordered further argument on implementing the Court's decision.

Warren had hoped that a forceful and unanimous opinion would quell any incipient resistance to the Court's ruling. Southern politicians quickly dashed his hopes; they needed no further argument on this issue. Governors and senators heatedly denounced the ruling. Georgia governor Eugene Talmadge claimed the Court had made the Constitution "a mere scrap of paper." Senator Harry Byrd of Virginia called the decision "the most serious blow that has yet been struck against the rights of the states in a matter vitally affecting their authority and welfare." Governor James Byrnes of South Carolina, a former Supreme Court justice, said he was "shocked" by the Court's action. Senator James Eastland of Mississippi vowed that the South "will not abide by or obey this legislative decision by a political court."

A few voices of moderation rose above the din. Governor Thomas Stanley of Virginia said the decision called for "cool heads, calm study, and sound judgment." The *Atlanta Constitution* urged Georgians to "think clearly" about their response and to ignore those who preached "violence and hatred." The first year after the Court's ruling was relatively calm and peaceful. Before any court actually ordered the admission of black children to white schools, those who counseled disobedience had nothing to disobey. One incident in Delaware, however, gave a preview of later conflict in Little Rock, Arkansas. In September 1954, fifteen hundred whites protested the enrollment of eleven black students at the Milford high school. After local officials closed the school, state officials ordered it reopened and police officers escorted the children inside, surrounded by hundreds of white protesters who had been whipped up by an "outside agitator" from the National Association for the Advancement of White People, a racist group that later caused trouble across the South. After NAACP lawyers filed a complaint against the Milford board in state court, Delaware's supreme court gave a preview of state resistance to federal authority, ruling that Milford officials had not followed proper procedure in admitting the black students and voiding their decision.

The Delaware incident did not influence school officials in other border states like Maryland and Kentucky, where most districts began integration without court orders. But the Deep South waited for federal judges to act, and the Supreme Court gave them plenty of time. The final round of arguments in the *Brown* cases began on April 11, 1955. Thurgood Marshall reminded the justices that there was "no local option on the Fourteenth Amendment" and urged them to order "forthwith" the dismantling of all dual-school systems. John W. Davis had died after his last tearful argument, and his replacement, S. Emory Rogers of Summerton, sorely tried Earl Warren's patience. Rogers requested an "open order" that would impose no time limit or conditions on Clarendon County. Warren asked if school officials would "immediately undertake to conform" to the Court's decree. "I am frank to tell you," Rogers answered, that he doubted whether "the white people of the district will send their children to the Negro schools." Warren pressed him: "You are not willing to say here that there would be an honest attempt to conform to this decree, if we did leave it to the district court?" Rogers replied, "No, I am not. Let us get the word 'honest' out of there." Warren shot back: "No, leave it in." Rogers remained defiant: "No, because I would have to tell you that right now we would not conform—we would not send our white children to the Negro schools." Lawyers saw Warren flush with anger. "We thought he might charge Rogers with contempt," one recalled.

Rogers was at least honest in expressing the contempt that whites in Clarendon County felt toward blacks. He actually won more from the Court than Marshall. Chief Justice Warren read the unanimous opinion—just seven paragraphs long—on May 31, 1955. He cited the "variety of obstacles" facing local school officials in giving them time to make a "prompt and reasonable start toward full compliance" with the *Brown* decision. But he said nothing about finishing the job. Warren simply handed federal district judges the task of framing such decrees "as are necessary and proper to admit to public schools on a racially nondiscriminatory basis with all deliberate speed the parties to these cases."

Two days after the second *Brown* decision, Thurgood Marshall called a friend to exult. "I think it's a damn good decision!" he said. Southern politicians had no choice. "They've got to yield to the Constitution! And yield means yield! Yield means give up!" And if they did not give up? "You can say all you want but those white crackers are going to get tired of having Negro lawyers beating 'em every day in court. They're going to get tired of it."

But southern white politicians did not give up, and did not get tired. They had no intentions of moving at *any* speed toward a destination their white constituents feared more than hellfire. Georgia's lieutenant governor, Ernest Vandiver, noted that "a 'reasonable' time can be construed as one year or two hundred." He clearly preferred the latter. In 1956, the vast majority of members of Congress from the former Confederacy signed a "Southern Manifesto" that denounced the Court for "substituting naked power for established law" in *Brown*. Senator Harry Byrd of Virginia called for "massive resistance" to integration. "The decision tortured the Constitution," one Alabama politician declared; "the South will torture the decision." And it did.

Senator James Eastland, racist to his core, was right when he called *Brown* a "legislative decision by a political court." The Court has always been a political body. Its historic opinions—in *Marbury*, in *Dred Scott*, in *Lochner*, in *West Coast Hotel*, in *Brown*—have all been legislative decisions; they "made" new law to replace old laws. To claim that justices simply "interpret" the Constitution denies reality; the Court necessarily plays a role in the political process.

The *Brown* case is a perfect example. The Constitution, the "supreme law of the land," guarantees every American "the equal protection of the laws." That provision of the Fourteenth Amendment was added by Radical Republican politicians during Reconstruction. Once the Radicals lost power and Reconstruction ended, southern legislators responded to political pressure from white voters and passed laws requiring racial segregation in public schools. Shut out from the political process, southern blacks took their grievances to federal judges after the Supreme Court promised "strict scrutiny" of discriminatory laws. Most of the judges they faced owed their positions to political sponsors who rewarded them for partisan loyalty with black robes. All the Supreme

Court justices who decided *Brown* had political experience; five had been elected to public office and the other four had worked closely with the president who picked them for the Court. The Constitution the justices "interpreted" in *Brown* was drafted by politicians, and the Court's decisions were made with frank recognition of their political impact.

The hostile reaction of southern politicians to the *Brown* decision in 1954, and their eager response to the "all deliberate speed" ruling in 1955 as an invitation to foot-dragging, confronted the Court with its greatest challenge since the *Dred Scott* decision of 1857. The country faced the prospect of a second Civil War, with race-baiting politicians like Georgia governor Eugene Talmadge and South Carolina senator Strom Thurmond playing the roles of antebellum firebrands like John C. Calhoun and Jefferson Davis in vowing to defend the "southern way of life" against Yankee meddlers. This time, of course, the Court had sided with black Americans in their freedom struggle, and Chief Justice Earl Warren was as determined to assert the Court's power to enforce federal authority over the states as Chief Justice Roger Taney had been to destroy it.

The Court over which Warren presided during the volatile and often violent years between 1954 and 1958 had changed in composition with the addition of four new members, all nominated by President Eisenhower, whose commitment to civil rights was lukewarm at best. Three of these justices, however, matched Warren's determination to enforce judicial authority over southern resistance to school integration. Even the most conservative of Eisenhower's nominees, Charles Whittaker, joined his colleagues in laying down the law to defiant southern officials.

The sudden death of Justice Robert Jackson in October 1954 gave President Eisenhower his first chance to shape the Court since he placed Earl Warren at its helm. He chose a lawyer with an impressive pedigree, Warren's opposite in many ways. The Chief's father came from Norway and worked on the railroads; John Marshall Harlan's father came from colonial stock and headed a prominent Chicago law firm. Not only that, Harlan was named for his illustrious grandfather, whose *Plessy* dissent in 1896 had been vindicated in *Brown*. Earl Warren spent most of his legal career in government service; John Harlan practiced for twenty years in a prestigious Wall Street firm. Eisenhower did not pick Harlan as a counterweight to Warren, but he served that role until the Chief's retirement in 1969.

John Harlan was a judicial conservative, but not in the reactionary mold of the "Four Horsemen of Reaction" who had frustrated the New Deal program of Franklin Roosevelt. Nor did he follow the "judicial restraint" doctrine with the dogmatism of Felix Frankfurter; Harlan voted to strike down state and federal laws in many free speech cases. His 1957 opinion in *Yates v. United States* reversed the Smith Act convictions of "second-tier" Communist leaders, without overruling the *Dennis* case. In 1961, Harlan dissented in *Poe v. Ullman* from the Court's refusal to hear a challenge to a state law barring doctors from giving contraceptives to married couples; his statement in that dissent that the Constitution protected a "right of privacy" placed him years ahead of the Court and miles apart from Frankfurter. The last justice born during the nineteenth century, in 1899, Harlan did not feel its tug in reading the Constitution. That document, he wrote in 1961, reflects the shifting "balance which our Nation, built upon postulates of respect for the liberty of the individual, has struck between that liberty and the demands of organized society." The second Justice Harlan retired in 1971 after sixteen years, a principled conservative with a libertarian streak, cast in the mold of his grandfather.

Justice Sherman Minton retired in October 1956, during the last month of President Eisenhower's second presidential campaign against Adlai Stevenson. This was a bad year for Democrats, with the exception of William J. Brennan, Jr., then a New Jersey supreme court judge. The popular president should not have worried about reelection, but he took the opening of Minton's departure to curry favor with Catholics, who had been unrepresented on the Court since Frank Murphy died in 1949. Cardinal Francis Spellman, an archconservative prelate who vocally supported Senator Joseph McCarthy, had pressed Eisenhower to fill the "Catholic seat" with his next appointment. Although Brennan had compared McCarthy's Red-hunting tactics to the Salem witch trials in several speeches, Eisenhower did not know this before he asked him to join the Court. "I never heard a man say 'yes' so fast," the president's press secretary told a reporter. McCarthy's loud "no" was not recorded when the Senate confirmed Brennan by voice vote.

The first justice born in the twentieth century, in 1906, Brennan learned about politics from his father, an Irish immigrant who settled in New Jersey and fired boilers in a Newark brewery. A union activist and city commissioner, Brennan's father gave him some career advice. "Lad, you argue well around the house and I've no doubt you'll make a fine lawyer. But as for politics, I think you'll be happier out than in." The junior Brennan also learned the Catholic "social gospel" from his church's encyclicals: "Workers are not to be treated as slaves," Pope Leo XIII wrote in 1891; "justice demands that the dignity of the human personality be respected in them."

Brennan applied these lessons during his entire career. After completing Harvard Law School in 1931, he spent eighteen years in private practice, interrupted by army service during World War II as a troubleshooter in labor disputes that disrupted wartime production; he won promotion to colonel. New Jersey's Republican governor tapped Brennan for the state trial court in 1949 and promoted him to the Supreme Court in 1952. Presiding at civil and criminal trials exposed Brennan to deficiencies in dispensing justice fairly and equally. His labors in court reform gained the attention of Herbert Brownell, Eisenhower's attorney general, who recommended him for Minton's seat.

Very few votes, if any, were swayed in 1956 by Ike's decision to place a Catholic Democrat on the Court. But the new justice swayed many votes on the

Court; Brennan's personal warmth, Irish charm, and legal brilliance combined to make him the most influential justice of the past half century. Justice Brennan served for thirty-four years and wrote dozens of landmark opinions. His judicial legacy includes opinions for the Court in *Baker v. Carr*, establishing the "one person, one vote" principle; *New York Times v. Sullivan*, shielding the press from vindictive libel suits; *Goldberg v. Kelly*, extending due process protections to welfare recipients; and *Texas v. Johnson*, wrapping the First Amendment around protesters who burned the American flag. All of Brennan's opinions rested on his bedrock commitment to "human dignity" as a guiding principle. He used this term in dozens of opinions and articles. Upholding the right of John Kelly, a disabled welfare recipient, to receive a hearing before officials cut off his benefits, Brennan cast the issue in broader terms: "From its founding, the Nation's basic commitment has been to foster the dignity and well-being of all persons within its borders."

Someone later asked Eisenhower if he had made any mistakes as president. "Yes, two," he replied, "and they are both sitting on the Supreme Court." Ike referred to Earl Warren and William Brennan, but his biggest mistake in picking justices came in his fourth nomination. Stanley Reed's retirement in February 1957 opened a seat that could be filled without national political considerations. Charles Evans Whittaker had practiced corporate law in Kansas City for thirty years and was a close friend of Eisenhower's brother Arthur, a Kansas City banker. Ike followed his brother's advice in placing Whittaker on the federal bench in 1954; three years later he again consulted Arthur and promoted the neophyte judge to the Supreme Court. Whittaker proved totally unfit for his new job; he developed a paralyzing writer's block and wrote no opinions of any significance. Rated as a judicial failure by scholars, Whittaker retired in 1962 as "disabled" and returned to corporate practice.

President Eisenhower's fifth and final nomination went to another midwestern corporate lawyer with a short tenure on the federal bench. Potter Stewart of Ohio replaced a fellow Buckeye, Harold Burton, who retired in October 1958. Born in 1915, Stewart was raised in a wealthy and staunchly Republican family in Cincinnati. After graduating from Yale Law School, he practiced law in Cincinnati and campaigned for Senator Robert Taft. Stewart risked his political future, however, by supporting Eisenhower over Taft at the 1952 Republican convention. He was rewarded in 1954 with a federal circuit court seat, and won respect for well-crafted opinions that stuck to the facts and bowed to precedent.

As an appellate judge, Stewart had followed the *Brown* decision without deviation, which provoked opposition to his Supreme Court nomination from Senator James Eastland of Mississippi. Praising Stewart as "an able lawyer" and "a man of integrity," Eastland nonetheless declared he would not support any judge who supported *Brown*. All seventeen votes against Stewart's confirmation came from Deep South senators. He confirmed their fears by consistently supporting civil rights plaintiffs, but he took a hard-line position in criminal cases.

Stewart avoided both the "rational basis" and "strict scrutiny" tests in his opinions; he would rather "balance" rights than place his thumb on either side of the judicial scale. During twenty-three years on the Court, Stewart wrote more than six hundred opinions, but just one contains a memorable phrase. Writing in a case that reversed an obscenity conviction for showing a French "art" movie called *The Lovers*, Stewart put the difficulty of defining "hard-core pornography" into these words: "I know it when I see it, and the motion picture involved in this case is not that." Looking at each case like a movie critic, Stewart cast his "thumbs up" or "thumbs down" votes without reference to any consistent judicial standard.

What good is the Constitution if government officials refuse to obey its commands? More to the point, what if they defy judicial orders to carry out these commands? The justices who served under Chief Justice Warren—including three who joined the Court after *Brown* was decided—faced that momentous question in 1958, a year after federal troops quelled an armed rebellion against the admission of nine black students to Central High School in Little Rock, Arkansas. The refusal of Arkansas officials to obey federal judicial orders produced a case, known as *Cooper v. Aaron*, that tested not only the Court's resolve but also the nation's commitment to the rule of law.

In a real sense, the greatest responsibility for the Little Rock insurrection in 1957 lay with President Eisenhower, who had pointedly declined in 1956 to support the *Brown* decision. "I think it makes no difference whether or not I endorse it," he told reporters. "It is difficult through law and through force to change a man's heart," he added. Statements like these created a vacuum of leadership, which demagogues quickly rushed to fill.

One southern politician, however, did not immediately join the Dixiecrats who urged "massive resistance" to the *Brown* decision. Arkansas governor Orval Faubus, elected as a racial "moderate" in 1954, added black members to state boards and Democratic Party committees. The rural Arkansas town of Hoxie ended its separate school system in June 1955. Even before the Supreme Court issued its second *Brown* opinion, the Little Rock school board adopted a plan for "phased" integration, beginning with the admission of black students to prestigious Central High in September 1957. Integration of other high schools, then junior highs, and finally elementary schools would be "phased in" over a ten-year period. The glacial pace of the Little Rock plan failed to satisfy the Arkansas NAACP, which filed suit against the board in February 1956. Six months later, federal judge John E. Miller endorsed the ten-year plan as a "good-faith" effort to "ultimately bring about a school system not based on color distinctions." The Eighth Circuit appellate court in St. Louis upheld Miller's decision and cleared a path for nine black students to enter Central High on September 3, 1957.

Although most whites in Little Rock supported the school board's "phased integration" plan, news reports of the judicial order to integrate Central High inflamed the city's racial bigots, who began waving Confederate battle flags and vowed to block the school's doors to black students. Holding his finger to political winds that had blown up to gale force, Governor Faubus shed his "moderate" mask and began railing against federal judges. The night before the "Little Rock Nine" were set to begin school, Faubus spoke to the state on television. Warning that "blood will run in the streets" if the black students entered Central High, Faubus announced that he had ordered National Guard troops to surround the school and keep them out. The next morning, eight of the nine gathered at the home of Daisy Bates, the young president of the state's NAACP chapters. They left in station wagons for the short drive to their new school. Fifteen-year-old Elizabeth Eckford did not show up at Daisy Bates's home. Walking alone, holding her head high, she tried to enter Central High and was turned away by soldiers with bayonets. A menacing crowd surrounded Elizabeth and began yelling, "Get her! Lynch her!" Someone hollered, "Get a rope and drag her over to this tree!" Protected by a white NAACP member, she finally escaped the mob on a city bus.

Americans across the country witnessed Elizabeth Eckford's dignity in the face of lynch-mob hysteria on their television screens. Many people had never seen the face of racism so clearly, and could not believe that "a man's heart" could hold so much hatred for anyone's child. The public also watched President Eisenhower playing golf in Newport, Rhode Island, unwilling to interrupt his vacation to deal with the most serious threat to federal authority since the Civil War. Pressure mounted on Eisenhower to intervene, but he took no action. National Guardsmen blocked Central High's doors to the Little Rock Nine until September 20, when a federal judge ordered Governor Faubus to remove the Guardsmen. Little Rock police then escorted the black students into the school, but an unruly mob stormed the building and the nine youngsters barely escaped with their lives. Facing the prospect of televised lynchings, Eisenhower finally ordered army airborne troops into Little Rock. The city's racists lacked the guts to battle paratroopers, and the Little Rock Nine finally began their classes. During the remainder of the school year, a band of white students harassed them unmercifully, while school officials turned their heads. On May 27, 1958, Ernest Green became the first black graduate of Central High; he later served as assistant labor secretary in Jimmy Carter's cabinet.

Also in May 1958, the Little Rock school board asked federal judge Harry Lemley to delay any further integration until January 1961. The board's lawyers argued that school integration "runs counter to the ingrained attitudes" of many Little Rock whites. They also pointed to Governor Faubus, who had persuaded the Arkansas legislature to pass laws authorizing him to take over local school boards that admitted any black students to white schools. Faubus had also issued statements that the *Brown* decisions had no force in Arkansas. Judge

Lemley heard the board's witnesses—all white—testify about the "chaos, bedlam, and turmoil" at Central High. He did not ask who had caused the chaos, but he granted the board's petition on June 20, 1958. Lemley's move precipitated a legal storm, as NAACP lawyers rushed between St. Louis, Little Rock, and Washington. They sought and obtained a stay of Judge Lemley's order from the Eighth Circuit appellate court, which reversed his order after a hearing. But the appellate judges later changed their minds and reinstated Lemley's order. The NAACP lawyers then asked the Supreme Court to step in and end the legal chaos. Although the justices had scattered around the country during their summer recess, Chief Justice Warren summoned them back to Washington for a "special term" on August 28. Little Rock schools were scheduled to open on September 15, and Warren wanted to decide the case before the class bells rang.

William Cooper, the Little Rock school board president, and John Aaron, first in alphabetical order of the black plaintiffs, gave their names to *Cooper v. Aaron*. But the real parties were Orval Faubus and Earl Warren; this case was really a contest for supremacy between the defiant governor and the determined Chief Justice. All nine justices had answered Warren's call and returned to Washington for the oral arguments, which began with an appeal for delay by Richard Butler, the board's lawyer. "All we're asking," he said, "is for time to work this thing out in a climate of calm rather than in a climate of hysteria." Earl Warren listened politely to Butler's assurance that he was not speaking for the "law defiers" in Little Rock. "I know you're not," Warren soothingly replied.

The Chief's soothing smile quickly faded when Butler spoke for the chief law defier in Arkansas. "The point I'm making is this," Butler said, "that if the governor of any state says that a United States Supreme Court decision is not the law of the land, the people of that state, until it is really resolved, have a doubt in their mind and a right to have a doubt." Warren exploded. "I have never heard such an argument made in a court of justice before," he shot back, "and I've tried many a case, over many a year. I never heard a lawyer say that the statement of a governor, as to what was legal or illegal, should control the action of any court." The former California governor now wore a black robe, and would not tolerate this challenge to his authority.

Russell Baker, covering the hearing for the *New York Times*, reported that Thurgood Marshall took the podium with "the hint of a scowl on his face, looking like Othello in a tan business suit." Marshall was just as angry as the Chief Justice, and his voice rose as he spoke for Little Rock's black children. "I think we need to think about these children and their parents," he said, "these Negro children that went through this every day, and their parents that stayed at home wondering what was happening to their children, listening to the radio about the bomb threats and all that business. I don't know how anybody under the sun could say, that after all those children and those families went through for a year to tell them: All you have done is gone. You fought for what you considered to be democracy and you lost. And you go back to the segregated school from which you came. I just don't believe it."

The justices did not believe it either, and they scolded Governor Faubus with a single voice. On September 12, the day after the Court heard a second round of arguments that largely rehashed the issues, the Court issued an unsigned order reversing Judge Lemley's two-year delay. Central High could now begin classes, with two thousand white and nine black students. On September 29, the Court handed down its written opinion in *Cooper v. Aaron*. Never before—or since—has every justice personally signed an opinion. Richard Butler had argued that Governor Faubus's claim that *Brown* had no effect in Arkansas left its citizens "in actual doubt as to what the law is." Warren proposed the collective opinion to remove any doubt.

The justices professed astonishment that Faubus and Arkansas lawmakers would claim "that they are not bound by our holding in the *Brown* case." The Court's opinion treated the defiant officials like schoolroom dunces. It was their "determination to resist this Court's decision in the *Brown* case" which had "brought about violent resistance to that decision in Arkansas," the justices stated. Had the Arkansas officials not read the Constitution? Article VI "makes the Constitution the 'supreme Law of the Land.'" Had they not all taken oaths "to support this Constitution?" The justices took out their rulers: "No state legislator or executive or judicial officer can war against the Constitution without violating his undertaking to support it." And who had the power to enforce the Constitution? "It follows that the interpretation of the Fourteenth Amendment enunciated in the *Brown* case is the supreme law of the land," the justices told the Arkansas officials. Looking beyond Little Rock, they demanded "the obedience of the States" to "the command of the Constitution" that federal court orders must be obeyed.

Despite this stern lecture, the Arkansas officials did not learn their lesson. Defying the Court once again, Governor Faubus and the state legislature closed down Little Rock's schools for an entire year. Going back to federal court, NAACP lawyers won a ruling in 1959 that reopened the schools. By spring 1960, Central High had fifteen hundred white students and just five blacks. Litigation dragged on for years, raising the question once again: What good is the Constitution if government officials refuse to obey its commands? What the Arkansas politicians finally obeyed was not the Supreme Court, but the commands of public opinion. Little Rock's voters finally tired of chaos and turmoil in their schools and voted in a new board that moved toward compliance with court orders.

But in the Deep South, racist governors continued to defy federal judges. Ordered to admit James Meredith to the University of Mississippi in 1962 as its first black student, Governor Ross Barnett refused to comply so many times that Fifth Circuit judges held him in contempt and committed him to "the custody of the Attorney General of the United States." President John Kennedy told the attorney general, his brother Robert, to ignore the court's order. Barnett continued to defy the courts, and Meredith began classes only after federal troops quelled a bloody riot that cost a news photographer his life. The violence began after the governor ordered state police to leave the Ole Miss campus, leaving the unarmed U.S. marshals who accompanied Meredith at the mercy of a howling mob. Barnett never spent a day in jail for his defiance. Emboldened by this example, Alabama governor George Wallace stood in a University of Alabama doorway in May 1963 to block the admission of two black students, Jimmy Hood and Vivian Malone. Only the presence of five hundred National Guardsmen prevented another Ole Miss riot. Wallace's stand did not keep the black students out, but it won him half a million white votes in the 1964 Democratic presidential primaries. And in 1968, running under the banner of the American Independent Party, Wallace received almost ten million votes for president. Politicians are more often rewarded than punished for defying the Supreme Court; Arkansas voters gave Orval Faubus four more terms as governor after the justices ordered him to end his "war on the Constitution."

31

"A Better Place

Because He Lived"

Southern defiance of the *Brown* decisions produced bloodshed and even death before the last redoubts of segregation capitulated to judicial orders in the late 1960s. But those decisions were not, in fact, the most widely defied of the Warren Court's many controversial rulings. That dubious honor goes to the school prayer decisions of 1962 and 1963. Striking down first a state-composed prayer and then Bible reading and the Lord's Prayer, the Court ruled that these practices violated the First Amendment's prohibition of any "establishment of religion" and breached the "wall of separation" between church and state. The Court's first batch of religion cases, decided in the late 1930s and early 1940s, had mostly involved Jehovah's Witnesses and raised claims under the First Amendment's clause that protects the "free exercise" of religion; the Court had ruled that licensing fees and other restraints placed on Witnesses had infringed their freedom to exercise their religious beliefs.

A second round of cases began after World War II and largely involved Roman Catholics, whose numbers grew rapidly with the postwar baby boom. Swelling enrollments in parochial schools created financial burdens on churches and parents, and several states responded with tax-funded subsidy programs. Some gave direct benefits to schools, such as textbooks and teacher salaries; others made it easier for parents to afford private schools. New Jersey, for example, reimbursed parents for their children's bus fares to both public and parochial schools. Illinois public schools brought Catholic, Jewish, and Protestant instructors into classrooms; parents chose between religion classes or secular courses for their children during "released-time" programs.

The Supreme Court decided the New Jersey and Illinois cases differently. Justice Hugo Black wrote for the majority in both, picking a careful path through unfamiliar terrain. His opinion in *Everson v. Board of Education,* decided in 1947, upheld the bus-fare subsidy. Black admitted that New Jersey helped Catholic children "get to church schools." But the state also helped children get to public schools, aiding "all its citizens without regard to their religious belief." The Establishment Clause, Black wrote, "requires the state to be a neutral in its relations with groups of religious believers and non-believers; it does not require the state to be their adversary." Despite this "accommodation" of religion, Black stressed that states cannot "pass laws which aid one religion, aid all religions, or prefer one religion over another." Nor can states "support any religious activities" that "teach or practice religion." Black looked for authority to President Thomas Jefferson's letter in 1802 to the Baptists in Danbury, Connecticut, who had complained about being taxed to support the established Congregational churches. Jefferson replied that the First Amendment had constructed "a wall of separation between church and state," a barrier that kept both preachers and politicians from trespassing on each other's domain.

Writing again in 1948 for the Court in *McCollum v. Illinois*, Black struck down the "released-time" program because tax-supported schools were "used for the dissemination of religious doctrine" in classrooms. Quoting Jefferson again, Black held that such "direct" benefits to religion breached "the wall of separation" that New Jersey's bus-fare subsidy had skirted as an "indirect" benefit to parochial schools. Later decisions tried to clarify the "direct-indirect" benefit distinction, but failed to provide a clear-cut standard. While the Court looked for a middle road, conflict between religious "separationists" and "accommodationists" mounted in the 1950s. John F. Kennedy's election in 1960 as the first Catholic president brought simmering religious disputes to a political boil. The Warren Court finally caught the heat over the emotional issue of school prayer.

"Almighty God, we acknowledge our dependence upon Thee, and we beg Thy blessings upon us, our parents, and our teachers." This prayer was adopted in the 1950s by the New York Regents, who control the state's education system. It would be hard to imagine more innocuous words. What parent could object to his or her child's reciting this prayer? Many people would be genuinely puzzled by this question, but others are offended by even this generic prayer. Atheists would reject any reference to "God," agnostics would be doubtful, and some devout believers—of many faiths—feel that vocal prayer should be confined to home and church and not imposed on children in public schools.

Steven Engel and nine other parents in the Long Island suburb of New Hyde Park, New York, challenged the "Regents' Prayer" in a suit against William Vitale, the school board president. Ruling in 1962, the Supreme Court struck down this daily religious practice. Justice Black again wrote for the Court in *Engel v. Vitale* and again cited Jefferson's "wall of separation" for support. Black stated that the Establishment Clause "must at least mean that in this country it is no part of the official business of government to compose official prayers for any group of American people to recite as part of a religious program carried out by government."

Back in the 1830s, when Alexis de Tocqueville visited America from France, he noted that "religious zeal is perpetually stimulated in the United States by the duties of patriotism" and remarked that "you meet with a politician where you expected to find a priest." Little had changed over the next century, and the *Engel* decision touched a live wire in American politics. Cardinal Spellman of New York was "shocked and frightened." Cardinal McIntyre of Los Angeles called the decision "positively shocking and scandalizing to one of American blood and principles." Evangelist Billy Graham was "shocked and disappointed." Alabama representative George Andrews complained that the Court had "put the Negroes in the schools, and now they've driven God out." Seventy-five congressmen of both parties introduced 147 bills to return prayer to classrooms through legislation or constitutional amendment.

The Court struck down another devotional ritual in 1963, banishing the Lord's Prayer and the Bible from classrooms. This case began in the high school attended by Roger and Donna Schempp in Abington Township, Pennsylvania, a suburb of Philadelphia. Classes began every morning with a reading of ten verses from the Bible and recital of the Lord's Prayer, a ritual commanded by state law, although children who objected could be excused from the classroom at their parents' request. The Schempp family belonged to the Unitarian Church, whose members reject the Christian Trinity and are not bound to any religious creed. Edward Schempp filed suit on his children's behalf, arguing that forcing Roger and Donna to stand in the hallway while their classmates prayed would carry "the imputation of punishment for bad conduct." Supported by the American Civil Liberties Union, the Schempps won the first two rounds in federal court and the school board appealed to the Supreme Court.

The justices could easily have denied review in *Abington Township v. Schempp*, which differed from *Engel* only in the text of the classroom prayer. Most likely, they wanted to tell the politicians who demanded a constitutional amendment to reverse *Engel* that the Court stood firm in the face of pressure. The Court heard oral argument in *Schempp* in February 1963. The school board's lawyer, Philip Ward, asserted that Pennsylvania schools used the Bible "to bring lessons in morality to the children." He admitted the Bible was a religious book, but claimed the state was "teaching morality without religion, cut adrift from theology." Pennsylvania lawmakers, Ward said, wanted to find the best source for teaching morality. "So what did they do? They picked a common source of morality, the Bible." Ward appealed to tradition. "Must the government rip out that document, that tradition, simply because it involves a religious book?"

The Schempps' lawyer, Henry Sawyer, scoffed at Ward's argument. "I think it is the final arrogance to talk constantly about 'our religious tradition' and equate it with the Bible," Sawyer responded. "Sure, religious tradition. *Whose* religious tradition? It isn't any part of the religious tradition of a substantial number of Americans." Sawyer concluded by suggesting that Pennsylvania schools "are a kind of Protestant institution to which others are cordially invited," so long as they stand in the hallway during morning devotions.

Hugo Black took a break from writing opinions in religion cases. Chief Justice Warren assigned the *Schempp* case to Tom Clark, perhaps thinking that an opinion from a conservative southerner might not spark the heated reaction that followed the *Engel* decision. With his respect for precedent, Clark followed the path his fellow Southern Baptist had cleared. "The place of religion in our society is an exalted one," he wrote, "achieved through a long tradition of reliance on the home, the church and the inviolable citadel of the individual heart and mind." Americans "have come to realize through bitter experience that it is not within the power of government to invade that citadel," Clark added. "In the relationship between man and religion, the State is firmly committed to a position of neutrality." Arguments that Bible reading and prayer were only "minor encroachments on the First Amendment" did not convert Clark. "The breach of neutrality that is today a trickling stream may all too soon become a raging torrent," he replied. Justice Potter Stewart complained in solitary dissent that Roger and Donna Schempp had infringed the "free exercise" rights of their classmates to pray, and that his colleagues had established a "religion of secularism" in place of Christianity.

The Court's decisions in the prayer cases do in fact run "counter to the ingrained attitudes" of many Americans. Polls have consistently shown a solid majority behind proposals to return prayer to the schools. Support for a constitutional amendment to accomplish this goal runs highest among southern white Protestants and lowest among northern Catholics and Jews. Well into the 1990s, close to half of the nation's public schools—and more than half in the South—continue to defy the Court's prayer decisions with such sectarian practices as classroom prayer, lunchtime grace, and Bible distribution.

As recently as 1992, the Court felt compelled to repeat its *Engel* and *Schempp* rulings that school prayer violates the Establishment Clause. But the "wall of separation" came perilously close to collapse in *Lee v. Weisman*, as four conservative justices dissented from a decision that struck down prayer at school graduations. Daniel and Vivian Weisman, who are Jewish, had complained about Christian prayer at the Nathan Bishop Middle School in Providence, Rhode Island, from which their daughter Merith graduated in 1986. A Baptist minister had thanked Jesus Christ for inspiring Merith and her classmates. Merith's sister Deborah was graduating in 1989. Principal Robert E. Lee assumed the Weismans would not object to having Rabbi Leslie Gutterman deliver the invocation. He was wrong; they did object and asked a federal judge to remove the rabbi from the program. The Weismans lost this round and attended the graduation, at which Rabbi Gutterman gave what Daniel called "a typical Jewish family blessing." Ironically, his prayer thanked God for America's "court system where all may seek justice." Just as ironically, Deborah received the award for "best school spirit" after her family had sued the school's principal to keep the rabbi from delivering this prayer.

The Weismans returned to court after Deborah's graduation and won a ruling against further prayer in Providence schools. The case reached the Supreme Court during a presidential election year in 1992. President George Bush endorsed a constitutional amendment to reverse the Court's prayer decisions, while his challenger, Bill Clinton, opposed this move. Bush sent his solicitor general, Kenneth Starr—who later became President Clinton's nemesis—to support Principal Lee at the Court. Justice Anthony Kennedy, a devout Catholic and former altar boy, wrote for the narrow majority; he followed *Engel* and *Schempp* in ruling that the Constitution "forbids the State to exact religious conformity from a student as the price of attending her own high school graduation." Justice Antonin Scalia, another devout Catholic and former altar boy, wrote for the four dissenters and accused the majority of driving a judicial "bulldozer" over an American tradition. Scalia noted that President Bush had asked the guests at his 1989 inauguration to "bow their heads" in prayer. But as Justice Kennedy noted, the "coercion" of a teenager to attend her graduation—from both family and friends—is far greater than any pressure on adults to participate in civic ceremonies.

Kenneth Starr lost the prayer case and George Bush lost the 1992 election to Bill Clinton. Supporters of a constitutional amendment to reverse the prayer decisions also lost their White House pulpit. But they have not given up the effort to "put God back into our schools." Voting in June 1998, a majority of House members supported the prayer amendment sponsored by Oklahoma Republican Ernest Istook, who said he wanted to overturn Supreme Court decisions that have "attacked, twisted, and warped" the First Amendment. Istook fell short of the two-thirds vote he needed, but vowed to bring the issue back to Congress. Proposals to amend the First Amendment continue to bedevil the political process.

Earl Warren became Chief Justice in 1953, but the "Warren Court" that liberals cheered and conservatives booed did not become a cohesive body until October 1962, when Arthur Goldberg took the seat occupied for thirty-three years by Felix Frankfurter. Goldberg was actually the second of President John F. Kennedy's two justices, but the first, Byron R. White, never joined the solid liberal bloc that extended constitutional protections to every "despised" group in American society, including Communists and criminals.

Byron White, who replaced Justice Charles Whittaker in April 1962, closely resembled John Kennedy in age, ambition, and aggressive pursuit of political goals. Born just ten days after Kennedy in 1917, White attended his home-state University of Colorado and earned both a Phi Beta Kappa key and All-American honors in football as a running back, earning him the nickname

"Whizzer," which he detested. He turned down a Rhodes scholarship to play professional football. After one starring season with the Pittsburgh Steelers, White took his Rhodes year at Oxford; on his return he combined studies at Yale Law School with games for the Detroit Lions. Enlisting in the navy in 1942, he became a PT-boat skipper in the South Pacific and formed a close friendship with another skipper, Jack Kennedy. White completed his Yale studies after the war and clerked for Chief Justice Vinson before returning to Colorado, where he practiced law and Democratic politics until President Kennedy named him as deputy attorney general in 1961.

White spent a turbulent year in the Justice Department, stamping out civil rights fires in the Deep South. His forceful role in dealing with bigoted southern officials like Sheriff "Bull" Connor in Birmingham, Alabama, impressed the president, who wanted to place the "Kennedy stamp" on the Supreme Court. Senate racists like James Eastland of Mississippi did not oppose White's confirmation, largely because Kennedy had appeased them by naming some notorious racists to the federal district bench. Once on the bench, White voted most consistently with Tom Clark, another former Justice Department official who shared his hard-line position in criminal cases. White dissented from Chief Justice Warren's opinion in the "right-to-remain-silent" *Miranda* case and consistently voted against abortion rights, from his *Roe v. Wade* dissent in 1973 to *Planned Parenthood v. Casey* in 1992, which upheld the "essential holding" of *Roe* against a ferocious political assault. Distressed by this final loss, "Whizzer" White hung up his cleats and retired from the Court in 1993.

Arthur Goldberg played on Earl Warren's team for just three seasons, but he gave the Chief his vote in almost every case. Born in Chicago in 1908, he raced through school and began practicing law at twenty, mostly representing labor unions. He became general counsel of the United Steelworkers and advised John Kennedy on labor issues during the 1960 presidential campaign. Goldberg was rewarded with the post of labor secretary and impressed the president with his mediating skills. When Justice Frankfurter retired in August 1962, Kennedy immediately named Goldberg to replace him. During his three years on the Court, Goldberg displayed little of the "judicial restraint" his predecessor had championed for three decades. He voted to strike down state laws in cases that dealt with coerced confessions, capital punishment, and contraception. Goldberg reluctantly left the Court in 1965 to become United Nations ambassador under President Lyndon Johnson; he hoped to mediate an end to the Vietnam War and then return to the Court. But the war ended Johnson's presidency in 1968, and Goldberg returned to private practice until his death in 1990.

John Kennedy died in November 1963 from an assassin's bullets in Dallas, Texas. Lyndon Johnson, who took the presidential oath with as little warning as Harry Truman, was a native Texan who fought Kennedy for the Democratic nomination in 1960 and took the vice presidency as his runner-up prize. Johnson succeeded where Kennedy had failed in pushing a sweeping civil rights bill through Congress in 1964, but he failed miserably in ending America's involvement in the Vietnam War. The Supreme Court decided several landmark cases that began with civil rights and antiwar protests, and President Johnson's two justices supported the protesters in almost every case.

Abe Fortas replaced Arthur Goldberg in 1965, capping a brilliant career in government legal service and private practice. Born in 1910 in Memphis, Tennessee, he became editor in chief of the *Yale Law Journal* and joined Yale's law faculty after graduation in 1933. Fortas became a New Deal lawyer and was working in the Interior Department when he met Lyndon Johnson, then a young Texas congressman, in 1937. Johnson owed his Senate election in 1948 to Fortas, who persuaded the Supreme Court to keep federal judges from opening the ballot boxes into which Johnson's eighty-seven-vote primary victory had been stuffed, which led wags to call him "Landslide Lyndon." In 1963, Chief Justice Warren appointed Fortas to argue for Clarence Earl Gideon, who was tried and convicted for a Florida pool-hall burglary without a lawyer, over his protest that the Constitution gave him the right to counsel. Fortas convinced a receptive Court that Gideon could not adequately defend himself against the state's lawyers, and the justices ruled in *Gideon v. Wainwright* that every indigent defendant must be given counsel. "Landslide Lyndon" finally rewarded his intimate adviser with the Supreme Court seat that Goldberg had hoped to reclaim.

Johnson added another experienced lawyer to the Court when he named Thurgood Marshall to replace Tom Clark in 1967. Marshall was already a legal legend, having served as the NAACP's chief counsel from 1939 to 1961 and having won all but three of the thirty-two cases he argued before the Supreme Court. In 1961, President Kennedy named him to the federal appellate bench in New York; he resigned in 1965 to become solicitor general, the first black to hold that post. The Senate's unrepentent Confederates donned their hoods at his confirmation hearings; Strom Thurmond of South Carolina demanded that Marshall answer sixty complicated questions, many about nineteenth-century cases. All but one of the eleven votes against him came from Deep South senators.

Marshall had been a forceful advocate before the Court, but on the bench he struck many observers as bored and detached. He focused on civil rights cases and wrote few opinions in areas like antitrust or tax law. Marshall reportedly allowed his law clerks to write his opinions; one story had Marshall responding to compliments about an important civil rights opinion: "Oh yeah? I'll have to read it." But other justices only lightly edit their clerks' opinions, and many never master fields of law they find boring. And the masterful advocate could tear apart lawyers whose oral arguments he found evasive or prejudiced. During argument in 1977 of the *Bakke* case, which challenged minority admissions programs in medical schools, Marshall questioned Allen Bakke's lawyer: "You're talking about your client's rights; don't these underprivileged people have some rights?" The lawyer replied: "They certainly have the rights to compete ..." Marshall cut him off: "To eat cake."

Earl Warren presided as Chief Justice from 1953 to 1969, and the *Brown* case—the most famous during his tenure—was decided in 1954. But the "Warren Court" that profoundly and lastingly reshaped the Constitution really existed only between 1962 and 1969, from the time Arthur Goldberg joined the Court until Earl Warren retired. Goldberg added the crucial fifth vote that gave Warren, William Brennan, Hugo Black, and William Douglas a solid majority on virtually every issue. The Warren Court remained intact after Abe Fortas replaced Goldberg and became even stronger when Thurgood Marshall replaced Tom Clark in 1967. Justice Brennan was fond of saying, "With five votes, you can do anything around here." And with five and then six sure votes, the Warren Court turned the Bill of Rights into a powerful weapon against government officials—from police officers to presidents—who failed to treat people fairly and equally and to respect their "human dignity."

We cannot give "close scrutiny" to more than a handful of the landmark Warren Court decisions. They mounted so rapidly that an entire book could hardly examine them in any detail. We can, however, look at snapshots of cases that raised issues dividing the American people and that gave the Warren Court opportunities to expand the Constitution's protection of the people's rights. Our five snapshots deal with disenfranchised voters, black travelers, accused rapists, student protesters, and newspaper editors. These groups have little in common, but they all looked to the Warren Court for protection.

After his retirement, Earl Warren was asked which of his opinions he considered the most significant. Most people would assume that *Brown* topped the list by far. Warren surprised his questioner by naming *Reynolds v. Sims*, a 1964 opinion that redrew the nation's entire political map, ending the grip of rural lawmakers on an increasingly urban society. Pressures on the Court to force the fair apportionment of state and federal legislative districts had mounted in the 1950s, as the population of cities and suburbs mushroomed. Voters in several states filed suits claiming that malapportionment violated the Fourteenth Amendment's Equal Protection Clause. But in 1946, the Court had decided in *Colegrove v. Green* that disgruntled urban voters should make their complaints in ballot boxes, not in courthouses. Justice Felix Frankfurter wrote for the Court in *Colegrove* that federal judges should stay out of this "political thicket."

The Warren Court decided in 1962 to cut down the brambles that surrounded the Congress and state capitals. The justices began with Tennessee, where the largest state legislative district had nineteen voters for each one in the smallest. Tennessee's constitution required a redistricting every ten years, but the rural-dominated legislature simply ignored this command. Writing in *Baker v. Carr*, Justice Brennan reversed *Colegrove* and ruled that federal judges had power to hear reapportionment cases. He stated that Tennessee's urban voters "are entitled to a trial and a decision" of their complaint. Hearing the news, urban voters in more than a dozen states quickly ran to federal courthouses to file similar complaints. Two years later, the Court decided six reapportionment cases at once. The lead case, *Reynolds v. Sims*, came from Georgia, where the largest senatorial district had forty-one times more voters than the smallest. Only Justice John Harlan dissented from Earl Warren's opinion. "Legislators represent people, not trees or acres," Warren wrote. "Legislators are elected by voters, not farms or cities or economic interests." The "one person-one vote" standard of the *Reynolds* opinion has reshaped America's political landscape, with both Congress and state legislatures now dominated by lawmakers who represent cities and suburbs; the 2 percent of Americans who still live on farms no longer hold the reins of power.

Shortly before the *Brown* decision, Chief Justice Warren set off with his black chauffeur to visit Civil War battlefields in Virginia. He heard echoes of those battles the next morning. Warren emerged from his nice hotel to discover that his driver had slept in the car. He asked why. "Well, Mr. Chief Justice," the driver began, "I just couldn't find a place—" Warren suddenly realized that nice hotels in Virginia did not admit black guests. "I was embarrassed, I was ashamed," he later recalled. Ten years later, in 1964, Congress passed a sweeping Civil Rights Act that outlawed racial segregation in "public accommodations" like hotels and restaurants. Congress based the law on its constitutional power to regulate "commerce among the several states." Back in 1883, the Supreme Court had struck down a federal civil rights law based on the Equal Protection Clause, and Congress feared the justices might feel bound by that precedent.

Owners of the Heart of Atlanta Motel, which filled most of its rooms with out-of-state guests, promptly challenged the law. The motel's lawyer asked the justices to listen to the "forty-three million white people in the South" who believed that a business owner's right to discriminate "is more important and more paramount than the commerce of the United States." Earl Warren listened to the echoing voice of his black chauffeur. He assigned the Court's unanimous opinion in 1964 to Justice Tom Clark, who wrote in *Heart of Atlanta Motel v. United States* that Congress may employ its commerce powers to legislate against "moral wrongs" like racial discrimination.

Racial discrimination is morally wrong, and so is rape. Society can punish both, but deciding who is guilty raises more difficult questions when the defendant is not a motel owner but a poorly educated drifter. Can the police force those charged with rape or murder to confess their crimes? Some methods of extracting confessions are clearly unlawful. The Supreme Court in 1936 threw out confessions obtained by whipping, and in 1958 the Warren Court ruled that police cannot tell suspects that a mob will "get them" if they refuse to confess.

Most suspects will talk without torture or death threats, but how many would confess if a lawyer advised them to keep their mouths shut? The Fifth Amendment says that no person "shall be compelled in any criminal case to be a witness against himself." Does this mean that police officers must act like defense lawyers in their squad cars and interrogation rooms? The Warren Court faced this question in the case of Ernesto Miranda, accused of raping a teenager in Phoenix, Arizona. The victim did not see his face, but witnesses saw his car's license plate. After two hours of questioning, Miranda gave police a signed confession. He was convicted over his lawyer's objection that police had violated his Fifth Amendment right to remain silent.

During oral argument in *Miranda v. Arizona*, a lawyer speaking for state prosecutors urged the Court not to "encourage" defendants to consult lawyers before talking to police. Earl Warren, a former prosecutor, had a question: "Are lawyers a menace?" Any defense lawyer, he was told, "is going to prevent a confession from being obtained." Warren knew from experience that most suspects will talk, even if they know they can remain silent. Speaking for a bare majority in 1966, Warren said that "incommunicado interrogation" was "destructive of human dignity." Word for word, he dictated the "Miranda warning" that police must now give all suspects. Justice Byron White, the most critical of the four dissenters, warned that Warren's opinion "will return a killer, a rapist or other criminal to the streets" to commit more crimes. But Ernesto Miranda did not return to the streets; jurors in his second trial—who did not hear his confession—convicted Miranda once again.

The Warren Court told criminal defendants they did not have to speak with police, but during the Vietnam War, many Americans wanted to speak out against American policies. The Court decided several cases that raised First Amendment issues. The hardest cases involved "symbolic speech" in which protest was expressed without words. For young men, the most visible symbol of the government's power over their lives was a small piece of cardboard. Federal law required men of draft age to carry their draft card at all times. When the war heated up, some protested by burning their cards. Congress promptly made it criminal to "destroy or mutilate" draft cards, but this law did not extinguish the protests. David O'Brien burned his card in 1966, and was sentenced to prison for his symbolic act. After a federal appellate court reversed his conviction on First Amendment grounds, the government protested to the Supreme Court. Warren wrote the opinion in 1968 that sent O'Brien to jail, placing the "smooth and efficient functioning" of the draft system ahead of his free-speech rights. This was one of the few cases in which the Chief Justice sided with the government in a First Amendment dispute, but Warren generally deferred to the military in clashes with civilians. William Douglas filed the sole dissent in *United States v. O'Brien*; his fellow First Amendment absolutist, Hugo Black, joined Warren's opinion.

The next year, the Court shifted positions in another "symbolic speech" case. Mary Beth Tinker did not have a draft card, but she displayed her opposition to the war by wearing a black armband to her eighth-grade classes at Warren Harding Junior High in Des Moines, Iowa. School officials had gotten wind of her plans and quickly issued an order banning armbands from the city's schools. Mary Beth was suspended when she wore her armband to school in December 1965. Her protest upset the "smooth and efficient functioning" of her algebra class, where the teacher argued with her about patriotism. Justice Abe Fortas, writing in *Tinker v. Des Moines*, admitted that "symbolic speech" like Mary Beth's armband "may start an argument or cause a disturbance." But "our Constitution says we must take this risk," he added. Fortas declared that schools "may not be enclaves of totalitarianism." Crotchety in his eighties, Justice Black dissented and lectured Mary Beth that "uncontrolled liberty is an enemy to domestic peace." He lumped Mary Beth, whose protest was totally quiet, with the "loudest-mouthed" students who "have too often violently attacked" their classmates. Only Justice Harlan, three months shy of seventy, joined Black in telling Mary Beth to sit down and shut up.

Our final Warren Court snapshot was taken in 1960, but was not developed until 1964. The "sit-in"movement against lunch counter segregation began in February 1960 in Greensboro, North Carolina, and rapidly spread across the South. Demonstrators filled local jails, and civil rights groups quickly ran out of bail money. Notable figures like Nat King Cole, Sammy Davis, Jr., and Jackie Robinson lent their names and prestige to a fund-raising effort that included a full-page advertisement in the *New York Times* on March 29, 1960. Under the headline "Heed Their Rising Voices," the ad detailed the "wave of terror" against sit-in protesters. "In Montgomery, Alabama, after students sang 'My Country 'Tis of Thee' on the State Capitol steps," the ad stated, "their leaders were expelled from school, and truckloads of police armed with shot-guns and tear gas ringed the Albany State College campus." The facts were slightly different: the students actually sang the national anthem, protest leaders were suspended but not expelled, and police were deployed but did not "ring" the campus.

The *Times* ad did not name any Montgomery officials, but police commissioner L. B. Sullivan brought a libel suit against the paper, claiming that readers would connect him with the police activities and that his reputation had been damaged. The ad's minor errors persuaded an all-white Montgomery jury to conclude that Sullivan had been libeled; they awarded him a $500,000 judgment against the *Times*. Justice William Brennan wrote for a unanimous Court in reversing the judgment. He delivered the most stirring defense of free expression since the time of Holmes and Brandeis. Brennan viewed the case of *New York Times v. Sullivan* "against the backdrop of a profound national commitment to the principle that debate on public issues should be uninhibited, robust, and wide-open, and that it may well include vehement, caustic, and sometimes unpleasantly sharp attacks on government and public officials." Brennan imposed on officials like Sullivan the high burden of proving that statements about them were published with "reckless disregard" of their truth or falsity. Few officials have met that burden since Brennan wrote his landmark opinion.

Earl Warren endured many vehement, caustic, and sharp attacks during the sixteen momentous years he presided over the Supreme Court. During the 1960s, the far-right John Birch Society launched a campaign to "Impeach Earl Warren," a response more to the Warren Court's rulings in cases that dealt with Communists than to its school segregation decisions. The efforts to impeach Warren failed, but they provided ironic evidence of his commitment—through the Court's First Amendment decisions—to the uninhibited debate on public issues on which the democratic process depends. Earl Warren's heart finally stopped beating on July 9, 1974, but his spirit lived on in the hearts of millions of Americans. For two days after his death, Warren's body lay in a flag-draped casket in the Supreme Court's rotunda, while thousands of people—most of them very ordinary Americans—filed by to honor this extraordinary American. Many of those who paid their respects were black, and most had never before entered the Court's imposing edifice. Mae Taylor, who was sixty-six and had worked on the cleaning staff of the Capitol, just across the street, came to say goodbye to a man she had never met. "We owe a lot to him, he wanted equal rights for all people," she told a reporter. "America is a better place because he lived."

America *is* a better place because Earl Warren lived, but during the two decades before his death, the American people witnessed—and many took part in—bitter conflicts over civil rights and the Vietnam War. Confrontations in scores of towns and cities—from Boston to Birmingham to Berkeley—erupted into battles that pitted angry demonstrators against police officers, state troopers, federal marshals, National Guardsmen, and army troops. The forces of "law and order" used clubs, dogs, tear gas, fire hoses, bayonets, even bullets to quell the disorder that swept the country.

Many people died in the struggles to end segregation at home and warfare abroad. We cannot list all the victims here, but some names still ring faint bells of remembrance. Four little black girls—Denise McNair, Addie Collins, Cynthia Wesley, Carole Robertson—died in their Sunday dresses when a bomb destroyed the Sixteenth Street Baptist Church in Birmingham, Alabama, in 1964. Three voter registration workers—James Chaney, Andrew Goodman, Michael Schwerner—were murdered that same year by Klansmen in Philadelphia, Mississippi. When the Vietnam War spilled into Cambodia in 1970, Ohio National Guard troops shot and killed four young people—Allison Krause, Jeffrey Miller, Sandra Scheuer, William Schroeder—during a protest rally at Kent State University. No monument like the Vietnam Memorial in Washington honors those who died in America's domestic wars, but the Warren Court's judicial opinions form a symbolic monument to their memory.

SECTION VI

"A Right of
Personal Privacy"

32

"You've Been Taking Pure

Thalidomide"

Richard Nixon won the presidency in 1968 by offering voters a "secret plan" to end the Vietnam War, while his Democratic opponent, Vice President Hubert Humphrey, could not untangle himself from Lyndon Johnson's disastrous Vietnam policies. Humphrey received twelve million fewer votes than Johnson had won in swamping Barry Goldwater in 1964. Almost ten million of the defectors, however, voted for George Wallace rather than Nixon, who barely squeaked past Humphrey at the finish line. In his last-ditch battle for wavering voters, Nixon turned his guns on the Warren Court, charging it with going "too far in weakening the peace forces as against the criminal forces in this country." There was some irony in the spectacle of one former Republican California governor attacking another, particularly since Earl Warren had been a tough prosecutor and Nixon—although he had a law degree—had never tried a criminal case. But many Warren Court decisions, including *Miranda* in 1966, had sparked public outcries, and Nixon knew that denouncing the Supreme Court had never cost a politician votes. George Wallace had proved that in running for president in 1964, and Nixon would not let Wallace outflank him on the right.

Before he left office, Lyndon Johnson handed Nixon the chance to replace Earl Warren as Chief Justice. Warren privately detested Nixon, but he shared the blame with Johnson and Justice Abe Fortas for this political and judicial blunder. Assuming that Johnson would run for a full presidential term in 1968, Warren had announced in June that he would retire when his successor was confirmed. Warren knew in advance that Johnson would name Fortas as Chief Justice, and heartily approved his choice. However, reports that Fortas had accepted large fees for short lectures quickly made headlines and prompted Republicans to hold up his confirmation hearings. The slow drip of news stories about Fortas's shady financial dealings finally eroded Johnson's resolve to stand behind his old friend, but Fortas stubbornly refused to withdraw until three weeks before the presidential election, too late for Johnson to make another nomination. Warren could have withdrawn his proffered resignation and remained as Chief Justice, but this would have looked duplicitous. The Chief was a man of his word, and he loyally allowed his political enemy Richard Nixon to appoint his successor. In truth, Warren Burger owed his nomination as Chief Justice to the greed and untruthfulness of Abe Fortas.

President Nixon had met Burger only on ceremonial occasions before choosing him to replace Warren as Chief Justice. But his attorney general, John Mitchell, recommended Burger as a "law and order" judge, just what Nixon ordered for the Supreme Court. Born in St. Paul, Minnesota, in 1907, Burger epitomized the Horatio Alger model for success. Raised in a working-class family, he worked during the day to pay his way through law school at night. Burger practiced law and Republican politics for more than twenty years, and swung his state's delegation behind Dwight Eisenhower at the 1952 GOP convention. Ike rewarded Burger in 1953 with an appointment to head the Justice Department's Civil Division. Two years later, the president placed Burger on the District of Columbia federal appellate court, one of the nation's busiest and most influential. Liberal judges dominated that court, and Burger wrote stinging dissents in many cases. He almost always upheld criminal convictions, and he publicly denounced the Supreme Court's *Miranda* decision in speeches and articles.

Richard Nixon hoped and expected that Warren Burger would preside over the dismantling of the Warren Court's liberal edifice. The great irony of Burger's seventeen years as Chief Justice is that he did little more than chip the marble of its sturdy walls. One scholar aptly called the Burger Court "the counter-revolution that wasn't." The Chief's inability to lead the Court was the primary reason for this failure. And Burger's lack of leadership allowed Justice William Brennan, the Warren Court's real leader, to minimize the damage and even to erect new walls that sheltered new rights, most notably the "right to privacy" that gave birth to *Roe v. Wade* in 1973.

Few Americans had any knowledge of the *Roe* case until the the Supreme Court announced its decision on January 22, 1973. Most lawyers would date *Roe*'s beginning to March 3, 1970, when a young lawyer named Linda Coffee entered the federal courthouse in Dallas, Texas, and filed a complaint for "Jane Roe" against Henry Wade, the county's district attorney, seeking to block enforcement of the state's abortion law. Historians would look back to 1854, when the Texas legislature made abortion a criminal offense except to save a pregnant woman's life. From another perspective, however, the *Roe* case began in Phoenix, Arizona, on July 20, 1962. On that day, a twenty-nine-year-old pregnant woman named Sherri Finkbine received a call from her doctor, warning that she faced a high risk of having a badly deformed baby. Sherri, the mother of four healthy children and the hostess of *Romper Room*, a popular children's television show, had been treating daily headaches with pills her husband, Bob, had brought with him from a trip to England. The label on the pill bottle read "Distaval," but Sherri had recently seen an article in the Phoenix newspaper, the *Arizona Republic*, about an epidemic of deformed babies in England and West Germany. Their mothers had taken a medication called thalidomide for headaches and morning sickness; Sherri wondered if Distaval might be the same thing, and called her doctor to find out. The call she got back confirmed her worst fears. "You've been taking pure thalidomide," he said.

The next day, Sherri and her husband visited the doctor, who showed them pictures in a medical journal of "thalidomide babies" with no arms or legs. Sherri had great misgivings about the morality of abortion, but the graphic pictures of babies with little fingers at their shoulders or toes at their hips overcame her qualms. "That did it," she later said. Sherri decided to have an abortion, and her doctor arranged one at Good Samaritan Hospital for the next week. Arizona law allowed abortions only to save the pregnant woman's life, but Sherri's doctor convinced the hospital's abortion committee that continuing her pregnancy might endanger her life. Most hospitals kept these questionable cases quiet, and Sherri's abortion would have passed without notice had she not called a friend at the *Arizona Republic* to thank him for the story that alerted her. Sherri then got a call from the paper's medical editor; she told him about the pictures her doctor had shown the Finkbines and her decision to end her pregnancy. The next morning's front-page *Republic* headline read, "Pill Causing Deformed Infants May Cost Woman Her Baby Here." The story did not identify Sherri by name, but the next day, hospital officials canceled her abortion after the county attorney warned them of legal action. The day after that, the Finkbines' lawyer asked a state judge to restrain state and county attorneys from intervening. Sherri's name became public, and the following day newspapers around the country informed their readers of her predicament.

Two weeks after Sherri called her doctor, *Life* magazine spread pictures of the Finkbines' healthy children and their mother across two pages, under the headline "Abortion—With the Future Grim, Should the Unborn Die?" The *Newsweek* headline over her story read, "Abortion: Mercy—or Murder?" Balancing opinions on the issue, *Newsweek* quoted two men on the issue. "No matter how praiseworthy the motives that inspire an abortion," stated Father Thurston Davis, editor of the Jesuit magazine *America*, "the answer must always be no. To deliberately terminate the life of an innocent being is, in one word, murder." Dr. Alan Guttmacher, chief of obstetrics at Mount Sinai Hospital in New York, answered that many women died from illegal abortions and warned that "criminal abortion will continue to be a serious medical-legal disease" until states repealed their laws. "Don't tell me your town doesn't have a criminal abortionist," Dr. Guttmacher said to opponents. "You're just too naive to know who he is."

The Good Samaritan Hospital closed its doors to Sherri Finkbine, and she had no intention of looking for a back-alley abortionist in Phoenix. Unwilling to wait until Arizona judges decided their suit, the Finkbines decided to seek an abortion outside the country. A Swedish newspaper offered to arrange their travel in return for interviews, and American reporters trailed Sherri and her husband to Stockholm. "We don't believe in abortions, really," she told one. "But the main thing is to do what is right for the baby. I don't feel it morally right to bring a deformed child into the world." Sherri finally ended her pregnancy on August 18, 1962. The doctors told her the fetus was "not a baby," and Bob Finkbine told reporters that "we both feel extremely relieved." But not everyone felt relieved. Speaking for the Roman Catholic Church, the Vatican radio called Sherri's abortion a "homicide" and said "the victim was a human being." However, the Gallup Poll reported in September 1962 that 52 percent of its respondents felt that Sherri had done the right thing, and only 32 percent disagreed. When they put down their newspapers and magazines, Americans began talking about abortion with friends and neighbors. Arguments over this emotional issue, mostly polite but sometimes heated, began moving from living rooms into courtrooms.

Rosa Parks had not planned in advance her decision in December 1955 to remain seated in the "whites-only" section of a bus in Montgomery, Alabama. But her arrest for defying the Jim Crow system of segregation helped to focus public attention on the plight of southern blacks and spurred a national campaign for civil rights. These efforts—which culminated in the Civil Rights Act of 1964 and its approval that same year by the Supreme Court—were led by the NAACP and defended in court by an experienced legal staff headed by Thurgood Marshall. Sherri Finkbine had also not planned in advance her decision in August 1962 to end her pregnancy outside a state that made abortion a criminal act. These two women—unlike in race, religion, and social class—shared one thing: their determination to defy laws they considered wrong. But unlike Rosa Parks, Sherri Finkbine could not turn for support to a large organization like the NAACP or a staff of experienced lawyers. In this respect, the campaign for abortion rights began with handicaps that only determination and persistance could overcome. There was, in fact, no abortion rights movement in the 1960s with any political clout or celebrity backers.

Although many women supported the suffrage movement in the early twentieth century and lobbied for laws to protect women workers, their campaigns largely disbanded after women won the vote in 1920. Abortion was not an issue that generated lobbying or litigation, although by 1910 all but one state had outlawed abortion. The birth control movement, led by Margaret Sanger, focused on contraception and stayed away from abortion. During the Great Depression and World War II, most women had more pressing concerns than abortion rights.

There was no visible women's movement during the Fifties, but many women supported the civil rights and antiwar movements in the Sixties. They were receptive to the message of Betty Friedan's 1963 book *The Feminine Mystique*, which documented and deplored the subordinate roles of women in families, jobs, and politics. Her book focused on bread-and-butter issues like "equal pay for equal work" and did not even mention abortion. In 1966, Friedan helped launch the National Organization for Women, whose members devoted most of their energy to lobbying for the Equal Rights Amendment to the Constitution, which provided that "equality of rights under the law shall not be denied or abridged by the United States or by any state on account of sex." First proposed in 1923, the ERA languished until the women's movement pushed it through Congress in 1972. However, after ratification by thirty-five states, the ERA became a victim of the abortion wars and finally died in 1982, falling short of adoption by three states. Although smaller groups like the National Abortion Rights League worked before 1973 to repeal criminal abortion laws, NOW did not make abortion rights a priority until the *Roe* decision sparked a "pro-life" backlash.

A decade before the Supreme Court docketed the *Roe* case in 1971, a few dedicated lawyers had begun planning a long-range campaign against criminal abortion laws. Sherri Finkbine's ordeal in 1962 had stirred Harriet Pilpel, a New York lawyer who acted as counsel for both Planned Parenthood and the American Civil Liberties Union. She raised the abortion issue at the ACLU's national conference in 1964, warning that abortion laws were "a dagger aimed at the heart of some of our most fundamental freedoms." Citing the Finkbine case, she argued that states deprived women of their liberty to make choices about childbirth when they compelled them "to have a baby when the medical testimony is that the baby may well be deformed." The ACLU's national board affirmed in 1967 "the right of a woman to have an abortion, and the right of a physician to perform, or refuse to perform, an abortion, without the threat of criminal sanctions." Supporting the right of doctors to refuse to perform abortions conformed to the ACLU's "conscientious objector" policy on military service.

Faced with criminal prosecution in every state for performing abortions, doctors who believed they and their patients should make these decisions began an effort in the 1960s to expand the loopholes in criminal abortion laws. Between 1967 and 1971, seventeen states had revised their laws, most to permit abortions for protection of the pregnant woman's physical and mental health as well as her life. With ACLU backing, Harriet Pilpel helped organize a campaign to repeal New York's criminal abortion law, which succeeded in 1970. In addition to New York, the District of Columbia and three states—Hawaii,

Alaska, and Washington—had adopted laws by 1971 that removed almost every restriction on abortion. Thirty states, however, still banned abortions unless the woman's life was endangered, and three—Louisiana, New Hampshire, and Pennsylvania—made every abortion unlawful.

The small band of lawyers who filed suits against restrictive laws in several states lacked the resources of the NAACP's Legal Defense and Education Fund, but they pooled their research and shared briefs. Unlike the lawyers who confronted in *Brown* the hostile precedent of *Plessy*, the abortion lawyers had no comparable obstacle in their path to the Supreme Court. But they also had few helpful decisions like *Sweatt* and *McLaurin*, the graduate school cases that NAACP lawyers had won in 1950 and cited as precedent in their *Brown* arguments. The feminist lawyers took whatever precedent they could find, and discovered some in the most unlikely places.

Jack Skinner was the most unlikely person to help American women gain the right to legal abortions. An Oklahoma jury sent him to jail in 1926 for the youthful crime of stealing chickens. Failing to learn that crime does not pay, Skinner went to prison in 1929 and again in 1934 for armed robbery. While he sat in the penitentiary, Oklahoma's attorney general brought proceedings in 1936 against the hapless "three-time loser" under the state's Habitual Criminal Sterilization Act. A judge ordered that Skinner undergo a vasectomy to protect Oklahoma from any further chicken thieves and robbers. Six years passed before the Supreme Court decided Skinner's appeal from this order.

Arguing before the Court, Oklahoma's attorney general claimed that criminal tendencies were inherited and defended his state's law as a "eugenic measure." But in 1942 this sounded too much like Nazi policies under which several hundred thousand "defective" people like criminals and the mentally retarded had been sterilized in Germany. Justice William Douglas wrote for a unanimous Court in *Skinner v. Oklahoma*. He made a veiled but pointed reference to the Nazis in striking down the law. "In evil or reckless hands," he wrote, the power to sterilize "can cause races or types which are inimical to the dominant group to wither and disappear." Douglas based his ruling on equal protection grounds, since the Oklahoma law exempted those convicted of white-collar crimes like embezzlement, even though they often stole more than robbers. But his opinion opened the door to future cases that raised broader issues. "We are dealing here with legislation which involves one of the basic civil rights of man," Douglas added. "Marriage and procreation are fundamental to the very existence and survival of the race."

The *Skinner* case established a "fundamental right" to procreate, allowing people to have children if they want them. Does the Constitution also include the right *not* to have children? The justices answered this question in 1965, ruling in a case that began in 1961 when Planned Parenthood opened a medical clinic in New Haven, Connecticut, the home of Yale University but also a heavily Catholic city. A Connecticut law, enacted in 1879 during the "moral purity" crusade of Anthony Comstock and his Society for the Suppression of Vice, made it illegal to use "any drug, medicinal article or instrument for the purpose of preventing conception." State officials had never prosecuted any doctors under this law, but the New Haven district attorney reluctantly followed up a complaint from an incensed Catholic neighbor of the New Haven clinic and arrested its director, Estelle Griswold, who greeted her arrest with delight. The Supreme Court had recently refused to hear a challenge to the Connecticut birth control law, on the ground that no person faced any penalty for violating its provisions. By arresting Griswold and Dr. Thomas Buxton, the clinic's medical director and a Yale medical professor, New Haven officials gave birth control advocates a better shot at Supreme Court review. After a brief trial in which the eager defendants admitted their guilt, a local judge fined them $100 each for giving contraceptives to married couples.

The justices heard arguments in *Griswold v. Connecticut* in March 1965. Thomas Emerson, who argued for Estelle Griswold and Dr. Buxton before the Court, was a Yale law professor and a close friend of Justice William Douglas. Emerson attacked the Connecticut law for infringing personal "liberty" under the Fourteenth Amendment's Due Process Clause, citing the opinion Douglas had written in the *Skinner* case for authority; he added that Connecticut lawmakers in 1879 believed "it's a religious principle that's being enacted into law." The state's lawyer, Joseph Clark, had trouble answering questions about the law's purpose, finally settling on the promotion of marital "fidelity" as the best reason. Access to contraceptives, he suggested, might plant thoughts of adultery in the minds of errant spouses. Given the state's weak argument, the Court could easily have struck it down under the "rational basis" test. But *Griswold* reached the justices at the height of the Warren Court's "activist" phase, and the liberal majority relished this chance to invalidate a law they viewed as a relic of Victorian morality.

Justice Douglas wrote for the Court in the *Griswold* case, and he eagerly walked through the door he had left open twenty-three years earlier in his *Skinner* opinion. Like his friend Tom Emerson, Douglas was a former Yale law professor, and his *Griswold* opinion read almost like a parody of academic jargon. He wanted to find a "right to privacy" in the Constitution, but that phrase does not appear in its text. So he scoured the Court's earlier decisions for precedent, turning up four cases that established a "right of association" under the First Amendment. Two upheld the rights of parents to make decisions about their children's education, and two protected the NAACP from harassment by southern officials. "The association of people is not mentioned in the Constitution nor in the Bill of Rights," Douglas conceded. Nonetheless, the cases he cited "suggest that specific guarantees in the Bill of Rights have penumbras, formed by emanations from those guarantees that help give them life and substance."

Douglas pointed to the First, Third, Fourth, Fifth, and Ninth Amendments as sources of the "emanations" whose "penumbras" created "zones of privacy" into which government cannot trespass without good reason. In other words, Douglas was comparing the Bill of Rights to an umbrella that shields the public from official snoopers, casting a wider shadow than its narrow words.

Although his arcane terms drew snickers from the legal cognoscenti, Douglas grounded his *Griswold* opinion on a solid foundation of precedent. He cited a dozen cases decided between 1886 and 1961—including his *Skinner* opinion of 1942—to argue that Dr. Buxton and his patients enjoyed "a relationship lying within the zone of privacy created by several fundamental constitutional guarantees." Oddly, the five amendments on which Douglas rested his "privacy" claim did not include the Fourteenth. In both *Skinner* and *Griswold*, he deliberately avoided reliance on the Due Process Clause, wary of raising the discredited *Lochner* decision from its judicial grave. Finding a "liberty" to use contraceptives might revive the "substantive due process" doctrine the Court had buried in 1937 in *West Coast Hotel*. "We do not sit as a super-legislature to determine the wisdom, need, and propriety of laws that touch economic problems, business affairs, or social conditions," Douglas wrote in *Griswold*. He feared that using the Due Process Clause to strike down Connecticut's ban on contraception might encourage more conservative justices, once they gained a majority, to wipe out the New Deal legacy of social legislation. Douglas did not want his *Griswold* opinion cited as precedent by lawyers who represented sweatshop owners and racial bigots. Grounding the "right to privacy" on the Bill of Rights would keep the Fourteenth Amendment out of the wrong hands.

Tom Clark was the only justice who did not quibble with Douglas in the *Griswold* case. John Harlan—the Warren Court's most principled conservative—had no qualms about finding the "liberty" to use contraceptives in the Due Process Clause. He wrote in concurrence that the Fourteenth Amendment "stands, in my opinion, on its own bottom" and does not depend on other amendments "or any of their radiations" for its meaning. Justice Harlan sounded like Harlan Fiske Stone in giving the Connecticut law "closer scrutiny" and concluding that it abridged the "fundamental liberties" of Dr. Buxton's patients to obtain contraceptives. Arthur Goldberg, joined by Earl Warren and William Brennan, chided Douglas for timidity. Goldberg fearlessly opened the Pandora's box of the Ninth Amendment, discovering "the right of privacy in the marital relationship" among those "retained by the people" when they handed powers to government officials. Byron White, skeptical of any "privacy" rights, joined the majority—but not Douglas—with a concurrence that stressed Connecticut's "total nonenforcement" of its contraceptive ban as grounds for striking down the law.

The two *Griswold* dissenters, Hugo Black and Potter Stewart, joined each other's opinions. "I like my privacy as well as the next one," Black wrote, "but I am nevertheless compelled to admit that government has a right to invade it unless prohibited by some specific constitutional protection." Consulting his well-thumbed copy of the Constitution, Black found no words that barred states from banning contraception. Admitting that Connecticut's law reflected Victorian morality, Black decried any effort to "keep the Constitution in tune with the times." Stewart also found no constitutional provision offended by the "uncommonly silly law" he voted to uphold. In his opinion, judges should not decide for voters which laws they considered "unwise, or even asinine."

Texas lawmakers—all men and all white—had enacted a criminal abortion statute in 1854, providing that "any person" who performed an abortion "shall be confined in the penitentiary not less than two nor more than five years." Fifty years later, the state legislature amended the law to permit abortions that doctors considered necessary to save a woman's life. Was the Texas criminal abortion statute an unwise or asinine law? Even if it was, did the law violate the Constitution? If so, which provision did it offend? Between them, the Supreme Court justices wrote six opinions on both sides of the *Griswold* case in 1965. Five years later, this judicial cacophony presented three federal judges in Dallas with several choices in deciding these questions at a hearing on May 22, 1970.

This judicial panel had convened to hear arguments on three separate lawsuits filed against the Texas abortion law. The first suit had been filed two months earlier, on March 3, on behalf of "Jane Roe." This legal pseudonym shielded the identity of a young woman named Norma McCorvey, who had asked her lawyers to keep her name out of the newspapers; the public did not learn her true name until 1984, when she finally took off her legal mask. Norma was twenty-two years old and three months pregnant when she first tried to get an abortion in January 1970. She was not another Sherri Finkbine, happily married with four children and her own television show. Norma Nelson McCorvey was a high school dropout from a broken home; she had been raped at an early age and spent much of her childhood in reform schools. She was sixteen and working as a carhop when she met "Woody" McCorvey, eight years older and twice divorced. They got married six weeks later and soon left Dallas for California, where Norma discovered she was pregnant. Woody flew into a rage, accusing his wife of sleeping around and punching her black and blue. She took a bus back to Dallas, got a job in a lesbian bar, and gave birth to Melissa in May 1965. Upset with Norma's bisexual lifestyle, her mother moved to Louisiana with Melissa and gained legal custody with her second husband.

Norma had a second daughter in 1967, the result of a brief affair, and willingly surrendered custody to the baby's father. She left Dallas in the fall of 1969 with a traveling circus, working as a ticket-taker. Sometime in October 1969, Norma discovered she was pregnant for the third time and returned home. She visited Dr. Frank Bradley, who had delivered her two daughters, and he confirmed her pregnancy; she later recalled that he was "absolutely appalled" when she told him she did not want another baby. Dr. Bradley would not give her any help, even the names of other doctors who might perform an abortion. Norma went to see an osteopath, Dr. Richard Lane, who said he could not help but referred her to a lawyer named Henry McCluskey. Time was running short for Norma to have an abortion, and she wanted help in arranging an adoption for her baby, which was due in July. McCluskey met with her in late January 1970 and agreed to help arrange an adoption with a good family who would pay her childbirth expenses. They talked about abortion, and Norma said that she wished it were legal in Texas. McCluskey had recently won a case before a federal judicial panel, challenging a Texas law under which a married couple had been prosecuted for committing acts of sodomy. Writing for the panel, district judge Sarah Hughes had cited *Griswold v. Connecticut* in holding that moral disapproval of sodomy "is not sufficient reason for the State to encroach upon the liberty of married persons in their private conduct." A young Dallas lawyer named Linda Coffee had helped McCluskey in this case, and had asked his help in finding a pregnant woman who might be willing to challenge the Texas abortion law.

After his meeting with Norma, McCluskey called Linda Coffee and said he might have found her a plaintiff. She was excited and asked him to arrange for her to meet with Norma. Coffee then called her friend Sarah Weddington, a law school classmate from the University of Texas who had set up practice in Austin after graduating in 1967. The two young lawyers had been working with a group of Dallas women at the First Unitarian Church, who were planning a public campaign to repeal the Texas abortion law. Coffee and Weddington thought a lawsuit might help the campaign and might even succeed in striking down the law in court.

Weddington agreed to come to Dallas for a meeting with Norma McCorvey, and the three women first met at Columbo's Pizza Parlor in late January. Norma had told another woman in Dr. Lane's waiting room that she wanted an abortion and was advised that doctors might be sympathetic if she told them she had been raped. This was not true, but she told the two lawyers that a group of men had gang-raped her in Florida while she walked late one night from the carnival to her motel room. Coffee and Weddington expressed sympathy, but the Texas abortion law did not include a rape-victim exception and they did not want to ask the courts to create one. They also did not want to help Norma obtain a late-term abortion before they filed suit; they needed a pregnant plaintiff who still wanted an abortion. Norma agreed, and they finished their pizza with an understanding that the suit would be filed without her name on the caption.

Linda Coffee did most of the work in February 1970 on the complaint for "Jane Roe." She and Sarah Weddington had decided it would be helpful to file another complaint on behalf of a married couple. They reasoned that judges might dismiss Jane Roe's case for "mootness" if she was no longer pregnant when the case was heard. Judge Hughes's decision in Henry McCluskey's sodomy case suggested that married couples might find more judicial sympathy than unmarried women. Giving the judges a choice of cases also increased the odds of getting a favorable decision in at least one. Linda Coffee knew a married couple, Marsha and David King, who agreed to become "John and Jane Doe." She filed the "Roe" and "Doe" complaints in federal court on March 3, 1970. They both asked for a "declaratory judgment" that the Texas abortion statute violated the First, Fourth, Fifth, Eighth, Ninth, and Fourteenth Amendments. Both also named Dallas County's district attorney, Henry Wade, as defendant and sought an injunction barring him from enforcing the statute. Jane Roe's complaint alleged that the law infringed her "right to safe and adequate medical advice pertaining to the decision of whether to carry a given pregnancy to term" and also infringed "the fundamental right of all women to choose whether to bear children." The Does' complaint alleged that the abortion law intruded on their "right to marital privacy" and that fear of an unwanted pregnancy had "a detrimental effect upon Plaintiffs' marital happiness."

Coffee had talked with a *Dallas Times-Herald* reporter about the lawsuit, and the paper ran a front-page story the evening she filed the complaints. A follow-up article reported estimates of three thousand illegal abortions in Dallas each year. The paper's editors evenhandedly deplored both the Texas abortion law, which they called "badly in need of an intelligent overhaul," and the suits against it, for "tossing an extremely sensitive and complex moral issue into the laps of a mere handful of individuals—the judges who are to decide the case."

Linda Coffee and Sarah Weddington drew a good panel of federal judges to decide the "sensitive and complex moral issue" of abortion. All three were elderly— their average age was sixty-six—but all had been appointed by Democratic presidents and were considered liberal by civil rights lawyers. Irving Goldberg, who presided at the hearing on May 22, 1970, was a native Texan with a Harvard law degree who had practiced in a powerhouse Dallas law firm before President Johnson named him to the Fifth Circuit Court of Appeals in 1966. District judge Sarah Hughes, born in Baltimore in 1896, had earned a law degree while she worked as a police officer in Washington, D.C. She moved to Dallas in 1922, was elected twice to the state legislature, and served as a state judge from 1935 to 1961, when President Kennedy named her to the federal bench. On November 23, 1963, Judge Hughes administered the presidential oath to Lyndon Johnson after Kennedy's assassination in Dallas. The third panel member, Judge William Taylor, had practiced law in Dallas from 1932 until President Johnson placed him on the bench in 1966.

Six lawyers sat at the counsel tables when Judge Goldberg opened the hearing. Linda Coffee and Sarah Weddington spoke for Jane Roe and the Does; John Tolle and Jay Floyd represented District Attorney Henry Wade and Texas attorney general Crawford Martin. Fred Brunner and Ray Merrill appeared for

Dr. James Hallford, an "intervenor" who had been indicted for performing illegal abortions. Dr. Hallford's patients included rape and incest victims, and women who had contracted German measles, or rubella, during their pregnancies and faced great risks of having deformed babies. His complaint asked that the state criminal charges be dismissed because the Texas abortion law violated the federal Constitution.

Linda Coffee led off, moving from questions of federal jurisdiction into the constitutional issues raised in the complaint. She spoke confidently, certain that Judge Hughes—for whom she had clerked the year after law school—and Judge Goldberg were sympathetic. Coffee started running down the list of five constitutional amendments—from the First to Ninth—that she claimed the Texas abortion law violated. Judge Hughes cut her off at the First and directed her to the Ninth. The judge had obviously read Justice Arthur Goldberg's concurrence in *Griswold* and liked his Ninth Amendment argument. Coffee agreed and sat down, sensing victory.

Sarah Weddington then stood up, nervous in her first court appearance. Judge Hughes "gave me a reassuring smile and a slight wink," she later recalled. More relaxed, Weddington addressed the question of the state's interests in limiting or preventing abortions; even a constitutional right can be overcome by a "compelling" state interest. Judge Goldberg interrupted, asking her to assume that the Ninth Amendment applied to abortion: Could Texas require that abortions be done in hospitals, or be limited to married women? Weddington's answers were superfluous; Goldberg and Hughes had already decided the case on Ninth Amendment grounds. The remaining lawyers went through the motions, but they also knew the inevitable outcome. Arguing for the state, Jay Floyd asked the judges to dismiss Jane Roe's complaint for lack of proof she was still pregnant. Judge Hughes was not impressed. "Apparently you don't think anybody has standing," she retorted. Floyd answered the question Judge Goldberg had asked Weddington by asserting that the state's "compelling" interest in banning abortion was to protect unborn fetuses. Asked for evidence that Texas lawmakers had ever asserted this interest, Floyd confessed he had none. The hearing ended with John Tolle's claim that "the right of the child to life is superior to that of a woman's right to privacy."

The panel's opinion came down on June 17, 1970, less than a month after the hearing. It was short and unsigned; all three judges agreed on the outcome. They dealt with the "sensitive and complex" issue of abortion in two words. Linda Coffee and Sarah Weddington, the judges wrote, claimed the Texas abortion laws "must be declared unconstitutional because they deprive single women and married couples of their right, secured by the Ninth Amendment, to choose whether to have children. We agree." The judges quoted Justice Goldberg's concurrence in *Griswold*, ignoring Justice Douglas's opinion for the Court. But they also declined to enjoin state officials from enforcing the abortion law, citing the "strong reluctance of federal courts to interfere with the process of state criminal procedure," a reference to the charges against Dr. Hallford. However, the judges had just declared unconstitutional the law under which he was prosecuted. This seemingly inconsistent ruling, giving both sides a partial victory, signaled the lawyers that either side could ask the Supreme Court to review the case. Just as Judge Hughes had winked at Sarah Wedding-ton, both sides got the message and promptly sent petitions for certiorari to Washington.

33

"The Raw Edges of

Human Existence"

The petitions for certiorari in *Roe v. Wade* arrived at the Supreme Court clerk's office in October 1970. But they languished there until May 21, 1971, when the Court issued a brief notice that *Roe* had been granted review along with a Georgia case, *Doe v. Bolton*. The latter case involved a more "liberal" abortion law than the Texas statute; Georgia allowed abortions to protect a woman's "health" and had a rape exception, but it required the approval of three-doctor panels and imposed restrictions on abortion procedures. A three-judge panel had struck down most of Georgia's law, but also denied injunctive relief; again, both sides asked the Supreme Court for review.

The Court set both abortion cases for argument on December 13, 1971. But only seven justices sat on the bench for that session. Hugo Black and John Harlan had resigned within six days of each other in September; both had cancer and both died before the year ended. Although President Nixon nominated both of their successors—Lewis F. Powell, Jr., and William H. Rehnquist—on October 21, the new justices did not take their seats until January 1972. Of the seven who did hear arguments, only four had voted in *Griswold* in 1965: Justices Douglas, Brennan, White, and Stewart. The first two were certain to vote against the Texas and Georgia abortion laws, along with Thurgood Marshall, who had joined the Court in 1967. Stewart had dissented in *Griswold* and White had written a narrow, almost-dissenting concurrence. The two newest justices, Warren Burger and Harry Blackmun, were questionable: both had been appointed by President Nixon, and both had displayed reluctance to strike down state laws, especially in criminal cases; the Texas and Georgia abortion statutes were, in fact, criminal laws. Justice Brennan, who learned to count votes at his father's knee, could tally only three sure votes against the Texas and Georgia abortion laws. Winning the crucial fourth vote—assuming the Court would decide the cases without Powell and Rehnquist—would take all of Brennan's persuasive skills. If the Court put off deciding the cases until the two new Nixon justices took their seats, the task would be even more daunting.

Justice Brennan decided to focus his efforts on Harry Blackmun, who had joined the Court after Abe Fortas resigned in disgrace in May 1969. Blackmun was the lucky beneficiary of Richard Nixon's political blundering. George Wallace, waving the Confederate flag, had almost cost Nixon the 1968 election. Determined to curry favor with southern whites, Nixon promised to fill the next Court vacancy with a southerner. He got his chance when Fortas resigned, but made a bad decision in choosing federal appellate judge Clement Haynsworth of South Carolina to succeed him. After the Fortas scandal, the Senate wanted squeaky-clean justices; investigators discovered that Haynsworth had serious financial conflict-of-interest problems, and his confirmation lost by ten votes. Nixon immediately vowed to find another "worthy and distinguished protagonist" of southern conservative views. His second nominee was far worse than the first. News reporters discovered that federal judge G. Harrold Carswell of Florida had affirmed his "firm, vigorous belief in the principles of White supremacy" in 1948. His later disavowal of that statement did not save Carswell from Senate rejection by six votes, but the fact that forty-five senators voted to confirm both of these tainted nominees speaks poorly for "the world's greatest deliberative body."

Nixon abandoned his "Southern strategy" with a final blast at the "vicious assaults" on judges who believed in "the strict construction of the Constitution." In April 1970, almost a year after Abe Fortas resigned, Harry Blackmun became the third nominee for his seat. Blackmun was born in 1908 in Illinois, but moved with his family in childhood to St. Paul, Minnesota. His major asset as a judicial nominee was his boyhood friendship with Warren Burger in St. Paul. Blackmun had other impressive credentials, including a Harvard law degree and nine years as counsel for the prestigious Mayo Clinic in Minnesota. President Eisenhower placed Blackmun on the federal appellate bench in 1959, where he almost always voted to uphold state laws and sided with government in conflicts over individual rights. But he impressed his fellow judges as "the most studious member of the court," looking closely at case records before he voted. Senator Strom Thurmond of South Carolina overlooked Blackmun's Yankee origin and proclaimed him a "strict constructionist," assuring his confirmation. Breathing a sigh of relief after the Haynsworth and Carswell debacles, the Senate approved Blackmun without dissent in June 1970. The press labeled Chief Justice Burger and Blackmun as the "Minnesota Twins," and during Blackmun's first term they agreed on more than 80 percent of the cases. However, Blackmun was modest and unassuming, in stark contrast to the pompous and self-important Chief Justice. Although he wrote some five hundred opinions before retiring in 1994, Blackmun will always be known as the author of the Court's *Roe* opinion. "I suppose I'll carry *Roe* to my grave," he once said.

Every news account of Blackmun's death in March 1999, at the age of ninety, began with his authorship of the *Roe* opinion, his legacy to American women.

Before the abortion case arguments, however, not even Harry Blackmun knew how he would vote. From the lawyers' podium, he sat in the far-right seat when the session began on Monday, December 13, 1971. Sarah Weddington recalled being "extremely nervous" before her first Supreme Court argument. "Once I was in motion and into the argument, I was fine." She first asked the justices to focus on her nameless client, fudging the facts slightly. "Jane Roe brought her suit as soon as she knew she was pregnant. As soon as she had sought an abortion and been denied, she came to federal court." Weddington widened the Court's focus. "In Texas, the woman is the victim," she said. The state's abortion laws forced thousands of pregnant women to undergo illegal abortions, "which certainly carry risks of death, all the side effects such as severe infection, permanent sterility, all the complications that result." Weddington argued that abortion "is a matter which is of such fundamental and basic concern to the woman involved that she should be allowed to make the choice" of childbirth or abortion.

Justice Stewart politely interrupted. "Mrs. Weddington, so far on the merits, you've told us about the important impact of this law and you've made a very eloquent policy argument against it. I trust you are going to get to the provisions of the Constitution you rely on." This proved to be a tough question. "We had originally brought the suit alleging the due process clause, equal protection clause, the Ninth Amendment, and a variety of others," Weddington began. Stewart broke in: "And anything else that might obtain?" The courtroom erupted in laughter as Weddington answered, "Yeah, right." She tried to salvage her argument. "One of the purposes of the Constitution was to guarantee to the individual the right to determine the course of their own lives." But she left the podium without showing the justices a clear constitutional path to the destination she urged them to find.

Jay Floyd argued for Texas as he had in Dallas. He first smiled graciously at Sarah Weddington and Linda Coffee at their counsel table. "It's an old joke," he said, "but when a man argues against two beautiful ladies like this, they're going to have the last word." No one laughed, and Chief Justice Burger looked annoyed. After an embarrassed silence, Floyd argued that the case was moot because Jane Roe was no longer pregnant. "What procedure would you suggest," Justice Stewart asked, "for *any* pregnant female in the state of Texas ever to get *any* consideration of this constitutional claim?" Floyd had lost this argument in Dallas, and he lost again in Washington. "I do not believe it can be done," he replied. This was a case in which "no remedy is provided" for Jane Roe to challenge the law, Floyd insisted. She could not choose between childbirth and abortion in Texas. "I think she makes her choice prior to the time she becomes pregnant," he stated. As he had with Weddington, Justice Stewart prompted laughter at Floyd's expense. "Maybe she makes her choice when she decides to live in Texas," he quipped.

Justice Blackmun quieted the chamber with a serious question. "In a constitutional case of this kind," he said, "it becomes quite vital sometimes to rather precisely identify what the asserted interest of the state is." Sarah Weddington had stumbled over the constitutional issues, and Floyd did no better, tripping over his words. "The protection of the mother, at one time, may still be the primary," he asserted. That did not satisfy Blackmun, who reminded Floyd that "it's important to know what the asserted interest of the state is in the enactment of this legislation." Floyd was still floundering. "I am, and this is just from my—I speak personally, if I may. I would think that even when this statute was first passed, there was some concern for the unborn fetus." Blackmun realized that Floyd had no idea what motivated the Texas lawmakers who adopted the criminal abortion statute in 1854.

Justice Marshall demanded to know when life begins in Texas. "We say there is life from the moment of impregnation," Floyd answered. Marshall made Floyd's life more difficult. "And do you have any scientific data to support that?" Floyd pointed to his brief, assuring Marshall that it documented "the development of the fetus from about seven to nine days after conception." Marshall poked his squirming victim. "Well, what about six days?" Floyd surrendered. "We don't know." Marshall poked again. "Well, this statute goes all the way back to one hour." Floyd waved his white flag again. "Mr. Justice, there are unanswerable questions in this field." The audience snickered, and Marshall ended Floyd's torment. "I withdraw the question." Expressing his relief, Floyd showed how rattled he had become. "Thank you. Or when does the soul come into the unborn, if a person believes in a soul? I don't know." Before he sat down, Floyd regained his composure. "There is nothing in the United States Constitution concerning birth, contraception, or abortion," he concluded. "We think these matters are matters of policy, which should be properly addressed by the state legislature."

Daniel Webster and John W. Davis had brought tears to many eyes in the Supreme Court chamber defending a "small college" in New Hampshire and segregated schools in South Carolina. But the arguments on the "sensitive and complex moral issue" of abortion raised more laughter than emotion. The seven justices who heard the arguments in *Roe v. Wade* left the chamber feeling annoyed at both Sarah Weddington and Jay Floyd. Neither lawyer had given them much help on the constitutional issues.

Three days after the arguments, the justices gathered in their conference room to discuss—and possibly decide—the abortion cases. There was considerable discussion but no decision. Chief Justice Burger led off, getting tangled in the facts of the Texas and Georgia cases, but he firmly supported both state laws. However, Burger reserved his vote. This practice, which Earl Warren had rarely used, infuriated Justice Douglas, who suspected that Burger wanted to see how the vote came out, so he could join the majority and assign the Court's opinion. If the Chief Justice was in the minority, Douglas would assign the opinion as the senior associate justice. Burger reserved his vote so often, joining the majority at the end, that Douglas had considered venting his anger in a published statement.

As the justices declared their positions, Douglas counted four votes to strike down most or all provisions of the Texas and Georgia abortion laws: himself, Brennan, Marshall, and Stewart. Although Blackmun voiced reservations about the laws, Douglas felt he would stick with his "Minnesota Twin" on this issue. Justice White counted differently; he tallied four votes to uphold the laws: himself, Stewart, Blackmun, and Burger. Obviously, Stewart and Blackmun were the swing votes, and both sides considered them sympathetic. Douglas was certain, however, that he had at least four votes to invalidate the laws, and equally certain that Burger was in the minority.

The next day, Douglas was astounded to receive Burger's assignment list, handing the abortion opinions to Blackmun. Burger had no right to assign the cases to anyone, and Douglas flew into a rage. He drafted a blistering memo, noting that Burger had assigned not one but four cases in which he voted with the minority. Douglas informed his colleagues that he would assign these cases. Burger professed surprise in his reply, conceding he was wrong in two cases. But he claimed the positions of several justices on the abortion cases had been unclear. "I therefore marked down no votes and said this was a case that would have to stand or fall on the writing, when it was done," Burger explained. "That is still my view of how to handle these two sensitive cases, which, I might add, are quite probable candidates for reargument."

Douglas suspected that Burger made his statement about reargument with an eye on the political calendar. If Blackmun, a notoriously slow writer, kept the assignment, the opinions would probably not be ready until the Court's term ended in June 1972. President Nixon was already running for reelection and clearly wanted to avoid being dragged into the abortion debate. Burger could—and did—argue that the Court's decision would have more weight if all nine justices voted. Reargument would allow Justices Powell and Rehnquist, whose confirmation hearings were underway, to participate in the abortion cases. This struck Douglas as disingenuous; he now counted five votes for striking down the abortion laws—himself, Brennan, Marshall, Stewart, and Blackmun. Barring an unforeseen switch, Powell's and Rehnquist's votes could not change the final outcome, but Douglas feared that Burger would pressure Blackmun to switch his vote.

Blackmun had secluded himself in the justices' private library, plowing through stacks of lawbooks and medical texts. He finally circulated a draft opinion in late May 1972. A few days later, Burger visited Blackmun's office and stayed for hours. Blackmun said nothing to his law clerks after Burger left. On June 3, Blackmun sent his colleagues a memo withdrawing his draft opinion. It was too late in the term to complete it and give any dissenters time to draft their own opinions, he explained. He felt the abortion cases should be reargued in the next term. Douglas exploded once more. He wrote a blunt memo to his colleagues. "This is an election year," he said. "Both political parties have made abortion an issue. What the parties say or do is none of our business. We sit here not to make the path of any candidate easier or more difficult. We decide questions only on their constitutional merits. To prolong these abortion cases into the next election would in the eyes of many be a political gesture unworthy of the Court." Douglas threatened to publish his statement if the justices voted for reargument.

Brennan and Blackmun pleaded with Douglas to reconsider. Their majority was solid, and it really *was* too late in the term to polish all the opinions. Douglas finally relented. On June 26, 1972, the Court's clerk sent a letter to Sarah Weddington: "This case is restored to the calendar for reargument. Mr. Justice Douglas dissents." But there was no dissent attached to the letter. Abortion would not become an issue in the presidential campaigns. Before the election in November, neither Richard Nixon nor his Democratic opponent, Senator George McGovern, made any mention of abortion.

The Supreme Court heard a second round of arguments in *Roe v. Wade* on October 11, 1972. Two new justices now sat behind the mahogany bench, Lewis Powell to the left of the lawyers' podium and William Rehnquist on the right. Their seating followed Court tradition, but Rehnquist was far to the right of his new colleagues in politics. He and Powell had been nominated together by President Nixon to fill the seats vacated in October 1971 by Hugo Black and John Harlan. Back in 1952, an older, hugely popular moderate politician— Dwight Eisenhower—had picked a young, highly partisan conservative—Richard Nixon—as his vice-presidential candidate. Although his hard-nosed political tactics had created several crises in Nixon's short career, he swept into office on Ike's coattails. Perhaps with this example in mind, Nixon filled Black's and Harlan's seats with an older, popular moderate and a young, partisan conservative. Nixon's strategy worked; although Rehnquist's hard-line political views cost him Senate votes, he rode to confirmation on Powell's coattails.

Lewis Powell's ancestors had landed in Virginia in 1607, three centuries before his birth in 1907. He graduated from Washington and Lee University's law school in 1931 and spent the next year in graduate law study at Harvard before returning to Richmond. During forty years in corporate practice, Powell devoted many hours to public service as chairman of both the Richmond and Virginia school boards. He declined Nixon's offer in 1969 to replace Abe Fortas, saying he was too old at sixty-two, but Hugo Black's death had left the Court's "southern seat" vacant. Besides, Powell's rejection of Nixon's first offer led to the Haynsworth and Carswell debacles, and accepting the second offer gave Powell the chance to repair the South's damaged reputation.

The only senator who voted against Powell, Fred Harris of Oklahoma, called him "an elitist who has never shown any deep feeling for little people." Harris was partly right. Powell did belong to elite Richmond society; but he worked hard after the *Brown* decision to ease the integration of Virginia's schools, and he supported legal services for the poor as president of the American Bar Association. Motivated less by deep feeling than noblesse oblige, Powell nonetheless displayed some concern for such "little people" as black children and welfare clients. Few of his law clients, however, were black or poor; Powell's firm represented Virginia's leading banks, insurance companies, and tobacco manufacturers. Announcing his nomination, a grateful Nixon told reporters that Powell "has received virtually every honor the legal profession can bestow upon him."

Nixon's choice to fill John Harlan's seat had not received many honors from the legal profession, although the president lauded William Rehnquist as "one of the finest legal minds in this Nation today." He later confessed that "Rehnquist's most attractive quality was his age; he was only forty-seven and could probably serve on the Court for twenty-five years." Rehnquist passed that milestone in 1997, in his eleventh year as Chief Justice. During that quarter century, the self-described conservative "partisan" remained on the Court's far right even after moving to the center seat in 1986. Rehnquist once said his political views "may have something to do with my childhood," which began in 1924 in Shorewood, Wisconsin, a solidly Republican suburb of Milwaukee with leafy streets and several Lutheran churches. His father, whose parents came from Sweden, made a comfortable living as a wholesale paper salesman.

Rehnquist entered college in 1942, but dropped out to join the Army Air Corps, serving as a weather observer in North Africa. He finished his studies in California, receiving undergraduate and law degrees from Stanford University; like Powell, he also did graduate work at Harvard Law School. Rehnquist always relished political debate and sent many letters to newspapers. During college, he argued in the *Stanford Daily* that "moral standards are incapable of being rationally demonstrated" and that "one personal conviction is no better than another." He never strayed from his position of moral neutrality. Rehnquist clerked after law school for Supreme Court justice Robert Jackson, during the year the Court first considered the *Brown* case. One memorandum he wrote for Jackson in 1953 surfaced during his Senate confirmation hearings in 1971. "I think *Plessy v. Ferguson* was right and should be reaffirmed," Rehnquist had written, adding that the Court should not consider "the moral wrongness" of school segregation. His later claim that these words reflected Jackson's thoughts and not his own prompted outraged denials by people who had worked closely with Jackson, who joined the Court's rejection of *Plessy* in the *Brown* case.

After his Supreme Court clerkship, Rehnquist practiced real-estate law and Republican politics in Phoenix, Arizona, working in Barry Goldwater's presidential campaign in 1964. That same year, he opposed the city's public accommodations law, defending in a letter to the *Arizona Republic* "the historic right of the owner of a drug store, lunch counter, or theater to choose his own customers." Three years later, he opposed a Phoenix school integration plan in another letter to the *Republic*, writing that "we are no more dedicated to an 'integrated' society than we are to a 'segregated' society." These opinions helped Rehnquist win a job in the Nixon administration, as director of the Justice Department's Office of Legal Counsel. In congressional testimony and public speeches, he defended "national security" wiretapping, the mass arrest of Vietnam War protesters, and the "preventive detention" of criminal suspects without bail. Democratic senators questioned his political views but not his legal skills, and Rehnquist won confirmation by a vote of sixty-eight to twenty-six.

The second round of arguments in *Roe v. Wade* took place before a full bench on October 11, 1972. Without knowing the score from the first round, the lawyers on both sides tried their best. Sarah Weddington, who had stumbled on the constitutional issues during her first argument, spent months polishing her second effort. She conceded at the outset that the Constitution did not provide, in clear words, "the right to an abortion." But it also did not provide other "very basic rights" that the Court had recognized. Weddington pointed the justices to "a great body of precedent" that supported abortion rights, rattling off case names like an eager law student. She included all the cases Douglas had cited in his *Griswold* opinion, adding that decision to her list. These cases "in the areas of marriage, sex, contraception, procreation, childbearing, and education of children," she asserted, all held that decisions in these fields "should be left to the determination of the individual."

Weddington spoke largely without interruption, normally a sign that justices have already made up their minds. Her only tough question came from Byron White, who asked whether a fetus was a "person" under the Fourteenth Amendment. Weddington knew the next question without being asked: If the fetus *was* a "person" with constitutional rights, why would Texas not have a "compelling interest" in protecting its life? Unwilling to concede this point, she dodged White's question, claiming that Texas "has not proved any compelling interest" in banning abortions. Potter Stewart helpfully offered Weddington an escape from White's trap. "If it were established that an unborn fetus *is* a person," he asked, "within the protection of the Fourteenth Amendment, you would have an almost impossible case here, would you not?" She missed the hint that she should say firmly that fetuses were *not* persons, the position Stewart had argued strongly to his colleagues. "I would have a very difficult case," she answered.

Robert Flowers argued for Texas in the second round, replacing the hapless Jay Floyd at the podium. He seized on Sarah Weddington's concession that fetal "personhood" might give the state a "compelling" interest in banning abortion. Flowers claimed that fetuses *were* persons in Texas. "We feel that this is the only question really that this Court has to answer," he added confidently. But Flowers had climbed too far out on this shaky limb. "Do you know of any case anywhere," Stewart inquired, "that held that an unborn fetus is a person within the meaning of the Fourteenth Amendment?" Flowers had none to offer. Justice White helpfully suggested that he move to a stronger branch. "You think the case is over for you?" he asked. "You've lost your case if the fetus or the embryo is not a person, is that it?" Flowers missed the hint that he should say no, and offer the Court a "compelling interest" to justify banning abortions. "Yes, sir, I would say so," he answered. White tried again to help the befuddled lawyer. "You mean the state has no interest of its own that it can assert?" Flowers beamed with relief. "Oh, we have other interests, Your Honor. Preventing promiscity, say." He mangled the word, but his linguistic slip made no difference. Even Daniel Webster at his best could not have saved the Texas abortion law.

Sarah Weddington recalled her feelings that day. "I left the courtroom with the sense that the justices had already decided the cases—but were not yet willing to tell us their decision." They *had* decided the abortion cases, in fact, and opinions had already been drafted. But none of the justices liked the opinions they had read, and final votes had not been tallied. Harry Blackmun had spent most of the summer of 1972 in the Mayo Clinic library in Rochester, Minnesota, plowing through more medical texts. He returned to Washington that fall with a second draft of the opinion he had circulated in May. This draft, the fruits of his summer research, exhaustively recounted the history of abortion, from the Greeks and Romans in antiquity to the 1970 statement of the American Medical Association urging that states allow doctors to use their best medical judgment about abortion. Blackmun's draft focused almost entirely on the doctor's professional interests and largely ignored the pregnant woman's personal concerns. He decided to withhold it from circulation until the justices held their conference after the second round of arguments.

Justices Brennan and Douglas had worried over the summer that Stewart might decide to uphold the abortion laws and that Powell might join him. They had already written off Rehnquist, and Burger and White appeared certain to sustain the statutes. What had been five votes against the laws in May 1972 looked very shaky in October. Brennan knew from Newark politics, however, not to concede the election before the ballots are counted. The justices cast their votes on October 12, 1972, the day after they listened to Sarah Weddington and Robert Flowers. Brennan and Douglas were delighted with the vote that followed Blackmun's lengthy and emotional appeal to his colleagues, urging them to strike down the abortion laws. Stewart stuck with his earlier vote, and Powell joined to make a majority of six. Powell later told his law clerk that he could find no constitutional objection to abortion laws, but voted from his "gut" because he felt the laws were "atrocious." Powell's vote left Burger, White, and Rehnquist in dissent.

The conference vote, however, did not end debate on the abortion cases. Brennan and Douglas had many criticisms of Blackmun's second draft, the most important that it did not place the "right to privacy" on any firm constitutional footing. They also felt that Blackmun had given the states too much power in allowing them to ban abortions after the point of fetal "viability," when the fetus could live outside the womb. This generally occurs after six months of pregnancy but varies in each case, depending on fetal weight and other factors. Brennan and Douglas feared that states would define "viability" at the earliest possible time, pushing it back as medical science progressed in keeping fetuses alive, even if they could never become normal, healthy babies. Brennan put his criticisms into a forty-eight-page memo to Blackmun, carefully phrased as "suggestions" for improving his opinion. Less politely, Chief Justice Burger had told Blackmun he would "never" join an opinion that permitted "abortion on demand" before fetal viability.

Blackmun devised a plan to satisfy both critics, who came at him from opposite sides. Going back to his medical texts, Blackmun divided pregnancy into three roughly equal "trimesters" of twelve weeks. His purpose was to "balance" the pregnant woman's right to abortion with the state's interests in protecting her health and assuring that no "viable" fetus was aborted. During the first trimester, Blackmun placed no restrictions on abortion; decisions were solely up to the woman and her doctor. States could regulate abortion procedures during the second trimester, but only to protect the woman's health. During the final trimester—the stage of fetal "viability" in most cases—states could prohibit abortions unless childbirth would endanger the woman's life. His trimester scheme, Blackmun wrote in his final opinion, would protect the pregnant woman's right to choose abortion over childbirth, but also leave "the State free to place increasing restrictions on abortion as the period of pregnancy lengthens, so long as those restrictions are tailored to the recognized state interests" in maternal health and fetal viability.

To answer criticisms that his "right to privacy" had no constitutional anchor, Blackmun dusted off his lawbooks and dug out nine cases that went back to the nineteenth century. None dealt with abortion—*Roe* was, after all, the first direct challenge to abortion laws on constitutional grounds. Blackmun put some odd cases in his grab bag of precedent. One stemmed from a railroad case in which a Pullman berth fell on a woman's head; another involved a police search for fraudulent customs declarations; a third upheld a Georgia man's right to own pornographic films; others dealt with wiretapping, police "stop and frisk" searches, and placing bets from telephone booths. They all, in some way, challenged governmental invasions of the "privacy" of individuals, even accused criminals. Some of these decisions ruled for the individual, some for the government. Some did not even mention the word "privacy." Piling up his cases, Blackmun found in them the Court's recognition "that a right of personal privacy, or a guarantee of certain areas or zones of privacy, does exist under the Constitution." Founded in the Fourteenth Amendment's "concept of personal liberty," Blackmun wrote in his final opinion, the right of privacy, "is broad enough to encompass a woman's decision whether or not to terminate her pregnancy."

Blackmun worked hard during January 1973 to satisfy all his critics. He agreed to Stewart's demand that his opinion make clear that fetuses were not "persons" under the Constitution. His trimester scheme met Brennan's concern that allowing states to ban abortions after "viability" would give them too much latitude, as well as Burger's fear that placing no restrictions on abortions before viability would give pregnant women too much control. Burger's last-minute agreement made the final tally seven to two for striking down the Texas and Georgia laws. Blackmun sent his *Roe* opinion to the Court's printshop in time for "Decision Day" on Monday, January 15, 1973. But the Chief Justice told Blackmun he wanted to write a short concurrence. "I'll get it to you next week," he promised on January 12. Blackmun now hoped to read his opinion on Wednesday, the 17th, but that day passed with nothing from Burger. Finally, on the 18th, a three-paragraph concurrence landed on Blackmun's desk. The next Court session was scheduled for the following Monday, January 22. Blackmun fumed when he realized that Burger had deliberately stalled, knowing the abortion opinions could not come down before he administered the presidential oath to Richard Nixon on Saturday, January 20. Burger did not want Nixon to know, as he swore to uphold the Constitution, that the Chief Justice had joined a decision granting women a constitutional right to have abortions, a practice the president had publicly deplored. All the justices knew that Burger had manipulated the abortion decisions to serve his personal interests.

The next Monday morning, January 22, 1973, Chief Justice Burger led his colleagues through the red velvet curtain behind the bench precisely at ten o'clock. He could hardly have enjoyed presiding over the Court's most momentous session since Earl Warren read his *Brown* opinion on Monday, May 17, 1954. Burger had joined the *Roe* decision at the last minute, reluctant to stand outside in dissent but equally reluctant to stand behind his boyhood friend's most important opinion. Harry Blackmun had asked his wife, Dottie, to come with him that morning. After the opening rituals, Burger told the audience in his deep voice that decisions in the abortion cases would be announced. He looked impassively at Blackmun, who smiled at his wife, then began reading from an eight-page summary of his abortion opinions. He started with *Roe v. Wade*, and with an unusual statement. "We forthwith acknowledge our awareness of the sensitive and emotional nature of the abortion controversy," Blackmun began, "of the vigorous opposing views, even among physicians, and of the deep and seemingly absolute convictions that the subject inspires."

Blackmun continued in this self-revelatory vein. "One's philosophy, one's experiences, one's exposure to the raw edges of human existence, one's religious training, one's attitudes toward life and family and their values, and the moral standards one establishes and seeks to observe, are all likely to influence and to color one's thinking and conclusions about abortion." This long sentence expressed the conflicts Blackmun had faced during the year he struggled with this opinion. He lived and worked in a comfortable, conservative world with happy, healthy children; but he knew that many pregnant women lived on "mean streets" where children went hungry, lacked medical care, and endured physical and emotional abuse. Harry and Dottie Blackmun had raised three daughters in their comfortable world, but he had learned a great deal about the "other America" during his year of reading and talking about abortion.

Justice Blackmun was not given to public displays of emotion. After reading his words about the "raw edges" of life and conflicting moral values, he glanced up briefly and continued. "Our task, of course, is to resolve the issue by constitutional measurement, free of emotion and of predilection." Blackmun then returned to the world of antiquity and began a lengthy historical account of abortion practices and procedures. When he finally emerged into the twentieth century, he noted the "wide divergence" of opinion on "the difficult question of when life begins." How could judges answer this question, Blackmun inquired, when doctors, philosophers, and theologians "are unable to arrive at any consensus" on life's first moment? Judges did know, however, that "the word 'person,' as used in the Fourteenth Amendment, does not include the unborn." Therefore, states could not ban abortions in the early stages of pregnancy; only when the fetus reaches the point of "viability" could they prevent its abortion.

Blackmun devoted twelve pages of his *Roe* opinion to history and twelve to medicine. He shoehorned his constitutional argument into two paragraphs, citing his grab bag of precedent on "the right of privacy" and concluding that the Fourteenth Amendment "is broad enough to encompass a woman's decision whether or not to terminate her pregnancy." By giving pregnant women the "liberty" to choose abortion over childbirth, Blackmun revived the "substantive due process" doctrine the Court had rejected in 1937 in *West Coast Hotel*, a decision reaffirmed by the Warren Court in 1963. Justice Douglas had carefully avoided the Fourteenth Amendment in his *Griswold* opinion, but Justice Stewart had insisted that Blackmun not open the Pandora's box of the Ninth Amendment or rely on the "penumbras" of the Bill of Rights. That left only the Fourteenth Amendment on which to ground abortion rights. Blackmun yielded to

Stewart, who argued in a brief concurrence that *Griswold*, despite its reliance on equal protection, really had been a "substantive due process" decision. Douglas grudgingly conceded in his own brief concurrence that many of the rights "retained by the people" under the Ninth Amendment "come within the meaning of the term 'liberty' as used in the Fourteenth Amendment." Stewart and Douglas did not read their concurrences aloud, and spectators had no inkling of their debates over doctrine.

Chief Justice Burger had used his three-paragraph concurrence as an excuse to delay the *Roe* decision until he left President Nixon's inauguration. Like Justice White's *Griswold* concurrence, it read more like a dissent. Burger faulted Texas for not allowing rape and incest victims to obtain abortions, hinting broadly that he would uphold laws with such exceptions. He wanted everyone— including the President—to know that he rejected "any claim that the Constitution requires abortion on demand."

The two actual dissenters raised very different objections to Blackmun's opinion. Justice White sounded like Mrs. Grundy in his peevish opinion. He suspected that many women were motivated by "convenience, family planning, economics, dislike of children, the embarrassment of illegitimacy," or even by "no reason at all" for ending their pregnancy. Accusing the majority of valuing "the convenience, whim, or caprice of the putative mother more than the life or potential life of the fetus," White blasted Blackmun's opinion as "an exercise of raw judicial power" that allowed women to "exterminate" human life.

Justice Rehnquist, in contrast, stuck to his principle of moral neutrality and expressed no opinion on abortion. Noting that Blackmun based his opinion on "substantive due process" grounds, Rehnquist complained that allowing judges to decide whether laws infringed the "liberty" of individuals would give them broad powers to nullify legislative judgments. He was, of course, entirely correct. The *Roe* majority nullified the 1854 judgment of Texas lawmakers because they felt a "fundamental right" had been denied to pregnant women. The Court had devised the fundamental rights doctrine and extended it to "the private realm of family life which the state cannot enter" some thirty years before the *Roe* decision. Rehnquist, however, could not find any "fundamental rights" in the Constitution that were "beyond the reach of majorities," as Justice Jackson had written in 1943. As Jackson's law clerk in 1953, Rehnquist had responded in his "*Plessy* was right" memorandum that "it is the majority who will determine what the constitutional rights of the minority are." In his *Roe* dissent, Rehnquist said the Court should have applied the "rational basis" test to abortion laws; he suggested that laws would flunk this test only if they failed to permit abortions when continued pregnancy or childbirth would jeopardize a woman's life. Since Texas allowed this exception, its law passed Rehnquist's test. All the constitutional questions on this issue, he concluded, had been settled "when the Fourteenth Amendment was adopted" in 1868.

Justice Blackmun's opinion in 1973 did not settle the abortion issue. Like the

Warren Court's prayer decisions, *Roe* struck a live wire. Catholic leaders were predictably upset; Cardinal Terence Cooke of New York found the decision "shocking" and "horrifying," while Cardinal John Krol of Philadelphia, president of the National Conference of Catholic Bishops, called it "an unspeakable tragedy for this nation." Abortion advocates were predictably happy; Dr. Alan Guttmacher of Planned Parenthood called the ruling "wise and courageous," and New York governor Nelson Rockefeller—whose family's foundation had generously supported Planned Parenthood—praised the decision as "a wonderful thing." The press almost uniformly endorsed the Court's ruling: the *New York Times* called it "a major contribution to the preservation of individual liberties," the *Washington Post* agreed that the decision was "wise and sound"; even the *Wall Street Journal*, while expressing "certain reservations," said the Court had "struck a reasonable balance on an exceedingly difficult question." Perhaps the most accurate barometer of the high pressure that would build up over the abortion issue was the first Gallup Poll after the Court's ruling. Asked whether abortion decisions should be left to women and doctors during the first three months of pregnancy, 46 percent of respondents said yes and 45 percent said no. This virtually even split guaranteed that arguments over abortion would continue in legislative halls and judicial chambers.

34

"Truly a Pandora's Box"

The abortion debate had flared up suddenly in American politics, and *Roe v. Wade* reached the Supreme Court without much public notice; the "abortion wars" that later engulfed the country and caused several deaths began only after the Court's 1973 decision. However, America's "race wars" had been waged for more than two centuries. The first large-scale slave rebellion took place in New York City in 1712, when black slaves killed nine whites; twenty-one blacks were executed for taking part in the revolt. The end of slavery did not end black resistance to segregation, the *Brown* decision did not end black complaints about inferior education, and the Civil Rights Act of 1964 did not end black anger over job discrimination. The list of black grievances included bad schools, bad jobs, and bad cops. During the hot summer of 1965, Los Angeles police officers in the city's Watts ghetto dragged a young black man from his car and clubbed a protesting bystander. The ensuing Watts riot left thirty-four people dead, hundreds injured, four thousand arrested, and whole blocks in flames.

As the smoke cleared over Watts, officials at all levels of government realized that drastic measures were needed to dampen racial tensions. The programs that emerged from the political process—like Head Start and the Job Corps—were hardly drastic in nature, but they did help many young blacks get better prepared for school and work. Another widely adopted program was "affirmative action" in education, designed to increase the numbers of "underrepresented minorities" in colleges and professional schools. The officials who drafted these programs usually spoke of "goals" for increasing minority enrollments, but some adopted "quotas" that set precise numbers and gave preferences to members of racial and ethnic minorities. Affirmative action programs worked, in the sense of putting more black and Hispanic students in classrooms. But they also raised questions about the quality of those students; many were admitted with lower grades and test scores than white applicants who were rejected. Proponents of affirmative action responded that grades and scores were not the only measures of academic "merit" and that racial "diversity" was a legitimate educational goal.

The 1960s were years of minority demands for more jobs and better education; the 1970s were marked by the white "backlash" against affirmative action programs that continues to roil American politics. Members of previously over-represented majorities—white males in particular—raised the cry of "reverse discrimination" and began filing lawsuits against schools that "gave away" their seats to minorities. The lawyers for these disgruntled applicants had two legal weapons and a slogan. Their primary weapon was the Fourteenth Amendment, which prohibits states from denying to "any person" the equal protection of the laws. White males fit the category of "any person" just as well as black males, or women. Backing up the Fourteenth Amendment was Title VI of the 1964 Civil Rights Act, barring discrimination "on the ground of race, color, or national origin" in any federally funded program, including universities. The favorite slogan of those who opposed affirmative action had been coined by Justice John Marshall Harlan in 1896. "Our Constitution is color-blind," he wrote in his *Plessy v. Ferguson* dissent, arguing that state laws could not discriminate against blacks. But the "reverse discrimination" lawyers argued that the color-blind principle applied equally to whites, and that officials who screened applicants for jobs and schools could take no account of their race or ethnicity.

The road to the Supreme Court for white males began on August 3, 1973, when Allan Bakke met with Peter Storandt in the admissions office of the University of California's medical school at Davis, near the state capital of Sacramento. Bakke was thirty-three, an aerospace engineer at a NASA research center close to Stanford University. Storandt was assistant dean of student affairs at the UC Davis medical school. One of these white males wanted to become a doctor; the other wanted to help him get into medical school. Bakke had applied twice to UC Davis, in 1972 and 1973, and had been rejected both times. In fact, Bakke had been turned away by more than a dozen medical schools across the country; most had frankly told him that he was too old. Even UC Davis officials had cited "your present age" as a factor in Bakke's rejection. But he was convinced he had lost his medical school place to a minority applicant with lower grades and test scores. After his first rejection in 1972, he discovered that the UC Davis medical school had an "affirmative action" program that set aside sixteen places in an entering class of one hundred for members of "disadvantaged" minorities. These sixteen places were known as Task Force seats, filled through a separate admissions process.

Before his meeting with Bakke, Peter Storandt studied Bakke's file carefully. Bakke certainly had good grades and test scores. His undergraduate average at the University of Minnesota, where he majored in engineering, was 3.46. His scores on the science, verbal, and math sections of the Medical College Admission Test were in the 97th, 96th, and 94th percentiles. Bakke's grades were higher than those of half the students admitted to the eighty-four places not filled by Task Force students, and his MCAT scores were considerably higher than average. Compared to the Task Force students, Bakke had higher grades than all but one of those admitted in 1973: their undergraduate grades averaged 2.88, and their MCAT scores on the science, verbal, and math sections averaged in the 46th, 24th, and 35th percentiles.

Bakke's numbers were impressive. So what had kept him out of the UC Davis medical school? The major reason was that he had received lukewarm reviews on his admission interviews with medical school faculty and students. The sole interviewer in 1972 had reported that Bakke was "tall and strong and Teutonic in appearance," not surprising for a former Marine Corps officer of Norwegian descent. The interviewer also wrote that Bakke's "main handicap is the unavoidable fact that he is now 33 years of age." But he considered Bakke "a very desirable applicant to this medical school and I shall so recommend him." However, his interview score, added to his grade and test scores, left Bakke two points shy of admission. When he applied again in 1973, after hinting that he might sue the university for giving preference to minority applicants with lower scores, his interview scores plummeted. The dean of student affairs, who had received Bakke's first complaint, interviewed him personally and called him "a rather rigidly oriented young man" who was "certainly not an outstanding candidate for our school."

At their meeting in August 1973, Peter Storandt explained the Task Force program to Allan Bakke in detail and gave him several documents about it. He later wrote Bakke and encouraged him "to pursue your research into admissions policies based on quota-oriented minority recruiting." Storandt also included several legal references and a Washington State court opinion, directing the state's law school to admit a rejected white applicant, Marco DeFunis. Ruling in 1974, the Supreme Court declined to hear the state's appeal on the ground the case was "moot" because DeFunis was nearing graduation. Justice William Brennan predicted in dissent that reverse discrimination cases "will not disappear" from the Court's docket. "They must inevitably return to the federal courts and ultimately to the Court," Brennan wrote. Allan Bakke did not disappear, and he turned to federal court after drawing the obvious conclusion that Storandt thought he should sue the UC Davis medical school. Through the material Storandt gave him, Bakke found a San Francisco lawyer, Reynold Colvin, who agreed to take his case. Colvin filed suit against the University of California Regents (who govern all UC schools) in state court in June 1974, alleging in his complaint that Bakke had been rejected "on account of his race, to-wit, Caucasian and white, and not for reasons applicable to persons of every race." Bakke won his case in the trial court, and the California supreme court upheld the ruling, striking down the UC Davis minority admissions program and ordering Bakke's admission to the medical school. Unlike the Washington court in the *DeFunis* case, however, the state court issued a stay of its order while the Regents asked the Supreme Court to review the ruling. This avoided any "mootness" problem when the Court granted the Regents' petition for certiorari in 1977.

The case of *Regents v. Bakke* confronted the Supreme Court with a dilemma. The justices had ruled for racial minorities in virtually all the job and school discrimination cases filed under Title VI of the Civil Rights Act. Would they make a "color-blind" decision in Bakke's case? The factual evidence was clear: Bakke had higher grades and scores than almost every minority student admitted to the UC Davis medical school under the Task Force program.

Did the Regents have any defense? They could—and did—argue that increasing the number of minority physicians in California offered a "compelling state interest" that overrode Bakke's interest in becoming a doctor. The Regents had numbers on their side as well: fewer than 2 percent of California's doctors came from minority groups. The only way to raise that number was to increase the number of minority medical students. Because their elementary and high school educations had generally been inferior, in ghetto or rural schools, minority applicants to medical school were burdened with lower college grades and test scores than whites. But this did not mean they were unqualified; more than 90 percent of minority medical students graduated and passed their licensing exams, only a slightly smaller percentage than white students. Setting aside sixteen places in the UC Davis entering class was a reasonable way, school officials felt, to achieve the goal of educating more minority doctors. Allan Bakke was not the only disappointed applicant; he was just one of 2,464 who competed for one hundred places at UC Davis. Bakke's argument, however, was that the Task Force program forced him to compete for one of just eighty-four places, which reduced his chances for admission. He might have been admitted if all one hundred places had been open to all applicants.

The justices heard argument in *Regents v. Bakke* on October 12, 1977. The dozens of amicus briefs piled on the bench testified to the high stakes in this case. The groups on the university's side included the ACLU, the Association of American Medical Colleges, the NAACP, and the National Council of Churches of Christ. Siding with Bakke were the American Federation of Teachers, the American Jewish Committee, the Fraternal Order of Police, the Sons of Italy, and Young Americans for Freedom. The civil rights coalition of blacks and Jews, who marched together for twenty years after *Brown*, had split over *Bakke* amid charges of racism on both sides.

The arguments inside the Court did not mention the acrimony outside its chamber. Archibald Cox took the podium first. The University of California

Regents had hired the noted Harvard law professor because their own lawyers, although they won the case in state court, lacked the Supreme Court experience that Cox, a former solicitor general under President Kennedy, had in abundance. Cox made a professorial appeal for the medical school's Task Force program. "There is no racially blind method of selection which will enroll today more than a trickle of minority students in the nation's colleges and professions," he asserted. But the Task Force quota of sixteen places raised judicial eyebrows. Justice Potter Stewart asked a skeptical question: "It did put a limit on the number of white people, didn't it?" Cox dodged the question, responding that "the designation of sixteen places was not a quota, at least as I would use that word." He preferred the word "goal." Justice John Paul Stevens, the Burger Court's newest member, tried to pin Cox down. "The question is not whether the sixteen is a quota; the question is whether the eighty-four is a quota." Cox wriggled away. "I would say that neither is properly defined as a quota." He explained that since minority applicants could apply through the "regular" admission process, the Task Force program did not place "a limit on the number of minority students." Pressed to provide a "compelling" interest for the program, Cox argued that "the minority applicant may have qualities that are superior to those of his classmate who is not minority." A Chicano doctor "certainly will be more effective in bringing it home to the young Chicano that he too may become a doctor."

Archibald Cox mentioned Allan Bakke just once, conceding that he "would be ranked above the minority applicant" under the "conventional standards for admission" to UC Davis. When he took the podium, Reynold Colvin talked *only* about Allan Bakke. "I am Allan Bakke's lawyer and Allan Bakke is my client," he reminded the justices. Colvin addressed the justices as if they were members of the UC Davis admission committee. "Look at the record in the case," he urged. "You'll find it on page 13 of our brief." He rattled off Bakke's impressive grades and scores, noting how much he outshone the minority applicants.

Justice Lewis Powell finally grew tired of Colvin's figures. "You have devoted twenty minutes to laboring the facts, if I may say so," he said. "I would like help, I really would, on the constitutional issues." But the dogged Colvin preferred talking about quotas. "What is the appropriate quota for a medical school? Sixteen, eight, thirty-two, sixty-four, one hundred?" Justice William Rehnquist tried to interest Colvin in the Constitution. Cox had argued, Rehnquist said, that UC Davis "could take race into account, and that under the Fourteenth Amendment there was no barrier to doing that, because of the interests that were involved. Now, what's your response to that?" Colvin answered that "race is an improper classification in this situation." Justice Thurgood Marshall wanted to know if UC Davis could reserve just one place for a minority student. Colvin's negative answer provoked Marshall. "So numbers are just unimportant?" he asked. "The numbers are unimportant," Colvin replied. "It is the principle of keeping a man out because of his race that is important."

How would the Burger Court resolve this dilemma? During their conference after the arguments, the justices split into two factions, each unwilling to compromise. It would take a Solomon to decide the *Bakke* case, with compelling interests on both sides and no clear-cut answer in the Constitution. As it happened, the Court had a Solomon on the bench, willing to cut the baby in half. With four justices on either side, Lewis Powell proposed giving Bakke and UC Davis what each wanted. Bakke would get into medical school, and minorities would receive a "plus" in the admissions process. The Davis quota of sixteen places would be replaced by a "race-conscious" program that could even exceed that number in admitting minorities.

Lewis Powell assumed his Solomonic role only because William Douglas had grudgingly left the bench in November 1975 after thirty-six years, the longest service of any justice. Crippled by strokes, Douglas tried to hang on, even writing opinions after his resignation. He finally gave up trying to be the "tenth justice" after his embarrassed colleagues ignored his memos. Douglas would certainly have voted to uphold the UC Davis program, but his replacement took Bakke's side. John Paul Stevens, a former clerk to Justice Wiley Rutledge, had practiced antitrust law in Chicago before President Nixon named him to the federal appellate bench in 1970. A judicial "moderate" in the Potter Stewart mold, Stevens would not have joined the Court if Nixon, crippled by Watergate, had not resigned in August 1974 after trying to hang on as president in the face of certain impeachment. Ironically, Warren Burger, who had administered the oath in which Nixon swore to "protect and defend the Constitution," wrote the unanimous opinion that forced him to hand over the "smoking gun" Watergate tapes revealing Nixon's contempt for the Constitution. Nixon would certainly have replaced Douglas with a more conservative justice than Stevens, who became Gerald Ford's sole nominee in November 1975.

It took Lewis Powell eight months to draft an opinion—actually two opinions in one—stating "the judgement of the Court" in the *Bakke* case. The first section of Powell's opinion also spoke for Burger, Rehnquist, Stewart, and Stevens. These five justices struck down the UC Davis quota system, ruling that it established "a classification based on race and ethnic background." Powell cited the Japanese American internment cases, *Hirabayashi* and *Korematsu*, in writing that "racial and ethnic distinctions of any sort are inherently suspect and thus call for the most exacting judicial examination." After examining Allan Bakke's skin, Powell stated that "discrimination against members of the white 'majority'" could not pass the "strict scrutiny" test. Speaking of minority groups, Powell wrote that the Equal Protection Clause does not permit "the recognition of special wards entitled to a degree of protection greater than that accorded others." Consciously or not, Powell echoed the words of Justice Joseph Bradley in 1883, writing in the *Civil Rights Cases* that the Fourteenth Amendment did not make blacks "the special favorite of the law."

At this point in Powell's opinion, the four justices who had been riding with him got off the train. They had achieved their goal of striking down racial quotas and had no desire to travel with Powell into "race-conscious" territory. For the final leg of this trip, four justices—Brennan, Marshall, White, and Blackmun—joined the excursion. In the second part of Powell's opinion, he asserted that "race or ethnic background may be deemed a 'plus' in a particular applicant's file," to be counted along with grades and test scores. The "plus" factors could also include "exceptional personal talents, unique work or service experience, leadership potential, maturity, demonstrated compassion, a history of overcoming disadvantage, ability to communicate with the poor, or other qualifications deemed important" to making good doctors. Powell's formula allowed UC Davis and other schools to "take race into account" in choosing students, although that factor could not be "decisive" in admissions decisions.

Unlike Solomon, who never cut the disputed baby in half, Powell sliced the *Bakke* case down the middle and handed each party what it wanted. But this compromise did not satisfy the four justices who supported the UC Davis quota system. They produced a separate opinion—drafted by William Brennan—disputing claims that officials must be "color-blind" in choosing between applicants for jobs and schools. Brennan's opinion noted that "race has too often been used by those who would stigmatize and oppress minorities." The American people, he wrote, cannot "let color blindness become myopia which masks the reality that many 'created equal' have been treated within our lifetimes as inferior both by the law and by their fellow citizens."

The Court's only black member, Thurgood Marshall, felt compelled to remind his colleagues—and those few Americans who actually read the opinions—that "the Negro was dragged to this country in chains to be sold into slavery." Marshall cited books by John Hope Franklin and C. Vann Woodward in presenting a brief but graphic history of slavery and its legacy. "The system of slavery brutalized and dehumanized both master and slave," he wrote. Marshall recalled the "Great Compromise" at the Constitutional Convention in Philadelphia, where "the Framers made it plain that 'we the people,' for whose protection the Constitution was designed, did not include those whose skins were the wrong color." Marshall linked this history to the present. "The position of the Negro today in America is the tragic but inevitable consequence of centuries of unequal treatment," he continued. "Measured by any benchmark of comfort or achievement, meaningful equality remains a distant dream for the Negro."

The justices produced five opinions in the *Bakke* case, spread over 153 pages of the Court's reports. Harry Blackmun's came last, and he spoke a final word on race and the Constitution. "In order to get beyond racism," he wrote, "we must first take account of race. There is no other way. And in order to treat some persons equally, we must treat them differently. We cannot—we dare not—let the Fourteenth Amendment perpetuate racial supremacy."

Chief Justice Charles Evans Hughes once said that "the Constitution is what the judges say it is." But what *did* they say in *Bakke*? The inability of nine justices to agree on a clear statement of what the Fourteenth Amendment says to UC Davis admissions officials speaks volumes about the continuing racial chasm in American society. The Supreme Court refused in 1997 to hear a challenge to the new policy of the University of California Regents, who voted in 1995 to remove any "plus" factors based on race or ethnicity in admissions decisions. Under the university's "color-blind" policy, the number of black and Hispanic students entering the nation's largest public university system has dropped by more than half. The first-year class at the UC Davis medical school in 1998 included just five black and three Hispanic students. That same year, not a single black student entered the university's prestigious law school at Berkeley. Allan Bakke, meanwhile, received his medical degree from Davis in 1982 and returned to Minnesota, where he practices anesthesiology.

The Burger Court dealt in *Roe* with women, and in *Bakke* with racial and ethnic minorities. Over the past century, members of these groups have often courted arrest to make a visible demand for their rights. Suffragettes chained themselves to the White House fence, and black students sat down at segregated lunch counters. These protestors sought public attention for their cause and welcomed reporters and photographers to their marches and picket lines. News reports and pictures of peaceful demonstrators being shoved into paddy wagons shocked the public and helped build support for their demands.

Before 1969, however, members of one minority group shied away from the media spotlight and rarely protested their mistreatment. America's homosexuals largely stayed in their closets, invisible to their neighbors but often harassed by hostile police officers. In many cities, cops invaded gay bars with impunity, closing them down on any pretext and shoving their patrons into the streets. Most gays and lesbians were afraid to resist; they feared arrest and exposure, which might cost them their jobs or even their families. But the example of civil rights and antiwar protesters inspired many gays who were fed up with constant harassment. New York City police made a serious mistake when they raided the Stonewall Inn on the hot summer night of June 29, 1969. Refusing to leave the gay bar in Greenwich Village, gays fought back in bloody battles that spilled into the streets and lasted for three nights. Out of the "Stonewall Riots" came the Gay Liberation Movement, which soon moved its agitation from the streets to council chambers and courtrooms.

Gays protested police abuse and worked against discrimination in jobs and housing. But their primary goal was to repeal or strike down sodomy laws, which threatened gays with long prison terms in most states. All the original thirteen states had made sodomy a criminal offense when the Bill of Rights was ratified in 1791. As late as 1961, all fifty states had outlawed sodomy, defined in Georgia's law—similar to those in other states—as "any sexual act involving the sex organs of one person and the mouth or anus of another." Georgia imposed a maximum penalty for sodomy of twenty years in prison. Studies indicated that more than 80 percent of all couples—gay and straight—engaged in sodomy, but police almost never charged straight people with this crime. (This form of sex between Monica Lewinsky and President Bill Clinton later made "sodomy" a household word, one that even children learned.) The quiet lobbying of gay organizations like the Mattachine Society had succeeded by 1975 in the repeal of sodomy laws in half the states. But none of those states was below the Mason–Dixon line, where hostility toward gays fed on the "good ol' boy" syndrome of exaggerated masculinity.

The road to the Supreme Court for gays began in Atlanta, Georgia, early in the morning of August 3, 1982. Officer K. D. Torick entered Michael Hardwick's house in the Virginia Highlands neighborhood, home to many of Atlanta's gays. Torick carried a warrant for Michael's arrest on a charge of failing to appear in court for drinking in public. Several weeks earlier, Torick had ticketed Michael outside the gay bar he worked in for carrying an open beer bottle. Michael had argued that the bottle was almost empty, but Torick gave him the ticket anyway. Although Michael had paid his $50 fine, Torick had not checked the record before he got the arrest warrant. He had a reputation for busting gays, and he wanted to bust Michael Hardwick for talking back. When Officer Torick entered Michael's home, someone pointed him upstairs; he pushed open a bedroom door and saw two men engaged in mutual oral sex. He arrested Michael and his friend, handcuffed them, drove them to the downtown police station, booked them for sodomy, and tossed them into the holding tank, informing both guards and prisoners in graphic terms of the charges against the two gay men, who were finally released on bail after twelve unpleasant hours in jail.

Several days after Michael's arrest, an ACLU lawyer contacted him with an offer of legal help. The ACLU staff had been checking the police blotter for sodomy arrests, hoping to find someone willing to challenge the Georgia law on constitutional grounds. Michael understood the risk in this effort; he faced a twenty-year prison term and the unwelcome glare of publicity. Michael had already been beaten up once—after he argued with Officer Torick—by three strangers who knew his name. But he told the ACLU lawyers he would take the risk; he was sick and tired of being harassed for being gay.

Getting wind of the ACLU's interest in Michael's case, the district attorney dropped the sodomy charge. The ACLU lawyer, Kathleen Wilde, promptly filed suit in federal court against Georgia's attorney general, Michael Bowers, asking for a judicial declaration that the sodomy law violated the Due Process Clause of the Fourteenth Amendment. After hearing argument on the constitutional issues, federal judge Robert Hall dismissed the suit, citing a 1975 ruling by a federal appellate panel in a Virginia case that homosexual sodomy was not protected by the Constitution because it "is obviously no portion of marriage, home or family life." Punishment of sodomy "is not an upstart notion," the appellate judges had ruled in *Doe v. Commonwealth's Attorney*; "it has ancestry going back to Judaic and Christian law." The Supreme Court had declined to review this decision.

Kathleen Wilde appealed Judge Hall's dismissal order to the federal appellate court in Atlanta, and waited two years for a decision. The result was worth the long wait. Judge Frank M. Johnson, who had endured much criticism for his consistent support of civil rights, held in Michael's case that "private consensual sexual behavior among adults" was protected from punishment. "For some," he added, "the sexual activity in question here serves the same purpose as the intimacy of marriage."

Georgia officials recoiled from Johnson's decision and asked the Supreme Court to reverse his ruling. Confronted with a rejection of *Doe*, the justices agreed to deal with gay rights for the first time. Georgia's brief in *Bowers v. Hardwick* rested on two millennia of Judeo-Christian morality. Homosexuality had been condemned throughout history, it argued, and the state's lawmakers had agreed in 1816—when the law was first passed—that "it is the very act of homosexual sodomy that epitomizes moral delinquency." Attorney General Bowers presented the Court with a "parade of horribles" in his brief, claiming that "homosexual sodomy leads to other deviate practices such as sado-masochism, group orgies, or transvestism, to name only a few." He brought the brief up to date by asserting that Georgia lawmakers "should be permitted to draw conclusions concerning the relationship of homosexual sodomy" to AIDS. Bowers neglected to note that his state's law was passed 150 years before the AIDS virus was discovered.

Among the numerous groups that filed amicus briefs in *Bowers v. Hardwick*, the most impressive was the joint brief of the American Psychological Association and the American Public Health Association, which included ninety-one citations to medical and social science literature. It noted that oral or anal sex was practiced by 80 percent of all married couples, and that 95 percent of American males—both gay and straight—had engaged in oral sex and violated sodomy laws. In fact, the brief claimed, "there are great similarities among homosexual and heterosexual couples—in emotional makeup, significance of the relationship to the individual, and in the role sexuality plays in the relationship."

The justices heard argument in *Bowers* on March 31, 1986. Michael Hobbs, a deputy to Attorney General Bowers, defended his boss and his state's law. He framed the question as "whether or not there is a fundamental right under the Constitution of the United States to engage in consensual private homosexual conduct." Hobbs argued that the "right of privacy" did not extend beyond "marriage, the family, procreation, abortion, childrearing and child education." Homosexual sodomy could not lead to pregnancy or childbirth, and therefore was not protected by the Constitution. Hobbs faced questions about Georgia's enforcement of its sodomy law. Had any married couple ever been prosecuted? "Not to my knowledge," he replied. Would such a prosecution be lawful? "I believe that it would be unconstitutional," he conceded.

Once Hobbs had fielded these questions, he urged the justices to avoid creating "a constitutional right which is little more than one of self-gratification and indulgence." He warned that Michael Hardwick's "crack-in-the-door argument is truly a Pandora's box" and that striking down sodomy laws would lead to attacks on laws "which prohibit polygamy; homosexual, same-sex marriage; consensual incest; prostitution; fornication; adultery; and possibly even personal possession in private of illegal drugs." Hobbs failed to note that Officer Torick had cracked open a bedroom door, behind which two gay men were engaged in sexual activity that straight couples could enjoy without fear of prosecution. "Georgia is not acting as a big brother," Hobbs concluded, but was simply "adhering to centuries-old tradition and the conventional morality of its people."

Laurence Tribe took the podium for Michael Hardwick. Professor of constitutional law at Harvard and author of the most influential treatise in the field, Tribe had appeared before the Court in a dozen important cases, with an impressive victory record. He began by reshaping the issue Hobbs had framed: "This case is about the limits of governmental power," Tribe said. Michael's case had nothing to do with bigamy or incest, but with Georgia's power to dictate "how every adult, married or unmarried, in every bedroom in Georgia will behave in the closest and most intimate personal association with another adult."

Justice Lewis Powell moved the discussion from bedrooms to "a motel room or back of an automobile or toilet or whatever." Could Tribe define the "limiting principles" of his claim that states could not prohibit consensual sodomy? Tribe reminded Powell that bedrooms in homes had special constitutional protection from police invasion, far more than public places. Arguing that "there is something special about a home," he added that "Robert Frost once said that home is the place where, when you go there, they have to take you in." Poetry has no force as precedent, but Tribe obviously hoped to focus the justices on Michael's bedroom and not on public toilets. Michael Hobbs had conceded that Georgia could not punish straight couples for sodomy, but Tribe did not make an equal protection argument, resting his case on the "liberty" interest of the Fourteenth Amendment.

Three months after the arguments, on June 30, 1986, a sharply divided Court ruled that Georgia could punish its gay citizens for sexual acts that straight couples could perform without fear of arrest. Justice Byron White, who had blasted the *Roe* decision in dissent as "an exercise of raw judicial power," wrote for the majority in *Bowers*. The former gridiron star had no desire to flex his judicial muscles in this case, expressing his deference to the "belief of a majority of the electorate in Georgia that homosexual sodomy is immoral and unacceptable." White based his opinion on the "ancient roots" of criminal penalties for sodomy. He agreed with Michael Hobbs, who argued that "the collective moral aspirations of the people" provide a legitimate basis for sodomy laws. "The law," White stated, "is constantly based on notions of morality, and if all laws representing essentially moral choices are to be invalidated under the due process clause, the courts will be very busy indeed."

Justice White's opinion did not answer the obvious question: To *whose* notions of morality should judges defer? Chief Justice Burger offered in a brief concurrence his opinion that sodomy laws were "firmly rooted in Judeo-Christian moral and ethical standards." To hold that sodomy "is somehow protected as a fundamental right would be to cast aside millennia of moral teaching," Burger concluded. In an even briefer concurrence, Justice Lewis Powell agreed that "there is no fundamental right" to practice sodomy, but he was troubled that Georgia allowed a twenty-year prison term "for a single private, consensual act of sodomy." Powell hinted that if Georgia had prosecuted Michael Hardwick, he might have voted against the law because it violated the Eighth Amendment's ban on "cruel and unusual punishment."

Harry Blackmun wrote for the four dissenters, who included William Brennan, Thurgood Marshall, and John Stevens. He accused the Court's majority of hiding their homophobia behind the mask of history. "Only the most willful blindness," he wrote, "could obscure the fact that sexual intimacy" is central to healthy personal relationships of all kinds. The majority refused to recognize that "a necessary corollary of giving individuals freedom to choose how to conduct their lives is acceptance of the fact that different individuals will make different choices." Blackmun deplored White's reliance on the "ancient roots" of hostility toward homosexuals as justification for modern-day sodomy laws. He quoted Oliver Wendell Holmes: "It is revolting to have no better reason for a rule of law than that so it was laid down in the time of Henry IV. It is still more revolting if the grounds upon which it was laid down have vanished long since, and the rule simply persists from blind imitation of the past."

The final paragraph of Blackmun's scathing dissent looked to more recent history for an ominous parallel and possible redemption. He pointed to the Court's 1940 decision upholding the expulsion of Lillian and William Gobitas from school for refusing to salute the flag. Justice Frankfurter's opinion in *Minersville v. Gobitis* had unleashed a wave of violence against Jehovah's Witnesses that shocked his colleagues. "It took but three years for the Court to see the error" of the *Gobitis* decision, Blackmun wrote, and to overrule it in *West Virginia v. Barnette*. "I can only hope that here, too, the Court will reconsider" its approval of sodomy laws, Blackmun urged, "and conclude that depriving individuals of the right to choose for themselves how to conduct their intimate relationships poses a far greater threat to the values most deeply rooted in our Nation's history than tolerance of noncomformity could ever do. Because I think the Court today betrays those values, I dissent."

It took the Court three years to confess the error of its *Gobitis* decision. It took Lewis Powell four years to confess his error in the *Bowers* case. He delivered a law school lecture in 1990, three years after retiring from the Court, and was asked during the question period how he could reconcile his support for *Roe* with his *Bowers* vote. "I think I probably made a mistake in that one," Powell said of *Bowers*. "When I had the opportunity to reread the opinions a few months later, I thought the dissent had the better of the arguments." Powell's vote had decided *Bowers* and kept alive the "ancient roots" that supported the sodomy laws of half the states. For gays and lesbians in those states, the Constitution means what one judge said it did, before he changed his mind, too late to change the outcome.

Two weeks before the Court handed down its *Bowers* decision, Chief Justice Burger announced that he would retire at the term's end in July 1986. Burger told President Ronald Reagan that he wanted to direct the preparations for the Constitution's bicentennial celebrations in 1987. He had grandiose plans for a birthday party in Philadelphia, complete with fireworks and brass bands. But did the American people have much cause in 1987 to celebrate after two centuries of constitutional government? Each person's answer, of course, depends on the perspective from which she or he views American society and the Constitution. The comments of two very different Americans on the constitutional bicentennial provide thought for reflection. One came to the birthday party in a celebratory spirit; the other declined the invitation in a critical speech.

Thirty-nine men had gathered at the State House in Philadelphia on September 17, 1787, to sign the Constitution they had spent four months drafting and debating. The first to place his name on that document was George Washington, who presided at the Constitutional Convention and then became the new nation's first president. On that same day, two hundred years later, the fortieth president came to the State House—now called Independence Hall—to praise the results of that hot summer's labors. Ronald Reagan said nothing in his bicentennial speech about the disputes that divided the Framers in 1787, most notably the conflict over slavery. The president had come to Philadelphia to sooth his listeners, not to remind them of the nation's unhealed wounds. He spoke of the Constitution in reverential words, attributing its genesis to divine inspiration. He called it "a covenant with the Supreme Being to whom our Founding Fathers did constantly appeal for assistance." Looking back, Reagan saw a "divine source" behind the Framers' deliberations and a "miracle" in their final agreement on a charter of government. From his perspective, the Constitution represented "the triumph of human freedom under God."

President Reagan invited Americans in 1987 to look "beyond distinctions of class, race, or national origin" in celebrating the Constitution. "I cannot accept this invitation," replied Justice Thurgood Marshall, whose grandfather was born into slavery. The first black American to sit on the Supreme Court reminded white Americans that "eloquent objections to the institution of slavery went unheeded" at the Philadelphia convention in 1787, and that the delegates who opposed slavery "eventually consented to a document that laid a foundation for the tragic events that were to follow." Marshall urged his fellow Americans to "commemorate the suffering, struggle, and sacrifice that triumphed over much that was wrong" with the Framers' compromises. The clauses in the Constitution that permitted and protected slavery have since been repealed, Marshall noted, "but the credit does not belong to the Framers. It belongs to those who refused to acquiesce to outdated notions of liberty, justice, and equality, and who strived to better them." From Marshall's perspective, "the true miracle was not the birth of the Constitution but its life, a life nurtured through two turbulent centuries of our own making, and embodying much good fortune that was not."

Justice Marshall spoke on the Constitution's bicentennial of those who "may observe the anniversary with hopes not realized and promises not fulfilled." The Supreme Court had given hope and made promises to several groups of Americans over the past half century in landmark cases, only to dash those hopes and break those promises in later decisions. The Court ruled unanimously in 1954 that school segregation violated the Constitution, but five justices decided in 1974 that "metropolitan" plans to reduce big-city segregation could not cross school district boundaries. By 1987 the schools in many northern cities had become almost totally segregated, as "white flight" to the suburbs left black and Hispanic students behind, crowded into poorly equipped schools with poorly trained teachers. The Court decided in 1973 that criminal abortion laws violated the Constitution, but five justices voted in 1980 to uphold a congressional ban on Medicaid funding for abortions. By 1987 the number of clinics offering abortions had dropped by half, and most poor women could not afford to end an unwanted or dangerous pregnancy. The Court held in 1965 that the Constitution protected a "right to privacy" in the "marital bedroom," but five justices decided in 1986 that homosexuals did not enjoy the right to sexual intimacy in their bedrooms. Half the states in 1987 still imposed criminal penalties for sodomy, but only gays and lesbians faced prosecution for acts that straight couples practiced with equal frequency.

35

"I Fear for the Future"

In 1987 the Chief Justice of the United States was William Rehnquist. As the Constitution entered its third century, the Supreme Court was headed by a man who had argued that *Plessy* was right and *Roe* was wrong. Only two sitting justices—Edward White in 1910 and Harlan Fiske Stone in 1941—had been elevated to the Chief's position before President Reagan nominated Rehnquist in June 1986 to succeed Warren Burger. A highly partisan Republican president, Richard Nixon, chose Rehnquist for the Court in 1971; fifteen years later, another partisan GOP president moved him into Burger's seat. Both presidents had been assured that Rehnquist—whom neither man knew well—would cast his judicial votes as a conservative "partisan," a label the new Chief Justice had proudly applied to himself. Rehnquist had survived a bruising confirmation battle when he first joined the Court; twenty-six senators considered his political and legal views too conservative in 1971. Since not one senator had opposed the promotions of White or Stone, one might expect that opposition to Rehnquist would have receded over fifteen years. But he won his second confirmation over thirty-three negative votes; seven more senators considered his judicial record too conservative in 1986.

The new Chief Justice did not command a conservative majority when he moved into Burger's center seat. Three justices remained from the Warren Court: William Brennan and Thurgood Marshall were staunch liberals, and Byron White joined them in most civil right cases. Harry Blackmun, Lewis Powell, and John Paul Stevens took "moderate" positions on most issues, along with the newest justice, Sandra Day O'Connor. President Reagan had named the first woman to the Court in 1981 to replace Potter Stewart, who retired after twenty-three years of movie-critic judging, deciding each case by his own standards of fairness. An honors graduate of Stanford Law School in 1952, O'Connor discovered that corporate firms hired women only as secretaries; she finally landed a job in a California county attorney's office and later moved to Arizona, where she practiced small-town law and Republican politics. O'Connor served in the Arizona senate for six years and in state judicial office for another six years before Reagan honored his campaign promise to place a woman on the Supreme Court. During her Senate confirmation hearings, O'Connor deflected questions about abortion and the *Roe* decision, pledging only to exercise judicial "restraint" and proclaiming that "I do not believe that it is the function of the judiciary to step in and change the law because the times have changed." Although the most fervent anti-abortion groups opposed O'Connor's confirmation, because she had once voted to liberalize Arizona's abortion law, the Senate approved her without dissent in September 1981.

When President Nixon nominated William Rehnquist and Lewis Powell for the Supreme Court in 1971, the younger, relatively unknown lawyer stood in the shadow of an older, respected leader of the American bar. When President Reagan announced Rehnquist's nomination as Chief Justice in 1986, he offered the Senate another team, with a younger—but hardly unknown—candidate for the opening that Rehnquist's promotion had created. Reagan picked Antonin Scalia, a fifty-year-old judge on the District of Columbia appellate court. The Harvard Law School graduate had earlier taught at the University of Virginia and University of Chicago law schools and served in the Justice Department post that Rehnquist had once held. The two lawyers were equally partisan in their conservative views, although Scalia was more combative in legal debate. During a decade of law teaching and four years on the federal appellate bench, "Nino" Scalia forcefully argued that the Equal Protection Clause mandated a "color-blind" Constitution and firmly denied that the Due Process Clause protected abortion rights. Given the rough treatment the Senate gave Rehnquist in 1971, it seems odd that Scalia's nomination sailed through by acclamation, even though he and Rehnquist agreed on most issues, particularly in denying any constitutional basis for abortion rights. The "pro-choice" lobby, however, did not mount a campaign against Scalia, despite his open desire to overrule the *Roe* decision.

Long before he joined the Supreme Court, William Rehnquist proclaimed his wish to dismantle the judicial legacy of the Warren Court. He and William Brennan differed in almost every case, but they agreed that "with five votes, you can do anything around here." Brennan had five votes more often, but Lewis Powell's retirement in June 1987 handed President Reagan the chance to shape a "Rehnquist Court" that could accomplish the new Chief's long-sought goal. Reagan's eagerness to find the crucial fifth vote against *Roe* proved his undoing, however. The pro-choice lobby woke up with a start when he nominated Robert Bork to replace Powell. Bork and Justice Scalia had both held Justice

Department posts and taught at prestigious law schools, and they had served together on the District of Columbia appellate court. They both opposed abortion rights with fire-breathing fervor, but the Senate confirmed Scalia without dissent and rejected Bork by a vote of fifty-eight to forty-two after a bruising and bitter campaign by partisans on both sides of the abortion issue.

The fact that forty-seven senators who voted for Scalia, knowing his opposition to abortion, turned around and voted against Bork the following year offers a striking illustration of the political nature of Supreme Court nominations. Bork's rejection, however, was hardly the first example of this phenomenon. The experience of Louis Brandeis in 1916 showed that conservatives could also mount partisan campaigns against nominees they considered too liberal. Charges that Brandeis held "radical" views on labor and civil liberties did not block his confirmation, but his opponents tried hard to keep him off the Court. And a coalition of labor and civil rights groups had successfully blocked President Hoover's nomination of Judge John Parker to the Court in 1930.

Bork's defeat only stiffened President Reagan's resolve to place the fifth vote against *Roe* on the Court. His advisers combed the federal appellate bench for potential justices and came up with two names: Anthony Kennedy of the Ninth Circuit in the West, and Douglas Ginsburg, who served for one year with Bork on the District of Columbia court after teaching antitrust law at Harvard. Ginsburg got the nod, largely because of his youth—he was just forty-one—and his rock-hard conservative views. Reagan announced his choice of Ginsburg on October 29, 1987. A week later, his nomination went up in smoke after former colleagues at Harvard—who opposed Ginsburg on political grounds—told reporters that the young professor had smoked marijuana at parties with students. The president could hardly say yes to Ginsburg while the First Lady conducted her "Just Say No" campaign against drug use.

Anthony Kennedy had much in common with Harry Blackmun. They were both the third choices for a seat whose new occupant was expected to be more conservative than his predecessor. Nixon and Reagan had both pledged to place a "strict constructionist" on the Court, and both looked to the federal appellate bench for candidates. And both presidents, twice foiled by the Senate in naming hard-line conservatives, had reluctantly turned to "moderates" whose judicial records would not trigger liberal opposition. Kennedy had all the right credentials. Born in Sacramento, California, in 1936, he graduated from Stanford and Harvard Law School, spent fourteen years in corporate practice in Sacramento, taught constitutional law at the University of the Pacific, and served for twelve years on the Ninth Circuit Court of Appeals. Kennedy also had an altar-boy reputation; he was a devout Catholic whose friends considered him totally square. Reagan's far-right supporters harbored suspicions about Kennedy's devotion to conservative dogma, but the president was convinced that he would vote "right" on *Roe.*

Leaders of the pro-choice lobby charged the Reagan administration with imposing a "litmus test" on all federal judicial appointments; the Republican platforms of 1980 and 1984 demanded that prospective judges affirm their opposition to abortion. Supreme Court nominees, who balked at explicitly promising senators they would vote to overturn the *Roe* decision, were expected to signal their willingness in code words like "judicial restraint." Sandra O'Connor used just those words at her Senate confirmation hearing, but that phrase also expresses the principle of following precedent, as well as deferring to legislative judgments. The first case that put the Reagan justices to the abortion test came in 1989, a busy year at the Supreme Court, which also handed down controversial decisions on flag-burning and affirmative action.

Confident they had five votes to overrule *Roe*, abortion opponents urged the Reagan administration to intervene in a Missouri case that involved drastic restrictions on access to abortion. State legislators passed a law in 1986 with four major provisions: the first proclaimed that "the life of each human being begins at the moment of conception" in Missouri; the second barred abortions in public hospitals except to save a pregnant woman's life; a third prohibited all state employees—including doctors—from "encouraging or counseling" women to have abortions; the last ordered all doctors—even those in private practice—to perform "viability tests" when they believed a woman had been pregnant twenty weeks or more. Several Missouri doctors and abortion providers sued the state's attorney general, William Webster, and federal judges struck down most of the law's provisions as violating *Roe*.

Arguing in *Webster v. Reproductive Health Services* as a "friend of the Court," Solicitor General Charles Fried stated the Reagan administration's position: "Today the United States asks this Court to reconsider and overrule its decision in *Roe v. Wade*." Fried assured the justices that he was not asking them "to unravel the fabric of unenumerated and privacy rights" that the Court had woven since *Griswold* in 1965. His adversary at the podium, Frank Sussman of St. Louis, replied that "when I pull a thread, my sleeve falls off." He accused Fried of wanting to shear off "the full range of procreation rights and choices" the Court had protected from state lawmakers.

Supporters of abortion rights feared the worst from the Court's ruling in *Webster*. But the justices did not cut *Roe* to ribbons, because Justice O'Connor declined "the state's invitation to reexamine the constitutional validity" of that decision. Chief Justice Rehnquist expressed "the judgment of the Court" in an opinion that upheld most of Missouri's restrictions on abortions in public hospitals. But he spoke for only three other justices: White, Scalia, and Kennedy. Justice O'Connor preferred to trim legal threads rather than take her shears to *Roe*. She noted that the Court had upheld the Missouri law's major provisions. "Precisely for this reason," O'Connor wrote, she would exercise "judicial restraint" and defer any final judgment on *Roe* until the Court faced a direct challenge to its rulings. When such a case arrived, "there will be time enough to reexamine *Roe*," she wrote. "And to do so carefully," she chided the Court's impatient tailors.

Justice Scalia responded to O'Connor's implied rebuke with scorn. Her invocation of "judicial restraint" as a reason "to avoid reconsidering *Roe* cannot be taken seriously," he wrote. Scalia's direct rebuke of his colleague broke the Court's unwritten rules of conduct and may have cost him the fifth vote in the final showdown over *Roe*. He certainly offended O'Connor, who never joined an opinion with Scalia in later abortion cases, even when they agreed on the outcome. Justice Harry Blackmun did not express relief that *Roe* had been spared by O'Connor's adherence to judicial restraint. "I fear for the future," he wrote in dissent. "I fear for the liberty and equality of the millions of women who have lived and come of age in the sixteen years since *Roe* was decided. I fear for the integrity of, and public esteem for, this Court." Blackmun also feared that the next Supreme Court justice would blow out the flickering candle of abortion rights. Among the four *Webster* dissenters, he and Thurgood Marshall were eighty years old, and William Brennan was eighty-three. John Stevens, at sixty-nine, was the youngest justice who firmly backed the *Roe* decision. "For today," Blackmun wrote despairingly, "the women of this Nation still retain the liberty to control their destinies. But the signs are evident and very ominous, and a chill wind blows."

Two of the Reagan justices—Antonin Scalia and Anthony Kennedy—voted as expected in the *Webster* case, and Sandra O'Connor surprised many people by refusing to overturn *Roe*. But another decision in 1989 surprised even more people. The case of *Texas v. Johnson* involved a criminal conviction for burning the American flag during the 1984 Republican convention in Dallas. Gregory Johnson headed a column of about a hundred members of the Revolutionary Communist Youth Brigade who marched through downtown Dallas, chanting slogans and spray-painting the walls of corporate buildings. One marcher pulled an American flag from its pole outside a bank and handed it to Johnson, who led his ragtag band to City Hall. Closely watched by Dallas police, Johnson doused the flag with kerosene and flicked a cigarette lighter. While the flag burned, the protesters chanted, "America, the red, white, and blue, we spit on you." No fights broke out, and the police did not intervene. One spectator, Daniel Walker, gathered the burned remains and buried them in his backyard. Police later arrested Johnson under a Texas law that punished anyone who "desecrates" a flag with knowledge the act will "seriously offend" an observer. Walker told a jury he was offended by the flag burning, and Johnson received a one-year jail term for putting a torch to Old Glory.

A panel of state judges reversed the conviction, holding that Johnson's act "was clearly 'speech' contemplated by the First Amendment." The Supreme

Court accepted the state's appeal for review, and most observers expected the justices to uphold the Texas law. Many were surprised when Justices Scalia and Kennedy joined Brennan, Marshall, and Blackmun to strike down the flag-desecration law. As the senior majority justice, Brennan assigned the Court's opinion to himself. A quarter century after his momentous *New York Times v. Sullivan* opinion, he reaffirmed the constitutional primacy of the First Amendment. Because "fundamental rights" of free expression were at stake, Brennan applied the "strict scrutiny" test; only laws that reflect "compelling state interests" can clear this judicial hurdle. The state's lawyers conceded that flag burning was symbolic speech, but they asserted two compelling interests: preventing breaches of the peace and protecting the flag as a symbol of national unity. Brennan quickly disposed of the first claim. Texas had not charged Johnson with breaching the peace, and states may not "ban the expression of certain disagreeable ideas on the unsupported assumption that their very disagreeableness will provoke violence."

Brennan addressed the "national unity" claim with agreement that the flag holds a "special place" in public sentiment, but he argued that Gregory Johnson's act "will not endanger the special role played by our flag or the feelings it inspires." Paraphrasing the *Abrams* dissent of Justice Holmes seventy years earlier, Brennan wrote that "nobody can suppose that this one gesture of an unknown man will change our Nation's attitude toward its flag." He summarized his Bill of Rights philosophy in one sentence: "If there is a bedrock principle underlying the First Amendment, it is that government may not prohibit the expression of an idea simply because society finds the idea offensive or disagreeable."

Brennan had no need to charm or cajole Scalia into the majority. In First Amendment cases, Scalia refuses to allow lawmakers to display any "content preference" for one opinion over another. At oral argument in the *Johnson* case, Scalia claimed that the flag could be flown "only in one direction" in Texas. "You can honor it all you like," he said of the state's argument, "but you can't dishonor it as a sign of disrespect for the country." Even with Scalia on his side, Brennan needed another vote to compensate for the defection of Justice Stevens from the liberal bloc; he found it in Justice Kennedy, the Court's newest member. In a brief concurrence, Kennedy stated that he was heeding the "pure command" of the First Amendment. But he confessed the personal toll the flag-burning case extracted from him. "The hard fact is that sometimes we must make decisions we do not like," Kennedy wrote. "We make them because they are right, right in the sense that the law and the Constitution, as we see them, compel the result."

Chief Justice Rehnquist viewed the Court's ruling as totally wrong. He reportedly glared at Brennan when the senior justice, sitting at his right hand, read portions of his majority opinion from the bench. Rehnquist accused Brennan of giving a "patronizing civics lecture" to the Court. But the Chief Justice delivered his own civics lecture, devoting six pages of his dissent to quotations from patriotic literature and poems, spanning American wars from the Revolution to Vietnam. He quoted Emerson's tribute to the "embattled farmers" who stood at the Concord bridge, "their flag to April's breeze unfurled." Rehnquist sang the first verse of "The Star-Spangled Banner" and recalled the sacrifice of the Marines who died on Iwo Jima, fighting "hand to hand against thousands of Japanese" while their flag was planted at the summit of Mount Suribachi. He argued that the "unique position" of the flag in American history "justifies a governmental prohibition against flag burning" to protect the nation's symbol. "Surely one of the high purposes of a democratic society," he wrote, "is to legislate against conduct that is regarded as evil and profoundly offensive to the majority of people—whether it be murder, embezzlement, pollution, or flag burning." In Rehnquist's mind, Gregory Johnson had murdered the American flag and deserved a prison term for his "evil" act.

Not since the school-prayer cases of the early 1960s had the Supreme Court ignited such a firestorm of public outrage. Newspapers printed thousands of heated letters, and hundreds were reprinted in the *Congressional Record*. President George Bush, whose 1988 campaign featured the flag, proposed a constitutional amendment to overturn the Court's ruling. The House of Representatives passed a resolution condemning the decision without one dissenting vote. In the Senate, leaders of both parties sponsored a similar resolution. "The Court's decision is wrong and should be corrected," said George Mitchell, the Democratic majority leader. Minority leader Robert Dole added that "there has been a lot of talk lately about how the Supreme Court has tilted right. Well, yesterday, the Court did not tilt right. It tilted wrong—dead wrong." Only three senators voted no on the bipartisan resolution, and Dole introduced a constitutional amendment to reverse the Court's decision.

The campaign to amend the First Amendment cooled off after the speeches ended and second thoughts began. Nebraska senator Bob Kerrey, who lost a leg in Vietnam and won a Medal of Honor, dampened the rhetorical flames with a dramatic speech against a constitutional amendment. "At first I was outraged by the Supreme Court's opinion," he said. Later, during the Senate's Fourth of July recess, he read the opinions. "I was surprised to discover that I found the majority argument to be reasonable, understandable and consistent with those values that I believe make America so wonderful." Kerrey responded to the "disappointing dissent" of Chief Justice Rehnquist with his own civics lecture. Recalling "the smell of my own burning flesh" on the battleground, he said that "I don't remember giving the safety of our flag anywhere near the thought that I gave the safety of my men."

When debate ended, Senator Dole's proposed amendment fell sixteen votes short of the two-thirds majority it needed for passage. Congress did, however, pass a Flag Protection Act that made it a federal crime to "knowingly mutilate, deface, physically defile, burn, maintain on the floor, or trample upon any flag of the United States." Gregory Johnson promptly burned another flag, this time on the Capitol steps, but a group of Seattle radicals won the race to the Supreme Court in 1990. Justice Brennan wrote for the same majority of five in *United States v. Eichman*, striking down the federal law. By this time, even Chief Justice Rehnquist seemed tired of the issue. "Surely there are not many people who burn flags in this country," he told a lawyers' group after the decision. Now that "it has finally been established it is legal, there will be far fewer." He was right; protestors against the Gulf War in 1991 did not burn flags but waved them under the banner "Support our Troops—Bring Them Home Alive." Forms of protest change, but the First Amendment endures the flames of controversy.

The Reagan justices were divided in the 1989 abortion and flag-burning decisions, but they stuck together in the most significant affirmative action case since the *Bakke* ruling in 1978. The issue in *City of Richmond v. J. A. Croson Co.* was a "minority set-aside" program designed to redress the historic imbalance in public funding of construction projects in Virginia's capital. During the Sixties and Seventies, many of Richmond's white residents fled to the suburbs to escape integration of the city's schools. By the early Eighties, blacks made up more than half of Richmond's population and controlled five of nine seats on the city council. In 1983, the council adopted a "Minority Utilization Plan" requiring contractors on public jobs to award at least 30 percent of their subcontracting dollars to "minority business enterprises," defined as those with at least 51 percent black, Spanish-speaking, Asian, Native American, Eskimo, or Aleut ownership.

Testimony before the council on the set-aside plan showed that between 1978 and 1983, fewer than 1 percent of the city's construction dollars went to minority-owned firms. However, the council received no evidence of past discrimination against any specific firm, which was not surprising. Blacks had been effectively shut out of the construction industry in Richmond—and most cities across the country—by lack of business training and start-up funding. Even with help from federal small-business programs, there were very few black-owned firms to discriminate against in Richmond. The council's set-aside plan, however, allowed contractors to meet their 30 percent quota with firms outside the city.

The J. A. Croson Company won a contract to install new plumbing fixtures at Richmond's city jail, but its purchasing agents could not find a minority-owned business to provide sinks and urinals anywhere between Richmond and the Aleutian Islands in Alaska. Croson requested a waiver from the set-aside requirements, but city officials refused. The company finally located a minority-owned firm, but its bid exceeded Croson's estimate by several thousand dollars; the city refused to raise the contract price and reopened bidding on the job. The company's lawyers filed suit in federal court, arguing that the city's program violated the Fourteenth Amendment's Equal Protection Clause. They relied for support on the Supreme Court's 1986 decision in *Wygant v. Jackson Board of Education*, a case that involved the layoffs of white teachers with more seniority than blacks in order to maintain racial balance in teaching staffs. The Court in *Wygant* had required evidence of past discrimination by government officials to support race-based remedial programs. Croson's lawyers argued that Richmond had not shown any such evidence. On their side, the city's lawyers cited the Court's 1980 ruling in *Fullilove v. Klutznick*, upholding a federal program that set aside 10 percent of public works contracts for minority-owned firms; Congress had found a past history of discrimination in the construction industry, but not against specific firms. Significantly, the Court spoke in both *Wygant* and *Fullilove* through plurality opinions, leaving the question of affirmative action in search of a majority.

All four Reagan justices voted against Richmond's set-aside program. Sandra O'Connor spoke for the *Croson* majority, which included Byron White and John Paul Stevens. Her opinion borrowed Earl Warren's language in *Brown v. Board of Education* to undermine the goals of affirmative action. "Classifications based on race carry a danger of stigmatic harm," she wrote. "Unless they are strictly reserved for remedial settings, they may in fact promote notions of racial inferiority and lead to a politics of racial hostility." The notions of racial inferiority that Warren deplored in *Brown* were those implanted in black children by their exclusion from white schools. O'Connor presumably assumed in *Croson* that black contractors would feel inferior because of their inclusion among members of their industry. This inverted reasoning left blacks in a no-win situation; keeping them out and putting them in both produced notions of racial inferiority.

Determined to promote the notion of a "color-blind" Constitution, Justice O'Connor shielded her eyes from historical reality. The dearth of black contractors in Richmond "is not probative of any discrimination in the local construction industry," she claimed. The "numerous explanations" for this obvious fact included "past societal discrimination in education and economic opportunities" for blacks. O'Connor's statement that "Blacks may be disproportionately attracted to industries other than construction" added to the unreality of her opinion. Given the "past societal discrimination" against blacks in almost every industry, it was hardly surprising they were not "attracted" to construction, long dominated by lily-white trade groups and unions. O'Connor did not list any industries to which blacks were "attracted" as owners, most likely because they own few businesses that do not primarily serve the black community. Not one of Richmond's largest construction firms had ever been owned by blacks. How, then, could the city council provide evidence of discrimination against black-owned firms that did not exist? This fact did not stop O'Connor from warning that allowing "past societal discrimination" to justify "rigid racial preferences" would "open the door to competing claims for 'remedial relief' for every disadvantaged group." But every group except whites was disadvantaged in Richmond. O'Connor chose *Wygant* as precedent for its reliance on evidence of "identified discrimination" against black teachers; she dismissed the evidence of nationwide construction-industry discrimination the Court had cited in *Fullilove* because it did not prove the existence of discrimination in Richmond.

Justice Thurgood Marshall, the Court's only black member, decried O'Connor's *Croson* opinion as a "cynical" effort to deny Richmond's "disgraceful history of public and private racial discrimination." Writing for Justices William Brennan and Harry Blackmun in dissent, Marshall accused O'Connor of ignoring both the city's ample "proof" of discrimination against blacks in construction and the "exhaustive" studies the Court had relied on in *Fullilove*. He called the *Croson* decision "a deliberate and giant step backward in this Court's affirmative action jurisprudence." Back in 1944, Justice Frank Murphy had dissented from the Court's "legalization of racism" in the *Korematsu* case, which upheld the wartime internment of Japanese Americans. Justice Marshall stopped just short of sticking the "racist" label on the *Croson* decision in 1989, but his dissent exposed the depth of his anger at the "armchair cynicism" of the Court's majority. The majority simply would not look at the evidence of "official racism" that pervaded Richmond and persisted long after slavery ended. Marshall spent more than sixty years fighting to end the racism that pervaded American society; he now despaired of stemming the Court's "full-scale retreat" from his cherished goal of racial equality.

On July 20, 1990, a steamy Friday in Washington, Justice William Brennan sat alone in his chambers and composed a brief letter to President George Bush. "The strenuous demand of court work and its related duties required or expected of a justice," he wrote, "appear at this time to be incompatible with my advancing age and medical condition. I therefore retire immediately as an associate justice of the Supreme Court of the United States." A gallbladder operation had weakened him, and a recent stroke had produced episodes of confusion. After thirty-four years on the Court, Brennan knew he could no longer function at full capacity. Fifteen years earlier, he had witnessed the agonizing slide into senility of his liberal ally William Douglas. Brennan was determined to leave the bench with the dignity that he consistently urged his colleagues to give every American.

Accolades poured in from Brennan's vast network of friends and former clerks, who now taught at virtually every top-notch law school. Professor Owens Fiss of Yale, who clerked for Brennan during the Warren Court era, wrote of this period that "it was Brennan who by and large formulated the principle, analyzed the precedents, and chose the words that transformed the ideal into law." Perhaps the most telling tributes came from Brennan's ideological adversaries, who uniformly spoke of his personal warmth and political acumen. Chief Justice Rehnquist, who rarely voted with Brennan in Bill of Rights cases, acknowledged that "the skills which Bill Brennan brought to the work of judging enabled him on numerous occasions to put together majorities espousing the side of individual rights in which he believed so deeply." Two former Reagan advisers wrote that "what Brennan has done has been to package and market his beliefs more attractively than have some of his ideological brethren." This was high praise indeed from officials of an administration that mastered the skills of packaging and marketing conservative policies. Perhaps the warmest tribute came from a former law clerk, Richard Posner, now a notably conservative federal judge. Justice Brennan's lasting influence, Posner wrote, stemmed less from his "commitment to a doctrine" than from "the emanation of a warm, generous, and good-hearted person."

In a real sense, Brennan's retirement marked the end of the Warren Court era, with its landmark decisions largely intact after thirty years of conservative leadership under Warren Burger and William Rehnquist. Brennan's vision of "human dignity" as the Constitution's animating principle remains alive, nurtured after his death in 1997 by a legion of admiring lawyers and judges. Justice Brennan also affected the lives of many ordinary Americans like Jacinta Moreno, John Kelly, Webster Bivens, Adell Sherbert, Steven Pico, Sharron Frontiero, and Leon Goldfarb. These are all people whose names appear in the captions of opinions Brennan wrote for the Court. Their cases raised issues of welfare rights, police brutality, religious practice, library censorship, sex discrimination, and social security benefits. In each case, Justice Brennan put together judicial majorities to give these Americans—and millions like them—the "dignity" they deserved from our Constitution.

Three days after he received Brennan's letter, President Bush announced his nomination of David Souter to replace the liberal icon. He picked an obscure federal appellate judge with only seven months' experience on the First Circuit bench in Boston. But Souter—like Brennan—had served for years on state courts, as a trial judge and supreme court justice in New Hampshire. Born in 1939, he attended Harvard Law School and spent a year in England as a Rhodes scholar. A bachelor who lived with his mother, Souter came to Washington with a country-bumpkin image, but he possessed a sharp legal mind. Because his political sponsors included fervent abortion opponents, liberals feared that Bush had nominated another Bork, without his scowl but equally determined to overturn *Roe*. During his Senate hearings, Souter resisted all efforts to pin him down on abortion, but he asserted his belief that the Constitution protected a "right to privacy" in matters of personal autonomy. Both sides in the abortion debate waited anxiously to see how Souter would vote when the time came to "carefully" reexamine *Roe*, as Justice O'Connor had promised in her *Webster* concurrence.

Brennan's departure left Thurgood Marshall feeling lonely on the bench, as the Court swung to the right under Rehnquist. Marshall had a big heart, but it labored to pump blood through his big body, and his lungs wheezed from years of smoking. After years of vowing that he would only leave the bench "feet first," he finally gave up on June 27, 1991, the last day of the Court's term. He sat grimly beside Rehnquist as the Chief Justice read an opinion upholding a death penalty imposed on a black man convicted of killing a white woman and her two-year-old daughter in Tennessee. Marshall and Brennan had consistently opposed capital punishment, and Rehnquist's eagerness to speed up executions offended Marshall's sense of fairness; the only justice who ever defended an accused murderer knew that blacks were far more likely than whites to die for the same crimes. In a scathing dissent to Rehnquist's opinion in *Payne v. Tennessee*, which overruled decisions just two and four years old, Marshall indicted the new majority for its disregard of precedent. "Power, not reason, is the new currency of this Court's decisions," he wrote. The Constitution had not changed in four years, "only the personnel of this Court did." In sending earlier decisions "to their graves," Marshall warned, "today's majority ominously suggests that an even more extensive upheaval of this Court's precedents may be in store. The majority today sends a clear signal that scores of established constitutional liberties are now ripe for reconsideration."

Marshall was unwilling to be a pallbearer as the new majority buried his offspring. When the justices returned to their conference room, he informed his colleagues that he was retiring. "I'm old and I'm coming apart," he told reporters the next day. But Marshall flashed his old spirit when a reporter asked whether President Bush should feel obligated to replace him with another black justice. "My dad told me way back," he replied, "that there's no difference between a white snake and a black snake. They'll both bite." Marshall did not name any black snakes, but he had one in mind. Four years earlier, Clarence Thomas—who then headed the federal Equal Employment Opportunity Commission—had criticized the speech in which Marshall noted the Constitution's acceptance of slavery. Thomas had assured a conservative audience that, unlike Marshall, he was "wild about the Constitution."

Four days after Thurgood Marshall announced his retirement, Clarence Thomas stood next to President Bush and heard himself lauded as "the best qualified" person to replace the first black justice. Thomas was then forty-three and had served for just over one year on the District of Columbia Court of Appeals. Born into poverty in Pin Point, Georgia, Thomas was raised by his grandfather after both parents abandoned him. Myers Anderson imposed rigid discipline on young Clarence, who still bears a scar from a whipping. His grandfather sent Thomas to Catholic schools, and he remained in them through elementary and high school, one year of seminary, and college at Holy Cross in Massachusetts. He won a scholarship to Yale Law School and graduated in

1974. The Supreme Court decided the *Roe* case during his second year at Yale, but Thomas later claimed he never discussed the Court's most controversial decision with classmates.

Thomas wound up in Washington in 1979, after five years of law practice in Missouri, first in the attorney general's office and then with the Monsanto chemical firm. He started as an aide to Republican senator John Danforth, his former Missouri boss, and moved into the Reagan administration in 1981, when he first told friends that Thurgood Marshall "wouldn't last forever" on the Supreme Court and that no one else "was in as good a position" to take his seat than Thomas, as the highest-ranking black lawyer in government. Thomas waited ten years for the nomination he felt was his reward for ducking liberal potshots as an outspoken black conservative.

During his confirmation hearings, Thomas dodged all questions on abortion. He displayed such a poor grasp of constitutional law that even a White House adviser who coached Thomas for the sessions called his performance "terrible." Erwin Griswold, the esteemed former Harvard Law School dean and solicitor general, bluntly told the senators that Thomas had "not yet demonstrated any clear intellectual or professional distinctions." But his confirmation seemed assured until Anita Hill, a University of Oklahoma law professor and former Thomas aide, charged that her former boss had propositioned her and made crude sexual remarks. Millions of Americans watched on television as Hill recalled Thomas asking if she had put a pubic hair on his Coke can, and describing the penis of "Long Dong Silver," a pornographic film star. Thomas later swore that he never made these remarks, although former law school classmates told reporters that he often showed them pornographic magazines. But Thomas won this "he-said-she-said" battle when the Senate narrowly confirmed him by a vote of fifty-two to forty-eight. Thomas once complained that civil rights leaders did little more than "bitch, bitch, moan, moan, and whine." He bitched during his confirmation hearings that he was the victim of a "high-tech lynching" by liberals. Thurgood Marshall, who had visited the sites of real lynchings as a civil rights lawyer, did not say a public word about his successor before he died in January 1993.

Clarence Thomas took his oath to "support and defend" the Constitution on October 23, 1991. Two weeks later, the case that gave the justices their chance to "carefully" reexamine *Roe* landed on the Court's docket. Hardly anyone doubted that Chief Justice Rehnquist now had at least five votes to overturn *Roe* and turn the abortion debate over to state lawmakers. "All lingering doubt has been erased," the *Wall Street Journal* assured its readers. "Conservatives have locked up control of the U.S. Supreme Court."

Even the most fervent pro-choice leaders expected to lose in *Planned Parenthood v. Casey*, which challenged restrictions that Pennsylvania lawmakers had placed on abortion access in 1989, heeding what Justice Blackmun had called the Court's "winks and nods" in the *Webster* ruling. The law required doctors to explain the "risks" of abortion to pregnant women, to provide them with information on "alternatives to abortion," and to obtain written consent for abortions. It also forced women to wait twenty-four hours for an abortion after signing the consent form, required unmarried women under eighteen to secure written consent from at least one parent, demanded that married women notify their husbands unless their pregnancy resulted from "spousal sexual assault" or they feared "bodily injury" from their husband, and opened all abortion consent forms to public inspection.

A coalition of abortion providers, headed by Planned Parenthood, sued Pennsylvania's anti-abortion governor, Robert Casey, to block the law's enforcement. A federal appellate panel upheld all but the spousal notification provision; the judges based their ruling on a finding that in *Webster* the Supreme Court had abandoned the "strict scrutiny" test in abortion cases. They applied instead Justice O'Connor's test: Did the Pennsylvania restrictions impose an "undue burden" on women seeking abortions? Like the question of what process is "due" under the Fourteenth Amendment, deciding what is "undue" requires judges to determine if lawmakers have made it too difficult for women to exercise their rights under *Roe*. Pro-choice leaders rushed *Casey* to the Supreme Court; anticipating a reversal of *Roe*, they wanted to make abortion rights the major issue in the 1992 presidential campaigns. Public opinion polls showed a pro-choice majority among the electorate, and voters would presumably back candidates—for both the White House and Congress—who vowed to protect abortion rights through the legislative process. The Supreme Court would become the whipping boy in this political scenario.

The justices heard argument in *Casey* on April 22, 1992. Kathryn Kolbert spoke for Planned Parenthood and challenged the Court to either flatly reverse or firmly uphold *Roe* and end the uncertainty about abortion rights. "Never before has this Court bestowed and taken back a fundamental right that has been part of the settled rights and expectations of literally millions of Americans for nearly two decades," Kolbert said. Taking back those rights, she added, "would be incompatible with any notion of principled constitutional decision-making."

Pennsylvania's attorney general, Ernest Preate, Jr., spent most of his twenty minutes at the podium fielding questions about the spousal-notification provision of his state's law. He argued that the Court could uphold the law "short of overruling *Roe*," but if the two cases could not be reconciled, then "*Roe*, being wrongly decided, should be overruled." Preate gave his remaining ten minutes to Solicitor General Kenneth Starr, who spoke for the Bush administration and urged the Court to overturn *Roe* without equivocation. Noting Starr's denial that the Constitution provided any "textual basis" for abortion rights, Justice Stevens asked to see the provision that made fetuses "persons" with legal rights. "I think it's in the nature of our system," Starr replied, and did not need to have any "basis in the Constitution." States have power under the Tenth Amendment, he added, to adopt laws "that reflect the morality of the people, within limits." Making abortion a criminal act would fit within Starr's limits on enforced morality.

Speculation about the outcome in *Casey* centered not on whether the justices would uphold the challenged provisions of the Pennsylvania law, but on whether *Roe* would live or die at their hands. As the Court's term neared its end in June 1992, the *New York Times* ran a front-page story under the headline "Changed Path for Court? New Balance Is Held by Three Cautious Justices." Linda Greenhouse wrote that "effective control of the Court has passed to a subgroup of the majority, a moderately conservative middle group of three justices." Pictured next to her article were Justices O'Connor, Kennedy, and Souter. "The group's hallmarks," Greenhouse continued, "appear to be a generally cautious approach to deciding cases, a hesitancy to overturn precedents and a distaste for aggressive arguments, whether those presented to the Court or those made by the Justices themselves in written opinions." Greenhouse made no mention of O'Connor's extreme distaste for Justice Scalia's sarcasm and hyperbole, but Court-watchers knew it well. "This group does not always vote together," Greenhouse noted of the centrist bloc, "but when it does, its views prevail."

Three days after this article appeared, "the judgment of the Court" in *Casey* was announced on June 29, 1992. Greenhouse had it right; O'Connor, Kennedy, and Souter voted together, and they prevailed. The headline came in the first sentence of their opinion: "Liberty finds no refuge in a jurisprudence of doubt." The centrist justices reassured those who had doubted that *Roe* would survive. "After considering the fundamental constitutional questions resolved by *Roe*, principles of institutional integrity, and the rule of stare decisis, we are led to conclude that the essential holding of *Roe v. Wade* should be retained and once again reaffirmed," they wrote.

The centrist justices frankly acknowledged the political factors that underlay their opinion. In a fascinating history lecture, they recalled the bad old days of *Plessy* and *Adkins*, which reflected a world "recognized everywhere outside the Court to be dead." The overruling of these decisions by *Brown* and *West Coast Hotel* had rested on new facts and new understandings of society. "In constitutional adjudication as elsewhere in life, changed circumstances may impose new obligations, and the thoughtful part of the Nation could accept each decision to overrule a prior case as a response to the Court's constitutional duty." The centrist troika evoked these "changed circumstances" to underscore "the terrible price that would have been paid if the Court had not overruled" its earlier decisions. Then why not overrule *Roe* when Justice Blackmun's opinion rested on "basic flaws" that slighted "the State's interest in potential life," as the three justices wrote? Because, they explained, the flaws in Blackmun's trimester system had not changed the "factual underpinnings of *Roe*'s central holding" that abortion is a protected "liberty" right under the Constitution. More important, a whole generation of women had come to rely on *Roe* and its protection of abortion rights. To upset their "settled expectations" by overturning *Roe* would provoke even greater political turmoil than the nation had experienced during two decades of abortion wars. The centrist justices feared that a "terrible price would be paid for overruling" a decision that had stood for so long. The demands of blacks and workers required that *Plessy* and *Adkins* be overruled; the demands of women required that *Roe* be affirmed. These are political calculations, pure and simple, but the centrist justices insisted they had not made any "compromises with social and political pressures having, as such, no bearing on the principled choices that the Court is obliged to make" in deciding cases.

Far below the headlines of their *Casey* opinion, the three justices who "reaffirmed" the "essential holding" of *Roe* joined with the four conservatives to sustain all but the spousal notification provision of the Pennsylvania law. They adopted O'Connor's "undue burden" test and found that none of the other provisions placed any "substantial obstacle in the path of a woman seeking an abortion of a nonviable fetus." But what restrictions on access to abortion *would* place a "substantial obstacle" in the entrances to doctors' offices and clinics? After promising "to clarify what is meant by an undue burden" on abortion, the plurality offered "unnecessary health regulations" as their only guideline. This mushy statement, and the Court's refusal to overturn *Roe*, left the four conservatives—Rehnquist, White, Scalia, and Thomas—fuming with frustration. Scalia turned once more to sarcasm—and the "fire" metaphor that justices love—in his dissent. "*Roe* fanned into life an issue that has inflamed our national politics in general, and has obscured with its smoke the selection of Justices to this Court in particular, ever since," he wrote. "And by keeping us in the abortion-umpiring business, it is the perpetuation of that disruption, rather than of any pax Roeana, that the Court's new majority decrees."

Justice Scalia obviously resented Justice Kennedy's defection in *Casey*, particularly since Kennedy had slipped onto the Court behind the smoke that billowed around the failed nomination of Robert Bork. Scalia was not the only justice who addressed the selection of justices in his opinion. Justice Harry Blackmun lauded O'Connor, Kennedy, and Souter for "an act of personal courage and constitutional principle" in giving his *Roe* opinion a reprieve from execution. But he also deplored their willingness to pardon the Pennsylvania legislators who had done everything but lock the doors of abortion clinics. Like everyone else, Blackmun knew that a presidential election was little more than four months away. "I am 83 years old," he wrote in a revealing personal statement. "I cannot remain on this Court forever, and when I do step down, the confirmation process for my successor may well focus on the issue before us today."

Justices Blackmun and Scalia differed profoundly on abortion, but they agreed on one crucial point: the Court's decisions in future cases would depend largely on changes in its personnel, which in turn would reflect political factors and currents in public opinion. This has always been true, but never before in American history had the Court been so narrowly divided on such a significant issue that the replacement of one justice would threaten to topple a long-standing decision. In a very real sense, what the Constitution means for all the American people would depend on the views of a single person. And who that person would be depended on which presidential candidate the American people chose in November 1992. The Republican incumbent, George Bush, proclaimed his desire to overturn the *Roe* decision, while his Democratic challenger, Bill Clinton, was committed to protecting it from judicial reversal. In casting their presidential ballots, American voters would probably be choosing at least one—and possibly several—Supreme Court justices who would likely serve well into the twenty-first century. This was an awesome responsibility, but one that few voters even considered before casting their ballots. In effect, the contest between Bush and Clinton became a national referendum on the Constitution, without any real debate over its provisions and their impact on the American people.

EPILOGUE

"How to Treat Other People"

During their campaigns for the presidency in 1992, neither George Bush nor Bill Clinton devoted a major speech to the Constitution or the Supreme Court. Bush did tell voters in Columbus, Ohio, just a week before the election, that he and Clinton had "a fundamental difference as to what should happen on the Supreme Court." All he said about that difference was that "I don't think the Supreme Court ought to legislate" but should "interpret the Constitution." Bush added that if voters wanted to "get somebody on there to legislate with a liberal point of view," they should vote for his opponent. Enough people took his advice to elect Clinton by a narrow margin and deny Bush a second term. Polls showed that many women who normally supported Republicans voted for Clinton because they feared a Bush-led assault on the *Roe* decision. To some degree, although hard to measure, concerns about the future of the Supreme Court affected the outcome of this closely contested election.

The Court now includes two justices named by President Clinton. Justice Byron White retired in June 1993 after thirty-one years as a civil rights liberal and criminal law conservative. His departure also removed one of the four sure votes for reversing the *Roe* decision, leaving Justices Rehnquist, Scalia, and Thomas with little prospect of gaining the necessary fifth vote to achieve their long-sought goal. Clinton named Judge Ruth Bader Ginsburg to succeed White and to join Justice Sandra O'Connor as the Court's second female member. Born in 1931, Ginsburg graduated Phi Beta Kappa from Cornell and became one of nine women in the 1956 class at Harvard Law School, where she was elected to the law review. But she followed her husband, a fellow law student, to New York when he landed a job there, and completed her law degree at Columbia, also making law review and graduating at the top of her class. These credentials did not impress any Wall Street firms, which then hired women only as secretaries, and Ginsburg taught law at Rutgers and Columbia before President Jimmy Carter named her to the District of Columbia appellate bench in 1980. During her teaching years, she also created and directed the ACLU's Women's Rights Project and argued six gender discrimination cases in the Supreme Court, winning five.

Assured by Ginsburg's confirmation that the *Roe* decision would survive his departure, Justice Harry Blackmun retired at the term's end in 1994. President Clinton named Judge Stephen Breyer of the First Circuit Court of Appeals to fill Blackmun's seat. Born in San Francisco in 1938, Breyer graduated from Harvard Law School, worked closely with Senator Ted Kennedy on issues like airline deregulation, and taught administrative law at Harvard before President Carter placed him on the federal bench in 1980. During their tenure on the Court thus far, Justices Ginsburg and Breyer have struck observers as cautious liberals, sticking to precedent whenever possible and writing careful, precise opinions that do not stake out any new constitutional ground.

One reason for ending this book with the *Casey* decision and the presidential election of 1992 stems from the fact that a thin line separates today's headlines from history. We tend to regard as current affairs those events whose outcomes are not yet known, or that happened so recently that full accounts are unreliable or unavailable. People change positions, break their silence, or disclose records that alter the "conventional wisdom" on disputed issues. Particularly when key participants still hold office (as President Clinton does at this writing), it is risky to consign them to history books or predict their future decisions. No one knows how many more—if any—Supreme Court nominations Clinton will make, or which current justices might depart through death or retirement. Another reason for ending with *Casey* is that the Court has not, in my judgment, decided any "landmark" cases since 1992. That does not mean the justices have busied themselves only with trivial cases. The Court has recently decided important cases dealing with gay rights, assisted suicide, gender discrimination, affirmtive action, and minority voting. But none of these decisions, however controversial, matched the impact on judicial doctrine—or more important, on people's lives—of *Casey* or earlier decisions we have examined. They are examples of the Court's normal business, smoothing the edges and patching the cracks in constitutional law. And there have been fewer jobs for judicial carpenters in recent years. Chief Justice Rehnquist, who took office in 1986, has successfully campaigned to cut back the Court's docket. During the term ending in 1987, the Court decided 175 argued cases; that number declined in 1997 to ninety.

There are other reasons for this drop than simply trimming legal deadwood. Conservative judges, mostly appointed by Presidents Reagan and Bush, now dominate the federal bench, and most current justices agree with their decisions. In consequence, the Rehnquist Court has fewer "bad" decisions from lower courts that a majority wants to reverse. Another factor is that groups like the ACLU and NAACP, faced with unfriendly or even hostile federal judges, now devote more effort to lobbying and education than to litigation, fearing that conervative judges might cut back legal rights their members have long enjoyed. The Court might also be joining the public in a "breather" between rounds of political battles over abortion and other controversial issues. Whatever the reasons, the sidewalks outside the Court are now rarely crowded with protesters. But this relative calm might be shattered at any time by economic disaster, racial explosion, or international crisis. Cutbacks in government programs or crackdowns on dissidents might well trigger another round of "rights litigation" that forces the Court to increase its caseload. The Great Depression, both world wars, and the civil rights revolution were all disruptive events in American history that spilled into the courts. It seems appropriate, as we end this journey through our Constitution's long and often turbulent history, to repeat the Court's admonition in 1866, in a case that stemmed from the nation's greatest crisis, the Civil War. "The Constitution of the United States is a law for rulers and people, equally in war and in peace, and covers with the shield of its protection all classes of men, at all times, and under all circumstances," the justices agreed without dissent in the *Milligan* decision.

It also seems appropriate to listen once again to a few of the people whose cases produced decisions that both harmed and helped the American people. Dred Scott appealed in 1854 for assistance with his suit for freedom. "My fellow-men, can any of you help me in my day of trial? Will nobody speak for me at Washington, even without hope of other reward than the blessings of a poor black man and his family?" The Supreme Court ruled that Dred and his family—and every black person in America—had "no rights which the white man was bound to respect." Eugene Debs told his Socialist followers in World War I that "it is extremely dangerous to exercise the constitutional right of free speech in a country fighting to make Democracy safe in the world." The Court upheld a ten-year prison term imposed on Debs for exercising his right to speak freely.

Lillian Gobitas was expelled from her seventh-grade class in 1935 for refusing on religious grounds to salute the American flag. "We were in the kitchen with the radio on," she recalled, "and they said, In Washington today, the Supreme Court decided the flag case. It was against us, eight to one. That just set off a wave of persecution. It was like open season on Jehovah's Witnesses." The Court overturned its 1940 decision in Lillian's case three years later, shocked by the explosive reaction to its ruling. Mary Beth Tinker was suspended from her eighth-grade class in 1965 for wearing a black armband to support a Christmas cease-fire in Vietnam. "We got all kinds of threats to our family, even death threats," she recalled. "People called our house on Christmas Eve and said the house would be blown up by morning." The telephone rang one morning and the caller told Mary Beth, "I'm going to kill you!" The Court upheld her peaceful protest, but her experience left Mary Beth wary of unknown callers.

Norma McCorvey hid behind the legal mask of "Jane Roe" until 1984, when she revealed her identity as the woman who had helped to secure abortion rights for all American women. The violent reaction when she took off her mask left her shocked and scared. "The first shot woke me up," she recalled of a terrifying night in her Dallas home. She and her partner, Connie Gonzalez, went to investigate. "The second shot went into our front door. And then there was another sound, another boom, much louder! The living room window exploded inward, in slow motion, like a horror movie. The pieces flew toward us." The FBI investigated, but never found the shooter. Michael Hardwick, a gay man who challenged Georgia's sodomy law, recalled his reaction to the ruling against him. "I was totally stunned. I just cried—not so much because I had failed but because to me it was frightening to think that in the year 1986 our Supreme Court, next to God, could make a decision that was more suitable to the mentality of the Spanish Inquisition."

Perhaps the best way to end this history of the Supreme Court and its varied readings of our Constitution is to listen to an American who will learn about the Court and Constitution as we enter a new century. Haley Fox—my older daughter—was born in 1991 in San Diego, California. She is bright and curious, and cares about the world around her, its people, its animals, and its oceans, deserts, and forests. She has helped at a homeless shelter, and marched in a Martin Luther King parade. Haley talked with me about some of the issues this book examines. She does not yet know what the Supreme Court or the Constitution are, but she understands their importance to her. Haley defines "rights" as "what you should be able to do." She believes that "everyone should be able to say what they believe in." Haley's closest friend, Tony Cardenas, is Catholic and she is Unitarian Universalist. "If you want to be Catholic, you should be able to," she says, "and if you want to be Unitarian, you should be able to." Haley's younger sister, Maya Grace IronFox, is African-American and is just becoming aware—at three—that her skin is darker. Haley thinks that people's skin color should not matter in how people treat them. "Whoever they are, they should be treated good and not badly," Haley says. "Everyone is the same inside; it's just the outside that's different." Haley thinks it would be a good idea to have our rights all written down, "so everybody would know how to treat other people."

History is always being made, and Americans like Haley—and others very much unlike her—will make the history of our Constitution as they learn how to treat other people.

UNITED STATES CONSTITUTION

We the People of the United States, in Order to form a more perfect Union, establish Justice, insure domestic Tranquility, provide for the common defence, promote the general Welfare, and secure the Blessings of Liberty to ourselves and our Posterity, do ordain and establish this Constitution for the United States of America.

ARTICLE I

Section 1. All legislative Powers herein granted shall be vested in a Congress of the United States, which shall consist of a Senate and House of Representatives.

Section 2. The House of Representatives shall be composed of Members chosen every second Year by the People of the several States, and the Electors in each State shall have the Qualifications requisite for Electors of the most numerous Branch of the State Legislature.

No Person shall be a Representative who shall not have attained to the age of twenty five Years, and been seven Years a Citizen of the United States, and who shall not, when elected, be an Inhabitant of that State in which he shall be chosen.

[Representatives and direct Taxes shall be apportioned among the several States which may be included within this Union, according to their respective Numbers, which shall be determined by adding to the whole Number of free Persons, including those bound to Service for a Term of Years, and excluding Indians not taxed, three fifths of all other Persons.][1] The actual Enumeration shall be made within three Years after the first Meeting of the Congress of the United States, and within every subsequent Term of ten Years, in such Manner as they shall by Law direct. The Number of Representatives shall not exceed one for every thirty Thousand, but each State shall have at Least one Representative; and until such enumeration shall be made, the State of New Hampshire shall be entitled to chuse three, Massachusetts eight, Rhode-Island and Providence Plantations one, Connecticut five, New York six, New Jersey four, Pennsylvania eight, Delaware one, Maryland six, Virginia ten, North Carolina five, South Carolina five, and Georgia three.

When vacancies happen in the Representation from any State, the Executive Authority thereof shall issue Writs of Election to fill such Vacancies.

The House of Representatives shall chuse their Speaker and other Officers; and shall have the sole Power of Impeachment.

Section 3. The Senate of the United States shall be composed of two Senators from each State, [chosen by the Legislature thereof,]² for six Years; and each Senator shall have one Vote.

Immediately after they shall be assembled in Consequence of the first Election, they shall be divided as equally as may be into three Classes. The Seats of the Senators of the first Class shall be vacated at the Expiration of the second Year, of the second Class at the Expiration of the fourth Year, and of the third Class at the Expiration of the sixth Year, so that one third may be chosen every second Year; [and if Vacancies happen by Resignation, or otherwise, during the Recess of the Legislature of any State, the Executive thereof may make temporary Appointments until the next Meeting of the Legislature, which shall then fill such Vacancies.]³

No Person shall be a Senator who shall not have attained to the Age of thirty Years, and been nine Years a Citizen of the United States, and who shall not, when elected, be an Inhabitant of that State for which he shall be chosen.

The Vice President of the United States shall be President of the Senate, but shall have no Vote, unless they be equally divided.

The Senate shall chuse their other Officers, and also a President pro tempore, in the Absence of the Vice President, or when he shall exercise the Office of President of the United States.

The Senate shall have the sole Power to try all Impeachments. When sitting for that Purpose, they shall be on Oath or Affirmation. When the President of the United States is tried, the Chief Justice shall preside: And no Person shall be convicted without the Concurrence of two thirds of the Members present.

Judgment in Cases of Impeachment shall not extend further than to removal from Office, and disqualification to hold and enjoy any Office of honor, Trust or Profit under the United States: but the Party convicted shall nevertheless be liable and subject to Indictment, Trial, Judgment and Punishment, according to Law.

Section 4. The Times, Places and Manner of holding Elections for Senators and Representatives, shall be prescribed in each State by the Legislature thereof; but the Congress may at any time by Law make or alter such Regulations, except as to the Places of chusing Senators.

The Congress shall assemble at least once in every Year, and such Meeting shall [be on the first Monday in December],⁴ unless they shall by Law appoint a different Day.

Section 5. Each House shall be the Judge of the Elections, Returns and Qualifications of its own Members, and a Majority of each shall constitute a Quorum to do Business; but a smaller Number may adjourn from day to day, and may be authorized to compel the Attendance of absent Members, in such Manner, and under such Penalties as each House may provide.

Each House may determine the Rules of its Proceedings, punish its Members for disorderly Behaviour, and, with the Concurrence of two thirds, expel a Member.

Each House shall keep a Journal of its Proceedings, and from time to time publish the same, excepting such Parts as may in their Judgment require Secrecy; and the Yeas and Nays of the Members of either House on any question shall, at the Desire of one fifth of those Present, be entered on the Journal.

Neither House, during the Session of Congress, shall, without the Consent of the other, adjourn for more than three days, nor to any other Place than that in which the two Houses shall be sitting.

Section 6. The Senators and Representatives shall receive a Compensation for their Services, to be ascertained by Law, and paid out of the Treasury of the United States. They shall in all Cases, except Treason, Felony and Breach of the Peace, be privileged from Arrest during their Attendance at the Session of their respective Houses, and in going to and returning from the same; and for any Speech or Debate in either House, they shall not be questioned in any other Place.

No Senator or Representative shall, during the Time for which he was elected, be appointed to any civil Office under the Authority of the United States, which shall have been created, or the Emoluments whereof shall have been encreased during such time; and no Person holding any Office under the United States, shall be a Member of either House during his Continuance in Office.

Section 7. All Bills for raising Revenue shall originate in the House of Representatives; but the Senate may propose or concur with Amendments as on other Bills.

Every Bill which shall have passed the House of Representatives and the Senate, shall, before it become a Law, be presented to the President of the United States; If he approve he shall sign it, but if not he shall return it, with his Objections to that House in which it shall have originated, who shall enter the Objections at large on their Journal, and proceed to reconsider it. If after such Reconsideration two thirds of that House shall agree to pass the Bill, it shall be sent, together with the Objections, to the other House, by which it shall likewise be reconsidered, and if approved by two thirds of that House, it shall become a Law. But in all such Cases the Votes of both Houses shall be determined by yeas and Nays, and the Names of the Persons voting for and against the Bill shall be entered on the Journal of each House respectively. If any Bill shall not be returned by the President within ten Days (Sundays excepted) after it shall have been presented to him, the Same shall be a Law, in like Manner as if he had signed it, unless the Congress by their Adjournment prevent its Return, in which Case it shall not be a Law.

Every Order, Resolution, or Vote to which the Concurrence of the Senate and House of Representatives may be necessary (except on a question of Adjournment) shall be presented to the President of the United States; and before the Same shall take Effect, shall be approved by him, or being disapproved by him, shall be repassed by two thirds of the Senate and House of Representatives, according to the Rules and Limitations prescribed in the Case of a Bill.

Section 8. The Congress shall have Power To lay and collect Taxes, Duties, Imposts and Excises, to pay the Debts and provide for the common Defence and general Welfare of the United States; but all Duties, Imposts and Excises shall be uniform throughout the United States;

To borrow Money on the credit of the United States;

To regulate Commerce with foreign Nations, and among the several States, and with the Indian Tribes;

To establish an uniform Rule of Naturalization, and uniform Laws on the subject of Bankruptcies throughout the United States;

To coin Money, regulate the Value thereof, and of foreign Coin, and fix the Standard of Weights and Measures;

To provide for the Punishment of counterfeiting the Securities and current Coin of the United States;

To establish Post Offices and post Roads;

To promote the Progress of Science and useful Arts, by securing for limited Times to Authors and Inventors the exclusive Right to their respective Writings and Discoveries;

To constitute Tribunals inferior to the supreme Court;

To define and punish Piracies and Felonies committed on the high Seas, and Offences against the Law of Nations;

To declare War, grant Letters of Marque and Reprisal, and make Rules concerning Captures on Land and Water;

To raise and support Armies, but no Appropriation of Money to that Use shall be for a longer Term than two Years;

To provide and maintain a Navy;

To make Rules for the Government and Regulation of the land and naval Forces;

To provide for calling forth the Militia to execute the Laws of the Union, suppress Insurrections and repel Invasions;

To provide for organizing, arming, and disciplining, the Militia, and for governing such Part of them as may be employed in the Service of the United States, reserving to the States respectively, the Appointment of the Officers, and the Authority of training the Militia according to the discipline prescribed by Congress;

To exercise exclusive Legislation in all Cases whatsoever, over such District (not exceeding ten Miles square) as may, by Cession of particular States, and the Acceptance of Congress, become the Seat of the Government of the United States, and to exercise like Authority over all Places purchased by the Consent of the Legislature of the State in which the Same shall be, for the Erection of Forts, Magazines, Arsenals, dock-Yards, and other needful Buildings;—And

To make all Laws which shall be necessary and proper for carrying into Execution the foregoing Powers, and all other Powers vested by this Constitution in the Government of the United States, or in any Department or Officer thereof.

Section 9. The Migration or Importation of such Persons as any of the States now existing shall think proper to admit, shall not be prohibited by the Congress prior to the Year one thousand eight hundred and eight, but a Tax or duty may be imposed on such Importation, not exceeding ten dollars for each Person.

The Privilege of the Writ of Habeas Corpus shall not be suspended, unless when in Cases of Rebellion or Invasion the public Safety may require it.

No Bill of Attainder or ex post facto Law shall be passed.

No Capitation, or other direct, Tax shall be laid, unless in Proportion to the Census or Enumeration herein before directed to be taken.[5]

No Tax or Duty shall be laid on Articles exported from any State.

No Preference shall be given by any Regulation of Commerce or Revenue to the

Ports of one State over those of another; nor shall Vessels bound to, or from, one State, be obliged to enter, clear, or pay Duties in another.

No Money shall be drawn from the Treasury, but in Consequence of Appropriations made by Law; and a regular Statement and Account of the Receipts and Expenditures of all public Money shall be published from time to time.

No Title of Nobility shall be granted by the United States: And no Person holding any Office of Profit or Trust under them, shall, without the Consent of the Congress, accept of any present, Emolument, Office, or Title, of any kind whatever, from any King, Prince, or foreign State.

Section 10. No State shall enter into any Treaty, Alliance, or Confederation; grant Letters of Marque and Reprisal; coin Money; emit Bills of Credit; make any Thing but gold and silver Coin a Tender in Payment of Debts; pass any Bill of Attainder, ex post facto Law, or Law impairing the Obligation of Contracts, or grant any Title of Nobility.

No State shall, without the Consent of the Congress, lay any Imposts or Duties on Imports or Exports, except what may be absolutely necessary for executing it's inspection Laws; and the net Produce of all Duties and Imposts, laid by any State on Imports or Exports, shall be for the Use of the Treasury of the United States; and all such Laws shall be subject to the Revision and Controul of the Congress.

No State shall, without the Consent of Congress, lay any Duty of Tonnage, keep Troops, or Ships of War in time of Peace, enter into any Agreement or Compact with another State, or with a foreign Power, or engage in War, unless actually invaded, or in such imminent Danger as will not admit of delay.

ARTICLE II

Section 1. The executive Power shall be vested in a President of the United States of America. He shall hold his Office during the Term of four Years, and, together with the Vice President, chosen for the same Term, be elected, as follows

Each State shall appoint, in such Manner as the Legislature thereof may direct, a Number of Electors, equal to the whole Number of Senators and Representatives to which the State may be entitled in the Congress: but no Senator or Representative, or Person holding an Office of Trust or Profit under the United States, shall be appointed an Elector.

[The Electors shall meet in their respective States, and vote by Ballot for two Persons, of whom one at least shall not be an Inhabitant of the same State with themselves. And they shall make a List of all the Persons voted for, and of the Number of Votes for each; which List they shall sign and certify, and transmit sealed to the Seat of the Government of the United States, directed to the President of the Senate. The President of the Senate shall, in the Presence of the Senate and House of Representatives, open all the Certificates, and the Votes shall then be counted. The Person having the greatest Number of Votes shall be the President, if such Number be a Majority of the whole Number of Electors appointed; and if there be more than one who have such Majority, and have an equal Number of Votes, then the House of Representatives shall immediately chuse by Ballot one of them for President; and if no Person have a Majority, then from the five highest on the list the said House shall in like Manner chuse the President. But in chusing the President, the Votes shall be taken by States, the

Representation from each State having one Vote; A quorum for this Purpose shall consist of a Member or Members from two thirds of the States, and a Majority of all the States shall be necessary to a Choice. In every Case, after the Choice of the President, the Person having the greatest Number of Votes of the Electors shall be the Vice President. But if there should remain two or more who have equal Votes, the Senate shall chuse from them by Ballot the Vice President.][6]

The Congress may determine the Time of chusing the Electors, and the Day on which they shall give their Votes; which Day shall be the same throughout the United States.

No Person except a natural born Citizen, or a Citizen of the United States, at time of the Adoption of this Constitution, shall be eligible to the Office of President; neither shall any Person be eligible to that Office who shall not have attained to the Age of thirty five Years, and been fourteen Years a Resident within the United States.

In Case of the Removal of the President from Office, or of his Death, Resignation, or Inability to discharge the Powers and Duties of the said Office,[7] the Same shall devolve on the Vice President, and the Congress may by Law provide for the Case of Removal, Death, Resignation or Inability, both of the President and Vice President, declaring what Officer shall then act as President, and such Officer shall act accordingly, until the Disability be removed, or a President shall be elected.

The President shall, at stated Times, receive for his Services, a Compensation, which shall neither be encreased nor diminished during the Period for which he shall have been elected, and he shall not receive within that Period any other Emolument from the United States, or any of them.

Before he enter on the Execution of his Office, he shall take the following Oath or Affirmation:—"I do solemnly swear (or affirm) that I will faithfully execute the Office of President of the United States, and will to the best of my Ability, preserve, protect and defend the Constitution of the United States."

Section 2. The President shall be Commander in Chief of the Army and Navy of the United States, and of the Militia of the several States, when called into the actual Service of the United States; he may require his Opinion, in writing, of the principal Officer in each of the executive Departments, upon any Subject relating to the Duties of their respective Offices, and he shall have Power to grant Reprieves and Pardons for Offences against the United States, except in Cases of Impeachment.

He shall have Power, by and with the Advice and Consent of the Senate, to make Treaties, provided two thirds of the Senators present concur; and he shall nominate, and by and with the Advice and Consent of the Senate, shall appoint Ambassadors, other public Ministers and Consuls, Judges of the supreme Court, and all other Officers of the United States, whose Appointments are not herein otherwise provided for, and which shall be established by Law: but the Congress may by Law vest the Appointment of such inferior Officers, as they think proper, in the President alone, in the Courts of Law, or in the Heads of Departments.

The President shall have Power to fill up all Vacancies that may happen during the Recess of the Senate, by granting Commissions which shall expire at the End of their next Session.

Section 3: He shall from time to time give to the Congress Information of the State of the Union, and recommend to their Consideration such Measures as he shall judge necessary and expedient; he may, on extraordinary Occasions, convene both Houses, or either of them, and in Case of Disagreement between them, with Respect to the Time of Adjournment, he may adjourn them to such Times he shall think proper; he shall receive Ambassadors and other public Ministers; he shall take Care that the Laws be faithfully executed, and shall Commission all the Officers of the United States.

Section 4. The President, Vice President and all civil Officers of the United States, shall be removed from Office on Impeachment for, and Conviction of, Treason, Bribery, or other high Crimes and Misdemeanors.

ARTICLE III

Section 1. The judicial Power of the United States, shall be vested in one supreme Court, and in such inferior Courts as the Congress may from time to time ordain and establish. The Judges, both of the supreme and inferior Courts, shall hold their Offices during good Behaviour, and shall, at stated Times, receive for their Services, a Compensation, which shall not be diminished during their Continuance in Office.

Section 2. The judicial Power shall extend to all Cases, in Law and Equity, arising under this Constitution, the Laws of the United States, and Treaties made, or which shall be made, under their Authority;—to all Cases affecting Ambassadors, other public Ministers and Consuls;—to all Cases of admiralty and maritime Jurisdiction;—to Controversies to which the United States shall be a Party;—to Controversies between two or more States;—between a State and Citizens of another State;[8]—between Citizens of different States;—between Citizens of the same State claiming Lands under Grants of different States, and between a State, or the Citizens thereof, and foreign States, Citizens, and Subjects.[8]

In all Cases affecting Ambassadors, other public Ministers and Consuls, and those in which a State shall be Party, the supreme Court shall have original Jurisdiction. In all the other Cases before mentioned, the supreme Court shall have appellate Jurisdiction, both as to Law and Fact, with such Exceptions, and under such Regulations as the Congress shall make.

The Trial of all Crimes, except in Cases of Impeachment, shall be by Jury; and such Trial shall be held in the State where the said Crimes shall have been committed; but when not committed within any State, the Trial shall be at such Place or Places as the Congress may by Law have directed.

Section 3. Treason against the United States, shall consist only in levying War against them, or in adhering to their Enemies, giving them Aid and Comfort. No Person shall be convicted of Treason unless on the Testimony of two Witnesses to the same overt Act, or on Confession in open Court.

The Congress shall have Power to declare the Punishment of Treason, but no Attainder of Treason shall work Corruption of Blood, or Forfeiture except during the Life of the Person attainted.

ARTICLE IV

Section 1. Full Faith and Credit shall be given in each State to the public Acts, Records, and judicial Proceedings of every other State. And the Congress may by general Laws prescribe the Manner in which such Acts, Records and Proceedings shall be proved, and the Effect thereof.

Section 2. The Citizens of each State shall be entitled to all Privileges and Immunities of Citizens in the several States.

A Person charged in any State with Treason, Felony, or other Crime, who shall flee from Justice, and be found in another State, shall on Demand of the executive Authority of the State from which he fled, be delivered up, to be removed to the State having Jurisdiction of the Crime.

[No Person held to Service or Labour in one State, under the Laws thereof, escaping into another, shall, in Consequence of any Law or Regulation therein, be discharged from such Service or Labour, but shall be delivered up on Claim of the Party to whom such Service or Labour may be due.]⁹

Section 3. New States may be admitted by the Congress into this Union; but no new State shall be formed or erected within the Jurisdiction of any other State; nor any State be formed by the Junction of two or more States, or Parts of States, without the Consent of the Legislatures of the States concerned as well as of the Congress.

The Congress shall have Power to dispose of and make all needful Rules and Regulations respecting the Territory or other Property belonging to the United States; and nothing in this Constitution shall be so construed as to Prejudice any Claims of the United States, or of any particular State.

Section 4. The United States shall guarantee to every State in this Union a Republican Form of Government, and shall protect each of them against Invasion; and on Application of the Legislature, or of the Executive (when the Legislature cannot be convened) against domestic Violence.

ARTICLE V

The Congress, whenever two thirds of both Houses shall deem it necessary, shall propose Amendments to this Constitution, or, on the Application of the Legislatures of two thirds of the several States, shall call a Convention for proposing Amendments, which, in either Case, shall be valid to all Intents and Purposes, as Part of this Constitution, when ratified by the Legislatures of three fourths of the several States, or by Conventions in three fourths thereof, as the one or the other Mode of Ratification may be proposed by the Congress; Provided [that no Amendment which may be made prior to the Year One thousand eight hundred and eight shall in any Manner affect the first and fourth Clauses in the Ninth Section of the first Article; and]¹⁰ that no State, without its Consent, shall be deprived of its equal Suffrage in the Senate.

ARTICLE VI

All Debts contracted and Engagements entered into, before the Adoption of this Constitution, shall be as valid against the United States under this Constitution, as under the Confederation.

This Constitution, and the Laws of the United States which shall be made in Pursuance thereof; and all Treaties made, or which shall be made, under the Authority of the United States, shall be the supreme Law of the Land; and the Judges in every State shall be bound thereby, any Thing in the Constitution or Laws of any State to the Contrary notwithstanding.

The Senators and Representatives before mentioned, and the Members of the several State Legislatures, and all executive and judicial Officers, both of the United States and of the several States, shall be bound by Oath or Affirmation, to support this Constitution; but no religious Test shall ever be required as a Qualification to any Office or public Trust under the United States.

ARTICLE VII

The Ratification of the Conventions of nine States, shall be sufficient for the Establishment of this Constitution between the States so ratifying the Same.

Done in Convention by the Unanimous Consent of the States present the Seventeenth Day of September in the Year of our Lord one thousand seven hundred and Eighty seven and of the Independence of the United States of America the Twelfth. IN WITNESS whereof We have hereunto subscribed our Names,

George Washington,
President and deputy from Virginia.

New Hampshire:	John Langdon, Nicholas Gilman.
Massachusetts:	Nathaniel Gorham, Rufus King.
Connecticut:	William Samuel Johnson, Roger Sherman.
New York:	Alexander Hamilton.
New Jersey:	William Livingston, David Brearley, William Paterson, Jonathan Dayton.
Pennsylvania:	Benjamin Franklin, Thomas Mifflin, Robert Morris, George Clymer, Thomas FitzSimons, Jared Ingersoll, James Wilson, Gouverneur Morris.
Delaware:	George Read, Gunning Bedford Jr., John Dickinson, Richard Bassett, Jacob Broom.
Maryland:	James McHenry, Daniel of St. Thomas Jenifer, Daniel Carroll.

Virginia:	John Blair,
	James Madison Jr.
North Carolina:	William Blount,
	Richard Dobbs Spaight,
	Hugh Williamson.
South Carolina:	John Rutledge,
	Charles Cotesworth Pinckney,
	Charles Pinckney,
	Pierce Butler.
Georgia:	William Few,
	Abraham Baldwin.

[The language of the original Constitution, not including the amendments, was adopted by a convention of the states on September 17, 1787, and was subsequently ratified by the states on the following dates: Delaware, December 7, 1787; Pennsylvania, December 12, 1787; New Jersey, December 18, 1787; Georgia, January 2, 1788; Connecticut, January 9, 1788; Massachusetts, February 6, 1788; Maryland, April 28, 1788; South Carolina, May 23, 1788; New Hampshire, June 21, 1788.

Ratification was completed on June 21, 1788.

The Constitution subsequently was ratified by Virginia, June 25, 1788; New York, July 26, 1788; North Carolina, November 21, 1789; Rhode Island, May 29, 1790; and Vermont, January 10, 1791.]

AMENDMENTS
AMENDMENT I
(First ten amendments ratified December 15, 1791)

Congress shall make no law respecting an establishment of religion, or prohibiting the free exercise thereof; or abridging the freedom of speech, or of the press; or the right of the people peaceably to assemble, and to petition the Government for a redress of grievances.

AMENDMENT II

A well regulated Militia, being necessary to the security of a free State, the right of the people to keep and bear Arms, shall not be infringed.

AMENDMENT III

No Soldier shall, in time of peace be quartered in any house, without the consent of the Owner, nor in time of war, but in a manner to be prescribed by law.

AMENDMENT IV

The right of the people to be secure in their persons, houses, papers, and effects, against unreasonable searches and seizures, shall not be violated, and no Warrants shall issue, but upon probable cause, supported by Oath or affirmation, and particularly describing the place to be searched, and the persons or things to be seized.

AMENDMENT V

No person shall be held to answer for a capital, or otherwise infamous crime, unless on a presentment or indictment of a Grand Jury, except in cases arising in the land or naval forces, or in the Militia, when in actual service in time of War or public danger; nor shall any person be subject for the same offence to be twice put in jeopardy of life or limb; nor shall be compelled in any criminal case to be a witness against himself, nor be deprived of life, liberty, or property, without due process of law; nor shall private property be taken for public use, without just compensation.

AMENDMENT VI

In all criminal prosecutions, the accused shall enjoy the right to a speedy and public trial, by an impartial jury of the State and district wherein the crime shall have been committed, which district shall have been previously ascertained by law, and to be informed of the nature and cause of the accusation; to be confronted with the witnesses against him; to have compulsory process for obtaining witnesses in his favor; and to have the Assistance of Counsel for his defence.

AMENDMENT VII

In Suits at common law, where the value in controversy shall exceed twenty dollars, the right of trial by jury shall be preserved, and no fact tried by a jury, shall be otherwise re-examined in any Court of the United States, than according to the rules of the common law.

AMENDMENT VIII

Excessive bail shall not be required, nor excessive fines imposed, nor cruel and unusual punishments inflicted.

AMENDMENT IX

The enumeration in the Constitution, of certain rights, shall not be construed to deny or disparage others retained by the people.

AMENDMENT X

The powers not delegated to the United States by the Constitution, nor prohibited by it to the States, are reserved to the States respectively, or to the people.

AMENDMENT XI

(Ratified February 7, 1795)

The Judicial power of the United States shall not be construed to extend to any suit in law or equity, commenced or prosecuted against one of the United States by Citizens of another State, or by Citizens or Subjects of any Foreign State.

AMENDMENT XII

(Ratified June 15, 1804)

The Electors shall meet in their respective states and vote by ballot for President and Vice-President, one of whom, at least, shall not be an inhabitant of the same state with themselves; they shall name in their ballots the person voted for as President, and in distinct ballots the person voted for as Vice-President, and they shall make distinct lists of all persons voted for as President, and of all persons voted for as Vice-President, and of the number of votes for each, which lists they shall sign and certify, and transmit sealed to the seat of the government of the United States, directed to the President of the Senate;—The President of the Senate shall, in the presence of the Senate and House of Representatives, open all the certificates and the votes shall then be counted;—The person having the greatest number of votes for President, shall be the President, if such number be a majority of the whole number of Electors appointed; and if no person have such majority, then from the persons having the highest numbers not exceeding three on the list of those voted for as President, the House of Representative shall choose immediately, by ballot, the President. But in choosing the President, the votes shall be taken by states, the representation from each state having one vote; a quorum for this purpose shall consist of a member or members from two-thirds of the states, and a majority of all the states shall be necessary to a choice. [And if the House of Representatives shall not choose a President whenever the right of choice shall devolve upon them, before the fourth day of March next following, then the Vice-President shall act as President, as in the case of the death or other constitutional disability of the President.—][11] The person having the greatest number of votes as Vice-President, shall be the Vice-President, if such number be a majority of the whole number of Electors appointed, and if no person have a majority, then from the two highest numbers on the list, the Senate shall choose the Vice-President; a quorum for the purpose shall consist of two-thirds of the whole number of Senators, and a majority of the whole number shall be necessary to a choice. But no person constitutionally ineligible to the office of President shall be eligible to that of Vice-President of the United States.

AMENDMENT XIII
(Ratified December 6, 1865)

Section 1. Neither slavery nor involuntary servitude, except as a punishment for crime whereof the party shall have been duly convicted, shall exist within the United States, or any place subject to their jurisdiction.

Section 2. Congress shall have power to enforce this article by appropriate legislation.

AMENDMENT XIV
(Ratified July 9, 1868)

Section 1. All persons born or naturalized in the United States, and subject to the jurisdiction thereof, are citizens of the United States and of the State wherein they reside. No State shall make or enforce any law which shall abridge the privileges or immunities of citizens of the United States; nor shall any State deprive any person of life, liberty, or property, without due process of law; nor deny to any person within its jurisdiction the equal protection of the laws.

Section 2. Representatives shall be apportioned among the several States according to their respective numbers, counting the whole number of persons in each State, excluding Indians not taxed. But when the right to vote at any election for the choice of electors for President and Vice President of the United States, Representatives in Congress, the Executive and Judicial officers of a State, or the members of the Legislature thereof, is denied to any of the male inhabitants of such State, being twenty-one years of age,[12] and citizens of the United States, or in any way abridged, except for participation in rebellion, or other crime, the basis of representation therein shall be reduced in the proportion which the number of such male citizens shall bear to the whole number of male citizens twenty-one years of age in such State.

Section 3. No person shall be a Senator or Representative in Congress, or elector of President and Vice President, or hold any office, civil or military, under the United States, or under any State, who, having previously taken an oath, as a member of Congress, or as an officer of the United States, or as a member of any State legislature, or as an executive or judicial officer of any State, to support the Constitution of the United States, shall have engaged in insurrection or rebellion against the same, or given aid or comfort to the enemies thereof. But Congress may by a vote of two-thirds of each House, remove such disability.

Section 4. The validity of the public debt of the United States, authorized by law, including debts incurred for payment of pensions and bounties for services in suppressing insurrection or rebellion, shall not be questioned. But neither the United States nor any State shall assume or pay any debt or obligation incurred in aid of insurrection or rebellion against the United States, or any claim for the loss of emancipation of any slave; but all such debts, obligations and claims shall be held illegal and void.

Section 5. The Congress shall have power to enforce, by appropriate legislation, the provisions of this article.

AMENDMENT XV
(Ratified February 3, 1870)

Section 1. The right of citizens of the United States to vote shall not be denied or abridged by the United States or by any State on account of race, color, or previous condition of servitude.

Section 2. The Congress shall have power to enforce this article by appropriate legislation.

AMENDMENT XVI
(Ratified February 3, 1913)

The Congress shall have power to lay and collect taxes on incomes, from whatever source derived, without apportionment among the several States, and without regard to any census or enumeration.

AMENDMENT XVII
(Ratified April 8, 1913)

The Senate of the United States shall be composed of two Senators from each State, elected by the people thereof, for six years; and each Senator shall have one vote. The electors in each State shall have the qualifications requisite for electors of the most numerous branch of the State legislatures.

When vacancies happen in the representation of any State in the Senate, the executive authority of such State shall issue writs of election to fill such vacancies: *Provided,* That the legislature of any State may empower the executive thereof to make temporary appointments until the people fill the vacancies by election as the legislature may direct.

This amendment shall not be so construed as to affect the election or term of any Senator chosen before it becomes valid as part of the Constitution.

AMENDMENT XVIII
(Ratified January 16, 1919)[13]

Section 1. After one year from the ratification of this article the manufacture, sale, or transportation of intoxicating liquors within, the importation thereof into, or the exportation thereof from the United States and all territory subject to the jurisdiction thereof for beverage purposes is hereby prohibited.

Section 2. The Congress and the several States shall have concurrent power to enforce this article by appropriate legislation.

Section 3. This article shall be inoperative unless it shall have been ratified as an amendment to the Constitution by the legislatures of the several States, as provided in the Constitution, within seven years from the date of the submission hereof to the States by the Congress.

AMENDMENT XIX
(Ratified August 18, 1920)

The right of citizens of the United States to vote shall not be denied or abridged by the United States or by any State on account of sex.

Congress shall have power to enforce this article by appropriate legislation.

AMENDMENT XX
(Ratified January 23, 1933)

Section 1. The terms of the President and Vice President shall end at noon on the 20th day of January, and the terms of Senators and Representatives at noon on the 3d day of January, of the years in which such terms would have ended if this article had not been ratified; and the terms of their successors shall then begin.

Section 2. The Congress shall assemble at least once in every year, and such meeting shall begin at noon on the 3d day of January, unless they shall by law appoint a different day.

Section 3.[14] If, at the time fixed for the beginning of the term of the President, the President elect shall have died, the Vice President elect shall become President. If a President shall not have been chosen before the time fixed for the beginning of his term, or if the President elect shall have failed to qualify, then the Vice President elect shall act as President until a President shall have qualified; and the Congress may by law provide for the case wherein neither a President elect nor a Vice President elect shall have qualified, declaring who shall then act as President, or the manner in which one who is to act shall be selected, and such person shall act accordingly until a President or Vice President shall have qualified.

Section 4. The Congress may by law provide for the case of the death of any of the persons from whom the House of Representatives may choose a President whenever the right of choice shall have devolved upon them, and for the case of the death of any of the persons from whom the Senate may choose a Vice President whenever the right of choice shall have devolved upon them.

Section 5. Sections 1 and 2 shall take effect on the 15th day of October following the ratification of this article.

Section 6. This article shall be inoperative unless it shall have been ratified as an amendment to the Constitution by the legislatures of three-fourths of the several States within seven years from the date of its submission.

AMENDMENT XXI

(Ratified December 5, 1933)

Section 1: The eighteenth article of amendment to the Constitution of the United States is hereby repealed.

Section 2. The transportation or importation into any State, Territory, or possession of the United States for delivery or use therein of intoxicating liquors, in violation of the laws thereof, is hereby prohibited.

Section 3. This article shall be inoperative unless it shall have been ratified as an amendment to the Constitution by conventions in the several States, as provided in the Constitution, within seven years from the date of the submission hereof to the States by the Congress.

AMENDMENT XXII

(Ratified February 27, 1951)

Section 1. No person shall be elected to the office of the President more than twice, and no person who has held the office of President, or acted as President, for more than two years of a term to which some other person was elected President shall be elected to the office of the President more than once. But this Article shall not apply to any person holding the office of President when this Article was proposed by the Congress, and shall not prevent any person who may be holding the office of President, or acting as President, during the term within which this Article become operative from holding the office of President or acting as President during the remainder of such term.

Section 2. This article shall be inoperative unless it shall have been ratified as an amendment to the Constitution by the legislatures of three-fourths of the several States within seven years from the date of its submission to the States by the Congress.

AMENDMENT XXIII

(Ratified March 29, 1961)

Section 1. The District constituting the seat of Government of the United States shall appoint in such manner as the Congress may direct:

A number of electors of President and Vice President equal to the whole number of Senators and Representatives in Congress to which the District would be entitled if it were a State, but in no event more than the least populous State; they shall be in addition to those appointed by the States, but they shall be considered, for the purposes of the election of President and Vice President, to be electors appointed by a State; and they shall meet in the District and perform such duties as provided by the twelfth article of amendment.

Section 2. The Congress shall have power to enforce this article by appropriate legislation.

AMENDMENT XXIV
(Ratified January 23, 1964)

Section 1. The right of citizens of the United States to vote in any primary or other election for President or Vice President, for electors for President or Vice President, or for Senator or Representative in Congress, shall not be denied or abridged by the United States or any State by reason of failure to pay any poll tax or other tax.

Section 2. The Congress shall have power to enforce this article by appropriate legislation.

AMENDMENT XXV
(Ratified February 10, 1967)

Section 1. In case of the removal of the President from office or of his death or resignation, the Vice President shall become President.

Section 2. Whenever there is a vacancy in the office of the Vice President, the President shall nominate a Vice President who shall take office upon confirmation by a majority vote of both Houses of Congress.

Section 3. Whenever the President transmits to the President pro tempore of the Senate and the Speaker of the House of Representatives his written declaration that he is unable to discharge the powers and duties of his office, and until he transmits to them a written declaration to the contrary, such powers and duties shall be discharged by the Vice President as Acting President.

Section 4. Whenever the Vice President and a majority of either the principal officers of the executive departments or of such other body as Congress may by law provide, transmit to the President pro tempore of the Senate and the Speaker of the House of Representatives their written declaration that the President is unable to discharge the powers and duties of his office, the Vice President shall immediately assume the powers and duties of the office as Acting President.

Thereafter, when the President transmits to the President pro tempore of the Senate and the Speaker of the House of Representatives his written declaration that no inability exists, he shall resume the powers and duties of his office unless the Vice President and a majority of either the principal officers of the executive department or of such other body as Congress may by law provide, transmit within four days to the President pro tempore of the Senate and the Speaker of the House of Representatives their written declaration that the President is unable to discharge the powers and duties of his office. Thereupon Congress shall decide the issue, assembling within forty-eight hours for that purpose if not in session. If the Congress, within twenty-one days after receipt of the latter written declaration, or, if Congress is not in session, within twenty-one days after Congress is required to assemble, determines by two-thirds vote of both Houses that the President is unable to discharge the powers and duties of his office, the Vice President shall continue to discharge the same as Acting President; otherwise, the President shall resume the powers and duties of his office.

AMENDMENT XXVI
(Ratified July 1, 1971)

Section 1. The right of citizens of the United States, who are eighteen years of age or older, to vote shall not be denied or abridged by the United States or by any State on account of age.

Section 2. The Congress shall have power to enforce this article by appropriate legislation.

Amendment XXVII
(Ratified May 7, 1992)

No law varying the compensation for the services of the Senators and Representatives shall take effect, until an election of Representatives shall have intervened.

Notes

1. The part in brackets was changed by Section 2 of the Fourteenth Amendment.
2. The part in brackets was changed by the first paragraph of the Seventeenth Amendment.
3. The part in brackets was changed by the second paragraph of the Seventeenth Amendment.
4. The part in brackets was changed by Section 2 of the Twentieth Amendment.
5. The Sixteenth Amendment gave Congress the power to tax incomes.
6. The material in brackets has been superseded by the Twelfth Amendment.
7. This provision has been affected by the Twenty-fifth Amendment.
8. These clauses were affected by the Eleventh Amendment.
9. This paragraph has been superseded by the Thirteenth Amendment.
10. Obsolete.
11. The part in brackets has been superseded by Section 3 of the Twentieth Amendment.
12. See the Nineteenth and Twenty-sixth Amendments.
13. This Amendment was repealed by Section 1 of the Twenty-first Amendment.
14. See the Twenty-fifth Amendment.

Source: U.S. Congress, House, Committee on the Judiciary, *The Constitution of the United States of America, as Amended,* 100th Cong., 1st sess., 1987, H Doc 100-94.

THE JUSTICES OF THE
SUPREME COURT

Appointment number/justice[a]	Position	Appointing president	Years of service[b]
1. John Jay	Chief justice	Washington	1789–1795
2. John Rutledge[c]	Associate justice	Washington	1789–1791
3. William Cushing	Associate justice	Washington	1789–1810
4. James Wilson	Associate justice	Washington	1789–1798
5. John Blair, Jr.	Associate justice	Washington	1789–1796
6. James Iredell	Associate justice	Washington	1790–1799
7. Thomas Johnson	Associate justice	Washington	1791–1793
8. William Paterson	Associate justice	Washington	1793–1806
9. John Rutledge[d]	Chief justice	Washington	1795
10. Samuel Chase	Associate justice	Washington	1796–1811
11. Oliver Ellsworth	Chief justice	Washington	1796–1800
12. Bushrod Washington	Associate justice	J. Adams	1798–1829
13. Alfred Moore	Associate justice	J. Adams	1799–1804
14. John Marshall	Chief justice	J. Adams	1801–1835
15. William Johnson	Associate justice	Jefferson	1804–1834

a. Ordered according to date of appointment.
b. Begin with date of Senate confirmation or date of recess appointment (whichever occurred first); end with date of service termination.
c. Served subsequently as chief justice.
d. Served previously as associate justice.

Appointment number/justice[a]	Position	Appointing president	Years of service[b]
16. Henry Brockholst Livingston	Associate justice	Jefferson	1806–1823
17. Thomas Todd	Associate justice	Jefferson	1807–1826
18. Gabriel Duvall	Associate justice	Madison	1811–1835
19. Joseph Story	Associate justice	Madison	1811–1845
20. Smith Thompson	Associate justice	Monroe	1823–1843
21. Robert Trimble	Associate justice	J. Q. Adams	1826–1828
22. John McLean	Associate justice	Jackson	1829–1861
23. Henry Baldwin	Associate justice	Jackson	1830–1844
24. James Moore Wayne	Associate justice	Jackson	1835–1867
25. Roger Brooke Taney	Chief justice	Jackson	1836–1864
26. Philip Pendleton Barbour	Associate justice	Jackson	1836–1841
27. John Catron	Associate justice	Jackson	1837–1865
28. John McKinley	Associate justice	Van Buren	1837–1852
29. Peter Vivian Daniel	Associate justice	Van Buren	1841–1860
30. Samuel Nelson	Associate justice	Tyler	1845–1872
31. Levi Woodbury	Associate justice	Polk	1846–1851
32. Robert Cooper Grier	Associate justice	Polk	1846–1870
33. Benjamin Robbins Curtis	Associate justice	Fillmore	1851–1857
34. John Archibald Campbell	Associate justice	Pierce	1853–1861
35. Nathan Clifford	Associate justice	Buchanan	1858–1881
36. Noah Haynes Swayne	Associate justice	Lincoln	1862–1881
37. Samuel Freeman Miller	Associate justice	Lincoln	1862–1890
38. David Davis	Associate justice	Lincoln	1862–1877
39. Stephen Johnson Field	Associate justice	Lincoln	1863–1897
40. Salmon Portland Chase	Chief justice	Lincoln	1864–1873
41. William Strong	Associate justice	Grant	1870–1880
42. Joseph P. Bradley	Associate justice	Grant	1870–1892
43. Ward Hunt	Associate justice	Grant	1872–1882
44. Morrison Remick Waite	Chief justice	Grant	1874–1888
45. John Marshall Harlan	Associate justice	Hayes	1877–1911

a. Ordered according to date of appointment.
b. Begin with date of Senate confirmation or date of recess appointment (whichever occurred first); end with date of service termination.

Appointment number/justice[a]	Position	Appointing president	Years of service[b]
46. William Burnham Woods	Associate justice	Hayes	1880–1887
47. Stanley Matthews	Associate justice	Garfield	1881–1889
48. Horace Gray	Associate justice	Arthur	1881–1902
49. Samuel Blatchford	Associate justice	Arthur	1882–1893
50. Lucius Quintus Cincinnatus Lamar	Associate justice	Cleveland	1888–1893
51. Melville Weston Fuller	Chief justice	Cleveland	1888–1910
52. David Josiah Brewer	Associate justice	Harrison	1889–1910
53. Henry Billings Brown	Associate justice	Harrison	1890–1906
54. George Shiras, Jr.	Associate justice	Harrison	1892–1903
55. Howell Edmunds Jackson	Associate justice	Harrison	1893–1895
56. Edward Douglass White[c]	Associate justice	Cleveland	1894–1910
57. Rufus Wheeler Peckham	Associate justice	Cleveland	1895–1909
58. Joseph McKenna	Associate justice	McKinley	1898–1925
59. Oliver Wendell Holmes, Jr.	Associate justice	T. Roosevelt	1902–1932
60. William Rufus Day	Associate justice	T. Roosevelt	1903–1922
61. William Henry Moody	Associate justice	T. Roosevelt	1906–1910
62. Horace Harmon Lurton	Associate justice	Taft	1909–1914
63. Charles Evans Hughes[c]	Associate justice	Taft	1910–1916
64. Edward Douglass White[d]	Chief justice	Taft	1910–1921
65. Willis Van Devanter	Associate justice	Taft	1910–1937
66. Joseph Rucker Lamar	Associate justice	Taft	1910–1916
67. Mahlon Pitney	Associate justice	Taft	1912–1922
68. James Clark McReynolds	Associate justice	Wilson	1914–1941
69. Louis Dembitz Brandeis	Associate justice	Wilson	1916–1939
70. John Hessin Clarke	Associate justice	Wilson	1916–1922
71. William Howard Taft	Chief justice	Harding	1921–1930
72. George Sutherland	Associate justice	Harding	1922–1938
73. Pierce Butler	Associate justice	Harding	1922–1939

a. Ordered according to date of appointment.
b. Begin with date of Senate confirmation or date of recess appointment (whichever occurred first); end with date of service termination.
c. Served subsequently as chief justice.
d. Served previously as associate justice.

Appointment number/justice[a]	Position	Appointing president	Years of service[b]
74. Edward Terry Sanford	Associate justice	Harding	1923–1930
75. Harlan Fiske Stone[c]	Associate justice	Coolidge	1925–1941
76. Charles Evans Hughes[d]	Chief justice	Hoover	1930–1941
77. Owen Josephus Roberts	Associate justice	Hoover	1930–1945
78. Benjamin Nathan Cardozo	Associate justice	Hoover	1932–1938
79. Hugo Lafayette Black	Associate justice	F. Roosevelt	1937–1971
80. Stanley Forman Reed	Associate justice	F. Roosevelt	1938–1957
81. Felix Frankfurter	Associate justice	F. Roosevelt	1939–1962
82. William Orville Douglas	Associate justice	F. Roosevelt	1939–1975
83. Francis William (Frank) Murphy	Associate justice	F. Roosevelt	1940–1949
84. Harlan Fiske Stone[d]	Chief justice	F. Roosevelt	1941–1946
85. James Francis Byrnes	Associate justice	F. Roosevelt	1941–1942
86. Robert Houghwout Jackson	Associate justice	F. Roosevelt	1941–1954
87. Wiley Blount Rutledge	Associate justice	F. Roosevelt	1943–1949
88. Harold Hitz Burton	Associate justice	Truman	1945–1958
89. Fred Moore Vinson	Chief justice	Truman	1946–1953
90. Tom Campbell Clark	Associate justice	Truman	1949–1967
91. Sherman Minton	Associate justice	Truman	1949–1956
92. Earl Warren	Chief justice	Eisenhower	1953–1969
93. John Marshall Harlan	Associate justice	Eisenhower	1955–1971
94. William Joseph Brennan, Jr.	Associate justice	Eisenhower	1956–1990
95. Charles Evans Whittaker	Associate justice	Eisenhower	1957–1962
96. Potter Stewart	Associate justice	Eisenhower	1958–1981
97. Byron Raymond White	Associate justice	Kennedy	1962–1993
98. Arthur Joseph Goldberg	Associate justice	Kennedy	1962–1965
99. Abe Fortas	Associate justice	Johnson	1965–1969
100. Thurgood Marshall	Associate justice	Johnson	1967–1991
101. Warren Earl Burger	Chief justice	Nixon	1969–1986

a. Ordered according to date of appointment.
b. Begin with date of Senate confirmation or date of recess appointment (whichever occurred first); end with date of service termination.
c. Served subsequently as chief justice.
d. Served previously as associate justice.

Appointment number/justice[a]	Position	Appointing president	Years of service[b]
102. Harry Andrew Blackmun	Associate justice	Nixon	1970–1994
103. Lewis Franklin Powell, Jr.	Associate justice	Nixon	1971–1987
104. William Hubbs Rehnquist[c]	Associate justice	Nixon	1971–1986
105. John Paul Stevens	Associate justice	Ford	1975–
106. Sandra Day O'Connor	Associate justice	Reagan	1981–
107. William Hubbs Rehnquist[d]	Chief justice	Reagan	1986–
108. Antonin Scalia	Associate justice	Reagan	1986–
109. Anthony McLeod Kennedy	Associate justice	Reagan	1988–
110. David H. Souter	Associate justice	Bush	1990–
111. Clarence Thomas	Associate justice	Bush	1991–
112. Ruth Bader Ginsburg	Associate justice	Clinton	1993–
113. Stephen G. Breyer	Associate justice	Clinton	1994–

a. Ordered according to date of appointment.
b. Begin with date of Senate confirmation or date of recess appointment (whichever occurred first); end with date of service termination.
c. Served subsequently as chief justice.
d. Served previously as associate justice.

NOTES

The notes for this book consist largely of citations to the source of quoted material. Each citation includes the name of the speaker or writer, the first few words of the quotation, and its source. For those readers who are not familiar with judicial citation form, material from the official reports of the Supreme Court, known as *United States Reports*, is cited by volume number and page. For example, the Supreme Court opinions in *Roe v. Wade* begin at page 113 of volume 410 of the *U.S. Reports*, and are cited as 410 U.S. 113. Full titles of cited books are listed in the Sources for Further Reading.

INTRODUCTION

xiv Tocqueville, "Scarcely any": David M. O'Brien, *Storm Center: The Supreme Court in American Politics*, 209.

xv Brennan, "We look": "The Constitution of the United States: Contemporary Ratification," 27 *South Texas Law Review* 433 (1986), 433–435.

CHAPTER 1

4 Avery, "surrounded with": Peter C. Hoffer, *Law and People in Colonial America*, 87.

5 Zenger trial: id. at 87–88.

5 Adams, "any feeling": id. at 88.

5 Body of Liberties: Edmund S. Morgan, *The Puritan Dilemma*, 169–173.

9 Roger Williams banishment: id. at 117–131.

10 Anne Hutchinson trial: id. at 147–153.

10 Madison, "There are": Robert S. Alley, *Without a Prayer*, 21.

11 Jefferson, "meant to comprehend": Sanford H. Cobb, *The Rise of Religious Liberty in America*, 498.

11 Saint Paul, "Wives, be subject": Ephesians 5:22–24.

11 "Eve, because": Marlene S. Wortman, *Women in American Law*, Vol. 1, 74.

12 "That if any": id. at 69.

12 "the wife of John Spring": id. at 71.

12 "It is not safe": id. at 71–72.

12 Abigail Adams, "I long to hear": id. at 74.

13 "Any married female": id. at 128.

13 "There shall never": *The Colonial Laws of Massachusetts* (Boston, 1889), 53.

14 "The obstinacy of many": Paul Finkelman, *The Law of Freedom and Bondage*, 17.

14 "if any number": id. at 19.

14   Slave Conspiracy of 1741: Howard Zinn, *A People's History of the United States*, 36; Hoffer,
     92–93.
15   Virginia Indian wars: Zinn, 12–13.
15   Plymouth Bay Indian wars: id. at 13–15.

CHAPTER 2

18   Webster, "So long as any": William Peters, *A More Perfect Union*, 5.
18   Jay, "Our affairs seem": Charles Mee, *The Genius of the People*, 39.
18   Franklin, "we discover": id. at 58.
19   Madison, "Temporizing applications": Peters, 13.
19   Madison, "I think with you": ibid.
19   Madison, "the most oppressive": id. at 62.
19   Madison, "thought it wrong": James Madison, *Notes of Debates in the Federal Convention of
     1787* (Adrienne Koch, ed.), (cited below as *Notes*), 532.
20   Mount Vernon and Annapolis meetings: Mee, 8–10.
21   Madison, "I have sought": id. at 68–69.
21   Randolph, "the Articles": *Notes*, 30.
21   Washington, "lamented his want": *Notes*, 24.
22   Madison, "unaware of the value": *Notes*, 17.
22   Madison, "I may be thought": *Notes*, ix.
22   Washington, "I know not": Peters, 79–80.
22   Virginia Plan: *Notes*, 30–33.
23   Madison, "with much diffuseness": *Notes*, 204.
23   Ellsworth, "a specimen": Peters, 223–224.
24   Sherman, "should have as little": *Notes*, 39.
24   Gerry, "The evils": *Notes*, 39.
25   Mason, "argued strongly": *Notes*, 39–40.
25   Mason, "Every master": *Notes*, 504.
25   Madison, "considered the popular": *Notes*, 40.
25   Dickinson, "he wished": *Notes*, 82.
26   Madison, "lost their influence": *Notes*, 83.
26   Gerry, "insisted that the commercial": *Notes*, 86.

CHAPTER 3

27   Randolph, "disclaimed any intention": Madison, *Notes*, 44.
28   Madison, "he had brought": *Notes*, 44.
28   Madison, "So vague a term": *Notes*, 605.
29   Gerry, "never expected": *Notes*, 476.
30   Paterson, "good breeding": Mee, 145.
30   Paterson, "he could regard": *Notes*, 259.
30   Madison, "reminded Mr. Paterson": *Notes*, 259.
31   Williamson, "a census": *Notes*, 267.
31   Butler, "the labor of a slave": *Notes*, 268.
31   Sherman, "thought the number": *Notes*, 270.
31   King, "great force": *Notes*, 270.
32   Butler, "the security": *Notes*, 286.
32   Wilson, "all men wherever placed": *Notes*, 287.
32   Madison, "expressed his apprehensions": *Notes*, 293–295.
33   Randolph, "The vote": *Notes*, 299.
33   Paterson, "it was high time": *Notes*, 299.
33   Randolph, "was sorry": *Notes*, 300.
33   Rutledge, "abandon everything": *Notes*, 300–301.

33   Madison, "The time was wasted": *Notes*, 301.
34   Butler, "to require": *Notes*, 545.
34   Sherman, "saw no more": *Notes*, 546.
34   Martin, "weakened one part": *Notes*, 502.
34   Rutledge, "Religion and humanity": *Notes*, 502.
34   Sherman, "disapproved of the slave trade": *Notes*, 503.
35   Mason, "infernal traffic": *Notes*, 503–504.
35   Ellsworth, "Let us not": *Notes*, 504.
35   Rutledge, "If the convention": *Notes*, 507.
35   Morris, "may form a bargain": *Notes*, 507.
35   Madison, "Twenty years": *Notes*, 530.

CHAPTER 4
36   Madison, "administered by one": Madison, *Notes*, 47, 112.
37   Wilson, "the executive consist": *Notes* 45.
37   Franklin, "observed that it was": *Notes*, 45.
37   Rutledge, "shyness of gentlemen": *Notes*, 45–46.
37   Randolph, "strenuously opposed": *Notes*, 46.
37   Wilson, "unity in the executive": *Notes*, 47.
38   Gerry, "would be most likely": *Notes*, 93.
38   Morris, "He ought": *Notes*, 306.
39   Sherman, "the people at large": *Notes*, 306.
39   Mason, "He conceived": *Notes*, 308–309.
39   Morris, "the executive magistrate": *Notes*, 322.
39   Madison, "seemed on the whole": *Notes*, 327.
39   Mason, "by those who know": *Notes*, 370–371.
41   Wilson, "opposed the appointment": *Notes*, 67.
41   Rutledge, "by no means": *Notes*, 67.
41   Franklin, "a point": *Notes*, 68.
41   Madison, "any numerous body": *Notes*, 68.
41   Madison, "who had displayed": *Notes*, 112–113.
42   Madison, "be appointed": *Notes*, 316–317.
42   Madison, "the spirit of compromise": *Notes*, 344.
43   Johnson, "all cases arising": *Notes*, 538.
43   Madison, "whether it was not": *Notes*, 539.
44   Mercer, "disapproved of the doctrine": *Notes*, 462.
44   Dickinson, "strongly impressed": *Notes*, 463.
44   Sherman, "unnecessary": *Notes*, 518.
44   Madison, "He had been": *Notes*, 518.
45   Williamson, "was a waste": *Notes*, 518.
45   Madison, "Mr. Mercer expressed": *Notes*, 405.
45   Gerry, "their exposition": *Notes*, 61.
45   New Jersey Plan: *Notes*, 118–121.
46   Paterson, "every act": Melvin I. Urofsky, *The Supreme Court Justices: A Biographical Dictionary*, 348.

CHAPTER 5
49   Pinckney, "propositions": Madison; *Notes*, 485–486, 503.
49   "The full and entire": *Notes*, 626–627.
49   Mason, "He wished the plan": *Notes*, 630.
49   Gerry, "concurred in the idea": *Notes*, 630.
49   Sherman, "The state Declarations": *Notes*, 630.

49 Mason, "The laws of the United States": *Notes*, 630.
50 Randolph, "dangerous power": *Notes*, 650–651.
50 Mason, "dangerous power": *Notes*, 651.
50 Pinckney, "These declarations": *Notes*, 651.
51 Gerry, "the Power of Congress": *Notes*, 652.
51 Madison, "All the states": *Notes*, 652.
52 Washington, "I wish the Constitution": Mee, 276; Craig R. Smith, *To Form a More Perfect Union*, 102.
52 Franklin, "I confess": *Notes*, 652.
53 Gorham, "of lessening objections": *Notes*, 655.
53 Madison, "On the question": *Notes*, 652.
53 Randolph, "apologized for his refusing": *Notes*, 655–656.
53 Franklin, "He expressed": *Notes*, 657.
53 Randolph, "He repeated": *Notes*, 657.
54 Gerry, "the painful feelings": *Notes*, 657–658.
54 Madison, "The members": *Notes*, 659.
54 Franklin, "I have, said he": *Notes*, 659.
55 Martin, "the people": *Notes*, 566.
55 Beard, "overwhelming majority": Leonard Levy, *Essays on the Making of the Constitution*, 6.
56 Warren, "patriotic sincerity": id. at 36.
56 Madison, "should it be adopted": Mee, 282.
56 Madison, "Begin with these": *Notes*, 650.
57 Randolph, "a respectable majority": *Notes*, 561.
57 Mason, "preferable": *Notes*, 565.
57 Madison, "the powers given": *Notes*, 563.
57 Madison, "a matter of form": *The Papers of James Madison*, Vol. 10, 180–181.
58 Congress, "be transmitted": id. at 182.
58 Madison, "A more direct": ibid.

CHAPTER 6

60 Washington, "if a weak state": Daniel A. Farber and Suzanna Sherry, *A History of the American Constitution*, 176.
61 "Their lodgings": id. at 176–177; Mee, 286–287.
61 Centinel, "most perfect system": Mee, 287–288.
61 Wilson, "such an idea": Craig R. Smith, *To Form a More Perfect Union*, 40–41.
61 "has always been tainted": Mee, 289.
62 Agrippa, "There is no bill": Farber and Sherry, 183–184.
62 Singletary, "These lawyers": Mee, 295.
63 Smith, "I am a plain man": id. at 296.
63 Heath, "ratify the Constitution": Smith, 64.
63 Hancock, "hazard a proposition": id. at 66.
63 Washington, "The decision": id. at 67.
63 Washington's secretary, "is a man": id. at 79.
64 Washington, "The plot": Smith, 97.
64 "Both sides": id. at 99.
64 Madison, "may depend": ibid.
65 Henry, "Who authorized them": Mee, 300–301.
65 Henry, "It seems to me": id. at 303.
65 Randolph, "I disdain": ibid.
65 Henry, "If I shall be": Farber and Sherry, 217.
67 Brutus, "it now contains": id. at 189.
67 Madison, "A landed interest": id. at 190–193.

67   Smith, "Can the liberties": id. at 206.
68   Lansing, "no person": Smith, 120–121.
68   Smith, "confidence": id. at 121.

CHAPTER 7

69   Jefferson, "I do not like": id. at 154.
69   Jefferson, "How it happened": id. at 154–155.
70   Jefferson, "a mere thing": Bernard Schwartz, *A History of the Supreme Court*, 53.
70   Jefferson, "There is a remarkable": Smith, 154–155.
71   Madison, "never thought": Levy, 279.
71   Washington, "decide how far": *Speeches of the American Presidents*, 4.
72   Madison, "mutilate": Levy, 280.
72   Madison, "wait with patience": Farber and Sherry, 226.
72   Madison, "I am sorry": id. at 227–231.
75   Gerry, "What, sir": Neil H. Cogan, ed., *The Complete Bill of Rights*, 186.
75   Madison, "No soldier": Farber and Sherry, 228.
76   Livermore, "it is sometimes": id. at 238.
76   Madison, "secured in their persons": id. at 228–229.
77   Madison, "the nauseous project": Levy, 284.
77   Jackson, "we ought not": Smith, 214.
77   Madison, "unfriendly to the object": ibid.
77   Sherman, "by a very great majority": id. at 216.
77   Madison, "compelled to beg": ibid.
78   Madison, "begged the House": Farber and Sherry, 231.
78   Burke, "not those solid": Levy, 285.
78   Vining, "the bill for establishing": Farber and Sherry, 232.
78   Sherman, "The Constitution": ibid.
78   Madison, "remain uniform": ibid.
78   Vining, "an act to amend": id. at 233.
79   Senate action: id. at 241–243.
80   Clinton, "has transacted": Smith, 161.
81   Lee and Grayson, "it is with grief": id. at 157.
81   Madison, "unnecessary and dangerous": Julius Goebel, Jr., *History of the Supreme Court of the United States: Antecedents and Beginnings to 1801*, 425.
81   Madison, "will kill the opposition": Levy, 285.
82   Jackson, "The very purpose": *West Virginia v. Barnette*, 319 U.S. 614, 638 (1943).

CHAPTER 8

87   Jay nomination: Abraham, 72; Urofsky, 263–269.
87   Jay, "those who own": Gustavus Myers, *History of the Supreme Court of the United States,* 37.
88   Rutledge nomination: Madison, *Notes*, 507; Abraham, 72–73; Urofsky, 389–390; Maeva Marcus and James R. Perry, eds., *The Documentary History of the Supreme Court of the United States, 1789–1800*, 813.
89   Cushing nomination: Abraham, 74–75; Urofsky, 127–129.
89   Blair nomination: Abraham, 74; Urofsky, 25–27.
89   Iredell nomination: Abraham, 75; Urofsky, 249–253.
89   Wilson nomination: Abraham, 73–74; Urofsky, 535–536.
89   Wilson, "I commit myself": Marcus and Perry, 613.
90   Washington, "I presume": id. at 618–619.
91   *Brailsford* case: 2 U.S. 402–408, 415–417 (1792).
91   *Gazette:* "Business": Marcus and Perry, 736.

 91 Johnson, "I cannot resolve": id. at 740.
 91 Jay, "takes me from": ibid.
 92 *Hayburn's Case:* David P. Currie, *The Constitution in the Supreme Court: The First Hundred Years, 1789–1888*, 6–9; 2 U.S. 408–414 (1792).
 92 Boudinot, "the first instance": Leo Pfeffer, *This Honorable Court*, 48–49.
 93 *Chisholm* case and reaction: Pfeffer, 50–52; Goebel, 723–741; Currie, 14–20; 2 U.S. 419, 479 (1793).
 95 Ellsworth nomination: Abraham, 77; Urofsky, 155–157.

CHAPTER 9
 96 Paterson nomination: Abraham, 75–76; Urofsky, 347–350.
 97 Chase nomination: Abraham, 76–77; Urofsky, 107–111; Marcus and Perry, 805, 833–836.
 98 Dwight, "our wives and daughters": Pfeffer, 61–62.
 98 "as we should": id. at 62.
 99 Lyon trial: Pfeffer, 64–65; Goebel, 638–639; Urofsky, 348.
 99 Fries trial: Urofsky, 110.
100 Peters, "I never sat": ibid.
100 Washington nomination: Urofsky, 511–513; Marcus and Perry, 868.
101 Moore nomination: Urofsky, 329; Marcus and Perry, 880, 882.
102 Marshall nomination: Abraham, 81–84; Urofsky, 301–306; Marcus and Perry, 904, 918–924.
105 *Marbury* case: Pfeffer, 66–67; Currie, 66–74; 5 U.S. 137, 152–180 (1803).

CHAPTER 10
108 Chase impeachment and trial: Urofsky, 110; Schwartz, 57; Pfeffer, 87.
110 Republican leader, "there should be": Pfeffer, 88.
110 Jefferson, "impeachment will not": ibid.
110 Jefferson, "judiciary of the United States": id. at 93.
110 Johnson, "I found": Urofsky, 273.
111 *Worcester* case: Currie, 181–183; 31 U.S. 515, 535–597 (1832).
112 "Trail of Tears": Zinn, 135–140.
112 Madison, "In the internal": Madison, *Notes*, 15.
112 *Fletcher* case: Myers, 181–187, 260–261; Pfeffer, 99; Currie, 128–136; 10 U.S. 87, 124–146.
115 Duvall nomination: Abraham, 90; Urofsky, 153–154.
115 Story nomination: Abraham, 89–90; Urofsky, 435–444.
115 *Martin* case: Myers, 23–28, 229–239, 270–281; Currie, 91–96; 14 U.S. 304, 323–362 (1816).
119 *Cohens* case: Currie, 96–102; 19 U.S. 264, 373–428 (1821).

CHAPTER 11
121 *McCulloch* case: Melvin I. Urofsky, *A March of Liberty: A Constitutional History of the United States* (cited below as Urofsky, *March of Liberty*), 211–215; Farber and Sherry, 198–199; Currie, 160–168; 17 U.S. 316 (1819).
126 *Dartmouth College* case: Pfeffer, 106–109; Myers, 286–293; Currie, 141–145; 17 U.S. 518 (1819).
130 *Sturges* case: Urofsky, *March of Liberty*, 240; Currie, 145–150; 17 U.S. 122 (1819).
131 *Gibbons* case: Pfeffer, 114–116; Urofsky, *March of Liberty*, 216–219; Currie, 168–176; 22 U.S. 1 (1824).
133 Thompson nomination: Abraham, 91–92; Urofsky, 477.
133 Trimble nomination: Abraham, 92–93; Urofsky, 483.
133 *Ogden* case: Urofsky, *March of Liberty*, 241–242; Currie, 150–156; 25 U.S. 213 (1827).
134 *Barron* case: Currie, 189–193; 3 U.S. 243 (1833).

CHAPTER 12

137 Missouri Compromise: Urofsky, *March of Liberty*, 350–352.
138 Tallmadge, "If a dissolution": Louis Filler, *Crusade Against Slavery*, 27–28.
138 Cobb, "We have kindled": id. at 28.
138 Marshall, "nothing portends": Jean Edward Smith, *John Marshall*, 489.
138 Marshall, "removal of our": id. at 489–490.
138 *The Antelope* case: 23 U.S. 66, 68–132 (1825).
140 Marshall's death and reaction: Jean Edward Smith, *John Marshall*, 523–524.
142 Story, "The reign": R. Kent Newmyer, *Supreme Court Justice Joseph Story*, 158.
142 McLean nomination: Abraham, 95–96; Urofsky, 293–295.
142 Baldwin nomination: Abraham, 96–97; Urofsky, 1–2.
143 Wayne nomination: Abraham, 98; Urofsky, 515–516.
143 Taney nomination: Abraham, 98–99; Urofsky, 465–473.
143 Barbour nomination: Abraham, 99–100; Urofsky, 3–4.
144 Webster, "Judge Story": Abraham 100.
144 *Charles River Bridge* case: Pfeffer, 123–124; Stanley Kutler, *Privilege and Creative Destruction*; Currie, 209–211; 36 P.L. 420 (1837).
148 Garrison, "monstrous evil": Louis Filler, *The Crusade Against Slavery, 1830–1860*, 55–62.
148 Calhoun, "Abolition and the Union": Don Fehrenbacher, *Slavery, Law, and Politics: The Dred Scott Case in Historical Perspective*, 57.
150 *Amistad* case: Paul Finkelman, *Slavery in Court*, 222–239; Howard Jones, *Mutiny on the Amistad*; 40 U.S. 592–597 (1841).
151 *Prigg* case: Finkelman, 60–64; Currie, 241–245; 41 U.S. 536–672 (1842).
153 Latimer Law: Finkelman, 64–65.
153 Anthony Burns arrest and trial: Finkelman, 107–119; Albert J. Von Frank, *The Trials of Anthony Burns*.
153 Garrison, "a covenant": Filler, 215–216.
154 "rivals *Dred Scott*": Fehrenbacher, 21–22.
154 Brightly, "resulted in the passage": 41 U.S. 541–542 (1842).

CHAPTER 13

159 Background of *Dred Scott* case: Fehrenbacher, 122, 129, 295.
160 *Strader* case: Finkelman, 35–38; 51 U.S. 82 (1850).
161 Missouri court decision: Fehrenbacher, 128–139.
162 Federal court decision: id. at 140–146.
162 Scott, "I have no money": id. at 147–148.
163 Catron nomination: Abraham, 101–102; Urofsky, 95–99.
163 Daniel nomination: Abraham, 104; Urofsky, 131–134.
163 Nelson nomination: Abraham, 106; Urofsky, 337–338.
164 Grier nomination: Abraham, 108–109; Urofsky, 203–204.
164 Curtis nomination: Abraham, 109–110; Urofsky, 125–126.
164 Campbell nomination: Abraham, 111–112; Urofsky, 89–90.
165 Blair, "emancipated": Fehrenbacher, 152.
166 *Scott* arguments: id. at 153.
166 Curtis, "will not decide": id. at 153–154.

CHAPTER 14

168 *Scott* arguments: Fehrenbacher, 156–163.
170 Grier-Buchanan correspondence: id. at 163–169.
171 *Dred Scott* decision: 60 U.S. 393 (1857).
172 "to grounds agreed": id. at 176.
173 Blackstone, "a slave or negro": Urofsky, *March of Liberty*, 354.

175 *American Insurance* decision: Fehrenbacher, 203–204; 26 U.S. 511 (1828).
176 "an argument": Fehrenbacher, 209.
177 *New York Tribune*, "mean and skulking": id. at 230.
177 *Constitutionalist*, "is now the supreme": ibid.
177 Cheever, "If the people": id. at 232.
177 "The right of property": id. at 247.
178 Hale, "to carry out": id. at 251.
178 Seward, "whisperings": ibid.
178 Benjamin, "principles": id. at 251–252.
178 Johnson, "mad and reckless": ibid.

CHAPTER 15
179 Lincoln, "we will submit": Philip van Doren Stern, ed., *The Life and Writings of Abraham Lincoln*, 399.
179 Lincoln, "the *Dred Scott* decision": id. at 418.
179 Douglas, "warfare": Fehrenbacher, 260.
179 Lincoln, "conspiracy": Stern, 456.
180 Lincoln, "set the niggers": id. at 468.
180 Lincoln, "I am not": id. at 492, 494.
180 Lincoln, "Douglas had the ingenuity": id. at 536.
180 "The *Dred Scott* decision": Fehrenbacher, 268.
182 Lincoln's inaugural address: Stern, 646–657.
182 Lincoln, "the power in me": id. at 660.
182 Clifford nomination: Abraham, 113; Urofsky, 123–124.
183 Swayne nomination: Abraham, 116–117; Urofsky, 455–456.
183 Miller nomination: Abraham, 117–118; Urofsky, 317–322.
183 Davis nomination: Abraham, 118–119; Urofsky, 135–137.
183 Field nomination: Abraham, 119–120; Urofsky, 159–167.
183 "has earned the gratitude": Fehrenbacher, 298.
183 *New York Times*, "an act of supreme folly": ibid.
184 "It is a pity": Abraham, 100–101.
184 Chase nomination: Abraham, 120–122; Urofsky, 101–106.
185 Lincoln, "With malice": Stern, 840–842.
185 Lincoln, "the constitutional": id. at 846–851.
186 Wade, "Johnson, we have faith": Eric Foner, *Reconstruction*, 177.
188 *Milligan* case: Currie, 288–292; 71 U.S. 2 (1866).

CHAPTER 16
190 "joined in the shouting": Foner, 66.
190 Seward, "The Constitution": ibid.
191 Lincoln, "the people": Stern, 477.
191 Giddings, "Let no man": Farber and Sherry, 263.
191 Hamlin, "must answer": id. at 266.
191 Adams, "over two thousand": Foner, 119.
191 "a sight that apaled me": ibid.
192 "the wholesale slaughter": id. at 261–263.
192 Civil Rights bill, "full and equal": id. at 243.
192 "then I demand": id. at 244.
192 Morrill, "I admit": id. at 245.
192 Johnson, "stride toward": id. at 250.
192 Bingham, "Congress shall": Farber and Sherry, 305.
192 Bingham, "for the enforcement": ibid.

193 Douglas, "zones of privacy": *Griswold v. Connecticut*, 381 U.S. 479 (1965).
194 "very unanimous": Foner, 268.
195 "sacrificed the moral power": id. at 265.
195 "Battle fought and won": Farber and Sherry, 322.
195 "Are we not": Foner, 269.
195 *New York Times*, "with so exclusive": id. at 267.
195 "If I was ever": id. at 261.
195 Reconstruction Act: id. at 316–319.
196 Klan violence: id. at 425–444.
198 Strong nomination: Abraham, 127; Urofsky, 445–447.
198 Bradley nomination: Abraham, 127–128; Urofsky, 33–37.
198 Hunt nomination: Abraham, 128; Urofsky, 247–248.
198 *Slaughterhouse Cases:* Charles Fairman, *Reconstruction and Reunion*, Part I, 1323; Currie, 342–351; 83 U.S. 36–130 (1873).
201 Waite nomination: Abraham, 130–131; Urofsky, 493–499.
202 *Cruickshank* case: Foner, 437; 92 U.S. 452 (1875).
205 "When the decision": Howard N. Meyer, *The Amendment That Refused to Die*, 87.

CHAPTER 17

206 "They are going around": Foner, 560.
207 "Is it possible": id. at 556.
207 Hawley, "I have been": ibid.
207 Douglass, "Do you mean": id. at 567.
208 "He is connected": id. at 568.
208 "Armed bands": id. at 571–572.
208 Hayes-Tilden election: id. at 579–581.
209 Harlan nomination: Abraham, 132–134; Urofsky, 205–23.
210 Harlan, "even upon grounds": 109 U.S. 3, 59 (1883).
210 Woods nomination: Abraham, 134; Urofsky, 539.
210 Matthews nomination: Abraham, 134–136; Urofsky, 315–316.
211 Gray nomination: Abraham, 137; Urofsky, 197–201.
211 Blatchford nomination: Abraham, 138; Urofsky, 29–31.
211 "may stand forever": Foner, 590.
211 Indictments in *Civil Rights Cases:* Philip B. Kurland and Gerhard Casper, eds., *Landmark Briefs and Arguments of the Supreme Court* (cited below as *Landmark Briefs*), Vol. 8, 307, 311–312, 355, 334–335.
213 Bradley votes: *Strauder v. West Virginia*, 100 U.S. 303 (1880); *Ex parte Virginia*, 100 U.S. 339 (1880); *United States v. Harris*, 106 U.S. 629 (1883)
213 *Civil Rights Cases:* 109 U.S. 3 (1883).
215 *Heart of Atlanta Motel* case: 379 U.S. 241 (1964).
215 Editorial reaction to decision: Charles Warren, *The Supreme Court in American History*, Vol. 2, 614.
216 *Yick Wo* case: 118 U.S. 356 (1886).
217 Industrial growth: Zinn, 247–260.
217 Lamar nomination: Abraham, 139–140; Urofsky, 283–284.
218 Fuller nomination: Abraham, 141–142; Urofsky, 183–188.
218 Brewer nomination: Abraham, 147–148; Urofsky, 61–65.
218 Brown nomination: Abraham, 148–149; Urofsky, 67–68.
219 Shiras nomination: Abraham, 149–150; Urofsky, 403–404.
219 Jackson nomination: Urofsky, 255.
219 White nomination: Abraham, 143–144; Urofsky, 525–531.
220 Peckham nomination: Abraham, 145–146; Urofsky, 351–353.

CHAPTER 18

221 McKinley, "We want a foreign": Zinn, 292.
221 "I give you": id. at 254.
222 *Plessy* case background: Charles Lofgren, *The Plessy Case*, 29–41; 163 U.S. 538–539 (1895).
222 Parks, "I was quite tired": Zinn, 442.
224 Martinet, "We'll make": Garraty, 161–163.
225 *Plessy* decisions in state courts: Lofgren, 44–60; 11 So. 948 (1892).
226 Tourgee, "Of the whole number": Lofgren, 149.
226 Tourgee brief in *Plessy: Landmark Briefs*, Vol. 13, 62–63.
227 Brown opinion in *Plessy:* 163 U.S. 537, 545–552 (1895).
229 Harlan dissent in *Plessy:* 163 U.S. at 554–559.
231 Tourgee, "virtually nullified": Lofgren, 201.
231 Harlan in *Cumming* case: 175 U.S. 528, 542–545 (1899).
232 Taft in *Gong Lum* case: 275 U.S. 78, 79–87 (1927).
232 Harlan in *Plessy:* 163 U.S. at 560.
232 Du Bois, "The problem": W. E. B. Du Bois, *The Souls of Black Folk* (Dover edition), 24.

CHAPTER 19

235 Goodwyn, "the crop lien system": Zinn, 278.
236 Grangers, "The State must": Warren, Vol. 2, 574.
236 "That it has": id. at 576.
236 Cooley, "legislative enactment": Sidney Fine, *Laissez-Faire and the General Welfare State*, 142–143.
237 Spencer, "The poverty": id. at 38.
237 Fine, "It would be difficult": id. at 44.
237 "found a new toy": id. at 45.
237 Fine, "It was in the courts": id. at 126.
237 Background of *Munn* case: Lee Epstein and Thomas G. Walker, *Constitutional Law for a Changing America: Institutional Powers and Constraints*, 439; Currie, 370–373.
238 "this assault": Warren, Vol. 2, 577–578.
238 *Munn* brief: 94 U.S. at 119.
238 Waite opinion in *Munn:* 94 U.S. 113, 123–136 (1877).
238 Field dissent in *Munn:* 94 U.S. at 136–154.
239 Pomeroy, "No other decision": Warren, Vol. 2, 583.
239 "the country": Zinn, 240.
239 Marx, "What do you think": id. at 245–246.
240 "When the great": id. at 246.
240 Haymarket Affair: id. at 264–266.
241 *Jacobs* case: 98 N.Y. 98, 104–115 (1885).
241 "in practically every case": Benjamin Twiss, *Lawyers and the Constitution*, 99–100.
241 "Socialism, Communism": Christopher Tiedeman, *Limitations on the Police Power*, 10.
242 Harlan opinion in *Mugler* case: 123 U.S. 623, 653–674 (1887).
242 Blatchford opinion in *Chicago, Milwaukee* case: 134 U.S. 418, 458 (1890).
243 Bradley opinion in *Chicago, Milwaukee* case: 134 U.S. at 461.
243 Larrabee, "further changes": Warren, Vol. 2, 593.
243 Sherman, "You must heed": Zinn, 253–254.
244 Fuller opinion in *E. C. Knight* case: 156 U.S. 1, 9–18 (1895).
244 Fuller opinion in *Pollock* case: 158 U.S. 601, 617–637 (1895).
245 Brown dissent in *Pollock* case: 158 U.S. at 686–695.
245 *Debs* case: Zinn, 272–275; 158 U.S. 564 (1894).
246 "all must applaud": Warren, Vol. 2, 700.

246 Pennoyer, "Our constitutional": id. at 704.
247 Debs, "I was": Zinn, 275.

CHAPTER 20

248 *Allgeyer* case: 165 U.S. 578 (1897).
249 *Holden* case: 169 U.S. 366 (1898).
250 Hughes, "apparently oblivious": Urofsky, 166–167.
250 McKenna nomination: Abraham, 152–153, Urofsky, 289–290.
251 Holmes nomination: Holmes, *The Common Law*, 1; Abraham, 156–161; Urofsky, 225–234.
252 Holmes opinion in *Buck* case: 274 U.S. 200, 205–207 (1927).
252 Later history of *Buck* case: J. David Smith, *The Sterilization of Carrie Buck*.
253 Day nomination: Abraham, 161–162; Urofsky, 139–140.
253 Moody nomination: Abraham, 162–163; Urofsky, 327.
254 Background of *Lochner* case: *Landmark Briefs*, Vol. 14, 663.
255 Wiesmann, "When I was young": *New York Times*, April 19, 1905.
256 Wiesmann brief in *Lochner*: *Landmark Briefs*, Vol. 14, 662, 674–675.
256 Mayer brief in *Lochner*: id. at 725, 733.
256 Peckham, "class against class": Fine, 135, 138; *People v. Budd*, 117 N.Y. 1, 30–34, 68–71.
256 Peckham opinion in *Lochner*: 198 U.S. 45, 55–64 (1905).
257 Harlan dissent in *Lochner*: 198 U.S. at 68–69.
257 Holmes dissent in *Lochner*: 198 U.S. at 75–76.
258 Brandeis brief in *Muller* case: *Landmark Briefs*, Vol. 16, 63–113.
259 Muller's brief in *Muller* case: id. at 3–35.
259 Brewer opinion in *Muller*: 208 U.S. 412, 419–422 (1908).
259 *Loewe* case: 208 U.S. 274 (1908).
259 *Adair* case: 208 U.S. 161 (1908).
260 Lurton nomination: Abraham, 165; Urofsky, 287–288.
260 Hughes nomination: Abraham, 166–168; Urofsky, 235–245.
260 Holmes, "How could you": Urofsky, 527.
260 Van Devanter nomination: Abraham, 170–171; Urofsky, 485–487.
261 Lamar nomination: Abraham, 171–172; Urofsky, 281–282.
261 Pitney nomination: Abraham, 172–173; Urofsky, 355–356.
261 Brandeis, "a first-rate": Urofsky, 460.
262 McReynolds nomination: Abraham, 175–178; Urofsky, 297–299.
262 Brandeis nomination: Abraham, 178–181; Urofsky, 39–48.
262 Clarke nomination: Abraham, 181–182; Urofsky, 121–122.
264 *Adkins* case: *Landmark Briefs*, Vol. 21, 636; 261 U.S. 525 (1923).

CHAPTER 21

265 Hofstadter, "rationalization": Zinn, 352.
266 Root, "We must have" and "there are men": id. at 359.
266 *Literary Digest*, "send to us" and "report the man," and Palmer, "It is safe": id. at 360.
267 *New York Herald* and *Minneapolis Journal*: id. at 361.
267 Hardwick, "general and widespread": ibid.
267 *United States v. Spirit of '76* and *Hall* cases: Richard Polenberg, *Fighting Faiths*, 26–29.
269 Background of *Schenck* case: id. at 212–216.
270 Hand opinion in *Masses* case: 244 Fed. 535 (1917).
270 Holmes on free speech: Polenberg, 211–212.
270 Holmes opinion in *Schenck*: 249 U.S. 47, 52 (1919).
272 Holmes, "The life": Holmes, *The Common Law*, 1.
274 *Debs* case: Polenberg, 314–315; *Landmark Briefs*, Vol. 19, 522–530, 249 U.S. 211, 213–216 (1919).

274   Debs, "Your honor": Zinn, 359.
275   Hand, "when the words," and Holmes, "I don't quite": Polenberg, 218–219.
275   Freund, "implied provocation," and Holmes, "I hated": id. at 219–222.
275   Chaffee, "where the line": id. at 222–223.
278   Background of *Abrams* case: id. at 42–53.
278   Briefs in *Abrams:* id. at 228–233.
278   Clarke opinion in *Abrams:* 250 U.S. 616, 623–624 (1919).
279   Holmes dissent in *Abrams:* 250 U.. at 627–630.
280   *Brandenberg* case: 395 U.S. 444 (1969).
281   Fate of *Abrams* defendants: Polenberg, 319–332, 341–370.

CHAPTER 22
283   Palmer raids: Samuel Walker, *In Defense of American Liberties*, 42–45.
283   *Washington Post*, "There is no time": id. at 44.
284   Background of *Gitlow* case: id. at 79–80.
285   Background of *Whitney* case: id. at 80.
286   Harding, "I am not fit": Abraham, 182.
286   Taft, "to prevent": id. at 184.
286   Sutherland nomination: Abraham, 186–187; Urofsky, 449–453.
286   Butler nomination: Abraham, 187–189; Urofsky, 81–85.
287   Sanford nomination: Abraham, 190–191; Urofsky, 395–396.
287   Stone nomination: Abraham, 192–196; Urofsky, 425–434.
288   Sanford opinion in *Gitlow:* 268 U.S. 652, 654–672 (1925).
289   Holmes dissent in *Gitlow:* 268 U.S. 672–673.
290   Sanford opinion in *Whitney:* 274 U.S. 357, 359–372 (1927).
290   Brandeis concurrence in *Whitney:* 274 U.S. at 372–380.
292   Hughes opinion in *DeJonge:* 299 U.S. 353, 356–366 (1938).
292   Roberts opinion in *Herndon:* 301 U.S. 242, 243–264 (1938).
292   Van Devanter dissent in *Herndon:* 301 U.S. at 264–278.

CHAPTER 23
294   Hoover, "We in America": Zinn, 378.
294   Ford, "There is plenty": ibid.
295   Wilson, "There is not": Peter Irons, *The New Deal Lawyers* (cited below as Irons, *New Deal*), 17.
295   "Indiana Harbor" and "Chicago, April 1": Zinn, 380–381.
295   Roosevelt, "The country needs": Urofsky, March of Liberty, 655.
295   Norris, "No man": Abraham, 197–199.
296   Parker, "The participation": id. at 43.
296   Roberts nomination: Abraham, 200–201; Urofsky, 383–387.
296   Cardozo nomination: Abraham, 201–205; Urofsky, 91–94.
298   Hughes opinion in *Blaisdell:* 290 U.S. 398, 426–427 (1934).
298   Sutherland dissent in *Blaisdell:* 290 U.S. at 473, 448.
299   Roberts opinion in *Nebbia:* 201 U.S. 502, 523–537 (1934).
299   McReynolds dissent in *Nebbia:* 291 U.S. at 558–559.
300   Wyzanski, "go so far," and Wagner, "It is true": Irons, *New Deal*, 24–27.
301   Background of *Schechter* case: Irons, *New Deal*, 86–90.
303   Hughes opinion in *Panama Refining:* id. at 58–73; 293 U.S. 388, 405–433 (1935).
303   Arguments in *Schechter:* id. at 94–99.
303   Hughes opinion in *Schechter:* 295 U.S. 495, 538–543 (1935).
303   Roosevelt, "what is happening": Leonard Baker, *Back to Back*, 116–117.
303   Roosevelt, "The implications," and *Time*, "was obviously": Irons, *New Deal*, 104–107.

305 Background of *Butler* case: Irons, *New Deal*, 181–183.
305 Brief in *Butler:* id. at 187–189.
305 Arguments in *Butler:* id. at 192–193.
306 Roberts opinion in *Butler:* 297 U.S. 1, 53–78 (1936).
306 Stone dissent in *Butler:* 297 U.S. at 78–88.
306 Early, "Please resist all": Irons, *New Deal*, 197.

CHAPTER 24

307 Roosevelt, "that the proposed": Irons, *New Deal*, 248.
307 Background of *Carter* case: id. at 248–250.
308 Sutherland opinion in *Carter:* 298 U.S. 278, 295–308 (1936).
308 Cardozo dissent in *Carter:* 298 U.S. at 317–341.
309 Epstein, "make the rule": 298 U.S. 587, 592–593.
310 "A social philosophy": 298 U.S. at 596–597.
310 Butler opinion in *Morehead:* 298 U.S. 602, 610–611 (1936).
310 Stone dissent in *Morehead:* 298 U.S. at 632–635.
310 Brant, "Because five": Irons, *New Deal*, 278.
311 Hoover, "regimented people": Bruce Ackerman, *We the People: Transformations*, 306.
311 Landon, "has been responsible": id. at 308.
312 Ickes, "there was" and Roosevelt, "is a mighty": Baker, 129–130.
313 McReynolds, "This will insure": id. at 134.
314 Roosevelt, "If we can pass": id. at 3–17.
314 Roosevelt, "The simple fact": Irons, *New Deal*, 275.
314 Hughes, "is fully abreast": id. at 276.
315 Sumners, "Boys, here's where": Baker, 7–8.
315 Roosevelt, "has improperly": Epstein and Walker, 296–300.
315 Background to *West Coast Hotel* case: John A. Garraty, ed., *Quarrels That Have Shaped the Constitution*, 266–284.
317 Hughes opinion in *West Coast Hotel:* 300 U.S. 379, 386–400 (1937).
317 Sutherland dissent in *West Coast Hotel:* 300 U.S. at 400–414.

CHAPTER 25

318 Background in *Labor Board* cases: Irons, *New Deal*, 203–214, 226–233, 254–267.
321 Arguments in *Labor Board* cases: id. at 283–286.
322 Emerson, "It was an amazing": id. at 287.
322 Hughes opinion in *Jones & Laughlin:* 301 U.S. 1, 30–45 (1937).
322 "Old McReynolds": Irons, *New Deal*, 288.
322 McReynolds dissent in *Jones & Laughlin:* 301 U.S. at 103.
324 Roberts, "I said I saw": Baker, 174–175.
324 "substantial 'favorite son' vote": *New York Times*, May 30, 1936, 3.
325 Reed, "threatened to 'pack' ": *New York Times*, August 6, 1936, 18.
326 Black nomination: Abraham, 211–216; Urofsky, 5–14.
327 Reed nomination: Abraham, 216–217; Urofsky, 367–372.
327 Frankfurter nomination: Abraham, 217–222; Urofsky, 171–181.
328 Douglas nomination: Abraham, 222–225; Urofsky, 141–151.
329 Murphy nomination: Abraham, 225–227; Urofsky, 331–336.

CHAPTER 26

334 *New York Times*, "2,000 Jewish lawyers," Goebbels, "Our racial theory," and *New York Times*, "eyes were gouged out": Irons, *Brennan vs. Rehnquist* (cited below as Irons, *Brennan*), 74–76.
334 Bilbo, "the lust": id. at 75.
334 Stone, "I have been": ibid.

334 Stone opinion in *Carolene Products:* 304 U.S. 144, 151–153 (1938).

336 *Lovell* case: 303 U.S. 444 (1938).

336 *Schneider* case: 308 U.S. 147 (1939).

336 *Cantwell* case: 310 U.S. 296 (1940).

337 Background to *Gobitis* case: Peter Irons, *The Courage of Their Convictions* (cited below as Irons, *Courage*), 15–27.

338 Gobitas, "He did it a lot": id. at 20–21, 30.

339 Hughes, "nothing to do": id. at 21.

339 Frankfurter opinion in *Gobitis:* 310 U.S. 586, 591–600 (1940).

340 Stone dissent in *Gobitis:* 310 U.S. at 601–607.

340 Gobitas, "We were": Irons, *Courage*, 30–31.

341 Attacks on Witnesses: id. at 22–23.

341 Roosevelt, "We will not," Willkie, "We must preserve," and Biddle, "essential at such": Walker, 135–136.

342 Reed opinion in *Jones:* 316 U.S. 584, 585–600 (1942).

342 Stone dissent in *Jones:* 316 U.S. at 600–611.

342 Black, Douglas, and Murphy in *Jones:* 316 U.S. at 623–624.

343 Douglas, "No, but he has": Irons, *Courage*, 23.

343 Byrnes nomination: Abraham, 228–229; Urofsky, 87.

343 Frankfurter, "I'd prefer Bob": Abraham, 230.

343 Rutledge nomination: Abraham, 234–236; Urofsky, 391–393.

345 Lower-court decision in *Barnette:* 47 F. Supp. 251 (1943).

346 Jackson opinion in *Barnette:* 319 U.S. 624, 632–642 (1943).

346 Frankfurter dissent in *Barnette* and diary entries: 319 U.S. at 646–647; Joseph Lash, ed., *From the Diaries of Felix Frankfurter*, 254.

347 Durkee, "I don't believe," and editorial: *San Diego Union-Tribune*, July 21 and 22, 1998.

CHAPTER 27

348 "thousands of Japanese": Peter Irons, *Justice at War: The Story of the Japanese American Internment Cases* (cited below as Irons, *Justice at War*), 6–7.

349 Ford, "all Japanese": id. at 7.

349 Lippmann, "the unwillingness": id. at 60.

349 Pegler, "The Japanese": id. at 61.

350 "We're charged": id. at 39–40.

350 DeWitt, "the very fact": id. at 59; Peter Irons, *Justice Delayed: The Record of the Japanese American Internment Cases* (cited below as Irons, *Justice Delayed*), 146.

350 Bendetsen, "the sheer military": Irons, *Justice at War*, 49–50.

350 DeWitt, "An American": id. at 30, 36.

351 Stimson, "We cannot": id. at 55.

351 McCloy, "To a Wall Street": id. at 46.

351 Cohen-Cox-Rauh, "Since the Occidental": id. at 53–54.

351 Burdell, "Jap citizens": id. at 140–141.

352 Background of *Hirabayashi* case: id. at 87–93.

352 Background of *Yasui* case: id. at 81–85.

353 Background of *Korematsu* case: id. at 93–99.

354 *Hirabayashi* trial: id. at 154–159.

354 *Yasui* trial: id. at 140–143.

355 *Korematsu* trial: id. at 151–154.

355 Briefs and arguments in *Hirabayashi* case: id. at 197–198, 219–227.

356 Stone opinion in *Hirabayashi:* 320 U.S. 81, 83–105 (1943).

357 Frankfurter-Murphy exchange: Irons, *Justice at War*, 246.

357 Debate over ending internment: id. at 269–277.

359 Brief in *Korematsu:* id. at 299–300.
359 Black opinion in *Korematsu:* 323 U.S. 214, 215–224 (1944).
359 Black, "People were": Irons, *Justice at War*, 356.
359 Murphy dissent in *Korematsu:* 323 U.S. at 233–242.
360 Roberts dissent in *Korematsu:* 323 U.S. at 225–233.
360 Jackson dissent in *Korematsu:* 323 U.S. at 242–248.
360 Douglas opinion in *Endo:* 323 U.S. 283, 284–307 (1944).
360 Roberts concurrence in *Endo:* 323 U.S. at 308–310.
360 War Department, "Those persons": Irons, *Justice at War*, 345.
360 *Los Angeles Times*, "Outbreak of Violence": id. at 345–346.
361 Warren, "all Americans": id. at 346.
361 "grave injustice": Irons, *Justice Delayed*, 120.
362 Reopening of internment cases: id. at 1–46, 243, 407.
364 Clinton, "A man of quiet bravery": Program for Medal of Freedom ceremony, the White House, January 15, 1998.

CHAPTER 28
365 Ho Chi Minh, "All men": Zinn, 460.
366 Truman, "Did you ever": Abraham, 237.
366 Burton nomination: Abraham, 238–240; Urofsky, 77–80.
366 Vinson nomination: Abraham, 240–242; Urofsky, 489–492.
367 Vinson dissent in Youngstown: 343 U.S. 579, 667–710 (1952).
367 Clark nomination: Abraham, 242–245; Urofsky, 113–119.
368 Minton nomination: Abraham, 245–247; Urofsky, 323–325.
368 "The Army": Zinn, 4110.
369 Woodward attack: *The Crisis*, Sept. 1946, 276; Richard Kluger, *Simple Justice*, 298–299.
369 Monroe killings: *New York Times*, July 27, 1946, 1.
369 NAACP, "Mob acts": *The Crisis*, Sept. 1946, 277; Jack Greenberg, *Crusaders in the Courts*, 61–62.
370 "Margold Report": Mark Tushnet, *The NAACP's Legal Strategy Against Segregated Education*, 25–28.
371 Hughes opinion in *Gaines:* 305 U.S. 337, 344–350 (1938).
371 *Sipuel* case: Greenberg, 63–67; 332 U.S. 631 (1948).
372 Background of *Sweatt* case: Greenberg, 64.
373 Background of *McLaurin* case: id. at 66–67.
373 *Corrigan* case: 271 U.S. 323 (1926).
374 Background of *Shelley* case: Irons, *Courage*, 65–69.
374 Vaughn argument: id. at 71.
375 Vinson opinion in *Shelley:* 334 U.S. 1, 4–23 (1948).
376 Rankin, "there must," and Shelley, "My little soul": Irons, *Courage*, 72.
376 Briefs in *Sweatt:* Greenberg, 72–76.
376 Vinson opinion in *Sweatt:* 339 U.S. 629, 631–636 (1950).
377 Vinson opinion in *McLaurin:* 339 U.S. 637, 638–642 (1950).
377 Background of *Dennis* case: Michal R. Belknap, *Cold War Political Justice*, 45–53.
378 Briefs and arguments in *Dennis: Landmark Briefs*, Vol. 47, 6–72; *New York Times*, Dec. 5. 1950.
379 Hand opinion in *Dennis:* 183 F.2d 201, 205–234 (1950).
381 Vinson opinion in *Dennis:* 341 U.S. 494, 495–517 (1951).
382 Frankfurter concurrence in *Dennis:* 341 U.S. 517–561.
382 Black dissent in *Dennis:* 341 U.S. at 579–581.
382 Harlan opinion in *Yates:* 354 U.S. 298, 300–338 (1957).

CHAPTER 29

383 Background on Clarendon County and *Briggs* case: Kluger, 3–26.
386 Clark doll tests: id. at 317–318, 330–331.
387 Trial and decisions in *Briggs:* id. at 297–301.
389 Waring death and funeral: id. at 364–366.
389 Trial and decision in *Brown:* Greenberg, 126–132.
390 Trial and decision in *Gebhart:* id. at 150–151; Kluger, 425–430.
390 Trial and decision in *Davis:* Kluger, 493, 506.
391 Trial and decision in *Bolling:* id. at 508–523.
391 First round of school case arguments: id. at 570–574; Greenberg, 169–171.
393 Frankfurter, "This is the first": Abraham, 251.
393 Warren nomination: Abraham, 252–259; Urofsky, 501–509.

CHAPTER 30

395 Second round of school case arguments: Greenberg, 189–191; Kluger, 670–673.
397 Drafting of *Brown* opinions: Kluger, 678–699.
397 Warren opinion in *Brown:* 347 U.S. 483, 486–496 (1954).
398 Reaction to *Brown* decision: Kluger, 710–711; Greenberg, 200.
399 Arguments in *Brown II:* Kluger, 729–732.
400 Warren opinion in *Brown II:* 349 U.S. 294, 298–301 (1955).
400 Reaction to *Brown II* decision: Urofsky, *March of Liberty*, 775–776.
401 Harlan nomination: Abraham, 259–262; Urofsky, 215–223.
402 Brennan nomination: Abraham, 262–265; Urofsky, 49–60; Irons, *Brennan,* 23–42.
403 Whittaker nomination: Abraham, 266–267; Urofsky, 533–534.
403 Stewart nomination: Abraham, 267–271; Urofsky, 419–424.
404 Eisenhower, "I think": Greenberg, 213.
406 Background of *Cooper* case: Greenberg, 228–243; Irons, *Courage*, 110–112.
406 Arguments in *Cooper:* Peter Irons and Stephanie Guitton, eds., *May It Please the Court* (cited below as Irons, *May It Please*), 250–256.
407 Supreme Court opinion in *Cooper:* 358 U.S. 1, 4–20 (1958).
407 Barnett and Wallace defiance: Greenberg, 318–332, 338–340.

CHAPTER 31

409 Black opinion in *Everson:* 330 U.S. 1, 3–18 (1947).
410 Black opinion in *McCollum:* 333 U.S. 203, 204–212 (1948).
410 Black opinion in *Engel:* 370 U.S. 421, 422–436 (1962).
411 Tocqueville, "religious zeal": Irons, *Brennan*, 119–120.
411 Reaction to *Engel* decision: Walker, 225.
411 Arguments in *Schempp:* Irons, *May It Please*, 62–68.
412 Clark opinion in *Schempp:* 374 U.S. 203, 205–227 (1963).
412 Stewart dissent in *Schempp:* 374 U.S. at 308–320.
412 Background of *Lee* case: Robert S. Alley, *Without a Prayer*, 128–138.
413 Kennedy opinion in *Lee:* 505 U.S. 577, 580–599 (1992).
413 Scalia dissent in *Lee:* 505 U.S. at 631–646.
413 Istook prayer amendment: *San Diego Union-Tribune*, June 5, 1998.
413 White nomination: Abraham, 272–277; Urofsky, 517–524.
414 Goldberg nomination: Abraham, 277–280; Urofsky, 193–195.
415 Fortas nomination: Abraham, 281–288; Urofsky, 169–170.
415 Marshall, "You're talking": Irons, *May It Please*, 313.
416 Warren opinion in *Reynolds:* 377 U.S. 533, 536–587 (1964).
417 "Well, Mr. Chief Justice": Kluger, 699.
417 "forty-three million": Irons, *May It Please*, 270.

417 Clark opinion in *Heart of Atlanta:* 379 U.S. 241, 242–262 (1964).
418 Warren, "Are lawyers": Irons, *May It Please*, 221.
418 Warren opinion in *Miranda:* 384 U.S. 436, 439–499
418 White dissent in *Miranda:* 384 U.S. at v526–545.
418 Warren opinion in *O'Brien:* 391 U.S. 367, 369–386 (1968).
419 Fortas opinion in *Tinker:* 393 U.S. 503, 504–514 (1969).
419 Black dissent in *Tinker:* 393 U.S. at 515–526.
419 Brennan opinion in *New York Times:* 376 U.S. 254, 256–292 (1964).
420 Taylor, "We owe a lot": *Washington Post,* July 1, 1974, B-1.

CHAPTER 32

424 Fortas withdrawal: Abraham 286–288; Laura Kalman, *Abe Fortas*, 327–358.
424 Burger nomination: Abraham, 297–301; Urofsky, 69–76.
425 Finkbine case: David Garrow, *Liberty and Sexuality*, 285–289.
427 Pilpel, "a dagger": Walker, 301.
427 ACLU, "the right": id. at 302.
428 Douglas opinion in *Skinner:* 316 U.S. 535, 536–543 (1942).
429 Background of *Griswold* case: Garrow, 196–229.
429 Arguments in *Griswold:* id. at 237–240; Stephanie Guitton and Peter Irons, eds., *Arguments on Abortion* (cited below as Guitton, *Arguments*), 2–10.
430 Douglas opinion in *Griswold:* 381 U.S. 479, 480–486 (1965).
430 Harlan concurrence in *Griswold:* 381 U.S. at 499–502.
430 Goldberg concurrence in *Griswold:* 381 U.S. at 486–499.
430 White concurrence in *Griswold:* 381 U.S. at 502–507.
430 Black dissent in *Griswold:* 381 U.S. at 507–527.
430 Stewart dissent in *Griswold:* 381 U.S. at 527–531.
431 Background of *Roe* case: Garrow, 402–407.
433 District court hearing and decision in *Roe:* id. at 433–444, 451–454.

CHAPTER 33

437 Haynesworth and Carswell rejections: Bob Woodward and Scott Armstrong, *The Brethren: Inside the Supreme Court*, 56–57, 74–75.
437 Blackmun nomination: Abraham, 301–305; Urofsky, 15–24.
438 Arguments in *Roe:* Garrow, 523–526; Irons, *May It Please*, 344–348.
440 Deliberations in *Roe:* Garrow, 528–538, 547–560.
441 Powell nomination: Abraham, 307–313; Urofsky; 357–366; Irons, *Brennan*, 45–46.
441 Rehnquist nomination: Abraham, 313–321; Urofsky, 357–366; Irons, *Brennan*, 43–64.
443 Second round of arguments in *Roe:* Garow, 567–571; Irons, *May It Please*, 349–354.
444 Weddington, "I left the courtroom": Sarah Weddington, *A Question of Choice*, 142.
445 Deliberations in *Roe:* Garrow, 573–588; Woodward and Armstrong, 271–280.
447 Blackmun opinion in *Roe:* 410 U.S. 113, 116–167 (1973).
448 Burger concurrence in *Roe:* 410 U.S. at 207–208.
448 White dissent in *Roe:* 410 U.S. at 221–223.
448 Rehnquist dissent in *Roe:* 410 U.S. at 171–178.
449 Reaction to *Roe* decision: Garrow, 605–606.

CHAPTER 34

451 Background of *Bakke* case: Joel Dreyfuss and Charles Lawrence III, *The Bakke Case*, 3–30.
452 Brennan dissent in *DeFunis:* 416 U.S. 312, 350 (1974).
453 Arguments in *Bakke:* Dreyfuss and Lawrence, 176–201; Irons, *May It Please*, 306–313.
455 Stevens nomination: Abraham, 323–328; Urofsky, 409–417.
455 Powell opinion in *Bakke:* 438 U.S. 265, 269–320 (1978).

456 Brennan opinion in *Bakke:* 438 U.S. at 324–379.

456 Marshall opinion in *Bakke:* 438 U.S. 387–402.

456 Blackmun opinion in *Bakke:* 482 U.S. 402–408.

459 Background of *Bowers* case: Irons, *Courage*, 381–403.

459 Brief in *Bowers:* id. at 387.

460 Arguments in *Bowers:* Irons, *May It Please*, 362–368.

460 White opinion in *Bowers:* 478 U.S. 186, 187–196 (1986).

461 Burger concurrence in *Bowers:* 478 U.S. at 196–197.

461 Blackmun dissent in *Bowers:* 478 U.S. at 199–214.

462 Powell, "I think": John C. Jeffries, Jr., *Lewis F. Powell, Jr.*, 530.

462 Reagan, "a covenant": *Public Papers of the Presidents*, Ronald Reagan, 1987, 1040–1043.

463 Marshall, "I cannot accept": *Harper's Magazine*, July 1987, 17–19.

CHAPTER 35

464 O'Connor nomination: Abraham, 330–339; Urofsky, 339–345.

465 Scalia nomination: Urofsky, 397–402.

466 Bork rejection: Michael Pertschuk and Wendy Schaetzel, *The People Rising;* Robert Bork, *The Tempting of America.*

466 Ginsburg withdrawal: David Savage, *Turning Right: The Making of the Rehnquist Court*, 176–180.

466 Kennedy nomination: Urofsky, 277–279.

467 Arguments in *Webster:* Guitton and Irons, *Arguments on Abortion*, 100–111.

467 Rehnquist opinion in *Webster:* 492 U.S. 490, 499–522 (1989).

467 O'Connor concurrence in *Webster:* 492 U.S. at 522–531.

468 Scalia concurrence in *Webster:* 492 U.S. at 532–537.

468 Blackmun dissent in *Webster:* 492 U.S. at 537–560.

469 Brennan opinion in *Texas:* 491 U.S. 397, 399–420 (1989).

469 Scalia, "You can honor it": Irons, *May It Please*, 155.

469 Kennedy concurrence in *Texas:* 491 U.S. at 420–421.

469 Rehnquist dissent in *Texas:* 491 U.S. at 421–435.

470 Reaction to *Texas* decision: Irons, *Brennan*, 161–165; *Eichmann*, 496 U.S. 310 (1990).

472 O'Connor opinion in *Croson:* 488 U.S. 469, 476–511 (1989).

473 Marshall dissent in *Croson:* 488 U.S. at 528–561.

473 Brennan, "The strenuous demand": Irons, *Brennan*, 321.

473 Accolades for Brennan: id. at 322–327.

474 Souter nomination: Urofsky, 405–407.

475 Marshall dissent in *Payne:* 501 U.S. 808, 844–856 (1992).

475 Marshall, "I'm old": Jane Mayer and Jill Abramson, *Strange Justice: The Selling of Clarence Thomas*, 14–16.

475 Thomas nomination: id. at 32–61.

476 *Wall Street Journal*, "All lingering doubt": id. at 16.

477 Arguments in *Planned Parenthood*: Guitton and Irons, *Arguments*, 188–195.

478 "Changed Path for Court? . . .": *New York Times*, June 2, 1991, 1.

478 O'Connor, Kennedy, and Souter opinion in *Planned Parenthood:* 505 U.S. 833, 843–901 (1992).

479 Scalia dissent in *Planned Parenthood:* 505 U.S. at 979–1002.

479 Blackmun concurrence and dissent in *Planned Parenthood:* 505 U.S. at 922–943.

EPILOGUE

481 Bush, "a fundamental": *Public Papers of the Presidents*, George Bush, 1992–1993, Vol. 2, 2053.

481 Ginsburg nomination: Urofsky, 189–192.

482 Breyer nomination: *Current Biography Yearbook*, 1966, 52–56.

483   "The Constitution": *Ex parte Milligan*, 71 U.S. at 120–121.

483   Dred Scott, "My fellow-men": Fehrenbacher, 147–148.

483   Debs, "it is extremely": *Landmark Briefs*, Vol. 19, 516.

483   Gobitas, "We were": Irons, *Courage*, 30–31.

483   Tinker, "We got all kinds": id. at 248.

484   McCorvey, "The first shot": Norman McCorvey, *I Am Roe*, 184–185.

484   Hardwick, "I was totally stunned": Irons, *Courage*, 400.

SOURCES FOR
FURTHER READING

The literature on the Constitution and the Supreme Court is vast and still expanding. For those readers who have developed from this book a desire to learn more about the issues, cases, and justices I have discussed, the works listed below should help. This is hardly an exhaustive bibliography, but it includes the books I have consulted and cited, and others with more extensive discussion of particular facets of constitutional history. These works vary considerably in their points of view; some authors are conservative, some are liberal, and others compile material or discuss issues from a supposedly "neutral" position. I have organized these suggested readings by topic, and by rough chronology within each category. I have included the original date of each work, but not the place and publisher; these details would clutter the text and are easily available by computer.

The book I have relied upon most heavily for American political and social history, and on which this book is modeled, is Howard Zinn, *A People's History of the United States* (1980; HarperPerennial edition, 1990). From the landing of Columbus to the Vietnam War, Zinn lets the people speak of their struggles, their triumphs, and their defeats. There are, of course, many other histories of the American people, but none match Zinn's eye for the telling fact and ear for the people's voices.

Histories of the Constitution and the Supreme Court abound. Leonard Levy and Kenneth Karst have edited an excellent four-volume *Encyclopedia of the American Constitution* (1986). Gustavus Myers pictured the Court as a den of thieves in his muckraking *History of the Supreme Court of the United States* (1912). In contrast, Charles Warren treated the Court reverentially in *The Supreme Court in United States History* (1922). Robert G. McCloskey offered a brief, admiring history through the early Warren Court period in *The American Supreme Court* (1960). Leo Pfeffer took a liberal's view in *This Honorable Court: A History of the United States Supreme Court* (1965). Two books published in the Constitution's bicentennial year were largely celebratory. Archibald Cox skimmed the surface in *The Court and the Constitution* (1987), and Chief Justice William H. Rehnquist did not reveal much of the Court's workings in *The Supreme Court: How It Is, How It Was* (1987). Two more recent books by prolific writers on the Court provide much more detail and analysis. Melvin I. Urofsky cites almost nine hundred Supreme Court decisions in more than 900 pages of *A March of Liberty: A Constitutional History of the United States* (1988). Urofsky provides excellent suggestions for further reading at the end of each chapter. Bernard Schwartz stays inside the Court's chambers in *A History of the Supreme Court* (1993). David M. O'Brien clearly explains the Court's operations in *Storm Center: The Supreme Court in American Politics* (4th ed., 1996).

Peter C. Hoffer provides a good, brief overview of the period before the Constitution in *Law and People in Colonial America* (1992). David H. Flaherty ranges over several topics in his *Essays in the History of Early American Law* (1969). Edmund S. Morgan discusses the legal systems of the Massachusetts Bay and Plymouth colonies in *The Puritan Dilemma: The Story of John Winthrop* (1958). The legal problems of religious dissenters in colonial America are discussed in Sanford H. Cobb, *The Rise of Religious Liberty in America* (1902, reprinted in 1958). Francis P. Prucha has collected and edited useful material in *The Indian in American History* (1971).

The drafting and ratification of the Constitution has attracted many scholars, and much documentary material is available. I have relied heavily on James Madison's *Notes of Debates in the Federal Convention of 1787* (ed. by Adrienne Koch, 1966). Two good popular accounts of the Constitutional Convention appeared in its bicentennial year: Charles L. Mee, *The Genius of the People* (1987), and William Peters, *A More Perfect Union* (1987). Max Farrand utilized a great many original records in *The Framing of the Constitution of the United States* (1913).

Two studies of the Constitutional Convention provide opposing viewpoints. Charles Beard attributed mercenary motives to the Framers in *An Economic Interpretation of the Constitution* (1913). Charles Warren offered a reverential view in *The Making of the Constitution* (1929). Leonard W. Levy compiled the best of his prodigious work in *Essays on the Making of the Constitution* (1969; 2d ed., 1987). Levy also wrote a masterful refutation of polemicists such as Robert Bork and Edwin Meese in *Original Intent and the Framers' Constitution* (1988). There is much useful documentation in the edited work of Daniel A. Farber and Suzanna Sherry, *A History of the American Constitution* (1990). Other documentary sources include Wilbourne E. Benton, ed., *1787: The Drafting of the United States Constitution* (Vol. II, 1986), and Craig R. Smith, *To Form a More Perfect Union: The Ratification of the Constitution and the Bill of Rights, 1787–1791* (1993). There are useful documents in Bernard Schwartz, *The Roots of the Bill of Rights* (Vol. II, 1980), and Neil H. Cogan, ed., *The Complete Bill of Rights: The Drafts, Debates, Sources, and Origins* (1997).

The Supreme Court's early years are chronicled in great detail in Julius Goebel, Jr., *History of the Supreme Court of the United States: Antecedents and Beginnings to 1801* (1971). Maeva Marcus and James R. Perry have collected many useful records in *The Documentary History of the Supreme Court of the United States, 1789–1800* (1985). Two volumes of the "Holmes Devise" series on Supreme Court history cover the period of the Marshall Court: George L. Haskins and Herbert A. Johnson, *Foundations of Power: John Marshall, 1801–1815* (1981), and G. Edward White, *The Marshall Court and Cultural Change, 1815–1835* (1988).

There are three excellent books on the slavery issue before the Civil War. Louis Filler focused on the political factors in *The Crusade Against Slavery, 1830–1860* (1960), and William M. Wiecek addressed the legal issues in *The Sources of Antislavery Constitutionalism in America, 1760–1848* (1977). David Potter put the two perspectives together in *The Impending Crisis, 1848–1861* (1976). Paul Finkelman has written many works on the law of slavery; he collected documents and court decisions in *Slavery in the Courtroom* (1985). Philip Van Doren Stern collected many of Lincoln's speeches and writings about slavery and the *Dred Scott* case in *The Life and Writings of Abraham Lincoln* (1940). Don Fehrenbacher produced a masterpiece in *The Dred Scott Case: Its Significance in American Law and Politics* (1978). He provided an abridged version in *Slavery, Law, and Politics: The Dred Scott Case in Historical Perspective* (1981). Carl B. Swisher covered the Taney Court period for the Holmes Devise series in *The Taney Period* (1974).

Scholars have produced several excellent accounts of law and politics during the Reconstruction period. Eric Foner provided a detailed and insightful account in *Reconstruction: America's Unfinished Revolution, 1867–1877* (1988). Charles Fairman offered much detail but little analysis in his contribution to the Holmes Devise series, *Reconstruction and Reunion, 1864–1888* (Part I, 1978).

Harold M. Hyman did an excellent job of analysis in *A More Perfect Union: The Impact of the Civil War and Reconstruction on the Constitution* (1975).

The last three decades of the nineteenth century have attracted several scholars. Sidney Fine wrote an excellent book in *Laissez Faire and the General-Welfare State* (1956). Arnold M. Paul combed the law-review literature for *Conservative Crisis and the Rule of Law: Attitudes of Bar and Bench, 1887–1895* (1960). Benjamin Twiss provided an early study in *Lawyers and the Constitution: How Laissez Faire Came to the Supreme Court* (1942).

There is, unfortunately, no good account of constitutional history during the first three decades of the twentieth century. The broader histories by Urofsky and Schwartz cover this period, and biographies of Chief Justices Edward White and William Howard Taft (cited below) add some detail. I wrote about law and politics during Franklin Roosevelt's first administration in *The New Deal Lawyers* (1981). Joseph Alsop and Turner Catledge offered a journalistic account of Roosevelt's "court-packing" plan in *The 168 Days* (1938), and Leonard Baker provided more detail in *Back to Back: The Duel Between FDR and the Supreme Court* (1967). Robert H. Jackson, Roosevelt's attorney general and later Supreme Court justice, wrote a partisan's account in *The Struggle for Judicial Supremacy* (1941).

We have several good studies by scholars and journalists of the Supreme Court since World War II. The best include two books by Bernard Schwartz: *Superchief* (1983), a detailed account of the Warren Court's deliberations in virtually every significant case decided during this period, and *The Ascent of Pragmatism: The Burger Court in Action* (1990). Bob Woodward and Scott Armstrong rifled through the Burger Court's hidden files in *The Brethren: Inside the Supreme Court* (1979). This book created a furor and remains the best account of the Court's internal politics. David Savage wrote an excellent book in *Turning Right: The Making of the Rehnquist Court* (1992). More recently, Edward Lazarus offered a former law clerk's account of Court politics in *Closed Chambers* (1998).

We can learn a great deal about constitutional law and politics from books about Supreme Court cases. The list below is just a sampling of the best and most important of these works, presented in chronological order of the cases. Stanley I. Kutler combined law, politics, and economics in *Privilege and Creative Destruction: The Charles River Bridge Case* (1971). I cited above Don Fehrenbacher's impressive book (and its abridgment) on the *Dred Scott* case. Charles Lofgren wrote a good study of Jim Crow laws in *The Plessy Case: A Legal-Historical Interpretation* (1987). Richard Polenberg produced a fine book on World War I cases in *Fighting Faiths: The Abrams Case, the Supreme Court, and Free Speech* (1987). I cited above my book on constitutional litigation during Franklin Roosevelt's first administration, *The New Deal Lawyers* (1981). David Manwaring provided a good study of the *Gobitis* and *Barnette* cases in *Render unto Caesar: The Flag-Salute Controversy* (1962). I have written one book on the wartime internment cases and edited another: *Justice at War: The Story of the Japanese American Internment Cases* (1983) and *Justice Delayed: The Record of the Japanese American Internment Cases* (1989). The latter book includes a 50-page account of the reopening of the internment cases in the 1980s. Slightly out of order, Maeva Marcus studied the collision of presidential and congressional power in *Truman and the Steel Seizure Case* (1977).

The cases dealing with racial segregation after World War II have generated many fine books. Clement Vose started filling this shelf with *Caucasians Only: The Supreme Court, the NAACP, and the Restrictive Covenant Cases* (1959). Richard Kluger produced a masterful study of the school segregation cases, both detailed and exciting, in *Simple Justice: The History of Brown v. Board of Education* (1976). Jack Greenberg, who succeeded Thurgood Marshall as the NAACP's legal director, offered an excellent insider's account of dozens of civil rights cases in *Crusaders in the Courts* (1994). Mark Tushnet, a prolific writer on constitutional history, adds background to these cases in *The NAACP's Legal Strategy Against Segregated Education, 1925–1950* (1987).

Other good case studies include Michal Belknap's book on the Communist Party cases, *Cold War Political Justice* (1977), and two books by Anthony Lewis: *Gideon's Trumpet* (1964), on the right to counsel, and his study of an important libel case in *Make No Law: The Sullivan Case and the First*

Amendment (1991). Robert S. Alley explored the school prayer cases in *Without a Prayer: Religious Expression in Public Schools* (1996). Joel Dreyfuss and Charles Lawrence III dealt with affirmative action in *The Bakke Case: The Politics of Inequality* (1979).

There are several excellent books on the abortion controversy and cases. The most detailed and important is David J. Garrow's *Liberty and Sexuality: The Right to Privacy and the Making of Roe v. Wade* (1994). Barbara H. Craig and David M. O'Brien present much useful data in *Abortion and American Politics* (1993). Sarah Weddington, who argued the Roe case before the Supreme Court, offers her account in *A Question of Choice* (1992); and Norma McCorvey, the real "Jane Roe," told her story in *I Am Roe* (1994), written before her "born-again" conversion to the pro-life position.

In addition to individual case studies, there are two books that recount the stories of several important cases. John Garraty edited a book with accounts of Supreme Court cases over two centuries in *Quarrels That Have Shaped the Constitution* (1964; expanded edition in 1987). I recorded the first-person stories of Supreme Court litigants between 1940 and 1986 in *The Courage of Their Convictions: Sixteen Americans Who Fought Their Way to the Supreme Court* (1988).

Philip B. Kurland and Gerhard Casper continue to edit another important source on significant Supreme Court cases, *Landmark Briefs and Arguments of the Supreme Court of the United States: Constitutional Law*. This series includes all the briefs and oral arguments (since 1955) in more than two hundred cases. I have produced (with Stephanie Guitton) three compilations of edited and narrated oral arguments in a series entitled *May It Please the Court*. The first set (in 1993) included arguments in twenty-three cases, including *Bakke*, *Miranda*, *Roe*, and the Pentagon Papers and Watergate tapes cases. The second set, *Arguments on Abortion* (1997), included arguments in eight cases dealing with contraception and abortion, from *Griswold* in 1965 to *Casey* in 1992. The third set, *The First Amendment* (1998), included arguments in cases that dealt with libel, obscenity, nude dancing, picketing, and other issues of free expression.

Judicial biography offers another perspective on the Constitution and Supreme Court. I have relied heavily on two sources in this book. Melvin I. Urofsky edited a collection of short (2- to 10-page) biographies of all Supreme Court justices from John Jay to Ruth Ginsburg in *The Supreme Court Justices: A Biographical Dictionary* (1994). I contributed a sketch of Justice Frank Murphy to this book. Appended to each essay are references for further reading. Henry J. Abraham recounts the details of each Supreme Court nomination in *Justices and Presidents: A Political History of Appointments to the Supreme Court* (1974; 2d ed., 1985). Abraham writes in a chatty style and offers his judgment on most justices. Leon Friedman and Fred L. Israel have edited a five-volume set of longer biographies in *The Justices of the United States Supreme Court, 1789–1978* (1969–1980).

The following list includes biographies of the Court's most important justices; Urofsky's collection offers material on those I have slighted here. There are more than twenty books about Chief Justice John Marshall. Albert J. Beveridge produced a monumental four-volume biography, *The Life of John Marshall* (1916–1919). Leonard Baker offered a shorter, more recent account in *John Marshall: A Life in Law* (1974). R. Kent Newmyer wrote of Marshall's devoted colleague in *Supreme Court Justice Joseph Story: Statesman of the Old Republic* (1985). Carl B. Swisher provided a largely admiring biography of Marshall's successor in *Roger B. Taney* (1935); Lewis Walker offered another, but still admiring view in *Without Fear or Favor: A Biography of Chief Justice Roger Brooke Taney* (1965). No biographer has yet revealed the hard core of Taney's racism.

Frederick J. Blue chronicled the career of Taney's successor in *Salmon P. Chase: A Life in Politics* (1987). Carl B. Swisher produced another admiring biography in *Stephen J. Field: Craftsman of the Law* (1930), and Charles Fairman had few criticisms of his subject in *Mr. Justice Miller and the Supreme Court* (1939). C. Peter Magrath did a fine job in *Morrison Waite: The Triumph of Character* (1963), but Willard L. King offered little analysis in *Melville Weston Fuller: Chief Justice of the United States, 1888–1910* (1950). Robert B. Highsaw took account of political factors in *Edward Douglass White: Defender of the Conservative Faith* (1981). Loren Beth wrote a good biography in *John Marshall*

Harlan: The Last Whig Justice (1992). Oliver Wendell Holmes has attracted several biographers; the most recent and most perceptive is Sheldon Novick in *Honorable Justice* (1989).

There are two good biographies of Justice Brandeis. Alpheus T. Mason wrote an early study in *Brandeis: A Free Man's Life* (1946); and Philippa Strum followed with *Brandeis: Justice for the People* (1984). A. L. Todd provided an account of Brandeis's confirmation battle in *Justice on Trial: The Case of Louis D. Brandeis* (1964). Alpheus T. Mason offered a large biography of his large subject in *William Howard Taft: Chief Justice* (1964). Mason had earlier written an excellent portrait in *Harlan Fiske Stone: Pillar of the Law* (1956), which made good use of Stone's papers. Richard Polenberg wrote an incisive biography of a reclusive justice in *The World of Benjamin Cardozo* (1997).

The justices named by Franklin Roosevelt have attracted numerous biographers. Gerald T. Dunne was largely uncritical in *Hugo Black and the Judicial Revolution* (1977). Felix Frankfurter has eluded a full-scale biography. Harry N. Hirsch portrayed him as an insecure judicial bully in *The Enigma of Felix Frankfurter* (1981), and Melvin I. Urofsky matched praise and criticism in *Felix Frankfurter: Judicial Restraint and Individual Liberties* (1992). James Simon tried without much success to explain his subject's personal and judicial wanderings in *Independent Journey: The Life of William O. Douglas* (1980). Bruce Allen Murphy is completing another biography of Douglas. Sidney Fine did an outstanding job in *Frank Murphy: The Washington Years* (1984).

G. Edward White stuck closely to the public record in *Earl Warren: A Public Life* (1982); in fairness, Warren's private life was fairly boring. Tinsley E. Yarbrough did an excellent job in *John Marshall Harlan: Great Dissenter of the Warren Court* (1992), although the second Justice Harlan hardly matched his grandfather (or Justice Holmes) as a dissenter. The only available biography of Justice William Brennan, Kim Isaac Eisler's *A Justice for All: William J. Brennan, Jr., and the Decisions That Transformed America* (1992), is thin and bland. Stephen Wermeil, who covered the Supreme Court for *The Wall Street Journal*, is completing an authorized biography that draws on Brennan's papers and many interviews. Abe Fortas has attracted two competent biographers. Bruce Allen Murphy focused on scandal in *Fortas: The Rise and Fall of a Supreme Court Justice* (1988); Laura Kalman looked more closely at her subject's legal and judicial career in *Fortas: A Biography* (1990). Thurgood Marshall, whose papers became available on his death in 1993, has not yet attracted a competent biographer. Marshall's close friend, Carl T. Rowan, offered no broad perspective in *Dream Makers, Dream Breakers: The World of Justice Thurgood Marshall* (1993).

Chief Justice Warren Burger, who detested reporters and distrusted scholars, has not yet attracted a full-scale biographer. Philippa Strum is working on a biography of Justice Harry Blackmun, and John C. Jeffries, Jr., a former law clerk, has produced a solid biography of his boss in *Justice Lewis F. Powell, Jr.* (1994). Chief Justice William H. Rehnquist still occupies the Court's center seat, and his judicial career has not yet concluded. I offered a comparison of two very different justices in *Brennan vs. Rehnquist: The Battle for the Constitution* (1994), based largely on their published opinions.

Let me emphasize once more that this is a highly selective compilation of books about the Constitution and the Supreme Court. The fact that libraries contain hundreds more worth reading attests to the importance of this document and this institution to our society.

INDEX

SMICA   347
         .7326
         09
         I71

IRONS, PETER
    A PEOPLE'S HISTORY
OF THE SUPREME COURT

SMICA   347
         .7326
         09
         I71

HOUSTON PUBLIC LIBRARY
SMITH

NOV   1999